RACIAL & RELIGIOUS VIOLENCE IN AMERICA:
A CHRONOLOGY

by Michael Newton and Judy Ann Newton

Garland Publishing, Inc.
New York and London 1991

Library of Congress Cataloging-in-Publication Data

Racial & religious violence in America: a chronology/edited by Michael Newton and Judy Ann Newton.

p. cm. – (Garland reference library of social sciences; vol. 501)

Includes bibliographical references and index.

ISBN 0-8240-4848-2

1. Violence – United States – History. 2. Hate crimes – United States – History. 3. Minorities – United States – Crimes against – History. I. Newton, Michael, 1951- . II. Newton, Judy Ann, 1952-. III. Title: Racial and religious violence in America. IV. Series: Garland reference library of social science; v. 501

HN90. V5R33   1991   90-22038

303.6 – dc20   CIP

Design by Marlon St. Patrick Mattis

Printed on acid-free, 250-year-life paper

Manufactured in the United States of America

CONTENTS

LIST OF ABBREVIATIONS

The following abbreviations are employed for organizations mentioned in the text.

AFL—American Federation of Labor

ADL—Anti-Defamation League of B'nai B'rith

AIM—American Indian Movement

APA—American Protective Association

BLA—Black Liberation Army

BSU—Black Student Union

CAWIU—Cannery and Agricultural Workers Industrial Union

CIO—Congress of Industrial Organizations

COFO—Council of Federated Organizations

CORE—Congress of Racial Equality

CSA—The Covenant, the Sword, and the Arm of the Lord

FALN—Armed Forces of National Liberation (Puerto Rico)

FBI—Federal Bureau of Investigation

FDP—Freedom Democratic Party

GOON—Guardians of the Oglala Nation

IRS—Internal Revenue Service

JDL—Jewish Defense League

KKK—Ku Klux Klan

NAACP—National Association for the Advancement of Colored People

NRP—National Renaissance Party

NSLF—National Socialist Liberation Front

NSRP—National States Rights Party

NSWPP—National Socialist White People's Party

OEO—Office of Economic Opportunity

OTO—Ordo Templi Orientis

PLP—Progressive Labor Party

RAM—Revolutionary Action Movement

RNA—Republic of New Africa

SCLC—Southern Christian Leadership Conference

SDS—Students for a Democratic Society

SLA—Symbionese Liberation Army

SNCC—Student Nonviolent Coordinating Committee

STFU—Southern Tenant Farmers Union

UNIA—Universal Negro Improvement Association

PREFACE

What follows is a time line of atrocity, acts of mayhem, murder, and intimidation perpetrated on the grounds of racial or religious prejudice, from the discovery of North America to modern times. In retrospect, it may not be precisely true—as H. "Rap" Brown alleged in 1967—that "violence is as American as cherry pie"; still, bloodshed based on race or creed is interwoven with the fabric of our culture from the first arrival of explorers to the present day. When Viking warriors landed on the shores of Greenland a millennium ago, they celebrated their arrival with the massacre of *skrellings*—natives later christened "Indians" by the *conquistadors* of Spain. The echoes of that slaughter could be heard at Wounded Knee in 1890 and in Howard Beach, New York, in 1988.

This present volume is designed to serve historians and sociologists by charting trends in racial and religious violence, placing so-called isolated incidents in their historical perspective, and demonstrating for the record that our modern spate of ethnic mayhem is by no means new, unprecedented, or unique. The neo-Nazis and survivalists of 1989 have much in common with the early Ku Klux Klan and the nineteenth century's gang of radical "Know-Nothing" bullies. Today's black militants and their counterparts in the barrios and on the reservations can trace their roots to Denmark Vesey, Pancho Villa, and Geronimo.

Racial or religious violence is defined here as any harmful or destructive action consciously directed at an individual or group primarily because of race or creed. Nonviolent demonstrations, telephone harassment, and the like are generally excluded in the absence of a confrontation or commission of a crime resulting in arrest. (Bomb threats, for example, *are* discussed when they mesh with other more substantial actions to reveal a pattern of harassment.) Likewise, accidents and other "neutral" incidents—the holdup of a black-owned store by whites, for instance, in the absence of a clear-cut racist motive—are omitted unless they serve as a trigger incident for a broader confrontation of a racial or religious nature. (For example, most of the explosive ghetto riots in the 1960s had their origin in minor confrontations with police.)

In short, the *motive* of an individual or group involved in violent acts has been a crucial factor in selecting entries. Once a racial or religious motive is established, many "unrelated" crimes take on a new perspective. The bombing of a department store in New York City or the holdup of an armored car in Idaho may qualify as racial crimes if they are perpetrated to advance a racist cause. The mercenary or political appearance of a crime does not exclude it from consideration when the perpetrators view themselves as chosen soldiers in a racial or religious war. The murder of a policeman by black militants in Harlem is a racial crime as surely as the lynching of a black by members of the KKK in Mississippi. When neo-Nazis rob a bank and have a shootout with policemen on the street, the neo-Nazis see themselves as being engaged in a guerilla war with blacks and Jews. The evident irrationality of that belief does not invalidate a racial motive in the case.

That said, it should not be supposed that racial or religious incidents are limited to clashes between whites and nonwhites, Protestants and Catholics, Christians and non-Christians. Violence between polygamous cults in Utah clearly qualifies, as does the urban warfare waged in recent years between Hasidic and Sephardic Jews in New York City. Violence within a given racist group also qualifies, such as when a group of Mississippi Klansmen or Connecticut Black Panthers torture and assassinate one of their own members suspected of informing. (Conversely, we do *not* include such incidents as the attempted murder of a Klansman who complained about his leader's obvious mismanagement of cash.) Struggles for the control of paramilitary racist groups or fringe religious cults frequently result in bloodshed, and police have been the targets of fanatic militants over the past three decades. Once again, the mood and published statements of the perpetrators are accepted here as prima facie evidence, despite denials from authorities that racial or religious motives are involved. (A survey of the data indicates such public statements are invariably aimed at polishing a state's or city's image by denying bigotry or violent cult activity exists.)

Despite the inclusion of over 8,000 entries spanning five centuries, the authors do not claim to offer a definitive chronology. Two years of concentrated research clearly demonstrates that no such final reckoning is possible for any given state, much less the nation as a whole. At least a dozen incidents will be reported, coast to coast, within the time required to read this preface, and perusal of existing records likewise leaves much to be desired by the scholar. It is absurd for anyone to claim that he has isolated each and every skirmish, incident of vandalism or intimidation, altercation, murder, bombing, beating, and the like sparked by actual (or fancied) ethnic insult. In many cases—and especially in the early days of the "Wild" West—reports can be sketchy, vague, or nonexistent. When a band of attacking Indians did their work efficiently, no witnesses remained, and published sources uniformly fill their pages with accounts of "numerous," "incessant," and "continuous" attacks, providing no specifics as to date or place. In modern times, who can pretend to to know of every confrontation on the countless urban battlefields? Below the Mason-Dixon Line, who monitors the victims of the Klan and racist individuals? So many incidents go unreported, even in our own computer age of satellite transmissions, that the present listing should be treated as a mere *suggestion* of the problem, rather than a final word immune to amendments and additions.

Certain racial and religious incidents are obviously catalogued with more precision than others. Black civil rights groups made a point of publicizing lynchings after 1898, and government commissions put the ghetto riots in the 1960s under intense scrutiny, but in many areas existing scholarship has barely scratched the surface, revealing a mere fraction of the incidents that mar our nation's history. When conflicts arise in the published literature—over names and dates, location of events or body counts, even the actual occurrence of an incident—the authors have attempted to determine the "truth" from an authoritative source. (A selected bibliography follows the main text.)

The work in hand is limited to incidents occurring on the soil of the United States, as currently defined, between the discovery of the New World and the latter part of 1989. (A few deliberate exceptions have been made, where violent border crossings were strategically inseparable from action in the United States.) A specific date is listed for an event when possible, although many chroniclers have been content with blurry references to a month, a season, or the year in which an incident occurred. When feasible, the location of an event is labeled with its modern name (Seekonk, Massachusetts, was named Rehoboth when hostile Indians attacked the settlement in colonial times). In cases where the disappearance of a town or other landmark renders transposition fruitless, the historic names remain in place. Incidents from declared wars fought on U.S. soil have been included only when minorities—primarily Indians, Hispanics, or blacks—were recognized as victims or significant combatants. (Thus, the 10,455 military engagements of the Civil War are not listed individually, except in cases in which Indians took part or blacks were singled out as special targets of Confederate Army reprisal.) Likewise, outbreaks of civilian violence during wartime are included where a racial or religious motive is evident.

A survey of racial and religious violence in the United States reveals certain notable trends, confirming the analyses of some historians while flatly contradicting others. The actions of European explorers in the fifteenth and sixteenth centuries belie their stated humanitarian motives, with massacres, enslavement raids, and widespread abuse of aboriginal people marking the advance of a "Christian" empire in the New World. The reputation for religious tolerance began with a slaughter of French Protestants in the 1500s, and the theocratic regime of colonial New England waged unceasing warfare against "heretics," "heathens," and "witches" in the form of Quakers, Catholics, Jews, and Indians. Indeed, Native Americans would remain a target of genocidal assault—openly touted as such—for four centuries, repaying cruelty and bloodshed in kind when the opportunity arose. Neither side held a monopoly on sadism or treachery in the United States' longest war, but it is fair to say that white invaders drew first blood and taught the Indian how to translate tribal conflicts into all-out racial persecution. Along the way, the government's policy of manifest destiny was periodically interrupted to allow the recruitment of Indians to serve as allies by one (or several) European powers in time of war, but these alliances would always end when the Europeans no longer required them.

The advent of black slavery created a new subject class in the United States, with thousands of African prisoners kept "in their place" by armed force, but a survey of history dispells the traditional myth of the smiling, long-suffering slave who accepted bondage as no more than his due. Historical records document more than 200 slave insurrections from the early eighteenth century to the final days of the Civil War, when blacks were "liberated" by presidential proclamation and constitutional amendments. Free blacks were a different sort of "problem" for the white population—particularly in the South—and violent solutions quickly developed. Lynching certainly predated the Civil War (and was never confined entirely to black or minority victims), but mob violence against blacks clearly accelerated after 1865, peaking with a virtual orgy of mayhem—some sources claim 5,000 victims—between the late 1880s and World War II. Southern politicians valiantly defended lynching as a necessary evil, a defense of "white womanhood" against sexual assault by lecherous blacks, but a careful analysis of lynchings in the South indicates that less than one in five black victims was slain for this reason. Other alleged offenses ranged from murder and assault to insulting a white man, with one in twenty victims slain for no apparent reason other than his or her race. In retrospect, it is apparent that lynching (along with the attendant riots, floggings, and other forms of terrorism) was primarily designed to intimidate blacks, allowing whites—sometimes outnumbered in the Black Belt counties of the South—to retain their antebellum dominance of politics and the economy.

Endemic nativism, expressed in violent hostility to non-Teutonic immigrants and non-Protestant religions, is another major theme of U.S. history illustrated by this chronology. Puritan colonists, persecuted in their own homeland, had barely put down roots in Massachusetts when they started banning, persecuting, and occasionally executing noncon- formists. In the nineteenth century, Mormons fled from persecution in Illinois and Missouri to the barren wastes of Utah, sometimes retaliating with mayhem of their own. Know-Nothing terrorists waged virtual guerilla war against U.S. Catholics in the 1830s and 1840s, while a later generation would witness the massacre of Chinese immigrants in several western states. Persistent cycles of anti-Semitism have marred U.S. history from colonial times to the depradations of the modern neo-Nazi movement, and there were retaliations, with members of the militant Jewish Defense League claiming credit in the 1970s and 1980s for various bombings, snipings, and assaults on actual or alleged anti- Semites. In the wake of the Vietnam War, Vietnamese refugees found themselves harassed and assaulted by organized racist groups in several states.

The historic expansion of the U.S. frontier—sanctified as manifest destiny with the assumption of divine approval—victimized Indians, Spaniards, Mexicans, and Hawaiians to varying degrees, from a "bloodless" coup in Honolulu to an all-out two-year war with Mexico, and conflict over slavery prior to 1860 guaranteed that contested territory would assume the aspect of a free-fire zone. "Bleeding Kansas" was the scene of civil war for years before secession and Fort Sumter's fall in 1861, with pro- and anti-slavery forces each persuaded that their cause was just. When neighbors to the south and west opposed U.S. advancement, they were driven from their homes by the force of arms, or else "permitted" to become servants of the victors. While Americans recall the Alamo, more Mexicans remember San Jacinto and the war of 1846 to 1848, a memory that turned angry, surfacing in violent border raids as late as World War I.

The years since 1945 have witnessed shifting patterns in domestic strife from coast to coast, both in the North and the South. The United States recorded its first lynch-free year in 1950, and while white segregationist violence remained a fixture of national headlines through the early 1970s, new trends in mayhem soon made themselves apparent. Urban riots, once the virtual monopoly of nativists and white supremacists, changed color in the 1960s, with blacks and Hispanics assaulting the symbols of white authority. As with the white riots of earlier generations, the triggering incidents were seemingly trivial—the arrest of a drunk driver or the failure of a local high school to select black cheerleaders—but the resulting violence was no less significant. While liberal apologists sought to differentiate between white and black violence—labeling white outbursts as "race riots," while minority eruptions were dubbed "commodity riots" or "ghetto rebellions"—racial motives were readily apparent in popular slogans such as "Get Whitey," "Black Power," and "Off the Pigs." At the same time, minorities created their own militant racist groups, seeking legitimacy in the guise of "revolutionaries." A critical review of rhetoric and group activities reveals few significant differences between the Ku Klux Klan or American Nazi Party and such groups as the Black Liberation Army, the Revolutionary Action Movement, the Young Lords, or the Republic of New Africa. Urban terrorism in the 1970s and 1980s was practiced with fine impartiality by anti-Semites, white supremacists, black militants, and Puerto Rican nationalists, with the identical results for the victims unfortunate enough to be caught in the crossfire.

The past two decades have been characterized by some analysts as the era of the "crazies," typified by explosions of random homicidal violence, serial and mass murders, the emergence of bizarre political splinter groups and murderous cults. In California, white members of the tiny Symbionese Liberation Army donned blackface makeup and targeted black politicians for murder in an effort to advance "people's liberation." Black "Death Angels" earn their "wings" by randomly slaughtering predetermined numbers of white men, women, and children. Policemen are imprisoned for murdering black and Hispanic prisoners, while nonwhite militants serve time for killing "racist pigs." In Washington state, the massacre of an entire family was blamed on a right-wing fanatic who mistook his victims for "communist Jews." White mobs in New York taunt black demonstrators with shouts of "Nigger go home" while brandishing placards that proclaim "We Are Not Racists."

This volume should not be regarded as "anti-American." The United States has no monopoly on racial or religious violence, as demonstrated by the gruesome record of the European witch hunts, the Inquisition and various Crusades, the colonial subjugation of Asia and Africa, racial decimation of the Polynesian peoples, the Spanish conquest of Latin America, persecution of various races and religions under both fascist and communist regimes, religious violence in Ireland and the Middle East . . . the list goes on, quite literally, forever. If anything, a review of U.S. weakness helps balance our history, tempering the traditional view of "God's chosen nation" and placing historical characters—both victims and villains—in a new, more human perspective. Only when a nation has come to terms with the truth of its past and the troubles of its present can citizens and leaders then chart a viable direction for the future.

1500

1501

August 8, Eastern Seaboard: After scrutinizing 700 miles of coastline, Portuguese explorer Gaspar Corte-Real departs for home with fifty kidnapped Indians destined to be sold as slaves. The ship disappears en route with Corte-Real's fate commonly attributed to an Indian mutiny on board.

1508

Eastern Seaboard: French explorers kidnap several Indians from the northeastern coastline, returning them to France for display as curiosities.

1513

April, Florida: Spanish explorers led by Ponce de Leon chart the coastline, landing at several points and clashing with hostile natives in each instance.

1520

Cape St. Helena, South Carolina: A Spanish expedition under Lucas Vasquez de Ayllon kidnaps thirty Indians. The Indians are transported to Haiti, where they are enslaved and soon die working in the mines.

1521

Florida: While searching for the Fountain of Youth, Ponce de Leon is wounded by an Indian arrow and a number of his conquistadors are killed in the same attack. Returning to Cuba, de Leon dies from the infection of his wound.

1524

March, North Carolina: Sailing for France, Giovanni Verrazano explores the coastline near modern Wilmington. His crew abducts an Indian child and attempts to kidnap a young squaw before they depart.

1525

St. Helena Sound, South Carolina: Returning to the scene of previous slave raids, Lucas Vasquez de Ayllon and over 200 of his men are massacred by Indians when their ship runs aground at the mouth of the Combahee River.

1526

November, Georgetown County, South Carolina: Black slaves revolt against their Spanish captors on the Waccamaw River, fleeing to live with local Indians, who instigated the uprising.

1528

April–July, Florida: A Spanish expedition led by Pánfilo de Narvaez lands at Pensacola Bay in April and spends the next three months marching eastward to the Apalachicola River, fighting numerous engagements with local Indians along the way. All but four or five of the 300 conquistadors are lost before their journey's end.

1539

May, Hawikuh, New Mexico: Estevanico, a black explorer sent by Spanish friars to locate the Seven Cities of Cibola in present-day Arizona, is killed by Zuñi tribesmen who refuse to believe he is the emissary of whites.

May 30, Florida: A Spanish expedition under Hernando de Soto comes ashore, fighting numerous battles with Indians in the following months, marching overland to discover the Alabama and Mississippi Rivers, and ending in the territory of modern Missouri. Along the way, Indian chiefs are held hostage to make tribesmen serve the Spaniards as porters and guides.

1540

March 24, Dougherty County, Georgia: Hernando de Soto's Spanish cavalry invades the Hitchiti Indian village of Toa, twenty-five miles west of modern Albany. His men erect a large cross and slaughter most of the village dogs for meat before they move on.

July, Hawikuh, New Mexico: Spanish troops led by Francisco Coronado attack and occupy the Zuñi pueblo, with unspecified losses reported for both sides in the battle. Some time later, at the village of Tiguex (above modern Albuquerque), Coronado orders 200 Indians burned at the stake in a show of force.

October18, Mobile, Alabama: Spanish troops assault a major Indian settlement, with eighteen men killed and 150 wounded in the clash. Eyewitness reports of 2,500 Indians slain in the fighting are currently dismissed as "doubtless greatly exaggerated."

1541

March 8, Yazoo River, Mississippi: Hernando de Soto's troops command local Chickasaw leaders to provide 200 Indian bearers for a new expedition. Tribesmen respond by torching the Spanish camp one night, killing eleven soldiers and an uncertain number of horses before retreating.

March 15, Yazoo River, Mississippi: Chickasaw warriors are repulsed in their second attack on the camp of Hernando de Soto's troops.

September, Kansas: Father Padilla, a Spanish friar, is killed by an Indian war party near the site of modern Lindsborg.

Fall, Washita River, Oklahoma: Hernando de Soto's expedition establishes a new base of operations, enslaving local Indians as porters and guides, and responding to any real or imagined defiance by leveling whole villages or cutting off the hands of individual offenders.

1543

January–July, Adams County, Mississippi: Hernando de Soto's expedition encamps on the Mississippi River, plundering Indian villages for supplies while a fleet of boats is constructed for their descent of the river. Local Indians starve to death as the conquistadors monopolize food for themselves.

1559

October, Alabama: Coosa tribesmen, armed by the Spaniards with superior weapons, initiate raids against members of the hostile Natchez tribe.

1564

Summer, Florida: French troops under Rene de Laudonniere launch their search for gold by helping members of the Apalachee tribe defeat rival warriors in contested territory.

1565

Spring, St. Mary's River, Florida: Indians launch raids against French explorers, killing an unspecified number of men and wounding twenty-two in a single engagement.

September 21, Nassau County, Florida: Spanish troops, acting under orders from King Phillip II, massacre a settlement of French Huguenots at Ft. Caroline, mutilating the dead by cutting out their eyes. The expedition's commander, Pedro Menendez de Aviles, rationalizes the slaughter by telling the victims in advance, "I do this not unto Frenchmen, with whom my king is at peace, but unto heretics."

September 29, St. Augustine, Florida: Captured fugitives from the massacre at Ft. Caroline are slaughtered by Spanish troops, a few Catholics being spared as the Huguenot death toll approaches 900 since September 21.

1567

August, Nassau County, Florida: French forces led by Dominic de Gourgues capture a Spanish garrison at San Mateo, near the former site of Ft. Caroline.

1568

May, Nassau County, Florida: Before abandoning the captured Spanish fort at San Mateo, Dominic de Gourgues hangs his prisoners in reprisal for the massacre at Ft. Caroline, declaring, "I do this not as unto Spaniards or mariners, but as unto traitors, robbers, and murderers."

1576

July, Parris Island, South Carolina: Indians demolish Ft. San Felipe, driving Spaniards south toward St. Augustine, Florida.

1581

October, Galisteo Valley, New Mexico: A Spanish priest, Father Juan de Santa Maria, is killed by Indians.

October, Malagon, New Mexico: After Indian raiders steal three Spanish horses, the Spaniards fire on the local pueblo in retaliation and arrest two suspects.

1582

December, Puaray, New Mexico: Two Spanish friars are killed by Indians.

1583

June, Puaray, New Mexico: Spanish troops set fire to an Indian pueblo in retaliation for the murder of two priests in December 1582. Sixteen prisoners are executed, with numerous other Indians reported killed in the fire.

1585

Roanoke Island, North Carolina: English colonists establish an ill-fated settlement. When reinforcements return in 1587, the camp is found littered with human bones and the stockade in ruins after an apparent Indian massacre.

September, St. Augustine, Florida: English forces under Sir Francis Drake raid the Spanish settlement, burning the fort, a warship in the harbor, and 250 homes.

1587

July 28, Roanoke Island, North Carolina: A leader of the new British settlement is murdered by Indian raiders. Colonists dispatch a punitive expedition, burning the nearest Indian village and the tribe's supply of corn. As relations with the natives deteriorate, armed force becomes the first resort of colonists in every situation. One member of the expedition writes: "Some of our company towards the end of the year, showed themselves too fierce, in slaying some of the people, in some towns, upon causes that on our part, might easily enough have been borne withall."

1590

Roanoke Island, North Carolina: After a three-year delay, supply ships arrive to find the British colony deserted. The cryptic legend "Croatoan," carved on a tree, leaves historians in disagreement about whether settlers were massacred or adopted by a nearby tribe of that name.

August, New Mexico: The Spanish Castano expedition, beginning the first effort to establish a permanent colony, enslaves local Indians as the trek proceeds.

December, New Mexico: Spanish soldiers attached to the Castano expedition raid an Indian village for supplies, killing several who resist.

1598

September, Rio Gallinas, New Mexico: Spaniards capture thirteen Apaches at gunpoint, forcing them to serve as guides for a party of explorers.

December 3, Acoma, New Mexico: Fifteen Spaniards are killed while trying to loot an Indian village for supplies.

1599

January, Acoma, New Mexico: Eight hundred Indian men, women, and children are slaughtered by Spaniards in retaliation for the death of fifteen Spanish soldiers the month before.

1600

1601

April, Texas: Two Spanish deserters bound for Mexico are killed by Jumano Apaches. Spaniards retaliate by destroying three Jumano towns, killing 600 men, women, and children. Each Spanish soldier is awarded a male Jumano slave.

October, Kansas: Spanish troops are routed in a battle with 1,500 Indians.

1605

Maine: An English expedition kidnaps several Indians for transport back to Europe.

Massachusetts: French explorers report clashes with natives while charting the coastline.

December, Savannah River, Georgia: Spanish troops capture several French corsairs.

1606

November 10, At Sea: Spanish warships capture and confiscate a British vessel en route to explore the American coastline for potential colonization.

1607

April 26, Jamestown, Virginia: English settlers fight their first skirmish with Powhatan Indians, twelve hours after coming ashore in the New World.

December, Jamestown, Virginia: Colonial leader John Smith is captured by Indians on a scouting expedition and marched to the seat of the Powhatan's confederacy. The chief's favorite daughter, Pocahontas, intervenes to save Smith's life in what some historians now describe as a mock execution, staged for the Englishman's benefit.

1608

New England: Several Indians are kidnapped and carried back to England by seamen.

1609

January, Jamestown, Virginia: John Smith launches military raids against nearby Indian villages, looting them for food and other supplies to sustain his failing colony.

July 29, Essex County, New York: Samuel de Champlain leads a force of Frenchmen and Ottawa braves against the hostile Iroquois near Ticonderoga. Champlain's first shot kills two Iroquois leaders and wounds a third, after which Ottawa warriors storm the Iroquois settlement, slaughtering captives and drinking their blood in celebration.

1610

Spring, Jamestown, Virginia: Indian warfare reaches a point where Alonso de Velasco, Spanish ambassador to England, informs his government that "the Indians hold the English surrounded in a strong place which they had erected there, having killed the larger part of them, and the others were left so entirely without provisions that they thought it impossible to escape." The colony is saved by the arrival of relief ships and reinforcements during May and June.

1611

Coastal New England: Capt. Edward Harlow kidnaps three Indians from Monhegan Island, New Hampshire, but one of his captives escapes. Continuing along the coast, he seizes another native before landing at Martha's Vineyard, where he captures two more natives. With his five prisoners secured, Harlow sails back to England.

Point Comfort, Virginia: Two Spaniards and one Englishman are captured by opposing sides after a Spanish scouting party enters Chesapeake Bay.

March, Cape Fear, North Carolina: Spanish forces rescue a Frenchman from Indians.

1613

Jamestown, Virginia: Capt. Samuel Argall engineers the kidnapping of Pocahontas, seeking to force the return of English prisoners and captured weapons and Indian payment of "a great quantity of corn." Pocahontas marries widower John Rolfe the following year and dies not long after her arrival in England in 1617.

New England: English seamen kidnap twenty-four Indians and sell them as slaves in Málaga.

1619

Martha's Vineyard, Massachusetts: Deaths are reported on both sides as local Indians attack the crew of a British ship.

August 20, Jamestown, Virginia: The first Africans kidnapped for enslavement in America arrive at Jamestown.

1620

November 15, Cape Cod, Massachusetts: Pilgrims from the *Mayflower* sight six Indians on shore, launching an immediate pursuit with guns and tracking dogs. The ten-mile chase is broken off at nightfall.

November 17, Cape Cod, Massachusetts: In their second foray, *Mayflower* colonists desecrate an Indian burial ground, opening graves and handling remains of the dead.

December 8, Wellfleet Harbor, Massachusetts: Indians fire arrows at a party of *Mayflower* explorers, who respond with musket fire.

1621

February 16, Plymouth, Massachusetts: A Pilgrim hunting party stumbles on an Indian village and pursues the inhabitants, losing them in the forest.

1622

March 22, Virginia: Powhatan raiders, led by Chief Opechancanough, attack seventy-four of the colony's eighty plantations, killing 347 persons (an estimated one-third of the white population). Violence continues sporadically until the signing of a truce in 1634.

1623

Fryeburg, Maine: Indian resistance in the area is crippled after Pequaket Chief Paugus dies in a clash with white settlers at Lovewell's Pond.

March 23, Massachusetts: Colonial leaders declare war on the local Indian tribes. A short time later, Miles Standish lures four Indians into his camp at Wessagusset and kills them. Several more Indians die in a subsequent skirmish near the camp.

May 22, Virginia: Capt. William Tucker concludes a "peace conference" by offering poisoned wine to 200 assembled Powhatans. Fifty of the Indians die. Chief Opechancanough escapes by ignoring his special invitation to the meeting.

1627

Spring, Santa Fe, New Mexico: Spaniards and Pueblo Indians attack a camp of Apaches visiting the city on a trading mission. At least twenty Apaches are killed, and more than forty are taken prisoner.

1630

Swanendael, New Netherland: Thirty-two white settlers die in a raid by Indian warriors.

October, Richmond, Maine: Indians stage their first recorded raid against a New England trading post, killing Walter Bagnall and burning his store. The victim had a reputation for cheating and robbing local Indians.

1633

Connecticut River, Connecticut: The officers and crew of a British ship are massacred by Pequot Indians after trying to abduct two tribesmen.

1634

Connecticut River Valley, Connecticut: Pequot Indians begin killing English and Dutch colonists, and declare war on the neighboring Narragansett tribe.

April, Kennebec, New Hampshire: One Puritan and one Plymouth Pilgrim die in a shootout sparked by religious animosity and economic rivalry.

1636

July, Block Island, Rhode Island: Narragansett Indians kill a white trader, and colonial troops mount a punitive expedition, destroying Indian crops and wigwams. On their return, the troops destroy a Pequot village, touching off new warfare with the Pequots, who retaliate by killing more settlers and livestock.

1637

May 1, Massachusetts: The colonial government declares war on the Pequot tribe, enlisting rival Mohegan warriors to assist in the campaign.

May 26, New London County, Connecticut: English colonists allied with Mohegan Indians sack Mystic Fort, slaughtering more than 400 Pequots in less than an hour. Another twenty-four Indian men and eighty women are captured; the men are summarily executed, the women are sold into slavery. The colonial forces lose two men, with sixteen wounded, repulsing a counterattack by 300 Pequots from another nearby fort.

June, Fairfield, Connecticut: The climactic battle of the Pequot war leaves numerous tribesmen dead or wounded, with 200 taken as prisoners. By August, the tribe is reportedly extinct.

1639

Jemez, Arizona: Navajos kill Father Diego de San Lucas, a Spanish priest.

1640

New Netherland: Gov. William Kieft sends troops to punish the Raritan for tax evasion and unlawful killing of pigs. Several Indians are killed, with the chief's brother captured and tortured by settlers. An estimated 1,000 Indians will die in combat over the next three years.

Virginia: A white man is forced to do penance in church for his love affair with a black woman. The woman is publicly flogged.

1641

Westchester County, New York: Wecquaesgeek Indians murder a Dutch settler.

New France: Iroquois warriors launch concerted attacks against Frenchmen and Indians allied with settlers throughout the Great Lakes region and Canada. Sporadic warfare drags on until 1660, when attrition finally defeats the Iroquois.

1642

Maryland: Indian warfare erupts, lasting for several years.

Union County, New Jersey: Hackensack Indians kill two Dutch farmers, across Newark Bay from New Amsterdam. Both victims are accused of letting their livestock trample Indian corn. Tribal custom is preserved with an offer of wampum to one victim's widow, in atonement, but tribal leaders refuse to surrender the killers.

1643

February, Westchester County, New York: Seventeen Wecquaesgeek are killed and others taken prisoner in a raid by hostile Mohicans from the Albany region. Survivors flee to New Amsterdam, where Dutch settlers encourage them to establish two camps near the town.

February 25-26, New Amsterdam: Dutch soldiers raid both Wecquaesgeek settlements, ignoring their orders to kill only men, murdering and mutilating Indians of both sexes and all ages. Officers report seeing infants dismembered and burned, with others bound to planks before being hacked and stabbed. Corpses are mutilated to such an extent that civilians initially blame hostile Indians for the massacre.

Summer, New Netherland: Indians launch raids against white settlers on Staten Island and Long Island in retaliation for recent attacks. Hostilities continue, with loss of life on both sides, until a treaty is signed in the summer of 1645.

1644

April 18, Virginia: After ten years of peace, Chief Opechancanough launches new surprise raids, killing 400 to 500 whites along the York and Pamunkey Rivers. This time, the war ends with Openchancanough's capture and death in captivity.

June 11, Delaware Valley, New Sweden: Gov. Johanx Printz requests troops to fight the local Indians, but his request is denied.

1645

August, New Netherland: Indians resume occasional raids against Dutch settlers in the region of modern New York, killing an estimated sixteen persons over the next decade.

1647

New Amsterdam: Dutch settler Simon Walingen is killed by Indian raiders near the site of modern New York City.

May 26, Windsor, Connecticut: Alse Young is hanged as a witch.

1648

August 21, Hartford, Connecticut: Mary Johnson is convicted of witchcraft and publicly flogged, with an order from the court that she be whipped again in one month.

December, Wethersfield, Connecticut: Mary Johnson is hanged as a convicted witch.

1651

Long Island, New York: Indian raiders kill the wife of Dutch settler Jan Pietersen.

March 6, Wethersfield, Connecticut: John and Joan Carrington are condemned as witches and hanged.

May, Stratford, Connecticut: Goody Bassett is hanged as a witch.

1652

Manhattan, New York: Four Dutch settlers are killed in an Indian raid.

1653

Staten Island, New York: Three Dutch settlers are killed in a raid by Indians.

December, Fairfield, Connecticut: Goodwife Knapp is convicted of witchcraft and hanged.

1654

New Amsterdam: Dutch settler Jochim Kuyter is killed by Indians in his home near the site of modern New York City.

November, Windsor, Connecticut: Lydia Gilbert is hanged as a witch.

1655

January, Providence, Maryland: Catholic troops assault a Puritan settlement on the site of present-day Annapolis. Six Puritans are killed in the engagement, with the attack force suffering fifty casualties. Ten Catholic leaders are captured and sentenced to die, six of whom later receive a reprieve.

September 17, New Amsterdam: Five hundred Indians invade the Dutch settlement, looting homes and assaulting colonists in an outburst that leaves two whites and three Indians dead, with three more colonists wounded.

1656

Massachusetts: The first Quaker immigrants, two women from Barbados, are jailed, stripped, and searched for signs of witchcraft, their books publicly burned before both are expelled from the colony. Subsequent punishments for Quakers include ear-cropping, whipping, branding, and tongue-boring.

March, Virginia: Col. Edward Hill murders five Powhatan chiefs who are sent to his camp on a peace mission, touching off a battle with colonial troops. Hill is found criminally guilty and removed from office for his treacherous action.

1657

Massachusetts: A Quaker woman, newly arrived from England, receives twenty lashes for her membership in "the accursed sect" and is afterward expelled from the colony.

1658

Massachusetts: The General Court invokes a standing death penalty for Quakers entering the colony.

Zuñi, New Mexico: Apaches raid a settlement of Pueblo Indians.

1659

New Mexico: Apache and Navajo Indians launch raids against several Pueblo settlements.

September, Boston, Massachusetts: Quakers Mary Dyer, Nicholas Davis, Marmaduke Stephenson, and William Robinson are ordered to leave the colony on pain of death. Dyer and Davis obey the order, but Dyer returns to Massachusetts in October.

October 27, Boston, Massachusetts: Quakers Marmaduke Stephenson and William Robinson are hanged on Boston Common. Mary Dyer is reprieved and deported, but she soon returns a second time and is executed.

1661

Massachusetts: A fourth Quaker is hanged while twenty-eight more remain in prison.

1662

Maryland: The Janodoa Indian War is fought and won by white settlers.

January, Hartford, Connecticut: Nathaniel and Rebecca Greensmith are hanged as witches.

January 6, Farmington, Connecticut: Mary Barnes is condemned for witchcraft and sentenced to hang at a later, unrecorded date.

June 13, Hartford, Connecticut: Mary Sanford is convicted of witchcraft and sentenced to hang. Her execution date is not recorded.

July, Bristol County, Rhode Island: Wamsutta, chief of the Wampanoag tribe, is arrested by British forces for plotting war against the colony. He dies, reportedly of "sudden illness," on the way back to Plymouth.

1663

Port Royal, South Carolina: A British vessel is wrecked along the nearby coast with surviving crewmen taken prisoner by local Indians.

September 13, Virginia: A scheduled revolt by slaves and indentured servants is betrayed to authorities. Several plotters are beheaded, their skulls displayed on chimney tops.

1666

New York: French raids against Iroquois villages prompt tribal leaders to sue for peace, inviting French priests to live among them and teach tribesmen the "true" religion.

1668

August 8, St. Augustine, Florida: British privateers capture a Spanish ship bound for the harbor, disguising themselves as crew members to stage a surprise assault on the town. Men, women, and children are slaughtered indiscriminately in the raid, and the attackers escape with their booty while surviving Spanish soldiers retreat to the safety of the fort.

1669

Massachusetts: King Philip's Wampanoag tribesmen fight a territorial war against hostile Mohegans, losing fifty warriors in the climactic battle before peace is restored with a Wampanoag victory.

1672

Hawikuh, New Mexico: Father Pedro de Arvila y Ayala, a Spanish priest, is dragged from his church by Navajos, stripped naked at the foot of a cross, and has his skull crushed beneath a bell.

1674

South Carolina: Colonists subdue the local Westo Indians with armed force, converting them into reluctant allies.

1675

Pennsylvania-New York: After defeating and absorbing members of the Susquehannock tribe, Iroquois warriors turn on local Jesuit missionaries, launching fierce assaults on the French seats of colonial power.

January 29, Middleboro, Massachusetts: John Sassamon, a "friendly Indian," is drowned in a local pond, reportedly murdered on orders from Wampanoag chieftain King Philip. His body is found in February, and two Indians are hanged for the crime on June 8.

June 18, Swansea, Massachusetts: An English farmer shoots and wounds an Indian found trespassing in his barn, touching off two years of conflict memorialized as "King Philip's War." The struggle will leave an estimated 600 whites and 3,000 Indians dead, with 1,200 homes burned and 80,000 head of cattle slaughtered by Indian raiders. Surviving tribesmen will be sold as slaves for thirty shillings each.

June 20, Swansea, Massachusetts: Indian warriors raid and ransack two white homes.

June 23, Swansea, Massachusetts: Twelve white homes are looted by Indians.

June 24, Fall River, Massachusetts: Indian raiders kill a white settler named Layton.

June 23, Swansea, Massachusetts: Twelve white homes are looted by Indians.

June 24, Fall River, Massachusetts: Indian raiders kill a white settler named Layton.

June 24, Swansea, Massachusetts: Indians fire on a meeting of white settlers, killing nine persons and mortally wounding two others. More colonists are killed the following day, with their homes burned by Indian raiders, as full-scale warfare erupts. Over the next week, attacks are also directed at the settlements of Seekonk and Taunton.

June 25, Mattapoisit Neck, Massachusetts: Colonial militiamen are routed by Indians, with six men killed as the troopers retreat into Swansea.

July, Virginia: A party of Doeg Indians attempts to steal hogs from a settler who has swindled them on a trade, and several braves are killed when colonists respond with gunfire. The Indians kill a number of whites in retaliation. Local planters respond in force, killing ten Doegs and fourteen friendly Susquehannocks in an ill-conceived attack. When the colonial government refuses compensation for the deaths of Susquehannock allies, tribesmen seek revenge with attacks on frontier settlements in Virginia and Maryland.

July 9, Middleborough, Massachusetts: Indian raiders burn most of the settlement's houses, forcing colonists to abandon the town a short time later.

July 14, Mendon, Massachusetts: Nipmuck men kill several whites in a surprise attack.

July 19, Pocasset Swamp, Massachusetts: Two soldiers die in a clash with Indians.

July 25, New London, Connecticut: Narragansett Indians deliver the severed head of a Wampanoag warrior to English colonists, demanding payment of a new coat under terms of a recent peace treaty.

July 26, Massachusetts: King Philip escapes from a trap set by the militia, fleeing across the Trenton River.

August 1, Nipsachuck, Massachusetts: Militia units and friendly Mohegan tribesmen raid King Philip's camp, but the Wampanoag chief escapes once more.

August 2, Brookfield, Massachusetts: Indians ambush militiamen near town, killing eight and wounding five. The Brookfield garrison is then besieged, and two more settlers are killed in the continuous fighting before troops arrive to break the siege on August 4.

August 22, Lancaster, Massachusetts: Indians attack a white settler's farm.

Late August, Hatfield, Massachusetts: Ten whites and twenty-six Indians die in a skirmish between tribesmen and militia units.

September, Maine: Tarratine Indians begin frontier raids against white settlers, apparently unrelated to King Philip's war in New England.

September, Essex County, Massachusetts: White troops burn a Pennacook Indian village in the Merrimac Valley.

September, Woburn, Massachusetts: A friendly Indian is "accidentally" killed by a white militiaman during practice maneuvers. Tribesmen respond by burning a local barn, and settlers from Chelmsford attack the nearest Indian camp, killing a boy and wounding five others.

September, Zia, New Mexico: A combined force of Spaniards and Pueblos attack the Navajos, killing fifteen, rescuing six Pueblo captives and one Spanish woman. Large amounts of corn are destroyed, and thirty-five Navajo Indians are taken as slaves.

September 1, Deerfield, Massachusetts: Indian raiders burn two homes and drive off a herd of cattle before being routed by settlers.

September 2, Northfield, Massachusetts: Indian raiders kill eight colonists and drive others into the garrison house before burning their homes.

September 4, Northfield, Massachusetts: Troops marching to relieve Northfield blunder into an Indian ambush nearby, leaving twenty-one soldiers killed.

September 6, Northfield, Massachusetts: Maj. Robert Treat is wounded by an Indian sniper after his troops bury mutilated victims of the September 4 militia massacre.

September 7, Boston, Massachusetts: Whites attempt to lynch an Indian prisoner, but they are prevented by an officer armed with a cudgel. On September 10, an Indian is lynched on suspicion of murder despite holding a safe conduct pass issued to him by local authorities.

September 18, South Deerfield, Massachusetts: Eighty-one whites are killed as Indian raiders attack a wagon train carrying goods between Deerfield and Hadley. Seventy militiamen assault a force of 1,000 Indians the same afternoon, the battle raging until nightfall.

between Deerfield and Hadley. Seventy militiamen assault a force of 1,000 Indians the same afternoon, the battle raging until nightfall.

October 5, Springfield, Massachusetts: Indians attack the town, burning thirty homes and barns and the mill.

October 16, Hatfield, Massachusetts: Indian raiders kill a party of scouts.

October 19, Hatfield, Massachusetts: Indians assault the town, with casualties recorded on both sides before the attack is repulsed.

October 25, Northampton, Massachusetts: Indians ambush a party of workers returning from the nearby fields, but the settlers escape with no casualties.

October 26, Westfield, Massachusetts: Indians kill three white men at a mill outside of town and then assault the settlement proper, burning several homes.

October 29, Northampton, Massachusetts: Several settlers returning from the fields are killed in an Indian ambush.

October 30, Dedham, Massachusetts: Friendly "praying Indians" are routed from their homes at midnight and driven into the wilderness reserve, where many will die from hunger and exposure. The action is reportedly taken in retaliation for the burning of an abandoned house in town.

November 2, New England: The United Colonies declare a "preventive" war against the then-peaceful Narragansett tribe.

November 15, Chelmsford, Massachusetts: Whites surround and attack a village of friendly "praying Indians," massacring the inhabitants reportedly as punishment for the burning of a white-owned barn in October.

Winter, Virginia: Frontier raids by Susquehannock warriors claim the lives of at least thirty-six colonists by early 1676. Angry white settlers strike back at the nearest available Indians, annihilating friendly members of the Appomattox and Pamunkey tribes, confiscating their land. Sporadic hostilities continue through May 1677.

December 2, Worcester, Massachusetts: The town is raided and burned by Indians.

December 6, Dedham, Massachusetts: Colonial militia units gather to launch an offensive against Narragansett Indians in Rhode Island, drawing an official protest from Rhode Island authorities on December 7.

December 10, Lancaster, Massachusetts: Indians stage an assault before dawn, burning most of the town.

December 14, Warwick, Rhode Island: Militiamen clash with Narragansetts, capturing thirty-five prisoners. On the following day, four Indians are killed and four are captured.

December 15, Pettaquamscot, Rhode Island: Troops discover the ruins of a local garrison, with seventeen whites killed by Indian raiders.

December 19, Petasquamscot, Rhode Island: One thousand colonial troops assault a nearby Narragansett settlement. Ninety soldiers die and over 125 are wounded in the three-hour battle. Indian casualties are disputed, but tribal spokesmen admit to 350 deaths, including many women and children.

1676

January 27, Pawtucket, Rhode Island: Indians stage an early-morning surprise attack, burning several buildings and escaping with a large number of livestock.

January 31–February 3, Rhode Island: Militia units pursue Narragansett warriors over a distance of sixty miles, killing or capturing "a considerable number" without ever waging a decisive battle.

February, Essex County, Massachusetts: Authorities foil a plot by residents of Lynn to massacre unarmed Indians living on nearby Deer Island.

February 10, Lancaster, Massachusetts: An estimated fifty settlers are killed or wounded in an Indian attack. Twenty settlers are taken prisoner, and several buildings are burned. The town is abandoned six weeks later.

February 21, Medfield, Massachusetts: Indian raiders burn an estimated forty to fifty settlers' homes.

February 25, Weymouth, Massachusetts: Indians burn several buildings during a surprise attack on the settlement.

March, Massachusetts: Indian raiders assault Hadley, Hatfield, Northampton, and Westfield, but in each case are unable to penetrate town defenses.

March 12, Plymouth, Massachusetts: Indians set fire to the garrison house on the Eel River, killing eleven whites.

March 13, Groton, Massachusetts: Indians mount a major attack on the settlement, burning the town meeting hall and several other buildings before being turned back.

March 17, Warwick, Rhode Island: Indian raiders burn the town, and then move on to sack Providence a few days later.

March 26, Longmeadow, Massachusetts: Indians ambush a party of white settlers en route to church. A man and a girl are killed, and two women and two infants are taken prisoner. A rescue party gives chase, and find the infants dead and the women gravely wounded. The raiders escape.

March 26, Marlborough, Massachusetts: The settlement is destroyed by Indians. Pursuers overtake the Indians that night, raiding their camp and inflicting an indeterminate number of casualties before escaping.

March 26, Central Falls, Rhode Island: Indians ambush a force of fifty white settlers and twenty friendly Indians, killing all of the settlers and many of their scouts.

March 26, Simsbury, Connecticut: Indians burn the abandoned town.

March 28, Seekonk, Massachusetts: An Indian attack leaves the town in smoking ruins.

April, Connecticut: Colonial troops raid an Indian camp, capturing Chief Canonchet. He is handed over to "friendly" Indians, who kill him on the spot and mutilate his body.

April 1, Hadley, Massachusetts: Soldier Thomas Reed is captured by Indians but escapes in early May.

April 9, Billerica, Massachusetts: Colonists repel an Indian assault.

April 9, Bridgewater, Massachusetts: Indian raiders attack the town.

April 15, Chelmsford, Massachusetts: Indians stage an attack on the settlement.

April 17, Marlborough, Massachusetts: Indians burn several abandoned homes. Over the next twenty-four hours, attacks are made against colonists in Weymouth, Hingham, and Wrentham.

April 18, Sudbury, Massachusetts: Twelve white settlers die in an Indian raid. A secondary thrust against the town of Scituate is repulsed.

April 18, Scituate, Massachusetts: Indian raiders are turned back after burning nineteen houses and barns.

April 21, Sudbury, Massachusetts: Twenty-nine white settlers and at least 120 Indians die during an engagement, with tribesmen routed by troops from Boston and surrounding towns.

May 8, Scituate, Massachusetts: Indians set fire to seventeen houses and five barns.

May 10, Scituate, Massachusetts: An Indian war party burns seven additional houses and two barns, and then moves on to destroy the remaining homes in Namasket.

May 13, Hatfield, Massachusetts: Indians raid the village herd and steal a large number of cattle.

May 18, Deerfield, Massachusetts: Colonial troops march twenty miles to assault an Indian camp. The colonials lose thirty-eight men and inflict heavy losses on the Indians.

May 30, Hatfield, Massachusetts: Indians stage another attack, setting fire to several buildings and rounding up the town's livestock before a counterattack drives them away.

June 12, Hadley, Massachusetts: Colonists repulse an Indian attack on the settlement, suffering few casualties. While the hostiles are thus engaged, a party of friendly Mohegans raid their camp, killing numerous women and children.

July 3, Dedham, Massachusetts: White settlers and Christian Indians ambush a party of Narragansetts, killing tribal leader Pomham in the engagement.

July 6–15, Bristol County, Massachusetts: A military expedition west of the Taunton River kills or captures numerous Wampanoag in a series of wilderness clashes. Precise Indian casualties are not recorded, although there is a record of twelve Indians killed in one skirmish.

July 11, Taunton, Massachusetts: King Philip's warriors are repulsed in an attack on the settlement.

July 11, Middleborough, Massachusetts: A party of Indians is surrounded and captured by militiamen.

July 15, Bridgewater, Massachusetts: Colonists defeat a party of Indian raiders.

July 27, Boston, Massachusetts: Nipmuck leader Sagamore John surrenders 180 members of his tribe to colonists, ending one phase of the recent Indian conflict. As a sign of good faith, the Nipmucks are required to execute their own sachem, Matoonas, and his son on Boston Common.

August 2, Bristol County, Massachusetts: King Philip narrowly escapes a white raid on his camp. His wife and son are among the Indians captured.

August 12, Mount Hope, Massachusetts: Troops assault King Philip's headquarters at dawn, killing the chief and 130 tribesmen. One white soldier is killed. Without Philip's leadership, Indian raids gradually taper off over the next year.

September, Seekonk, Massachusetts: Surviving Wampanoag raiders harass local settlers by raiding their livestock. The resultant military expedition captures twelve of the raiders, two of whom direct the troops to their camp six miles west of Taunton. A nocturnal surprise attack captures the remaining Indian raiders, ending King Phillip's War.

September 6, Dover, New Hampshire: Colonial authorities treacherously seize 400 Indians who have already signed peace treaties with the government. Several are later hanged in Boston as participants in recent hostilities, and 200 are sold into slavery.

September 13, Boston, Massachusetts: Eight Indians are publicly executed, and three are hanged later the same week.

September 26, Boston, Massachusetts: Four leaders of the Nipmuk tribe are publicly executed on Boston Common.

October 12, Boston, Massachusetts: Two Indian men are executed before cheering crowds.

1677

February, Lincoln County, Maine: A peace conference in Pemaquid between local Indians and British colonists erupts into violence, leaving ten Indians dead and several held prisoner.

June 19, Black Point, Rhode Island: Indians ambush a party of sixty-one British colonists and 200 friendly Indians, killing sixty persons in a brisk engagement.

1678

July, Chama Valley, New Mexico: A combined force of Spaniards and Ute Indians attack the Navajos, killing an unspecified number and taking fifty prisoners. Two female captives are rescued from the tribe. Thirteen horses are seized and large areas of crops are laid to waste.

1680

South Carolina: Settlers employ Shawnee mercenaries to attack, defeat, and enslave members of the Westo tribe.

Illinois: Tribesmen of the Five Nations invade French territory, razing settlements and forts and capturing French canoes and furs along the river routes leading east.

October 10, New Mexico: Pueblos and Apaches launch a war against the Spaniards, killing twenty-one priests and more than 400 colonists. Santa Fe is besieged until October 20, with defenders killing an estimated 300 attackers and executing forty-seven Indian prisoners. Spaniards abandon the city, retreating to Mexico on October 21.

1681

November, New Mexico: Spanish troops launch an abortive campaign to recapture the colony from native Indians, but give up and return to El Paso, Texas, in January 1682.

1683

May, St. Augustine, Florida: A combined force of British and French privateers stage an abortive attack on the city and then continue their campaign with raids against Spanish missions in Georgia.

1684

Illinois: Raiders from the Five Nations launch new attacks against French forts and villages.

1686

August, Beaufort County, South Carolina: Spanish forces destroy the English settlement of Stuart's Town near modern Beaufort.

1687

Virginia: The leader of an aborted slave uprising is betrayed and executed.

New York: French raiders invade Seneca tribal territory south of Lake Ontario, provoking violent reactions from local Indians.

March, Colleton County, South Carolina: A combined force of Spaniards, Indians, and blacks overruns the British settlement in Stewart's Town, pushing eastward to the Edisto River and raiding plantations along the way, abducting slaves and killing the brother of South Carolina's governor.

May 7: King William's War is declared between Britain and France, and its violence soon spreads to the New World. The war continues until September 20, 1697.

1688

Cumberland County, Maine: British incursions on territory claimed by France prompt Frenchmen to send their Indian allies against

British settlers. The violence begins in North Yarmouth with the slaughter of livestock, which initiates a series of wars that will claim an estimated 30,000 British lives by 1775.

1689

Illinois: Members of the Five Nations stage new attacks against French troops and settlers, exacting revenge for the 1687 invasion of Seneca lands in New York.

Cia, New Mexico: Spanish soldiers assault a Pueblo village and kill more than 600 Indians in one afternoon.

Dover, Massachusetts: Twenty-three settlers are killed and twenty-nine are captured when Indians raid the settlement. The attack is made in retribution for the 1676 arrest of 400 Indians in Dover. Surviving prisoners are transported to Canada and sold to the French.

1690

January, Schenectady, New York: Indians, incited and armed by the French governor of Canada, launch the first of many raids against British settlers. Sixty settlers are killed in the attack, and ninety are taken prisoner. Of those who escape on foot, twenty-five lose arms or legs to frostbite on the overland trek to Albany. Other raiding parties strike at Salmon Falls and destroy the settlement of Casco, Maine.

May, Newington, Connecticut: Indian raiders assault the nearby settlement of Fox Point, killing several settlers and taking others prisoner.

July 6, Wheelright's Pond, Connecticut: Colonial troops clash with Indians. Fifteen soldiers are killed and several others wounded.

1691

October–November, Rappahannock County, Virginia: An escaped slave, Mingoe, leads other runaways in raids on plantations for food and weapons over a two-month period. The outcome of the uprising is not recorded.

1692

January 25, York, Maine: A combined force of Frenchmen and Indians raze the settlement, killing seventy-five British settlers and capturing almost as many.

May 10, Salem, Massachusetts: Sarah Osburne dies in prison while on trial for witchcraft. Her death is the first in Salem's outbreak of witch hysteria, which ultimately claims the lives of twenty-one persons and several domestic animals suspected of dealing with the Devil.

June 10, Salem, Massachusetts: Bridget Bishop is hanged as a witch.

June 10, Wells, Maine: French troops with Indian support are repulsed in an attack on the British garrison.

July 19, Salem, Massachusetts: Five women are hanged for witchcraft on Gallows Hill. The condemned include Goody Good, Elizabeth How, Susanna Martin, Rebecca Nurse, and Sarah Wild.

August 19, Salem, Massachusetts: Four men and one woman are hanged for witchcraft. Victims include Rev. George Burroughs, Constable John Willard, George Jacobs, John Proctor, and Martha Carrier.

September 19, Salem, Massachusetts: Suspected warlock Giles Cory is pressed to death by the local sheriff in an effort to make him confess. Cory's only recorded comment during the torture is a defiant call for "more weight."

September 22, Salem, Massachusetts: seven women and one man are hanged in the colony's last public execution for witchcraft. Victims include Samuel Wardwell, Martha Cory, Alice Parker, Mary Esty, Margaret Scott, Mary Parker, Wilmot Redd, and Ann Pudeator (alias "The Hag of Hell").

1693

December, Santa Fe, New Mexico: Spanish troops recapture the city after a two-day battle with Indians. Seventy-two of the Indian prisoners are hanged.

1694

June 17, Dover, New Hampshire: French troops and 250 Indians surprise the British settlement, burning twenty houses and killing or capturing an estimated ninety to one hundred settlers. Emboldened by their victory, the Indian warriors launch further raids as far west as Groton, Connecticut, in the weeks that follow. Others cross the Piscataqua River into York County, Maine, and kill several persons on outlying farms.

June 26, Portsmouth, New Hampshire: Fourteen settlers are killed and four are captured in an Indian raid on homes two miles from town.

July 26, Dover, New Hampshire: Indians ambush settlers returning home from church service. Three are killed, three wounded, and three are taken prisoner.

1695

June, *New Mexico*: Indians launch a new offensive against Spanish colonists, but it is crushed by October.

1696

August 14, Lincoln County, Maine: British troops surrender the fort at Pemaquid to a superior force of French troops and Indians.

1697

June, Exeter, New Hampshire: Indian raiders are repulsed during a surprise attack against the settlement.

July 4, Kittery, Maine: Maj. Frost, a British officer known for his battles with Indians, is ambushed and killed by Indians.

1700

1702

Tallapoosa River, Alabama: Choctaw tribesmen, urged on by French officers, raid settlements of Creek Indians known for their tentative friendship with British settlers.

April, Alabama: Violence erupts when Creek Indians ambush and kill four Frenchmen in the southwestern part of the state. A punitive expedition is launched, with fifty French soldiers leading 1,800 Choctaw and Mobile Indians against the enemy. Sporadic engagements continue through the winter, with a number of Creek braves killed, their women and children captured and sold into slavery. These initial forays broaden into intermittent violence between Creeks and Frenchmen over the next seven years.

May, Florida: With the outbreak of Queen Anne's War, British traders persuade Lower Creek tribesmen to attack Spanish Apalachee settlements in the vicinity of modern Tallahassee. At the same time, Spanish officers organize an expedition of 900 Apalachees to attack British colonists in South Carolina. Forewarned of the attack, friendly Creeks lay an ambush on the Flint River in southwestern Georgia and turn back the enemy force with heavy losses. A joint force of Carolina colonists and Creeks retaliate with an attack on St. Augustine, burning the town but failing to capture the fort.

Fall, St. Augustine, Florida: A British blockade of the harbor compels Spanish occupants of the city to surrender, while troops remain secure behind their nearby fortifications. Public buildings are occupied, looted, vandalized, and burned by the invaders, as the British initiate a siege of the garrison.

December 26, St. Augustine, Florida: British occupation forces set fire to the town and retreat when Spanish reinforcements arrive.

1703

June–July, Maine: Frenchmen and Indians spend six weeks raiding British settlements from Casco to Wells, in the southern part of the state, killing or capturing 130 colonists.

August 17, Hampton, New Hampshire: French-backed Indian raiders loot two British homes, killing five people before they are driven away.

Fall, Cumberland County, Maine: British troops from Casco kill six Indians and capture six more in a clash at Pigwacket.

1704

January, Florida: Fifty British colonists and 1,000 friendly Creeks raid Apalachee missions in the northwestern part of the state, capturing Spanish Ft. St. Lewis and destroying several Apalachee towns. Hundreds of Indians are killed and more than 1,000 are taken prisoner. The missions are decimated, Apalachee survivors are sold as slaves in Carolina or forced to resettle near Savannah, Georgia. Only four British soldiers are killed in the campaign. Similar raids over the next six years enslave an estimated 12,000 Appalachees, Guales, and Timucas.

Spring, Berwick, Maine: Indians kill two white men in successive days of raiding isolated homes, and capture a woman and boy as hostages. Other raiders strike along Maine's Cocheco River, wounding a British officer's maid.

Summer, Maine: British expeditions destroy the Indian villages of Minas and Chiegnecto and attack combined French and Indian garrisons in Penobscot and Passamaquody. One strike force ranges as far south as Port Royal, South Carolina. Indians retaliate with lethal raids around Dover, New Hampshire, and in neighboring Rockingham County.

1705

Texas: Spanish troops mount three campaigns against the Navajo during the year.

March, New Mexico: Navajo raiders attack the pueblos of San Juan, Santa Clara, and San Ildefonso. Spanish troops pursue the raiders, but in vain.

August 11–14, Dinetah, New Mexico: Spanish troops fight several engagements with the Navajo in the vicinity of a tribal stronghold.

Navajo ranchos are burned by the troops, and thirty-nine Indians are reported dead, with several women and children taken prisoner.

1706

Wayne County, Michigan: Ottawa warriors slaughter Miami and Huron tribesmen along the Detroit River.

April, Rockingham County, New Hampshire: Indians raid a rural homestead, killing eight people and wounding two. A family of eight is attacked as the warriors retreat, four of whom are killed while the other four escape.

July, New England: French-backed Indian warriors kill British livestock in Kingston, New Hampshire, and Amesbury, Massachusetts. Near Exeter, New Hampshire, an Indian ambush kills three colonial soldiers, with one wounded and three taken prisoner. Two more whites are attacked in Dover, Maine, with one killed and one captured. British authorities estimate that the government is spending 1,000 pounds for each Indian killed in battle.

August, Pueblo, Colorado: Apaches defeat a party of French explorers and Pawnee Indians, killing two Frenchmen and a Pawnee chief.

1707

Pensacola, Florida: Tallapoose tribesmen burn the town and launch attacks against the local Spanish fort, failing to capture the garrison.

Georgia: Carolina colonists induce friendly Catawbas to attack trade-dependent Savannah Indians, thus preventing a planned exodus of the Savannahs to Maryland and Pennsylvania.

Winter, Black Point, Rhode Island: British soldiers kill four Indians and capture one squaw, who leads them to another camp of eighteen Indians. Staging a dawn attack on the camp, the British kill seventeen and take one prisoner.

July, Port Royal, South Carolina: British forces attack the French garrison, but disease and harassment by Indians combine to break the siege in late August. The British retreat with sixteen men dead and an equal number wounded.

Summer, New Hampshire: While a British expedition makes ineffectual attacks on Port Royal, South Carolina, French-backed Indians kill settlers near the settlements of Dover, Exeter, and Kingston. Raids continue through September, with the worst raid claiming seven lives in Rockingham County.

1708

Long Island, New York: A small band of slaves revolts at Newton, leaving seven whites dead. Four slaves, including an Indian and a woman, are sentenced to death; the three men are hanged, while the black woman is burned alive.

Wayne County, Michigan: Miami warriors kill three French missionaries, prompting a reprisal by French troops against their principal settlement. Driven from the area, they resettle in Ohio and invite trade with competing English colonists to spite the French.

Georgia: Carolina settlers lead Catawba Indians on new raids against the outnumbered Savannah Indians, justifying their attacks as a method of "thinning the barbarous Indian natives."

Spring, Haverhill, Massachusetts: A French-Indian thrust is repulsed by colonial troops, blunting the year's New England offensive.

October, Pensacola, Florida: Tallapoose Indians renew their assault on the Spanish fort, killing several Spaniards and numerous local Indians before being driven away.

1709

February, Santa Clara, New Mexico: Navajos mount raids around the Pueblo, provoking the first of six retaliatory campaigns by Spaniards in this year.

March, Virginia: Authorities uncover plans of a slave revolt in the counties of Surry, James City, and Isle of Wight. Two rebel leaders remain at large until their capture and execution in June 1710.

Spring, New England: French-backed Indians capture two white prisoners in Exeter, New Hampshire, and then move on to kill a white man nearby.

May, Mobile, Alabama: Creek Indians attack the French settlement, inflicting several casualties before a counterattack turns them back.

June 8, Jemez, New Mexico: A raid by Navajos leads to armed retaliation by Spanish troops.

1710

September, Exeter, New Hampshire: Indians kill two men and capture a third. On the same day, another war party kills two men and captures two in Kingston. The summer's final victim is ambushed and slain in Cocheco, Maine, after a church service. Colonial forces pursue the raiders, killing five Indians in a clash on the Saco River.

1711

Alabama: British colonists from Carolina lead 1,300 Lower Creek Indians into battle against the French-allied Choctaw tribes.

Spring, Rockingham County, New Hampshire: Small Indian war parties resume their frontier attacks around Cocheco, killing several settlers.

April, New England: French-backed Indians murder British settlers near Dover, Exeter, and Kingston, New Hampshire.

May, South Carolina: A black slave named Sebastian leads other blacks in a series of armed raids against whites. The revolt ends when Sebastian is tracked down and killed by an Indian hunter.

July, Dover, New Hampshire: An Indian war party is routed near the settlement, where an ambush has been prepared for British colonists. While militiamen pursue the enemy, other raiders abduct and decapitate two white children near town.

December, North Carolina: The Tuscarora Indian War begins with a massacre of white settlers by Indians, claiming 137 lives in the vicinity of Roanoke.

1712

New Hampshire: French-backed Indians increase their raids against British colonists, ceasing only when the treaty of Utrecht ends Queen Anne's War.

January, North Carolina: Settlers and friendly Indians launch an expedition against the Tuscarora tribe, defeating one band and capturing thirty, to be used as slaves. The settlers' Indian allies then abscond with all but one of the prisoners, leaving only a girl behind.

March, North Carolina: Thirty-three white settlers and 900 friendly Indians storm the Tuscarora stronghold at Nooherooka, slaughtering several hundred Tuscaroras in the battle. One hundred sixty-six of the prisoners, deemed useless as slaves, are executed, and 392 captives are transported to the Charleston, South Carolina, slave markets. Colonial losses in the battle include twenty-two white settlers and thirty-five friendly Indians killed or wounded. Historians estimate that the brief war killed 1,000 Tuscaroras and enslaved some 700, the survivors driven north, away from their ancestral lands.

April 9, New York City: An estimated thirty slaves, including two Indians, launch an ill-fated revolt, setting fire to a downtown building and lying in wait for settlers who respond to the alarm. Nine settlers are killed and six others are wounded before the uprising is crushed. One of the rebels commits suicide after killing his wife, but twenty-seven of the rebels are captured and sentenced to die. Authorities pardon six of the condemned, including a pregnant black woman, but the remaining twenty-one die on schedule.

1713

Spring, Goose Creek, South Carolina: A slave revolt is betrayed and crushed in the planning stage.

1714

March, Jemez, New Mexico: Navajo raiders strike at the pueblo, killing one of its leading citizens. Spanish troops retaliate in force, killing thirty Navajos and capturing seven, as well as gaining supplies of corn and livestock.

1715

Mississippi: Natchez Indians murder four Frenchmen in retaliation for the mistreatment they have suffered at the hands of traders. French troops retaliate in force to crush Indian resistance.

April 15, Pocataligo, South Carolina: Yamasee Indians, encouraged by members of the related Creek tribe, launch their war against British settlers with an attack that claims ninety lives. The Yamasee war will continue through November 1717.

May, Salkehatchie, South Carolina: Colonial troops defeat a combined force of Yamasee and Shawnee warriors.

June, South Carolina: Creek Indians openly join the Yamasee war effort, attacking British traders in their frontier settlements through the fall.

August, New Mexico: Spaniards and Pueblo Indians launch a campaign against native Apaches, but they fail to locate any targets.

August, Goose Creek, South Carolina: A French-backed invasion force of Creek and Apalachee warriors is routed in a fierce battle with British colonists. A short time later, the final defeat of the Yamasee at Stone Ferry leaves the Creeks to carry on alone against superior forces.

1716

January, Georgia: The Creek war effort is broken when British colonists join forces with Cherokee Indians on the Ocmulgee River, forcing hostile Creeks back to the Chattahoochee region. Several Creeks serving as ambassadors, dispatched in preparation for a planned surprise attack, are taken prisoner and executed by the Cherokees.

October, Jemez, New Mexico: Spanish troops launch another punitive campaign against the Navajos.

1718

New Orleans, Louisiana: An incipient slave rebellion is exposed. The leader, Samba, and seven others are broken on the wheel as punishment. A black woman, who betrayed the plot in a fit of anger, is hanged.

1719

August 14, Nebraska: Pawnee raiders armed by the French attack a party of Spanish explorers and Pueblo Indians, killing thirty Spaniards and eleven Pueblos.

1720

June, Charleston, South Carolina: Two white settlers and a young slave are killed as black rebels try to seize the town. Fourteen conspirators are captured in Georgia while en route to sanctuary in Spanish Florida and they are returned to South Carolina for trial. Six of them are convicted and sentenced to die, but three escape before the scheduled execution.

1721

May, South Carolina: British agents negotiate a treaty with Creek Indians, breaking the Creek-Yamasee alliance and inducing the Creeks to scalp several Yamasee and deliver their scalps to Charleston for a reward.

Winter, Norridgewock, Connecticut: A British expedition fails in its attempt to capture Ralle, a French Jesuit advisor to local tribesmen, at his home. The raiders seize correspondence proving Ralle's complicity with French Canadian officials in a plot to murder British colonists.

1722

Mississippi: New fighting erupts between Natchez Indians and French settlers. Governor Bienville burns three Natchez villages, demanding that the tribal emperor, Tattooed Serpent, deliver the head of a minor chieftain, and thereby violating a Natchez custom that exempts all chiefs from the death penalty.

Summer, New England: Indians retaliate for the attempt to seize Ralle by launching concerted raids against British settlements. Nine white families are taken prisoner in Merrymeeting Lake, New Hampshire, and the town of Brunswick, Maine, is destroyed. An attack on Ft. George, Maine, is repulsed by colonial troops.

August 16, Massachusetts: The colonial government authorizes payment of a bounty for Indian scalps. Claimants include Capt. John Lowell and his men seeking rewards for the scalps of ten Indians killed while asleep.

November 2, Virginia: Three rebel slaves, convicted of plotting to kill whites in a tri-county area, are sentenced to three years in prison or sale outside the colony.

1723

New Hampshire: Indian raiders kill three and capture at least five in the southeastern corner of the state.

Charleston, South Carolina: A vigilante posse led by Justice Symmons storms the fortified commune erected near town by a "free love" cult. Symmons is killed by a gunshot in the second charge before the cultists are overpowered and disarmed. Leader Christian George, a religious fanatic from Switzerland, is convicted of murder and hanged with two of his disciples.

May 17, Virginia: The House of Burgesses sentences seven slaves to sale outside the colony, following abortive uprisings in Middlesex and Gloucester Counties.

July 4, Boston, Massachusetts: A black man is executed for setting fire to a home with the white family sleeping inside. The case caps a two-year string of arson incidents, popularly blamed on slaves.

October, New Haven, Connecticut: A yearlong string of arson incidents culminates in the arrest and confession of a black suspect. The defendant's penalty is not recorded.

1724

Spring, Rockingham County, New Hampshire: Indian raiders kill six whites and capture eight others near Kingston and Londonderry. One Indian is killed and two wounded in a clash with the militia. Prisoners are sold to the French, prompting a British retaliatory raid against Norridgewock, Maine, where the Jesuit Ralle and eighty Indians are killed.

June, South Carolina: Colonial authorities launch a trade embargo against the Creek tribes in an effort to get stronger action from the Creeks against Yamasee hostiles. Tallapoose tribesmen deliver Yamasee scalps to Charleston, and Apalachee settlements in Florida are broken up by friendly Indians. Upper Creeks join Cussita Indians in war against the Yamasees, but Lower Creeks remain stubbornly neutral, edging toward a tribal civil war.

Summer, Alabama: Yamasee warriors kill Ouletta, the pro-British son of Brim, a Lower Creek chieftain. A short time later, Tallappose raiders attack a trading post in Toogaloo, wounding a British trader and carrying off goods and three black slaves.

Summer, New Hampshire: Frontier raiding by Indians continues, with three settlers killed in Dunstable and Kingston. The ambush of a militia company results in one Indian being killed and four wounded. The rest are driven off. Two Indians are killed at a camp on Lake Winnipesaukee.

August 2, Coweta County, Georgia: Creek Chief Brim, enraged by the recent death of his son, accepts fifty Cherokee scalps while ordering new raids against the Yamasee.

1725

Wakefield, New Hampshire: Colonial troops surprise a sleeping camp of warriors at Lovell Lake, killing all ten braves. Emboldened by their victory, the raiders blunder into an Indian ambush at Pigwacket, Maine, losing their commander and seven other men, with sixteen wounded.

1726

McIntosh County, Georgia: Indian raids, endemic disease, and a disastrous fire compel British troops to abandon Ft. King George. They retreat to Port Royal.

March, Georgia: Five hundred Cherokees and Chickasaws bearing British colors march into Lower Creek territory. Forty Cussita braves ambush the army and kill sixty warriors, capturing the British flag.

1727

July, Wheeler County, Georgia: A Yamasee-Creek war party raids a trading post at the fork of the Altamaha River, killing six and capturing several others.

Fall, Pon Pon, South Carolina: A Yamasee raid on the settlement kills several colonists.

1728

Savannah, Georgia: Rebel slaves plot to kill all of the town's white citizens, but they fall out in an argument over methods, and a white posse scatters them with gunfire.

February, St. Augustine, Florida: A combined force of South Carolina colonists and friendly Indians destroy Yamasee Indian settlements within sight of the Spanish garrison.

1729

Mississippi: French settlers demand new land cessions from Natchez Indians without compensation, including the site of a major Natchez Indian village. Tribesmen respond with a new offensive, in an attempt to drive all Frenchmen from the area.

June, Blue Ridge Mountains, Virginia: A settlement of armed runaway slaves is raided by white settlers, who seize their weapons and return them to bondage.

November 28, Ft. Rosalie, Louisiana: Natchez Indians attack and destroy the French fortress, killing several hundred Frenchmen and capturing an equal number of women, blacks, and enslaved Indians. Further depradations are recorded along the lower Mississippi, with British colonists blamed as the instigators.

1730

Louisiana-Mississippi: French troops and friendly Choctaws retaliate against the Natchez Indians in force, killing more than 1,000 and burning many of their prisoners at the stake. Four hundred of the captured Natchez Indians are sold as slaves in Santo Domingo.

Summer, Williamsburg, Virginia: Several slaves are sentenced to "severe whipping" after they hold meetings to discuss their possible freedom. Six weeks later four abolitionist spokesmen are executed, as the illicit meetings continue. Rumors of impending slave revolts in Norfolk and Princess Anne Counties result in a government order requiring all white men to carry weapons to church.

Summer, New Orleans, Louisiana: Nine rebel slaves are arrested and tortured with burning matches for information on rumored uprisings. One prisoner confesses, whereupon eight men are broken on the wheel and one woman is hanged.

August, Wisconsin: French troops and friendly Indians attack the Fox Indians, driving survivors to the southeast. The Fox make their last stand a few miles south of Lake Michigan.

August 15, Charleston, South Carolina: A slave revolt is betrayed to authorities and crushed on the scheduled day of the uprising.

1730–1734

Georgia: Creeks wage sporadic war against the Cherokee Indians and raid Yuchi settlements along the Savannah River. In 1733, the murder of two British traders on the Creek Trail leads to a brief suspension of trade, but relations are soon normalized, with the murders blamed on Yuchi or Yamasee tribesmen.

1731

At Sea: Black captives revolt and massacre the crew of a ship returning to Rhode Island from the Guinea coast.

1732

New Orleans, Louisiana: Authorities crush a plot involving slaves and Natchez Indians. Four male conspirators are broken on the wheel and one woman is hanged; their severed heads are mounted on poles at the city limits.

At Sea: Capt. John Majors, of Portsmouth, New Hampshire, is killed by mutinous slaves, his crew and cargo seized.

1734

Burlington, Pennsylvania: In the wake of a failed slave revolt, two blacks are hanged, two have their ears severed, and twenty-five are flogged.

Summersville, New Jersey: A slave uprising is betrayed by a white "friend," who informs the authorities.

Georgia: Yamasee raiders from Florida attack a hunting party from the Creek tribe, killing the brother of headman Umpechy.

March, South Carolina: Rewards are paid to a white servant and several slaves who captured and killed the leader of a local slave outlaw gang.

1735

March, Georgia: British emissaries encourage Licka, headman of the Lower Creeks, to seek revenge against the Spaniards for killing his brother and drinking wine from the dead man's skull. Licka leads a war party into Florida, killing one Spaniard and several Yamasee tribesmen.

1736

Mississippi: Chickasaw warriors repulse—and several times destroy—large French military expeditions sent against them. French officers try a new tack over the next three years by inciting friendly Choctaws to make war against the pro-British Chickasaws.

1737

Eufala, Alabama: Creek Indians complain to the authorities that a British trader deliberately killed the tribe's cattle.

February, Georgia: Pro-British Creeks massacre a party of Spaniards and Yamasee south of the Altamah River and transport their horses to Savannah for sale.

1738

Spring, Prince Georges County, Maryland: Several imprisoned slaves escape from jail, arm themselves, and launch a localized guerilla campaign against white settlers.

1739

Mississippi River: Chickasaw attacks on French river convoys threaten communications between New Orleans and Illinois, forcing the French to open peace negotiations.

January, South Carolina: A planned slave revolt is exposed by authorities and prevented.

January, Prince Georges County, Maryland: An incipient revolt by 200 slaves is betrayed, and the leader executed.

January, Duval County, Florida: British troops and Indians attack the Spanish post at St. Francis, in the area of modern Jacksonville.

February, Purysburgh, South Carolina: Two white planters are accused of fostering a slave uprising.

March, South Carolina: Two white men lead a group of rebel slaves in attacks against their masters. One person is killed and three others wounded before the raiders are driven away by gunfire from neighbors. None of the conspirators is captured.

September 9, Stono, South Carolina: A slave named Cato leads twenty blacks in a raid on the local arsenal, where they kill two guards and arm themselves for a march to Spanish Florida. Their numbers swell to seventy-five or eighty along the way. They burn several buildings and kill twenty-three whites before they meet the militia, south of town. Fourteen rebels are killed in the initial clash, and twenty more are hunted and shot over the next ten days. An estimated forty blacks are captured and executed for their part in the uprising.

Fall, Alabama: The murder of a Choctaw headman leads to scalping raids against the Creeks.

Winter, Amelia Island, Florida: A combined force of Spaniards and Indians attack a British outpost, killing two Highlanders and escaping with their severed heads.

1739–1741

Atlantic Coast: Spanish privateers capture at least 300 British ships in a series of raids between New England and the Caribbean.

1740

Stone River, South Carolina: An incipient slave revolt is crushed by whites.

Berkeley County, South Carolina: Authorities expose and disrupt a scheduled slave uprising.

January, St. Johns County, Florida: British colonists and Indians capture the Spanish outposts of San Francisco de Pupo and Picolata, burning the latter settlement and retreating into Georgia with several prisoners.

May, St. Johns County, Florida: A combined force of British troops and friendly Indians again capture the Spanish settlements at Picolata and San Francisco de Pupo, moving on to occupy Ft. Mosa, north of St. Augustine. At Ft. Mosa, Spaniards stage a nocturnal counterstrike, decimating the British detachment and killing several Yamacraw tribesmen. British forces lay siege to St. Augustine, then end the effort in July.

May 3, Charleston, South Carolina: War is declared against Spain.

June, Charleston, South Carolina: A revolt by 150 slaves is betrayed and crushed in the planning stage before they can acquire weapons. Fifty blacks are arrested, condemned, and publicly hanged in groups of ten a day.

1741

February 28, New York City: Unidentified blacks are blamed for a robbery and for various arson fires over the following months. Hysteria over the burnings will prompt the arrest of 150 blacks and twenty-five whites, including seventeen soldiers. Four whites and eighteen slaves are eventually hanged. Thirteen blacks are burned alive and seventy are banished from the colony. The seven blacks indicted for arson are never captured.

May 5, Hackensack, New Jersey: Two slaves are burned alive for allegedly participating in a month-long series of arson incidents.

July, Charleston, South Carolina: A female slave is condemned and executed for arson.

August, Charleston, South Carolina: A black man is burned at the stake for arson.

December, Charleston, South Carolina: Two slaves are convicted of setting fire to the town's powder magazine.

1742

July 4, St. Simons Island, Georgia: Spanish warships launch their attack on the British garrison at Ft. Frederica with a four-hour bombardment. Creek warriors aid the British colonists in defense of the island as the siege proceeds. The tide of battle turns on July 7, when a combined force of Highlanders and Indians stages a brisk counterattack, with Creek headman Tooanabey personally killing the Spanish commander.

Fall, Wayne County, Georgia: Spanish-backed Yamasee Indians raid the trading post at Mt. Venture, on the Altamaha River, killing several Creeks and destroying the outpost. Creeks, wanting to avenge the killings, sign on for raids against St. Augustine in 1743.

Winter, Alabama: British traders persuade Creek tribesmen to murder two Choctaw hunters, deepening tribal rifts and weakening the French-Choctaw military alliance.

1743

St. Johns County, Florida: Creek headman Tooanabey is killed when his warriors attack a party of Spanish cavalry. He is the only Indian casualty of the battle.

1744

February, St. Simons Island, Georgia: Spanish and Indians raid the British garrison, capturing several prisoners. U.S. troops pursue the invaders, overtaking and destroying the war party on the St. John River, in Duval County, Florida.

1747

Alabama: Upper Creeks warring with the Cherokees buy or steal ammunition from both French and British traders. Meanwhile, Choctaw war parties trap the French in Mobile.

June, Wayne County, Michigan: Hurons ambush and kill five French traders, who were en route to Detroit.

June, Emmet County, Michigan: Inspired by pro-English Iroquois, Ottawa and Chippewa raiders kill several Frenchmen, threatening Ft. Michilimackinac.

1748

The Southwest: Apaches launch a war of attrition against Spanish colonists, killing an estimated 1,000 soldiers and settlers by 1770.

January, South Carolina: A "horrid insurrection" by slaves is discovered and crushed.

August, Florida: Creek flirtations with the Spanish end when British spokesmen persuade a party of Creeks to kill Chickillalee, a Yamasee chief on the Spanish payroll. Spaniards and Yamasee raiders retaliate by killing fifteen Creeks, provoking several Lower Creek tribes to launch new attacks in Florida.

1749

May, Arkansas River, Arkansas: Creek and Chickasaw raiders join forces to attack a French trading post, killing several whites and taking a number of prisoners.

Fall, Charleston, South Carolina: Creeks suspect British duplicity when several of their leaders die from disease after a strategy meeting with British leaders. French agitators insist that the deaths are deliberate murder.

Winter, Alabama-Georgia: New hostilities erupt between the Creek and Cherokee. Lower Creeks suspect a conspiracy between Upper Creeks and Cherokees in the murder of several hunters and the abductions of some of their families. Upper Creeks respond by killing fourteen Lower Cherokees in the neutral territory of eastern Alabama. In reprisal, Lower Creeks assemble a force of 500 men and move westward, killing numerous Cherokees and burning two settlements.

1750

Perth Amboy, New Jersey: Two blacks are burned alive after their conviction for murder.

1751

Spring, Georgia: New violence flares in the Creek-Cherokee war, as Cherokee and Seneca raiders kill nine warriors in the Lower Creek towns. The victors pursue fleeing survivors to Clement's trading post on the Oconee River, killing two white men and several Chickasaws. The latest outbreak leads to an embargo on British trade with the Cherokees until new accords are reached in the fall.

1752

April, Charleston, South Carolina: A party of Cherokees are ambushed and massacred by Creek tribesmen outside of town. In August, the leader of the raid, Acorn Whistler, is assassinated by other Creeks in an effort to preserve peace with British colonists, who had forbidden fighting in the area. Acorn Whistler's killer is then murdered to insure his silence.

June, Miami County, Ohio: Two hundred and forty Frenchmen and Ottawa warriors assault the main Miami settlement at Pickawillany, near the site of modern Piqua, capturing five English traders and burning the town. La Demoiselle, the Miami chief, is boiled and eaten by his Ottawa enemies.

1754

Charleston, South Carolina: Two female slaves are burned alive as punishment for setting fire to plantation outbuildings.

July 4, Fayette County, Pennsylvania: A combined force of French troops and Indians assault Ft. Necessity, with 200 attackers and fifty-eight defenders killed or wounded before the garrison surrenders. Indians harass the retreating British column en route to Monongahela, killing or wounding a "considerable number" of the survivors in repeated attacks.

1755

Charleston, South Carolina: Planter John Cadman is killed by two slaves, who believe that his will provides for their freedom. On conviction, one of the blacks is hanged, the other burned alive.

July 9, Allegheny County, Pennsylvania: A force of 200 Frenchmen and 600 Indians engage 1,300 British troops in a battle near the Monongahela River. Four hundred fifty-six British are killed, another 421 wounded, against estimated French losses of sixty-five dead and injured. British officers report at least twenty men and women captured by the enemy, most of whom were tortured to death and cannibalized in the ensuing victory celebration.

September 8, Essex County, New York: British troops, with 300 friendly Indians in support, attack a French military camp, inflicting 700 casualties before the enemy escapes to nearby Ft. Ticonderoga.

1755–1763

The South: Cherokee wage sporadic war against white settlers in the South.

1756

Pennsylvania: The colonial government responds to recent Indian raids by approving a bounty on Indian scalps, in addition to a bonus of $700 each for the heads of two Delaware chiefs.

April, Mobile County, Alabama: Creeks murder two Cherokees in the woods near Mobile, inspired by British traders who hope to break the pro-French Creek-Cherokee alliance.

May 17: King George II declares war on France, beginning the French and Indian War, which lasts until February 10, 1763.

August 14, Oswego County, New York: British troops and their Indian allies capture the French garrison at Ft. Oswego after a siege of several days. Many of the 1,500 defenders are slaughtered by pro-British Indians after their surrender.

1757

January, Alabama: Choctaw warriors, pursuing a French-inspired vendetta against the Chickasaw tribe, accidentally kill two Shawnee braves, believing them to be Chickasaws.

August, Florida: A Creek war party attacks Spanish plantations, capturing four Spaniards and killing a number of friendly Indians. Spanish cattle are also slaughtered during the raids, and a Creek headman dies in one attack.

August 9–15, Warren County, New York: A combined force of French troops and friendly Indians besieges Ft. William Henry, leading to the garrison's surrender on August 15. The defenders are promised safe passage to nearby Ft. Edward, but Indian troops are unleashed as soon as the British emerge, with at least 1,500 men killed or carried into captivity. A small number of pro-British Indians are slowly tortured to death by their captors.

1758

July 6, Essex County, New York: British troops advancing on Ft. Ticonderoga are ambushed by pro-French Indians, the British commanding officer and numerous soldiers are slain as the skirmish becomes a rout.

July 8, Essex County, New York: British troops attack a combined force of French Canadians and Indians near Ft. Ticonderoga. The attackers are turned back, with 2,000 men killed or captured.

August 27, Oswego County, New York: British attackers capture Ft. Oswego after the French garrison's Indian allies desert their posts.

September 14, Ft. Duquesne, Pennsylvania: French and Indian defenders kill 270 British soldiers, wound forty-two, and capture 100 on the site of modern Pittsburgh.

November 24, Ft. Duquesne, Pennsylvania: French and Indian forces burn their garrison in the face of a massive British advance, retreating up the Allegheny River to Ft. Machault, at the site of modern Franklin, Pennsylvania. British troops erect Ft. Pitt on the site of old Ft. Duquesne.

1759

South Carolina: Authorities record a "serious attempt at revolt" by slaves.

July 7, Niagara County, New York: British troops, supported by colonial irregulars and 900 Iroquois warriors, lay siege to the French garrison at Ft. Niagara.

July 24, Niagara County, New York: British and Iroquois forces ambush a French relief party bound for Ft. Niagara, killing an estimated 500 men and capturing 120.

September, Virginia: Settlers ambush a party of Cherokee horse thieves, killing at least a dozen. Cherokee respond with new raids along the frontier, including clashes that kill several soldiers near Ft. Loudon, Tennessee.

September 28, Elmore County, Alabama: While meeting with Creek leaders at the tribal settlement of Tuckabatchee, British spokesman Edmund Atkin is attacked and wounded with a tomahawk.

November–December, South Carolina: A colonial campaign against local Cherokee ends with a hastily drawn treaty on December 26.

1760

January, Pickens County, South Carolina: Angered by colonists holding Cherokee prisoners at Ft. Prince George, the Indians once more launch raids against British settlers.

February, Georgia: British authorities announce generous rewards for Cherokee scalps. British guides lead Creek raiding parties against the Lower Cherokee towns, ambushing and scalping three Cherokees in Oconee County, South Carolina, and carrying the trophies back to Savannah.

February 16, Pickens County, South Carolina: Soldiers massacre Cherokee hostages imprisoned at Ft. Prince George.

April, Georgia: A British military expedition raids the Lower Cherokee towns, killing sixty Indians and capturing forty others before marching to aid Ft. Prince George in neighboring South Carolina.

May 16, Clay County, Alabama: Eleven British traders and two black servants are killed when Creek raiders burn several frontier trading posts. Several others escape with help from their Indian wives.

June 27, South Carolina: Members of a British expedition against the Cherokees are ambushed and driven back toward Charleston.

August 8, Macon County, North Carolina: The besieged British garrison at Ft. Loudon is starved into surrender. On August 9,

Cherokee warriors massacre the defenders, sparing only Capt. John Stuart.

September, Augusta, Georgia: Creek war chief Handsome Fellow delivers a Cherokee scalp to British officers as a gesture of good will.

October, Alabama: Seeking to disrupt trade between British colonists and Choctaws, Frenchmen persuade a Choctaw warrior to murder a British trader. Creeks and pro-British Choctaws retaliate by killing a Frenchman near Ft. Tombigbee.

November 29, Wayne County, Michigan: British troops, supported by an estimated 700 Iroquois, occupy the French garrison at Ft. Detroit.

1761

South Carolina: Widespread reports of slaves poisoning their masters prompt new legal crackdowns on blacks.

February, Alabama: French-inspired Creeks murder a Choctaw peace emissary. Choctaws respond by killing two Creeks before a settlement is arranged.

March 20, Charleston, South Carolina: Colonial troops, reinforced by British soldiers from New York, launch a new expedition against hostile Cherokees.

June 7, Georgia: Troops from Ft. Prince George, South Carolina, launch a month-long campaign against Cherokee settlements in the northern part of the state. On June 11, the column suffers sixty casualties in a clash with Indians, sinking their dead in a river to prevent later scalping and mutilation. Before returning to Carolina, the soldiers burn the Indian town of Echota, in Gordon County.

July, Florida: Creek warriors skirmish with Spaniards near Pensacola and St. Augustine, touching off a war that claims nine Creek lives by January 1762.

December 27, Edgefield County, South Carolina: Creek warriors attack and kill fourteen whites, bringing the total number of settlers slain since May 1760 to thirty.

1762

March, Florida Keys: Creek warriors attack a Spanish ship traveling from Cuba to St. Augustine, seizing one Spaniard and holding him for a ransom of 10,000 pounds. Other war parties drive pro-Spanish Indians inland, occupying the Florida coast to prey on passing ships.

April 10, Charleston, South Carolina: A new war against Spain is declared.

May, Florida: Creeks capture two Dutch schooners, slaughtering the crews and looting the cargos of rum, ammunition, and other goods. British raids against Spanish and Indians wreak such havoc that whole tribes are evacuated to Cuba.

June, Atlantic Coast: Spanish and French privateers based in St. Augustine, Florida, attack British ships as far north as Newfoundland.

1763

January, Florida: Creek and Yuchi harass Spanish forces, carrying trophy scalps to colonial officers in Savannah, Georgia. Before the end of the year, British forces have taken possession of Florida, lowering the Spanish flag at St. Augustine for the first time in two centuries.

May, Tallapoosa River, Alabama: Creek warriors kill John Spencer, a British trader.

May 6, Saginaw County, Michigan: Pontiac's rebellion begins as Chippewa raiders ambush a British party in Saginaw Valley, killing four soldiers, capturing six and also capturing a friendly Pawnee scout. One of the dead, Lt. Charles Robertson, is devoured by the victors, with skin from one arm used to make a tobacco pouch.

May 9, Wayne County, Michigan: Ottawa tribesmen launch raids around Ft. Detroit, killing nine whites and capturing five and seizing British livestock on Belle Isle.

May 12, Wayne County, Michigan: Indian raiders attack Ft. Detroit, wounding three whites while suffering losses of four warriors killed, with nine injured. Further south, on the lower Detroit River, Huron tribesmen kill two white traders carrying a quantity of rum and seventeen barrels of gunpowder. After one week of war, white casualties stand at fifteen dead, five wounded, and fifteen captured. The Indian siege of Ft. Detroit will continue through the fall.

May 16, Erie County, Ohio: Ft. Sandusky is overrun in a surprise attack by Huron and Ottawa warriors. Fourteen soldiers and several resident merchants die in the raid, with one white man taken prisoner. Hostage Christopher Pauli is forced to run the gauntlet before a widowed squaw adopts him as her second husband. He escapes to Ft. Detroit on July 3.

May 23, Paulding County, Ohio: Indian raiders, en route to attack Ft. Miamis in Indiana, capture an English trader named Welch.

May 25, Niles, Michigan: Potawatomi Indians capture Ft. St. Joseph, killing all but six of the British soldiers inside and looting the garrison.

May 25, Allen County, Indiana: Indians capture three soldiers from Ft. Miamis, near the site of modern Ft. Wayne.

May 27, Ft. Wayne, Indiana: A soldier is lured outside Ft. Miamis by a squaw and killed by Indian snipers. Indians capture a sergeant who comes to investigate the gunfire, and the rest of the garrison—eleven men—surrender on demand from the surrounding warriors. Only four of the prisoners survive their trek to Detroit, where they are to be displayed before Chief Pontiac.

May 28, Pelee Point, Ontario: A party of ninety-six Queen's Rangers are ambushed by Indians. Six members of the group escape by canoe, eluding pursuit after a mile-long chase.

May 28, West Newton, Pennsylvania: Delaware and Mingo tribesmen massacre five whites, including two women and a child.

May 29, Macomb County, Michigan: Indians capture two boats containing nineteen soldiers and one white woman on the St. Clair River.

May 29, Ft. Pitt, Pennsylvania: Delaware raiders kill two soldiers at a saw mill outside the stockade, laying siege to the fort.

May 30, Niagara County, New York: Warriors parade their prisoners from a May 28 engagement past Ft. Niagara in canoes. Four soldiers dive into the river in an escape attempt; one is pulled under water and drowned by Indians, the other three disappear into the woods. The remaining prisoners are tortured to death near the fort in a three-day victory celebration.

May 31, Lafayette, Indiana: Lt. Edward Jenkins is lured from Ft. Ouiatenon for "peace talks" with Indians and is taken prisoner. Under threat of death, he orders his twenty-man command to surrender. All are eventually released.

June, Clay County, Alabama: Creek tribesmen kill a British trader named Pierce.

June 2, Emmet County, Michigan: Chippewas capture Ft. Michilimackinac, killing twenty soldiers and one English trader, mutilating some of the victims while they are still alive.

June 2, Westmoreland County, Pennsylvania: Indian snipers fire on Ft. Ligonier, inflicting no casualties.

June 4, Ft. Michilimackinac, Michigan: Jealous Ottawa tribesmen invade the garrison, seizing eighteen British survivors from the Chippewa raiders. Two days of negotiation between the tribes results in a division of spoils and hostages.

June 7, Bedford County, Pennsylvania: Indians launch raids around Ft. Bedford.

June 8, Cross Village, Michigan: Chippewas kill four of their prisoners from Ft. Michilimackinac, devouring one of the dead soldiers.

June 16, Franklin, Pennsylvania: Seneca tribesmen attack Ft. Venango, annihilating the garrison and slowly roasting the commanding officer.

June 18, Waterford, Pennsylvania: Senecas assault Ft. Le Boeuf with flaming arrows. Soldiers hold off the attackers until nightfall, then escape into the woods.

June 19–20, Erie, Pennsylvania: A combined force of Seneca, Ottawa, Huron, and Chippewa warriors erect breastworks on two hills overlooking Ft. Presque Isle, peppering the garrison with gunfire and flaming arrows over the next two days. The garrison surrenders on June 22, with a promise of safe passage, but the occupants are taken prisoner instead, and divided among several tribes. Most of the hostages are never seen again.

June 21, Fighting Island, Michigan: Fourteen Indians are killed and many others wounded during a night assault on the sloop *Michigan*, near the mouth of the Detroit River.

July, Greenbrier County, West Virginia: Shawnee raiders pose as friendly Indians to infiltrate the rural homes of several white families, afterwards killing the men in each house before taking the women and children prisoner.

July 4, Ft. Detroit, Michigan: British troops attack nearby entrenchments held by Indians and French supporters. Two Indians are killed during the inconclusive fight, one of them scalped by a British soldier who was once held captive by Indians.

July 6, Wayne County, Michigan: The sloop *Michigan* shells Chief Pontiac's camp, upriver from Ft. Detroit.

July 7–16, New York City: Gen. Jeffrey Amherst writes to Col. Henry Bouquet: "Could it not be contrived to send the small pox among the disaffected tribes of Indians? We must on this occasion use every stratagem in our power to reduce them." Bouquet replies that he will try to spread an epidemic among the hostile Indians warriors with infected blankets. On July 16, Amherst orders Bouquet to proceed, further urging him "to try every other method that can serve to extirpate this execrable race."

July 9, Ft. Detroit, Michigan: Huron warriors kill two of their captives from Ft. Presque Isle. Pontiac's men fail in a nocturnal attempt to sink ships anchored near the fort with a burning raft.

July 10–13, Cumberland County, Pennsylvania: Indians raid homes in the Tuscarora Valley, killing twenty-five whites and wounding four or five during four days of violence. At least six warriors are slain in clashes with white residents of the county.

July 11, Ft. Detroit, Michigan: Pontiac sends two more fire rafts against ships anchored at the fort, but neither strike their targets. British sailors respond with cannon fire and scatter the attackers.

July 13–15, Cumberland, Maryland: Two white men are killed and another wounded during three days of Indian raids against homes east of town.

July 24, Wayne County, Michigan: Indians fire on British soldiers in canoes scouting the river near Ft. Detroit. The skirmish forces the Indians to abandon construction on six more fire rafts.

July 27–August 1, Ft. Pitt, Pennsylvania: Indians stage repeated attacks on the garrison but are repulsed by rifle fire and grenades.

July 31, Wayne County, Michigan: British troops from Ft. Detroit, intending a surprise attack on Pontiac's camp, are met by Ottowa warriors at Parent's Creek, in the battle of Bloody Bridge. Twenty-three soldiers die in the engagement, with thirty-four wounded. Indian losses are estimated by the British at seven killed and a dozen wounded.

August 5–6, Westmoreland County, Pennsylvania: A combined force of Hurons, Delawares, Mingoes, and Shawnees pin down a British advance party at Edge Hill. A surprise counterattack scatters the Indians, who flee after one brief attack on the new army camp at Bushy Run. British losses include fifty men killed, sixty wounded, and five missing. Although unverified, Indian casualties are thought to equal those of British troops.

August 31, Ft. Detroit, Michigan: A Chippewa chief is killed in fighting at the garrison.

September, Elmore County, Alabama: Creek raiders kill two Cherokees. Cherokees respond by capturing the Creek killer of a white man and delivering him to British authorities.

September 1, Ft. Detroit, Michigan: British riflemen kill the nephew of an Ottawa chief, further alienating Pontiac's Indian allies in the long-running siege.

September 2, Wayne County, Michigan: Indians attack a British schooner on the Detroit River, killing two members of the crew and wounding four. Fifteen Indians die in the assault, with thirteen others wounded.

September 3, Wayne County, Michigan: Frustrated Indians torch a French-owned barn near Ft. Detroit, destroying 1,000 bushels of wheat to prevent it from falling into British hands.

September 3, Erie County, New York: Ottawas and Chippewas attack a camp of officers and men from the grounded sloop *Michigan*, killing three soldiers before being driven away.

September 14, Erie County, New York: Five hundred Indians ambush a military wagon train at Devil's Hole, between Ft. Schlosser and Ft. Niagara. Troops from a nearby camp, rushing to support their comrades, stumble into a secondary ambush and are nearly annihilated. British losses for the day include seventy-two men killed, and eight of the survivors wounded.

September 24, Ft. Detroit, Michigan: Indians kill two soldiers outside the stockade.

Fall, Augusta County, Virginia: A detachment of sixty militiamen is ambushed by Indians on the Jackson River, with thirteen men killed. Punitive expeditions are launched, killing several Indians.

October, Northampton County, Virginia: Delaware Indians attack four rural homes, killing eleven white settlers.

October, Wyoming, Pennsylvania: Delaware Indians raid the small settlement, torturing nine men and one woman to death.

October 2, Belle Isle, Michigan: Indian warriors attack a scouting party from Ft. Detroit, suffering thirteen casualties before the warriors retreat in disarray.

October 20, Niagara County, New York: Indians attack a British expeditionary force, killing eight soldiers and wounding eleven.

November 5, Niagara County, New York: Indian raiders assault a party of ten British soldiers, killing seven and capturing two others in the last action of Pontiac's Rebellion.

November 11, Ft. Detroit, Michigan: Chief Pontiac abandons the area on a march to Illinois, leaving allies to continue the siege for a few more days before they retreat.

December 14, Shawanee Creek, Pennsylvania: A white gang, the Paxton Boys, destroy a peaceful Conestoga village, murdering six unarmed Indians.

December 24, Edgefield County, South Carolina: Seven Creek warriors kill fourteen white settlers in an unprovoked attack.

December 27, Lancaster, Pennsylvania: The Paxton Boys invade a local workhouse and slaughter fourteen Conestoga survivors housed there under official "protection." Rewards are issued for the killers, but none are prosecuted. The leader of the gang, Lazarus Stewart, is later killed by Indians in 1778.

1765

December, South Carolina: Authorities report the exposure of a slave insurrection around Christmastime.

1766

March 15, Washington County, Alabama: Creek warriors murder a Choctaw brave, and British spokesmen use the incident to agitate for war between the tribes.

April, Escambia County, Florida: Urged on by British advisers, Choctaws attack a party of Creeks near Pensacola.

May, Escambia County, Florida: Angry Creeks retaliate for British agitation by killing a trader near Pensacola.

September, Tallapoosa River, Alabama: Creeks kill two British traders, bringing the number of dead to six within the last year.

November, Tallapoosa River, Alabama: After negotiating with British authorities, Creek leaders publicly execute the warrior who killed two traders in September.

1767

April, Cleburne County, Alabama: Indians kill a British traveler named Thomas in territory occupied by the Hillabee tribe.

July, Oconee River, Georgia: White settlers are fired on when they enter a Creek settlement to reclaim stolen horses. On their return with reinforcements, they find the town deserted, looting it of hides and clothing before burning it to the ground.

September, Satilla River, Georgia: Creeks kill two white men, but British authorities dismiss the incident, deciding that the attack may have been justified.

1768

January, Georgia: Chickasaw warriors join Choctaws in attacking Creek hunting parties.

January 12, Middle Creek, Pennsylvania: Frederick Stump, a German settler, murders six Indians at his home and conceals their bodies in a nearby creek. The next day Stump travels to a nearby Indian settlement and kills four to prevent news of the murders from spreading. Arrested and jailed at Carlisle pending trial on murder charges, Stump is freed by an armed mob on January 29.

April, Satilla River, Georgia: Reversing their stand on a September 1767 incident, British authorities persuade Creek leaders to execute one of the warriors responsible for killing two white men.

December, Alexandria, Virginia: A slave conspiracy is exposed and thwarted by authorities, and the eight ringleaders are beheaded in January 1768.

1769

April 20, St. Clair County, Illinois: Chief Pontiac is assassinated by a Peoria Indian brave, near his home, at the French settlement of Cahokia.

December 22, Kentucky: Daniel Boone and a companion named Stuart are captured by Indians. After a week they escape and are pursued toward North Carolina, with Stuart killed along the way.

1769–1782

Kentucky: Indians wage sporadic war against white settlers over a span of fourteen years.

1770

August, Putnam County, Georgia: Creek raiders steal horses from settlers along the Little River. Militiamen pursue them to their rebuilt settlement on the Oconee River and burn the settlement for the second time in three years.

1771

January, Georgia: New warfare erupts between the Creek and Choctaw tribes.

April, Augusta, Georgia: Tension flairs between settlers and Indians after a Creek visitor is killed by a white man.

April, Clarke County, Alabama: Tallapoose warriors drive Andrew Hamilton from his home, threatening to kill him if he returns.

July, Augusta, Georgia: A Creek headman is killed in a drunken brawl with a Cherokee, who escapes. War between the tribes is narrowly averted.

July, Alabama: Two British traders are ambushed and killed by Creek warriors while returning to Tallapoosa County from Pensacola, Florida.

Fall, Randolph County, Alabama: Creeks stage a horse-stealing raid on the Georgia frontier. One of them is killed by a white posse. Tribal leaders agree to accept the death as punishment for the Creek slayings of two whites on the Oconee River in 1769.

November, Georgia: Reports are logged of widespread violence by runaway slaves, between Savannah and Ebenezer. Incidents include the setting fire of a rural home in which a white child is burned to death.

Winter, Queensborough, Georgia: A white man named Carey is killed by a Creek warrior. Tribal leaders execute the murderer and display his body to colonial authorities.

1772

New Mexico: The Navajo and Apache form an alliance against the Spaniards, launching concerted raids in 1774.

Spring, Hawkins County, Tennessee: Cherokee tribesmen kill six whites on the Holston River.

Summer, Kanawha River, West Virginia: White vigilantes retaliate for the murder of a local family by annihilating the peaceful Indian village of Bulltown.

October, Perth Amboy, New Jersey: Authorities expose and crush a slave conspiracy.

1773

October 10, Clark County, Kentucky: A pioneer party is attacked by Indians, leaving six men dead and one wounded. Daniel Boone's son is among the dead.

December, Burke County, Georgia: Thirteen settlers and four militiamen die in a series of Creek raids, reportedly launched after one Indian killed another and blamed the murder on a white man.

1774

May, Columbiana County, Ohio: Indians rob a party of whites on the Ohio River. A punitive expedition fights two brief skirmishes, killing several Indians. Several relatives of Mingo Chief Logan are among the dead.

May 24, Columbiana County, Ohio: A party of whites, pretending friendship, ply several Indians with rum and then murder them. A brother and sister of Chief Logan are among those killed. The massacre provokes an immediate war, with Mingos, Delawares, Wyandots, Cayugas, and Shawnees united against the white settlers.

July, Chattahoochee County, Georgia: Seeking to appease British colonists, Creek leaders order the execution of three tribesmen who recently killed whites in Florida and Georgia.

July 12, Muskingum County, Ohio: Chief Logan's warriors attack a party of whites on the Muskingum River, killing one and capturing two others.

September, New Mexico: Spanish troops launch two expeditions against the Navajos, reporting twenty-one Indians killed and forty-six captured.

October 1, Point Pleasant, West Virginia: Troops clash with Chief Logan's warriors in an all-day battle, climaxed by an Indian retreat across the Ohio River. Thirty-three warriors lie dead on the field, with others having been dumped in the river by their fellow tribesmen. The colonial troops lose fifty-five men, with eighty-seven wounded.

October 5, Laguna, New Mexico: Navajos raid nearby ranches, killing four Spaniards, abducting two others, and slaughtering herds of sheep.

November, St. Andrew's Parish, Georgia: Rebel slaves kill four whites and wound three others. After their capture, two of the black leaders are burned alive.

November, Alabama River, Alabama: Mortar, a Creek headman, is ambushed and killed by Choctaws while traveling to New Orleans for a strategy session with French military leaders.

1775

New York: Delancey's Rangers, a Tory organization, recruits blacks for guerilla warfare that will plague the colony throughout the revolution.

July, North Carolina: A slave conspiracy is exposed, spanning the counties of Beaufort, Pitt, and Craven. Five blacks are sentenced to eighty lashes each, with their ears cropped for good measure.

August 18, South Carolina: Whites hang and burn a free black named Jerry, on suspicion of instigating a slave revolt.

1776

Summer, Kentucky: Indians stage repeated raids along the frontier.

July, Nassau County, Florida: A small U.S. detachment raids Creek settlements along St. Mary's River. Creeks retaliate by killing a white man on the Ogeechee River, in eastern Georgia.

July, Tennessee: Angered by white incursions in Cocke and Hawkins Counties, Cherokees mount a new offensive against British settlers from eastern Tennessee through the Carolinas.

November 1–3, Hominy Creek, North Carolina: White troops ambush and scalp a Cherokee hunter. On November 3, soldiers raid the Cherokee town of Too Cowee, killing and scalping two more Indians, looting and burning the settlement.

1777

Spring, Point Pleasant, West Virginia: One white man and two Indian men are killed in a confusing altercation at the local garrison, sparking new hostilities by Shawnees. Warriors led by white renegade Simon Girty stage repeated attacks around Wheeling through midsummer.

May, Logan County, Kentucky: One man is killed, with two others wounded, in an Indian raid on a frontier stockade.

June, Mississippi River: Spanish forces crack down on illicit trade, and seize a dozen British vessels.

August 6, Oriskany, New York: A combined force of British troops and Indians clash with colonial militiamen near Ft. Schuyler, killing or capturing an estimated 400 Americans. Ft. Schuyler is besieged until August 22, when the British are forced to withdraw after their Indian allies desert.

September, Washington County, New York: Colonists are enraged after Indians attached to a British advance column murder a young white woman near Ft. Edward.

September 19, Elmore County, Alabama: Creek warriors attack British advance parties, driving the redcoats back toward Pensacola.

September 26–28, Wheeling, West Virginia: Simon Girty's Indian raiders stage repeated assaults along the Ohio River, striking at Grave Creek and Ft. Henry. Twelve defenders are killed in one clash on September 27, and several Indians die the same afternoon when Girty's cannon explodes outside Ft. Henry. In the climactic battle of September 28, Indians kill twenty-five defenders against an estimated loss of 100 warriors slain.

1778

January, Florida: Spanish officers open negotiations with local Indians, plotting the overthrow of British forces and the recapture of Florida for Spain.

March, Beaver Creek, Pennsylvania: Troops from Ft. Pitt ambush a party of Indian "warriors," killing a man and a woman and wounding a second woman before they discover their error. In fact, the victims are innocent travelers, with only the one man in their party.

July 4, Wyoming, Pennsylvania: A party of Tories and pro-British Indians destroy the settlement, killing at least 360 colonial militiamen. U.S. captives are beheaded or burned at the stake, with some thrown on beds of hot coals and pinned down with pitchforks.

July–August, Florida-Georgia: Creek war parties side with the British in various moves against U.S. troops. Indian raids tie up colonial forces on the Georgia frontier, and Creeks help repulse a U.S. thrust in east Florida. Forty horses are captured when Creeks burn a U.S. fort on the Satilla River. Creek raids along the Broad River, in eastern Georgia, kill thirty settlers and numerous head of livestock.

August 8, Boonesboro, Kentucky: A combined force of Canadians and Indians surrounds the fort, laying siege until August 20, when the attackers retreat with known casualties of thirty-seven.

October, Pennsylvania: Tory forces burn pro-American Indian settlements in the eastern part of the state, between the Delaware and Susquehanna Rivers.

November 9, Cherry Valley, New York: Tories and pro-British Indians surprise the settlement, killing an estimated forty persons and capturing an equal number.

1779

April 19, Onondaga County, New York: Colonial troops destroy the Onondaga tribal settlements, killing twelve Indians and capturing another thirty-four.

July 23, Minisink Ford, New York: A party of Tories and Indians attack the settlement, burning several houses and barns. A detachment of colonial militia gives chase and defeats the raiders in a brisk engagement.

July 31, Easton, Pennsylvania: U.S. troops inaugurate a seven-week campaign against the Cayuga, Mohawk, and Seneca tribes in eastern Pennsylvania and New York. Forty Indian towns are destroyed by mid-September, with 160,000 bushels of corn destroyed. Tories and Indians harass the U.S. force at various points, but the only serious clash occurs at Newtown, Pennsylvania. Of the 5,000 Americans involved in the campaign, less than forty die.

August, Ohio River: Colonial forces from Pittsburgh launch a month-long campaign against the Mingo and Seneca Indians, destroying several settlements and 500 acres of corn.

August 22, South Carolina: Troops destroy the grain supplies of eight Indian settlements. Native Indians are uprooted at gunpoint and ordered to resettle further inland.

August 29, Hamilton County, New York: Colonial forces launch their campaign against pro-British Mohawk tribesmen with a two-hour battle that routs the Indians and leaves their villages open to pillage and destruction.

October, Licking Creek, Kentucky: Indian warriors ambush a party of seventy white soldiers, killing fifty-seven and seizing $600,000 in Spanish coin.

1779–1780

Taking advantage of the ongoing American Revolution, Spanish forces capture the British outposts at Manchac and Natchez on the Mississippi River, forcing the stronger garrisons at Mobile and Baton Rouge to surrender after protracted sieges.

1780

Albany, New York: Two whites and several slaves are held for plotting insurrection and the burning of the nearby Half-Moon settlement.

Canajoharie, New York: A war party of Tories and pro-British Indians destroy the settlement, moving on to kill several more Americans in raids along the Mohawk River.

April, Botetourt County, Virginia: A slave named Jack is hanged after his conviction for recruiting blacks for the British army.

June, St. Louis, Missouri: Spanish defenders repulse a determined assault by several hundred British troops and 1,000 Indians. Residents of outlying farms are massacred, some tortured to death, as the assault force retreats.

June, Rock River, Illinois: Colonial troops assault a mixed force of British traders and their Indian allies.

June 22, Harrison County, Kentucky: A combined force of 600 British Canadians and Indians captures the settlement at Riddle's Station, on the south fork of the Licking River.

July, Ohio: U.S. troops raze Indian settlements on the Mad and Little Miami Rivers, depriving Canadian troops of food stores as grain and other supplies are destroyed.

September 14, Augusta, Georgia: U.S. troops assault a nearby Creek village in the largest Indian battle of the Revolutionary War, inflicting heavy losses before they are beaten back by warriors.

1781

Williamsburg, Virginia: One white man is killed as slaves set fire to several buildings, including the state capitol.

Prince William County, Virginia: A slave is hanged for leading maroons on raids against local plantations.

Johnstown, New York: Tory Walter Butler, a leader of the November 1778 massacre at Cherry Valley, is captured and executed by Oneida tribesmen.

Greenwood County, South Carolina: Cherokees stage raids around the settlement of Ninety-Six, killing several families and burning their homes. Colonial troops respond with a two-week foray into Georgia, destroying thirteen Cherokee towns and killing more than forty Indians, with several others captured.

Spring, Muskingum River, Ohio: U.S. troops mount a campaign against Delaware tribesmen, razing various settlements. Indian raiders still remain active on the Kentucky frontier, however.

August, Berrien County, Michigan: A combined force of Spaniards, Frenchmen, and Indians stage a dawn attack on the British garrison at Ft. St. Joseph, looting the fortress and raising the Spanish flag before leaving.

December 16, Sullivan County, Tennessee: White militiamen attack seventy Cherokees, killing thirteen.

December 25–31, Tennessee: A state militia campaign against the Cherokees destroys the Indian towns of Chote, Scittigo, Chilhowee, Togue, Micliqua, Kai-a-tee, Sattoogo, Telico, Hiwafee, and Chistowee, as well as "some small ones and several scattering settlements." An estimated 1,000 Cherokee homes are burned. Twenty-nine Indians are killed and seventeen are captured. Militia losses include one man killed in combat and two more wounded "by accident."

1782

Cebolleta, New Mexico: Repeated raids by Navajo warriors drive Laguna Indians from the vicinity.

January, Savannah, Georgia: Creek warriors try to break the U.S. siege in a fierce hand-to-hand battle. While most of the warriors break through, headman Emisteseguo is killed in the fighting, removing a major pro-British voice from the tribal leadership.

February, Gnadenhutten, Ohio: Ninety-six peaceful Delaware Indians are murdered and scalped by whites. The victims, all of whom are Christian converts, include thirty-five men, twenty-seven women, and thirty-four children.

May, Kentucky River, Kentucky: Indians raid Estill's Station, killing one man, capturing a black slave, and slaughtering a number of cattle. A posse gives chase, overtaking the raiders near Little Mountain, and kill ten to twelve Indians before they are forced to retreat. Four wounded survivors of the posse of twenty-two escape.

Spring, Licking River, Kentucky: Indian raiders sack Hoy's Station, capturing several white prisoners. A posse overtakes the raiders the next day, at Blue Licks, and lose four men before being driven back.

August, Mississippi: Mixed bands of British Loyalists and Indians conduct sporadic guerilla warfare against Spanish forces, raiding supply lines between New Orleans and St. Louis, and capturing the Spanish governor's wife in one attack.

August 15–18, Scott County, Kentucky: Indians lay siege to Bryant's Station, on the Elkhorn River. An estimated thirty Indians are killed, with many others wounded, before the siege ends August 18. White losses include four men killed, three wounded, and a large number of cattle slaughtered.

August 19, Blue Licks, Kentucky: Pursuers overtake the Indians who raided Bryant's Station and a battle ensues. Sixty of the pursuers and sixty-four of the Indians are killed. Seven of the pursuers are captured as the shaken survivors retreat.

September 1, Jefferson County, Kentucky: Indian raiders assault Kinchloe's Station, killing several whites and capturing others before nightfall permits a few of the survivors to escape.

November 10, Chillicothe, Ohio: George Rogers Clark, commanding 1,100 mounted riflemen, routs a party of Shawnee Indians who served the British in the revolutionary war.

1782–1787

Fugitive slaves, used as troops by British commanders in the American Revolution, wage guerilla warfare in the South for five more years. White militia units finally destroy the rebel fort in Bell Isle Swamp, twenty miles north of Savannah, Georgia, in 1786. The guerilla war ends after other camps are razed in 1787.

1783–1790

An estimated 1,500 men, women, and children are slain or captured by Indians along the Ohio River. During the same period, an estimated 2,000 horses are stolen from white settlers, with an unspecified "immense" number of homes and frontier settlements burned.

1785

June 16, Sierra Azul, New Mexico: A combined force of Navajo and Pueblo Indians attacks rival Apaches, killing an estimated forty persons, with light casualties on the attackers' side.

1786

July, New Mexico: A slave raid conducted by Spanish troops, with support from Commanche and Pueblo warriors, leaves one Apache woman dead and fourteen women and children held captive. The Apaches intensify their own raiding in retaliation.

September 10, Gila Mountains, Arizona: A combined force of Spaniards and Commanches kill eighteen Apache braves and capture four women.

October 6, Logan County, Ohio: Kentucky militiamen raid a Shawnee camp on the Mad River, killing ten Indians. After the clash, Shawnee King Moluntha is axed to death by Capt. Hugh McGary. Tried for murder on March 21, 1787, McGary is convicted and punished with a one-year suspension from rank.

1787

March 28: The foreign slave trade is banned for a period of three years; the ban is continuously renewed until 1803. Illegal smuggling of slaves continues on a reduced scale, while many slave dealers turn to the domestic breeding of slaves.

1788

Spring, Ohio River: Indian raiders capture a river boat and slaughter the occupants, cooking and eating the heart of passenger John Ashby.

May, Blount County, Tennessee: Cherokee raiders strike at a homestead on the Little River, killing eleven members of the Kirk family. Militiamen respond with attacks on Indian villages along the Tennessee River, destroying several settlements and killing an unspecified number of Indians. Six Cherokees are lured to a "peace conference," then confined and tomahawked to death by a surviving son of the Kirk family while soldiers look on.

July 12, Muskingum River, Ohio: Chippewa raiders attack an army camp, killing two soldiers and wounding three. One Indian is killed in the skirmish and two are wounded.

1789

March 20–21, Ohio River: Shawnee raiders ambush several river boats, capturing six white men and burning four of them at the stake.

Spring, Kentucky: A three-month Indian rampage leaves seventeen whites dead, fifteen wounded, and five held as captives.

June, Ft. Knox, Kentucky: Indian raiders kill and mutilate a sentry.

June, Ohio River: Indian warriors capture Charles Builderback, a leader of the 1782 Gnadenhutten massacre, and torture him to death.

August 9, Knox County, Indiana: Kentucky troops attack a Shawnee camp on the Wabash River, killing three men, three women, one boy, and one infant, carrying their scalps downriver to Vincennes.

1790

July, Posey County, Indiana: Indian snipers kill three white men on a boat traveling the Ohio River.

October 15, Allen County, Indiana: Miami Indians abandon a major settlement as white troops advance, burning the town to prevent its occupation. Soldiers invade and pillage the town as it burns, capturing two Indians.

October 17–18, Allen County, Indiana: Miami raiders drive off 100 packhorses from an army camp. Troops are sent in pursuit on October 18, and kill two Indians.

October 19, Allen County, Indiana: Troops clash with Miami warriors on the Eel River, and twenty-eight soldiers die during the fierce battle.

October 20, Allen County, Indiana: Troops burn five Indian camps along the Maumee River, killing two braves and decapitating one of them.

October 22, Allen County, Indiana: Troops and Miami tribesmen clash in a series of battles throughout the day, leaving an estimated 118 whites and forty Indians dead, and at least twenty-nine whites wounded.

October 29, Piqua, Ohio: An army detachment is ambushed and scattered by Indian raiders.

1791

Louisiana: Twenty-one slaves are hanged, with three whites expelled in the wake of a slave insurrection.

January 2, Morgan County, Ohio: Indians raid a settlement on the Muskingum River, killing twelve whites and capturing four. Two settlers escape to report the attack.

January 8, Butler County, Ohio: Indians ambush a four-man survey party on the Great Miami River, killing one and capturing another.

January 10, Hamilton County, Ohio: Indian raiders, led by the white renegade Simon Girty, assault Dunlap's Station on the Great Miami River, capturing one resident who tries to escape and torturing him to death. The raiders depart on the morning of January 11.

April, Scioto County, Ohio: A military expedition finds twenty white men killed and mutilated by Indian raiders. Crossing the Ohio River into Kentucky, the troops discover three dead Indians and scalp their decomposing corpses. Returning home along the Scioto River, they find the remains of Jacob Greathouse and his wife, tortured to death by Indians who slit their abdomens, tied their intestines to a tree, and forced them to run in circles until they were disemboweled.

April, Snag Creek, Ohio: Whites ambush an Indian war party returning from raids in Kentucky. Five warriors are killed, scalped, and otherwise mutilated, one of whom is decapitated and has his head mounted on a pole.

June 1, Lafayette, Indiana: Troops attack two Indian villages four miles away, killing thirty-eight tribesmen and capturing fifty-two.

June 2, Putnam County, Indiana: Troops burn several Indian villages along the Eel River, capturing an unspecified number of prisoners.

August 7, Putnam County, Indiana: Militiamen raid an Indian village on the Eel River, killing six braves, and capturing thirty-four women and children. Two militiamen are killed in the clash, with one wounded.

November 3–4, Mercer County, Ohio: Indian snipers fire on an army camp beside the Wabash River, losing one during the skirmish. A battle ensues on November 4, with twenty-one Indians killed and forty-four wounded in an assault that leaves 630 whites dead or missing, with nearly 300 wounded.

1792

April 3, Hamilton County, Ohio: Indian warriors kill four white men dispatched as peace emissaries.

May, Northampton County, Virginia: Five blacks, armed with clubs, attack a white militia unit designated to keep slaves off the road after dark. All five are convicted and hanged, although no whites had been injured in the attack.

May 29, Hamilton County, Ohio: Peace emissary Alexander Trueman is killed by Indians.

June, Henry County, Ohio: Col. John Hardin and a companion are ambushed and killed by Indians along the Maumee River.

June 25, Darke County, Ohio: Indians attack a hay-cutting party outside Ft. Jefferson, killing four soldiers and capturing eleven.

July 7, Ohio River: Indian raiders capture Oliver Spencer, a white youth.

September 29, Ft. Jefferson, Ohio: Indians attack the garrison's beef herd, killing several guards.

November 6, Preble County, Ohio: Indian raiders attack a military camp near Ft. St. Clair. Six soldiers are killed in the clash, with four missing and five wounded. Of the 100 pack horses in the camp, Indians kill twenty-six, wounding ten and steal forty-one. Two Indians are killed in the raid.

1793

July, Richmond, Virginia: Authorities expose and crush a slave conspiracy.

August 17, Petersburg, Virginia: A slave revolt is revealed in the planning stage.

August 24, York County, Virginia: Aborted slave uprisings are reported by white authorities.

September, Powhatan County, Virginia: Several blacks are flogged after authorities discover 300 slaves meeting to discuss a revolt.

October, Big Bead Mesa, New Mexico: Apaches launch raids against several Spanish ranches. A combined force of Spaniards and Navajo warriors pursue the raiders, killing several Apaches. A Navajo leader, Antonio el Pinto, is wounded by an arrow during the clash, dying of an infection on October 26.

October, Norfolk, Virginia: Police expose an arson conspiracy involving eighty slaves and thirty-four white abolitionists.

October 17, Preble County, Ohio: Indians ambush a military column traveling between Ft. St. Clair and Ft. Jefferson. Fifteen soldiers are killed and ten are captured before the remainder of the column escapes.

1794

Albany, New York: Five blacks, including two women, are executed for lighting a series of fires that caused $250,000 damage the year before.

June 28, Greenville, Ohio: A party of friendly Choctaws, sent out as military scouts, retreat back to the settlement after a clash with local Indians.

June 30, Ft. Recovery, Ohio: Indians assault a military column nearby, inflicting forty casualties and pursuing the survivors as they retreat to the garrison. Seventeen Indians are reported dead in the clash. Sniping at the fort resumes on July 1, with a punitive expedition dispatched to scatter the Indians. Soldiers return to the fort with six scalps.

August 11, Ft. Defiance, Ohio: A scouting party clashes with Indians, killing one Indian woman.

August 18, Lucas County, Ohio: Army scout William May is captured by Indians along the Maumee River.

August 20, Lucas County, Ohio: The Indian ambush of an army patrol erupts into the Battle of Fallen Timbers, with troops under Gen. Anthony Wayne losing thirty-three men and 100 wounded before they rout an estimated force of 2,500 Indians.

August 25, Lucas County, Ohio: Troops fire on a party of eight mounted Indians, killing one and wounding two.

September, Darke County, Ohio: Indians lie in ambush along the road connecting Greenville with Ft. Recovery, killing three soldiers and capturing two white civilians.

October 6, Darke County, Ohio: Robert Elliot is ambushed and killed by Indians.

1795

St. Landry Parish, Louisiana: A slave revolt is crushed by whites.

November, Charleston, South Carolina: Slaves are blamed for a major outbreak of arson in the city.

1796

Pointe Coupe Parish, Louisiana: An aborted slave revolt leads to the execution of two dozen blacks, with several whites jailed for complicity.

New Jersey: Black arson conspiracies are exposed in Newark and Elizabethtown.

Charlotte, North Carolina: A grand jury blames Quakers for recent unrest and outbreaks of violence among local slaves.

1799

Virginia: Black arsonists kindle serious fires in Richmond and Frdericksburg.

Southampton County, Virginia: A party of slaves rebels in transit, killing two white escorts. Ten blacks are executed for their role.

1800

1800

April, Cebolleta, New Mexico: Navajos launch repeated strikes against the Spanish settlement. Spaniards launch a retaliatory expedition on May 13, but the Indians agree to make restitution in lieu of fighting.

August 30–October 7, Richmond, Virginia: A scheduled slave revolt under Gabriel Prosser is betrayed by two of the plotters, and troops mobilize to prevent the seizure of a local armory scheduled for that night. Twenty-one conspirators have been executed by September 25, when authorities capture Gabriel. He is hanged on October 7, with nineteen other alleged participants in the revolt. Another imprisoned black commits suicide in his cell.

September 7, Whitlock's Mills, Virginia: Authorities raid a gathering where 150 blacks and several whites are meeting to plan a slave revolt. Numerous persons are arrested, but punishment stops short of executions.

November, Petersburg, Virginia: Unrest and disturbances among local slaves are reported.

December, Virginia: Slave rebellions in Norfolk, Richmond, and in Nottoway County lead to the arrest of several dozen blacks through January 1801.

1801

January, Nottoway County, Virginia: Following the exposure of a slave conspiracy, white panic spreads to neighboring Amelia County, where numerous blacks are arrested and two are executed.

February 15, Petersburg, Virginia: A scheduled slave uprising is betrayed by one of the plotters.

1802

January 2, Nottoway County, Virginia: An incipient slave revolt is exposed by authorities.

January 18, Norfolk, Virginia: A slave conspiracy is crushed in the planning stage.

January 22, Powhatan County, Virginia: Authorities discover and disrupt a scheduled slave revolt.

February 12, Brunswick, Virginia: Two blacks are executed for plotting a slave revolt.

April, Virginia: Numerous blacks are arrested for participating in slave conspiracies in Norfolk and Princess Anne. One suspect in the latter city is hanged. Another black is hanged for the same offense in Hanover County, and a second is banished from the area.

April 3, Richmond, Virginia: Four blacks are shot at after hurling bricks at the state capitol. None of them are hit, however.

April 23, Halifax, Virginia: Two rebel slaves are hanged.

June 4, Warrenton, North Carolina: One hundred blacks are jailed for participating in a slave conspiracy against their owners.

June 8, Hertford, North Carolina: A scheduled slave revolt is betrayed.

June 10, North Carolina: Armed slave uprisings are reported in a nine-county area, and blacks are executed in Camden and in Currituck County. In Elizabeth City, six blacks on horseback attempt to rescue other slaves from jail, but four are captured by authorities.

June 13, Halifax County, Virginia: One slave is hanged for his part in a local rebellion.

June 15, Raleigh, North Carolina: Authorities crush a budding slave revolt. The alleged ringleader is hanged on June 28.

June 28, Halifax, North Carolina: Two slaves are convicted of plotting against local whites.

June 30, Elizabeth City, North Carolina: Several rebel slaves are hanged.

July 1, Halifax County, Virginia: One black is sentenced to hang for plotting a slave revolt.

July 14, Henrico County, Virginia: Authorities hang a rebel slave.

Fall, Madison County, Virginia: Exposure of a slave conspiracy leads to the arrest of numerous blacks. All are sentenced to be "severely flogged."

1803

February, York, Pennsylvania: The conviction of a female slave for trying to poison two whites sparks violence. Eleven buildings are burned by arsonists over the next three weeks, with numerous arrests recorded through March. Twenty blacks are convicted of arson.

February, Charleston, South Carolina: Two blacks are jailed for attempting to burn the city.

April 24, Warrenton, North Carolina: Authorities report that a black revolt has forced some white residents to flee the area.

December 17: The foreign slave trade is resumed. More than 40,000 slaves are imported during the next four years.

1804

February, Isle of Wight County, Virginia: Authorities report evidence of a local slave conspiracy.

February 25, Norfolk, Virginia: Blacks are blamed for an arson fire that destroys six ships and hundreds of homes.

April, Cebolleta, New Mexico: Navajo raiders kill nine Spanish shepherds, abducting one boy and stealing large numbers of livestock.

April 24–25, Cebolleta, New Mexico: Two hundred Navajos swarm the plaza, sacking three houses and stealing twelve horses and fifty cattle. They also raid a nearby shepherd's camp, killing three men and abducting one captive. Spaniards pursue the warriors on April 25, recapturing several stolen sheep.

July, Georgia: Slave conspiracies are exposed by police in Augusta and Savannah.

August, Lincoln County, Missouri: Three or four whites are killed by Sauk warriors at a settlement on the Cuivre River after an Indian father is beaten while defending his daughter from an attempted rape by a white man.

August 3, Cebolleta, New Mexico: One thousand Navajos raid the settlement, killing three residents and wounding fifteen. Indian losses include twenty-two killed and forty-four wounded.

December 3, Zuñi, New Mexico: Spanish troops raid a nearby Navajo ranch, killing two men and capturing one woman and two children.

1805

Wayne County, North Carolina: Authorites expose a slave conspiracy to poison white masters. Two black women are burned alive for their part in the plots, two women and a man are hanged, and twelve other slaves receive lesser penalties.

January 17–18, Canyon de Chelly, Arizona: Spanish troops assault a Navajo stronghold, killing 115 Indian men, women, and children and capturing thirty-three. Troops slaughter 350 Navajo sheep after the battle.

April, Stafford County, Virginia: One black is hanged and another banished from the area for their convictions of participation in a slave revolt.

July, Cambridge, Maryland: Two blacks are convicted of plotting a local slave rebellion. One is sentenced to hang; the other draws a seven-year prison term.

September, New Orleans, Louisiana: Authorities report that a slave conspiracy has been exposed in the planning stage.

September, North Carolina: Slave conspirators poison several whites in Johnston, Sampson, and Wayne Counties, resulting in at least two deaths. Twenty blacks are arrested—one woman is burned alive, four are hanged, one is "pilloried, whipped, his ears nailed down and then cut off," thirteen are flogged, and one is banished from the area.

1806

April, Williamsburg, Virginia: Authorities report the discovery of a local slave rebellion being planned.

Fall, Savannah, Georgia: A slave conspiracy to seize the city is uncovered.

1808

November–December, Virginia: Authorities report evidence of budding slave insurrections in Norfolk and Richmond, along with the counties of Abbemarle, Chesterfield, and Nelson.

1809

November, New Orleans, Louisiana: A "serious" slave uprising is crushed by armed whites.

1810

March, Halifax County, North Carolina: Authorities discover correspondence between slave conspirators in Georgia, Tennessee, and Virginia discussing strategy for an April 22 uprising in four states.

May, Smithfield, Virginia: A local black, after receiving twenty lashes, confesses to participation in a slave conspiracy spanning Virginia and North Carolina.

June, Isle of Wight County, Virginia: A slave named Sam is convicted of conspiracy to rebel against his owners. Slaves from Nansemond County are implicated in the plot. As his punishment, Sam is sold to a trader in South Carolina.

June, Norfolk, Virginia: Authorities report disturbances among local slaves.

June, Culpeper, Virginia: Three slaves, including two women, are accused of arson. On conviction, the man is hanged, and one of the women receives fifteen lashes.

November, Lexington, Kentucky: Wholesale arrests crush an impending slave revolt. Panic induced by the incident prompts state legislators to pass a new law in January 1811 making conspiracy among slaves a capital offense.

1811

January, Virginia: Authorities blame white abolitionists for a planned slave revolt, alleging that blacks were promised $25 each once Richmond was taken.

January 8–10, Saint John the Baptist Parish, Louisiana: A slave revolt involving more than 500 blacks leaves sixty-eight slaves dead after one clash with the militia. The rebels are hunted down and killed during the week that follows. Sixteen leaders of the rebellion are executed, their heads mounted on poles.

March, Cabarrus County, North Carolina: Whites raid a fugitive slave settlement, killing two men, wounding a third, and capturing two black women.

November 7, Prophetstown, Indiana: Eleven hundred Shawnee warriors attack William Henry Harrison's camp, touching off the battle of Tippecanoe. Forty Indians are found dead on the field, with officers estimating 150 killed or wounded in the clash. Troops proceed to destroy the nearby Indian town in the wake of their victory.

December, New Orleans, Louisiana: Outbreaks of slave unrest are reported by authorities.

1812

January, Lexington, Kentucky: Slaves are blamed for a series of arson fires in the city. Several blacks are arrested. Three are finally convicted, and one is executed.

March 26, Kittome, Mississppi: Thomas Meredith is murdered by Creek Indians on a rural road. His alleged killer is executed on July 19.

April, Mongomery County, Virginia: John Smith is killed by one of his slaves, who confesses to the crime before escaping from custody and fleeing the state.

May, Bedford County, Tennessee: Creek Indians massacre two white families along the Duck River.

May 23, Creek Agency, Alabama: William Lott is murdered by four Creek braves, eight miles from agency headquarters.

July, Mississippi: Several blacks are imprisoned for their roles in a planned slave revolt.

July 25, St. Johns County, Florida: A combined force of Seminoles and blacks raid American-owned plantations, killing nine whites and liberating a number of slaves.

August 18, New Orleans, Louisiana: Lewis Bolah, a slave, confesses his role in a local conspiracy against whites, implicating several white abolitionists. One of the white defendants, Joseph Wood, is executed on September 13.

September, Oconee River, Georgia: Creek warriors attack a militia company, waging an inconclusive skirmish before they are forced to retreat.

September 3, Clark County, Indiana: Indians raid a frontier outpost on Pigeon Roost Creek.

September 4, Marion County, Indiana: Indian raiders stage an attack on Ft. Harrison.

September 5, Ft. Madison, Iowa: Indians assault the army garrison.

September 6, Wayne County, Michigan: Indian warriors attack Ft. Wayne, on the Detroit River.

September 12, St. Johns County, Florida: Seminoles and blacks ambush a military wagon train at Twelve Mile Swamp, killing two whites and wounding seven before survivors of the escort mount a successful counterattack.

September 25, Maumee River, Ohio: Indian scouts employed by the British capture and kill several Americans.

September 27, Alachua County, Florida: U.S. troops attacked by Seminole warriors kill King Payne, their chief in the initial clash.

Troopers erect a hasty stockade, where they are besieged for the next six days, inflicting at least fifty enemy casualties before they evacuate and retreat to St. Johns under cover of night on October 2.

November 11, Warren County, Indiana: Troops destroy two Indian villages on the Wabash River.

1813

Florida: Lt. Col. Thomas Smith reports that his troops have destroyed a fortress manned by runaway slaves.

Illinois: Kickapoo warriors massacre a white family named Lively, leaving the youngest boy disemboweled and decapitated. A detachment of rangers fails to locate the killers.

January 22, Monroe County, Michigan: Indian warriors join British troops in an assault on a U.S. military camp at Frenchtown, on the north side of the River Raisin. Of 1,000 Americans in camp, roughly 100 escape, with an estimated 400 killed and 500 captured in the battle.

February 9, Alachua County, Florida: Troops level a deserted Seminole town, and clash with Indians at a second settlement. One soldier is killed in the battle, with seven wounded. Fifty to sixty Indians are reported dead. Soldiers burn 386 houses and thousands of bushels of corn, capturing 300 horses and 400 head of cattle.

March 30, Gloucester County, Virginia: Ten slaves are jailed for their roles in an aborted insurrection. Three are later sentenced to death.

April, Virginia: Another outbreak of slave violence is recorded.

May 1, Lucas County, Ohio: A combined force of British troops and Indians capture a U.S. expedition from Ft. Meigs, with a number of the prisoners killed by Indians after they surrender. Surviving captives are transported to Ft. Miami, where Indian "guards" use them for target practice until Chief Tecumseh arrives and orders a halt to the carnage.

June 6, Sackets Harbor, New York: British troops scatter U.S. forces in a surprise attack, capturing fifty soldiers and 400 Indians.

July, Norfolk, Virginia: Slaves rebel against their owners for the third time in four months.

July, Coosa, Florida: Civil war erupts among Creeks when followers of Tecumseh murder three chiefs friendly with white settlers. The friendly Indians retaliate by tracking the killers to Lake Ocfuskee, killing the nine murderers and several more of Tecumseh's disciples.

July, Escambia County, Florida: Creeks burn the home of James Cornells at Burnt Corn Spring, abducting his wife and selling her for the price of a blanket to a French woman in nearby Pensacola. En route to the city, the raiders stage several attacks on Indians friendly with whites.

July, Lucas County, Ohio: British troops and Indians briefly lay siege to Ft. Meigs, but dissension between the British and the Indians aborts the campaign.

July 27, Escambia County, Alabama: The first battle of the Creek War is fought at Burnt Corn Creek, half a mile below the Conecuh County line. White troops are repelled by the Indians, suffering casualties of two men dead and fifteen wounded. A general massacre is prevented when white survivors manage to outrun their pursuers.

July 31, Menominee County, Michigan: A combined force of British troops and Indian warriors assault Ft. Stephenson, suffering losses of 150 men killed or wounded against U.S. casualties of one man killed and seven injured.

August 30, Baldwin County, Alabama: Creek warriors overrun Ft. Mimms, near the Alabama River, in a battle lasting through the day and after nightfall. Of 500 whites in the fort, an estimated fifty escape.

September, Richmond, Virginia: Summer ends with another report of slave insurrections.

September 1–2, Clarke County, Alabama: Muscogee Indian raiders strike at the residence of the Kimbell and James families in Bassett's Creek Valley. Twelve women and children are killed in the attack, along with various domestic animals. One woman miraculously survives being clubbed and scalped by the warriors. On September 2, the Muscogees attack nearby Ft. Sinquefield during a funeral service for the massacre victims. A pregnant woman is killed, scalped, and mutilated outside the stockade, with one man killed and one boy wounded inside. At least eleven Indians die in the attack.

September 6, Clarke County, Alabama: Creek warriors attack Josiah Fisher's farm, along the Alabama River near Ft. Madison. Fisher and one of his sons are wounded, but both escape.

September 29, Clarke County, Alabama: Creeks abduct a black worker from a local mill and hold him prisoner. He escapes five days later.

October, Clarke County, Alabama: Sixteen year old Ben Arundel is killed by Creeks at Ft. Madison. Raiders also attack a white party north of Wood's Bluff, killing two men and wounding two. The white party returns fire, without visible effect.

October 28, Ft. Madison, Alabama: A soldier named Beard is ambushed and shot by Creeks near the stockade, scalped, and his skull crushed.

November, Alabama River, Alabama: Three white soldiers are pursued by nine Indian warriors in canoes and kill all nine in hand-to-hand combat.

November 3, Etowah County, Alabama: Troops raid the Creek Indian village of Tallussahatchee, killing 186 men and capturing eighty women and children. The settlement and tribal crops are burned in Gen. Andrew Jackson's first example of "total war" against the Indians. Five Americans are killed and forty wounded in the battle.

November 4–5, Escambia County, Florida: White settlers shoot and scalp an Indian for digging potatoes near Burnt Corn Spring. At dawn on November 5, his tribesmen open fire on the white camp, killing one man and wounding another.

November 9, Talladega, Alabama: White troops relieve 154 friendly Indian families besieged by 1,000 Creeks. Two hundred ninety-one Creeks are dead on the field in the wake of the battle, but white commanders insist the numbers "fall considerably short" of the true body count. Fifteen whites are killed and eighty wounded in the battle.

November 18, Talladega County, Alabama: Troops from Ft. Strother raid a settlement of Hillabee Indians at Ten Islands, on the Coosa River. The attack, officially described as "a mistake," enrages the Indians who are already negotiating peace terms with the government. Sixty Hillabees are killed in the attack, with 250 taken prisoner. Survivors go on to battle white troops in subsequent engagements.

November 29, Elmore County, Alabama: White troops and friendly Indians attack the Creek settlement of Autosee, on the south bank of the Talapoosa River, killing an estimated 200 Indians and burning 400 homes.

December 23, Butler County, Alabama: White troops clash with Creek Indian warriors on the tribal holy ground, losing one soldier and twenty wounded. Twenty-one Indians and twelve black guerilla fighters die in the battle, with an unknown number of wounded escaping.

December 24, Monroe County, Alabama: Choctaw tribesmen attack a Creek camp on the west bank of the Alabama River, killing three warriors before the rest escape. On the same afternoon, white troops engage a Shawnee party on Pintala Creek and kill the Indians in a two-hour battle.

December 25–31, Niagara County, New York: A British force, including 600 Indians, slips across the river from Canada, assaulting Ft. Niagara in the midst of Christmas celebrations and slaughtering sixty-seven before surrender is accepted. The Indians are then unleashed to raid the countryside at will. By December 31, warriors have razed the towns of Buffalo, Black Rock, Lewiston, Manchester, Schlosser, Tuscarora, and Youngstown.

1814

Louisiana: State legislators pass a new law requiring the death penalty for any slave who wilfully sheds a white person's blood.

January 22, Emuckfau Creek, Alabama: White troops and Indians wage an all-day battle with 500 Creeks, finally routing the force. An unspecified "great number" of Indian dead are left on the battlefield.

January 24, Elmore County, Alabama: Hillabee Indian warriors clash with a military expedition at Enitachopco, forcing soldiers to retreat across the Coosa River.

January 27, Macon County, Alabama: White troops and Indians are repulsed in a battle with Creek tribesmen in the Calabee Valley, seven miles from Tuskegee.

March 27, Tallapoosa County, Alabama: Troops under Gen. Andrew Jackson clash with a combined force of 1,000 Muscogee and Hillabee on the Tallapoosa River in the Battle of Horseshoe Bend. Five hundred fifty-seven Indians are killed, with 300 women and children captured, before Chief Red Eagle surrenders, bringing the Creek War to a close. White losses in the battle include fifty-five men killed and 146 wounded. A treaty signed on August 9 cedes most of the Creek tribal lands to the U.S. government.

July 3–5, Buffalo, New York: A combined force of U.S. troops and Indians cross the Niagara River to capture the British garrison at Ft. Erie, Ontario. Pushing north along the river, the invaders meet with stiff resistance on July 5, defeating the British in a battle that leaves 500 redcoats killed or wounded, against U.S. losses of 300 men.

July 14, Prairie du Chien, Wisconsin: A combined force of British Canadians and Indians fire on U.S. troops on the Mississippi River, forcing their retreat.

July 17, Crawford County, Wisconsin: British and Indian forces lay siege to the U.S. garrison at Ft. Shelby, near Prairie du Chien. Five Americans are wounded by artillery fire before the fort capitulates on July 20.

July 21, Rock Island County, Illinois: Sauk tribesmen attack a party of U.S. keelboats at Campbell's Island, killing sixteen men and wounding twenty before remnants of the U.S. force escape. One Sauk brave and one squaw are killed in the battle.

September 6, Rock Island County, Illinois: Sauk warriors rout a combined force of U.S. troops and Chemokemon Indians under Maj. Zachary Taylor, driving the survivors back from Saukenuk.

September 15, Mobile County, Alabama: Troops under Gen. Andrew Jackson successfully defend Ft. Bowyer from a combined force of British gunships and Creek tribesmen attacking on land.

November 7, Pensacola, Florida: Gen. Andrew Jackson's troops capture the city, launching expeditions the following day against Indian tribes in the swamps of the Escambia and Choctahatibee Rivers.

December 24, Kaskaskia, Illinois: The territorial government authorizes a $50 reward for each male Indian killed, with the same bounty allotted for women and children captured.

1816

February, Virginia: Slaves in Louisa and Spottsylvania Counties attempt a revolt, led by George Boxley, a white merchant. Six blacks are hanged, with six others transported out of the area, but Boxley escapes from jail and disappears before his trial in May.

Summer, Mt. Taylor, New Mexico: Commanche tribesmen, urged on by Spanish settlers, launch fierce raids against the Navajos.

Summer, Ashepoo, South Carolina: Militia units destroy a nearby community of runaway slaves, who are blamed for various crimes against whites recorded the preceeding several months.

June, Camden, South Carolina: Six leaders of an incipient slave revolt are hanged.

July, Fredericksburg, Virginia: A slave conspiracy is betrayed, and its organizers are hanged.

July 17, Apalachicola, Florida: Fugitive blacks ambush a U.S. gunboat, killing and scalping five members of the crew. One sailor escapes.

July 26, Negro Fort, Florida: U.S. troops under Gen. Andrew Jackson destroy a fortified settlement of runaway slaves and Seminole Indians in Spanish territory, near the site of modern Blountstown. Two hundred seventy men, women, and children are killed in the assault, with another sixty-four wounded—most of them mortally. None of the white attackers are lost, although one soldier has been killed by Indians the previous day while fetching water. News of the massacre is suppressed by Washington, but it becomes the trigger incident for full-scale war with the Seminoles.

1817

April 7, St. Mary's County, Maryland: Two hundred blacks run amok in a series of slave uprisings. Two homes are sacked before authorities restore order.

Autumn, St. Marys, Florida: Seminole raiders kill a white woman and her two children.

November 19, Fowltown, Georgia: U.S. troops seek to arrest Indian Chief Neamathla, accused of threatening white woodcutters in the area. Violence erupts when he refuses to surrender, and four Indian men and one woman are killed. The other inhabitants flee before troops occupy and burn the town on November 23.

November 30, Apalachicola River, Florida: A strike force of Seminoles and blacks ambushes a boat on the river, killing thirty-eight soldiers, six women, and four children. A seventh white woman is taken captive by the raiders.

December, Apalachicola River, Florida: Three boats loaded with military supplies are pinned down by Seminole snipers and immobilized for several hours until help arrives.

1818

Charleston, South Carolina: Authorities uncover a slave revolt in the planning stage.

March 10, Florida: Retaliating for December's attack on the Apalachicola River, 1,500 U.S. troops invade the western part of the state, destroying the homes and property of any Indians or blacks they find.

April 1, Mikasuki, Florida: Troops raze Seminole villages, burning 300 houses and capturing cattle and large stores of grain.

April 8, St. Marks, Florida: Three Seminole leaders and two of their white arms suppliers are tricked into captivity and executed by military authorities.

April 16, Suwanee River, Florida: A combined force of white troops and Creek Indians clashes with a band of Seminoles and blacks, killing nine blacks and two Indians, and capturing two blacks. A sweep of the area results in the burning of 300 Seminole homes, with three more Indians killed, as troops capture five black men and nine Seminole women and children.

May 24, Pensacola, Florida: Gen. Andrew Jackson's troops surround the Spanish garrison and commence a three-day bombardment, leading to the fort's surrender on May 27. The fall of Pensacola leaves St. Augustine as the only Spanish fort on the North American continent.

June, Charleston, South Carolina: One hundred forty blacks are arrested for attending an abolitionist rally, with thirteen of the defendants fined, imprisoned, or flogged. Maroon guerillas are reported active in the state.

June, Princess Anne County, Virginia: A band of outlawed slaves, traveling with several renegade whites, are blamed for various local crimes.

November, North Carolina: Attacks by maroon guerillas make headlines across the state. Militia units are organized in Wake County, where armed whites repulse a raid on a local store.

1819

Philadelphia, Pennsylvania: Three white women stone a black woman to death on the street.

February – March, New Mexico: Spanish raids against the Navajos kill thirty-three Indians and capture fourteen, and take livestock.

Spring, Augusta, Georgia: One white man is killed in an aborted slave revolt, for which the black leader, Coco, is hanged. Another slave, Paul, is sentenced to be branded on one cheek, his ears cut off, and 250 lashes administered over a period of thirty days, in three-day intervals.

July, Williamsburg County, South Carolina: Whites attack a fugitive slave community, killing three blacks and capturing several others. One white man is wounded in the clash.

1820

Philadelphia, Pennsylvania: Black homes are burned by rioting whites.

Raleigh, North Carolina: A white man is executed for the "willful and malicious" murder of a slave.

Galveston Bay, Texas: Caranchua Indians capture and loot a schooner driven into the bay by inclement weather. A short time later, tribesmen skirmish with white treasure hunters on Galveston Island, killing three of them and losing fifteen of their own and several wounded.

February, Petersburg, Virginia: A slave insurrection is reported, including several attempts to burn the town. Numerous blacks are jailed, along with several "suspicious" whites.

March, Florida: Slaves newly imported from Jamaica rebel against their owners but are quickly subdued by a detachment of U.S. troops.

Spring, Gates County, North Carolina: Outlaw maroons kill one white man before they are routed by armed locals. A posse tracks and kills the reputed leader, a runaway named Harry, earning a $200 reward for his head.

December 20, South Carolina: New legislation forbids the freeing of any slave without formal consent of the state legislature. Free blacks are also barred from entering the state.

1821

Kennett Square, Pennsylvania: A mob prevents the recapture of a fugitive slave, killing his owner and overseer.

June, Georgetown, South Carolina: Fugitive maroons kill one slave owner in a local outbreak of violence. Three of the outlaws are captured a short time later.

August–September, North Carolina: Militia units are deployed to crush slave uprisings in Bladen, Carteret, Jones, and Onslow counties. Twelve whites are wounded in a bungled engagement in which two militia companies open fire on each other.

1822

January–July, New Mexico: At least twenty-seven Spanish settlers are killed by Navajo raiders.

April 8, Philadelphia, Pennsylvania: An anti-Catholic riot leaves several persons seriously injured.

May, Jemez, Arizona: Spaniards kill thirteen Navajo tribesmen.

June 14, Charleston, South Carolina: The Denmark Vesey slave revolt is exposed, involving several thousand blacks. Arrests begin on June 17, with 131 slaves jailed in the following month. Of those arrested, thirty-seven are executed, forty-three are transported out of the area, and forty-eight are discharged after flogging.

1823

Spring, Norfolk County, Virginia: Outlaw maroons kill several white men in raids on rural homes. In early May a militia unit is organized to track the renegades.

April 29, Rio Abajo, New Mexico: Navajos launch a series of raids that kill sixteen Mexicans by June 1. Eight of the victims die in a single attack on the village of Sabinal.

May 28, Norfolk County, Virginia: Militiamen clash with fugitive maroons, inflicting several casualties.

June 5, Norfolk County, Virginia: The press reports another armed clash between maroons and local militiamen.

June 25, Norfolk County, Virginia: Maroon leader Bob Ferebee is captured by the militia, facing execution in late July.

July, Charleston, South Carolina: Bishop Moses Brown, founder of the local African Methodist Church, is driven from the state by white militia leaders.

July 8, Crystal, New Mexico: Mexican troops clash with Navajos in the mountains nearby, killing fourteen Indian men and women, capturing one girl and five horses.

July 13, Canyon de Chelly, Arizona: Mexican troops pursue two Navajo riders, killing one.

July 15, Low Mountain, New Mexico: One Navajo is killed in a skirmish with the militia.

July 16, Polacca Wash, New Mexico: A running battle between Mexicans and Navajos leaves eight Indians dead and eight more in custody.

July 22, Canyon de Chelly, Arizona: Troops assault a Navajo ranch, killing five women and capturing nine Indian men and women. Soldiers also seize twelve horses and mules, along with seventy sheep and goats.

August 9, Klethla Valley, New Mexico: Four Mexican soldiers are wounded in a clash with Navajos. The Indians lose eighty-seven cattle and over 400 sheep and goats.

August 10, Monument Valley, Arizona: Mexican troops attack a Navajo settlement, killing one man and capturing twelve Indians of various ages.

August 14, Lukachukai Wash, New Mexico: Navajos assault a column of troops, killing four soldiers. The attack resumes the next day, with snipers harassing the retreating column.

October, Pineville, South Carolina: Armed whites attack a party of fugitive slaves, killing one woman and one child, capturing several other blacks. One maroon is beheaded, his skull mounted on a pole as "a warning to vicious slaves."

1824

Colorado River, Texas: Trader John White and several Mexican companions are captured by Caranchua Indians, with White released on his promise to travel upriver and obtain various goods for trade. Instead, he returns with armed reinforcements, and several tribesmen are killed before the Caranchuas sue for peace.

May, Cape Fear, North Carolina: Isam, a fugitive slave named as the leader of statewide insurrections in August 1821, is publicly flogged to death.

Summer, Guadalupe County, Texas: A settler named Tumlinson is ambushed and killed by Waco Indians near the site of modern Seguin. A short time later, pursuers led by Tumlinson's brother and nephew surprise a party of thirteen Wacos in Colorado County, near present-day Columbus, killing twelve of the Indians.

September, Philadelphia, Pennsylvania: Blacks numbering 150 attack white officials escorting a runaway slave to jail.

October, Providence, Rhode Island: Five hundred white rioters level a district where blacks have settled.

1825

Greenville, South Carolina: Whites burn a black man alive outside of town.

April 7, Abiquiu, New Mexico: Mexican troops surprise a Navajo camp, killing eleven Indians and capturing twenty.

December, Edgecomb County, North Carolina: Authorities crush a revolt by local slaves, who erroneously believe that they have been liberated by the U.S. government.

1826

Cincinnati, Ohio: Six hundred ninety blacks are driven out of town by rioting whites.

January, Petersburg, Virginia: Slaves are blamed for a series of local arson fires.

March 20, Belen, New Mexico: Navajo raiders steal eight horses and mules from a local ranch.

May, At Sea: Twenty-nine slaves en route from Maryland to Georgia on the ship *Decatur* kill two members of the crew and command another to take them to Haiti. The ship is captured and taken to New York, where all of the blacks manage to escape. One, William Bowser, is recaptured and executed in New York City on December 15.

July, Charleston, South Carolina: Authorities blame local slaves for an outbreak of arson.

July, Mobile, Alabama: Slaves are believed responsible for recent incidents of arson.

September, Union County, Kentucky: Seventy-seven slaves rebel on an Ohio River boat bound for the deep South, killing five white men on board. The fugitives flee into Indiana, but all are recaptured. Five are publicly executed on November 29, while the rest are sold into captivity across the South.

October 6, New Orleans, Louisiana: A detachment of U.S. troops is sent upriver to suppress slave revolts on three plantations.

December 21, Nacogdoches, Texas: Two hundred Anglo settlers led by Hayden Edwards forcibly seize the town, proclaiming the Republic of Fredonia. The revolt is crushed by Mexican authorities, with the support of Anglo leaders that include Stephen Austin.

1827

Illinois: White settlers invade and burn a Sauk Indian village while the Indians are away on a communal hunt. Unprovoked violence against the Sauk and Fox tribes continues unabated until the Indians flee northward, into Wisconsin.

Burleson County, Texas: Local whites attack a Commanche camp, killing all but two of the Indians, leaving one of the survivors wounded. Furious Comanches respond with a raid that leaves one rancher gravely wounded.

January, South Carolina: White patrols kill two runaway slaves in separate shooting incidents.

April 2, St. Johns River, Florida: Troops pursue two Seminoles accused of killing two white men.

June, Macon, Georgia: A "French immigrant from the Mississippi" is blamed for instigating a local revolt by some 300 slaves. Authorities arrest one of the rebels, while the rest escape.

June, Mobile County, Alabama: Whites assault a fugitive slave community at the junction of the Alabama and Tombigbee Rivers, killing three blacks and capturing several others.

November, St. Johns River, Florida: White gunmen ambush and kill an Indian traveling with a couple who have a pass to visit relatives in the area.

1828

Baltimore, Maryland: Abolitionist Benjamin Lundy suffers repeated assaults on the public street. One beating, administered by slave trader Austin Woolfolk, leaves Lundy in critical condition.

November, Mobile, Alabama: Slaves are blamed for a serious local arson fire.

1829

Philadelphia, Pennsylvania: Abolitionist orators are met with rioting, which soon evolves into a general assault on blacks.

Boston, Massachusetts: Rioting nativists spend three days stoning Irish Catholic homes.

January, Mobile, Alabama: Slaves are blamed for a series of arson fires.

February, Huntsville, Alabama: Several suspicious fires are blamed on black arsonists.

March, Iberville Parish, Louisiana: Two blacks are hanged for leading a slave revolt forty miles upriver from New Orleans.

April, Savannah, Georgia: Authorities blame local slaves for several arson incidents.

April, Brazos River, Texas: Cherokee warriors raid the villages of rival Wacos accused of stealing Cherokee horses in forays north of the Red River. Casualty figures are uncertain from the several battles, but Cherokee raiders returned to their settlements in Oklahoma with fifty-five Waco scalps.

April, Georgetown, South Carolina: Twenty blacks are held for trial after local authorities crush a slave uprising.

April, Augusta, Georgia: A series of arson fires blamed on rebel slaves climax with a disastrous blaze late in the month, destroying most of the town arsenal. One female slave, convicted in that case, is "executed, dissected, and exposed." A second black woman, pregnant at the time of her conviction, is sentenced to hang after giving birth.

Summer, South Carolina: Authorities report various clashes with "a large gang of runaway Negroes." One of the blacks is killed, and several others captured, when they are surprised by a party of deer hunters in late August.

July, Bastrop County, Texas: Four Indians die when a white posse attacks their camp, driving them off a white settler's farmland.

July, Schleicher County, Texas: Texas volunteers assault a camp of Waco and Tehuacana Indians, finding it deserted except for one brave, whom they kill. Nearby, a running skirmish with Indians results in the capture of several Indian horses.

July–August, Cincinnati, Ohio: White attacks on local blacks are climaxed by an August 22 mob assault on the black quarter, with numerous casualties. By the end of the year, racist violence has prompted at least 1,200 blacks to desert the city, many of them bound for Canada.

July 4, Hanover County, Virginia: One white man is killed, and another wounded, in an attack by eight rebel slaves.

August, Greenup County, Kentucky: Ninety slaves, in transit from Maryland to sale in the South, revolt and kill two of their white guards, and scatter into the countryside. All are soon recaptured, with five men and one woman sentenced to die as the ringleaders. The men are executed on November 20; the woman's hanging is delayed until May 25, 1830, after the birth of her child.

October, Frankfort, Kentucky: Slaves are blamed for a local outbreak of arson.

October–November, Augusta, Georgia: A new series of arson incidents is blamed on rebellious blacks.

December, Camden, South Carolina: Slaves are blamed for an incendiary fire that destroys eighty-five buildings.

1830

Matagorda County, Texas: Indians attack a rural homestead, killing one woman and wounding two girls. A posse overtakes the raiders on the Colorado River, killing an estimated forty to fifty Indian men, women, and children.

Fayette County, Texas: Indian war parties raid white homes, killing several persons and plundering their houses, driving off horses, cattle, and sheep. Pursuers are unable to trace the raiders.

April, New Orleans, Louisiana: Two blacks are executed as the leaders of a local slave insurrection.

May, Prairie du Chien, Wisconsin: Eighteen Fox Indians, invited to a government conference, are ambushed by a mixed war party of Menominee and Sioux. All but one of the Fox are slaughtered; the survivor is placed in a canoe, both arms broken, and set adrift to carry news of the defeat to his tribe at Dubuque, Iowa.

May 28, Washington, D.C.: President Andrew Jackson signs the Indian Removal Act, requiring eastern tribes to be resettled west of the Mississippi River.

Summer, Fayette County, Texas: Indians raid Jesse Burnham's ranch on the Colorado River, stealing several horses. Burnham gives chase and attacks the band of thieves, scattering the stolen animals and escaping with his life in a running battle across the prairie.

Summer, Rock Island County, Illinois: Settler Rennah Wells reports an "attempted stabbing" by an Indian brave surprised in his corn-field. No one is injured in the encounter.

Summer, McLennan County, Texas: Cherokee warriors stage raids against the villages of rival Tehuacana tribesmen, accused of stealing horses from their tribe.

July, Cambridge, Maryland: Fifty blacks are jailed on arson charges after two homes are burned to the ground.

September, Wilmington, North Carolina: Authorities crush a local slave rebellion.

September, Nashville, Tennessee: A slave insurrection is exposed and foiled by authorities.

September–December, North Carolina: Violence by fugitive maroons is reported from Bladen, Dublin, Jones, New Hanover, Onslow, and Sampson Counties. A fugitive leader named Moses, captured in November, directs authorities to a rebel camp in Dover Swamp, where white raiders kill several blacks and burn eleven homes.

Fall, Red River County, Texas: William Cooper is pursued by Indians while hunting near his rural home. A posse is organized to pursue the warriors, who are overtaken on Caney Creek in a skirmish that leaves one white man and one Indian dead.

October, Plaquemines Parish, Louisiana: Militia units arrest the leaders of a revolt involving 100 slaves and some free blacks.

December, New Bern, North Carolina: Armed whites surround and annihilate a band of fugitive maroons in a nearby swamp.

1831

Memphis, Tennessee: A slave revolt is betrayed and crushed in the planning stage.

Louisville, Kentucky: Several blacks are arrested as police expose a planned slave revolt.

January 7, Wilmington, North Carolina: The press reports that "there has been much shooting of Negroes in this neighborhood recently, in consequence of symptoms of liberty having been discovered among them." Two companies of militia are stationed in the area to crush local slave revolts.

May, Cimarron River: Trapper and explorer Jedediah Smith is killed by Indians near the present Kansas-Oklahoma border.

July, Crawford County, Wisconsin: Fox warriors surprise a party of twenty-five drunken Menominee tribesmen, killing them all in revenge for the April 1830 massacre at Prairie du Chein.

July 28, Rock Island County, Illinois: Militia units raid a Sauk village at Saukenuk but find it deserted, Sauks having made their escape across the Mississippi River into Iowa.

August, Sussex County, Virginia: Several blacks are jailed on charges of plotting a revolt, one of whom manages to escape.

August 20–22, Southampton County, Virginia: Nat Turner's slave revolt claims an estimated sixty lives before armed whites mount a counterattack. More than 100 blacks are killed in the fighting, with an equal number of innocent blacks massacred for revenge after the uprising is crushed. Of fifty-three blacks arrested, twenty are hanged, twelve are sold out of state, and twenty-one are acquitted. Nat Turner and three of his trusted lieutenants are hanged on November 11. (Other slave revolts were reported in Virginia and North Carolina at the same time, but details have not survived.)

August, Botetourt County, Virginia: A male slave is executed on charges of conspiring with Nat Turner in a slave revolt.

September 4, North Carolina: Slave conspiracies are uncovered in the counties surrounding Raleigh. Virginia newspapers report that seventeen white families have been slaughtered by blacks. In Wilmington, four blacks are whipped until they confess to conspiracy, whereupon they are hanged. Twelve blacks are shot in Duplin, with several others hanged as alleged ringleaders of the plot.

September 21–23, Providence, Rhode Island: A fight between blacks and white sailors that leaves one white man dead sparks a bloody race riot, with several more persons killed. Violence continues until September 23, when militiamen fire on the rioters, killing four persons and wounding fourteen. At least eighteen black homes are destroyed in the outbreak.

Fall, DeWitt County, Texas: One Texan and two Waco Indians die in a clash between settlers and Indian horse thieves.

October 3, Sussex County, Virginia: Numerous blacks are arrested as authorities crush a slave revolt.

October 4, Milledgeville, Georgia: Four blacks are arrested for plotting a slave uprising. All are later released without trial.

October 7, Prince George County, Virginia: A slave is executed for his role in an aborted uprising.

November, New York City: St. Mary's Roman Catholic church is robbed and burned by nativist rioters.

November 23, San Saba County, Texas: Eleven white prospectors battle with Indians, outnumbered twelve to one. One white man is killed in the clash, with three others wounded and five horses shot. The Indians carry their dead and wounded away, but white survivors count forty-eight patches of blood where enemy bodies have lain on the field.

1832

Shelbyville, Tennessee: Several blacks are flogged after a scheduled slave revolt is betrayed by one of the plotters.

March 25, Hiram, Ohio: Mormon leaders Joseph Smith and Sidney Rigdon are beaten, and tarred and feathered by a mob. The incident encourages Smith's followers to relocate to Missouri.

Spring, Indian Creek, Illinois: Settler William Davis beats a Potawatomie tribesman found tampering with a dam on his property. Neighbors are furious with Davis for letting the Indian live, afraid that the incident may spark reprisals. As one farmer explains, "Had he killed the Indian, it might have ended the affair."

April 6, Illinois: The Black Hawk War begins, as Sauks cross the border from Wisconsin to plant corn in their traditional fields. In a panic settlers kill one tribesman holding a truce flag, whereupon warriors retaliate in kind. By the end of the conflict, in August, over seventy whites have been killed, while Indian losses are estimated at 450 to 600.

Spring, Jackson County, Wyoming: Residents inaugurate a guerilla campaign lasting until July against Mormon settlers, smashing windows in their houses, firing into their homes, and burning haystacks.

May, Kane County, Illinois: Rev. Adam Payne is ambushed and killed by Potawatomie raiders, his head mounted on a pole near the Fox River.

May 2, New York City: Anti-Catholic rioting erupts at a meeting of the New York Protestant Association.

May 14, Ogle County, Illinois: Isaiah Stillman's raiders overtake Black Hawk's Sauk warriors at Old Man's Creek, with twelve soldiers killed and mutilated. Forty raiders desert under fire. Black Hawk admits to three warriors killed, but no Indian dead are found on the battlefield.

May 19, Carroll County, Illinois: One traveler is killed when Indians ambush a party of six near Buffalo Grove, west of modern Polo.

May 20, Indian Creek, Illinois: Sauk raiders attack the settlement, killing fifteen persons and looting their homes.

May 24, Stephenson County, Illinois: Winnebago warriors attack a party of white travelers near Kellogg's Grove, killing three men in a running fight.

June 14, Lafayette County, Wisconsin: Kickapoos attack a party of six workmen near Ft. Hamilton (now Wiota), killing five.

June 15, Stephenson County, Illinois: Military sentries fire on Sauk horse thieves outside camp at Kellogg's Grove. The next morning, troops pursue the Indians for twenty miles, killing and scalping four in a skirmish that leaves one soldier badly wounded. Indians retaliate with sniper fire as the troops retreat to Kellogg's Grove, wounding two more soldiers.

June 16, Lafayette County, Wisconsin: Settler Henry Appel is ambushed and killed by Kickapoo raiders near Ft. Hamilton. Troops overtake the war party on the Pecatonica River, killing and scalping eleven Kickapoos, against losses of three soldiers wounded (all of them fatally). Friendly Indian mercenaries arrive late for the battle and vent their frustration by dismembering the Kickapoo dead and scattering their remains.

June 20, Iowa County, Wisconsin: Emerson Green and George Force are ambushed and killed by Sauk raiders near Blue Mounds. A watch stolen from Force is found on the body of a Sauk killed at Four Lakes on July 21.

June 24, Jo Daviess County, Illinois: Sauk snipers besiege a fort on the Apple River for three hours, killing one white youth with rifle fire while other braves loot surrounding homesteads. No other casualties are reported on either side.

June 25, Stephenson County, Illinois: Troops pursue a Sauk raiding party, losing two men to Indian sniper fire before the rest are surrounded and besieged until nightfall at Kellogg's Grove. Authorities report nineteen whites killed since the Sauk offensive began on June 14.

July, Jefferson County, Wisconsin: A blind, elderly Sauk is captured by Illinois volunteers and then tortured, shot, and scalped.

July 2, Green River, Wyoming: Grose Ventre Indians raid a trappers' supply camp and steal ten horses.

July 7, Jefferson County, Wisconsin: Indian snipers fire on soldiers fishing along the Bark River, leaving one man gravely wounded. A search party fails to locate the Indians.

July 17–18, Pierre's Hole, Wyoming: Whites corner the Grose Ventre raiders in a battle that leaves twenty-six Indians dead and five trappers and seven friendly Indians dead.

July 20, Independence, Missouri: A mob of 500 "gentiles" destroys the printing office of a Mormon newspaper, inflicting $6,000 in damage. Raids on the homes of leading Mormons leave two men tarred and feathered, with warnings to evacuate the area. Mormons react by staging an armed demonstration in town on July 23.

July 21, Dane County, Wisconsin: U.S. troops overtake Black Hawk's war party at Wisconsin Heights, killing an estimated forty Indians before the rest escape under cover of nightfall. Four more braves are killed and scalped in a skirmish at nearby Four Lakes.

August 1, Crawford County, Wisconsin: One hundred fifty Sauk warriors approach the steamboat *Warrior* at the mouth of the Wisconsin River, three miles below Prairie du Chien. Indians display two white flags of truce, but crewmen open fire on orders from their captain. One white man is wounded in the clash and twenty-three are killed, with numerous Sauk wounded. On the same day, troops near the Kickapoo River invade a Sauk camp, capturing one invalid man and executing him as an act of "mercy."

August 2, Vernon County, Wisconsin: Volunteer forces assault Black Hawk's camp at Bad Axe, inflicting an estimated 300 casualties against white losses of eight men killed and eighteen wounded. Indian women and children are deliberately killed in the attack, on the theory that "nits make lice." A number of the women are stripped and raped before they are killed. Sauk refugees crossing the Mississippi River are met by Sioux warriors, who lift at least sixty-eight scalps. By the time regular troops arrive, militiamen are looting the camp and dancing with scalps around the mutilated bodies of their victims.

October 31, Big Blue, Missouri: "Gentile" raiders damage several Mormon homes, flogging two men and driving Mormon families out of the region.

November 1, Independence, Missouri: Rioters sack a store owned by Mormons, hurling merchandise into the street.

November 4, Jackson County, Missouri: Several persons are wounded, one of them fatally, when "gentile" nightriders clash with armed parties of Mormons. Church spokesmen estimate that 1,500 Mormons are driven out of the county by raiders, with more than 200 homes destroyed.

November 23, Jackson County, Missouri: Vigilantes rout another Mormon settlement, fifteen miles from Independence.

1833

Wilmington, North Carolina: The ringleaders of an aborted slave uprising are executed.

Independence, Missouri: Mormon settlers are driven from the area, on suspicion of plotting to free local slaves.

Detroit, Michigan: The rescue of Thornton Blackburn and his wife from slave-catchers touches off a riot against blacks.

Wharton County, Texas: A white posse assaults the camp of Caranchua Indians, who have recently visited outlying ranches demanding food at gunpoint. Several Indians are killed or wounded in the raid, with no white casualties.

August, Travis County, Texas: Indians attack a party of four whites, killing three. One wounded member of the group survives by feigning death while he is scalped.

Fall, Houston County, Texas: Four white men flee from an Indian assault on an isolated settlement, leaving their wives and children to be slaughtered in what historians have called "the only instance of such shameful cowardice recorded in the bloody annals of Texas."

October 2, New York City: White rioters prevent a scheduled speech by abolitionist spokesmen Arthur Tappan and William Lloyd Garrison.

December 6, Charlestown, Massachusetts: A white protestant male is beaten to death by Irish immigrants. Rioting mobs retaliate against Catholics in general, destroying several homes.

1834

Authorities record fifteen mob attacks on abolitionist groups and speakers during the year, all in Northern states.

Utica, New York: A white mob drives abolitionist speakers out of town.

Jefferson Parish, Louisiana: A runaway slave named Squier is shot and wounded by slave hunters in a swamp outside New Orleans. As soon as his wound has healed, Squier again flees the plantation, gathering a band of fugitive blacks and renegade whites to terrorize New Orleans and environs for the next three years. Taking the name of Bras Coupe, Squier becomes a fearful legend in his own time, leading bloody raids against outlying homes and plantations.

Columbia, Pennsylvania: Several black homes are destroyed by rioting whites.

March, Baltimore, Maryland: Immigrants disrupt an anti-Catholic gathering, assaulting the speaker.

April, Brazos River, Texas: Indians attack a Texas garrison, slaughtering several horses for meat. A posse pursues the Indians for sixty-five miles before wounding one brave, who afterward makes good his escape.

April 18, New York City: Protestant and Catholic voters clash in an election free-for-all.

May, New York City: Whites stage a riot against local abolitionists.

June, Clay County, Texas: Judge Gabriel Martin and a black servant are tortured to death by Pawnee raiders, their bodies mutilated.

Summer, Philadelphia, Pennsylvania: Five hundred whites raid a black amusement area, running amok before they are driven away. Violence continues over the next two days, with at least one black man, Stephen James, murdered by whites. Rioters destroy thirty-one black homes and two churches during the outbreak.

July 4-11, New York City: Violence by white racist rioters destroys sixty homes and six churches, inflicting serious damage on other churches and meeting halls before National Guardsmen restore order. Trouble begins on Independence Day, when hecklers disrupt an abolitionist rally. On July 5 two men are arrested for fighting following an argument about slavery. On the night of July 7, rioters storm a black meeting at Chatham Street Chapel, forcing the blacks to flee. The next day, arsonists set fire to a building housing a store owned by abolitionist John Rankin, and rioters disrupt an integrated meeting at Clinton Hall. Three outbreaks of nocturnal violence are reported on July 9, with major rioting on July 10 and 11. Black-owned property valued at $20,000 is destroyed in the riots, along with a store owned by abolitionist Lewis Tappan. The churches damaged or destroyed have all issued statements supporting the abolition of slavery.

August, Philadelphia, Pennsylvania: Local anti-Semites stage a violent "Passover riot" against Jews.

August 11, Charlestown, Massachusetts: An Ursuline convent is burned to the ground by a mob of anti-Catholic rioters.

September, Canterbury, Connecticut: White rioters wreck a black school run by local abolitionists.

October, Philadelphia, Pennsylvania: Pro-slavery rioters destroy four homes in the black community.

October 13, Santa Fe, New Mexico: A Mexican campaign against the Navajos is launched, killing sixteen Indians and leading to the capture of three others over the following five weeks. Troops also seize fifteen horses and mules and 3,000 sheep.

1835

Abolitionists suffer thirty-seven incidents of mob violence in Northern states during this year.

Washington, D.C.: A white mob tries to lynch Reuben Campbell, held for distributing abolitionist papers, then vents its frustration by destroying the homes and churches of free blacks. A second riot, sparked by disputes at the local navy yard, results in the destruction of more black homes, churches, and schools.

Nashville, Tennessee: Amos Dresser, a black abolitionist, is beaten and run out of town by vigilantes.

Fannin County, Texas: An Indian war party, including at least one fugitive black, assaults Kitchens's Station. One settler and at least two of the attackers are killed, with survivors decapitating a black corpse and mounting its head on a pole outside.

Philadelphia, Pennsylvania: White rioting is sparked by reports of a black man assaulting a white woman.

St. Louis, Missouri: A black man named McIntosh is burned alive for killing a policeman. A second mob destroys abolitionist Elijah Lovejoy's printing press, after Lovejoy prints an editorial denouncing the lynching.

Pittsburgh, Pennsylvania: Whites mob a black-owned barber shop, and then move on to launch a general assault on local blacks.

Van Zandt County, Texas: One white man dies when Indians attack a party of travelers.

Coryell County, Texas: Surveyor James Coryell is captured and killed by Indians in the area that now bears his name, ten miles from the site of modern Gatesville.

Gonzales County, Texas: An Italian traveler and his Mexican guides are ambushed by Indians, and all are killed and scalped following a day-long battle.

Falls County, Texas: David Ridgeway is ambushed and killed by Indians along the Brazos River, with a companion escaping unharmed. War parties move on to kill several white settlers in the vicinity of Ft. Marlin.

February 17, New York City: Catholics disrupt a nativist rally, assaulting the speaker.

February 28, Washington Pass, New Mexico: Navajos ambush Mexican troops in a box canyon, with heavy (but unspecified) Mexican losses. Thirty-five Indians are reported killed in the clash.

June, Mississippi: Members of a white vigilance committee in Hinds and Madison Counties expose a local slave conspiracy, using torture to obtain confessions from various blacks. The investigation culminates in the July executions of fifteen blacks and six white accomplices.

June 5, Lemitar, New Mexico: Navajo raiders strike on the west bank of the Rio Grande, kidnapping a shepherd and driving off 1,000 sheep and goats. One Mexican is killed and two others wounded in a futile pursuit of the warriors.

June 7, Socorro, New Mexico: Navajos kidnap a shepherd and seize his entire herd.

June 26, New York City: One person is killed in a riot between Catholics and Protestants.

Summer, Fayette County, Texas: James Alexander and his son are ambushed and killed by Indians while traveling from Austin to

Columbus. Local whites retaliate by raiding an Indian camp on Little River, killing five.

Summer, Lavaca County, Texas: Young DeWitt Lyons is captured by Comanches, who kill and scalp his father. Adopted by the tribe, he lives with them for several years.

Summer, Grimes County, Florida: Texans raid a Keechi Indian village on the Navasota River, tracking suspected horse thieves. Two Indian men are killed in the clash, with several Indian women and children captured for sale as slaves.

July, Madison County, Mississppi: Fifteen blacks and several white abolitionists are executed for plotting a slave revolt.

July 4, Detroit, Michigan: Catholics and Protestants clash in street rioting.

July 25, Nashville, Tennessee: Abolitionist Amos Dresser receives twenty lashes from members of a local pro-slavery vigilance committee.

July 29–30, Charleston, South Carolina: Mobs raid the local post office to prevent circulation of abolitionist literature through the mail.

August, Worcester, Massachusetts: An abolitionist minister is mobbed and beaten.

August, Charlestown, Maryland: Authorities report evidence of a local slave conspiracy against whites.

August, Philadelphia, Pennsylvania: A mob seizes large quantities of abolitionist literature, shreds it, and dumps it in the Delaware River.

August, Charleston, South Carolina: A white man named Brady is jailed for attempting to incite a slave rebellion.

August, Lynchburg, Virginia: A white abolitionist is hanged after conviction of inciting a slave insurrection.

August, New Hampshire: An abolitionist minister is beaten by rioters, then jailed by local authorities as a "brawler."

August 6, Hillsborough County, Florida: A mail carrier, Dalton, is ambushed and killed by Seminole raiders en route to Tampa.

September, Aiken, South Carolina: A white abolitionist is lynched.

September, Jefferson County, Georgia: Two whites are lynched for "seditious activity" among local slaves.

September, Twigg County, Georgia: A white abolitionist is driven from the area for inciting rebellion among slaves.

September 5, Florida: Nativist rioters harass immigrants in an anti-Catholic outbreak.

September 19, Texas: Reversing his stance of 1826, Stephen Austin issues a call to arms for Anglo settlers to rise against the Mexican government, proclaiming, "War is our only recourse. There is no other remedy."

Fall, Williamson County, Texas: Members of the McLennan family, en route to their new home, are ambushed by Indians and robbed and stripped of their clothing before they escape.

Fall, Bexar County, Texas: Anglo settlers rebel against Mexican rule, laying siege to the garrison at San Antonio.

October, Elizabeth City, North Carolina: Several slaves are imprisoned after exposure of a planned uprising. Free blacks involved in the plot are ordered to leave the state by November 1.

October, Georgia: A "considerable number" of rebel slaves are jailed in Jones and Monroe Counties, with two leaders hanged and a third "whipped, branded, and cropped."

October 21, Utica, New York: Rioters demolish the office of an abolitionist newspaper.

October 21, Boston, Massachusetts: Abolitionist William Lloyd Garrison is dragged through the streets with a rope by pro-slavery rioters. Police rescue him from the mob and place him in jail for his own protection.

November, Bell County, Texas: Indians attack the Taylor homestead, losing two braves, with four severely wounded in the fighting.

December, Clarkesville, Tennessee: A revolutionary plot is exposed among slaves at the local iron works.

December, Georgia: Aborted slave revolts are reported from several counties.

December, East Feliciana, Louisiana: Local blacks betray a planned rebellion by forty armed slaves.

December 18, Micanopy, Florida: The second Seminole war begins, started after a skirmish in which Indians assault a military wagon train, killing eight soldiers and wounding six more.

December 26–27, St. Johns River, Florida: A combined force of blacks and Seminoles raids area plantations.

December 28, Pasco County, Florida: Two Indians are killed in an attack on the garrison at Camp King. Meanwhile, twelve miles away, 109 soldiers are killed during a battle with Seminole warriors near the site of modern Dade City.

December 31, Withlacoochee River, Florida: A troop of Seminoles and blacks fires on soldiers building a bridge across the river. Five U.S. soldiers are killed and fifty-one are wounded.

1836

Authorities record sixty-four incidents of mob violence against abolitionists in Northern states during the year.

Alabama: Creeks open renewed hostilities against white settlers.

San Saba River, Texas: A surveyor named Harvey is captured by Waco Indians and is later liberated when the tribe is raided and conquered by rival Comanches.

Bell County, Texas: Indian raiders decimate a white settlement on the Little River.

Marblehead, Massachusetts: Abolitionist Amos Dresser is mobbed by racists. A few days later, he is struck in the head by a rock while addressing an abolitionist church meeting in Circleville, Ohio.

Kendall County, Texas: Three white travelers are ambushed by Indians along the Guadalupe River. Two of the travelers die in the skirmish.

Berlin, Ohio: Abolitionist Marius Robinson is stripped and tarred and feathered before being driven naked into the woods by a mob.

Lavaca County, Texas: Comanche raiders massacre the Creath and Hibbins families, taking one woman prisoner.

Washington County, Texas: John Edwards is ambushed by Indians, lanced to death, and scalped. A male companion escapes.

Grimes County, Texas: John Taylor is killed and mutilated by Indians near his rural home. A short time later, visiting the murder site, his wife is killed by warriors at the same place.

Fayette County, Texas: Indian raiders abduct a white woman and her two sons from a settlement on Cummins Creek. The boys are never seen again.

January, Colorado River, Texas: Indians assault DeWitt's Colony, killing two whites, and capturing a woman and two children.

January 6, New River, Florida: Indian raiders massacre five whites, including a woman and three children, in an assault on a rural homestead.

January 22, Indiana: Nativist rioters attack Catholic immigrants.

February 23, San Antonio, Texas: Mexican troops under Gen. Santa Ana lay siege to the Alamo, with 182 Anglo defenders inside. Skirmishes, sniper fire, and artillery bombardments continue for the next thirteen days, until Mexican shock troops stage three assaults on the Alamo, annihilating the garrison on March 6. Mexican forces lose 1,544 men during the siege.

February 27–March 6, Withlacoochee River, Florida: U.S. troops are pinned down by Seminole raiders in their makeshift barracks, with the siege lasting until March 5. Two U.S. soldiers are killed and two wounded during a battle on February 28. One soldier is killed and thirty-three wounded during a clash on February 29. Skirminshing ends after officers and Indian leaders hold a parley on the morning of March 6

March, Bell County, Texas: Indians massacre Laughlin McLennan's family on the San Gabriel River.

March 4, Lavaca County, Texas: Indians raid a small settlement, slaughtering eight members of the Dougherty and Douglas families.

March 17, Volusia, Florida: Seminoles ambush U.S. troops, killing three soldiers and wounding six.

March 17, Pilatkilaha, Florida: Troops burn an Indian village, killing one occupant.

March 19, Goliad, Texas: Mexican Gen. Jose Urrea orders the execution of 350 Texans in a move designed to crush the latest Anglo rebellion.

March 27, Ft. Alabama, Florida: Indians attack this outpost on the Hillsborough River, killing one soldier. Fighting resumes the next day, with another soldier killed and two more wounded.

March 28, Withlacoochee River, Florida: Indian snipers kill two members of a military expedition, harassing the rest of the troops as they retreat.

April 4, Maverick County, Texas: The latest in a series of Indian raids against the settlement of Dolores on the Rio Grande leaves twelve whites dead and two women captured and carried away. Survivors abandon the town a few days later.

April 21, San Jacinto, Texas: Relaxing after an indecisive skirmish with Anglo troops on April 20, Gen. Santa Ana allows himself to be surprised by Sam Houston's counterattack. Six hundred thirty Mexicans are killed in the assault, some of them reportedly while trying to surrender. Two Texans die. Santa Ana is captured, and spends more than six months in various prison camps before his release.

Spring, Missouri: Authorities crush a budding slave revolt, selling the identified conspirators out of state.

Spring, Texas: Three woodcutters are attacked by Indians at an unrecorded location, killing four braves before their assailants retreat.

Spring, Burleson County, Texas: Joseph Reed is ambushed and slain by Indians. His brother leads a posse in pursuit, losing his life in a brisk engagement that also claims the lives of several other whites before the Indians are routed. Vengeful settlers scalp the dead chief of the war party.

Spring, Travis County, Texas: Indian raiders rob the home of Nathaniel Moore, and resurface the next day to ambush and kill settler John Rover.

May, Micanopy, Florida: Seminoles attack two white-owned plantations in the area. Troops abandoning nearby Ft. Defiance are harassed by Indian snipers.

May, Brazos River, Texas: Two whites are killed when Indians attack a rural homestead.

May 19, Limestone County, Texas: Indian warriors attack Ft. Parker, killing five persons, wounding three, and capturing five. Four more whites are captured in a skirmish near the fort, but escape when armed comrades intervene on their behalf. One of the women captured at Ft. Parker watches her infant child murdered by the Indians, and remains a captive of the Indians until February 1838. Her surviving son is held prisoner until the latter part of 1842.

May 19, Alabama: Gen. Thomas Jesup receives orders from Washington for the immediate removal of Creek Indians from their ancestral homelands to the "Indian Territory" of Oklahoma. By late summer, a few hundred stragglers have been collected and penned in concentration camps near Mobile Bay.

June, Gates County, North Carolina: Gangs of fugitive maroons terrorize local whites.

June, Jefferson Parish, Louisiana: Authorities track a gang of outlaw fugitive slaves into the Cypress Swamp, near New Orleans.

Summer, Nacogdoches County, Texas: Cherokee warriors massacre two white families.

Summer, San Gabriel River, Texas: Three Indian warriors are killed in a clash with Texas militiamen.

June 4, Bell County, Texas: Indian warriors attack a party of travelers, killing two white men.

July, New Mexico: Mexican troops launch a new campaign against the Navajos. Casualties are not recorded.

July 12, Cincinnati, Ohio: Rioters demolish the press of an abolitionist newspaper.

July 31, Cincinnati, Ohio: A mob destroys the press of an abolitionist paper, moving on to attack several interracial brothels. Sporadic violence continues over the next two nights, with attacks on local blacks.

August, Sandy Creek, Texas: Indians surround a Texas militia camp by night, killing eight whites and wounding most of the eight survivors in a brisk firefight.

August, Boston, Massachusetts: Nativist rioters demonstrate outside a new Catholic church, firing shots at a statue of Bishop Benedict Fenwick.

September, Boston, Massachusetts: An effigy of the Pope is carried through the streets by a nativist mob, then used for target practice.

October 19, Withlacoochee River, Florida: Indian snipers harass an army camp, and troopers respond with artillery. Under cover of darkness, Indians invade the camp and slit the throats of six horses.

Fall, Brazos River, Texas: Three white travelers are ambushed and killed by Indian raiders who then scalp, dismember, and disembowel their bodies.

November, Robertson County, Texas: Indians kill three members of the Harvey family and abduct a young girl, who is sold in Mexico.

December, Ojo del Oso, New Mexico: Mexican troops assault four Navajo ranches, killing twenty men and capturing one woman and fourteen children. Soldiers also seize eighty mules and horses, and 5,300 sheep.

December, Withlacoochee River, Florida: U.S. troops capture sixteen Indians in one engagement. A few days later, soldiers kill two

Seminole chiefs, capturing eleven Indians and nine blacks. Another expedition captures seventy-seven blacks.

December 11, Winchester, Virginia: Slaves are blamed for an attempt to burn the town. Other fires are started on December 14 and 15, with two blacks subsequently jailed on suspicion.

December 24, Jackson, Louisiana: A slave revolt involving forty blacks is crushed in the planning stage. Two whites are hanged as ringleaders in the plot.

1837

Abolitionists are the target of forty-one mob incidents in Northern states during the year.

Alexandria, Louisiana: Eleven blacks are hanged and thirty others jailed when a scheduled slave uprising is exposed.

Boston, Massachusetts: Authorities suppress a nativist riot against Catholic immigrants.

Bastrop County, Texas: Indians massacre a family of six in their rural home, taking a woman and three children prisoner. The captives are traded for beads and blankets in 1839. Later in the year, one Comanche is killed by a posse of whites and Indians pursuing alleged horse thieves.

January 5, Milam County, Texas: Texas Rangers clash with Indians along Elm Creek, with two whites mortally wounded in the exchange.

January 16, Milam County, Texas: Texas Rangers and white volunteers wage a battle with Indians, routing the inhabitants of a local Indian village.

January 28, Anderson County, Texas: Indians attack a party of five white men on the Trinity River, killing three.

February, Gulf of Mexico: The Mexican government equips several small ships as gunboats, declaring a blockade of the Texas coastline.

February 8, Ft. Mellon, Florida: Seminoles attack the stockade, killing one officer and wounding seventeen soldiers.

April, Gulf of Mexico: A Texas gunboat, the *Independence*, is captured after a fierce battle with two Mexican warships, her crewmen taken as prisoners to Matamoros.

April 6, Jefferson Parish, Louisiana: Fugitive slave leader Bras Coupe is shot and wounded in an ambush by two white hunters outside of New Orleans.

April 22, Hidalgo County, New Mexico: White bounty hunters massacre a band of peaceful Apaches, lifting their scalps for sale to the governor of Sonora, Mexico.

July 6, New Orleans, Louisiana: The corpse of Bras Coupe is delivered to local authorities by one of his cohorts, Francisco Garcia. Despite a standing $2,000 reward for the slave, Garcia receives only $250 and an order to leave town at once. Coupe's body is placed on public display for two days.

August 26, Gulf of Mexico: The Texas "navy"—consisting of two gunboats—is attacked by Mexican vessels en route to Galveston. The *Brutus* escapes, but the *Invincible* is grounded on a sand bar and destroyed by Mexican gunfire.

September, St. Johns County, Florida: Troops stage a dawn attack on a Seminole camp south of St. Augustine, capturing twenty-one Indians. At dawn the following day, a second camp is raided, with one soldier and one Seminole killed, and twenty-six Indians taken prisoner.

September 5, Pennsylvania: Catholic rioters attack a Lutheran church.

Fall, Travis County, Texas: Joseph Rogers is killed when Indians ambush a white work party on Walnut Creek, six miles from the site of modern Austin. Soldiers from Ft. Prairie pursue the raiders, without success.

Fall, Cherokee County, Texas: White settlers return to their homes after being driven away by Indians. A short time later, hostilities are renewed by a mixed party of Indians and Mexican renegades, with an ambush that leaves six persons dead and ten taken prisoner. In separate incidents, Indian raiders massacre seven members of the Allen Killough family and murder a settler named Wood, while abducting his wife and children.

October, Rapides Parish, Louisiana: Authorities expose a local slave conspiracy, rounding up an estimated sixty slaves and at least three free blacks. Twelve of the prisoners are hanged, including all of the free blacks, with others sentenced to life imprisonment. U.S. troops are deployed to restore order among blacks.

October, Travis County, Texas: Ten whites and fifty-six Indians are killed and three white men wounded in a battle near Walnut Creek.

October 18, Ft. Moultrie, South Carolina: Seminole war chief Osceola is lured to a "peace conference" and then captured. He dies of illness on January 30, 1838, and the post doctor removes his head as a personal trophy before the body is buried.

October 28, Palo Pinto County, Texas: William "Big Foot" Wallace is attacked by an Indian war party. He kills one of his pursuers before he manages to elude the rest.

November, Bastrop County, Texas: Indian warriors fire on a party of woodcutters, killing a man named McCollum.

November 7, St. Louis, Missouri: Abolitionist Elijah Lovejoy is shot and killed in a mob assault on his newspaper office. The incident marks the third attack on Lovejoy's presses since July 4.

November 20, Palo Pinto County, Texas: William "Big Foot" Wallace is captured by Indians. First condemned to be burned at the stake, he is adopted by an elderly Indian woman, and then escapes from the tribe months later.

December 25, Lake Okeechobee, Florida: Seminole warriors ambush a volunteer force in the swamps nearby, killing twenty-six whites and wounding 112. Indian losses in the clash are presumed to be roughly equal.

1838

Four incidents of mob violence against abolitionists are reported in Northern states during the year.

Navarro County, Texas: Three surveyors are killed by Indians near the site of modern Corsicana. A posse gives chase, killing several warriors and losing one of their own before recapturing property valued at $4,000.

Fannin County, Texas: Texas volunteers assault an Indian village, killing and scalping an unspecified number, against losses of one white man wounded.

Corpus Christi Bay, Texas: Comanche raiders attack the settlement founded by Col. H.L. Kinney, killing three whites and wounding eight, against Indian losses of seven warriors dead and ten wounded.

January, Bastrop County, Texas: Indians stage repeated raids for livestock around the town of Bastrop. John Eagleston is shot with an arrow in one nocturnal foray, and dies three days later. Indians also attack a camp near Young's settlement, stealing sixty horses and some laundry after a skirmish with whites.

January, Grayson County, Texas: Josiah Washburn is shot and scalped by Indians, touching off a long series of raids and harassment against rural homesteads.

January 10, Jupiter River, Florida: Seminole warriors pursue an army patrol, killing five soldiers and wounding twenty-two.

Spring, Goliad County, Texas: Indians attack two white campers at night, but find dummies placed in the travelers' bed rolls.

Spring, Nacogdoches, Texas: Vincente Cordova receives a commission from the Mexican government to recruit East Texas Indians as auxiliaries to the Mexican army for a war against Texas.

Spring, Milam County, Texas: Two Indians are killed when they attack a survey party.

May, Philadelphia, Pennsylvania: White rioters burn a shelter for black orphans, stoning one black church and attempting to burn another. Violence against blacks quickly spreads to other Pennsylvania cities.

May, Washington, D.C.: Police and white vigilantes break up some "infamous dens" where local slaves have recently plotted a revolt.

Summer, Bell County, Texas: Comanche raiders attack a wagon train, killing thirteen men, burning the wagons, and escaping with two white prisoners. One, a Mrs. Webster, remains in captivity through the spring of 1840.

Summer, Kendall County, Texas: Indians attack a party of ten surveyors on the Guadalupe River, killing all of them.

Summer, Bastrop, Texas: Samuel Robertson is ambushed and killed by Indians near town. A male companion escapes.

July 23, Caloosahatchee River, Florida: Seminoles stage a dawn raid on an army camp, killing most of the soldiers present.

August 4, Nacogdoches, Texas: A white posse traces several stolen horses to a nearby Mexican settlement. While returning home with the animals, they are ambushed by Cordova's gunmen, with one of their number killed.

August 8, Gallatin, Missouri: Several persons are injured as riotous "gentiles" prevent Mormon settlers from voting in a state elections.

August 9, Angelina County, Texas: A company of Texas volunteers report being fired on by a troop of 100 Mexicans near Gonzales. By the following day, a combined force of 600 Mexicans and Indians has been organized along the Angelino River. Cordova announces his rebellion in a formal letter to the Texas government.

August 10, Arroyo Seco, Texas: A party of twenty-two white men is ambushed by 100 Comanches. The party repulses the Indians with one man wounded.

Fall, Yuma County, Arizona: A two-month Mexican campaign against the Navajos ends with sixty-eight Indians reported dead and fifty-six men and women captured. Troops also seize 226 horses and 2,060 sheep.

Fall, Grayson County, Texas: Indian raiders kill one man and wound a boy when they attack an outlying farm.

October, Navarro County, Texas: Members of a survey party clash with Indian raiders in a bloody engagement at Battle Creek.

October 6, Dewitt, Missouri: Troops intervene as 300 armed "gentiles," complete with artillery, besiege a small Mormon settlement. Over the next three weeks, Mormon raiders retaliate against real and suspected enemies in Daviess and Caldwell counties, slaughtering livestock and burning an estimated 150 homes. An armed assault by eighty Mormons on the town of Gallatin results in two stores being looted, with several dwellings set afire.

October 12, Nacogdoches County, Texas: Anglo militiamen pursue a force of Cordova's Mexicans and Indians, blamed for an assault on the Killough family. Most of the renegades escape after a disorganized battle.

October 16, Trinity River, Texas: Two hundred Texans assault a Mexican-Indian camp, routing the enemy forces and pursuing them for over a mile. Cordova's troops and Indian allies sustain unspecified "heavy" casualties, leaving eleven Indians dead on the field as they escape, retreating to Mexico.

October 20, Bexar County, Texas: Comanche raiders attack a survey party, killing two men. A posse of thirteen men is sent to investigate, clashing with an estimated 100 Indians in a skirmish that leaves eight surveyors dead and four wounded.

October 24, Crooked River, Missouri: Four men are killed and at least seven wounded when Mormons stage a pre-dawn assault on a "gentile" militia encampment.

October 25, Young County, Texas: Texans clash with Comanche warriors at the village of Jose Maria, leaving an unspecified "large number" of Indians dead on the field of battle.

October 30, Haun's Mill, Missouri: A mob led by three state militia captains attacks a Mormon settlement, killing nineteen persons and wounding several others.

November, Florence, Kentucky: A local slave conspiracy is exposed, but the leaders escape to Canada.

November 29, Missouri: Militia units are dissolved in the wake of the "Mormon insurrection." Authorities estimate that forty Mormons have been killed since October, versus a loss of one "citizen" killed and fifteen badly wounded.

Winter, Gonzales County, Texas: Tonkawas encouraged by Texans attack a camp of rival Comanche and Waco Indians, killing and scalping ten and carving pieces from their bodies for subsequent use in a cannibalistic victory feast.

December, Tennessee: Authorities crush a slave insurrection in Rutherford and Williamson Counties.

1839

Northern states are the scene of four mob attacks on abolitionist groups and speakers during the year.

New York: White riots, sparked by the hiring of black laborers, are reported in several cities.

Lavaca County, Texas: A white settler named Henseley survives two "close calls" with Indians during hunting trips near his rural home.

Denton County, Texas: Rev. John Denton is ambushed and killed by Indians in the region that now bears his name.

Erath County, Texas: A young settler named Saunders narrowly escapes from an ambush by Indians.

Gonzales County, Texas: A posse pursues Indian horse thieves to their camp, killing all but one brave, who manages to escape.

Grayson County, Texas: Indians ambush, kill, and scalp three travelers, three miles west of modern Denison. A few days later, Indians surprise a black man working in the fields near Ft. English. One of the Indians is wounded when he opens fire with a revolver.

January, Burlington, Massachusetts: Arsonists cause serious damage to St. Mary's Roman Catholic church, the fire spreading to destroy surrounding homes.

January, Gonzales County, Texas: A party of five whites and thirty-five Tonkawa Indians clash with Comanche and Waco Indians, killing five of the enemy and wounding several more. One Tonkawa warrior is slain.

January 1, Falls County, Texas: Indian raiders loot a home near Morgan's point, killing six persons and wounding a seventh.

January 10, Falls County, Texas: Seven Indians die in a raid against a rural homestead.

January 16, Falls County, Texas: Texas volunteers discover two rural homes abandoned and looted by Indians. A subsequent clash with the Indians kills an estimated thirteen Texans, with at least five wounded before the posse retreats in disarray. Indian casualties are unknown.

February, Macon, Georgia: Several arson fires are blamed on slaves.

February, Iberville Parish, Louisiana: Patrols are mounted in response to local slave uprisings.

February 14, San Saba River, Texas: A combined force of Texans and friendly Lipan Indians attack a Comanche village at dawn, indiscriminately killing Indians of both sexes and all ages.

February 18, Colorado River, Texas: A war party of 300 Indians attack the settlement at Well's Prairie, killing a white woman and her son. Three or four braves die in the skirmish. A posse gives chase on February 19, but its leader is killed and the other members routed in a clash with Indians near the settlement of Brushy. Indians pursue the retreating whites to Brushy, where a pitched battle leaves four settlers dead or mortally wounded and an unspecified "great number" of Indians slain or injured.

March, Memphis, Tennessee: Authorities expose a plot by several slaves to poison their masters.

March 29, Guadalupe County, Texas: White volunteers wage a running battle with a Cordova's force of Indians, Mexicans, and fugitive blacks, killing an estimated eighteen of the enemy, with five captured and an uncertain "considerable number" wounded. The Texans suffer no casualties.

Spring, Grayson County, Texas: Indian raids terrorize local settlements, with patrols mounted to little or no effect.

May 15, Travis County, Texas: Texans clash with a party of Mexicans at Onion Creek, south of Austin, continuing their pursuit into the following day. The Texans are nearly routed in a clash on May 17, before William "Big Foot" Wallace kills the Mexican commander with a single, well-placed shot.

May 27, Bell County, Texas: Texas Rangers skirmish with Comanches, pursuing the Indians until they meet an ambush near the site of modern Belton. Fourteen Rangers are killed or wounded, against estimated Comanche losses of 100 dead.

June, Burnet County, Texas: One man is wounded when Indian warriors ambush a surveyor's party.

July, Florida: Indians attack travelers and plantations along the coastal areas of Sarasota and Charlotte Counties. Twenty-four soldiers are killed at Charlotte Harbor when warriors raid their sleeping camp.

July 15, Neches River, Texas: Texas militia units attack a Cherokee war party, killing eighteen braves. Three militiamen are killed and five wounded. Fighting is renewed on July 16, with an estimated 100 Indians killed; five Texans die in the second battle, and twenty-seven are wounded. Pursuit of the Indians continues until July 25, with a skirmish near modern Grand Saline, before the survivors escape.

August 30, Pennsylvania: Ten white men are shot by the militia, as authorities suppress rioting between Irish Catholics and German Protestant workmen on the Chesapeake and Ohio Canal.

September 24, Cebolleta, New Mexico: A Navajo warrior kills one Mexican rancher and drives away his livestock.

Fall, Travis County, Texas: A black slave is ambushed and killed by Indians on Walnut Creek, near Austin.

October 13, New Mexico: A military campaign against the Navajos is launched, extending through January 1840. Mexican troops kill sixteen Indians and capture two, along with 145 horses and 10,000 sheep.

Winter, Austin, Texas: Indians kill several persons within the town limits.

December, Wolcott, Connecticut: Rioters burn an abolitionist meeting house.

December 3, Tome, New Mexico: Two Mexicans are killed by Navajo raiders.

December 4, Belen, New Mexico: Sixteen Mexicans die in a Navajo raid.

December 7, Tome, New Mexico: Navajo warriors kill another Mexican.

December 25, Schleicher County, Texas: Cherokees attack a party of white travelers, killing several men before they are driven back, with unspecified casualties. Twenty-seven Indian women and children are captured in the engagement.

1840

Authorities report four incidents of mob violence against abolitionists in Northern states during the year.

Bastrop, Texas: Indians raid surrounding settlements for livestock, then flee into nearby Lee County with a posse on their heels. The thieves are overtaken near the Yegua River. Six Indians die, the rest escape.

Robertson County, Texas: A posse pursues Indian horse thieves, with two Indians killed in a skirmish that leaves one white man seriously wounded.

Grayson County, Texas: Indians attack a rural homestead, killing three and capturing a child. Sporadic raids continue throughout the year.

March 19, San Antonio, Texas: Violence erupts when U.S. authorities try to arrest sixty-five Comanches who have entered the town to treat for peace. Seven Texans are killed and eight wounded during the outbreak. Thirty-seven Comanche die and twenty-seven are captured. One Comanche escapes.

Spring, Fayette County, Texas: Henry Earthman is surprised and killed by a band of Indians.

Spring, DeWitt County, Texas: Indian raiders kill two white men and one boy, taking another child prisoner.

June, Virginia: Slave unrest is reported from Southampton and Westmoreland Counties.

July, Texas: An estimated 1,000 Comanche raiders, encouraged by the Mexican government, launch a series of raids in the southwestern part of the state.

August, Craven County, North Carolina: Authorities crush a slave revolt.

August, Travis County, Texas: Indians assault the settlement at Brushy Creek, eighteen miles from modern Austin. One white man is wounded in the siege before reinforcements arrive; Indian casualties are unknown. Indian attacks continue around Brushy Creek, with one settler wounded and nearly scalped in an ambush nearby. A cowboy named Foley is captured on the range, tortured, then lanced to death.

August, Petersburg, Virginia: Armed patrols are mounted in response to a slave insurrection.

August, Charles County, Maryland: Several slaves are arrested for plotting an armed attack on nearby Washington, D.C.

August 6, Victoria, Texas: Several whites are killed or wounded in a surprise attack by Comanche raiders. The Indians escape with an estimated 2,000 head of livestock.

August 7, Key Island, Florida: Indians attack the settlement, killing several whites.

August 8, Calhoun County, Texas: Comanche raiders sack the seaport town of Linnville, killing or capturing most of the inhabitants before setting the town on fire.

August 12, Travis County, Texas: A combined force of Texans and Tonkawa Indians clash with Comanche warriors on Plum Creek, south of Austin. An estimated fifty to eighty Comanches die in the clash, with several hundred stolen animals captured, against Texan losses of no one killed and only a few men wounded. Three dead hostages from Linnville are found on the battlefield, while Tonkawa warriors cut off the hands and feet of their fallen enemies for use in victory dances.

August 22, Sabinal, New Mexico: Navajo raiders kill two men and a woman, wound three people, and drive off ninety horses and mules.

September, Cebolleta, New Mexico: Mexican civilians raid local Navajo ranches, capturing several women and children and freeing one Mexican hostage. Elsewhere in the state, Mexican troops kill thirty-three Navajos and capture fourteen in two separate battles.

September–October, Louisiana: Large-scale conspiracies involving hundreds of slaves are reported from Avoyelles, Iberville, Lafayette, Tapides, St. Landry, St. Martin, and Vermillion Parishes. Many blacks are jailed, along with a few white suspects; some are flogged, with "a considerable number" executed or lynched. At least two of the alleged leaders commit suicide in jail.

Fall, San Antonio, Texas: A war party of 200 Comanches steal a large number of horses, fleeing northward toward the Guadalupe River with Texas Rangers in pursuit. The Indians are routed and most of the stock is recovered in a skirmish in which the Comanche leader is shot and killed.

October 2, St. Louis, Missouri: One person is reported killed in anti-Catholic rioting.

October 24, Runnels County, Texas: Texas volunteers assault and burn a Comanche village on the Colorado River, killing 128 Indians and capturing thirty-four. Two Texans are wounded.

November, The Everglades, Florida: Troops stalking Seminoles report killing four warriors and capturing thirty-six Indian men, women, and children. One soldier is killed and six wounded in the campaign.

December, Williamson County, Texas: Texas volunteers clash with a party of Comanches at Opossum Creek.

December 6, Red River, Texas: Indians attack the sleeping camp of a surveying party, killing thirty-nine men in their bedrolls.

December 8, New York City: Anti-Catholic rioting erupts at a meeting of the Public School Society.

December 28, Alachua County, Florida: An army detail is ambushed by Indians between Fort Micanopy and Watkahoota. Twelve soldiers and one woman are killed in the attack, and one man escapes to tell about the ambush.

1841

Louisiana: A planned slave revolt is exposed in St. Landry and Lafayette Parishes. Nine blacks are hanged and four white conspirators are flogged and expelled from the state by vigilantes.

Fannin County, Texas: Two white boys are captured by Indians, who then kill a one-armed man, scalping him, and cutting his good arm off at the elbow before dumping his corpse in a creek.

Mississippi, Louisiana: A widespread slave conspiracy is uncovered along the Gulf coast, with one black leader and a number of his followers hanged.

January 4, Wilmington, North Carolina: Whites are repulsed in their assault on a nearby community of runaway slaves. One attacker is killed. Three maroons are captured and taken to jail in Wilmington, where one escapes and the others are lynched by a mob on January 5.

January 9, Travis County, Texas: Judge James Smith is ambushed and killed by Indians north of Austin. A young son is taken prisoner, while his brother escapes.

January 19, Travis County, Texas: The father-in-law of Judge James Smith—murdered by Indians on January 9—is killed by Indians south of Austin.

February, Augusta, Georgia: The leader of a slave uprising is hanged.

February 16, Philadelphia, Pennsylvania: An anti-Catholic orator is mobbed by Irish adversaries.

March, Alachua County, Florida: U.S. troops fight two inconclusive skirmishes with Indians.

Spring, Bandera Pass, Texas: Three hundred Commanches clash with forty Texas Rangers in a battle that leaves sixty Indians dead, with five Rangers killed and six wounded.

Spring, Kimble County, Texas: Texas volunteers stage a dawn raid on an Indian camp, killing four braves and capturing a number of horses and mules.

June, Florida: Troops destroy every Seminole village found between the Withlacoochee River and the Everglades, seizing a handful of prisoners and an abundance of supplies.

June 19, Austin, Texas: A paramilitary expedition of 321 Texans with twenty-one wagons—dubbed the "Santa Fe Pioneers"—start north on a mission "to induce New Mexico to become an integral part of Texas."

July, Grayson County, Texas: Daniel Dugan and William Kitchens are ambushed and killed by Indians. On the Sunday following their funeral, tribesmen assault the Kitchens homestead, wounding one boy before they are driven off with several casualties.

August, West Feliciana, Louisiana: Authorities suppress a local slave revolt, jailing several blacks.

August, Woodville, Mississippi: A slave conspiracy is exposed, and several blacks are imprisoned.

August 31, Cincinnati, Ohio: Blacks and whites clash in street brawl.

September, Mobile County, Alabama: Two companies of militia are sent to track a gang of forty-five fugitive slaves who have terrorized local whites with thefts and arson.

September 1, Cincinnati, Ohio: White men armed with clubs attack a boarding house for blacks.

September 2, Cincinnati, Ohio: Racial street fighting breaks out after white boys throw gravel at a group of blacks. Two whites are stabbed in the incident.

September 3, Cincinnati, Ohio: A major race riot erupts after three days of street clashes between blacks and whites. Violence continues until the predawn hours of September 5, with "dozens" of persons reported killed and 300 blacks jailed for their own protection.

September 8, Massachusetts: While traveling by train from Newburyport to Providence, Rhode Island, Frederick Douglass is roughed up by five railroad employees, who drag him from a "white" car to the Jim Crow compartment reserved for blacks.

September 28, Massachusetts: Traveling between Lynn and Newburyport, Frederick Douglass and two white abolitionists are beaten by eight men and thrown off the train for sitting together in a white railroad car.

September 29, Woonsocket Falls, Rhode Island: White racists armed with stones and rotten eggs disrupt an abolitionist gathering.

Fall, Bexar County, Texas: Indians suffer several casualties in an attack on an armed survey party.

Fall, Grayson County, Texas: Members of a volunteer posse raid an Indian camp, killing one Indian and recapturing several stolen horses.

October, New Orleans, Louisiana: A local newspaper cites "the late repeated attacks of the Negro upon the white man in our city" as evidence of mounting slave unrest.

October, Terrebonne Parish, Louisiana: Authorities report frequent attacks on whites by a band of fugitive slaves.

October 5, Quay County, New Mexico: Mexican troops capture the "Santa Fe Pioneers" near Tucumcari.

October 20, Big Cypress Swamp, Florida: Two soldiers die in a Seminole ambush.

November, Big Cypress Swamp, Florida: Troops raid two Seminole camps, killing eight Indians and capturing forty-seven.

November 7, At Sea: Slaves mutiny on board the brig *Creole*, bound from Hampton Roads, Virginia, to New Orleans. The captain is wounded as blacks take control and sail to Nassau, where they are freed by British authorities.

Winter, Grayson County, Texas: Indians assault the Dugan homestead, killing one person and losing three of their own number mortally wounded. Texans retaliate with a raid into Oklahoma, attacking an Indian camp north of the Red River and killing twelve allegedly hostile Indians. Indian raids continue in Grayson County, with one settler killed in Warren before the end of the year.

December 20, Mandarin, Florida: Five whites are killed when Indians assault and burn the settlement.

1842

Louisiana: Authorities uncover a revolutionary plot hatched by runaway slaves dwelling in the swamps of Carroll, Concordia, and Madison Parishes. More than twenty blacks are arrested, and several are hanged.

Dallas County, Texas: An immigrant settler named Clubz is ambushed and killed by Indian raiders. Local whites retaliate by attacking a nearby Indian camp, killing one brave.

Pennsylvania: Sporadic violence breaks out between black and Irish miners in the coal fields.

Collin County, Texas: Two white farmers are killed, scalped, and mutilated by Indians.

Philadelphia, Pennsylvania: Two persons die as white mobs attack a peaceful parade, celebrating the abolition of slavery in the West Indies. Black-owned stores are razed before the violence is suppressed.

Milam County, Texas: Texans pursue a party of Indian horse thieves near the site of modern Cameron. Three Indians are killed and scalped in the ensuing skirmish, including a chief known as Big Foot.

Bastrop County, Texas: Settler Matthew Jett surprises three Indians looting his cabin and kills all three.

Winter, Colorado River, Texas: One white man and at least six tribesmen die in a series of Indian raids on white settlements.

January, Mandarin, Florida: Seminole warriors burn a white settlement, killing two women and one child.

February, Suwanee County, Florida: Seminole raiders attack a white family, killing a woman and one child, and leaving four other children for dead. Troops pursue the warriors and surprise them with a dawn raid on their camp, but the raiders escape, leaving the soldiers with four women and three children.

March, Texas: An estimated 1,500 Mexican troops cross the Rio Grande, stopping at Goliad and Victoria to raise Mexican flags before invading San Antonio on March 5. The army withdraws two days later, after inflicting minor damage on the town.

Spring, Gonzales County, Texas: Indians raid outlying homes and settlements, stealing livestock and killing several whites. One, a doctor named Witter, is scalped and mutilated on a country road.

April 12, New York City: Nativist mobs stone a Catholic bishop's home and hound Irish immigrants through the streets.

April 18, Lake Ahapopka, Florida: Seminoles ambush a military party but are routed by the troops, with two Indians killed, two more wounded, and one captured at the scene. Two soldiers die in the clash, and three others are injured. Sporadic skirmishes continue until July 14, when military commanders announce the cessation of Seminole hostilities.

May 6, Independence, Missouri: Gov. Lilburn Boggs, an enemy of Mormonism, is shot and gravely wounded by a sniper at his home. Mormon O.P. Rockwell is tried and acquitted in the case, and afterward boasts of his role in the attack.

June 28, Marshall County, Tennessee: The press reports an outbreak of slave revolts, which are quickly suppressed by authorities.

Summer, Austin, Texas: Indians abduct two white children, a boy and a girl. The girl is killed six miles from town, the boy is held captive for eighteen months before he is traded for supplies.

Summer, Alabama: Slave uprisings are reported in the northern part of the state.

September, San Antonio, Texas: Mexican troops capture the town, taking several prominent citizens prisoner.

Fall, Llano County, Texas: William "Big Foot" Wallace is surprised by an Indian while watering his horse, and kills the brave with his knife in a hand-to-hand encounter.

Fall, Austin, Texas: Indians invade the town, killing one man, wounding one boy, and abducting another.

Fall, Bastrop County, Texas: A settler named Lance is ambushed, killed, and scalped by Indians.

September 11, San Antonio, Texas: Fourteen hundred Mexican soldiers, led by a French mercenary officer, invade the town. Three members of the Lone Star congress and various other officials are among the prisoners seized.

September 18, Bexar County, Texas: Texas volunteers clash with Mexican troops at Salado Creek, killing sixty Mexicans against losses of one Anglo slain. Retreating toward San Antonio, the Mexicans overpower a smaller troop of volunteers, killing most of the Texans and carrying a few survivors back to Mexico as the invaders withdraw.

October 26, Fulton, Missouri: Authorities report the suppression of a local slave revolt.

November 17, Louisiana: A New Orleans newspaper reports incidents of slave unrest in Carroll, Concordia, and Madison Parishes, instigated by a band of 300 fugitives dwelling in the nearby swamps.

December 15, Laredo, Texas: Anglo forces cross the border into Mexico, seeking revenge on Mexican troops for their attack on San Antonio.

December 23, Mier, Mexico: Texans capture the hamlet, taking the mayor and local priest hostage as they demand supplies and then retreat across the Rio Grande into Texas.

December 25, Mier, Mexico: Two hundred sixty-one Texans cross the river a second time, clashing with 2,000 Mexican troops in a battle lasting past nightfall. An estimated 600 Mexicans die in the clash, with an equal number wounded. Thirty Texans are slain. Unaware of the body count, the outnumbered Texans are bluffed into surrendering. Sentenced to prison on December 26, the survivors are marched first to Matamoros, then to Mexico City.

1843

Pendleton, Indiana: Black abolitionist Frederick Douglass is severely beaten by local racists.

January 1, Travis County, Texas: Two white men are killed, and a white boy and a black servant abducted in Indian raids south of Austin. A posse corners the raiders at Walker Creek and inflicts an unspecified number of casualties before the surviving Indians escape.

February 11, Salado, Mexico: Texan prisoners from the Mier raid overpower their Mexican guards and scatter in a vain attempt to reach the Rio Grande. Of 230 beginning the chaotic trek, 176 are recaptured alive. President Santa Anna orders all prisoners executed, but the governor of Coahuila refuses to obey, and the order is changed to death for one man out of every ten, with the selection to be done by drawing colored beans. Seventeen of the prisoners draw black beans—the rest being white—and are summarily executed by firing squad. Those who survive captivity in Mexico are released on September 16, 1844.

April, Ft. Johnson, Texas: A new paramilitary expedition goes north, acting under orders to ambush Mexican wagon trains in the disputed area of modern Kansas.

Spring, Arkansas River, Oklahoma: An expedition from Texas, hoping to intercept the Mexican governor of New Mexico on his way home from Independence, Missouri, clashes with an advance detachment, killing eighteen Mexicans and capturing seventy to eighty. The prisoners are subsequently freed, with horses for the wounded.

June 20, Kansas: Members of a Texan expeditionary force clash with Mexican soldiers, killing seventeen and capturing eighty-two in a battle that leaves the Anglos unscathed.

June 30, Oklahoma: A party of Texans are surrounded and disarmed by U.S. troops for trespassing on U.S. soil in their pursuit of Mexican caravans.

July, Oklahoma: While trailing the New Mexico governor's caravan, Texan forces are attacked by Comanches at Owl Creek. Two men are killed and several are wounded. Indian losses total ten to fifteen warriors dead. Ten days later, near the Canadian River, the Texans are ambushed again, thus preventing them from overtaking the Mexican column.

1844

Blanco County, Texas: Fifteen Texas Rangers clash with seventy-five Comanches on the Pedernales River, leaving thirty Indians dead, and two Rangers dead and five wounded.

Milam County, Texas: Two white men and seven Indians die when settlers attack a tribal war party at Cedar Creek.

February, Hanesville, Mississippi: One fugitive slave is killed and two others wounded when white planters ambush a group of runaways near town.

March 3, Abiquiu, New Mexico: Navajo warriors raid the settlement, driving away fourteen oxen and several head of cattle.

May 7–8, Philadelphia, Pennsylvania: At least one person is killed and more than fifty injured as nativist mobs riot against Catholics. A second mob gathers in the evening to threaten a Catholic school, but disperses after armed guards kill two rioters and wound several more. Violence continues on May 8, with a Catholic church and school burned, together with a row of Irish homes. Troops arrive to scatter the mob before it can demolish two more churches.

June 10, Nauvoo, Illinois: Mormon raiders, acting under orders from "prophet" Joseph Smith, destroy the presses of a critical newspaper. Smith and his brother are subsequently jailed on charges of inciting a riot.

June 27, Carthage, Illinois: A lynch mob invades the local jail, murdering Mormons Joseph and Hyrum Smith in their cell.

July 5–7, Philadelphia, Pennsylvania: New anti-Catholic riots break out, with mobs sacking one church in a quest for nonexistent weapons. Troops restore order on July 8, at a cost of two soldiers killed and twenty-six wounded.

July 11, New Mexico: Utes join Navajos in raiding various settlements.

1845

Charles County, Maryland: A scheduled revolt by slaves and free blacks is discovered and crushed by authorities. One slave is hanged, with several others sold out of state. The free blacks are sentenced to forty-year prison terms.

Massachusetts: After helping a fugitive slave escape, Capt. Jonathan Walker is branded on his hand with the letters "SS"—for "slave stealer"—and thrown into jail.

Franklin County, Idaho: Texan Jim Kinney, traveling with an emigrant party west of Ft. Hall, captures a passing Indian, and flogs and binds him for use as a personal slave. Kinney threatens to track the Indian with dogs and kill him if he flees, "to show the other Indians the superiority of the white man. He said he had killed plenty of Negroes, and an Indian was no better than a Negro." Other members of the train are frightened to oppose Kinney, but the captive escapes with Kinney's best Kentucky rifle and a quantity of food.

Bexar County, Texas: A war party of 300 Comanches attack white settlements west of San Antonio, killing several persons. Texas Rangers pursue the raiders into Kendall County, overtaking their quarry on the Guadalupe River. A battle ensues, leaving roughly half of the Indians dead. One Ranger is killed and three wounded.

June, Travis County, Texas: Daniel Hornsby and William Adkisson are killed by Indians while fishing on the Colorado River.

July, Rockville, Maryland: Whites intercept a party of armed slaves from Charles, Prince Georges, and St. Mary's Counties before they can reach their destination in the free state of Pennsylvania. At least five slaves are wounded by gunfire, and thirty-one are jailed. A free black implicated in the revolt is sentenced to forty years imprisonment, while one slave is hanged and most of the others are sold out of state.

August 28, Campti, Louisiana: Authorities suppress a local slave revolt.

September 9, Green Plain, Illinois: Nightriders fire on a local school where an anti-Mormon meeting is in progress. "Gentile" raiders retaliate by driving Mormon settlers out of Hancock County, burning their homes, outbuildings, and grain stores.

September 11, Sligo, Louisiana: Local whites suppress a slave uprising fifteen miles south of town.

September 16, Nauvoo, Illinois: Phineas Wilcox, suspected as a "gentile" spy, is murdered and secretly buried by Mormon militants.

November 17, Warsaw, Illinois: Local citizens rally to condemn recent vigilante raids against Mormons that have resulted in one murder and the burning of several homes in the area.

1846

Comal County, Texas: Seventy-five Comanches attack a party of six travelers, including William "Big Foot" Wallace, charging their position several times without inflicting any casualties.

February 12, New Orleans, Louisiana: Local slaves are foiled in an attempt to revolt.

April 9, Cameron County, Texas: Col. Truman Cross disappears on a routine horseback ride near Ft. Texas, on the Rio Grande. Murdered by Mexican troops from Matamoros, he is found by his comrades on April 22.

April 20, Cameron County, Texas: Lt. David Porter leads a patrol in search of Col. Truman Cross. The expedition is ambushed by Mexican forces on the U.S. side of the Rio Grande, with Porter and three Mexicans killed before nine survivors fight their way clear of the trap.

April 23, Cameron County, Texas: Capt. Seth Thomas leads a force of sixty-three dragoons to intercept a Mexican army crossing the Rio Grande into Texas. The patrol is ambushed, with sixteen men killed and the remainder captured.

May, Pensacola, Florida: Local authorities crush a slave rebellion in its planning stage.

May 2–5, Cameron County, Texas: Mexican artillery bombards Ft. Texas, killing one soldier and wounding several others. Another of the wounded dies on May 9.

May 8, Cameron County, Texas: U.S. troops clash with Mexican forces in the Battle of Palo Alto. Five hundred Mexican dead are left on the field. U.S. losses total two soldiers killed and forty-two wounded.

May 9, Cameron County, Texas: U.S. forces fight another battle with Mexican troops at Resaca de la Palma. Mexican forces are routed and driven back across the Rio Grande. Casualties are estimated at 700 killed or wounded in combat and 300 drowned while swimming the river. U.S. losses total thirty-two dead and seventy-one wounded.

May 16, Richmond, Virginia: A budding slave revolt is crushed by armed whites.

July 11, Nauvoo, Illinois: Three Mormon farmers are flogged by their "gentile" neighbors outside of town. A Mormon posse arrests seventeen suspects, with enemies of the church seizing five Mormon hostages in retaliation.

September 12, Nauvoo, Illinois: A "gentile" raiding party, complete with artillery, besieges the Mormon settlement. Four persons die in the battle, with at least seven more wounded, before the attackers are driven away.

September 17–18, Nauvoo, Illinois: A "posse" of 2,000 men invades the settlement, commanding all Mormons and their sympathizers to leave the state. The order is enforced on September 18, as raiders loot homes and drive settlers from the area by force.

September 27, Laguna, New Mexico: Trackers return with the scalps of four Navajos who earlier had raided the settlement, killing one man and two children and driving away a herd of sheep.

September 30, Bernalillo County, New Mexico: Navajo raiders kill several settlers on the west bank of the Rio Grande, seven miles south of Albuquerque, driving away 2,000 sheep.

October, Blanco County, Texas: Indians kill two members of a survey party near the Pedernales River.

October 3, Polvadera, New Mexico: Navajo warriors raid the settlement, driving residents from their homes, and escaping with cattle and horses.

October 8, San Pedro, California: U.S. troops come ashore for an advance on Los Angeles. They are met by Mexican cavalry and a single field gun, repulsed in a skirmish that leaves four U.S. soldiers dead and ten wounded.

October 13, Cubero, New Mexico: Mexican troops burn a deserted Navajo village, prompting the Indians to retaliate with a raid against settlers ten days later.

October 25, Los Lunas, New Mexico: Two shepherds are killed by Navajos, who escape with 6,000 sheep.

November, Oregon: Klamath Indians attack a wagon train from California, killing two white men and wounding one.

November, St. Landry Parish, Louisiana: Slave owners attack "a considerable gang of runaway Negroes," killing a man and a woman, and leaving two women badly wounded. The other fugitives escape.

November 26, Socorro, New Mexico: Two unarmed Mexican volunteers are sent to recover 800 sheep stolen from the army by Navajo raiders. Both are later found dead, their bodies bristling with arrows and their skulls crushed by stones.

December, Memphis, Tennessee: Several blacks are arrested as authorities quell an aborted slave revolt.

December 6, San Diego County, California: U.S. troops under Col. Stephen Kearny clash with a superior force of Mexican lancers at San Pascual. Eighteen die and thirteen are wounded. The survivors are surrounded and besieged by Mexicans until reinforcements arrive on the night of December 10.

December 25, Dona Ana County, New Mexico: U.S. troops clash with Mexican forces on the Brazita River, inflicting casualties of 100 Mexicans killed or wounded in the forty-minute skirmish. No U.S. soldiers are injured.

1847

Harrisburg, Pennsylvania: Rioters disrupt a speech by Frederick Douglass, throwing stones, firecrackers, cayenne pepper, garbage, and rotten eggs around the auditorium.

Humboldt River, Nevada: Indians steal six horses from an emigrant party. Leader Chester Ingersoll says, "After that we shot at every Indian we saw. This soon cleared the way."

January 8, San Gabriel, California: Mexican troops defending Los Angeles are defeated by U.S. forces in a ninety-minute battle.

January 18–19, Taos, New Mexico: Mexican and Indian rebels stage an assault on the Anglo capital, killing Gov. Charles Bent and five other leading members of the U.S. bloc.

February 3, Taos, New Mexico: U.S. troops recapture the settlement, killing 150 rebels. U.S. losses number seven men dead and forty-five wounded (some of them mortally). Sixteen leaders of the revolt are sentenced to death and hanged in April. One rebel leader is murdered in jail, by a relative of his victims, before he can be tried and sentenced.

1848

San Marcos, Texas: White settlers and Tonkawa Indians pursue a party of Comanche horse thieves, killing two of them in a clash that leaves one friendly Tonkawa slightly wounded.

January 8, The Dalles, Oregon: Troops clash with Cayuse Indian cattle rustlers, killing three and wounding one, with one soldier wounded. The Indians escape with 300 head of stock. On January 9, troops retaliate by capturing sixty Cayuse horses.

January 29, Deschutes River, Oregon: Soldiers kill one Cayuse man and capture two women and several horses.

January 30, Deschutes River, Oregon: Troops surprise a Cayuse village, destroying the settlement and killing thirty Indians in a running battle. Three soldiers are killed in the fight, with two others wounded.

February 24, Umatilla Valley, Oregon: Eight Cayuse warriors are killed, and five are wounded in a clash with troops. The soldiers report five of their men wounded.

March, Abiqua Creek, Oregon: Whites kill Klamath Chief Red Blanket and twelve of his eighty braves. The surviving Indians agree to leave the area.

March 14–15, Tuscannon River, Oregon: Troops wage an overnight battle with Indian warriors, killing four and wounding fourteen. One soldier is killed and several others injured.

April, Dismal Swamp: Armed whites attack a fugitive slave community in the marshy wilderness spanning the Virginia-North Carolina border. Several runaways are captured in the raid.

May 7, Pena Blanca Creek, New Mexico: Four Navajos are killed and several others wounded as troops seek to recover sheep stolen in recent raids.

July, New River, Florida: Seminole raiders strike at a white-owned plantation, killing one man.

July, Pease Creek, Florida: Seminoles raid a rural trading post, killing two men before they loot and burn the complex.

August 5, Fayette County, Kentucky: Led by a white college student named Patrick Doyle, seventy-five slaves arm themselves and march toward the Ohio River, seeking freedom in Indiana. The group fights two battles with white pursuers, leaving one man dead on each side. Doyle and most of the rebels are later captured, and three blacks are hanged in October. Doyle, convicted the same month, is sentenced to twenty years.

September 19, Nauvoo, Illinois: Arsonists destroy an abandoned Mormon temple.

October, Woodford County, Kentucky: Authorities crush a slave revolt patterned on Doyle's rebellion in August.

October 8, Gonzales County, Texas: Indians murder a white man and a child in separate raids. Another war party kills two men in neighboring Karnes County before joining forces with the first group on the San Antonio River. A company of volunteers pursues the raiders, striking their trail thirty miles above Goliad. Three Texans die in the resultant skirmish, before both sides tire of the fighting and the Indians retreat.

1849

Philadelphia, Pennsylvania: White thugs, calling themselves the "Killers of Moyamensing," lead armed raids against local blacks. Three whites and one black man are killed, with twenty-five people hospitalized, before militia units restore order.

New York City: German immigrants, armed with guns and stones, prevent Jews from holding a funeral ceremony in a local cemetery.

Oneida County, Idaho: An emigrant party led by a Capt. Walker murders several Indians for their horses near the Malad River. The Indians retaliate with raids against other wagon trains.

Elko County, Nevada: Two whites are killed and four wounded—one of them mortally—when Indians attack an emigrant wagon train. Survivors retreat to winter in Salt Lake City after their wagons and provisions are destroyed.

Schleicher County, Texas: Comanches ambush a party of travelers near Devil's River, wounding one man and killing a pack mule before the concentrated fire of six-shooters forces them to retreat.

February 28, Utah Valley, Utah: A military force clashes with Ute Indians accused of killing cattle and stealing horses from the settlement at South Willow Creek. Four Indians are killed during the four-hour battle, with women and children from the tribe being "warned and fed" by white troops.

Spring, Utah Valley, Utah: Indian raiders begin stealing grain and livestock from white settlers, and occasionally fire arrows at the ranchers. Five Indians are killed in a skirmish with the Deseret Militia at Battle Creek, in Tooele County, but raiding continues through the fall, with Ft. Utah falling under a virtual state of siege.

June 15, San Francisco, California: A racist gang, known as the Hounds, attacks the Chilean barrio, killing one woman and raping two others, and looting and vandalizing immigrant property.

July, Jemez, Arizona: Navajos kill herder Vincente Garcia outside the settlement and escape with his herd. On the Rio Abajo a second war party kills another shepherd and steals his flock.

July, St. Mary's, Georgia: Three hundred slaves are foiled in their plot to capture a steamboat and sail to freedom in the British West Indies.

July, Charleston, South Carolina: Authorities report the suppression of a local slave uprising.

August 1, Provo, Utah: Three white settlers kill an Indian named Old Bishop for allegedly stealing a shirt. Afterward, his body is weighted with stones and dropped in a river. Fellow tribesmen find the remains twenty-four hours later and begin raids to kill livestock when they are denied access to the murderers.

August 31, Tunicha Creek, New Mexico: Troops open fire on Navajos gathered for a peace conference, killing seven. One of the victims, a headman named Narbona, is scalped by his killers. Navajos retaliate with sniper fire from the surrounding hills, killing several army horses as the troopers retreat.

September, Provo, Utah: One settler is killed and eight wounded in a three-day battle with local Indians.

September 6, Chaco Canyon, New Mexico: U.S. mail carrier Charles Malone and his Mexican guide are killed by Navajos.

September 21, Sandia, New Mexico: Navajos kill five Mexicans and loot their homes.

September 29, Santa Fe, New Mexico: Navajo raiders kill one Mexican, firing eighteen arrows into his body.

Fall, Lake County, California: A group of Pomo Indians, enslaved by two white men named Stone and Kelsey, kill their captors and retreat to an island in nearby Clear Lake. Whites retaliate by storming the island and slaughtering most of the tribe, stabbing women and children to death, hanging one Indian, and tying one to a tree and burning him alive. The following day, white soldiers assault another Indian village in neighboring Mendocino County, leaving a number of women and children among the dead.

October, Ft. Steilacoom, Oregon: Six Indians are placed on trial for the murder of Leander Wallace, a white settler. Two of the defendants are convicted and executed.

October, Humboldt River, Nevada: Indians stage repeated raids on settlers and emigrant parties. Members of one train lose twenty-seven mules, and finish their trip to California on foot.

October, Las Vegas, New Mexico: Troops open fire on a peaceful band of Apaches, wounding several. The tribe swiftly retaliates by raiding a nearby wagon train, killing all the white men and capturing a woman and a child.

October 5, Le Bugarito, New Mexico: Navajos attack a Mexican village, killing two men and wounding one and escaping with a female hostage.

1850

New York City: A racist mob disrupts an abolitionist meeting led by William Lloyd Garrison.

La Salle County, Texas: A party of Texas Rangers, including William "Big Foot" Wallace, clash with Indians near the Nueces River, killing or wounding an unspecified number of Indians.

January, Lewis County, Missouri: A revolt by thirty armed slaves spreads panic among local whites. The rebellion's leader is shot and killed by vigilantes; his followers are captured and sold to buyers in distant areas.

January 12, Chuska Valley, Arizona: Navajos fire on a military camp. Warriors assault the camp in force the next day, losing one during the battle.

February 8-9, Wasatch County, Utah: One white man and four or five Indians die during a two-day battle at Ft. Utah. Several other persons are wounded on each side before the Indian attackers retreat. Militiamen pursue the attackers on February 10, fighting brief skirmishes at Spanish Fork and Payson, before the Indians are overtaken on February 11 at Table Mountain, near the south end of Utah Lake. The Indians are nearly annihilated in a battle fought largely on ice.

April 23, Yuma County, Arizona: John Glanton and his gang of professional scalp hunters are surrounded and annihilated by Yuma Indians. Authorities estimated that Glanton's pack of "border scum" have slaughtered at least 1,000 Indians in the past two years, earning an estimated $100,000 selling scalps to the Mexican government. Rewards totaling $75,000 have been posted for Glanton and company since U.S. officers discovered their penchant for scalping Mexicans and dark-skinned Anglos, selling the hair in Mexico as "Apache" scalps. The Yumas receive no payment for ending Glanton's reign of terror, but Ft. Yuma is named in their honor.

May 8, New York City: White rioters disrupt a speech by Frederick Douglass.

May 29, Sanpete County, Utah: Indian raiders kill a white settler named Barker.

June–July, California-Nevada-Utah: Indians launch numerous raids for horses and cattle across three states. A detachment of Utah militia surprises renegade Gosiute Indians in the Cedar Mountains, Tooele County, Utah, killing most of the Indian men.

July 10, Sonora, California: Four Mexican prisoners, charged with murdering white men, are lynched by a mob.

August, Zuñi, New Mexico: Navajo raiders attack the pueblo.

August, Ogden, Utah: Shoshoni tribesmen deliberately stampede their ponies through grain fields and melon patches cultivated by Mormon settlers.

August 20, San Patricio County, Texas: One white man is killed and another wounded in a skirmish with Indians.

September, Zuñi, New Mexico: Zuñi Indians kill thirty Navajos in a tribal clash nearby.

September, Oklahoma-Texas: Several hundred former Florida maroons flee the Oklahoma Territory for Mexico, routing a force of Creek Indians who try to stop them.

September 17, Ogden, Utah: Shoshoni Chief Terrikee is shot and killed while trying to retrieve ponies from settler Urban Stewart's cornfield.

September 22, New York City: Inflamed by false rumors that Jews have killed a gentile girl, 500 white men raid a Jewish-occupied tenement on Yom Kippur, vandalizing the apartments, and beating and robbing their victims.

October, Zuñi, New Mexico: Navajos again raid the settlement, destroying crops in the adjacent fields.

October 5, Salt Lake City, Utah: A Mormon party arrives from California and reports that Indians are holding at least 1,000 stolen animals in Elko County, Nevada, at the head of the Humboldt River.

November, Black Mesa, Arizona: U.S. troops mount a campaign against Navajos, capturing fifty-two Indian men, women, and children. Soldiers also capture more than 5,000 head of sheep, horses, and oxen.

Winter, Utah: Hostilities between whites and local Indians increase when Mormon settlers usurp Shoshoni winter camps in Weber and Cache Counties, near the present sites of North Ogden, Willard, and Brigham City.

December, La Salle County, Texas: Ten Texas Rangers clash with sixteen Comanche warriors near the Nueces River. This desperate battle, lasting a mere three minutes, leaves every member of both parties dead or wounded. Scouts later retrieve more than 200 Comanche arrows from the half-acre battleground.

December 17, Madera County, California: Mariopsa Indians raid a cattle herd along the Fresno River, killing three white men. The next day, a party of white men pursues the raiders and finds an Indian village near Aqua Fria Creek, deserted except for one dead woman and two children. Later that morning, the volunteers overtake their quarry and hear a formal declaration of war against all whites from Mariposa Chief Baptiste.

1851

Maryland: A white man is ambushed and killed on his way home to Nottingham, Pennsylvania, while transporting a free black woman kidnapped from her Baltimore residence.

New Orleans, Louisiana: A riot breaks out against Spanish residents of the city.

January, Cajon Pass, California: The Lugo brothers, pursuing Indians who rustled stock from their San Bernadino ranch, are accused of killing a white man, Patrick McSwiggin, and his Creek Indian companion. A lynching is narrowly averted, and the brothers require armed protection until their acquittal in October 1852.

January 7, Madera County, California: A half-breed Mexican is hanged on suspicion of murder.

January 11, Madera County, California: White volunteers fight an inconclusive battle with Indians.

January 18, Mariposa County, California: Troops assault an Indian camp near the headwaters of the Merced River, killing twenty-six and driving away the rest in a battle lasting nearly four hours. One white officer dies in the clash.

February, Boston, Massachusetts: A mob rescues Shadrach, a fugitive slave, from mercenary slave hunters.

February 1, Pajarito, New Mexico: Navajos stage a surprise raid, driving off 1,000 sheep and a large number of horses, mules, and oxen.

March 3, San Joaquin County, California: Indians kill four white miners at Fine Gold Gulch, moving on to drive other whites from a trading post on the San Joaquin River.

March 6, San Joaquin County, California: Wiley Cassidy is killed by Indians near his ranch, shot with several arrows, one leg amputed, and his tongue cut out. At least one Indian dies in the fight.

March 16, Stanislaus County, California: White troops kill and scalp ten Indians and capture two, in a clash along the San Joaquin River.

Spring, Tooele County, Utah: A settler named Custer is killed while escorting several captive Indians from Richville to Tooele. The prisoners escape and a short time later steal and butcher a herd of cattle stolen in Black Rock. Settlers retaliate with a raid against the nearest Indian camp, killing nine men.

April, Boston, Massachusetts: Federal marshals prevent an abolitionist mob from freeing Thomas Sims, a runaway slave.

April 27, Stanislaus County, California: Troops raid an Indian camp on the San Joaquin River, killing two and wounding two.

May, Rogue River, Oregon: David Dilley, a white traveler, is ambushed and killed by Indians; his companions escape.

May, Ferron, Utah: James Lemmon, a twenty-month-old boy, is killed by an Indian named Squash Head, who tortures the child by cutting off his toes and fingers, then swings him by the heels and smashes his skull against a rock. Arrested and taken to Provo, Squash Head confesses the crime to one of his jailers, who promptly slashes the prisoner's throat in a fit of rage.

May 17, San Joaquin County, California: A group of white men capture six Indians at Coarse Gold Gulch and kill two when they try to escape.

May 26, Hoboken, New Jersey: Four people die and dozens are wounded when a nativist mob assaults German immigrants during their celebration of Pentecost.

June 1, Rogue River, Oregon: Indian warriors attack a party of whites, losing one of their own. On June 2 three separate parties are attacked at the same crossing, with four white men killed in one ambush. By the end of the summer, at least thirty-eight persons are murdered by Rogue tribal raiders.

June 3, Rogue River, Oregon: Two hundred Indians attack a party of thirty-three white men. The battle continues for several hours, ending only when the tribal chief is killed.

June 15, Cebolleta, New Mexico: Navajos stage three attacks on travelers in the vicinity, wounding two of their six chosen targets.

June 17, Table Rock, Oregon: Troops raid a Rogue Indian camp, killing eleven and wounding several others. No soldiers die in the clash, but several are wounded.

June 23, Table Rock, Oregon: A renewed battle between white troops and Rogue Indians rages throughout the day. Several whites are wounded, but none are killed.

June 25, Rogue River, Oregon: Indian raiders escape a military ambush, eluding troops in a running fight along the river.

July 2, Valle Grande, New Mexico: Troops clash with Navajo warriors in a two-hour battle.

July 5, Downieville, California: A Mexican woman named Juanita stabs and kills a white man who broke down the door of her home. Although pregnant, she is taken from jail and hanged by a mob of 2,000 Anglos.

July 12, Ojo del Gallo, New Mexico: Navajos attack a party of fourteen hay cutters, wounding all but one.

July 12, Cubero, New Mexico: Four haycutters are wounded by arrows in a Navajo attack.

July 18, Franklin County, Idaho: The night guard for a camped wagon train fires on Indians suspected of trying to steal horses and oxen. The Indians—described as "Diggers"—escape without casualties.

August 26, Pena Blanca, New Mexico: Navajos strike at a nearby ranch, killing a Mexican girl and escaping with a flock of sheep.

August 28, Santa Fe, New Mexico: Hopi Indians complain to the white governor that Navajo raids are leaving them destitute.

August 30, Pescado Springs, New Mexico: Navajo raiders strike under cover of darkness, driving away mules from an army camp.

September, Tule Lake, California: Modoc Indians attack a wagon train, killing seventy-nine teamsters and mutilating their bodies. One white man escapes to report the massacre.

September 11, Christiana, Pennsylvania: Slave owner Edward Gorsuch is killed and several members of his party wounded by an interracial mob while attempting to recapture fugitive slaves. Thirty-eight members of the mob are charged with treason under the Fugitive Slave Act, but all are acquitted on December 11.

September 14, Coquilla River, Oregon: Indians massacre five whites; five others escape, with one badly wounded in the attack.

October, Syracuse, New York: Black abolitionists rescue a slave called Jerry, on trial for running away, from a crowded courtroom.

October, Willow Creek, California: Indians massacre a wagon train, sparing only two young sisters, both of whom later die in captivity.

November 18, Ft. Defiance, Arizona: Navajos set fire to fifty tons of hay, the army's winter feed supply.

November 21, Rogue River, Oregon: Troops clash with Rogue Indians, leaving fifteen Indians dead and many others wounded.

December, Massachusetts: Nativist mobs riot against Catholic immigrants.

1852

Ft. Boise, Idaho: Travelers find six dead Indians hidden in brush near an emigrant camp. Investigation shows that members of a passing wagon train deliberately left poisoned stock on the trail, "to prove a disputed point about whether or not the Indians would eat cattle left dead by travelers."

April, Josephine Creek, Oregon: Four white trappers are besieged at their camp by Rogue Indians, fighting off attacks for two days before help arrives.

April 8, Klamath River, Oregon: Calvin Woodman, a white settler, is killed by Klamath Indians. The local sheriff is wounded while leading a posse on a punitive raid.

May, Humboldt River, Nevada: Absalom Woodward, holder of the mail contract between Sacramento and Salt Lake City, is murdered by Indians.

June, Table Rock, Oregon: Six Indians are killed when a white posse attacks their village, acting on an erroneous report of white hostages.

June 12, Salt Lake City, Utah: The *Deseret News* denounces a recent emigrant party for setting grass fires and murdering several Snake Indian women and stealing their ponies.

July 19, Jacksonville, Oregon: Whites and Indians clash in a battle that leaves one white man and two Indians dead, with several more

Indians wounded. They retaliate by slaughtering several white miners downstream.

August, Ashland, Oregon: Whites attack a band of Indians without apparent provocation, killing six. Within the next two weeks Indian raiders kill two white men and wound four others at a nearby immigrant camp. Four days later a white militiaman is killed when warriors ambush a patrol.

August 4, Stuart's Creek, Oregon: Settler Richard Evans is killed by Indian raiders at his home.

August 5, Rogue River Valley, Oregon: Two white men are killed and two are wounded in Indian raids. Two Shasta men are hanged for the murders on August 7, and an innocent Indian bystander is lynched for "good measure."

August 15, Table Rock, Oregon: Whites raid an Indian village five miles to the north, but the Indians escape after setting the prairie on fire.

August 17, Evans Creek, Oregon: Six white soldiers are killed and four wounded during a four-hour battle with Indian warriors.

August 24, Evans Creek, Oregon: Four whites are killed and three wounded in a battle against Indians. Indian losses are eight killed and twenty wounded.

September, Tule Lake, California: Modoc Indians assault a wagon train, killing all but three of the sixty-five travelers. Two girls are taken prisoner but later manage to escape.

September 3, Tule Lake, California: Modoc raiders attack two different parties of white men near the same site. Four white men are slain and mutilated and a fifth is wounded in the second raid.

September 7, Natural Bridge, California: White volunteers assault the Modoc capital, killing the tribal chief and at least forty other Indians before the survivors escape.

Fall, Utah: Harrison Sever is robbed of his oxen and briefly held captive by Indian raiders in Salt Lake County. In neighboring Tooele County, raiders steal a hundred horses and, ironically, sell them for cash to U.S. troops at Ft. Bridger.

1853

California records more homicides than all other states combined during this year, with the majority of victims listed as Mexicans or Indians killed by whites.

March, Charlestown, Massachusetts: Enraged by false rumors of a local girl's abduction, nativist rioters menace a Catholic church where the nonexistent kidnappers are thought to be hiding.

March, Shasta County, California: Lt. Edmund Russell is ambushed and killed with arrows while leading an army patrol against Indians in the Sacramento River valley.

Spring, Wichita County, Texas: Indians kill several members of a white scouting party.

April 6, Cincinnati, Ohio: Catholic rioters destroy a Protestant church where a nativist rally is in progress.

May, Boston, Massachusetts: A nativist street preacher incites riots against Catholic citizens.

May 3, Vallecito, New Mexico: Navajos raid Ramon Martin's grazing camp, killing one of his sons and abducting two others, stealing several horses in the process.

May 22, Zuñi Mountains, New Mexico: Navajo raiders drive off 5,600 sheep.

June 13, New Orleans, Louisiana: Twenty blacks are arrested and several hanged after a planned slave revolt is exposed.

July, Manchester, New Hampshire: Catholic homes are assaulted by nativist rioters.

July, Lawrence, Massachusetts: Nativist mobs damage several Catholic homes.

July 17, Springville, Utah: Settler James Ivie and three Utes are injured in a brawl at Ivie's cabin, sparked by an argument over the proper ratio of fish to flour in an exchange of food. Chief Walker, of the Ute tribe, is furious when the settlers refuse to surrender Ivie for "trial."

July 18, Payson, Utah: Chief Walker's men kill settler Alexander Keele on the outskirts of town, vowing war against the settlers until all are exterminated.

July 19, Springville, Utah: One settler is wounded in an attack by Utes.

July 19, Nephi, Utah: Cattle are stolen from the settlement by Utes, with shots fired at the guard.

July 19, Sanpete County, Utah: Utes raid the settlements at Manti and Pleasant Creek for livestock, exchanging fire with guards on duty.

July 23, Payson, Utah: Ute raiders exchange fire with sentries guarding the settlement's livestock herds. One of the sentries suffers a severe leg wound.

July 24, Santaquin, Utah: Clark Roberts and John Berry are wounded in an ambush by Ute snipers. Both men escape.

July 24, Springville, Utah: Sentries fire on Ute warriors scouting the settlement.

July 28, Sanpete County, Utah: Militiamen clash with a party of forty Utes, killing several in the brief skirmish.

August 5, Juab County, Utah: Indians attempt to steal horses from a military camp north of Nephi. Sentries fire on the raiders, and blood is found on the ground next morning.

August 8, South Easton, New York: A Catholic student is severely punished with a ferule, then expelled from public school. The state superintendent of education describes the teacher's action as "not only unwarrantable, but barbarous."

August 10, Mona, Utah: Indians attack a military camp on Willow Creek, wounding one soldier and killing two horses. One of the raiders is killed by return fire.

August 17, Willard, Utah: John Dixon and John Quail are killed by Shoshoni raiders at nearby Parley's Canyon. A short time later, 150 Shoshoni and Bannock gallop through town, raiding cultivated fields for food and turning their horses out to eat the Mormon crops.

September 13, Fillmore, Utah: William Hatton is shot and killed by Indians while guarding the settlement's livestock.

September 26, Salt Lake County, Utah: Troops stage a dawn raid on an Indian camp at Salt Creek, in Goshen Valley. Nineteen Indians are killed, with one soldier and one army horse wounded.

Fall, Palmyra, Utah: Indians steal seventy cattle from grazing land near the settlement.

October, Millard County, Utah: Violence erupts when an emigrant party, camped near Fillmore, tries to disarm a small group of Pahvant Indians. The Indians resist and whites open fire, killing the father of Pahvant war chief Moshoquop and wounding two others.

October 1, Fountain Green, Utah: Four white men are killed when Indians attack their camp and steal a shipment of grain bound for Salt Lake City.

October 2, Nephi, Utah: Eight Indians are killed and three captured in a clash with troops.

October 4, Sanpete County, Utah: William Mills and John Warner are killed by Indian raiders near Manti.

October 5, Jacksonville, Oregon: Settler Thomas Wills is killed by Indian raiders.

October 6, Ft. Lane, Oregon: Settler James Kyle is killed in an Indian attack on his home.

October 14, Santaquin, Utah: A white man, Furnee Tindrel, is killed and scalped when Indians raid the settlement.

October 25, Illinois River Valley, Oregon: Two white soldiers are killed and four wounded in a clash with Indians who have been harassing miners in the area.

October 26, Millard County, Utah: Pahvant Indian warriors attack a military scouting expedition, killing all twelve members in their camp.

November 6, Sanpete County, Utah: Indians burn Chase's sawmill.

November 9, Santaquin, Utah: Indian raiders burn six vacant houses.

1854

Authorities in Los Angeles, California, report a murder a day during this year, with the majority of victims listed as Mexicans or Indians.

Boston, Massachusetts: An abolitionist mob fails to prevent the recapture of fugitive slave Anthony Burns. Two thousand troops are deployed to restore order in the city.

Kendall County, Texas: Rancher Jesse Lawhorn is killed in an ambush by Indians. A black servant narrowly escapes the trap.

January, Illinois River Valley, Oregon: Casualties are reported on both sides, as white miners clash with a party of Indians suspected of theft.

January, Coos County, Oregon: Violence erupts between local Indians and white miners at Coos Bay and Port Orford. U.S. troops raid an Indian village in reprisal, killing sixteen persons, wounding four, and capturing twenty before the rest of the Indians escape.

January 6, Spring City, Utah: Indians burn a settlement abandoned by Mormons the previous summer.

January 18, Cottonwood Creek, Oregon: Indians steal horses from a mining camp. Miners pursue the thieves in vain, falling back to demand help from the army.

January 27, Klamath River, Oregon: Troops assault a cave occupied by Indian horse thieves, losing one of their officers in the attack.

January 27, New York City: An anti-Catholic mob descends on the waterfront, menacing a visiting Italian dignitary.

March–April, New Mexico: Jicarilla and Ute warriors ravage the northern plains, killing forty-one white soldiers in a single ambush.

April 15, Applegate River, Oregon: Settler Edward Phillips is killed in his home by Indians.

May, Campti, Louisiana: Authorities report an outbreak of violence by local slaves.

May 28, New York City: A nativist mob marches on city hall, assaulting suspected Irish Catholics along the way.

June, Nashua, New York: A nativist mob attacks Catholic homes.

June, Bath, Maine: A Catholic church is burned by Protestant rioters.

June, Grappes Bluff, Louisiana: A short-lived slave rebellion is crushed by whites.

June, Oregon Territory: Modocs kill at least four whites in scattered raids.

June, Eagle Springs, New Mexico: Mescalero Apaches raid several wagon trains in the vicinity.

June 4, Brooklyn, New York: A mob of 20,000 storms the Irish district, inflicting numerous injuries before troops arrive to quell the violence and make sixty arrests.

June 11, Brooklyn, New York: A mob of 10,000 gathers after two Irishmen hurl paving stones at a nativist orator. Troops are deployed and twenty-three persons are arrested in the rioting.

June 24-25, Klamath River, Oregon: Two whites are killed in clashes with local Indians.

Summer, Humboldt River, Nevada: An emigrant party carrying twelve scalped travelers makes it a point to "shoot and kill every Indian they meet on sight." Indians retaliate with raids against other parties. In one raid on seven travelers, four are killed and the three survivors stripped of their clothing and forced to walk naked in search of help.

Summer, Ellsworth, Maine: Father John Bapst is seized by order of a town meeting. He is robbed, stripped, beaten, and tarred and feathered for advising local Catholics to challenge the recent expulsion of their children from public school based on failure to participate in Protestant ceremonies.

July, Sidney, Ohio: A Catholic church is destroyed with gunpowder charges.

July, Dorchester, Massachusetts: Nativist bombers destroy a Catholic church.

July, San Buenaventura, California: Anglo vigilantes raid the home of Encarnacion Berreyesa, hanging him in an effort to force his confession to the murder of a white man found dead on his land. When he refuses to confess, the mob leaves him for dead and moves on to lynch his brother, Nemesio.

July 3, Manchester, New Hampshire: Nativist rioters attack a Catholic church.

July 4, Lexington, Kentucky: The Knights of the Golden Circle are organized to protect slavery inside the United States or, failing that, to propagate the institution elsewhere. Its headquarters is moved to San Antonio, Texas, in the fall of 1860, as the leaders consider incursions into Mexico.

July 7, Palmyra, New York: A Catholic church is burned by nativist rioters.

July 8, Bath, Maine: Nativist rioters burn a Catholic church.

July 11, Lawrence, Massachusetts: Rumors circulate that an Irishman has inverted the U.S. flag, threatening to kill anyone who fixes it. A Know-Nothing mob armed with pistols attacks the Irish neighborhood, wrecking twenty homes.

July 13, Buffalo, New York: Irish Catholics disrupt a nativist rally, touching off a riot.

August, Charlestown, Massachusetts: Nativist rioters try to free an anti-Catholic agitator from jail.

August, Ft. Meigs, Alabama: A slave is burned alive for killing his white master.

August 6–7, Louisville, Kentucky: Twenty persons die during two days of anti-Catholic rioting. Discouraged by the mayor from sacking a church, Know-Nothings armed with knives, muskets, and a cannon assault the Irish quarter, burning homes.

August 7–8, St. Louis, Missouri: Rumors of weapons hidden in a Catholic church touch off forty-eight hours of nativist rioting, leaving ten people killed, thirty more gravely wounded, and "a large number" suffering minor injuries.

August 8, Cedar Valley, Utah: Brothers Warren and William Weeks are killed by Indians.

August 19–20, Owyhee County, Idaho: An emigrant wagon train, split into three parties, receives Indian attacks twenty-five miles west of Ft. Boise. In the first raid, white men painted as Indians reportedly lead the attack, killing one traveler outright and mortally wounding two. Two Indians are wounded before the raiders escape with five horses. The same day, a second party is nearly decimated when thirty Indians approach the train and one is shot to death while trying to steal a horse. The resultant battle leaves eighteen of the twenty travelers dead; two boys escape, both wounded with arrows, to report the incident. On August 20 the third group arrives to find Indians torturing wounded captives at the battle site, and one settler dies in a futile rescue attempt. Troops later find the women and girls raped and mutilated, including one pregnant woman who has been dismembered. A piece of hot iron has been run through another woman's body, while several children are hung by their hair above a fire and burned to death. The raiders flee with five wagons, forty-one head of cattle, five horses, an estimated $3,000 in cash, and some guns.

September, Oregon Territory: One white man is reported dead in raids by Modoc warriors.

September, Provo, Utah: Eighty Shoshoni warriors raid a Ute camp nearby, killing five of the rival tribesmen. Frustrated Utes vow revenge against all residents of the territory, leading the sheriff of Utah County to request state troops to "kill every damned rascal" in both tribes.

September 8, Newark, New Jersey: Armed members of the U.S. Protestant Association invade St. Mary's German Church and vandalize the building, fatally wounding a Catholic pedestrian nearby.

September 12, Ft. Boise, Idaho.: Authorities report that soldiers have killed three or four Indian suspects in the August massacre, all while trying to resist arrest. Two more Indians are subsequently killed, and twenty ponies are seized.

Fall, Goshen County, Wyoming: Thirty-one soldiers and a drunken civilian interpreter invade a Sioux village, demanding the surrender of the Indians who slaughtered a Mormon emigrant's cow. The resultant argument erupts into gunfire, with several Indians killed and Chief Conquering Bear mortally wounded. Furious tribesmen overwhelm the patrol, killing thirty at the scene. One soldier, mortally wounded, survives long enough to reach Ft. Laramie and report the battle.

October, Boston, Massachusetts: Anti-Catholic mobs take to the streets on three successive Sundays.

October 7, Ft. Defiance, Arizona: Pvt. Nicholas Hefbiner is wounded by an arrow while cutting hay outside the stockade. He dies the next day. Navajos surrender a wounded Indian, alleged to be Hefbiner's killer, on November 5. The suspect is quickly tried, convicted, and hanged.

October 15, Pecos River, New Mexico: Navajo raiders spear a shepherd, wounding him, and slaughter several of his sheep before they are frightened away by approaching soldiers.

October 25, Ellsworth, Maine: A Catholic priest is tarred and feathered and then ridden out of town on a rail.

November, Maine: Nativist rioters destroy a Catholic church, toppling and defacing statues of priests. Another mob prevents the laying of a cornerstone for a new church.

November, Williamsburg, New York: Nativist rioters attack Irish immigrants at the polls on election day. The next afternoon, gunmen fire indiscriminately on suspected Catholics in the streets, peppering the Church of Sts. Peter and Paul with musket fire. Rioters are attempting to demolish the church when the mayor arrives, leading a company of police and militia to quell further violence.

November 15, New York City: Police disperse a mob surrounding a local Catholic church.

November 29, Kansas Territory: Violence marks a special election held to determine whether Kansas will enter the Union with or without legalized slavery. Armed pro-slavery forces from Missouri invade the territory to stuff ballot boxes and intimidate free-soil voters. At least one murder is recorded at the polls, as the pro-slavery votes narrowly swing the election.

December 11, New York City: A nativist mob surrounds the mayor's home, compelling him to order the release of a jailed anti-Catholic agitator.

1855

January, Texas: Fifteen Mescalero warriors and three white soldiers die in a running battle.

January, Kansas: Pro-slavery settlers are accused of organizing armed bands and illegally cutting timber on property owned by free-soilers.

March 20, Providence, Rhode Island: Aroused by rumors of "captive women" in a local Catholic church, nativist rioters nearly demolish the building before armed Irishmen intervene.

March 30, Leavenworth, Kansas: William Phillips, a free-soil attorney working to have November's pro-slavery vote overturned on grounds of fraud, is seized by a mob, who shave his head, coat it with tar and feathers, and then "sell" him in a mock slave auction.

Summer, Garden County, Nebraska: Seeking revenge for the 1854 annihilation of an army patrol in Wyoming, U.S. troops assault a village of innocent Sioux on blue creek. Eighty-six Indians die in the assault, many of them women and children, with an unspecified number wounded.

August, Klamath River, Oregon: Drunken Indians assault a mining camp, killing ten miners and losing several of their own during the battle.

August, Gerlandsville, Mississippi: A planned slave revolt is discovered.

August, Rogue River, Oregon: Settler James Buford is shot and wounded by Indian snipers. Two suspects are being transported by canoe under military guard when Buford and two friends open fire, killing both Indians. Soldiers return the fire, killing two of the gunmen.

August 1, Louisiana: A white patrolman kills a slave for not stopping when he was called. Authorities rule that the killing was justifiable.

August 6, Louisville, Kentucky: Twenty persons are killed and a large number wounded as nativist rioters attack Catholic immigrants on election day.

September, Sidney, Ohio: A Catholic church is destroyed with gunpowder by nativist bombers.

September, Bangor, Maine: Fr. John Bapst, a Catholic priest, is attacked a second time. He is tarred, feathered, and run out of town on a rail.

September 2, Curry County, Oregon: One white man is killed and two wounded when vigilantes invade an Indian reservation to search for stolen horses.

September 21, Grand County, Utah: Two boys from the Mormon Elk Mountain Mission are killed by Indians while hunting. Indians assault the mission on September 22, killing another Mormon and losing six men.

September 24, Siskiyou Mountains, California: Indian raiders kill Calvin Fields and John Cunningham and wound two others before slaughtering their oxen. Samuel Warren is wounded by Indians near the same site on September 25.

October, Texas: A band of "defeated" Mescalero Apaches resume their raids against white settlements.

October 2, Pisco River, Oregon: U.S. troops clash with a force of 1,500 Indians, and find themselves surrounded until October 4, when they launch a fighting retreat toward The Dalles. Five soldiers are killed and seventeen wounded before reinforcements arrive. Indian losses are estimated at forty dead.

October 8, Butte Creek, Oregon: Troops assault an Indian village, killing twenty-three persons and wounding many more, most of them old men, women, and children. One officer is killed in the raid, and eleven soldiers are wounded.

October 8, Jewett's Ferry, Oregon: Indian raiders kill two white men.

October 9, Evans Ferry, Oregon: Isaac Shelton is killed by Indian raiders, who then proceed downstream to murder J.K. Jones and his wife and burn their home. Four other settlers are killed before the raiding party strikes the home of John Wagoner, where they burn his house and abduct his wife and daughter. Fifteen whites are killed between Evans Ferry and Grave Creek, and two more are slain between Indian Creek and Crescent City.

October 11, Jacksonville, Oregon: Five soldiers are killed when Indians ambush a troop bound for Ft. Orford.

October 17, Rogue River, Oregon: A skirmish between troops and Indians leads to a full-scale Indian assault on a camp of soldiers and miners at Skull Bar. One third of Company E is dead before nightfall.

October 23, Rogue River, Oregon: One white man is killed, and four wounded by Indian warriors at a river ford. The raiders move on to burn several homes in Cow Creek Valley.

October 28, King County, Washington: Indian raiders kill several settlers in the White River Valley.

October 31, Grave Creek, Oregon: Troops assault an Indian village, sustaining thirty-seven casualties before the Indians flee.

November 9, Grave Creek, Oregon: Soldiers force Indians back to the reservation, where, infuriated, the Indians burn their own possessions and slaughter tribal livestock, and then launch raids against nearby white settlements.

November 21, Hickory Point, Kansas: Free-soiler Charles Dow is shot and killed by pro-slavery neighbors in a boundary dispute. The killers flee as anti-slavery forces arm and vow revenge.

November 23, Ft. Kitchen, Oregon: Sentries fire on Indians near the garrison, killing one.

November 25, King County, Washington: One soldier is killed and forty horses are stolen when Indians raid an army camp in the White River Valley.

November 26, Rogue River, Oregon: Indians repulse a military assault, firing on a raft loaded with soldiers as it nears their village.

December, Umpqua River, Oregon: Indian raiders destroy fifteen homes along the river's south fork.

December 4, King County, Washington: Lt. W.A. Slaughter is killed by an Indian sniper at the junction of the Green and White Rivers.

December 6, Lawrence, Kansas: Thomas Barber, a free-soiler, is killed in a skirmish with pro-slavery forces near town.

December 7, Walla Walla County, Washington: Indians clash with an army patrol, pursuing the soldiers for ten miles until they make a stand beside the Walla Walla River. Indian reinforcements bring the attacking force to an estimated total of 1,000 and the battle continues through October 10. Eight soldiers are killed in the fighting and eighteen are wounded before 100 Indian casualties prompt their retreat.

December 11, Ft. Kitchen, Oregon: Two sentries fire on Indian Chief Long John, killing him instantly.

December 25, Little Butte Creek, Oregon: Troops raid an Indian camp, killing eight and capturing several horses.

December 25, Rogue River, Oregon: U.S. troops kill all the warriors in an Indian settlement and captures the women and children.

1856

Maryland: A state law is enacted, requiring that any black convicted of murder shall have his head and right arm severed and his body cut in four parts, with the head and quarters displayed in the most public place near the crime scene.

North Carolina: Maroon guerillas terrorize whites in Bladen and Robeson Counties.

January–April, Florida: Troops report three skirmishes with Seminole war parties.

January 2–4, Jackson County, Oregon: Troops besiege a party of Indians barricaded in cabins along the Applegate River and greet them with artillery. Most of the braves escape under cover of darkness January 4, leaving three dead and an uncertain number of wounded behind. One soldier is killed in the siege, and three are wounded.

January 23–24, Jackson County, Oregon: Pursuit of Indians who have escaped from Applegate River on January 4 leads to renewed fighting, with one soldier killed and several wounded.

January 25, Seattle Harbor, Washington: Indians fire on the warship *Decatur*, killing two whites before they are driven back by return fire.

February, Josephine County, Oregon: Rogue Indians kill three settlers and wound three more in raids on homes along the Illinois River, fighting an inconclusive skirmish with troops before they escape.

February 21, Cedar Fort, Utah: A Mormon posse, pursuing Utes who have raided local herds for livestock, clashes with an Indian war party. One white is killed; five Indians die and several are wounded. That night, Utes murder three shepherds in Cedar Valley, near the western shore of Utah Lake. The Ute war chief, Tintic, wounded in the afternoon skirmish, is reported dead on March 5.

February 23, Gold Beach, Oregon: Indians raid a local militia camp at dawn, killing eight of the ten soldiers present. Later in the day, an Indian agent and a militia captain are killed while trying to make an arrest at a nearby Indian village. The agent's heart is cut out, cooked, and eaten by his killers.

February 25, Miner's Fort, Oregon: Soldiers repulse an Indian assault, inaugurating a thirty-day siege by Indians.

March, Seattle, Washington: Twenty-seven Indians are killed and twenty-one wounded in an attack by troops landed from warships in the harbor.

March 4, Pierce County, Washington: One soldier is killed and nine wounded when Indians attack a road-building crew near the Puyallup River.

March 8, Chelan County, Washington: One hundred fifty Indians assault a party of white volunteers. Thirty warriors are killed, with an unknown number wounded, against volunteer losses of four men injured.

March 17, Pistol River, Oregon: A group of whites settlers burn an abandoned Indian village, leading Indians to retaliate that evening with an attack on Miner's Fort. Fighting continues through March 19, when regular troops arrive. One settler is killed and one wounded. Indian losses total twelve dead and an equal number injured.

March 23, Slate Creek, Oregon: Indian raiders kill two white men at a rural home. A force of fifty white men intercepts 200 braves en route to raid another farm, waging a brief skirmish that leaves two settlers dead and one wounded.

March 23, Deer Creek, Oregon: Indians clash with troops, killing two soldiers and wounding two more, against estimated losses of three Indians slain.

March 24, Douglas County, Oregon: One white man dies and another is wounded in a clash between volunteers and Indians at Cow Creek. The warriors are pursued for six days, with sporadic skirmishes along the way that result in one more Indian death.

March 26, Yakima County, Washington: Indians attack a trading post on the Yakima River, killing fifteen and wounding twelve before survivors escape in two steamers and retreat to a fortified outpost nearby. The stockade is besieged until reinforcements arrive on March 28, routing the Indians in a skirmish that leaves one man dead on each side.

March 27, McKinley County, New Mexico: Navajos raid two grazing camps west of the Puerco River, killing three shepherds and driving off 11,000 sheep.

March 30, Coos County, Oregon: Militiamen assault an Indian camp on the Coquille River, killing fifteen persons, and capturing thirty-two women and children. The troopers move upstream for a second skirmish, killing three Indians and capturing several others. Forty-eight more Indians are captured as the column enters the Umpqua Valley.

Spring, Humboldt River, Nevada: Numerous Indian raids against emigrant trains are reported across the state. At Gravelly Ford, in Elko County, travelers find the bodies of three white men killed by Indians. Nearby, in a separate incident, Indians attack an emigrant camp and kill one horse, with snipers firing in retaliation for the beating of an Indian who had asked for food.

April, Alabama: A slave is publicly burned to death after his conviction of killing his owner.

April, Box Elder County, Utah: Carlos Murray and his family are massacred by Indians in the Goose Creek Mountains, an act of retaliation for Murray's killing of an Indian in 1855.

April 13, Ft. Lane, Oregon: Troops cross the Rogue River to assault an Indian camp.

April 19, Lawrence, Kansas: A mob gathers to liberate the officers of an unofficial free-soil "government" being held on charges of treason. Authorities return in greater force on April 20 and are met by an even larger mob. Troops arrive to serve the warrants on April 23, by which time the fugitives have escaped. That night, free-soilers harass the encamped soldiers with sniper fire.

April 21, Ft. Henrietta, Oregon: Indian raiders steal forty-five horses.

April 21, Little Meadows, Oregon: Indian snipers fire on sentries at an army camp. Troops pursue the raiders, without result.

April 22, Rogue River, Oregon: An army patrol is pinned down by Indian snipers, who flee before reinforcements arrive.

April 26, Rogue River, Oregon: Troops clash with Indians who shot several head of army cattle.

April 26, Gold Beach, Oregon: One soldier is killed when troops attack and raze an Indian camp.

April 27, Rogue River, Oregon: Soldiers clash with Indians leaving one trooper wounded, with Indian losses reported as "heavy."

April 27, Ellsworth, Maine: A Catholic church, stoned by rioters on several previous occasions, is destroyed by arsonists.

April 28, The Dalles, Oregon: Indians stampede a herd of army horses five miles from the settlement.

April 28, Rogue River, Oregon: Soldiers and Indians clash two miles downstream from their engagement of April 27, leaving two Indian men dead on the field after a three-hour battle.

April 28–29, Josephine County, Oregon: Indians repeatedly assault an army camp on the Illinois River. In the second day of fighting, one-third of the eighty-man troop is killed. Reinforcements arrive, and the troopers pursue the Indians in vain, with five men reported missing after the chase. Their mutilated bodies are found hanging from nearby trees on April 30.

April 29, Rogue River, Oregon: Troops surround an Indian camp, capturing numerous prisoners.

April 29, Josephine County, Oregon: Indians raid an army pack train on the Chetcoe River, killing one soldier and wounding three before they are repulsed. Six Indians die.

May, Gold Beach, Oregon: Soldiers pursue and kill forty Indians accused of harassing local miners.

May 6, Sherman County, Oregon: Indian raiders attack an army camp at Ahtanahm Creek, twenty-five miles east of The Dalles, setting the prairie afire before they are repulsed.

May 17, Spokane County, Washington: Indians attack a column of troops southbound, toward Walla Walla. Eight soldiers are killed in the clash and eleven wounded. Nine braves are killed.

May 19, Lawrence, Kansas: A free-soiler named Jones is killed by a pro-slavery patrol outside of town; a second man dies when three of his friends retaliate. A pro-slavery militia lays siege to the town, invading the community on May 21. Cannons are used against the offices of a free-soil newspaper and a hotel owned by abolitionists. Numerous shops and homes are looted, vandalized, and burned.

May 21, Washington, D.C.: Sen. Charles Sumner is assaulted and beaten with a cane on the Senate floor, two days after delivering a speech against slavery. His assailant, Rep. Preston Brooks of South Carolina, resigns from office but is immediately reelected by the voters of his district, receiving dozens of canes in the mail from grateful Southerners.

May 24, Potawatomie, Kansas: John Brown's raiders murder and mutilate five pro-slavery men and boys, touching off a guerilla war that will claim more than 200 lives in "Bleeding Kansas" by January 1861.

May 26, Osawatomie, Kansas: Pro-slavery gunmen raid John Brown's farm, arresting two of his sons and burning his home in retaliation for the Potawatomie massacre.

May 31, Palmyra, Kansas: A pro-slave posse seizes and tortures two free-soilers. One of the prisoners, a Baptist minister, has whiskey forced down his throat with a funnel. On June 1, free-soilers kill pro-slavery gunmen during another raid.

June 3, Wakarusa, Kansas: John Brown's raiders attack a pro-slave encampment, killing four men in a three-hour battle.

June 25, Encinal, New Mexico: Navajos raid a nearby grazing camp, killing one shepherd and wounding another, who dies on June 26.

August 1, North Carolina: One white man is killed when units of a volunteer militia assault a maroon settlement in the wilderness between Bladen and Robeson counties. The fortress remains unscathed.

September, Colorado County, Texas: Authorities expose a slave conspiracy, supported by Mexican elements, designed to result in a massacre of whites on September 6. Two blacks are whipped to death, three are hanged, and an estimated 200 are flogged. The alleged instigators, inluding one white man and all of the local Mexicans, are given five days to leave the county.

August 11, Franklin, Kansas: Free-soil raiders assault a pro-slavery stronghold, scattering defenders and setting fire to part of the town with a wagonload of burning hay. The raiders move on to Ft. Sanders, southwest of Lawrence, where "Major" David Hoyt is killed by pro-slavery snipers. Another man is killed on August 12 during a night battle at Ft. Sanders. A cease-fire is declared on August 17.

August 25, Middle Creek, Kansas: Pro-slavery troops from Missouri attack and rout a free-soil detachment, wounding two men and capturing military supplies. Free-soilers retaliate on August 26, killing one man. Raiding by free-soldiers continues over the next two days, with numerous head of livestock seized from pro-slavers.

August 29, Osawatomie, Kansas: Pro-slavery forces clash with free-soil guerillas led by John Brown. One of Brown's sons is killed in the skirmish, with at least forty-nine other persons. The free-soilers scatter when their opponents open fire with artillery.

August 30, Salt Lake City, Utah: David Burr, surveyor general for Utah Territory, reports a near-fatal assault on one of his aides by three Mormons. The incident marks a beginning to the "war" between Mormon leaders and the U.S. government for political control of Utah.

September 1–3, Bourbon and Linn Counties, Kansas: Pro-slavery gunmen raid thirty-one free-soil farms, looting, burning homes, and stampeding livestock.

October, Arkansas: Slave uprisings are reported in Ouachita and Union counties.

October, Louisiana: Authorities report slave rebellions in Claiborne and Union parishes.

November, Tennessee: A Fayette County slave revolt is betrayed in the planning stage, leading to the arrests of one white man and thirty blacks. Two weeks later, more disturbances and arrests are reported in Montgomery and Obion counties.

November, Fulton, Kentucky: Authorities report the exposure of an aborted slave rebellion.

November, Missouri: Outbreaks of slave violence are recorded in New Madrid and Scott counties.

November 7, Texas: An "extensive" slave conspiracy is exposed, spanning De Witt, Lavaca, and Victoria counties. One white man is severely flogged as the alleged instigator.

November 14, St. Mary Parish, Louisiana: Several blacks are whipped after a planned slave revolt is exposed.

November 19, Cedar Spring, New Mexico: Henry Dodge, a civilian scout attached to an army expedition, is killed by Apaches while hunting.

December, Dover, Tennessee: Four slaves are executed for their role in a conspiracy against whites.

December, Cadiz, Kentucky: Exposure of a scheduled slave revolt leads to the hanging of one free black and one slave, with another slave flogged.

December, Murfreesboro, Tennessee: Free blacks are driven from the town as a hedge against future slave rebellions.

December, Paducah, Kentucky: Whites drive free blacks from the area en masse, blaming them for provoking slave revolts.

December, Charles County, Maryland: Two free blacks are hounded from the area by nervous slave owners.

December, Montgomery, Alabama: The entire population of free blacks is evicted as insurance against slave uprisings.

December, Obion, Tennessee: A free black man is jailed on suspicion of inciting slaves to rebel against their owners.

December, Waxahachie, Texas: Rev. Thomas Donegan, a white abolitionist, receives 500 lashes for agitating against slavery.

December, Arkansas: A white man named Hurd receives 1,000 lashes for inciting slaves to desert their owners.

December, Lavaca County, Texas: A white abolitionist named Davidson gets 100 lashes for speaking out against slavery.

December, the South: In addition to incidents detailed above, outbreaks of slave rebellion are also reported during this month in

Florida, Georgia, Louisiana, Mississippi, North Carolina, South Carolina, and Virginia. No details are available.

1857

El Monte, California: Four Mexicans are lynched by Anglos.

Texas: Anglo settlers launch a systematic campaign of terrorism designed to force Mexican freighters out of the lucrative transportation business between San Antonio and Chihuahua, Mexico. The so-called cart war rages for over a year, with Texans ambushing wagon trains, killing the Mexican drivers, and stealing the cargos. Federal troops are dispatched to protect the Mexican drivers after repeated complaints from the Mexican ambassador in Washington, D.C.

Cumberland, Tennessee: A planned revolt by slaves employed at the local iron works is found to include conspirators in Arkansas, Kentucky, Louisiana, Missouri, and Texas, with more than sixty blacks implicated in the plot. Nine slaves are hanged in Tennessee— four of them legally, the remaining five lynched by a mob.

Los Angeles, California: Anglo mobs lynch eleven Mexicans during the year.

Bosque, Texas: Indian raiders kill at least eleven people, taking several others captive. Texas volunteers fight several battles with the Indians, losing two men while the Indians lose ten in their first engagement. Indian warfare in the county continues through the early 1860s.

Burnet County, Texas: Rancher Robert Adams is ambushed, killed, and mutilated by Indians.

January, Alabama: A slave is burned alive after his conviction for killing his owner.

Feb 14, California: Mexican rebel Juan Flores is convicted by a vigilante court and hanged, thus ending a revolt against Anglo authority that began with his 1856 escape from San Quentin prison. Leading an "army" of fifty Mexicans, Flores is blamed for murdering the Los Angeles sheriff and countless other crimes.

March, Salt Lake Valley, Utah: Two men die when Mormon raiders seek to punish a defector from the church.

March, San Buenaventura, California: Encarnacion Berreyesa, nearly the victim of a lynching in July 1854, is charged with banditry and hanged by Anglo vigilantes.

March, Bovina, Mississippi: Slave owners clash with a band of fugitive blacks and capture three men and a woman.

March, Dickinson County, Iowa: Forty white settlers are massacred in a Sioux uprising around Spirit Lake and the neighboring Okoboji Lakes. Defeat of the Indians marks the end of Sioux warfare in Iowa.

March 3, Comanche County, Texas: Comanches raid homes along the Leon River, killing one man and capturing two children, one of whom is tortured to death. His sister is abandoned with grievous wounds. Volunteers clash with the war party the next day, but the volunteers are routed, with one man killed and another seriously injured.

March 27, Johnson's Station, Texas: Two hundred fifty Comanches assault the Overland Mail depot, with six men and one woman inside. Two whites are wounded in the battle, with an unknown number of Indian casualties, before the arrival of a coach prompts the attackers to retreat.

May, Kayesville, Utah: Four travelers from California who are suspected of being "federal spies" are attacked in their camp and murdered by Mormon guerillas. Two other members of the party are briefly taken into custody and executed by their captors while en route to Salt Lake City.

Summer, California Trail, Nevada: Authorities report that Shoshoni warriors kill eighty-five whites during the peak travel season for wagon trains, stealing an estimated 1,100 cattle and horses.

June, Grant County, New Mexico: U.S. troops clash twice with Apache warriors along the upper Gila River, killing forty-two Indians in one battle and seven in another.

July, Florida: Troops capture nine Seminole women and six children in one engagement.

July–August, Douglas County, Nevada: Indians repeatedly stop emigrant trains in the vicinity of Genoa, demanding ammunition and other supplies.

August, Florida: A clash between soldiers and Seminoles leaves one Indian dead and one child in military custody.

August, Texas: Comanche warriors launch a series of raids from Palo Pinto to Burnet, killing several whites and stealing an estimated 500 horses.

August, Pershing County, Nevada: Indian raiders attack an emigrant party on the Humboldt River, wounding a traveler named Wood and killing his wife and infant child. The family's wagon is looted, including a loss of English coins valued at $1,500. At least one white renegade joins in the attack; identified at Humboldt Sink, he is killed while resisting arrest.

August 13, Elko County, Nevada: Indians stage a dawn raid on an emigrant camp, killing six of the travelers. Three wounded white men escape while an injured woman feigns death and is scalped but survives. Her two-year-old daughter is killed when one of the raiders swings the child by her feet against a wagon wheel.

September, California Trail, Nevada: An armed patrol of thirty men from Marysville, California, moves west toward Salt Lake City, tracking Indians and repelling one attack en route. Shoshoni raids against emigrant trains continue, with one party robbed of everything "except the clothing on their backs." Caroline Jones is shot, mutilated, and scalped by Indians at Rocky Point, near the Carson River Valley, but she survives her wounds. Traveler S.G. Gibson is stopped at Stony Point by three Indians who demand powder, whereupon he draws his pistol and kills two of them.

September 7, Mountain Meadows, Utah: A mixed band of Mormons and Indians besiege an emigrant wagon train bound for California, slaughtering 120 men, women, and children. The victims had previously drawn attention to themselves with blatant anti-Mormon comments, and by allowing their stock to devastate cultivated fields. When residents of Cedar City had refused to sell them food, the party threatened to form a military expedition of reprisal as soon as they reached California.

Fall, Coryell County, Texas: Two Baptist ministers are ambushed and severely wounded by Indians.

October 3–4, Utah: Acting under orders from Brigham Young, Mormon raiding parties loot three federal supply trains. In one attack at Sandy Fork, federal officers are held at gunpoint and are forced to burn their own supplies, including more than 350,000 pounds of food.

November, Florida: Soldiers surprise a Seminole party, killing one man and capturing eighteen women and children.

November, Mills County, Texas: Settlers and Indians clash at Pecan Bayou, recording the first Indian fatality since raids began in 1856. A short time later, a settler named Lewis becomes the regions first white fatality in Indian warfare.

November, Coryell County, Texas: Two white men are killed and scalped in an ambush by Indians.

November, Comanche County, Texas: A white posse surprises five Indian horse thieves camped near the Leon River, killing two before the others escape. Two members of the posse are wounded in the skirmish.

1858

White County, Tennessee: A slave owner sues the members of a lynch mob that murdered one of his slaves.

Eastland County, Texas: One settler is killed and another wounded in an ambush by Indians near the Leon River.

Parker County, Texas: Indian warriors launch a series of raids that continue through 1875, killing or capturing an estimated 400 settlers in eighteen years, and stealing or destroying property valued in excess of $6 million.

Palo Pinto County, Texas: Indian raiders kill seven-year-old John Edwards.

January, Comanche County, Texas: Indians ambush a black slave, lancing him several times before leaving him for dead.

January, Hamilton County, Texas: John Bune and a black servant are killed by Indian raiders, marking the area's first fatalities in Indian warfare.

January, Bosque County, Texas: Indians kill Peter Johnson and capture his ten-year-old son.

February, Dona Ana, New Mexico: Nine peaceful Mescalero Apaches are murdered by drunken white men calling themselves the "Mesilla Guards."

February, Arkansas: Twenty-three whites and seven blacks die in a "fearful insurrection" of slaves, reportedly inspired by white abolitionists. Eighteen blacks are imprisoned.

February 28, Ft. Lemhi, Idaho: A force of Bannock and Shoshoni Indians attack the Mormon settlement, killing two herders, wounding four missionaries, and driving off 220 cattle and thirty-five horses. The settlers abandon their outpost and return to Utah.

March 27, Little Osage River, Kansas: Free-soiler Isaac Denton is shot and killed at his home by nightriders; a second victim is killed on another ranch, and a third home is fired on by pro-slavery gunmen.

Spring, Texas: Indians launch a series of concerted raids, lasting through the fall in Brown, Comanche, and Erath Counties.

April, New Mexico: Mesilla Guard vigilantes raid a peaceful Mescalero Apache camp, killing more than twenty Indians before soldiers arrive to halt the slaughter.

April 1, Little Osage River, Kansas: A pro-slaver named Travis is killed and two men wounded when free-soilers retaliate for earlier raids.

April 4, Power County, Idaho: Indians ambush a Mormon party at Bannock Canyon, thirty miles southwest of Pocatello. One white man is killed in the clash. The party loses three saddle horses and sixteen pack animals.

April 23, Marmaton River, Kansas: Shots are fired and two horses stolen during a pro-slavery raid on a free-soiler's farm. Two more farms are raided in similar fashion on April 25.

April 26, Ft. Scott, Kansas: A young free-soiler named Potts is killed by pro-slavery gunmen. The killers leave threatening notes for other free-soilers at a local hotel before leaving town.

May, Laguna Negra, New Mexico: Soldiers raid a Navajo camp, killing forty-eight cattle and eight horses. One cavalry horse is killed in a running fight with Indians. No human casualties are reported.

May 11, Willow Springs, Kansas: Free-soil militiamen rob a store and post office owned by a pro-slavery resident.

May 11, Hickory Point, Kansas: Free-soilers rob a pro-slavery farmer of his horse and mule.

May 12, Canadian River, Texas: Texas Rangers and friendly Indians clash with Comanches in the battle of Antelope Hill, killing Chief Iron Jacket and seventy-five of his men, and capturing eighteen women and children. One Ranger and one friendly Indian die in the battle.

May 14, Johnson County, Kansas: Free-soilers rob two local men, including the sheriff.

May 19, Marais de Cygnes, Kansas: Southern guerillas gun down eleven free-soilers, killing five, in the continuing dispute over slavery.

May 17, To-Hoto-Nim-Me, Washington: U.S. troops clash with Spokane Indians. Twelve whites are killed and ten are wounded, with three friendly Indians slain. Indians admit nine men killed and thirty to forty wounded.

May 19, Blooming Grove, Kansas: Pro-slavery gunmen invade a free-soil settlement, standing eleven men before a firing squad. Four of the victims are killed, six wounded, and one unharmed, having feigned death. Abolitionists retaliate with raids to the north, looting stores owned by pro-slave proprietors around Lecompton.

June, Arizona-New Mexico: Apache warriors launch raids against white settlers in the area of the Gadsden Purchase.

June 4, Juab County, Utah: Four Mormon travelers, including two women, are ambushed and killed by Indians in Salt Creek Canyon, near Nephi.

July 7, Ft. Defiance, Arizona: Soldiers fire on a Navajo brave collecting spent bullets on the post's rifle range. Later the same day, Navajos fire arrows at army haycutters in nearby Canoncito Bonito, killing a dog.

July 12, Ft. Defiance, Arizona: A black slave named Jim, owned by a major assigned to the fort, is killed by a Navajo bowman. The alleged killer's body is delivered by tribesmen September 7.

August, Coffeesville, Mississippi: Fifty-five slaves revolt and attack their overseer on the plantation owned by President James Polk's widow. One white man is severely injured in the fighting, and blacks roam the plantation for several days before white volunteers crush the revolt. Two slaves are hanged after their conviction of insurrection; the other fifty-three are flogged.

August, Comanche County, Texas: Indians attack a ranch on Resley's Creek. One Indian is killed.

August 16, Pershing County, Nevada: Shoshoni warriors attack a party of four Overland Mail guards on the Humboldt River, killing three.

August 20, Pershing County, Nevada: A mail coach is attacked by Shoshoni raiders at a Humboldt River crossing. Three guards hold the Indians off for a day and a half before escaping into the nearby mountains.

August 29, Bear Spring, New Mexico: Soldiers raid a Navajo camp, killing ten Indians and capturing four, and burn several hogans and seize various items of booty. The captain in charge of the raiding party is wounded.

September, Texas: Comanche warriors raid settlements in Denton, Jack, and Montague Counties.

September 1, Four Lakes, Washington: U.S. troops report no casualties in a battle that leaves eighteen to twenty Indians dead.

September 5, Spokane Plains, Washington: Four Indians are known dead and "many others" killed or wounded in a running fight between Four Lakes and Spokane. One soldier is wounded in the clash, and several Indians are captured. One of the prisoners is hanged on September 8, and soldiers slaughter tribal livestock over the next two days.

September 10, Canyon de Chelly, Arizona: Troops dispatched from Ft. Defiance kill one Navajo on the second day of a punitive expedition against the tribe.

September 13–14, Apache County, Arizona: Navajo warriors harass a military column bound for Ft. Defiance over two days, killing a bugler on September 14.

September 14, Ft. Defiance, Arizona: Navajos attack at the fort before dawn, killing one soldier and wounding three. At least ten braves are killed in the running battle, as the troops give chase.

September 24, Stevens County, Washington: Qualchin, son of Yakima Chief Owhi, is hanged after surrendering himself at an army camp sixteen miles above Spokane Falls.

September 25, Laguna Negra, New Mexico: Soldiers raid a Navajo camp, killing six Indians and burning the tribe's supply of wheat.

September 26, Snake River, Washington: Yakima Chief Owhi is shot and killed while trying to escape from military custody.

September 30–October 2, Apache County, Arizona: Troops from Ft. Defiance mount a three-day expedition against local Navajos, losing one of their number to hostile fire.

October, Spanish Fork, Utah: Utes capture and rape a white woman and child. Troops are sent to arrest the raiders, killing one Indian and transporting two others to jail in Salt Lake City.

October, Texas: Comanche raiders strike at settlements in Brown and Lampasas counties.

October 1, Mesa de los Lobos, New Mexico: Navajos ambush a military patrol in a box canyon, killing two soldiers and wounding one. Seven Indians are reported dead in the clash.

October 1, Rush Springs, Oklahoma: Texas volunteers assault a Comanche encampment, killing seventy Indians, including some women. Eleven volunteers die in the battle, with five wounded.

October 6, Ft. Defiance, Arizona: Three Navajos are shot while trying to stampede horses at the garrison. Tribesmen raid the fort's beef herd on October 7, then attack a military camp twenty-five miles to the south that night.

October 7, Juab County, Utah: Josiah Call and Samuel Brown are killed by Indians near Chicken Creek, their bodies discovered on October 15.

October 9, Walla Walla, Washington: Soldiers hang four Walla Walla Indians randomly selected from thirty-five prisoners who admit participating in recent clashes with U.S. troops.

October 17, Canoncito Bonito, Arizona: Three hundred Navajos attack a herd of army horses sent from Ft. Defiance to graze. Two soldiers are killed in the clash, and four are wounded. At least three Indians die before the raiders escape with sixty-two mules.

November 5, Isleta, New Mexico: A Navajo youth is killed on suspicion of leading raids to steal sheep in the area.

November 6, Carrizo Mountains, Arizona: Utes defeat Navajo opponents in a tribal clash, capturing one Navajo woman and forty horses.

November 7, Salt Creek, New Mexico: Soldiers kill one Navajo and capture Indian livestock.

November 16, Cienega Juanico, New Mexico: Navajo warriors approach an army camp with a white flag, then launch an attack. One officer is wounded, and twelve Indians are killed and another fifteen reported injured.

November 16, San Juan County, New Mexico: Utes raid Navajo ranches along the San Juan River, killing ten and capturing six women and children for sale as slaves. Five hundred horses are also seized in the raids.

December 20, Missouri: John Brown's guerillas raid several plantations, killing one slave owner and liberating eleven slaves, and stealing horses and other property.

December 28, Palo Pinto County, Texas: White vigilantes attack a party of Indians who have left the Brazos reservation with the Indian agent's permission. Four men and three women die in the attack, with most of the other Indians wounded. The governor and district attorney order arrests, but the county sheriff refuses to cooperate. A grand jury commends the killers for performing "a public service."

1859

Cincinnati, Ohio: A mulatto woman wins her civil suit on charges of assault and battery against a white streetcar conducter who forcibly expelled her from his car.

Texas: Settlers along the Llano River are driven from their homes by Indian raiders. One settlement, twenty-five miles from Fredericksburg, is annihilated.

Burnet County, Texas: Two Indians are killed and one white man wounded as settlers pursue a tribal war party.

Uvalde County, Texas: John Bowls is ambushed and killed by Indians near his rural home.

January 15, Young County, Texas: Five Indians are killed as settlers clash with a band of tribal rustlers.

January 21, Leavenworth, Kansas: Free-soilers riot after Southern slave-catchers try to abduct Charles Fisher, a free Negro, at gunpoint.

March, New Mexico: Navajos raid the Zuñi Pueblo, along with Hopi villages near Laguna, Acoma, and Jemez, Arizona.

March, Bell County, Texas: Indians attack the Riggs homestead, killing three persons and abducting two girls.

Spring, Jack County, Texas: Indian raiders attack several homesteads, killing at least nine people and carrying off four children. A posse recovers one of the hostages, killing an Indian woman in the process.

May, New Mexico: Navajo raiders stage two attacks on Abiquiu. Two shepherds are killed in a raid at Agua Azul.

May 13, Cimarron County, Oklahoma: Troops clash with Comanches at Crooked Creek, killing forty-nine Indian men and thirty-two women. Two white soldiers die in the battle.

May 23, Llano County, Texas: Rev. Jonas Dancer is ambushed and killed by Indian raiders.

May 23, Palo Pinto County, Texas: Two hundred fifty armed whites appear at the reservation, intent on either destroying the Indians or driving them out of Texas. Determined resistance by U.S. troops prevents a massacre. The governor responds by placing 100 militiamen under the command of the mob's leader, with orders to execute any Indian found off of the reservation without a white escort.

Summer, Hood County, Texas: Nathan Holt is killed by Indians on his farm, pierced by a dozen arrows while resisting his assailants.

July, Brownsville, Texas: Juan Cortina shoots and wounds a white marshal for beating a drunken Mexican. Fearing that he will be lynched, Cortina escapes to Mexico, collecting a band of outlaws and guerillas that will cross the border repeatedly over the next sixteen years, raiding towns and outlying ranches. Texas Rangers and militiamen respond in kind, often against innocent Mexicans, in a war that finally ends with Cortina's arrest by Mexican authorities in 1875.

July, Clarksburg, West Virginia: Ten slaves are jailed after a black woman betrays their plot against local whites.

July, Daviess County, Kentucky: Seven slaves are banished from the area for plotting a rebellion.

July 18, Bernalillo County, New Mexcio: Navajos raid cattle herds on the Puerco River, west of Albuquerque, killing two herdsmen and escaping with 100 head of stock.

July 27, Sweetwater County, Wyoming: Indian raiders attack an emigrant wagon train, acting in retaliation for the previous murder of two Flathead Indians. One white man is killed in the first raid. Indians escape with nine cattle and two horses. A second attack leaves two Indians dead and eight wounded, the warriors driving off twenty-one head of stock. A few miles further on, the travelers encounter a full-scale ambush, which leaves four men killed and three others wounded, one of them mortally. An eighteen-month-old girl suffers a broken leg when one of the Indians picks her up and dashes her against a stone.

August, Patagonia, Arizona: Apaches raid the town, killing one white man and wounding several others.

August 14, Cache County, Utah: Twenty Indians are killed and six soldiers wounded in a two-hour fight at Sardine Canyon.

August 20, Cache County, Utah: A wagon train is attacked by Shoshoni men near Marsh Creek, with one white traveler killed and three wounded. The Indians escape with sixty-eight cattle and a mule.

August 31, Bingham County, Idaho: Indian raiders attack an emigrant party twenty-five miles west of Ft. Hall. The Indian leader is killed, but the attack continues, leaving five men, one woman, and two children killed and mutilated.

September, Uvalde County, Texas: Louis Thompson is killed by Indians along the Frio River.

September 28, Brownsville, Texas: Juan Cortina invades the town with a troop of armed Mexicans, killing five Anglos and rescuing several Mexican prisoners from jail. By 1860 Cortina's men raided the countryside from Brownsville to Rio Grande City and inland as far as Arroyo Colorado, killing at least fifteen Anglos and eighty "friendly" Mexicans, with losses of at least 100 renegades slain. Innocent peons are caught in the middle of the struggle, with Texans burning the homes of alleged Cortina sympathizers and Cortina executing suspected "traitors." Texas Rangers cross the Rio Grande against orders, defeating Cortina's men at the battle of Las Cuevas, but Cortina defeats Rangers and Mexican troops in other engagements. The war finally ends after Cortina's arrest in 1875.

October, Chester, Illinois: One black man is killed and two white men wounded when slave owners and fugitive slaves from Missouri battle.

October, Uvalde County, Texas: A settler named White is killed by Indians on Hondo Creek.

October, Nash County, North Carolina: Three fugitive slaves are wounded in a battle with slave owners.

October 16, Harper's Ferry, Virginia: John Brown's abolitionist raiders seize a U.S. arsenal, hoping to touch off a massive slave revolt across the South. By the time marines retake the arsenal on October 18, twelve of Brown's men are dead, along with one marine and five local civilians. Brown is transported to Charleston and hanged on December 2.

October 28, Uvalde County, Texas: John Davenport is killed by Indians near the Sabinal River. A posse overtakes the Indians on October 29, killing three in a running fight and recovering Davenport's scalp.

November, San Tomas, Arizona: Apache raiders kill three settlers at a nearby ranch.

November, Berryville, Virginia: Two blacks are jailed for life after a series of arson fires blamed on slaves.

November, Juab County, Utah: Indians raid the Overland Mail station at Deep Creek, stealing wheat raised to feed their tribe through the winter.

November, Tooele County, Utah: Bannock Indians send word that they are coming to raid the Overland Mail station at Schell Creek for livestock, but the actual attack falls on an emigrant train near Egan Canyon. Several horses are stolen, and the lone rider sent in pursuit is captured by Indians, stripped naked and forced to go back on foot.

November 6, Pena Blanca Creek, New Mexico: Soldiers fire on a party of five Navajos, killing one and wounding another.

November 8, Chuska Mountains, Arizona: Troops kill three Navajo men, wound one woman, and capture 600 sheep.

December, Berea, Kentucky: Thirty-six abolitionist missionaries are stripped of their belongings and deported to Ohio, on charges of fomenting slave revolts.

December, Bolivar, Missouri: One white man is killed, with several injured during a local slave revolt. Recaptured slaves are flogged for their participation in the action.

December, Parker County, Texas: One white man is killed and a woman tortured and left for dead when Indian raiders attack several outlying ranches. Several horses are stolen.

1860

Canby, California: Modoc Indian raids leave three white men dead, one wounded, and steal 910 head of cattle.

Colorado River, Texas: One Texan and several Indians are killed when militiamen assault an Indian camp on Wolf Creek.

Tooele County, Utah: One soldier is shot and several horses stolen in an Indian raid on a military post at Deep Creek.

San Saba County, Texas: Settler Chancy Couch is killed and mutilated by Indians near his home.

Hamilton County, Texas: Indians pursue a white scout named Hamilton. Rangers retaliate by raiding a nearby Indian camp, inflicting several casualties.

January 5, New Mexico: Navajos launch a ten-week series of raids along the Rio Grande, capturing four shepherds, thirty head of cattle, 500 mules, and 18,500 sheep by March 16.

January 17, Ft. Defiance, Arizona: Navajo raiders overrun guards assigned to the garrison's beef herd, killing three soldiers and firing 130 arrows into their bodies. Two Indians are later killed in a second raid on the herd. Nearby, one soldier is killed and one teamster wounded when Navajos attack a wagon train.

February 7, Ft. Defiance, Arizona: Five hundred Navajo raiders attack the U.S. cavalry's herd of horses, suffering thirty casualties before being driven off by armed guards. One soldier is wounded during the two-hour battle.

March, Nevada-Utah: Gosiute, Shoshoni, and Bannock Indians launch repeated attacks on mail stations, looting food and horses. Most of the rural stations are abandoned by mid-May, but sporadic raids continue through October.

March, Medina County, Texas: Indian raiders kill a rancher named Schoon near D'Hanis and return the next day and murder a Mexican boy at a nearby farm. Pursuers track the raiders to the Sabinal River, where they discover two more white men and an Indian dead at the scene of a recent skirmish. Overtaking their quarry, the Texans recapture several head of stolen cattle without getting a clear shot at the Indians.

March, Uvalde County, Texas: Eighteen-year-old Henry Shane is captured by Indian raiders and flogged with leather straps several times over the next two days. On his third day of captivity, the war party is attacked by U.S. troops, allowing Shane to make his escape.

March 22, Tooele County, Utah: Indians raid Eight-Mile Station, killing stagecoach driver Henry Harper and wounding one of his passengers.

Spring, Nevada: Indians launch concerted raids against stations on the Pony Express route. Within the space of a few days, rider James Ouldcart is killed, Simpson's Park Station is burned, and two men are killed in an attack at Dry Creek. Two others escape, stripping to their underwear in an effort to outdistance their pursuers.

April, Cedar Springs, Utah: A local Indian held in police custody is shot and scalped, his body dumped in the Sevier River by the arresting officer.

April 30, Ft. Defiance, Arizona: One thousand Navajo warriors stage a dawn raid against white troops, with twelve Indians verified as dead before the raiders fall back.

April 30, Young County, Texas: A rancher named Newhouse and one of his Mexican cowboys are ambushed and killed by Indians. A posse pursues the raiders, without result.

May, Chuska Mountains, Arizona: Six Navajos are killed and one woman captured in a clash with rival Indians.

May, Pershing County, Nevada: Station owner Tom Anderson kills an Indian on the lower Humboldt River. Anderson is forced to flee the area when tribesmen begin killing cattle in retaliation.

May 7, Williams Station, Nevada: Five whites are killed and several shanties burned when Paiute warriors raid a settlement to rescue kidnapped Paiute women.

May 12, Pyramid Lake, Nevada: Maj. William Ormsby and forty-two soldiers are killed and thirty soldiers are reported missing after a clash with Paiutes. The Indians admit losing two men and three horses in the engagement.

May 28, Tooele County, Utah: Indians attack the mail station at Deep Creek, wounding one man and stealing several horses.

May 29, Williams Station, Nevada: Troops clash with a band of 150 Indians and report seven Indians killed.

June, Laguna Grande, New Mexico: Thirty Mexicans and five friendly Indians die in a clash with Navajo warriors. Another thirteen Mexicans are wounded in the battle, which leaves fifteen Navajos dead and an uncertain number injured.

June 2, Pinnacle Mount, Nevada: A punitive expedition clashes with Paiute raiders, killing forty-six Indians, and leaving eleven soldiers killed and wounded.

June 8, Tooele County, Utah: A group of white men open fire on a party of fifty Gosiute Indians at Shell Creek, killing three or four of them.

June 13, Malheur County, Oregon: Indians attack a mining camp and skirmish with prospectors for a day and a half. Two whites are wounded in the clash, while the raiders suffer five fatalities before they flee, taking forty-three horses and mules.

June 23, Stephens County, Texas: Josephus Browning is ambushed and killed by Indians, his brother narrowly escaping from the trap. A posse overtakes the Indians on June 28 at Paint Creek, killing thirteen Indians and scalping nine of the corpses.

July, Waxahachie, Texas: Two white men and two blacks are hanged for their roles in a planned slave revolt.

July, Black Mesa, Arizona: Mexican volunteers kill one Navajo, wounding seven or eight in a clash that leaves one Mexican wounded and four horses dead.

July, Elko County, Nevada: Seven Shoshoni approach the trading post at Willow Creek, seeking food. Dissatisfied with the twenty pounds of flour they are given, members of the party kill a cow, whereupon the station keeper shoots and kills two of their group. Survivors stage attacks throughout the night. Three more die before they finally withdraw.

July–August, Texas: Renegade slaves are blamed for an eight-week rash of arson fires in the counties of Anderson, Austin, Dallas, Denton, Ellis, Grimes, Hempstead, Lamas, Milan, Montgomery, Rusk, Tarrant, Walker, and Wood.

July 6, Tooele County, Utah: Indians burn the mail station at Shell Creek. A few days later, pony express rider Elijah Wilson is killed by Indians near Deep Creek station.

July 8, Texas: Arson fires are reported in seven northern Texas towns, with the Dallas business district nearly destroyed. A widespread slave conspiracy in the northern counties is suspected, and poison is confiscated from numerous blacks. In Henderson, a white man is hanged for supplying poison to slaves, and another is hanged at Ft. Worth for providing blacks with firearms. At Tennessee Colony two white abolitionists are hanged on a charge of inciting a revolt. Eighty stores are set afire in Austin before the plot is revealed, and blacks are whipped or hanged in almost every northern county of the state.

July 20, Tooele County, Utah: Indian raiders set fire to the military post at Butte Valley.

July 22, Smithfield, Utah: Shoshoni Chief Pagunap is shot and killed while resisting arrest for horse theft. His ten companions kill two whites and wound four others in a running battle. Pagunap's death sparks two years of sporadic warfare in the Cache Valley region.

August, Georgia: Slave revolts are reported in Cobb, Floyd, and Whitfield Counties. Following outbreaks of black violence in Floyd County, the revolt's leader is convicted and exiled from the state. Slaves reportedly plan to burn the town of Dalton, seize a train, and crash into Marietta, seventy miles away. Thirty-six alleged leaders of the outbreak are imprisoned.

August, Talladega County, Alabama: Armed whites crush an incipient slave revolt.

August, Winston County, Mississippi: One white man and one black man are hanged after a black woman betrays the plotters of a planned slave revolt. Other blacks are sentenced to floggings, with several dying from their injuries.

August, Montgomery, Alabama: Authorities suppress a slave revolt, sparing the white instigator's life because of his advanced age.

August, Mobile, Alabama: A white man is sentenced to thirty-nine lashes for inciting slaves to revolt.

August, Tooele County, Utah: Four soldiers ambush a party of Indians at Deep Creek, killing two. The next day, angry tribesmen attack Shell Creek station, pinning down the occupants for an hour before troops arrive and kill seventeen braves. The same afternoon, four Shoshoni are killed by soldiers escorting a mail shipment through Shell Creek Canyon.

August, Alexandria, Louisiana: White patrols break up a planned slave revolt.

August, Henderson, Texas: An arson fire nearly destroys the town. Investigation leads to the confession of a female slave, who implicates her owner in the plot. An estimated seventy-five to 100 blacks die in the ensuing outbreak of vigilante mayhem.

August 1, Elko County, Nevada: Troops in Egan Canyon clash with Indians who have been harassing the local pony express station. Three Indians die in the fight, and three soldiers are wounded.

September 6, Cassia County, Idaho: Indians stage a series of raids around City of Rocks, on the Raft River. Pursuit of the raiders proves fruitless.

September 7, California Trail, Nevada: Indians assault an emigrant camp, driving away thirty cattle after a battle that lasts an hour and a half. The attack is renewed on September 9, with warriors seizing wagons and 150 head of livestock. The travelers escape.

September 9, Twin Falls County, Idaho: Shoshoni raiders strike a wagon train west of Salmon Falls, killing six men, one woman, and four children.

September 12, Cassia County, Idaho: Shoshoni and Bannock Indians fight a twenty-mile running battle with members of an emigrant train, killing six whites and wounding two more. Authorities report that it is the sixth train attacked in as many weeks.

September 24, Laguna Negra, New Mexico: Navajo headman Agua Chiquita is shot and wounded, then executed, after approaching U.S. troops on a mission of peace. His death sparks a war that will last through the first week of November.

October, Virginia: Several arrests are made as planned slave revolts are uncovered in Norfolk and Princess Anne counties. In Norfolk, one white abolitionist and one free black are killed by local whites.

October, Patagonia, Arizona: Apaches stage a series of raids in the area, abducting an eleven-year-old boy during one raid.

October, Elko County, Nevada: Eighty Paiute warriors attack Egan Station and capture two white men. The Indians are preparing to burn their hostages when troops arrive, killing eighteen Indians in the ensuing fight.

October, Plymouth, North Carolina: Numerous blacks are jailed as authorities crack down on a planned slave revolt.

October 13, Ojo del Oso, New Mexico: Capt. George McLane is killed as his troop engages Navajo warriors.

October 15, Sagebrush Spring, Arizona: Navajo chief Sarcillo Largos is killed in an ambush by Mexicans and Zuñi Indians.

October 20, Apache County, Arizona: Troops from Ft. Defiance clash with Navajos at Pueblo Colorado Wash, killing five Indians and capturing four.

October 22, Socorro County, New Mexico: Troops kill five Navajos, wound six, and capture four in a clash at Jornado del Muerto.

October 24, Black Mesa, Arizona: Troops kill five Navajo men and capture three women and two children.

November, Georgia: Slave conspiracies are discovered in Crawford and Habersham counties. One white abolitionist is executed in Crawford County, with several blacks sentenced to "severe whipping."

November 8, Arizona–New Mexico: U.S. troops officially terminate their ten-week campaign against Navajos, reporting thirty-four Indians killed and 860 horses and 7,000 sheep captured since September 24.

November 18, Calites Canyon, New Mexico: U.S. troops clash with Navajos, killing four men and capturing four women.

Winter, Delta County, Texas: Two Indians are killed in a skirmish with Texas Rangers.

December, Alabama: Slave insurrections are reported in Autaugaville, Hayneville, Pine Leve, and Prattville.

December 3, Boston, Massachusetts: White rioters drive abolitionists from Tremont Temple.

December 10, Independence, Missouri: Kansas free-soilers raid a plantation seven miles from town. One person is killed and another wounded in the skirmish. Two of the raiders are soon killed by a vengeful posse.

December 18, Hardeman County, Texas: Texans surprise a Comanche camp on the Pease River, killing an unspecified "considerable number" of them. Four hundred fifty Indian horses are captured in the raid, which effectively crushes Comanche resistance to white settlers in the area.

1861

Brown County, Texas: Rangers attack an Indian camp near Pecan Bayou, killing one man and scattering the rest, recovering thirty-six stolen horses.

Colorado: Three Mexican brothers—Felipe, Julian, and Victorio Espinosa—invade the territory with the announced intention of killing 600 Anglos to avenge the loss of their family in the Mexican-

U.S. War. Preying on isolated prospectors, soldiers, and travelers, they manage to kill and rob twenty-six people by mid-1863, when Victorio is captured and lynched by vigilantes. A few weeks later Felipe and Julian are cornered and shot by an army detail near Indian Springs.

Lampasas County, Texas: A party of Rangers clash with Indian horse thieves, killing one man and capturing several animals. A month later, in another fight with Texas Rangers, two Indians are killed and four are severely wounded.

Hayneville, Alabama: One white and six blacks are hanged for plotting a local slave revolt.

Greensboro, Alabama: Four whites and sixteen blacks are executed as authorities crush a scheduled slave uprising.

January, Apache Pass, Arizona: Apache leader Cochise is surprised by armed troops during a meeting with military leaders and is wounded when he escapes from custody. Tribesmen retaliate with an attack on the Overland Mail coach.

January, Eastland County, Texas: Indian raiders attack a rural homestead, killing two women and abducting two others, abusing both captives before releasing them naked in the wilderness.

January 8, Pensacola, Florida: Federal sentries fire the first shots of the Civil War, repulsing a party of twenty Confederates at Ft. Barrancas. War between the Union and the Confederacy will not become official until the shelling of Ft. Sumter, South Carolina, on April 12. Leaders of both sides publicly reject assertions that the abolition or defense of black slavery is a primary issue in the war that lasts until through April 1865. In four years the opposing sides will engage in 10,455 military actions, ranging from brief skirmishes to battles involving thousands of troops. Final body counts reveal at least 623,026 soldiers killed in the Civil War, with another 471,427 wounded.

February, Taos, New Mexico: Mexican civilians kill seven Navajos, six of whom are women and children. Four Indian women are captured in the attack.

February 1, Apache Pass, Arizona: Eight teamsters are captured and burned to death when Apaches raid their wagon train, and three escape. Apaches besiege the local army camp from February 2 until reinforcements arrive on February 9.

March, Tohgaii, New Mexico: Two days after the murder of a Mexican man, civilian forces clash with Navajos suspected of the killing. A second Mexican expedition raids Navajo ranches at Herrero, Vincente Baca, and El Chupador, killing or capturing fifteen Indians.

March 7, Uvalde County, Texas: Henry Robinson and Henry Adams are killed by Indian raiders at Chalk Bluff on the Nueces River. The same war party next attacks Robinson's home, seven miles away, killing one boy and scalping a girl, who survives her wounds.

Spring, Parker County, Texas: After a brief skirmish with Texas Rangers, Indians murder and scalp settler William Youngblood. Rangers overtake the Indians and kill their chief and recover Youngblood's scalp.

April, Walker River, Nevada: Troops break up an effort to reorganize the Paiute tribes.

April, Charleston, South Carolina: Seven leaders of a local slave rebellion are hanged.

April, Lexington, Kentucky: Authorities suppress a slave revolt.

April 21, at Sea: An illegal slave ship, the *Nightingale*, is captured by the *USS Saratoga*, with 961 Africans on board.

May, Delaware: Muskets and ammunition are seized from slave conspirators in the southern part of the state.

May, Kentucky: Slave insurrections are reported in Owen and Gallatin Counties.

May, Jefferson County, Mississippi: Five white abolitionists are implicated in a slave revolt that ends with the hanging of several blacks.

May, Brown County, Texas: Ten Indians ambush a pair of white travelers, killing both men.

May, Charles City County, Virginia: Several participants in a local slave rebellion are sentenced to receive thirty lashes each.

May, New Orleans, Louisiana: Black arsonists are blamed for burning a dozen ships anchored in the harbor.

June, Monroe, Arkansas: Authorities execute three leaders of a local slave revolt.

June 10, Butte Creek, California: White settlers call for troops to protect them from raids by Modoc and Klamath Indians.

Summer, Tooele County, Utah: Overland Mail agents at Eight Mile Station are besieged by Indians for two days before troops arrive.

Summer, Parker County, Texas: Indians raid isolated homes along Grindstone Creek, killing one man and wounding another, and then murder and scalp a woman in a separate incident.

Summer, Young County, Texas: A settler named Butoff is ambushed and killed by Indians along Elm Creek. A second white man is pursued by the Indians, but escapes.

Summer, Hamilton County, Texas: Samuel Kuykendall is ambushed, killed, and scalped by an Indian war party.

July, Knox County, Texas: Three Texans and seven Indians die in a battle.

August 7, Hampton, Virginia: Confederate troops burn the village after learning that Union Gen. Benjamin Butler plans to quarter runaway slaves in some of the abandoned buildings. Residents are given fifteen minutes to leave before the houses are set on fire.

August 8, Tooele County, Utah: Indians attack an emigrant wagon train near Great Salt Lake.

August 25, Ft. Stanton, New Mexcio: Confederate troops launch military operations against Indians, which continue through September 8.

September 13, Ft. Fauntleroy, New Mexcio: Troops open fire on a crowd of drunken, rioting Navajos, killing twelve.

September 27, Pinos Altos, Arizona: Apaches raid the town, but are driven back by white settlers. The next day armed whites foil an Indian strike on a wagon train leaving town.

Fall, Brown County, Texas: Indians massacre five members of the Jackson family near Pecan Bayou, taking two children prisoner.

November 19, Oklahoma: Creek Indians en route to Kansas defeat a combined force of Confederate Texans and pro-Southern Cherokees at the Battle of Round Mountain. Twenty Texans are killed in the clash, their bodies grossly mutilated after death.

Winter, Pecos River, Texas: Texas volunteers loot an Indian camp, overtaking the occupants the next day in a running battle that kills most of the Indians. Two volunteers are wounded.

December, Charleston, South Carolina: A fire blamed on black arsonists razes 600 buildings, causing an estimated $7 million damage.

December, Red Butte Station, Utah: Indians kill an Overland Mail agent, looting his wagon and stealing his mules.

December, Henry County, Kentucky: Slaves are blamed for a series of arson fires that destroy "numerous houses and barns."

December 26, Oklahoma: Texans and Confederate Indians overwhelm the Creek rear guard at Chustenahlah, inflicting heavy losses and capturing the tribe's supply train. Survivors, virtually stripped of supplies, continue their trek to Kansas through a blizzard.

December 29, Oklahoma: Skirmishing between Union and Confederate Indians continues in the wake of the Creek exodus to Kansas.

1862

New York City: Black women and children employed at a local tobacco factory are mobbed by white rioters.

Edisto Island, South Carolina: Runaway slaves open fire on Confederate troops. Five of the slaves are captured; one is hanged, one is sent to prison, and three are released.

Richmond, Virginia: Confederate leaders decree that captured black soldiers shall be executed or put to work in irons. Union generals employing black troops are subject to hanging, if captured.

San Saba County, Texas: Ranchers Ben Linn and Tom Cabinass are killed by Indians in separate incidents.

Burnet, Texas: John McGill is ambushed and killed by Indians five miles from town.

Texas: Widespread Indian raids kill several white families on the frontier west of the Brazos River.

January, Weber Canyon, Utah: Gov. J.W. Dawson, fleeing the territory fearing for his life, is ambushed by Mormon raiders and suffers "shocking and almost emasculating injuries." Two of the attackers are killed by deputies while resisting arrest on January 16 and 17, respectively.

January, Snake River, Idaho: Indians begin a series of raids that will claim the lives of at least fifteen whites by September.

January 20, Chillicothe, Ohio: Col. W.O. Jennings, commander of the Hawn's Mill anti-Mormon raid in 1838, is shot and wounded on the street by persons unknown. Mormon "avengers" are suspected in the attack.

February, Utah: Indians stage repeated attacks against Overland Mail stations. Two white men are killed and fourteen mules stolen at Split Rock Station, while another raid nets thirteen mules from Horse Creek Station the same night. Twenty-five horses and mules are stolen from Granger's Station, and the violence continues through May, with attacks at Split Rock, Rocky Ridge, and Dry Sandy accounting for another twenty mules stolen. In Cache Valley, Shoshoni Indians begin killing settlers' livestock in a series of raids that continue through June.

February 13, Wheeling, West Virginia: The state constitutional convention adopts a provision that no blacks, free or slave, may enter the state as permanent residents.

February 21, New York City: Convicted slave trader Nathaniel Gordon is hanged.

March 7, Pea Ridge, Arkansas: Indian troops under Stand Watie join Confederate forces against Union troops in the Civil War's largest battle west of the Mississippi River, leaving more than 2,300 men killed, wounded, or missing in action. Reports of Confederate Indians scalping Yankee corpses are generally discounted by historians.

March 24, Cincinnati, Ohio: Abolitionist Wendell Phillips, delivering a lecture, is pelted with eggs and stones before the meeting dissolves into general brawling.

Spring, Parker County, Texas: Rancher Marion Tacket is attacked and killed by Indians on the open range.

Spring, Burnet County, Texas: Two ranchers are killed by Indians along the San Gabriel River.

April, McCulloch County, Texas: Militiamen clash with an Indian war party on the San Saba River, killing several Indians. One of the Indians slain is wearing a silk dress stolen from the homestead of a recently murdered family.

April 17, Split Rock, Utah: A band of forty to fifty Indians attacks two stagecoaches, wounding six of the nine passengers in a four-hour fight.

April 19, Green River, Utah: Twenty-four Indians attack the Overland Mail station, killing John Mallory, stealing five horses, and leaving the station in ruins.

April 21, Box Elder County, Utah: A dozen whites are killed in an Indian raid on Devil's Gate Station, an outpost for the Overland Mail.

May, Llano County, Texas: A rancher named Denyer is mortally wounded by Indian raiders, dying the day after their attack.

June, Idaho: Shoshoni raiders attack various wagon trains in the southeastern part of the state. One emigrant party has only two survivors, one of whom is wounded, from an attack east of the Raft River. Three different trains are raided in the area of Soda Springs, with several travelers killed.

June 13, Kington Fort, Utah: Mormon troops besiege a settlement of dissidents, the Morrisites, killing two women in the first barrage. The siege continues until June 16, when the Morrisites run out of ammunition. Two dissident leaders and two of the women are summarily executed by the victors. In March 1863 seven Morrisite survivors are convicted of killing possemen and sentenced to prison terms of five to fifteen years each.

June 29, Renville County, Minnesota: Sioux braves, angered after two of their tribesmen are killed by Chippewas, set out to raid. U.S. troops at Ft. Ridgely placate the Sioux with barrels of crackers, while civilians make sport of the Indians.

July, Adams County, Mississippi: Authorities report at least one white man implicated in a local slave revolt.

July 15–16, Cochise County, Arizona: Three hundred U.S. troops clash with 500 Apaches during two days of fierce combat at Apache Pass. Fourteen soldiers die in the battle, which marks the first use of artillery against Apaches. War chief Mangas Colorado is critically wounded on the second day of action, forcing the Apaches to halt their attack.

July 18, Green River, Utah: Martin Moran is killed by Indians west of town. Over the next week, another white man is killed in the area and two are wounded.

July 27, Cassia County, Idaho: G.W. Sanders dies of exposure while pursuing Indians who stole his horses along the Raft River.

August, Box Elder County, Utah: Travelers find the bodies of three white men, murdered by Indians, beside their looted and abandoned wagons.

August 2, St. John the Baptist Parish, Louisiana: An armed slave revolt fails after the Union commander of New Orleans threatens to suppress it with military force.

August 4, Marshall County, Minnesota: Troops intervene as Sioux warriors armed with tomahawks and clubs loot an Indian agency warehouse on the Yellow Medicine River.

August 8, Cassia County, Idaho: Indians attack a party of twelve Californians, wounding four men and killing fourteen horses.

August 9, Cassia County, Idaho: Searchers find four white men dead and scalped, "with indications of a hard fight" at the scene.

August 9–10, American Falls, Idaho: Indians attack a wagon train, then clash with a nearby military force. Five whites are killed in the two engagements, with a sixth mortally wounded. On August 11 members of another emigrant wagon train recover some looted property during a three-mile running battle with the Indians, losing four in the process.

August 13, Utah: A military detachment finds the dead body of an unknown white man, shot by Indians.

August 17, Acton, Minnesota: Drunken Sioux warriors invade the home of Howard Baker, killing Baker, his wife, and his mother.

August 18–19, Minnesota: A Sioux uprising leaves 100 whites dead by noon of the first day. Most of the early victims fall in Redwood and Yellow Medicine counties, but the Sioux also mount an attack against the settlement of New Ulm, where eighty settlers die in two days of fighting. By nightfall on August 19, an estimated 1,000 persons have been slain by warriors in the southern half of the state. Casualties include twenty-seven soldiers killed in a Sioux ambush at Redwood Ferry on August 19.

August 19–October 11, Idaho: U.S. Troops launch an expedition against the Snake Indians.

August 19–22, Ft. Ridgley, Minnesota: Sioux warriors besiege the military garrison. Five occupants of the fort are killed and five are wounded. Sioux casualties are unrecorded.

August 20, Murray County, Minnesota: An estimated twelve white settlers die in Sioux raids around Lake Shetak.

August 21–23, Minnesota: Attacks on whites by Sioux raiding parties, beginning at Acton, leave an estimated 500 settlers dead in three days. Warriors stage a second assault at New Ulm on August 23, killing twenty-six and wounding more than thirty. Forty Sioux are killed.

August 22, California Trail, Nevada: An emigrant party reports the loss of four cattle to Indian raiders. The same Indians return to steal a pony from the travelers on August 26.

August 24, Ft. Hall, Idaho: Ferry operator Charles Hall, seriously wounded by Indians and stripped of his clothing, escapes by feigning death. Thirty-two ferrymen and traders in the area abandon their posts in the wake of the attack.

August 24, Breckenridge, Minnesota: Sioux raiders attack the one-building settlement, killing three men and wounding a woman, stealing horses, and slaughtering or driving off cattle. Sioux warriors remain in the vicinity on August 25, clashing with a white reconnaissance party nearby. A search of the surrounding area reveals two farmers and a stagecoach driver killed by the war party.

August 25, Sioux Falls, South Dakota: Seven Sioux warriors die in a clash with U.S. troops.

August 26, Box Elder Canyon, Utah: Five white prospectors, en route to the Salmon mines in Idaho, are killed and scalped by Indians, their livestock butchered and wagons looted.

September, Cassia County, Idaho: A white man named Phillips is captured and tortured to death by Indians near Goose Creek.

September, Cache County, Utah: An emigrant party suffers three separate Indian raids in a matter of days. Four whites die in the attacks, with the train losing eleven wagons and most of its livestock.

September, Pershing County, Nevada: Twelve emigrants are killed when Indians assault a wagon train on the Humboldt River eight miles from Gravelly Ford.

September 2, Hutchinson, Minnesota: U.S. troops clash with Sioux raiders outside of town, leaving six men dead and fifteen wounded before they retreat to the settlement.

September 2–3, Renville County, Minnesota: Sioux warriors assault an army burial detail at Birch Coolie and sustain heavy losses during a thirty-six hour battle. Thirteen soldiers die in the engagement, with sixty wounded.

September 3, Richmond County, North Dakota: Sioux raiders cross the Red River from Minnesota to attack Ft. Abercrombie, killing one soldier and wounding two, suffering two casualties themselves.

September 3, McLeod County, Minnesota: U.S. troops retreat to Hutchinson after Sioux attacks at Cedar Falls and Forest City. Army losses are listed as three men dead and fifteen wounded, with Indian casualties estimated at two to three times that number.

September 6, Ft. Abercrombie, North Dakota: A second assault on the fort is staged by the Sioux, who retreat with their dead and wounded after a three-hour battle. Sporadic sniper fire is directed at the garrison over the next few days, but no new assault is attempted. A total of eight soldiers are listed as killed in the Indian siege.

September 12, Cassia County, Idaho: Fifteen whites clash with forty Indians near the Raft River, losing six during the all-day battle.

September 19, Washington, D.C.: The Commissioner of Indian Affairs issues a public warning about Indian raids along the Oregon Trail.

September 23, Wood Lake, Minnesota: The climactic battle of the Sioux revolt leaves nine whites dead and fifty wounded, with sixteen dead braves recovered from the battlefield. Statistics for the month-long conflict show forty-two Indians and 737 whites killed. Over the next five weeks, 425 Sioux are brought to trial, with 303 sentenced to death, but most are later pardoned by President Abraham Lincoln. Thirty-eight warriors are hanged at Mankato on December 26.

Fall, San Saba County, Texas: A rancher named Williams is killed and scalped by Indians in the southern part of the county.

October, New Mexico: Gen. James Carleton issues an order concerning Apaches, commanding that "All Indian men of that tribe are to be killed whenever and wherever you can find them." Women and children are to be imprisoned at Ft. Stanton. Troops in Santa Fe County fire on Apaches traveling to the territorial capital for a peace conference. Chief Manuelito and nine other braves are killed and several women are mortally wounded and left to die in the desert.

October, Parker County, Texas: Indians attack three homesteads, killing several whites and capturing ten prisoners, holding their hostages until 1864, when a new treaty wins their release.

October, Culpeper County, Virginia: Seventeen slaves are executed for participating in a revolt against their owners.

October, Surry County, Virginia: Fugitive blacks kill three white men sent to investigate their wilderness camp.

October 5, Pershing County, Nevada: A troop of California Volunteers lure three Indians into their camp at Gravelly Ford, killing all three when they resist arrest. Over the next two days the troops kill twenty-one more Indians, thirteen of whom are prisoners captured in the vicinity and then executed or shot "while trying to escape."

October 10, Mercer County, North Dakota: Sioux battle a boatload of miners on the Missouri River below Ft. Berthold.

October 22, Old Ft. Wayne, Indian Territory: Kansas militiamen rout a detachment of pro-slavery Indians and capture their field artillery.

November, New Mexico: Several scores of Apaches are killed by soldiers in various engagements, including a group trapped and massacred at Dog Canyon. Indian casualties include men, women, and children.

November, St. James Parish, Louisiana: Authorities report a slave uprising fifteen miles north of Thibodeaux.

November, Taos, New Mexico: White ruffians tempt a Ute man with liquor, waiting until he is drunk before they douse him with turpentine and set him on fire, inflicting fatal injuries.

November 12, New Ulm, Minnesota: Settlers armed with axes, clubs, and stones assault a military column moving Sioux prisoners to their scheduled point of execution near Mankato.

November 23, Providence, Utah: U.S. troops assault a nearby Shoshoni camp, killing only three Indians despite their standing orders to massacre "every Indian they could see."

December 4, Mankato, Minnesota: Soldiers clash with a mob bent on lynching Sioux prisoners held at Camp Lincoln, outside of town. A show of force prevents the lynching, and the Indians die, the day after Christmas, on schedule.

December 5, Arkansas River, Colorado: Cheyenne warriors attack a stage station maintained by U.S. mail carriers and burn it to the ground.

December 5, Franklin County, Idaho: Soldiers capture four Indians at a camp near the Malad River. All four are executed December 6.

December 24, Cache County, Utah: Shoshoni retaliate for the December 6 executions by stealing an estimated twenty horses from area farms.

1863

Young County, Texas: Three Indians die in a clash with Texas Rangers.

Bosque County, Texas: Two Indians are killed when a raiding party tries to steal horses from a militia camp.

Hood County, Texas: Cattlemen ambush a party of seven peaceable Indians on the Paluxy River. Two whites are killed and several are wounded when the Indians fire back in self-defense, but all the Indian men are killed. A second skirmish between whites and Indians is fought on the Paluxy a short time later, with several men wounded on each side.

Coryell County, Texas: Indians attack two travelers, killing a man named Williamson.

Parker County, Texas: Indian warriors kill four settlers and critically wound a fifth in one afternoon of raiding homesteads.

Burnet County, Texas: Three members of the Waford Johnson family are killed and an infant child is wounded by Indian raiders.

Winter, Concho County, Texas: Militiamen overtake a party of Kickapoo Indians at Dove Creek, with an estimated fifty men killed on each side before the surviving Indians escape.

January, Ft. McLean, New Mexico: Apache war chief Mangas Colorado, held in military custody, is tortured with hot bayonets, riddled with bullets, scalped, and beheaded by his army captors.

January 4, Arizona-New Mexico: U.S. troops launch a series of continuous operations against Navajos that last until May.

January 5, Box Elder County, Utah: Indians ambush and kill ten prospectors returning to Utah from Nevada.

January 6, Cache County, Utah: Indians attack a party of eight travelers, killing John Smith and escaping with several head of livestock.

January 14, Marsh Valley, Utah: Settlers George Clayton and Henry Bean are killed by Indians.

January 29, Franklin County, Idaho: U.S. troops assault a Shoshoni camp on the Bear River, killing an estimated 250 men, women, and children. Fourteen soldiers die and fifty are wounded in the battle.

February, Burnet, Texas: Two white men die in an Indian ambush six miles from town.

February 28, Palo Pinto County, Texas: Settlers Bejamin Baker and William Peters die in separate Indian attacks.

March, New Mexico: Troops kill an estimated forty Apache men and an uncertain number of women in various clashes.

March, Brown County, Texas: One white man is killed and three more are wounded in a clash with Indians near Pecan Bayou.

April, Benson County, North Dakota: Sioux clash with Arickaree Indians, with eight men and one woman killed in a battle lasting several hours.

April 2, Camp Finegan, Florida: Confederate troops uncover a plot by slaves in the eastern part of the state to revolt and join Union forces.

April 4–5, Utah County, Utah: U.S. troops fight a two-day engagement with Ute Indians at Spanish Fork Canyon.

April 12, Pleasant Grove, Utah: Soldiers and Ute warriors clash in another battle.

April 15, Utah County, Utah: One white officer and thirty Utes die in a battle at Spanish Fork Canyon.

April 16, Watonwan County, Minnesota: Indians raid a small settlement on the Watonwan River, killing two whites and wounding three before stealing some horses.

May, Richmond, Virginia: Authorities mete out unspecified punishment to the leaders of a slave revolt at the Tredegar Iron Works.

May, Humbolt, Kansas: Twenty-one Confederate scouts, dispatched on a mission to recruit Indians for the Southern cause, are massacred and scalped by Ossage warriors.

May, Utah: U.S. Troops report the death of fifty-three Gosiute Indians in various engagements.

May 1, Richmond, Virginia: The Confederate Congress passes a resolution that captured Union officers in charge of black troops shall be put to death or otherwise punished at the discretion of a court-martial for inciting rebellion.

May 1, Franklin County, Idaho: Shoshoni raiders attack two Mormon woodhaulers in the Cub River Canyon.

May 3, Erath County, Texas: Rancher Samuel Rogers is killed by Indian warriors.

May 4, Idaho: U.S. troops launch an expedition against Indians in the Snake River region that lasts until October 26.

May 5, Utah: U.S. Troops from Camp Douglas track Indians as far north as Soda Springs, Idaho, in a campaign that lasts through May 30.

May 14, Brown County, Minnesota: Tribesmen kill a farmer and steal four of his horses.

May 18, Box Elder Canyon, Utah: William Thorpe is killed and mutilated by Shoshoni.

June, Nine Mile Ridge, Colorado: Travellers in a wagon train are massacred by Indians, seventy-five miles west of Ft. Larned. One white teamster survives the attack.

June, Pine County, Minnesota: Two white men are ambushed and killed by Indians.

June, Government Springs, Utah: Soldiers kill ten Indians.

June 1, Elko County, Nevada: Gunfire is exchanged between two white travelers and a party of three Indians at Willow Creek, Washington. No casualties are reported.

June 5, Florida: Confederate officers report another plot by area slaves to escape their owners and join Union troops.

June 7, Wright County, Minnesota: Indian raiders steal several horses at Silver Creek. A posse gives chase on June 8, but fails to recover the animals.

June 7, Milliken's Bend, Louisiana: An estimated 650 Union troops are lost in a clash with Confederate forces, including a number of black troops who are massacred when the rebels, enraged by the Union's arming of former slaves, order the prisoners killed.

June 10, Utah County, Utah: Indians attack a stagecoach between Ft. Critenden and the Jordan River. Two whites are killed and mutilated by the raiders.

June 16, North and South Dakota: U.S. troops inaugurate a campaign against Sioux Indians that lasts until September 13. Despite the deployment of 6,300 soldiers, the Sioux avoid major contact with their pursuers, slipping away after a few inconclusive skirmishes.

June 24, Charleston, South Carolina: Authorities foil a slave conspiracy to revolt and join the Union forces.

June 29, Hennepin County, Minnesota: Six members of the Amos Dustin family are slaughtered by Indians.

July, Hood County, Texas: Five white travelers are ambushed by Indians, with one man killed in the resultant running battle.

July, Juneau County, Wisconsin: Winnebago Indians raid the home of a whiskey dealer named Salter, killing his wife and consuming a great deal of liquor in his absence. Salter returns home to find a drunken Indian on the premesis. He kills and decapitates the brave, mounting his severed head on a stake. The subsequent ax murder of an innocent Indian traveler prompts tribesmen to declare war on Salter and sporadically snipe at him around his home.

July 3, Hutchinson, Minnesota: Little Crow, a Sioux chieftan, is shot and killed by whites. His killers receive a $500 reward in addition to the normal bounty offered for Indian scalps by the state government.

July 4, Socorro County, New Mexico: U.S. troops skirmish with Navajos near Ft. Craig.

July 6, Minnesota: State records indicate payment of a $25 bounty for an Indian scalp.

July 7–19, Arizona: Col. Christopher "Kit" Carson leads military expeditions against the Navajo.

July 11–14, New York City: A draft riot by Irish laborers, unable to afford the $300 needed to avoid military conscription, turns into a bloody pogrom against blacks. Rioters burn two provost marshal offices, a black orphan's home, and an entire block of buildings on Broadway. The mob kills three policemen and at least eighteen others—mostly blacks—before troops react in force. Casualty estimates run as high as 1,200 killed and wounded before the riot subsides.

July 17, Delaware County, Oklahoma: Union forces, including black troops, clash with Confederate soldiers and pro-Southern Indians at Elk Creek, near Honey Springs, in the largest engagement fought in the Indian Territory. The Confederates are ultimately forced to retreat for lack of ammunition.

July 25, Bonito River, New Mexico: Cavalry troops burn Navajo food stores and confiscate livestock. Maj. Joseph Cummings is killed by an Indian marksman a short time later, and Navajos raid Ft. Canby, recapturing some of their livestock.

July 28, Sully County, South Dakota: Sioux assault an army camp at Stone Lake, are repulsed, and flee toward the Missouri River. The U.S. commander estimates that his men have killed or wounded at least 150 Sioux in the preceding month.

July 30, Missouri River, North Dakota: Lt. Frederick Beever and Pvt. Nicholas Miller are killed by Sioux while hunting near their army camp.

July 31, Griggs County, North Dakota: Lt. George Brackett is killed and a civilian companion wounded in an ambush by a band of fifteen Indians.

August, Tooele County, Utah: U.S. troops assault an Indian camp twenty miles north of Shell Creek Station, killing twelve to fourteen Indians. Surviving tribesmen retaliate with a raid on Canyon Station, killing six whites and burning all the buildings.

August, Missouri River, North Dakota: Indians decimate a party of prospectors, losing several men in the attack.

August 3, Ft. Canby, New Mexico: Gen. James Carleton orders troops from Albuquerque to mount expeditions against local Indians, killing "every male Navajo or Apache Indian who is large enough to bear arms." On August 18 Carleton posts a cash bounty for each head of Indian livestock seized and returned to the fort by his troops.

August 7, Minnesota: State records indicate the payment of a $75 reward for the death of a Sioux warrior.

August 20, Pueblo, Colorado: Kit Carson leads a new military expedition toward Canyon de Chelly, Arizona, in reprisal for Indian depredations in the area. Operations against the local tribes continue through December 16.

August 21, Lawrence, Kansas: Quantrill's raiders sack the town in a move against abolitionist forces, killing more than 150 civilians.

August 28, Burleigh County, North Dakota: U.S. troops kill fifty-eight Sioux in a battle at Apple Creek.

August 29, New Mexico: Operations against the Navajos are intensified, with the aim of moving them to a reservation at Bosque Redondo on the Pecos River.

August 31, Minnesota: State records indicate payment of a $5 bounty for an Indian scalp.

September, Colorado: Kiowa and Commanche raiders attack three wagon trains near Cimarron Crossing. Other assaults are staged near Ft. Larned and Ft. Lyons.

September, Chattanooga, Tennessee: Union troops demolish a Catholic cathedral to obtain materials for their own fortifications. The federal government later pays $18,729 in damages to the congregation.

September 3, Burleigh County, North Dakota: U.S. troops fight a major battle with the Sioux, and sporadic skirmishes continue through the next day. One hundred dead Indians are left on the field and 156 are captured, and commanders estimate the total number of Indians killed may reach 200. The army suffers twenty dead and thirty-eight wounded in the engagement.

Fall, Young County, Texas: Texas Rangers kill three Indians in a running battle.

Fall, San Saba County, Texas: Settler Beardy Hall is killed by Indian raiders.

Fall, Llano County, Texas: Brazilla Payne dies at the hands of an Indian war party. Volunteers pursue the raiders, killing one Indian in a brief skirmish. A second Indian is met and killed as the posse is returning home.

October, Hancock County, Georgia: Eighteen slaves are imprisoned for their roles in a conspiracy against their white owners.

October, Provo Canyon, Utah: Indians massacre a party of eight white men.

October 9, Minnesota: State records indicate the payment of a $25 bounty for the killing of a Sioux brave.

November, Siskiyou County, California: Skookum John, a Modoc chief, is killed while resisting arrest.

November 10, Palo Pinto County, Texas: Rancher Henry Welty is slain by Indians.

December, Ft. Whipple, Arizona: U.S. troops ambush a party of Apaches, killing twenty immediately after tribal leaders have signed a treaty with the government.

December 9, Jefferson Parish, Louisiana: White Union officers suppress a mutiny of black troops at Ft. Jackson, sparked by the alleged mistreatment of the black soldiers by one racist officer.

December 13, Canyon de Chelly, Arizona: Navajo raiders capture a herd of cavalry pack mules and elude the pursuers under cover of a driving snow storm.

December 18, Kansas: Confederate Cherokee troops under Stand Watie are repulsed in their invasion of the territory by a Union force composed of blacks and Indians. The Cherokees afterward turn their attention to raids in Missouri.

1864

Richmond, Virginia: A black arsonist sets fire to the official residence of Confederate President Jefferson Davis.

Jack County, Texas: John Reasnor is ambushed and killed by Indians.

Yavapai County, Arizona: White vigilantes, led by a Tasmanian escaped convict, raid and burn an Apache village, killing twenty-four Indians and wounding many others. One white man dies in the clash and several others are injured.

Clifton, California: Indians kill three soldiers assigned to guard an Overland Mail station.

Burnet, Texas: Sam Binion is killed and scalped by Indians north of town. A short time later, J.T. Hamlin is attacked near the same place, but makes his escape.

January 6, Ft. Canby, New Mexico: U.S. troops launch a new offensive against the Navajos that lasts through the end of the month.

January 12, Canyon de Chelly, Arizona: U.S. troops led by Kit Carson skirmish with Navajo warriors, killing eleven.

February 16–23, Washington: Soldiers campaign against Indians between Ft. Walla Walla and the Snake River.

March 13, Ft. Canby, New Mexcio: The first party of defeated Navajo begin their "long walk" to confinement at Ft. Sumner. By May 11, 4,776 men, women, and children will make the overland trek, with soldiers recording 320 deaths along the way. Another 126 are reported dead in captivity, at Ft. Canby, before the long march begins.

April, John Day River, Oregon: Modoc warriors clash with a mixed force of U.S. troops and white civilians.

April 12, Morgan County, Colorado: U.S. troops clash with a party of Indians blamed for the theft of horses. Two soldiers are killed and four are wounded, two of them mortally. The officer in charge of the patrol reports eight to ten Indians killed and twelve to fifteen wounded, but no bodies are recovered.

April 12, Ft. Pillow, Tennessee: Rebel troops under Gen. Nathan Bedford Forrest, Confederate cavalry leader and later Grand Wizard of the KKK, capture the Union garrison with Southern losses of fourteen men killed and eighty-six wounded, and Yankee casualties of 231 dead, 100 wounded, and 226 captured. Forrest orders the mass execution of black Union troops, along with several black women and children. Victims are killed in various ways; there are reports of some crucified, burned at the stake, and buried alive "as a lesson" to other blacks serving the North.

April 13, Cedar Bluff, Colorado: Soldiers "chastise" Cheyenne Indians for recent raids, inflicting sixty casualties and burning tribal property. One soldier is killed and one is wounded as Indians try to defend themselves.

April 18, South Platte River, Colorado: U.S. troops respond to a report of Cheyenne warriors raiding a nearby ranch. After searching a fifty-mile area, no trace of Indians—or a ranch—can be found.

May, Poison Springs, Arkansas: Retreating from an invasion of central Louisiana, 1,200 Union troops, mostly black, are ambushed by Confederate forces. Blacks who attempt to surrender are killed.

May 16, Smoky Hill, Colorado: Indians clash with cavalry troops in a battle that leaves four whites dead and three wounded, and Indian losses of three chiefs and twenty-five warriors killed.

May 17, Colorado: Indians raid a ranch thirty miles east of Ft. Larned, killing one settler. Two supply trains are raided nearby on the same day.

May 18, Crooked River, Oregon: Three white soldiers are killed and seven are wounded in a clash with Modoc Indians.

May 30, Smoky Hill, Colorado: A clash with Indians leaves four white men dead and three wounded, with Indian losses of twenty-eight known dead.

June 11, Adams County, Colorado: Arapahoes raid a farm twenty miles east of Denver, killing Ward Hungate, his wife, and their two young children, mutilating their bodies after death.

June 15, Arkansas: Stand Watie's Confederate Cherokees attack a Union stern-wheeler on the Arkansas River twenty miles from Ft. Smith. Driving the boat ashore with cannon fire, the Indians kill one man, then loot and burn the vessel.

June 24, Ft. Klamath, Oregon: Modoc warriors raid a wagon train nearby, wounding three whites, stealing six oxen, and destroying 3,000 pounds of flour.

Summer, Burnet County, Texas: A settler named Benson is killed and scalped by Indians and his son is captured and held prisoner for three years.

July, Young County, Texas: Alfred Lane is killed and mutilated by Indians ten miles from the site of modern Graham.

July 1, Minnesota: U.S. troops launch a new campaign against Indians.

July 6, Ft. Larned, Colorado: Kiowa raiders drive away a group of cavalry horses. One sentry is critically wounded by arrows.

July 18, Colorado: Indians raid a rural farm to steal cattle. Two white men are killed and scalped nearby on Beaver Creek Road.

July 25, North and South Dakota: U.S. troops launch an expedition against the Sioux that continues through October 8.

July 28, Dunn County, North Dakota: Soldiers clash with Sioux warriors in the Killdeer Mountains.

August, Brooks County, Georgia: One white man and three black men are hanged for their roles in an aborted slave rebellion.

August, Florida: Union officers report that roving bands of Yankee deserters and fugitive blacks are terrorizing Alachua, Lafayette, Levy, and Taylor counties and that scattered incidents are reported in other areas. The renegade bands have reportedly threatened attacks on the cities of Madison, Marianna, and Tallahassee.

August, Sanpete County, Utah: Indian harassment and threats drive Mormon settlers from Thistle Valley. Cattle and sheep are killed in the vicinity of Fairview, with one settler wounded in an altercation over sheep.

August 7, Ft. Lyon, Colorado: Kiowas raid a Mexican wagon train seven miles from the fort, killing one teamster. Four white men die in another attack at Cimarron Crossing the same day.

August 8, Colorado: Nine white men are killed during an Indian raid at Plum Creek. Three wagon trains are attacked east of Ft. Kearney, with one entirely destroyed and all of the white men killed. Indians also strike at settlements along the Little Blue River, killing fifteen whites, and abducting three women and four children.

August 11, Nebraska: U.S. troops launch a campaign against Indians that lasts through late October.

August 16, Beaver Creek, Colorado: Arapahoes raid the Indian Agency office and steal twenty-eight horses.

August 17, Colorado: Indians kill a white man and boy at Running Creek. U.S. troops find a settlement burned on the Arkansas River, with three white men scalped and a woman missing. The female captive hangs herself before she can be rescued, after being gang-raped by her Arapaho kidnappers.

August 19, Cimarron Springs, Colorado: A wagon train is burned, and ten white men are killed and mutilated by Indian raiders.

August 21, Colorado: Two white men are scalped by Indians west of Ft. Lyons. Two hundred Indians attack a wagon train near Ft. Larned, killing the wagon master and wounding several teamsters.

August 27, Idaho: U.S. troops begin a campaign against Indians from Ft. Boise to Salmon Falls, fighting several skirmishes before the operation ends in the late autumn.

September, Ft. Klamath, Oregon: One soldier is wounded in a raid by Modocs. A few days later, the Indians attack a wagon train nearby.

September, Jack County, Texas: Sheriff State Cox is killed and one of his companions is badly wounded during an Indian assault.

September, Parker County, Texas: A settler named Berry is killed by Indians on Sanches Creek.

September 11, Oklahoma: Sporadic operations against local Indians continue through the end of the month, including skirmishes between Union and Confederate Indians.

September 16, Ft. Gibson, Oklahoma: Confederate Cherokees under Stand Watie raid a Union outpost, killing several black haycutters and burning 3,000 tons of hay.

Fall, Coryell County, Texas: Indian raiders capture the son of Capt. Gideon Graham. A posse gives chase, killing one Indian, but the child is lanced and mortally wounded before his captors escape.

Fall, Parker County, Texas: Indians kill two boys and capture a woman, two children, and several horses in raids on isolated farms. A posse overtakes one war party, liberating the two children following a brisk skirmish.

October 11, Stewart County, Tennessee: Confederate troops are repulsed after attacking a black Union recruiting detachment near Ft. Donelson.

October 13, Young County, Texas: One thousand Comanche warriors invade the area near Ft. Belknap, killing five Texas Rangers and eleven civilians, and abducting seven women and children before they withdraw.

November 25, Hutchinson County, Texas: Cheyenne and Arapaho warriors repulse a punitive expedition led by Kit Carson, near the site of modern Borger.

November 29, Sand Creek, Colorado: Col. John Chivington's militia attacks a Cheyenne village and follow their commander's order to "kill and scalp all Indians, big and little." Soldiers massacre fifty-three Indian men, 110 women and children, mutilating their bodies after death. The attacking force loses nine men and thirty-eight are wounded, due in large part to indiscriminate fire by other soldiers.

November 25, Adobe Walls, Texas: U.S. troops raid a Kiowa village, inflicting sixty casualties. Two soldiers are killed and twenty-one wounded.

December 1, Troy, Alabama: Several whites are implicated in a local slave conspiracy.

1865

Kerr County, Texas: A white woman named Mrs. Joy and her daughter are ambushed by Indian raiders, with the girl decapitated. Mr. Joy swears eternal vengeance against red men in general, soon killing three in a one-man attack on a nearby camp.

Davidson County, Tennessee: Rev. J.T. Nealis, a Catholic priest, is ambushed and killed by Confederate guerillas near Nashville.

Parker County, Texas: Henry Maxwell is killed by Indians near his home, on the Brazos River. A male companion escapes from the ambush, after a fight that leaves several Indians dead or wounded. Rancher Hugh Blackwell, his son, and a neighbor's child are killed in subsequent Indian raids.

San Saba County, Texas: Settler C.C. Carter is mortally wounded in a running fight with Indian warriors.

Tehama County, California: White settlers retaliate for recent Indian raids by razing a village of the Mill Creek Indians, killing and scalping the inhabitants regardless of sex or age. One child—a boy with six toes on each foot—is allowed to live, adopted by one of the raiders as a curiosity.

January, South Platte River, Colorado: An alliance of Cheyenne, Arapaho, and Sioux warriors declare open war on whites, attacking wagon trains, stage stations, and small military posts. The town of Julesburg is burned, with settlers scalped in retaliation for the Sand Creek massacre in 1864.

January, Llano County, Texas: Indians attack an isolated farm, killing one child.

January 8, Dove Creek, Texas: State troops attack a party of 1,400 friendly Kickapoo en route from Oklahoma to Mexico, mistaking them for Comanches. The Texans are soundly defeated, with thirty-six men killed and sixty wounded. Indian losses total eleven dead and thirty-one injured. After settling safely in Mexico, the revenge-minded Kickapoos will join Apaches and Mexicans in launching an eight-year war against white Texans, inflicting an estimated $50 million in property damage by 1873.

January 11, Colorado: U.S. troops launch a campaign against Indians between Julesburg and Denver, continuing through the end of the month and fighting several skirmishes.

February, Robeson County, North Carolina: Members of the white Home Guard clash with armed mulattoes and execute three of the mulattoes' leaders.

February, Gillespie County, Texas: Two women are killed and scalped by Indians near the Pedernales River.

March 7, Finney County, Kansas: U.S. troops skirmish with Indians eighty miles west of Ft. Larned.

April, Richfield, Utah: Ute raiders steal several herds of cattle, driving them into Salina Canyon and laying in ambush for pursuing troops. Two soldiers and nine army horses die in the clash.

April 10, Sanpete County, Utah: Peter Ludvigsen is killed and mutilated in a clash with Utes at an Indian ranch near Twelve-Mile Creek.

April 10, Soldier Fork, Utah: Barney Ward and James Andersen are captured and tortured by Utes, their bodies left bristling with arrows.

April 12, Sevier County, Utah: Indian raiders ambush a cavalry detachment, killing two soldiers and wounding two.

April 15, Sevier County, Utah: U.S. troops fight "a spirited engagement" with Utes near Fish Lake, repulsing the Indians with unspecified heavy losses.

April 20, Piute County, Utah: Indians kill a member of the local militia at Ft. Sanford on the Sevier River.

April 21, Circleville, Utah: Whites respond to news of the Piute County murder the day before by arresting a band of local Indians and killing one before the rest submit to incarceration. On the evening of April 22, several Indians assault two of their jailers and whites open fire, killing all but a handful of Indian children.

May 25, Fairview, Utah: Utes kill shepherd Jens Larsen north of town.

May 26, Sanpete County, Utah: Utes massacre six members of the John Given family at Thistle Valley. Two other white men escape with their lives.

May 29, Fairview, Utah: David Jones is murdered by Ute raiders three miles north of town.

June 23, Choctaw County, Oklahoma: Brig. Gen. Stand Watie surrenders his battalion of Cherokee, Creek, Osage, and Seminole soldiers to Union commanders near Ft. Towson, marking the last formal submission of a significant Confederate force.

July, Colorado: Gen. Patrick Connor instructs his troops that Indians north of the Platte River "must be hunted down like wolves."

July 13, Sanpete County, Utah: Utes ambush and kill Robert Gillespie at Lost Creek. A male companion escapes and saves himself by hiding nearby.

July 14, Sevier County, Utah: Ute warriors kill and scalp Anthony Robinson on the Sevier River near Monroe.

July 18, Grass Valley, Utah: Several Utes are killed in a skirmish with troops that leaves one soldier wounded. After the clash, a number of captured Ute women and children are shot to death in an alleged escape attempt when one of the women strikes a guard with a stick.

July 26, Platte Bridge Station, Colorado: Cheyenne and Sioux warriors attack a military outpost, with casualties on both sides. At the height of the battle, an army wagon train is attacked nearby, with all its soldiers killed.

July 26, Glenwood, Utah: Indians attack the settlement. One white man is wounded and one Indian dies.

August 8, Kimble County, Texas: Kiowa raiders attack the Mathew Taylor homestead, killing two persons and taking six as captives after a two-hour battle.

August 16, Johnson County, Wyoming: Indian raiders ambush and harass an emigrant wagon train, retreating after troops open fire with howitzers. Sporadic harassment continues for several days as the train proceeds along the Powder River.

August 29, Rosebud County, Montana: U.S. troops burn an Arapaho village on the Tongue River, seizing 1,000 ponies from the tribe. Indians retaliate the next day by attacking a nearby wagon train.

September 1, Johnson County, Wyoming: Soldiers fire on a Sioux truce party, despite the Indians' display of a white flag, killing several men and wounding others. Retreating to their village, the survivors retaliate by stealing several army horses. A reinforced band of Sioux assault the local garrison and harass troops for several days along the Powder River.

September 8, Johnson County, Wyoming: Cheyenne warriors attack U.S. troops along the Powder River, staging several assaults before they are driven away by superior firepower.

September 8, Uvalde, Texas: A.H. Robinson is killed by Indians while collecting wood near town. His brother escapes unharmed.

September 21, Fish Lake, Utah: Eight Utes are reported dead and at least four are wounded in a clash with troops that lasts until dusk. Two soldiers and two army horses are wounded in the battle.

Fall, Ft. Ephraim, Utah: U.S. troops pursue Utes, who harassed a party of lumbermen, into Strawberry Valley, but the small detachment is repulsed by a superior Indian force. While pursuing their enemies back toward the fort, Ute warriors pause to kill Martin Kuhre, his wife, and his sister-in-law at a nearby ranch.

October 17, Sanpete County, Utah: Seven Mormon settlers are killed and two more are wounded in an Indian attack near Ephraim.

October 28, Warner Lakes, California: Modocs ambush a detachment of U.S. troops.

October 31, Camp Alford, California: Snake Indian raiders kill one military guard and steal sixteen horses.

November 26, Circleville, Utah: Utes raid the settlement, killing two white boys and stealing some cattle. The Utes also strike a party of travelers returning from Salt Lake City, killing and mutilating four.

December, Blanco County, Texas: A settler named Jackson is killed and mutilated by Indians while hunting game near his home.

1866

Hamilton County, Texas: Settler William Jenkins is fatally wounded by an arrow while pursuing Indian horse thieves.

Shackelford County, Texas: Thomas Eubank dies in a skirmish with Indians and kills one of his attackers before he dies.

January 11, Washington County, Utah: Ute warriors raid a ranch at Pipe Springs, abducting and killing two white men. Local authorities suspect the raiders may have acted under orders from a more powerful tribe of Arizona Navajos known to harass and enslave Utes at will.

January 20, Washington County, Utah: White vigilantes kill seven Indians in retaliation for the Pipe Springs raid on January 11.

March 12, Juab County, Utah: U.S. troops kill one Indian and capture twelve others near Nephi. Four of the twelve are summarily shot for complicity in local raids. The eight survivors are jailed at Manti.

Spring, Jack County, Texas: Five members of the McKinney family are killed and mutilated by Indians.

Spring, Texas: Frontier raids by Comanche and Kiowa raiders leave an estimated four-fifths of all West Texas settlements unoccupied by early April.

April, Salina, Utah: Utes raid the settlement, wounding one boy and driving off most of the cattle. Residents abandon the town on April 21.

April 2, Washington County, Utah: Utes capture three white men and one woman near Short Creek and torture and kill all four.

April 3, Salt Lake City, Utah: O.N. Brassfield, a non-Mormon who married the second wife of a local church member, is shot and killed by Mormon gunmen at his home.

April 13, Sanpete County, Utah: Utes attack a party of three wagons near Saline, capturing nine oxen as the teamsters escape. The same raiders kill a shepherd named Johnson in the foothills northeast of town. Another Mormon herdsman is killed on the Sevier River, his brother surviving despite severe wounds.

April 14, Manti, Utah: Several Indian prisoners escape from the local jail, slashing a guard's throat in the process. One Indian is killed during the break and a second is gunned down by a posse that tracks him to Birch Creek. The other escapees are later hunted down and killed on September 18 and 19.

April 21–22, Utah: Ute warriors stage a series of raids in Sevier, Piute, and Iron Counties. The first clash, at Ft. Sanford, leaves one soldier dead, and one Indian killed and another wounded. Next, an Indian is shot and killed after firing on whites at Circleville. Eleven Indian captives held in a cellar are afterward removed and executed, one by one. Tribesmen are repulsed in an attempt to steal livestock at Monroe, but they turn the tables by laying an ambush for pursuers, killing one militiaman and wounding two.

April 29, Fairview, Utah: One white sentry is killed and another wounded when Indians raid the community. A posse sights the killers but is unable to catch them.

April 30, Memphis, Tennessee: Rioting breaks out among local whites, with violence continuing through May 2. Forty-six blacks and two "radical" whites are killed during the riot. Ninety black homes, twelve schools, and four churches are destroyed.

May, Heber City, Utah: Four armed whites pursue a party of Ute cattle thieves. They surprise the raiders in the act of skinning a cow, and two Indians are killed by gunfire at the scene.

May 16, Utah County, Utah: Indians raid a livestock herd at Spanish Fork Canyon, killing and scalping Christian Larsen before taking his cattle and 200 horses. A short time later, whites retaliate by assaulting an Indian camp at Diamond Fork, but the vigilantes are repulsed by a fierce counterattack, losing one man. U.S. troops intervene, and the Indians flee after their chief is wounded.

June 10–11, Scipio, Utah: Two white men are killed and 500 cattle and horses stolen when Utes raid the town. U.S. troops give chase on June 11, scattering the raiders with rifle fire.

June 10, Sevier County, Utah: Militiamen wage a running battle with Indians between Glenwood and Gunnison. One Indian is killed and another has his horse shot out from under him.

June 24, Thistle Valley, Utah: Indian warriors attack a milita camp, killing one man and wounding another. Survivors pursue the Indians, wounding several in a skirmish at the head of the Spanish Fork River, but they escape.

June 26, Utah County, Utah: Indian raiders steal fifty horses and twenty head of cattle from outlying ranches. A militia detachment pursues the raiders to Maple Canyon, where the Indians spring an ambush, killing one soldier and wounding another before they are forced to retreat, and abandon their camp and the stolen livestock.

June 28, Circleville, Utah: Whites abandon their settlement in the face of continuing Indian raids.

Summer, Salt Lake City, Utah: Dr. J. K. Robinson, a non-Mormon who married the daughter of a deceased church member, is targeted for violent harassment. Arsonists first burn his clinic, after which he is lured from home on the pretext of treating a patient and is shot to death on the street.

Summer, Glenwood, Utah: Ute raiders launch a series of local raids by killing Merritt Staley and stealing a quantity of livestock.

July, Heber City, Utah: Indians steal two oxen and a cow, touching off a pursuit that leaves one Indian dead. Snipers fire on troops sent to apprehend the thieves.

July, Parker County, Texas: A.J. Gorman dies in a skirmish between whites and Indians on the open range.

July 17, Sheridan County, Wyoming: Oglala warriors launch guerilla warfare against white troops at Ft. Philip Kearny, stampeding 175 horses and mules from the garrison's herd and wounding several troopers during a fifteen-mile running skirmish. Over the next five months, Indians will conduct fifty-one verified raids near the fort.

July 30, New Orleans, Louisiana: A white riot against blacks leaves thirty-eight persons dead and 146 wounded before federal troops intervene.

August, Heber City, Utah: Indian raiders steal several mules and horses from grazing land east of town.

August 20, Heber City, Utah: Indians stage their fourth raid for livestock, but settlers give chase and recapture the stolen horses.

August 21, Garfield County, Utah: One man is killed when Indians ambush a party of six soldiers bound for St. George.

September, Heber City, Utah: A fifth raid by Indians results in the theft of two horses and several oxen.

Fall, San Saba County, Texas: Comanche raiders assault a rural homestead, wounding two people before they escape with stolen horses. A posse surprises the raiders in camp the next morning, killing and scalping seven Indians, with several others wounded. One posse member is killed and one injured.

Fall, Parker County, Texas: A settler named Leeper is killed and scalped by Indians at his home.

October, Uvalde County, Texas: Indians attack the Robert Kinchloe homestead, killing one woman and wounding another with eleven arrows before ending the assault.

October 1, Texas: The governor reports that Indian raids in fourteen counties over the preceding twelve months have left seventy-eight whites dead, seven wounded, and eighteen abducted.

October 23, Beaver County, Utah: Indian raiders attack a farm on South Creek, wounding one white youth.

November, Parker County, Texas: Bohlen Savage is killed by Indians while plowing his field, and his daughter is abducted (and held prisoner until 1868). The warriors kill Savage's brother and two of his children at a nearby homestead.

November 5, Kane County, Utah: Indians ambush a party of travelers at Kolob Mountain, wounding one white man and stealing several horses.

December 6, Sheridan County, Wyoming: Oglalas kill two soldiers and wound several others in a series of skirmishes.

December 19, Sheridan County, Wyoming: Indians attack a wagon train near Ft. Philip Kearny, baiting soldiers in an effort to provoke a decisive battle.

December 21, Sheridan County, Wyoming: A combined force of Cheyenne, Arapaho, and Sioux warriors annihilate eighty-one white soldiers in a battle memorialized as the "Fetterman Massacre." Indian forces suffer an estimated 200 men killed or wounded. The soldiers' corpses are dismembered and otherwise mutilated after death.

1867

Loving County, Texas: Oliver Loving is ambushed and killed by Indians along the Pecos River in the county that now bears his name.

Mason County, Texas: Allen Gentry is killed, scalped, and mutilated by Indian warriors.

January 18, Washington County, Utah: Navajo raiders capture a herd of horses from Shoal Creek. Mounted troops are dispatched from St. George, killing eleven Indians before the animals are recovered.

February 12, Newnanville, Florida: Cooley Johnson, a black man, is murdered by the KKK.

March 21, Glenwood, Utah: Ute warriors ambush two white men outside of town, killing both men and stealing their livestock. Other whites give chase and recapture the stock after a brief skirmish. While searching for strays, the posse finds the bodies of James Peterson, his wife, and a teenaged girl, all killed and mutilated by the Utes.

Spring, San Saba County, Texas: Two settlers attacked by Indians on a country road kill several Indians in a skirmish that leaves the two men with a total of forty-eight nonfatal wounds.

April, Nashville, Tennessee: A year-old social club, the Ku Klux Klan, is reorganized along military lines by a convention of Confederate veterans. Within a year the KKK will be active in twelve states, attempting to overthrow Radical Reconstruction by armed force. No accurate body-counts are available, but congressional hearings indicate that Klansmen, riding from 1868 to 1871, have murdered at least seventy-four persons in Georgia, 109 in Alabama, and 235 in Florida. A single Mississippi county, Kemper, accounts for thirty-five Klan murders between 1869 and 1871. A six-month tabulation during 1871 credits the South Carolina Klan with thirty-five murders, 262 floggings, two rapes, and another 101 victims wounded, mutilated, or driven from their homes.

April 16, Pawnee County, Kansas: U.S. troops under Gen. George Custer raze an abandoned Cheyenne village after the Indians ignore military demands for unconditional surrender.

April 20, Utah: Mormon settlers abandon the settlements of Glenwood and Monroe after continuing Indian raids.

May, Louisiana: Militant whites organize the Knights of the White Camellia in St. Mary Parish to frustrate Radical Reconstruction and prevent blacks from obtaining their civil rights. In many parts of the

South, the Knights will work hand in hand with Klansmen to preserve white supremacy.

June, Texas: Indian raiders assault the homestead of a settler named Rabb in the western part of the state, killing one woman and capturing another and two children.

June 1, Fountain Green, Utah: Utes kill one man and wound another and escape with an estimated 200 cattle and horses. A posse trails the raiders toward Thistle Valley and recovers the stolen animals.

June 2, Sanpete County, Utah: Indians ambush four militiamen at Twelve-Mile Creek, killing two.

June 22, Iron County, Utah: Indian raiders sweep through the Paragonah Range, stealing livestock from isolated farms. U.S. troops give chase and recapture the animals and a Mexican held prisoner by the Indians for several years.

Summer, Erath County, Texas: Indian raiders ambush a party of cowboys, killing two.

July, Young County, Texas: Three cowboys are killed by Indians while branding cattle near Ft. Belknap.

July, Buffalo Springs, Texas: Responding to reports of Indian raids in the area, Maj. B.O. Hutchins leads a company of troops "in pursuit," detouring past Ft. Belknap, where they spend two days playing poker. Meanwhile, Indian warriors steal most of the horses in the vicinity, besieging sixty men at the army post for two days before they withdraw.

July 21, Parowan, Utah: Indians attack a herd of stock at nearby Little Creek. The warriors are repulsed after an all-night battle with cavalry troops and civilians.

August 1, Big Horn County, Montana: Cheyenne warriors surprise thirty soldiers and civilians in a hay field near Ft. C.F. Smith. At least twenty Indians are killed before they retreat, setting the field ablaze as they go. Three soldiers die in the attack and three are wounded.

August 2, Sheridan County, Wyoming: Cheyenne raiders assault a party of woodcutters near Ft. Philip Kearny, suffering heavy losses from the combined fire of modern, rapid-fire weapons. Three whites are killed in the attack and two are wounded. Indian casualties are estimated at sixty dead and 120 injured.

August 5, Texas: The governor issues a report summarizing Indian attacks between May 1865 and July 1867, listing 162 whites killed, twenty-four wounded, and forty-three abducted. The report does not include casualties from Young and Wise counties, two of the hardest hit by Indian attacks, where statistics remain incomplete.

August 13, Spring City, Utah: Ute warriors attack a grazing herd, killing two men and wounding another. Local whites give chase but lose their quarry after a skirmish at Horseshoe Mountain.

September, Silver Lake, Oregon: U.S. troops destroy two Modoc Indian camps, killing twenty-four braves and capturing nineteen women and children. Two soldiers are wounded in the clash.

September 4, Sanpete County, Utah: Indian snipers fire on a military camp near Fayette, killing one soldier.

Fall, Mason County, Texas: Settler Francis Johnson is killed and scalped by Indian raiders.

1868

January, Pulaski, Tennessee: An argument between a white man and a former slave concerning a black girl erupts in a riot, with gunfire in the streets. At least one black is killed and several are badly wounded. Whites, including several prominent Klansmen, emerge unscathed.

January, Marshall County, Tennessee: Eight blacks are abducted by Klansmen, marched into an open field, and forced at gunpoint to swear that they will never vote the Republican ticket.

February, Utah: Navajo raiders steal herds of stock from Harrisburg and Washington. A militia party gives chase, recovering some of the stock and driving the Indians across the Colorado River.

February, Maury County, Tennessee: KKK nightriders confiscate at least 400 guns from black citizens in raids on private homes. Late in the month, a Klansman named John Bicknell is murdered by a black robber. His killer is taken from jail by members of the KKK and hanged outside Columbia.

February, Burnet County, Texas: A rancher named Smith is killed, scalped, and mutilated by Indians.

February 5, Llano County, Texas: Indians raid an isolated home in Legion Valley, killing three persons, wounding a fourth, and escaping with four prisoners.

March, Tennessee: Klansmen across the state threaten blacks to keep them from voting in scheduled county elections, afterward punishing some who defiantly exercise their rights.

March 20, Eutaw, Alabama: Klansmen burn down the Greene County courthouse.

March 21, Greensboro, Alabama: KKK members are foiled in their attempt to burn the Hale County courthouse.

March 21, San Bernadino County, California: Utah merchant Franklin Woolley is killed by Indians near the Mojave River while returning from a business trip.

March 31, Columbus, Georgia: Klansmen invade the home of Republican George Ashburn after midnight, killing him in his bedroom.

April, Malheur River, Oregon: U.S. troops from Ft. Klamath clash with Modoc Indians.

April, Danville, Kentucky: An agent for the Freedmen's Bureau reports that Klansmen are terrorizing blacks in the surrounding countryside.

April, Murfreesboro, Tennessee: Republican Sheriff J.S. Webb is dragged from his home by Klansmen and threatened with lynching if he does not resign. Webb's brother was later flogged by the KKK in a related incident.

April 1, Wellsville, Utah: A three-year-old white girl is abducted and presumed killed by Indians.

April 5, Millard County, Utah: Charles Williams is killed in an ambush by Indian warriors near Rocky Ford. A male companion escapes. Indians are still at the scene when a militia company arrives, and two more whites are wounded—one of them fatally—in the hour-long battle that ensues.

May, Woodruff County, Arkansas: A black man named Bluffkins, held for vagrancy, is taken from jail and lynched by Klansmen. Raiders also visit the home of a black couple, giving the husband and wife 200 lashes each.

May, Louisiana: Beginning this month and lasting through the summer, crimes against blacks are reported from Bienville, Bossier, Caddo, Claiborne, Franklin, Jackson, Morehouse, Richland, and St. Landry parishes. In Bienville Parish, a black Republican is dragged from his home and decapitated by whites.

May 1, Kane County, Utah: Indians kill three Indians from a rival tribe and steal eighteen horses.

May 6, Claiborne Parish, Louisiana: William Meadows, a black delegate to the state constitutional convention, is ambushed and killed by whites.

May 7, Scipio, Utah: Indian raiders drive off fifteen horses.

June, Washington, D.C.: Congress reports that racial violence in the South has claimed the lives of 373 blacks and ten whites since January 1866.

June 29, Pulaski, Tennessee: A mob of more than 100 Klansmen remove a black rape suspect from jail, riddle him with bullets, and leave his body lying in the street.

Summer, Hamilton County, Texas: White settlers clash with a raiding party of eight Indian men, killing seven before the only survivor escapes.

July, Columbia, Tennessee: A mob of fifty Klansmen drag a black child from his home, strangle him to death, and dump his body in the Duck River.

July 1, Texas: Authorities report a minimum of 1,053 murders in the state since the end of the Civil War, with one third committed in 1867 and another third in the first half of 1868. At least 833 of the slayings have been perpetrated by whites; nearly half of the victims are black, although whites hold a three-to-one majority in the state population.

July 4, Maury County, Tennessee: Thirty armed blacks ambush a nocturnal KKK procession, wounding several Klansmen before they are driven back by superior numbers and firepower. By mid-July, at least three of the blacks have been lynched, while others have fled to Nashville for safety.

July 4, Cornersville, Tennessee: Black leader William Burk dies in a shoot-out with nightriding Klansmen at his home.

July 4, Jefferson, Texas: Three hundred armed whites take control of the town to prevent a Republican rally. Mounted posses scour the surrounding countryside, gunning down blacks or jailing them on charges of "insurrection" and hanging white Republicans.

July 4, Shelbyville, Tennessee: Fifty masked Klansmen invade the town, dragging two men from their homes to be flogged. Victim J.C. Dunlap, a white teacher at a school for blacks, receives 200 lashes.

July 5, Gunnison, Utah: Seth Childs is "accidentally" shot and wounded by a "friendly" Indian outside town.

July 8, Homer, Louisiana: A white Republican is flogged by militant racists shortly before a mob destroys the presses of the local Republican newspaper.

July 14, Woodruff County, Arkansas: The KKK launches a reign of terror that will claim twenty lives by August 28, including eight persons murdered in one day.

July 23, Blanco County, Texas: Thomas Phelps and his wife are surprised while fishing on Cypress Creek and murdered by Indians. Striking at nearby homesteads, the raiders kill another man and capture a child. The prisoner and several Indian ponies are abandoned when pursuers overtake the Indians in a skirmish near Ft. Mason.

July 30, Big Horn County, Montana: Cheyenne warriors burn Ft. C.F. Smith, one day after its abandonment by U.S. troops.

August, Johnson County, Wyoming: Cheyenne Indians burn Ft. Philip Kearny after it is vacated by the military.

August, Kansas: Cheyenne and Arapaho warriors launch concerted attacks on white settlers between the Solomon and Saline Rivers in the northern part of the state. One hundred seventeen people are killed in the raids, with seven women captured and numerous buildings burned.

August, Crittenden County, Arkansas: E.G. Barker, a Republican state legislator and agent of the Freedmen's Bureau, is ambushed and seriously wounded by Klansmen.

August, Louisiana: The governor reports 150 racist murders in the preceeding six weeks. Democrats brand the statement "a willful Radical fabrication."

August, Georgia: Klansmen launch a terror campaign that lasts through October. Thirty-one people are killed, forty-three shot and wounded, five stabbed, fifty-five beaten, with eight flogging victims receiving 300 to 500 lashes each.

August, Parker County, Texas: Jacob Lopp is killed and scalped by Indians at his home.

August 15, Wayne County, Tennessee: Sixty Klansmen confront a party of black militiamen in the countryside, ordering them to disband. On their way back to Waynesboro, the Klansmen are met and fired on by the county sheriff, who is then pursued into town and beseiged in his fortified jail.

August 26, Mississippi County, Arkansas: Klansmen assassinate a state legislator, Dr. A.M. Johnson. Raiders will murder six blacks in the county by September 20.

August 29, Columbia County, Arkansas: A state legislator informs the governor that Klansmen have murdered ten blacks in the county since August 9.

September, Trinity County, Texas: Masked whites are blamed for several murders in a pre-election campaign designed to intimidate black voters.

September, Paris, Texas: Lamar County farmers arm and organize to suppress Klan violence in the area, but the terrorism continues into November.

September, Searcy, Arkansas: Detective Albert Parker vanishes after infiltrating the White County KKK. He is never seen again, and the facts of his murder by Klansmen are not revealed until March 1870.

September 10, Northport, Alabama: Klansmen raid a black man's home, killing his wife while he hides in the chimney.

September 17, Republic County, Kansas: Cheyenne and Sioux warriors assault a military camp on the Republic River, touching off a three-day battle. Five soldiers are killed in the fighting and eighteen are wounded. The Indians sustain heavy casualties, including the loss of Roman Nose, a Cheyenne war chief.

September 19, Bennett's Bayou, Arkansas: Capt. Simpson Mason is shot and killed by KKK members while trying to register black voters.

September 19, Camilla, Georgia: Armed whites disperse a Republican rally with gunfire and then devote the rest of the day to a "nigger hunt" that leaves seven blacks dead and thirty to forty wounded. Six whites are slightly injured by blacks defending themselves from attack.

September 22, New Orleans, Louisiana: Rioting breaks out after white Democrats fire on a Republican political parade.

September 28, Opelousas, Louisiana: Emerson Bentley, a white teacher at a school for blacks, is beaten in front of his class by three members of the militant Seymour Knights.

Fall, Columbia County, Florida: Whites fire on a black social gathering, trying to assassinate Republican activist Prince Weaver. They miss their target, instead killing Weaver's thirteen-year-old son and severely wounding three other persons.

Fall, Erath County, Texas: Nathan McDow is killed by Indians while cutting timber.

Fall, Young County, Texas: Herdsman Charles Rivers is mortally wounded by Indians while grazing his stock. He survives for six days before infection claims his life.

October, Louisiana: A full-scale race war erupts in the month preceding the presidential election. Members of the KKK and other groups scour the countryside for black voters and white Republicans, leaving an estimated 1,723 killed or wounded by November 8. In St. Landry Parish, more than 200 are killed during a two-day purge; a pile of twenty-five bodies is found half-buried in the woods. Another 162 corpses are reported from Bossier Parish, in the wake of a local "nigger hunt." Two hundred ninety-seven political murders are reported from the parishes around New Orleans. Forty-two victims are known dead in Caddo Parish, and twenty-five to thirty black corpses are counted during the month as they float past Shreveport on the Red River. In Alexandria a white mob demolishes the office of a Republican newspaper. In Franklinton hooded Klansmen raid the homes of three black Republicans, seizing and destroying their Republican ballots.

October, Monticello, Arkansas: Deputy Sheriff William Dollar and Frederick Reeves, a black man, are murdered by Klansmen.

October, Live Oak, Florida: A black man, Doc Rountree, and his wife and four children are abducted by Klansmen. All are flogged for the offense of owning land and are warned to go back to work for their pre-war slave owner.

October, Weakley County, Tennessee: Armed Klansmen invade the voting registrar's home, seeking to prevent registration of blacks and Republicans, but an argument erupts among the raiders, leading to blows and gunfire. The Klansmen finally retreat, with several self-inflicted wounds.

October 1, Cache Bottom, Arkansas: Two white Republicans, D.P. Upham and F.A. McClure, are ambushed and wounded by Klansmen while trying to organize a militia detachment to use against nightriders.

October 1, Cokesbury, South Carolina: Republican State Senator B.F. Randolph is shot and killed on a railroad platform by three Klansmen.

October 1, Sumter County, Alabama: Ben Brown, a black Republican activist, is murdered by the KKK.

October 1, Jefferson, Texas: George Smith, a New York "carpetbagger," is ambushed by white supremacists at a black home, and wounds two of his attackers in an exchange of gunfire. Jailed on trumped-up charges of assault that night, Smith is shot and killed in jail on October 4 by members of the Knights of the Rising Sun.

October 11, Newnanville, Florida: Cesar Sullivan, a black man, is killed by the KKK.

October 15, Crittenden County, Arkansas: Klansmen on the tug boat *Netty Jones* open fire on the steamer *Hesper*, forcing their target ashore and seizing arms intended for the Arkansas militia and dumping the weapons overboard.

October 17, Franklin, Louisiana: Sheriff Henry Pope and Judge Valentine Chase are assassinated by white supremacists.

October 22, Monroe County, Arkansas: Klansmen ambush and kill Congressman James Hinds. Future governor James Brooks is wounded in the same attack.

October 23, Jefferson Parish, Louisiana: Knights of the White Camellia provoke blacks into attacking several of their members, using the excuse of "self-defense" to launch raids that leave five blacks dead, nine wounded by gunfire, and thirty-three beaten or otherwise injured.

October 24, Rocky Comfort, Arkansas: Maj. Porter Andrews, U.S. revenue assessor, and Lt. Hiram Willis, of the Freedmen's Bureau, are killed in a KKK ambush. Other victims of the same ambush include one black man killed and two persons wounded, one of them the local sheriff.

October 24, New Orleans, Louisiana: Whites fire on a Republican parade, leaving several blacks dead or wounded. The mob next turns its wrath on white Republicans and members of the metropolitan police, ambushing beat patrolmen and laying siege to the police station. Sixty-three persons die during the outbreak before order is restored.

October 25, Eutaw, Alabama: A pre-election race riot erupts, with whites firing on blacks. Two white men are slightly wounded in the outbreak, and four blacks are killed and fifty others are injured.

October 25, Algiers, Louisiana: Authorities report that members of the Knights of the White Camellia and the Wide Awakes have killed seven blacks in recent days.

October 29, Augusta, Arkansas: Klansmen shoot up the town, killing George McElum and wounding Bill Cincinnati, narrowly missing the sheriff. Outside of town, two black families are disarmed and terrorized at their rural homes.

October 29, Tangipahoa, Louisiana: Forty Klansmen raid the home of John Kemp, the black coroner, shooting him to death and beating his wife. The same raiders strike at several other homes, wounding two more blacks and robbing a third.

October 31, Huntsville, Alabama: Participants in a KKK parade clash with blacks, and shooting erupts, leaving two persons dead and several wounded.

November, Gainesville, Florida: A black man named Stephens is murdered by Klan raiders.

November, Tuscaloosa, Alabama: Twenty Klansmen attack a Republican gathering shortly before the November 3 elections.

November 1, Monticello, Arkansas: Klansmen stage multiple raids to frighten blacks from voting in a scheduled election. Rev. Abraham Boler is flogged, with a pistol forced down his throat. Another black minister, Rev. Wesley Ridgwell, is also beaten, and James Manees narrowly escapes from a party of would-be lynchers.

November 1, Gordon, Florida: Klansmen murder Moses Smith, a black man.

November 1, Warrenton, Georgia: One Klansman dies and three are wounded in a shoot-out at the home of Perry Jeffers, a black man and intended victim. A larger raiding party strikes on November 5, shooting one of Jeffers's sons to death and burning the boy's body on a bonfire constructed of the family's furniture. His wife is hanged, but neighbors cut her down while she is still alive. Days later, while attempting to flee the state, Jeffers and three of his sons are taken from a train at Dearing, shot to death in the woods nearby, and their bodies dumped in a well.

November 2, Franklinton, Louisiana: Klansmen visit the board of election supervisors to warn them not to distribute any Republican ballots on November 3.

November 2, Tennessee: KKK nightriders launch raids against blacks and Republicans in Franklin, Giles, Lincoln, and Shelby Counties on election eve.

November 3, South Carolina: Klansmen in the northwestern third of the state launch an orchestrated terror campaign to prevent blacks from voting. In Anderson and Lauren counties, roughly half the registered blacks cast their ballots, while only one-fifth of the registered blacks vote in Abbeville County.

November 3, Pulaski, Tennessee: A Confederate veteran who cast a Republican ballot is seized by a mob and placed on an auction block for mock sale as a "white nigger."

November 5, Greenville, Florida: Klansmen board a train carrying arms for the militia from Jacksonville to Tallahassee, scattering weapons along the tracks where they are later destroyed.

November 10, Beaver County, Utah: William Allred pursues Indian horse thieves near Buckhorn Springs, killing two of the raiders and recovering his stock.

November 14, Sumter County, Alabama: A Klansman fires into the yard of Republican Gerard Choutteau, narrowly missing his children.

On November 15 raiders fire guns around his rural home through the night, terrorizing the family. Harassment continues through December, with four blacks whipped on Choutteau's plantation. When he moves his family to the county seat in Linvingston, shots are fired at their new home.

November 14, Center Point, Arkansas: State militiamen clash with 400 armed whites, suffering one man killed and five wounded before the racist forces are scattered.

November 15, Alexandria, Louisiana: A racist mob makes its second assault on the local Republican newspaper, destroying new equipment and hurling brickbats at the editor.

November 27, Washita River, Oklahoma: Gen. George Custer's cavalry attacks a Cheyenne encampment, acting under orders to "destroy their villages and ponies, kill or hang all warriors, and bring back all women and children." Of the one hundred three Indians killed, only eleven are warriors, including Chief Black Kettle, a Sand Creek survivor. Custer's force loses twenty-one men, and fourteen are wounded in the battle. Two white captives are killed by Indian women to prevent their rescue. In fulfillment of their orders, the troops also kill 875 ponies.

November 30, Lewisburg, Arkansas: George Washington, a black man, is shot and killed by Klansmen at his home. On December 1, Klan arsonists burn one-third of the town, destroying court dockets required for the prosecution of nightriders. Three KKK members are arrested and one of them killed while "trying to escape."

December, Augusta, Arkansas: Militia officers seize fifteen white hostages, threatening to destroy the town if a force of 200 whites proceeds with its plan to attack the troops.

December, Warren County, Georgia: Sheriff John Norris is ambushed and seriously wounded by Klansmen.

December, Overton County, Tennessee: Armed blacks rout a KKK raiding party, capturing three horses and three Klan disguises. A few nights later, 100 Klansmen return to the scene, outnumbering blacks, and retrieve their animals. One Klansman is killed in a raid on a black home, after which his fellow Klansmen kill and disembowel the man responsible. In a separate incident, Klansmen reportedly hang one of their own for killing "the wrong Negro" in a nocturnal attack.

December, Chatham County, North Carolina: Caswell Holt, a black man suspected of theft, is taken from his home by Klansmen and is beaten and tortured in a fruitless effort to extract his confession. He is left alive, with a warning to leave the area within ten days.

December 15, Lewisburg, Arkansas: One week after declaration of martial law, Klansmen kill an elderly Republican merchant and burn down his store.

December 18, Pulaski, Tennessee: A black prisoner is dragged from jail and lynched by masked whites.

December 25, Parker County, Texas: Edward Rippey and his wife are killed by Indian raiders at their home, fourteen miles west of Weatherford.

1869

Sitka, Alaska: Several U.S. soldiers are drummed out of the service for looting a Russian Orthodox church.

Wichita County, Texas: One man is severely wounded when Indians clash with a party of white prospectors.

January, Palestine, Texas: Nightriders terrorize local blacks, shaving heads and flogging, shooting several persons, and burning homes.

January, Georgetown, Kentucky: KKK nightriders invade a black man's home, shooting him several times.

January 11, Columbia, Tennessee: Detective Seymour Barmore, hired to infiltrate the KKK, is removed from a train, hanged, and riddled with bullets, his body afterward dumped in the Duck River.

January 24, Kinston, North Carolina: Members of the Constitutional Union Guard remove five black prisoners from jail at gunpoint and take them outside of town, where they are executed.

February, Hernando County, Florida: Two black men, charged with killing a young white man, are taken from police custody and hanged by Klansmen.

February 26, Marianna, Florida: Republican State Senator W.J. Purman is ambushed and wounded by Klansmen while walking home from a concert. A bullet passes through his body and kills his companion, county clerk John Finlayson.

March, Stephens County, Texas: Settler George Hazlewood is killed by a mixed party of Indians, blacks, and Mexicans. U.S. troops overtake the renegades, killing twenty-two and wounding an estimated forty in the ensuing battle.

March, Alamance County, North Carolina: Forty masked Klansmen invade the county seat in Graham, firing into several black homes. Also, Joseph Harvey, a black man, receives 150 lashes from nightriders, and his infant child is clubbed to death. Elsewhere, a black woman defends her home against Klansmen with an ax, severely wounding one of the raiders before they retreat.

March, Jessamine County, Kentucky: One Klansman is killed when a prospective victim defends himself with gunfire.

March, Warrenton, Georgia: Democratic newspaper editor Charles Wallace is shot and killed on the street by Republican Dr. G.W. Darden. That night, a mob of black-robed Klansmen remove Darden from jail and riddle him with bullets. Soon after the lynching, in one night of violence, KKK members kill one black man, beat eleven others to the point of death, and gang-rape a teenage black girl.

Spring, Columbia County, Florida: Lishur Johnson, a black Republican, is abuducted by the KKK. His clothes are found in the woods, but his body is never recovered.

April, Tuscaloosa County, Alabama: A quarrel between blacks and whites sparks raiding by the KKK, with one Klansman killed in an exchange of gunfire. The next day, every black home on a local plantation is burned in retaliation. Klan violence continues for two more days. Two blacks and a Klansmen are killed, and several blacks are wounded.

April, Garrard County, Kentucky: A black prisoner is lynched by members of the KKK.

May, Sumter, Alabama: Klansmen kill two blacks and gravely wound a third. The gunmen flee into Mississippi for sanctuary.

May, Jefferson County, Georgia: Dr. Benjamin Ayer, a Republican state legislator, is murdered by Klansmen near his home.

May 10, Warren County, Georgia: Republican State Senator Joseph Adkins is ambushed and murdered by Klansmen near Dearing.

May 28, Jones County, North Carolina: The KKK lies in ambush for O.R. Colgrove, the "carpetbag" sheriff, killing Colgrove and a black companion.

June, Lincoln County, Kentucky: Klansmen raid the home of a local Unionist. Finding him absent, they flog his wife and burn his house to the ground.

June, Lawrence County, Alabama: Eight Klansmen are jailed in the wake of a lynching and several arson fires. A few days before their scheduled trial, masked men liberate the prisoners and execute those who have confessed. Three are finally recaptured, convicted, and sentenced to prison, but on July 14 the Klan again frees them from the Athens jail.

June, Tuscaloosa County, Alabama: Klansmen murder four persons during the month, with numerous other victims assaulted, beaten, and otherwise abused.

Summer, Lincoln County, North Carolina: Klansmen burn the home of Rev. J.R. Peterson.

July, Harrodsburg, Kentucky: Authorities report that more than twenty-five persons have been hanged by local Klansmen, with at least 100 flogged or otherwise outraged, in the preceeding two years. All of the attacks have taken place within a twenty-mile radius of town.

July, Marion, Arkansas: Militia Capt. A.J. Haynes is ambushed and murdered on a public street in broad daylight. His killer, a known Klansman, is allowed to flee without interference.

July, Jackson County, Alabama: KKK harassment of James Weir, a British subject, produces official protests in Washington.

July 4, Parker County, Texas: Three members of the James Light family are killed in an Indian ambush while returning from an Independence Day celebration.

July 31, Huntsville, Alabama: Three hundred Klansmen invade the town, hunting white Unionists and driving blacks from their evening church services at gunpoint.

August, Tennessee: Klansmen terrorize blacks in Rutherford, Sumner, and Wilson counties, killing at least two persons and whipping, raping, or robbing numerous others. Scores of blacks abandon their farms to seek refuge in Nashville. A separate outbreak in Dyer and Weakley counties results in one black prisoner being lynched, one white man shot to death, and three blacks whipped.

August, Hillsborough, North Carolina: One hundred masked Klansmen remove two black arson suspects from jail, lynching one of them. A few nights later, Alamance County Klansmen lynch two relatives of the victim, and a fourth black is hanged a short time later on charges of trying to rape a white girl.

August 12, Livingston, Alabama: Nightriders storm the home of white Republican Gerard Choutteau, killing a security guard and losing one of their own in the shoot-out. During the same raid, black legislator George Houston is shot and wounded in his home.

August 16, Lenoir County, North Carolina: Republican leader M.L. Shepard is shot and killed by Klansmen at his sawmill.

September, Chapel Hill, North Carolina: Parties of fifty to 100 masked Klansmen repeatedly invade the town at night, beating blacks and driving white "enemies" from their homes. One visitor, suspected of being a state detective, is dragged from his hotel and flogged in the street. Beatings are also administered to many black inmates of the county poorhouse.

September 11, Hood County, Texas: Indians steal horses and laundry from several outlying homes. On the morning of September 12, seven Indians are trapped by eighty whites in a gully near Thorp Spring, and all seven are killed and scalped by the posse. Two white men are wounded, one of them mortally.

September 28, Robinson Spring, Florida: Whites fire on a black picnic, killing Wyatt Young and two-year-old Stewart Livingston. Calvin Rogers, a black constable, is slightly wounded while returning the fire.

Fall, Columbia County, Florida: Klansmen and other whites mount a campaign of terror against blacks and "radicals." Thomas Jacobs, a black Republican, is called to the door of his home and shot dead by nightriders. Another black victim, Timothy Francis, is chased from the area and then killed two weeks later by Klansmen at Sanderson. James Green, a black Republican activist, is abducted from home and tortured and shot to death, his body then dumped in a pond. Another black Republican, Ike Ipswich, is shot by a white man. His murderer is arrested and eventually acquitted by an all-white jury in a courtroom packed with armed Klansmen.

October 1, Marianna, Florida: Shots are fired into a local hotel, killing a white woman, Maggie McClellan, and wounding her father. Whites blame constable Calvin Rogers, a black man, for the incident, calling it retaliation for the September 28 picnic shooting.

October 2, Marianna, Florida: M.L. Stearns, a "carpetbag" state assemblyman, is threatened on the street by armed men, who blame him for instigating the Maggie McClellan murder the day before. Oscar Granbury, a black man, is killed by a mob tracking constable Calvin Rogers.

October 4, Jackson County, Florida: Klansmen raid a black home, killing Henry Reed, his wife, and his son, dumping their bodies in a nearby lime pit.

October 5, Jackson County, Florida: White gunmen wound Jerry Pridgeon, a black man, on a rural plantation. Samuel Fleishman, a

Jewish Republican, is abducted and escorted to the state line and ordered to leave the state. When he returns to the county October 11, he is ambushed and killed by Klansmen.

October 6, Marianna, Florida: Richard Pooser, a black man, escapes from would-be lynchers who had abducted him from home.

October 8, Jackson County, Florida: Klansmen abduct a black man, Matt Nickles, and his wife and son. All three are shot to death and dumped at a lime sink a mile from their home.

October 23, Jackson County, Florida: Nightriders fire into the homes of two black men, George Harvey and Alexander Bell.

October 24, Jackson County, Florida: Klansmen raid the home of a black woman, Adeline Failey.

October 24, Marianna, Florida: Lucy Griffin, a black woman, is assaulted three times on the street by whites.

October 29, Wrangel, Alaska: Leon Smith and two other drunken whites assault an Indian on the street, beating him for an alleged insult.

November, Lincoln County, North Carolina: At least four floggings are blamed on KKK raiding parties.

November, Alamance County, North Carolina: A black man flogged by the KKK identifies a justice of the peace and a deputy sheriff as two of his five assailants.

November 26, Burlington, North Carolina: Alonzo Corliss, a crippled "carpetbag" teacher at a school for blacks, is whipped by Klansmen, who also shave half his skull and paint it black.

December, Marianna, Florida: A black man named Pousser is ambushed at his home and wounded by Klansmen.

December, Montana: Acting on complaints from settlers and miners, U.S. troops launch a winter campaign against the local Piegan tribe.

December, Pulaski, Tennessee: Fifty masked Klansmen invade the town to rescue a barrel of moonshine seized by revenue agents.

December, Alamance County, North Carolina: Klansmen raid a party at a black home, flogging three men and fatally injuring a four-month-old child. Numerous other blacks are whipped in later raids.

December, Orange County, North Carolina: KKK members from Alamance County lynch two blacks accused of barn-burning.

December, Obion County, Tennessee: Klansmen raid the plantation of William Jones. One man is killed and several wounded as

Jones and his black field hands respond with gunfire. Authorities arrest Jones and several of his workers, but the party is ambushed by Klansmen en route to jail. Two blacks are killed and three are wounded.

December 25, Wrangel, Alaska: An Indian assaults Mrs. Jacob Muller on the street, biting off one of her fingers.

December 26, Wrangel, Alaska: Leon Smith is shot and killed in apparent retaliation for beating an Indian on October 29. When tribal leaders refuse to surrender the alleged killer, U.S. troops fire on their settlement with artillery, destroying the chief's home before a suspect is delivered.

December 29, Wrangel, Alaska: The Indian charged with killing Leon Smith is executed by military authorities, and his body is left hanging until sundown as a lesson to his fellow tribesmen.

1870

Burnet County, Texas: Eighteen Comanche raiders attack outlying homesteads and steal a number of horses. Volunteers pursue the raiders, killing one Indian and wounding five before recovering all the livestock.

Llano County, Texas: Four members of the Whitlock family are killed by Indians, with one child taken prisoner.

January, Dallas, North Carolina: Black members of the Union League are blamed for fires that have destroyed nine barns owned by white Democrats in the space of one week.

January, Greene County, Alabama: Klansmen launch a campaign of terrorism lasting through March. Seven persons are murdered and several black schools are burned, primarily in the area of Union.

January 23, Chouteau County, Montana: U.S. troops under Maj. Eugene Baker, pursuing suspected Indian horse thieves, surround a village of Piegan Blackfeet on the Marias River and shoot thirty-three men, ninety women, and fifty children. Due to a military cover-up, the Commission of Indian Affairs hears nothing of the massacre until late April, when a young army officer goes public with his report. Forced to explain why only one soldier died in the "battle," commanders finally admit to raiding a friendly village by mistake.

February, Kentucky: Klansmen lynch two victims in Richmond and Winchester on successive nights.

February 10, York County, South Carolina: Fifty Klansmen raid the home of militia captain John Farris, seizing rifles and ammunition.

February 12, Rutherford County, North Carolina: Klansmen raid the home of a white Republican named McGahey and abuse his wife. The same nightriders also strike at two other homes, flogging black Republican Almon Owens and the black female cook employed by an elderly white widow. Aaron Biggerstaff helps track the raiders back to the home of his half-brother, Samuel, and shots are exchanged. Victim McGahey later kills one of the raiders, a Klansman named William DePriest.

February 26, Graham, North Carolina: Klansmen abduct Wyatt Outlaw, a black town councilman, and hang him near the county courthouse.

March, Alamance County, North Carolina: Nightriders murder William Puryear, a black man who witnessed the Wyatt Outlaw lynching on February 26.

March, Jacinto, Mississppi: A mob of 100 invade the local jail, abducting one black and one white prisoner. The black victim is literally shot to pieces; his companion is mutilated with knives, then hanged.

March 18, Morgan County, Alabama: Klansmen murder Judge Charlton, a leading Republican and co-founder of an anti-Klan action squad.

March 31, Eutaw, Alabama: A band of thirty to forty Klansmen drag county solicitor Alexander Boyd from his home and shoot him to death.

March 31, Union, Alabama: Klansmen murder Jim Martin, a prominent black Republican.

Spring, Jackson County, Florida: Black constable Calvin Rogers is murdered by a group of white men.

April 1, Tuscaloosa, Alabama: A street duel between Klan leader Ryland Randolph and one of his opponents leaves an innocent bystander dead. Randolph suffers a leg wound that results in amputation.

April 30, Pinal County, Arizona: U.S. troops dispatched from Camp Grant to warn an Apache village of impending attack by white settlers finds the settlement in flames and more than 100 Indians killed and mutilated.

May, Franklin County, Kentucky: Klansmen raid black homes in the neighborhood of Frankfort, threatening occupants with death if they vote in the August elections.

May 11, Lincoln County, North Carolina: Local blacks report a wave of KKK violence that includes sixteen attacks since late March. Incidents include robbery, whipping, flogging, and gang rape.

May 12, Cleveland County, North Carolina: Aaron Biggerstaff is beaten by Klansmen for a second time, his arm broken, en route to give testimony regarding the raids on February 12.

May 30, Washington, D.C.: Congress passes the first so-called Force Act, designed to suppress racist terrorism in the South.

June, Live Oak, Florida: Doc Rountree, a black farmer who was also attacked in October 1868, narrowly escapes a Klan ambush.

June, Tuskegee, Alabama: James Alston, a leading black Republican, is driven from the county by KKK intimidation.

July, New York City: Five persons are killed and many others wounded during a riot between Irish Catholics and Protestant Orangemen.

July, Belmont, Alabama: Two hundred armed blacks organize a militia troop and threaten to burn the town after several attacks by white racists, including the disruption of a local Republican meeting. Whites respond by arming themselves and scouring the countryside for "insurrectionists" and importing KKK reinforcements from Meridian, Mississppi. One white man is killed by a black in self-defense; the black man spends nearly a year in jail before he is lynched in September 1871.

July 11, Cross Plains, Alabama: A fight between black and white youths results in scattered gunfire but no casualties on either side. On July 12, three blacks and the white teacher of a black school are arrested on charges of assault. That night Klansmen remove the four defendants from jail and a black prisoner held on separate charges. As they leave town, the Klansmen abduct a black from the street, and eventually lynch all six men.

August, Versailles, Kentucky: Klansmen invade the town and murder two blacks during a nocturnal foray.

August 1, Kentucky: Blacks are forcibly prevented from voting by white Democrats in several towns. Klansmen riot on election day in Harrodsburg and afterward threaten to hang the U.S. commissioner and any other Republicans who attempt to prosecute any violent demonstrators.

August 18, Gainesville, Alabama: Richard Burke, a black legislator, is killed by Klansmen at his home.

September, Greene County, Alabama: Guilford Coleman, a black Republican, is dragged from his home by Klansmen, shot to death, and mutilated almost beyond recognition.

Fall, Moore County, North Carolina: A black school is burned by the KKK.

Fall, Chatham County, North Carolina: Klansmen flog Henderson Judd, a black man, at his home.

Fall, Hale County, Alabama: Members of the KKK lynch a black man suspected of arson.

October, Madison County, Florida: Klansmen attempt to kill "radical" Sheriff David Montgomery and wound his horse in an ambush. Days later, a Klansman named Bryant is stabbed to death by blacks in Montgomery's store. During this month federal authorities reject a plea from Florida's governor, who had asked for troops to control Klan terrorism. On December 17, Montgomery's store is burned down by arsonists.

October, Cookeville, Tennessee: One night after a KKK parade, local whites riot against blacks and Republicans, beating two Unionists and driving them from town.

October, Spartanburg County, South Carolina: Klansmen whip a Republican election manager and a black couple, forcing the former to perform degrading acts before the Klansmen sever part of the black man's ear with a knife. Several of the raiders are arrested, then released on bond without further prosecution. Those responsible for arresting them are flogged by the KKK. In a subsequent raid, sixty-nine year old John Genobles is flogged and ordered to renounce publicly his Republican membership.

October 5, Eastland County, Texas: Henry Martin is surrounded and killed by Indians near Palo Pinto Creek.

October 19–22, Clinton, South Carolina: A group of whites drive a state constable from the polls and prevent blacks from voting on election day. U.S. troops arrive in time to prevent a racial clash, but general rioting breaks out within hours of their departure on October 20. A dozen Republicans are killed, most of them black, over the next two days; victims include a white probate judge and black state legislator Wade Perrin.

October 25, Eutaw, Alabama: Four blacks are killed and fifty wounded when whites fire on a local Republican gathering. Two of the attackers report slight injuries.

November, Union County, North Carolina: Klansmen murder a white justice of the peace whose home was used as a meeting place for black Republicans. Soon afterward, several blacks are killed and scores beaten, and a white probate judge is flogged. At least 200 blacks flee the county to escape Klan violence.

November, York County, South Carolina: Klan nightriders launch a terror campaign lasting through September 1871. Best estimates reveal at least eleven murders, 600 serious beatings, and numerous lesser assaults and abuses. Five black schools or churches are destroyed, including one that has been rebuilt and demolished four times.

November, Spartanburg, South Carolina: Fifty masked Klansmen demand the release of a white man jailed for killing a black. They depart unsuccessfully after the sheriff threatens to shoot anyone entering the jail.

November, Wickenberg, Arizona: Apache raiders attack a stagecoach, killing seven of the eight passengers.

November, Spartanburg, South Carolina: Fifty Klansmen demand the release of a white man jailed for killing a black. The sheriff turns them away with threats of armed force.

November, Noxubee County, Missississppi: Klansmen flog and murder black tenant farmers throughout the county, and whip three black women accused of serving as mistresses of local whites.

November, White County, Georgia: Local Klansmen murder a federal revenue agent.

November, Coosa County, Alabama: KKK members launch a campaign of terrorism around Nixburg that lasts through the summer of 1871. At least one black church is burned by the raiders, with victims whipped, shot, or hanged.

November 7, Lake City, Florida: Whites riot on election eve. The next morning, 100 men armed with pistols surround State Senator E.G. Johnson, a "radical," and threaten his life, placing him under house arrest. Republicans estimate that whites have prevented 250 blacks from voting.

November 8, Quincy, Florida: Armed whites bar blacks from the polls on election day.

November 8, Monticello, Florida: White mobs prevent blacks from voting.

November 15, Marianna, Florida: Klansmen assault Richard Pousser, a black Republican constable, stripping him and threatening him with pistols.

December, Alachua County, Florida: A black man is taken from jail and lynched for allegedly shooting a white.

December, Columbia County, Florida: Robert Jones, a black Republican, is ambushed and killed en route to a meeting with white Democratic leaders.

December, Kewaunee, Mississppi: Frank Diggs, a black mail agent on the railroad line between Selma, Alabama, and Meridian, Mississppi, is murdered by Klansmen.

December, York County, South Carolina: Sixty Klansmen surround the rural home of Tom Roundtree, a black man, shooting him and then slashing his throat.

December 16, Palo Pinto County, Texas: Indians kill and mutilate three white travelers in the northeast corner of the county.

December 21, Chatham County, North Carolina: Klansmen raid the home of Essic Harris, a black man, to confiscate his guns. Two of the nightriders are wounded in an exchange of gunfire.

December 24, Arizona: Mexicans kill Charles Reed, James Little, and Thomas Oliver and wound Reed's wife during an armed dispute over the alleged theft of horses and furniture. The killers flee to Mexico, claiming that they had been falsely accused and violently assaulted by the deceased. Anglo vigilantes cross the border and raid the ranch of Francisco Gandara, brother of Sonora's ex-governor. Gandara and one of the raiders are killed in a shoot-out before the posse moves on, remaining south of the border long enough to murder a Mexican who swore to avenge Gandara.

December 26, Floyd County, Georgia: Klansmen raid the Waltemire plantation and whip two black men and an old woman, and rape two or three girls.

December 31, Union County, North Carolina: Members of a black militia unit murder Mat Stevens, a one-armed Confederate veteran and local bootlegger.

1871

Colorado: The state's first anti-Chinese incident is recorded as vandals burn a Chinese man's home.

Montague County, Texas: Indians attack the Keenon ranch, killing two women and five children.

January, Rutherford County, North Carolina: Several blacks are convicted and sentenced to prison for burning a series of white-owned barns since December 1870.

January, Marion, Alabama: Klansmen are frustrated in their attempt to rescue a comrade from the county jail.

January, Stamping Ground, Kentucky: Klansmen raid several black homes, losing one of their own in an exchange of gunfire. A black church is burned in retaliation for the killing.

January, Chatham County, North Carolina: Nightriders visit the home of Essic Harris, a black man, for a second time, shooting at the house and wounding Harris in the arm. One Klansman is hit by return fire.

January, Parker County, Texas: Three black settlers are ambushed, killed, and mutilated by Indians near Weatherford.

January, Frankfort, Kentucky: Abducted by Klansmen, two blacks are robbed of a watch and $30, then forced to lie in ice until their clothes are stiff. Upon their release, they are warned to leave the county or they will be killed.

January, Big Poplar, North Carolina: Klansmen burn a black church, flog Stokes Judd, and whip one of his relatives, William Judd, on two separate occasions.

January–February, York County, South Carolina: Blacks retaliate for Klan violence by burning at least a dozen white-owned farm buildings. By early summer, nearly two dozen buildings have been set afire. A January 22 announcement from the KKK threatening to kill ten prominent blacks and two white Republicans if the fires continue has no effect.

January 4, Union, North Carolina: Fifty hooded Klansmen invade the county jail, removing five blacks suspected of killing Mat Stevens on December 31, 1870. Transported into the woods, all five are shot, but three survive their wounds and two are subsequently rearrested.

January 7, Lexington, Kentucky: A black man is shot and killed by KKK raiders outside of town.

January 7, Shelbyville, Kentucky: Klansmen whip and shoot a local man, but he survives his wounds.

January 12, Union, North Carolina: Five hundred robed Klansmen again try to abduct and murder the killers of Mat Stevens, turning out for the single largest KKK demonstration of Reconstruction days. Ten black prisoners are taken from jail, with two hanged and six shot to death outside of town. Two blacks escape from the mob. Both are later rearrested, convicted of murder, and legally executed.

January 14, Louisville, Georgia: Klansmen remove nine black prisoners from jail, executing one accused arsonist, cropping the ears of seven men charged with misdemeanors, and releasing one inmate unharmed.

January 14, Gainesville, Florida: Alexander Morris, a black man, is taken from jail and lynched by whites.

January 25, Yorkville, South Carolina: Random shots are fired from the hotel headquarters of the anti-Klan militia. Moments later, arsonists set fire to three gin houses, a mill, and a barn. Local whites accuse the militia of collusion with black incendiaries.

February, Shelby County, Kentucky: Klansmen hang one of their comrades, lately released from jail on bond, for turning state's evidence against the KKK.

February, Colfax Township, North Carolina: A black school is burned.

February, Rutherford County, North Carolina: Light Hall, a white "radical," is whipped by Klansmen. Raiders also visit the home of Henry Houser, a black man, on two occasions, robbing and beating him the first time, and whipping members of his family on the second raid.

February, Kewaunee, Mississppi: John Coleman, the white successor of murdered black mail agent Frank Diggs, is accosted by Klansmen and warned to stay out of Mississippi.

February, Chattooga County, Georgia: Klansmen murder a black tenant on the Robert Foster plantation. Foster and his sons suffer KKK harassment when they try to prosecute the killers.

February, Cleveland County, North Carolina: Dick Beam, a black man, is shot and wounded by the KKK.

February, Meridian, Mississppi: Adam Kennard, a black deputy sheriff from Alabama, is abducted and whipped while searching for fugitive Klansmen in the area.

February, Chattooga, Georgia: Klansmen kill a black man on a local plantation.

February 6, Floyd County, Georgia: Klansmen, including some from Alabama, wound one black and whip at least two others in a series of nocturnal raids around Rome.

February 24, Frankfort, Kentucky: Seventy-five Klansmen liberate a white prisoner jailed for killing a black man.

February 25, Yorkville, South Carolina: Klan nightriders tear up the railroad tracks outside town to delay the arrival of federal troops, and then move on to murder Anson Brown, a black accused of arson. The next morning, raiders invade and ransack the office of Republican county treasurer E.M. Rose, then target the home of black county commissioner Thomas Wright. The Klansmen retreat when they are met by gunfire, but two more blacks are shot during the next week, one suspected of arson and the other accused of living with two white women.

February 28, Washington, D.C.: Congress passes the second Force Act designed to fight racist terrorism in the South.

March, Rutherford County, North Carolina: Klansmen whip the daughter of Ben Maize, a black man, for fighting with a white girl. Another black, Thomas Wood, evades nightriders on their first visit to his home, but a week later he is captured and whipped. After blacks complain of repeated attacks on their schools, federal authorities jail the county sheriff as a participant in the Klan raids.

March, Arizona-New Mexico: Apache raiders led by Cochise plunder wagon trains, sack ranches, and murder settlers throughout the territory. By late spring, an estimated thirty white settlers have died in Indian raids.

March, Jackson County, Florida: The county sheriff resigns after numerous threats from the KKK and at least one assault against him.

March, Walton County, Georgia: Local Klansmen issue a ban on black schools, publicly burning one teacher's collection of books.

March, Gwinnett County, Georgia: A black woman is whipped by Klansmen, who return to flog her again in October.

March, Locksville, North Carolina: Nightriders flog Frances Gilmore, a black woman, then slash her with a knife and burn off her pubic hair.

March, Sandersville, Georgia: Two hundred Klansmen invade the town and lynch a black man accused of arson. One of the raiders is convicted and sentenced to die in June, but other KKK members liberate him from jail in Milledgeville.

March 4, Meridian, Mississppi: Scattered acts of violence are reported as white supremacists disrupt a Republican rally. A store owned by Meridian's mayor is set afire that night, leading to the arrest of Republican activists William Dennis and Warren Tyler, and black legislator Aaron Moore on charges of making incendiary speeches.

March 4, Chester County, South Carolina: Militiamen repulse a KKK attack on the home of black Capt. Jim Woods. A second, larger assault is beaten back the following night. By March 6, Klan reinforcements from neighboring counties and North Carolina swell the local ranks, and a skirmish is reported that evening. Near dawn on March 7, Klansmen rout the black militia in a battle west of Chester, the county seat.

March 6, Meridian, Mississippi: Gunfire erupts at a court hearing for several blacks and Republicans arrested during the March 4 disturbance. The judge and two black bystanders are killed. A riot ensues, leaving three blacks and two white Republicans dead. More blacks are killed and mutilated over the next several days. Klan reinforcements arrive from Eutaw, Alabama, and intermediate points. Six local whites are held on various charges, but a grand jury refuses to indict them. The only person convicted is an Alabamian who is charged with raping a black woman during the riot.

March 6, York County, South Carolina: Klansmen hang former militia captain Jim Williams. A short time later, black militiaman Alex Leech is shot to death and dumped in a local creek.

April, Rutherford County, North Carolina: Klansmen whip the same black man on two different occasions for "running after white women." A black woman, Adeline Beam, is also flogged for bearing a "white" child. Other flogging victims include J.P. Gillespie, a white "radical," and Henry Houser, a black man who was also attacked in February.

April, Clarendon County, South Carolina: Klansmen assassinate a black county commissioner.

April, Newberry County, South Carolina: A Klansman and a black county commissioner are seriously wounded in a Klan raid on the latter's home.

April, Washington County, Georgia: Klansmen raid the home of Scipio Eager, a local black, whipping him and fatally wounding one of his brothers.

April 3, Marianna, Florida: J.Q. Dickinson, the Republican county clerk, is ambushed and killed by Klansmen.

April 13, San Pedro, Arizona: Four whites die in an Apache raid.

April 16, Young County, Texas: Twelve Texans are killed or wounded in a clash with Indians at Rock Creek, near Ft. Belknap.

April 20, Washington, D.C.: President U.S. Grant signs into law a third Force Act, aimed at curbing KKK activities and other racial terrorism.

April 23, Parker County, Texas: Fifteen-year-old Linn Cranfill is killed by Indians near his home, thirteen miles from Weatherford.

April 29, Chatham County, North Carolina: Klansmen flog a sixty-year-old black woman and shoot her in the leg. Four other blacks are beaten in the same raid, with one man shot and fatally wounded.

April 30, Pima County, Arizona: White vigilantes from Tucson raid an Apache village, slaughtering 144 men, women, and children. The bodies of the dead are then stripped and mutilated. Twenty-seven children captured in the raid are taken to Mexico and sold into slavery by Christianized Papago tribesmen.

May, Haralson County, Georgia: Klansmen murder a black man accused of consorting with white women. Three black women are whipped in a separate attack, with Klansmen instructing them to stay home and mind their families. Several other black homes are raided, with weapons confiscated by the nightriders.

May, Baker County, Florida: Black men named Griffis and Smith are whipped at their homes by the KKK.

May, Gwinnett County, Georgia: Klansmen visit a local plantation, disarming and whipping several black tenants.

May, Rutherford County, North Carolina: Nightriders storm the home of an interracial couple, Silas Weston and Polly Steadman. Weston and his three oldest children are killed before Klansmen torch the house. Steadman and her youngest child are wounded, but escape with their lives.

May, Parker County, Texas: Henry Helerin is ambushed and murdered by Indians.

May, Attalla, Alabama: Klansmen from Etowah and St. Clair counties commandeer a train, then ride into town and beat several blacks before forcing the train crew to return them home.

May, Choctaw County, Mississppi: The local probate judge resigns after Klansmen threaten his life, shoot up his home, and wound him in an ambush on the road.

May, Clay County, Florida: Samuel Tutson and his wife, a black couple, are flogged at their home by Klansmen.

May 5, York County, South Carolina: Klansmen raid the home of Elias Hill, an invalid black Republican, and beat him with fists and a buggy whip.

May 12, Pontotoc County, Mississppi: Klansmen searching for school superintendent Robert Flournoy are met by a posse of his friends. One nightrider is mortally wounded during the exchange of gunfire.

May 18, Jack County, Texas: Kiowa Indians attack a wagon train en route to Jacksboro, killing seven of the eleven teamsters and plundering the wagons.

May 21, White County, Georgia: Klansmen raid the home of Mary Brown, a black witness to the November 1870 murder of a federal revenue agent. Brown, her mother, and her daughter are beaten, tortured, and then humiliated by Klansmen.

June, Arizona: Apache warriors continue their raids against white settlers, raiding ranches in Williamson Valley and stealing 2,000 sheep within a mile of Ft. Whipple. Twelve soldiers are reported killed in clashes with the Apache warriors, including a corporal who is tied to a burning tree and tortured to death at Davidson Canyon. In Sonoita Valley thirteen Mexicans are killed when Apaches raid their ranch.

June, Jack County, Texas: Rancher Charles Rivers is mortally wounded by Indians while gathering stock.

June, Bartow County, Georgia: Nightriders murder a local black. A Klansman is convicted and sentenced to life imprisonment in August.

June 16, Sanpete County, Utah: Ute Indians kill Niels Heiselt and wound several other whites in a series of livestock raids near Twelve-Mile Creek. The Utes kill or mutilate the animals they are unable to steal.

July, Jackson County, Georgia: Twenty to thirty Klansmen storm the home of J.R. Holliday and lose two men in a furious hand-to-hand battle before retreating. Holliday's mill and cotton gin are later burned and all of his black workers are driven away after he files charges against thirteen of his attackers.

July, Washington County, Georgia: Klansmen again raid the home of Scipio Eager and chase him through the woods with hounds. Eager escapes.

July, White County, Georgia: White Unionists ambush a party of Klansmen on the highway, effectively halting local terrorism by the KKK.

July 12, New York City: Protestant Orangemen clash with Irish Catholics in a bloody riot that leaves thirty-nine people dead and ninety-one injured.

July 22, Yorkville, South Carolina: Republican Rep. Alexander Wallace is assaulted by a drunken racist in a local restaurant. Later in the evening, a black man is shot five times by a town constable known to be a member of the KKK.

August, Wilkinson County, Georgia: Sheriff Mat Deason is beaten and shot to death by Klansmen for allegedly keeping a black mistress. The woman is also killed and their bodies are weighted with iron bars and dumped in a local creek. In the same month, Republican Henry Lowther flees the county after threatening visits from the KKK. Local Klansmen castrate at least three blacks—one with fatal results—on suspicion of having affairs with white women.

August 7, Frankfort, Kentucky: Whites riot against blacks on election day. Two whites are killed during the outbreak and several persons of both races are wounded. A black man is jailed on charges of firing the first shot, and Klansmen invade the jail that night and lynch the prisoner along with another black being held on suspicion of rape.

September, Aspalaga, Florida: A black ferryman is shot and killed by Klansmen.

September, Belmont, Arkansas: Zeke High, a black man jailed for killing a white rioter in self-defense, is taken from jail and lynched.

September, Greene County, Alabama: Guilford Coleman, a black Republican leader, is taken from his home and killed by Klansmen, his body mutilated almost beyond recognition. Raiders kill a second black man days later.

September, Gwinnett County, Georgia: Klansmen burn the county courthouse and thus destroy evidence against twelve members held on various charges.

September, Morgan County, Georgia: Charles Clarke, a black accused rapist, is lynched by Klansmen.

September 14, Gainesville, Florida: Sandy Hocock, a black man, is murdered by the KKK.

Fall, Hood County, Texas: Settlers pursue an Indian war party of seven men and one woman in an effort to recapture fifteen stolen horses. All eight Indians and one settler are killed and one settler is wounded.

Fall, Kimble County, Texas: Indians attack outlying homesteads, killing two white men. One Indian dies during the attack.

October, Jackson County, Florida: Abram Hall, a black man, is shot dead at his home by Klansmen. A second black victim is killed at the "murder ford" on the Florida-Alabama border.

October, Gadsden County, Florida: A black ferryman is shot dead by whites on the Apalachicola River.

October, Texas: U.S. troops and Tonkawa scouts kill two Comanches during a brief skirmish. The Tonkawas scalp and partially flay their enemies, while soldiers decapitate the corpses and boil the heads "for future scientific knowledge."

October, Yavapai County, Arizona: An Apache is murdered and buried outside a tavern in Kirkland Valley by three white men. The following day, a party of twenty Apaches is ambushed by whites near the same tavern, with several Indians killed or wounded before the survivors escape.

October 7, Alachua County, Florida: Henry Washington, a black man, is shot and mortally wounded by Klansmen.

October 8, Newnanville, Florida: Nightriders kill W.M. Lucy, a black merchant.

October 8, Archer, Florida: Tom Williams, a black man, is shot and wounded by the KKK.

October 24, Los Angeles, California: Enraged by a white man's death at the hands of Chinese "Celestials," 500 whites attack the Chinese quarter in Negro Alley, hanging fifteen and killing another three. (A nineteenth victim dies of gunshot wounds on October 27.) White looters steal an estimated $30,000 in cash and personal property from their victims.

November 7, Marianna, Florida: Black constable Richard Pousser is attacked and beaten on the street while escorting a white prisoner to jail.

November 24, Crittenden County, Arkansas: Klansmen drag a black man, Alexander Farmer, from his home and shoot him. He dies on November 25, after local doctors refuse to treat him.

1871–1875

Texas: The region between the Nueces and Rio Grande Rivers, long known as "the dead-line of sheriffs," explodes for four years of brutal violence between Texans and Mexicans. U.S. troops cross the border dozens of times, and Mexican forces respond in kind. Near-anarchy prevails in the region, with historians unable to tabulate the precise number of raids, skirmishes, and individual murders.

1872

Young County, Texas: Brothers Henry and Willie Dillard are attacked by thirty Comanches near Ft. Griffin, killing or wounding eleven Indians before their assailants retreat, leaving five horses dead on the field.

March, South Carolina: Federal troops begin arresting members of the KKK for terrorist activities. Of 500 nightriders held for trial, only fifty-five are finally convicted and punished.

March 14, Parker County, Texas: Thomas Landrum is killed by Indian snipers. Local settlers pursue the Indians, killing one.

June 16, Sanpete County, Utah: Niels Heislet is killed by Indian raiders at Twelve-Mile Creek. Raids for livestock result in several more whites being shot over the next two months.

June 26, Palo Pinto County, Texas: Chesley Dobbs is killed by Indian warriors near his home.

Summer, Utah: Indians steal horses from Richfield and Fountain Green.

July 4, Weatherford, Texas: Teenagers Jackson Hale and Martin Cathy are killed by Indians on their way home from an Independence Day celebration in town.

August 9, Manti, Utah: The *Deseret News* reports that Indians have stolen livestock "every night during the week." One farmer's wife has reportedly been beaten by Indians for refusing to give them food.

August 10, Moroni, Utah: Armed Indians rob two Mormon boys of their horses.

August 10, Fairview, Utah: Two men are fatally wounded and a third beaten in an ambush by Indians.

August 16, Mt. Pleasant, Utah: Telegraph operator Jeremiah Page is fatally wounded by Indians outside his office.

September, Wilkinson County, Georgia: Nightriders resume local raids after a period of inactivity, flogging several black Republicans.

September 26, Sanpete County, Utah: The last known death in Utah's Indian war is recorded when Utes ambush and kill Daniel Miller at Oak Creek. Miller's son escapes the trap with a minor wound. On the same day, Indians briefly lay siege to Spring City, but they are repulsed by gunfire without inflicting any casualties.

September 29, Carson County, Texas: U.S. troops raid a Comanche village on McClellan's Creek, killing twenty-three persons, capturing 124 women and children, and burning 262 lodges. Two soldiers are killed in the attack, and two are wounded. Indians stampede and recapture several hundred horses seized in the raid. Eight Indian captives die en route to Ft. Concho, including a baby born along the way.

Fall, Grass Valley, Utah: Three Navajos are killed and another wounded in a dispute over the killing of a white settler's calf.

November 28, Linkville, Oregon: Several Modoc Indians are wounded during a skirmish with whites.

November 29, Klamath County, Oregon: U.S. troops surprise a Modoc camp on the Lost River, killing one Indian and wounding six. Over the next two days, while retreating toward Tule Lake, California, the Modoc survivors raid every farm in their path, killing at least fifteen settlers.

December, Arizona: U.S. troops and Apaches clash a number of times, with both sides suffering losses. Eleven Apache warriors are killed in the Chino Valley, and thirteen die and several are captured on the Verde River. Several women and one elderly man are captured on the Gila, but the warriors escape. Seventy-six Apache men and women are killed by soldiers in the Salt River Canyon, with another twenty women and children wounded "more or less severely."

December 4, Willow Creek, California: A white mob threatens peaceful Modoc Indians traveling with rancher John Fairchild.

December 21, Siskiyou County, California: Modoc raiders attack a wagon with a cavalry escort near Tule Lake. One soldier is killed and his body mutilated, and a second is mortally wounded.

1873

Lincoln, New Mexico: Constable Juan Martinez dies in a gun battle with the Harrell clan, a band of racist marauders. Three members of the gang are also killed, prompting them to shoot up the town at random, and kill four Mexicans at a local dance hall. U.S. troops chase the Harrells out of Lincoln County, but they stop long enough to execute Jose Haskell for the "crime" of marrying a Mexican woman.

January, Arizona–New Mexico: U.S. troops report 100 Apaches killed, with light military losses. The number of Indians killed since early 1872 is estimated at over 600.

January 17, Siskiyou County, California: U.S. troops are routed near Tule Lake by Modoc warriors in the Battle of the Lava Beds. Two soldiers are killed in the fighting and thirteen are wounded.

February 25, Palo Pinto County, Texas: Jesse Veale is ambushed and killed by Indians. A male companion escapes.

April, Maricopa County, Arizona: Delshay's Apache warriors are forced to surrender after U.S. troops surround their camp at Tonto Basin.

April, Colfax, Louisiana: Armed whites storm the county courthouse, routing black Republican defenders and killing more than 100 persons, including twenty prisoners, who are shot the night after the battle.

April 11, Siskiyou County, California: Modoc leader Captain Jack shoots and kills Gen. E.R.S. Canby while visiting an army camp at Tule Lake under a white flag of truce. Rev. Eleazar Thomas is also killed in the attack, and Indian Superintendent A.B. Meacham is wounded and partially scalped. The shooting signals a coordinated Modoc assault on soldiers at nearby Hospital Rock, where one trooper is killed. Indian snipers later harass soldiers carrying caskets to Hospital Rock.

April 15–17, Siskiyou County, California: U.S. artillery shells Modocs in the Lava Beds near Tule Lake, beginning a three-day battle on rugged terrain. Three soldiers are killed and ten are wounded in the first day of fighting. U.S. troops assault Captain Jack's stronghold on April 16 and 17, but they are repulsed. Four Indian deaths are confirmed in the action. Military losses total fifty men killed.

April 26, Siskiyou County, California: Renewed fighting in the Lava Beds leaves six soldiers dead and twenty-three wounded, after Modocs assault an army patrol. Indian raiders suffer no casualties in the three-hour battle.

May 9, Siskiyou County, California: Modoc warriors raid an army supply train near Tule Lake, wounding three soldiers, burning four wagons, and escaping with eleven horses and three mules.

May 10, Sorass Lake, California: U.S. troops repulse a Modoc assault on an army camp, capturing twenty-one Indian ponies and three pack mules bearing most of Captain Jack's spare ammunition. One dead Indian is dragged back to camp behind a horse following the rout. Eleven soldiers are wounded in the raid, three of them fatally.

May 17, Texas: Four hundred U.S. soldiers and twenty Seminole scouts cross the Rio Grande into Mexico and storm a Kickapoo village near Remolino on May 18. Nineteen Indians die in the clash and one soldier is killed and two wounded. The Kickapoo chief is captured, along with forty women and children, all of whom are returned to Texas as prisoners. Kickapoo raids along the Rio Grande come to an end by early summer.

June, Siskiyou County, California: White vigilantes execute four Modocs traveling in the company of rancher John Fairchild. An Indian woman is also wounded by the firing squad, her injury dismissed as "an accident."

Summer, San Carlos, Arizona: Lt. Jacob Almy is killed in an uprising at the local Indian agency.

July 3, Phoenix, Arizona: Mariano Tisnado is lynched by Anglos.

July 4, Cottonwood, Idaho: Nez Percé raiders ambush two civilian scouts near the settlement, killing one. A posse of eleven volunteers is decimated when they pursue the Indians.

August, Parker County, Texas: John Hemphill and George McCluskey die in separate Indian raids, and the Indians escape with a number of stolen horses.

August 4, Tucson, Arizona: A white mob lynches Mexicans Leonardo Cordoba, Clement Lopez, and Jesus Saguaripa. A coroner's jury defends the lynching.

August 10, Llano County, Texas: A party of cowboys pursue Indian rustlers to their camp on Packsaddle Mountain, where a hand-to-hand battle leaves four whites wounded, three Indians dead, and several more Indians presumed killed or injured. The engagement ends Indian raids in Llano County.

August 16, Tres Pinos, California: Mexican bandits led by Tiburcio Vasquez rob a white-owned store, escaping with $1,200. Over the next year, raids by Vasquez and his men will be sensationalized in the Anglo press, attaining the status of a "revolution," while portions of California are transformed into armed camps.

October, Jack County, Texas: A settler named Walker and his son are killed by Indians on the Salt Fork of the Keechi River.

October, Kimble County, Texas: Peter Hazelwood is killed when settlers find themselves outnumbered in a clash with Indian horse thieves.

November, Jack County, Texas: Indians kill a settler named Harris on the Keechi River.

1874

Arizona: Military expeditions in Pinal County kill an estimated 136 Apaches and capture close to 100. Near Tucson, in Pima County, Chief Cochinay is killed while raiding farms. His head is severed and carried to San Carlos as a trophy.

Coushatta, Louisiana: Members of the White League lynch five "radical" Republicans.

Texas: Comanche chiefs Big Tree and Satanta leave the reservation to lead one last raid in the northwestern part of the state. Arrested on their return, Big Tree manages to escape, but Satanta is imprisoned at Huntsville, where he commits suicide on October 11, 1878.

January, Texas: The state legislature authorizes the creation of a ranger battalion to combat Indians on the western frontier. By September 1875, the commander reports nineteen engagements with Indians, killing an estimated thirty-nine. Militia losses total two men killed and six wounded.

January 27, Lincoln County, New Mexico: Statewide newspapers report that the county has exploded into an "unfortunate war between the Texans and the Mexicans."

March, Nederland, Colorado: A white mob threatens 160 Chinese laborers with harm.

May 8, Penascal, Texas: Mexican bandits murder four Anglos.

May 20, Jack County, Texas: Settler James Wright is killed by Indians on the open range.

June 27, Hutchinson County, Texas: Comanche warriors besiege a party of buffalo hunters at Adobe Walls, losing fifteen warriors to the concentrated fire of long-range hunting rifles before they retreat. Four whites are killed—one by an accidental self-inflicted gunshot—before the defenders abandon their outpost in the first week of July.

July, San Carlos, Arizona: Two mercenary Apaches deliver severed heads, each purportedly belonging to the war chief Delshay. Both hunters receive the promised bounties, with the heads displayed separately at San Carlos and Rio Verde.

July 10, Jack County, Texas: Cowboy John Heath is shot and killed by Indian warriors.

August, Anadarko, Oklahoma: Arguments erupt into gunfire when a band of Comanches try to surrender to military authorities. Each side blames the other for an outburst that leaves four white civilians dead and several soldiers wounded. The Comanches loot a reservation store and burn a school and several homes before they retreat. A war party renews the attack the next morning, but the Comanches are repulsed by armed force. This incident launches the so-called Red River War, with fourteen battles recorded between Indians and U.S. troops by spring 1875.

August 24, Wheeler County, Texas: U.S. troops clash with an Indian war party on Sweetwater Creek.

August 30, Armstrong County, Texas: Soldiers attack an Indian camp at Battle Creek, killing seventeen and burning the village, and pursuing the Indians onto the Staked Plains before dwindling supplies force a retreat.

September, Smoky Hill River, Kansas: Cheyenne warriors attack a rural homestead, killing four members of the German family and taking four girls prisoner. Two of the captives are recovered in Oklahoma following an army skirmish with Indians in early November.

September 14, New Orleans, Louisiana: Three thousand members of the White League stage an armed coup against the elected government, seizing city hall in a bloody clash that leaves twenty-seven persons dead and 105 wounded. Federal troops restore order and the rebellion is crushed by September 19, but white supremacists will regain control of state government within two years.

September 25, Briscoe County, Texas: A captive comanchero is tortured by U.S. troops until he reveals the location of a large Indian camp at Palo Duro Canyon. On September 26, Indian raiders strike at the military camp, making a futile attempt to stampede the horses.

September 28, Armstrong County, Texas: Four hundred fifty soldiers accompanied by Tonkawa scouts attack a settlement of Cheyenne, Comanche, and Kiowa in Palo Duro Canyon, routing the Indians with light casualties on either side. In the aftermath of the attack, more than 1,400 Indian horses and mules are gunned down and the village burned in an effort to leave the Indians destitute.

October 9, Donley County, Texas: U.S. troops attack and completely disperse a large Kiowa village on the Salt Fork of the Red River.

October 17, Texas: Soldiers surprise another Kiowa camp near the Red River, scattering the inhabitants before they have time to collect their personal belongings.

November, Oklahoma: U.S. trroops escorting a military wagon train between the Red and Washita Rivers engage Cheyenne in a twelve-mile running battle, routing the Indians with light casualties.

November 3, Eufala, Alabama: Armed whites ambush black voters on election day, killing two and wounding forty. Six whites are wounded, two of them mortally, by blacks firing in self-defense. White Democrats easily carry the election.

November 3, Mobile, Alabama: Whites open fire on black voters en route to the polls, killing one person and wounding four others. Federal troops dismiss the incident as a "drunken brawl," leaving local police in charge as white Democrats carry the election at gunpoint.

November 18, Brown County, Texas: Texas militiamen clash with Indians, killing three and wounding one. Two soldiers are wounded and one militia horse is killed in the battle.

November 21, Menard County, Texas: A militia detachment kills six Indians and wounds a seventh, capturing most of the war party's equipment in a running battle.

December 7, Vicksburg, Mississippi: One hundred twenty-five armed blacks march into town, demanding reinstatement of a black sheriff recently forced to surrender his office at gunpoint. Whites retaliate in force, shooting several of the blacks and scattering the survivors. An estimated 300 blacks are lynched or shot to death over the next several days, with only two whites reported killed.

1875

March, Texas: A band of 150 Mexicans cross the border at Eagle Pass, raiding Anglo homes and settlements as far east as Corpus Christi. Texans retaliate by forming armed posses and attacking Mexican homes and settlements throughout South Texas, killing numerous innocent persons. Merchants in Corpus Christi complain that the reign of terror is hurting business, preventing "good Mexicans" from traveling to market.

April 9, Canadian County, Oklahoma: Cheyenne prisoners clash with their military guards at the Darlington agency, with several men killed on each side before reinforcements arrive from nearby Ft. Reno. Two hundred fifty warriors desert the agency, taking their families and fleeing into Kansas.

May, Decatur County, Kansas: U.S. troops accompanied by twenty-five buffalo hunters annihilate a band of fugitive Cheyenne on the Sappa River, slaughtering men, women, and children. Two soldiers die in the fighting, and reports of Indian casualties remain disputed.

Army officers acknowledge the death of nineteen Indian men and eight women and children; buffalo hunters involved in the battle refer to 100 or more Indian dead, with women and children accounting for most of the body count.

May 1, Young County, Texas: Militiamen clash with a combined force of Comanches, Kiowa, and Apaches at Lost Valley, killing three Indians and wounding three more. Militia losses total two dead, two wounded, and fourteen horses killed or injured.

September 4, Clinton, Mississippi: A race riot erupts during a local Republican rally, and twenty to thirty blacks are murdered by whites.

September 14, Colfax County, New Mexico: Rev. T.J. Tolby, outspoken critic of the Santa Fe land speculation ring, is murdered. Mexican constable Cruz Vega is accused of the crime and lynched by a white mob.

November 16, Texas: U.S. troops cross the Rio Grande into Mexico at Las Cuevas crossing, pursuing Mexican bandits and retrieving a herd of stolen cattle.

November 19, Texas: Thirty-two Texas Rangers illegally cross the border into Mexico, assaulting a ranch suspected of harboring Mexican troops. No soldiers are found, but the Rangers massacre innocent civilians, covering their error by naming the victims as "bandits."

1876

January 25, Salt Lake City, Utah: A local newspaper, the *Tribune*, estimates that Mormon gunmen have murdered at least 600 persons in the territory since 1848, acting "in nearly every case at the instigation of their priestly leaders."

March, Cochise County, Arizona: Apache warriors continue sporadic raids from their base camps in the Dragoon Mountains, sometimes crossing the border into Mexico.

March 17, Powder River County, Montana: U.S. troops stage a surprise assault on a peaceful Oglala village, routing the inhabitants and burning their lodges. The Indians retaliate by stealing army horses after nightfall.

April, Cochise County, Arizona: Apache raiders kill two prominent ranchers, eluding pursuit in the Dragoon Mountains.

May 18, West Feliciana Parish, Louisiana: Federal officers report the massacre of thirty-eight blacks, shot and hanged by whites along the Louisiana-Mississppi border.

June 25, Big Horn County, Montana: Surrounded by 3,500 Sioux and Cheyenne braves on the Little Big Horn River, Gen. Custer and 266 of his troopers are annihilated to the last man.

June 29, Horn Lakes, Mississippi: Black Republicans complain to Congress that local whites have threatened to murder all Republican voters in forthcoming elections.

July, Cochise County, Arizona: A series of raids by Apache warriors leave two miners dead near Bowie, with more than twenty victims along the Mexican border. U.S. troops pursue the Apaches into the Florida Mountains of southwestern New Mexico, killing an estimated twenty members of the band.

July 8, Hamburg, South Carolina: Three hundred white supremacists clash with a black militia unit, besieging the local armory. An estimated forty blacks die in the outbreak, including the town marshall and at least five captives shot after the militiamen surrender. One white man is killed in the riot.

September 9, Slim Buttes, South Dakota: Soldiers trap twenty Sioux in a cave. Two men are killed and nine are wounded before the Indians surrender. A counterattack by other tribesmen fails that afternoon, due to a shortage of ammunition.

October 16, Charleston County, South Carolina: Five whites are killed in an ambush by militant blacks at Cainhoy.

November 25, Hot Springs County, Wyoming: U.S. troops surprise a Cheyenne village, killing a number of Indians and driving away the survivors. During the next two nights fourteen Cheyenne infants freeze to death in their mothers' arms.

1877

February, Sonoita, Arizona: Fifteen whites are killed and more than 100 horses are stolen by Apache raiders who escape into Mexico.

June 14, Idaho County, Idaho: Nez Percé Indians kill four settlers in raids along the Salmon River.

June 17, White Bird Canyon, Idaho: U.S. troops attack a Nez Percé camp, but they are routed by Chief Joseph's warriors with thirty-four men killed and four wounded.

June 26, Cottonwood, Idaho: Nez Percé clash with a troop of white volunteers, killing two men and wounding several others before the Indians are repulsed with heavy losses.

July 4, Cottonwood, Idaho: Nez Percé warriors ambush two civilian scouts near the settlement, killing one. A posse of eleven volunteers gives chase, but all are killed.

July 11, Idaho County, Idaho: U.S. troops clash with Nez Percé Indians on the Clearwater River. Fighting resumes on July 12, with Indians suffering sixty casualties before they retreat. Soldiers pursue their enemies through that day and the next, but lose the tribe near Kamiah.

July 28, Mineral County, Montana: U.S. troops fight several inconclusive skirmishes with Nez Percé warriors near Lolo Creek.

August 9, Madison County, Montana: U.S. troops, acting under orders to take no prisoners, surprise a sleeping Nez Percé village on the Big Hole River. Eighty Indians are killed, two thirds of whom are women and children, before the rest of the tribe escapes. Thirty-three soldiers are killed and thirty-eight are wounded in the battle.

August 20, Camas Meadows, Montana: Nez Percé raiders strike an army camp by night, running off most of the horses and mules and stealing 250 animals.

September, San Juan County, New Mexico: Apache warriors raid isolated ranches south of Ft. Wingate, killing six or seven settlers and driving off herds of livestock.

September 5, Ft. Robinson, South Dakota: Chief Crazy Horse is fatally wounded with a bayonet while scuffling with his military jailers.

September 13, Natrona County, Wyoming: Two hundred ninety-seven Cheyenne men, women, and children escape a trap laid by U.S. troops. Fleeing through Nebraska, they are pursued by 10,000 soldiers and 3,000 white vigilantes, fighting five battles during the last two weeks of September.

September 30–October 4, Hill County, Montana: U.S. troops assault Nez Percé in the Bear Paw Mountains, near the Canadian border. Twenty-four soldiers are killed during the first day of fighting, with forty-two wounded; eighteen Indian men and three women die in the initial clash. On October 1, Chief Joseph is arrested during peace negotiations with the troop commander, but his warriors manage to rescue him on October 3. Sporadic fighting continues until Joseph voluntarily surrenders on October 4, ending the Nez Percé's long flight.

October 10, El Paso, Texas: The short-lived Salt War erupts after land baron Charles Howard excludes Mexicans from a salt mine that they have utilized since 1862. Howard shoots and kills Luis Cardis, spokesman for the Mexicans, and Cardis's followers storm the town, killing three Anglos and committing property damage estimated in the thousands of dollars. "Law and order" is restored with several Mexicans shot in the street and others lynched, bringing the outbreak to a close.

November 24, San Elizaro, Texas: One hundred armed Mexicans besiege Charles Howard and thirteen Texas Rangers in the local Ranger station. Howard surrenders on November 25, to spare the others, and he is summarily executed by firing squad.

December, Hidalgo County, New Mexico: Apache raiders capture a wagon train and kill the teamsters, moving on to raid area ranches, murdering several more whites and stealing herds of livestock. U.S. troops follow the warriors to their camp in the Animas Mountains, where they kill fifteen, capture one brave, and recover many of the stolen animals.

December 17, El Paso, Texas: County judge Charles Howard is murdered by Mexican gunmen, acting on orders from Father Antonio Borajo. The slaying touches off a "war" for control of the profitable salt beds near town. Anglo attempts to punish Howard's killers provoke rioting, which is violently suppressed by Texas Rangers, deputized posses, and Anglo vigilantes who kill and rape Mexicans at random.

1878

January 9, Ft. Robinson, Nebraska: One hundred fifty captive Cheyenne stage a desperate breakout from a military stockade. Only thirty-eight escape after an hour-long battle that leaves forty-seven Indians dead and twenty-three wounded. Soldiers pursue the main party of thirty-two fugitives to Hat Creek Bluffs, killing twenty-three when the Indians resist capture.

June 8, South Mountain, Idaho: U.S. troops clash with a Bannock Indian raiding party, suffering casualties of two soldiers killed and three wounded. Chief Buffalo Horn is critically wounded in the skirmish, dying on the trail two days later.

June 10, Malheur County, Oregon: Bannock warriors ambush an Overland Mail coach on the Owyhee River, killing the driver and burning the coach.

June 23, Harney County, Oregon: Soldiers stage a dawn raid on a Bannock camp on Silver Creek, killing 100 Indians and wounding a greater, unspecified number.

Summer, Wyoming: U.S. troops clash with Bannocks on the eastern side of the Continental Divide, killing several with rifle and artillery fire. In a later engagement, soldiers ignore a Bannock party's efforts to surrender, responding with heavy gunfire.

July 8, Birch Creek, Oregon: U.S. troops defeat an Indian war party, losing the survivors in a deep pine forest. A second fight occurs near the Umatilla reservation, with several Indians killed and no whites injured.

July 10, Umatilla County, Oregon: Indians ambush three white travelers between Meacham and Pendleton, killing one and wounding another.

July 15, Meacham, Oregon: Umatillas attack Bannock Indians at a peace conference three miles from town. Chief Egan and thirty other Bannocks die in the ambush.

September, Ft. Reno, Oklahoma: Three hundred twenty Cheyennes desert the reservation to begin a long trek north to their ancestral homeland. Along the way, they fight four major battles with U.S. troops, defeating the cavalry each time, killing five soldiers and losing six of their own men. Indian raids for livestock leave twenty-six settlers dead, while newspapers spread reports of a general massacre in progress.

October: Military authorities declare the Bannock Indian war at an end, with an official body count of nine soldiers, thirty-one white civilians, and seventy-eight Indians killed since the spring.

October 3, Dawes County, Nebraska: A party of Cheyenne led by Dull Knife meets U.S. troops in the midst of a blizzard, with 148 Indians surrendering after two days of negotiation. A second party of reservation fugitives under Little Wolf have already evaded U.S. troops to the east, continuing their long march.

1879

U.S. troops mount over 100 expeditions against Apaches across the Southwest.

Crio Canyon, Texas: Anglo residents post warnings for all Mexicans to leave the area within three days, with threats of violent reprisals if they do not leave.

Bee County, Texas: Congressional investigators report that whites have brutally murdered a Mexican man "because he would not go and play the fiddle for them."

January 3, Sioux County, Nebraska: One hundred forty-nine Cheyenne prisoners at Ft. Robinson reject orders to prepare for a return trip to the Oklahoma reservation, demanding that soldiers kill them instead. The camp commander responds by denying the Indians food, water, and firewood as a raging blizzard continues.

January 9–11, Sioux County, Nebraska: After six days of hunger, thirst, and freezing cold, Cheyenne prisoners escape from their prison barracks at Ft. Robinson, fleeing into the blizzard with soldiers and civilian vigilantes in pursuit. By dawn on January 10, sixty-five dead or wounded Indians have been returned to the fort, some of the thirty corpses scalped and mutilated by white civilians. More Indians are killed, wounded, or captured on January 10, while the main party pushes westward, covering seventeen miles through the snow before they are overtaken by soldiers. Two cavalrymen are killed in the skirmish that quickly becomes a siege, with the Cheyenne escaping once more under cover of nightfall.

January 21, Sioux County, Nebraska: U.S. troops surround the thirty-one remaining Cheyenne fugitives in a wash near War Bonnet Creek, forty-five miles from Ft. Robinson. Seven women and children survive this last-ditch stand, five of whom are seriously wounded.

March 25, Carter County, Montana: Soldiers finally surround and capture Little Wolf's band of 112 Cheyenne fugitives from the Oklahoma reservation.

Spring, Idaho County, Idaho: Sheepeater Indians raid a Chinese mining camp in the Payette Forest, killing several of them.

May, Mississippi: Alarmed by a mass exodus of black labor, which will strip the area of 40,000 workers by year's end, armed whites "close" the Mississippi River, threatening to sink any vessels carrying blacks to the North.

Summer, Phoenix, Arizona: Local Mexicans convene a public meeting to air their grievances against Anglos. A mob reacts by dragging two white prisoners from the jail and lynching them within sight of the gathering, speakers afterward warning that the same may happen to Mexicans if the angry speeches continue. The Mexican meeting disperses at once.

July, Bear River, Colorado: White settlers complain that Ute tribesmen are deliberately lighting forest fires to cripple the lumber industry.

July 29, Idaho County, Idaho: Sheepeater marksmen harass a column of U.S. troops along the Salmon River, wounding two soldiers.

August 15, Idaho County, Idaho: Sheepeater Indians raid a farm on the South Fork of the Salmon River, wounding two settlers and burning several buildings.

August 19, Idaho County, Idaho: Military scouts exchange fire with Sheepeaters on the Middle Fork of the Salmon River. One soldier is mortally wounded in the skirmish and dies on August 20.

September 29, Rio Blanco County, Colorado: U.S. troops clash with Ute Indians on the White River, touching off a week of fighting that leaves thirty-seven Utes and twelve soldiers dead, with another forty-three soldiers wounded. In a separate but related incident, Utes attack the local Indian agency run by Nathan Meeker, killing Meeker and all his white workmen. Three white women are taken as hostages and raped by their captors.

Fall, New Mexico: Mescalero raiders led by Victorio kill two shepherds in Temporal Canyon, butchering several sheep and stealing their horses. The same band invades Gila River country, killing five soldiers and three more herdsmen, stealing close to fifty horses. Their trail across the Black Mountains and San Andreas range is marked by other murders, ravaged farms, and thefts of livestock. Victorio's ambush of U.S. troops at Animas Creek sparks a battle that lasts through the night. Eight soldiers, two civilians, and two Indian scouts die in the clash, with fifty-three army horses killed or stolen. Further running skirmishes kill an additional thirty-five soldiers and civilians before the Apaches retreat into Mexico.

October 1, Idaho County, Idaho: Thirty-nine Sheepeaters are captured by U.S. troops on the Middle Fork of the Salmon River.

October 6, Chamberlain Basin, Idaho: U.S. troops capture twelve more Sheepeaters, effectively crushing tribal resistance in the state.

October 31, Ft. Reno, Wyoming: Big Snake, a chief of the Ponca tribe, is pistol-whipped then "accidentally" shot and killed during the course of his arrest by eight soldiers.

1880

April 12, West Point, New York: James Smith, the military academy's first black cadet, is dragged from his bed, bound and gagged, severely beaten, and has his ears slit. White cadets insist that the wounds were self-inflicted.

May, New Mexico: Apache raiders under Victorio terrorize the western half of the state. Thirteen Mexican shepherds are killed in the Black and Mogollon mountain ranges, along with ranches burned and livestock stolen. Warriors raid a camp at Mineral Creek, killing two whites and stealing a number of horses. Several teamsters are killed when Apaches capture a wagon train on the Gila River. U.S. troops track Victorio to a camp on the Palomas River, killing several of his men before the rest escape. A subsequent clash in Cook's Canyon kills ten Apaches, including Victorio's son. Authorities estimate that fifty Apaches have been killed during the month, against a loss of seventy-eight white soldiers and civilians.

July, New Mexico: U.S. troops fight a half dozen skirmishes with Victorio's raiders along the Rio Grande. Retreating across the border, the Apaches are confronted by Mexican-U.S. troops in Chihuahua, and sixty Apache men and more than twenty women are killed in the battle. Victorio is one of the dead, but another war chief, Nana, escapes with thirty men to continue the raids.

October 31, Denver, Colorado: An argument between a white man and two Chinese men sparks an anti-Chinese riot by 3,000 whites and a handful of blacks. Fire hoses fail to disperse the mob, and a Chinese laundryman, Sing Lee, is lynched before violence subsides. More than 100 other Chinese are jailed for their own protection during the outbreak. Sing Lee's lynchers are acquitted by a jury in February 1881.

1881

April, El Paso, Texas: Seventy-five armed Mexicans invade the town, demanding an inquest into the recent murder of two Mexican cowboys by persons unknown. On April 15, with the hearing in progress, two local racists murder the town's Spanish-speaking constable, Gus Krempkau, who has served as interpreter at the inquest. Marshal Dallas Stoudenmire kills both gunmen in a shoot-out memorialized as the Battle of Keating's Saloon. The killers of the two Mexican cowboys are never identified.

July, Cochise County, Arizona: Members of the outlaw Clanton gang ambush a pack train carrying gold bullion through Guadalupe Pass in the Chiricahua Mountains, murdering nineteen Mexicans and escaping with loot valued at $75,000. The massacre leaves Mexicans along the border hungry for revenge.

July–August, New Mexico: Apache war chief Nana directs a six-week campaign against white settlers in the state, beginning with the murder of several ranchers in the Sacramento Mountains. Before retreating into Mexico, Nana's raiders fight at least a dozen skirmishes with U.S. troops, killing an estimated fifty soldiers and civilians, wounding more than 100 others, burning homes and killing stock at twenty ranches, stealing more than 200 horses, and kidnapping two white women as hostages. The campaign's final clash, an ambush of U.S. troops in the Black Range, leaves six soldiers dead and three wounded.

August, Gila County, Arizona: Warriors attack a column of U.S. troops escorting The Dreamer, an Apache medicine man, to nearby Ft. Apache. Nine soldiers are killed, twenty are wounded, and The Dreamer is shot to death by his guards while trying to escape. The raiders kill or capture sixty army horses.

August, Cochise County, Arizona: Mexicans ambush six members of the Clanton gang in Guadalupe Canyon when the outlaws attempt to pass through with a herd of stolen Mexican cattle. Five of the gang are killed and one escapes. Later in the month, survivors of the gang trap a Mexican trail herd in the San Luis Pass, killing six and capturing eight, who are then slowly tortured to death.

September, Arizona: Apache raiding continues in the vicinity of Gila and Graham Counties. A war party strikes Ft. Apache, killing three soldiers, wounding several others, and setting two buildings afire. Four Mormon ranch hands are captured and then burned to death within sight of the fort. Other ranches are raided in Pleasant Valley, with several whites killed, homes burned, and livestock stolen.

October, Graham County, Arizona: Apache raiders led by Geronimo strike a wagon train at Cedar Springs, killing seven whites. U.S. troops arrive while the wagons are being looted, and the Apaches engage soldiers in a twelve-hour battle. Retreating through the Arivaipa Valley, the Indians raid several ranches, burning homes and killing settlers, stealing 600 cattle and a herd of horses valued at $20,000.

1882

Forty-eight black people are lynched by whites during the first year when records are kept.

April, Graham County, Arizona: Troopers from Ft. Thomas find three prospectors murdered by Apaches. The Indians raid a ranch near Clifton, killing seven men, one woman, and two children—one of whom is thrown alive into a roaring fire. A large herd of sheep is also butchered at the massacre site.

April, Cochise County, Arizona: U.S. troops attack an Apache camp, south of the Chiricahua Mountains. Half a dozen Indians die in the attack, but the Apaches stand firm in a six-hour fight, killing one soldier and wounding another before the troops run out of ammunition. Retreating across the border, the Indians are ambushed by Mexican troops in a battle that claims the lives of twenty-one soldiers and seventy-eight Apaches, most of them women and children.

April, Hidalgo County, New Mexico: Apache raids in the vicinity of Lordsburg and along the Southern Pacific Railroad lines leave ten whites dead and a large number of livestock stolen.

May–June, Arizona: Apache raiding continues around the state. Fifteen white volunteers pursue Indians near Globe, but the Apaches double back and steal their horses when the posse stops for a noon siesta, leaving the trackers on foot in the desert. In Pima County, Tucson Rangers fire on an elderly Indian gathering mescal, but their target escapes. Frustrated and restless, the Rangers illegally cross into Mexico, killing thirty-seven Indian women and children they "hope" belong to a hostile tribe. The massacre victims are never clearly identified.

July, Coconino, Arizona: Arizona's last major Indian battle is fought when U.S. troops overtake Apache warriors at Big Dry Wash, on the Mogollon Rim. Twenty-six Indians are killed and roughly the same number wounded. Two soldiers are slain and several are injured.

August 11, Bisbee, Arizona: A Mexican is lynched by Anglos.

October 22, Sitka, Alaska: An Indian shaman is accidentally killed by careless gunfire from a whale boat. Indians capture two whalers and their boat and equipment valued at several thousand dollars, demanding a payment of 200 blankets from the whaling company for the shaman's death. U.S. Customs officers respond by arresting four tribal leaders and imposing a fine of 400 blankets, to be paid by the next morning. When no blankets are delivered by noon on October 23, government forces shell and burn the Indian village, also destroying all of the tribe's canoes.

1883

Fifty-two blacks have been lynched by year's end.

March, Arizona: A band of twenty-six Apache raiders from Mexico stage random attacks on white settlers during a six-day rampage. Twenty-five white men and one woman are killed in the raids, and a six-year-old boy is kidnapped. The Indians also seize arms, ammunition, and several hundred head of livestock.

May, Chihuahua, Mexico: U.S. troops pursue Apache raiders across the border, into the Sierra Madre Mountains. Indian sentries forewarn tribesmen of a surprise attack on their camp, with most of the band escaping before soldiers kill nine men, capturing one woman and four children.

June, New Mexico: Apache warriors resume attacks in the western part of the state, striking isolated ranches, killing a family of four outside of Silver City. (One three-year-old child is found hanging on a meat hook still alive, but later dies of internal injuries.) As a final gesture of defiance, the Apaches raid an army supply camp at Guadalupe Canyon, near Ft. Huachuca, killing five soldiers and wounding three before they retreat to Mexico.

July–August, Chichuahua, Mexico: U.S. troops cross the border again to stalk Apaches. Three Indians are killed and thirty are captured in the Sierra Madre Mountains.

August, San Antonio, Texas: Mexican protestors march on San Pedro Park, assaulting lessee Fred Kerble because he excluded Hispanics from using his dance floor.

1884

Fifty blacks are lynched during this year.

Taos, New Mexico: Mexican shepherd Teofilo Trujillo is beaten to death by Anglo cattlemen.

1885

Seventy-four blacks are lynched nationwide by year's end.

February 6, Eureka, Washington: City councilman David Kendall is accidentally killed and a white child is wounded in a street shooting between Chinese Tong members. A riot and near-lynching result, as whites call for expulsion of all Chinese.

Spring, Colorado: Three dozen Apache warriors, led by Geronimo, desert their reservation in the southwestern part of the state, escaping into Arizona and Mexico before launching a ten-month guerilla war against whites.

September, Cochise County, Arizona: Apache raiders strike from Mexico, killing three whites in the Chiricahua Mountains.

September 2, Rock Springs, Wyoming: Whites attack a Chinese settlement, killing twenty-eight persons and wounding fifteen, driving several hundred from the area. Property damage is calculated at $147,000.

September 7, Issaquah Valley, Washington: Seven whites and two Indians raid a Chinese camp, murdering three men and wounding two. Thirty-two Chinese survivors of the incident evacuate the area next day.

September 10, Pierce City, Idaho: Merchant D.M. Frazier is found murdered and dismembered in his shop. Vigilantes seize two Chinese competitors, torturing both until each accuses the other of Frazier's murder. That night a white mob lynches the two suspects, along with three other "undesirable" Chinese—a gambler, a barber, and a prostitute. The incident triggers wholesale expulsion of Chinese from several Idaho settlements, with the tacit approval of governing authorities.

September 11, Coal Creek, Washington: A band of masked whites raid a settlement of Chinese coal miners, assaulting one man, burning clothes and dwellings, and ordering Chinese out of the area at gunpoint.

September 19, Black Diamond, Washington: Nine persons are injured as white miners drive Chinese from the community.

November, Luna County, New Mexico: Ten Apache warriors cross the Mexican border, killing two white civilians and an Indian scout and wounding one soldier in the Florida Mountains.

November 3, Tacoma, Washington: A mob of 300 whites begin the "peaceable expulsion" of Chinese from their city. Chinese residents are routed from home by whites armed with clubs and placed aboard waiting wagons with any belongings they can carry. On November 4 and 6, two arson fires destroy the Chinese quarter of Tacoma.

November 6, Seattle, Washington: The governor summons U.S. troops to protect Chinese residents following a series of boisterous rallies by white racists. U.S. troops remain in town until November 17.

December, Graham County, Arizona: Apaches from Mexico attack peaceful tribesmen near Ft. Apache, killing five men, eleven women, and four children when the victims refuse to join in raids against whites. Before retreating into Mexico, the raiders abduct two women and kill two wranglers on the reservation's beef herd, and steal several horses.

1886
Seventy-four blacks are lynched during the year.

January, Cochise County, Arizona: U.S. troops attack an Apache renegade camp, capturing several women and children, and most of the band's horses. The warriors escape. Two days later, Mexican irregulars assault a nearby army camp, wounding four soldiers. Four Mexicans are killed and five others are wounded in the battle. Surviving Mexicans describe the incident as a mistake, claiming that they mistook the white U.S. troops for Apaches.

February 7, Seattle, Washington: A white mob drives 400 Chinese from their homes, forcing 100 to board a steamer bound for San Francisco. Federal troops are summoned because the local police sympathize with the mob. Leaders of the riot are arrested on February 8, but the damage is already done. All but fifteen of Seattle's Chinese "voluntarily" evacuate the city that day, harassed and assaulted by a riotous mob as they march out of town. Martial law is declared, lasting until February 22.

1887
Seventy blacks are lynched during the year.

1888
White mobs lynch sixty-nine blacks nationwide during the year.

New Mexico: Authorities estimate that 1,500 Mexicans have joined the militant *Gorras Blancas* (White Caps), launching sporadic guerilla warfare against Anglos in the territory. Numerous murders and other acts of violence are charged against the group, with no specific body count available. Infiltration and betrayal by informants, however, dooms this loose-knit group within a year.

1889
Arizona: Cowboys employed by the Chiricahua Cattle Company raid a Mexican sheep ranch, murdering three shepherds.

January 15, Pratt Mines, Alabama: George Meadows, a black accused rapist, is lynched.

January 15, Arkansas: Dean Reynolds, a black man accused of jilting a girl, is lynched by a mob.

January 21, Bolar, Missouri: Henry Thomas, a black charged with murder, is lynched.

January 25, New Iberia, Louisiana: Samuel Wakefield, a black suspected of murder, is lynched.

January 26, Wadis Station, South Carolina: William Brewington, a black charged with murder, is lynched.

February 1, New Iberia, Louisiana: Whites lynch a black man named Rosemond, on an accusation of stealing cattle.

February 7, Amite County, Mississippi: An unknown black man is charged with rape and lynched.

February 10, Houghton, Louisiana: Hayward Handy, a black who defended himself against white assailants, is lynched by a mob.

February 19, Liberty, Texas: Two unnamed black men are lynched on an accusation of murder.

February 22, Artesia, Mississippi: D.H. Smith, a black man who founded a commune for members of his race, is lynched by whites.

February 23, Port Gibson, Mississippi: Whites lynch Thomas Wesley, a black accused of attempted rape.

February 28, Port Gibson, Mississippi: A black man named Perkins is lynched by whites, without apparent cause.

March 8, Texarkana, Arkansas: J.E. Robinson, a black accused rapist, is lynched by whites.

March 14, Tasley, Virginia: Whites lynch Magruder Fletcher, a black accused of rape.

April 3, Abingdon, Virginia: Martin Roland, a black charged with murder, is lynched.

April 15, Hempstead, Texas: George Driggs, a black accused rapist, is lynched.

April 18, New Iberia, Louisiana: Whites lynch a black man named Hector, who is suspected of murder.

April 19, Bayou Desard, Louisiana: An unidentified black man is lynched on an accusation of rape.

April 23, Oklahoma: An unknown black man, charged with murder, is lynched.

April 23, Halifax, Virginia: Whites lynch Scott Bailey, a black accused of rape.

May 17, Mt. Carmel, South Carolina: A black man, Tut Danford, is lynched for turning state's evidence against a white criminal.

May 17, Millican, Texas: Whites lynch an unidentified black man suspected of rape.

May 18, Columbia, Louisiana: An unknown black accused of burglary is lynched by whites.

May 19, Forrest City, Arkansas: A.M. Neeley, a black man, is lynched as a result of "political troubles."

May 20, Wickliffe, Kentucky: Joseph Thornton, a black accused rapist, is lynched.

May 21, Kosciusko, Mississippi: Whites lynch James Mitchell, a black charged with rape.

May 22, Walnut Grove, Alabama: Whites lynch Noah Dickson, a black accused of rape.

May 27, Port Huron, Michigan: Albert Martin, a black charged with rape, is lynched by whites.

May 31, Thomastown, Mississippi: An unknown black man accused of rape is lynched.

June 1, Eureka, Mississippi: Whites lynch Robert Herron, a black man, without apparent motive.

June 5, Tangipahoa, Louisiana: Two blacks, Dick Conley and a man called Huey, are lynched without apparent motive.

June 11 Petersburg, Virginia: John Forbes, a black rape suspect, is lynched by whites.

June 13, Pine Bluff, Arkansas: Armstead Johnson, a black man, is lynched on an accusation of theft.

June 21, Tiptonville, Missouri: Whites lynch Alfred Grizzard, a black man, for gambling.

June 22, Ridgewater, South Carolina: Andy Caldwell, a black accused rapist, is lynched.

June 28, Union County, South Carolina: A black man, A. McNight, is lynched for quarreling with whites.

July 1, Irwinville, Georgia: An unidentified black man is lynched on an accusation of rape.

July 1, Gravity, Iowa: An unidentified Indian is lynched on an accusation of rape.

July 11, Tunnel Hill, Georgia: Martin Love, a black accused rapist, is lynched by whites.

July 11, Iuka, Mississippi: Whites lynch Prince Luster, a black charged with rape.

July 11, Lafayette, Louisiana: Felix Keyes, a black accused murderer, is lynched.

July 11, Waco, Texas: Henry Davis, a black man, is lynched without apparent motive.

July 11, Iuka, Mississippi: Swan Burres, a black charged with murder, is lynched by whites.

July 20, Warsaw, Indiana: Willis Peter, a black charged with rape, is lynched by whites.

July 20, Clinton, Mississippi: Three unidentified blacks, suspected of killing a white man, are mobbed and lynched.

July 23, Covington, Kentucky: Whites lynch Daniel Malone, a black accused rapist.

July 23, Paris, Kentucky: James Kelly, a black charged with rape, is lynched.

July 26, Belen, Texas: George Lewis, a black accused of poisoning a well, is lynched.

July 28, Greenville, Texas: Whites lynch George Lindley, a black man, for no apparent reason.

July 30, Honolulu, Hawaii: One hundred fifty armed Americans occupy the royal palace, waging a battle with the militia that leaves seven men dead and twelve wounded. The white revolt against native rule is temporarily suppressed.

July 31, Clinton, Mississippi: Whites lynch Thomas Talbot, a black accused rapist.

August 3, La Plata, Missouri: Benjamin Smith, a black accused rapist, is lynched.

August 14, Aberdeen, Mississippi: Keith Bowen, a black suspected of rape, is lynched.

August 14, Orange, Texas: A black accused rapist, James Brooks, is lynched by whites.

August 23, Luccalena, Mississippi: Whites lynch Sherman Lewis, a black charged with rape.

August 30, Fayetteville, West Virginia: John Turner, a black accused murderer, is lynched.

September 2, Montevallo, Alabama: Two unidentified blacks, charged with murder, are taken from jail and lynched.

September 4, East Point, Georgia: Warren Powers, a black accused rapist, is lynched.

September 9, Hiawatha, Kansas: Richard Fisher, a black charged with stealing a horse, is lynched by whites.

September 9, Le Flore County, Mississippi: Whites lynch George Allen, a black suspected of arson.

September 9, Stanley Creek, North Carolina: John Sigmond, a black accused rapist, is lynched.

September 11, Morganton, North Carolina: A mob lynches David Boone, a black man suspected of murder.

September 12, Shell Mound, Mississippi: Lewis Mortimer, a black charged with murder, is lynched.

September 16, Bluefield, Virginia: Whites lynch Samuel Garner, a black accused rapist.

September 17, Columbia, Missouri: A black accused rapist, George Burke, is lynched by whites.

September 27, Birmingham, Alabama: John Steele, a black accused killer, is lynched by whites.

October 1, Spring Place, Georgia: John Duncan, a black man who lived with a white woman, is lynched by whites.

October 4, Alabama: A black man named Stark is lynched on a charge of suspected murder.

October 12, Jesup, Georgia: William Moore, a black accused of throwing stones in public, is lynched by a mob.

October 12, Hernando, Mississippi: Whites lynch Robert Biggs, a black accused rapist.

October 21, Lake Cormorant, Mississippi: An unidentified black man, suspected of rape, is lynched by whites.

October 26, Columbus, Mississippi: A black accused rapist, Joseph Harrold, is lynched outside town.

November 8, Leesburg, Virginia: A mob lynches Owen Anderson, a black man charged with attempted rape.

November 10, Midville, Georgia: John Thomas, a black charged with rape, is lynched by whites.

November 15, Hazelhurst, Mississippi: Whites lynch two black brothers named Stanford on an accusation of murder.

November 16, Magnolia, Mississippi: A black accused rapist, George Washington, is lynched by whites.

November 16, Lincolnton, Georgia: Whites lynch John Anthony, a black accused of attempted rape.

November 16, Hazelhurst, Mississippi: An unknown black man is lynched on an accusation of murder.

November 18, Vidalia, Louisiana: An unidentified black man, accused of arson, is lynched by whites.

November 23, Petersburg, Virginia: Robert Bland, a black man, is lynched without apparent motive.

December 19, Owensboro, Kentucky: Doc Jones, a black charged with murder, is lynched by whites.

December 26, Jesup, Georgia: Two blacks, William Hopps and Peter Jackson, are lynched by a white mob without apparent motive.

December 27, Tuscaloosa, Alabama: Bud Wilson, a black charged with attempted rape, is lynched by whites.

December 28, Barnwell, South Carolina: Eight blacks are lynched on suspicion of murder.

1890

January 1, Phillips County, Arkansas: An unidentified black man is lynched as an accessory to murder.

January 3, Bossier Parish, Louisiana: Whites lynch Henry Holmes, a black man, without apparent motive.

January 8, Bayou Sara, Louisiana: Henry Ward, a black murder suspect, is lynched.

January 11, Barnwell, South Carolina: Whites lynch William Black, a black burglary suspect.

January 15, Iowa: George Smith, a black man, is lynched without apparent motive.

February 8, Blountsville, Indiana: Eli Ladd, a black "desperado," is lynched.

February 14, Camden, Arkansas: William Larkin, a black accused killer, is lynched.

February 19, Heiskell's Station, Tennessee: Whites lynch Jacob Staples, a black rape suspect.

February 28, Athens, Georgia: Washington Brown, a black rape suspect, is lynched by whites.

March 2, Greenville, Mississippi: Burke Martin, a black charged with murder, is lynched.

March 15, Napoleonville, Louisiana: Black rape suspect Philip William is lynched.

March 16, Gadsden, Tennessee: Henry Williams, a black charged with rape, is lynched by whites.

March 22, Huntsville, Alabama: Whites lynch Robert Moseley, a black accused rapist.

March 24, Wrightsville, Georgia: Samuel Martin, a black charged with murder, is lynched.

March 27, Hedsville, Texas: An unidentified black man is lynched on suspicion of murder.

March 29, Marianna, Florida: Simmons Simpson, a black murder suspect, is lynched by whites.

March 31, Stanton, Alabama: Frank Griffin, a black charged with rape, is lynched.

April 2, Brantley, Alabama: An unidentified black man, accused of murder, is lynched by whites.

April 5, Kosse, Texas: A black man named Williams is lynched on suspicion of rape.

April 5, Thornton, Texas: An unidentified black man is charged with rape and lynched.

April 18, Auburn, Kentucky: A mob lynches Samuel Moody, a black murder suspect.

April 20, Fay, Texas: Stephen Jacobson, a black arson suspect, is lynched.

April 20, San Augustine, Texas: Simeon Garrette, a black, is lynched for attempting to kill a white man.

April 24, San Augustine, Texas: Whites lynch Jerry Teel, a black man, on an accusation of attempted murder.

May 5, Lexington, South Carolina: Willie Leaphart, a black man accused of rape who is later proved innocent, is lynched.

May 12, Hearne, Texas: Edward Bennett, a black rape suspect, is lynched.

May 22, Columbus, Mississippi: A black accused rapist, Grant Anderson, is lynched by whites.

May 30, Arkansas: Robert Weaver, a black man, is lynched without apparent motive.

June 1, Hooks Ferry, Texas: Thomas Brown, a black murder suspect, is lynched.

June 3, Hattiesburg, Mississippi: George Stevenson, a black charged with rape, is lynched.

June 10, Eastman, Georgia: Whites lynch Jesse Poke, a black murder suspect.

June 10, Elbert County, Georgia: George Prince, a black man charged with rape, is lynched by whites.

June 10, Marion County, Georgia: Rich Perry, a black unpopular with local whites, is murdered by a mob.

June 13, Elberton, Georgia: A black rape suspect, George Penner, is lynched.

June 16, East Feliciana, Louisiana: George Swayey, a black man, is lynched for "political causes."

June 20, Livingston, Texas: An unidentified black man is charged with murder and is lynched.

June 28, Waycross, Georgia: Whites lynch Andrew Roberts, a black charged with rape.

June 28, Antlers, Texas: An unknown black man is lynched without an apparent motive.

June 29, Shreveport, Louisiana: John Coleman, a black accused killer, is lynched.

July 3, Nechesville, Texas: Patrick Henry, a black man, is lynched for gambling.

July 10, Lebanon, Virginia: A black man is lynched for threatening whites.

July 11, Social Circle, Georgia: James Harmon, a black rape suspect, is lynched.

July 13, Anniston, Alabama: A mob lynches John Jones, a black man, on an accusation of robbery.

July 18, Ft. White, Florida: Green Jackson, a black murder suspect, is lynched by whites.

July 22, Red River County, Texas: Andy Young, a black man, is lynched without apparent motive.

July 25, Riverton, Alabama: Accused of miscegenation, an unknown black man is lynched by a mob.

July 30, Cypress, Texas: A black man, William Hawkins, is lynched on an accusation of theft.

August 4, Navasota, Texas: John Brown, a black accused rapist, is lynched.

August 8, Anderson, Texas: An unidentified black rape suspect is lynched.

August 12, Montgomery, Alabama: Isaac Cook, a black "desperado," is lynched by whites.

August 14, Mexia, Texas: Two unidentified black men are lynched on suspicion of rape.

August 17, Midway, Kentucky: John Henderson, a black murder suspect, is lynched.

August 18, Humboldt, Tennessee: A black robbery suspect, Thomas Woodward, is lynched.

August 21, Trenton, Tennessee: Fox Henderson, a black charged with robbery, is lynched by whites.

August 22, Baton Rouge, Louisiana: A mob lynches William Alexander, a black man charged with attempted rape.

September 3, Poplar Bluff, Missouri: Whites lynch Thomas Smith, a black charged with murder.

September 4, Water Valley, Mississippi: John Rogers, a black charged with attempted rape, is lynched.

September 11, Amory, Mississippi: Two black accused rapists, Stephen Crump and George Bolter, are lynched.

October 2, Princeton, Kentucky: Ernest Humphreys, a black accused murderer, is lynched by whites.

October 12, Homer, Georgia: Whites lynch Frank Wosten, a black charged with arson.

October 24, Waynesboro, Georgia: John Williams, a black murder suspect, is lynched.

October 31, Barton, Georgia: A mob lynches two black rape suspects.

October 31, Valdosta, Georgia: A black prisoner named Polasco, accused of rape, is lynched by whites.

November 1, Pulaski, Georgia: Owen Jones, a black rape suspect, is lynched.

November 14, Water Valley, Mississippi: A black man named McGregory, accused of rape, is lynched by whites.

November 17, Savannah, Tennessee: Edward Stevens, a black murder suspect, is lynched.

November 18, Indiana: Henry Smith, a black accused rapist, is lynched.

November 18, Longstown, Mississippi: Whites lynch Sandy Wallace, a black accused rapist.

November 19, Cairo, Georgia: John Simmons, a black charged with rape, is lynched by a mob.

December 3, Rome, Georgia: An unidentified black man is lynched on an accusation of rape.

December 3, Central, South Carolina: Whites lynch Henry Johnson, a black accused rapist.

December 7, Roebuck Landing, Mississippi: A mob lynches black murder suspect Dennis Martin.

December 9, Roebuck Landing, Mississippi: Moses Lemon, a black man, is lynched on accusation of threatening whites.

December 11, Florida: Whites lynch Daniel Williams, a black man accused of arson.

December 15, Corson County, South Dakota: Sioux Chief Sitting Bull is shot and killed by Indian police. Six officers and eight tribesmen are killed in the resultant fighting before white U.S. troops arrive to rescue the killers.

December 24, Winton, North Carolina: Kinch Freeman, a black murder suspect, is lynched.

December 24, Mecklenburg, Virginia: Five black murder suspects are lynched by whites.

December 29, Wounded Knee, South Dakota: Shooting breaks out after U.S. troops discover hidden weapons on the Sioux reservation. In the resultant massacre, soldiers fire with rifles and artillery into a crowd of 350 Indian men, women, and children, leaving 153 dead on the field. Many others crawl away to die alone, and only fifty-one survivors are identified. Twenty-five soldiers are killed in the "battle," and thirty-nine are wounded—most of them struck by "friendly fire" or shrapnel from exploding shells.

1891

January 1, Lang, Texas: A mob lynches Charles Bealle, a black rape suspect.

January 2, Neshoba County, Mississippi: A black man named Sharp, accused of robbery, is lynched.

January 10, Neshoba County, Mississippi: Whites lynch an unidentified Indian murder suspect.

January 20, Glasgow, Missouri: Olli Truxton, a black accused rapist, is lynched by whites.

February 6, Greenville, Mississippi: Green Jackson, a black suspected of murder, is lynched.

February 7, Knickerbocker, Texas: Whites lynch Jesus Salceda, a Mexican, without apparent motive.

February 16, Roxie, Mississippi: A black murder suspect, William Brown, is lynched.

February 16, Hendersonville, Tennessee: Frinch Haynie, a black charged with rape and arson, is lynched.

February 17, Douglas, Texas: Thomas Rebin, a black "desperado," is lynched.

February 18, Gainesville, Florida: A black outlaw named Champion is lynched by whites.

February 19, Battlefield, Mississippi: John Bull, an Indian murder suspect, is lynched by a white mob.

February 21, Georgia: Whites lynch Wesley King, a black murder suspect.

February 21, New Mexico: An agent of the Santa Fe land speculation ring is murdered, presumably by Mexicans, and the company retaliates by unleashing a racist posse to track down his killers. Mexicans resist by burning crops, cutting fences, slaughtering livestock, and torching buildings. The violence escalates through spring.

February 23, Blackstone, Virginia: Scott Bishop, a black accused robber, is lynched by whites.

February 24, Douglas, Texas: Thomas Rowland, a black robbery suspect, is lynched.

February 26, Abbeville, Georgia: Allen West, a black accused rapist, is lynched.

March 3, Woodward, Oklahoma: An unidentified black man is charged with rape and lynched.

March 7, Louisville, Mississippi: Louis Hodge, a black accused of attempted rape, is lynched.

March 10, Pinson, Tennessee: Whites lynch Bradford Scott, a black man, without apparent motive.

March 13, Lavernia, Tennessee: Henry Sanders, a black accused rapist, is lynched.

March 14, New Orleans, Louisiana: Eleven Italians, alleged to be members of the Mafia, are lynched on suspicion of conspiracy to murder the local police chief.

March 26, Cumberland Gap, Tennessee: Thomas Huntley, a black charged with murder, is lynched by whites.

March 28, Russellville, Oklahoma: Elrod Hudson, a black arson suspect, is lynched.

April 2, Whistler, Alabama: Whites lynch Zachioli Grohan, a black accused rapist.

April 2, Bryant Station, Tennessee: Martin Mayberry, a black rape suspect, is lynched.

April 13, Princeton, West Virginia: Alexander Foote, a black murder suspect, is lynched.

April 15, Centerville, Alabama: Roxie Elliott, a black woman, is lynched without apparent motive.

April 16, Old Union, Kentucky: Whites lynch William Skapp, a black murder suspect.

April 21, Liberty, Mississippi: Charles Curtis, a black prisoner charged with rape, is lynched.

April 25, Winfield, Alabama: A black man named Randall is lynched on accusations of robbery and murder.

April 30, Franklin, Tennessee: William Taylor, a black jailed on charges of robbery and murder, is lynched.

May 2, Hudson, Mississippi: Black murder suspect Monroe Walters is lynched by whites.

May 11, Loundes County, Mississippi: Three black murder suspects—John Barrentine, Wesley Lee, and Monroe Walker—are lynched.

May 12, Centerville, Maryland: Whites lynch Asbury Green, a black rape suspect.

May 22, Indiana: James Jennings, a black rape suspect, is lynched.

May 26, Tennessee: A black murder suspect, Green Wells, is lynched by whites.

May 30, Claiborne, Louisiana: Turnip Hampton, a black man, is lynched, on an accusation of larceny.

June 2, Point Cenpee Parish, Louisiana: Three blacks are lynched on charges of involvement in a murder.

June 13, Bristol, Tennessee: Robert Clark, a black man, is lynched, on accusations of rape.

June 15, Bridgeport, California: Whites lynch Ah Anong Ti, a Chinese murder suspect.

June 15, Brookhaven, Mississippi: An unknown black man is lynched on an accusation of rape.

June 17, Ft. White, Florida: An unidenditifed black man is lynched without apparent motive.

June 22, Florida: A mob lynches Charles Griffin, a black murder suspect.

June 25, Hamburg, Arkansas: Henry Jones, a black charged with murder, is lynched by whites.

June 28, Cass County, Texas: Two blacks, William Hartfield and Munn Sheppard, are lynched for "being troublesome."

July 1, Bluffton, Georgia: Whites lynch Daniel Buck, a black charged with rape.

July 1, West Point, Mississippi: William Gates, a black rape suspect, is lynched.

July 5, Dyer, Tennessee: A black man named Thompson is lynched on suspicion of murder.

July 6, Alabama: Two blacks, Calvin and Robert Brown, are lynched on an accusation of rape.

July 6, Vicksburg, Mississippi: Henry Centry, a black charged with murder, is lynched outside town.

July 7, Beebe, Arkansas: A mob lynches black accused killer James Bailey.

July 7, Whitaker Station, Mississippi: Whites lynch Wallace Douglas, a black robbery suspect.

July 14, De Soto, Mississippi: Sam Gillespie, a black man, is lynched without apparent cause.

July 19, Decaturville, Tennessee: Ben Walling, a black accused rapist, is lynched.

July 20, Shelbyville, Kentucky: Mark Brown, a black rape suspect, is lynched.

July 22, Henderson, Texas: William Johnson, a black accused rapist, is lynched.

July 25, Franklin, Kentucky: A black man, John Grange, is lynched on a charge of threatening whites.

July 26, Jackson, Tennessee: John Brown, a black murder suspect, is lynched by whites.

July 26, Tuscumbia, Alabama: Whites lynch Jesse Underwood, a black suspected of arson.

August 1, Henry County, Alabama: Two black couples are lynched on suspicion of arson.

August 21, Clanton, Alabama: Ray Porter, a black man, is lynched without apparent motive.

August 24, Magnolia, Mississippi: Lucius Andrews, a black man, is lynched on the basis of his "bad reputation."

August 25, California: Lee Oman, a Chinese rape suspect, is lynched by whites.

August 25, Tullahoma, Tennessee: William Lewis, a black man, is lynched on charges of drunkenness.

August 25, Gainesville, Florida: Andy Ford, a black man with a "bad reputation," is lynched by whites.

August 28, Georgetown, Kentucky: Whites lynch James Dudley, a black murder suspect.

August 29, Jesup, Georgia: William Owens, a black accused rapist, is lynched.

August 30, Conway, Arkansas: Whites lynch Charles Mulligan, a black man charged with murder.

September 2, Maybee Station, Michigan: Two black hobos are lynched on suspicion of murder.

September 5, Oxford, Mississippi: An unidentified black man is lynched on allegations of rape.

September 8, Nearland, North Carolina: Mack Bess, a black charged with attempted rape, is lynched.

September 25, Asheville, North Carolina: Whites lynch Hezekiah Rankin, a black murder suspect.

September 26, Swainsboro, Georgia: A mob lynches Charles Mack, a black prisoner charged with rape.

September 28, Hollandale, Mississippi: Louise Stevenson, a black woman jailed as an accessory to murder, is lynched.

September 29, Georgiana, Alabama: Two unidentified blacks are lynched on suspicion of murder.

September 29, De Land, Florida: Whites lynch Lee Barley, a black accused rapist.

October 1, Hackette, Arkansas: Ben Patterson, a black man, is lynched for participating in labor violence.

October 1, Childersburg, Alabama: John Brown, a black man, is lynched for testifying against whites in court.

October 1, Marianna, Arkansas: Edward Peyton, a black union activist, is lynched outside town.

October 9, Omaha, Nebraska: Joseph Coe, a black rape suspect, is lynched.

October 15, Helena, Alabama: Sam Wright, a black accused rapist, is lynched by whites.

October 17, Clifton Forge, Virginia: James Scott, a black held on charges of rioting, is lynched.

October 26, Linden, Texas: Whites lynch Leo Green, a black murder suspect.

October 30, Monroe, Louisiana: A black man named Snowden is lynched on suspicion of arson.

October 30, Abitz Springs, Louisiana: Jack Parke, a black murder suspect, is lynched by whites.

October 31, Poole's Landing, Louisiana: An unidentified black man is lynched, without apparent motive.

November 8, Arkansas: William Rice, a black man, is lynched without apparent motive.

November 10, Homer, Louisiana: John Hagle, a black, is lynched for no apparent reason.

November 13, McConnell, Tennessee: Joseph Mitchell, a black rape suspect, is lynched.

November 13, Burnet, Texas: Two unidentified blacks are lynched without apparent motive.

November 20, Gurdon, Arkansas: Whites lynch Nat Hadley, a black accused murderer.

November 21, Baton Rouge, Louisiana: An unidentified black man is lynched outside town, with no motive given by the killers.

November 22, Atlanta County, Mississippi: Daniel Gladney, a black man, is lynched without apparent motive.

November 22, Moscow, Texas: William Black, a black man, is lynched for insulting whites.

November 27, Many, Louisiana: A black accused rapist, named Mixy, is lynched by whites.

November 30, Meridian, Mississippi: A black man, Arthur Rainsey, is lynched by whites without apparent cause.

December 10, Edgefield, South Carolina: Whites lynch Richard Lundy, a black murder suspect.

December 14, Waycross, Georgia: Robert Kingut, a black man, is lynched for participating in a riot.

December 14, Newton County, Arkansas: An unidentified black man is lynched without apparent motive.

December 15, Live Oak, Florida: Two black murder suspects are lynched by whites.

December 15, Camak, Georgia: An unidentified black man is lynched on suspicion of burglary.

December 15, Florida: Two black men are lynched on suspicion of robbery.

December 16, Waycross, Georgia: Welcome Golden, a black man, is lynched by whites on an accusation of rioting.

December 17, Holloway, Louisiana: John Ely, a black murder suspect, is lynched.

December 20, Meridian, Mississippi: An unidentified black man is lynched on suspicion of rape.

December 21, Dewitt, Arkansas: Whites lynch Moses Henderson, a black accused of rape.

December 30, Blackwater, Louisiana: An unidentified black man is lynched for suspicion of murder.

1892

January 7, Rayville, Louisiana: Two blacks, Calvin Foster and L.N. Descharner, are lynched on accusations of murder.

January 9, Caddo Parish, Louisiana: A black murder suspect, Nathan Andrews, is lynched by whites.

January 12, Micanopy, Florida: Henry Henson, a black charged with murder, is lynched.

January 14, Oxford, Ohio: Whites lynch Henry Corbin, a black murder suspect.

January 28, Owenton, Kentucky: Lee Gibson, a black accused murderer, is lynched.

February 3, Sumner County, Tennessee: A black woman named Martin is lynched without apparent cause.

February 9, Wilmar, Arkansas: Henry Beavers, a black man, is lynched for assaulting a white woman.

February 10, Arkansas: A black family—Hamp Brisco, his wife and son—is lynched without apparent motive.

February 12, Roanoke, Virginia: Whites lynch William Lavender, a black charged with attempted rape.

February 13, Sylvan, Alabama: Two unidentified blacks are lynched on a charge of arson.

February 14, Pine Bluff, Arkansas: Two blacks, John Kelly and Gulbert Harris, are lynched for their alleged participation in a murder.

February 14, Selma, Alabama: Wiley Webb, a black accused rapist, is lynched.

February 18, Arcadia, Florida: Whites lynch Walter Austin, a black murder suspect.

February 20, Texarkana, Arkansas: Ed Coy, a black accused rapist, is lynched by whites.

February 23, Varner, Arkansas: Whites lynch George Harris, a black man charged with murder.

February 28, Shaw Station, Mississippi: A black robbery suspect, John Robinson, is lynched by whites.

March 4, Waynesboro, Tennessee: An unidentified black man is charged with robbery and lynched.

March 8, Boyle Station, Mississippi: Two black arson suspects, John Rice and Richard Center, are lynched.

March 8, Memphis, Tennessee: Three black murder suspects—Calvin McDonnell, Thomas Moss, and William Stuart—are lynched by whites.

March 10, Macon County, Alabama: An unknown black man is lynched for assaulting a white.

March 13, Rayville, Louisiana: A black woman is lynched on a charge of attempted murder.

March 18, Farquhar County, Virginia: Two black murder suspects, Lee Heplin and Joseph Dye, are lynched.

March 28, Gretna Parish, Louisiana: Jack Tillman, a black man, is lynched without apparent motive.

March 30, Arcadia, Florida: Denniss Cobb, a black man, is lynched for no apparent reason.

April 1, Millersburg, Ohio: An unidentified black man is lynched without apparent motive.

April 5, Lithonia, Georgia: Five black rape suspects are lynched outside town.

April 6, Fishville, Louisiana: Four blacks are lynched on suspicion of murder.

April 9, Charles City, Virginia: Isaac Brandon, a black charged with attempted rape, is lynched.

April 14, Georgia: William West, a black murder suspect, is lynched.

April 19, Inverness, Alabama: Four blacks are lynched on an accusation of murder.

April 26, Riesil, Texas: An unidentified black man is lynched on suspicion of murder.

April 27, Clarkton, Missouri: Whites lynch David Sims, a black man, without apparent reason.

April 28, Goodlettsville, Tennessee: Henry Griggard, a black rape suspect, is lynched by whites.

April 30, Nashville, Tennessee: Ephraim Griggard, brother of Henry, is lynched on accusations of rape.

May 3, Elizabethtown, North Carolina: Black murder suspect Lyman Purdee is lynched.

May 8, Butler, Alabama: George Hoes, a black accused rapist, is lynched by whites.

May 9, Berkley County, South Carolina: Whites lynch an unidentified black murder suspect.

May 12, Greenville, Mississippi: An unidentified black man is lynched on charges of rape.

May 13, Little Rock, Arkansas: James Henry, a black man, is lynched on suspicion of rape.

May 13, Mercer County, West Virginia: Whites lynch Luther Mills, a black murder suspect.

May 15, Naugatuck, West Virginia: "Red" Smith, a black charged with murder, is lynched by whites.

May 16, Childersburg, Alabama: Three blacks are lynched by a mob, on suspicion of robbery.

May 16, Berkley County, South Carolina: An unidentified black man is charged with murder and lynched.

May 17, Clarksville, Georgia: Whites lynch three blacks on suspicion of robbery.

May 18, Chestertown, Maryland: James Taylor, a black accused rapist, is lynched.

May 19, Manchester, Tennessee: Charles Everett, a black charged with attempted robbery, is lynched.

May 21, Morrillton, Arkansas: A mob lynches Charles Stewart, a black charged with murder.

May 21, Covington, Georgia: Serborn Smith, a black accused rapist, is lynched by whites.

May 22, Monroe, Louisiana: A black murder suspect is lynched outside town.

May 23, Bastrop, Louisiana: Whites lynch a black accused murderer.

May 25, Florida: Whites lynch two black prisoners, James Williams and an unidentified man, on accusations of murder.

May 27, Logan County, West Virginia: James Smith, a black accused murderer, is lynched.

May 31, Gray Court, South Carolina: Whites lynch David Shaw, a black man charged with larceny.

May 31, Lebanon, Tennessee: A black rape suspect, Heck Willis, is lynched.

June 1, Sparta, Louisiana: A black man named Walker, accused of rape, is lynched by whites.

June 2, Port Jervis, New York: Robert Lewis, a black rape suspect, is lynched.

June 7, Apalachicola, Florida: Whites lynch William Kaneker, a black rape suspect.

June 8, Grayson, Kentucky: Austin Porter, a black man, is lynched for killing his wife.

June 10, Paducah, Kentucky: Charles Hill, a black rape suspect, is lynched by whites.

June 10, Bastrop, Texas: Tobe Cook, a black accused rapist, is lynched.

June 11, Forsythe, Georgia: Anderson Moreland, a black charged with rape, is lynched.

June 12, Albermarle, North Carolina: A group of whites lynch J.A. Burris, a black murder suspect.

June 16, Seattle, Washington: Four Italian murder suspects are lynched outside town.

June 19, McComb, Mississippi: John Johnson, a black murder suspect, is lynched.

June 28, Spurger, Texas: Three black rape suspects—Prince Wood, Thomas Smith, and Henry Gaines—are lynched.

July 1, Woodbury, Tennessee: Thomas Lillard, a black charged with rape, is lynched by whites.

July 2, Wynne, Arkansas: An unidentified black man is lynched on an accusation of rape.

July 2, Union Township, Arkansas: Whites lynch Robert Donnelly, a black accused rapist.

July 5, Jasper, Alabama: Whites lynch an unidentified black man charged with attempted rape.

July 5, Vicksburg, Mississippi: Tooley Smith, a black accused of murder, is lynched.

July 6, Weston, West Virginia: Edgar Jones, a black murder suspect, is lynched.

July 8, Clay County, Alabama: Edward Prater, a black accused rapist, is lynched.

July 8, Orlando, Florida: A mob lynches Henry McDuffie, a black man charged with theft.

July 9, Louisa Court House, Virginia: William Anderson, a black rape suspect, is lynched.

July 14, Arkansas City, Arkansas: Julian Moseley, a black charged with rape, is lynched by whites.

July 19, Jackson, Mississippi: Doc Davis, a black rape suspect, is lynched outside town.

July 21, Jesup, Georgia: An unidentified black man is lynched for committing an unspecified offense.

July 29, Oaks Crossing, Kentucky: Lee McDaniels, a black charged with attempted rape, is lynched.

July 30, Monticello, Arkansas: Eugene Baker, a black man, is lynched for defending himself against white assailants.

August 1, Dresden, Tennessee: Loeb Landers, a black man charged with attempted rape, is lynched.

August 4, Wynne, Arkansas: Whites lynch Allen Carter, a black charged with rape.

August 10, Camden, Arkansas: Robert Jordon, a black man, is lynched for "insulting a white woman."

August 14, Westville, Mississippi: Port Magee, a black jailed on suspicion of rape, is lynched by whites.

August 16, Mt. Sterling, Kentucky: A mob lynches Logan Murphy, a black murder suspect.

August 20, Santa Ana, California: Francisco Torres, a Mexican charged with killing his Anglo foreman in an argument over wages, is taken from jail and lynched by a white mob.

August 23, Gurdon, Arkansas: A black man named Bowles is lynched on suspicion of rape.

August 25, Josselin, Georgia: Whites lynch Benjamin Howard, a black murder suspect.

August 27, Alamo, Tennessee: Dennis Blackwell, a black accused of attempted rape, is lynched by whites.

August 30, Forsythe, Georgia: John Jess, a black accused rapist, is lynched outside of town.

September 2, Edmonton, Kentucky: John Wilcoxson, a black charged with murder, is lynched by whites.

September 6, Bunkie, Louisiana: Two blacks, Edward Laurent and Gabriel Magloire, are lynched for allegedly threatening whites.

September 6, Paris, Texas: Three blacks—John Walker, William Armor, and John Ransom—are lynched for participating in a riot.

September 7, Waldo, Florida: An unidentified black man is lynched on accusations of arson.

September 8, Eastman, Georgia: Jesse Williams, a black charged with attempted rape, is lynched.

September 8, Kenner, Louisiana: Sam Dixon, a black accused of attempted murder, is lynched by whites.

September 14, Larned, Kansas: James Thompson, a black rape suspect, is lynched by whites.

September 15, Bonita, Louisiana: James Patton, a black charged with murder, is lynched.

September 19, Paris, Texas: Whites lynch an unidentified black rape suspect.

September 20, Champagnolle, Arkansas: A black man named Harrison is lynched without apparent motive.

September 23, Plantersville, Texas: William Sullivan, a black accused rapist, is lynched.

October, Georgia: Fifteen blacks are murdered by whites during a statewide election campaign. Whites also stuff the ballot boxes on election day, and twice the number of legally registered voters in Augusta are recorded.

October 5, Beandon, Mississippi: Four black "desperados" are lynched outside of town.

October 5, Mt. Pelia, Tennessee: Alex Bell, a black man, is lynched for "insulting a woman."

October 6, Concordia, Louisiana: Whites lynch Benjamin Walker, a black man jailed for attempted rape.

October 6, Copiah County, Mississippi: Two black "desperados" are lynched.

October 13, Monroeville, Alabama: Four blacks are lynched on suspicion of murder.

October 16, Big Horn, Wyoming: J.S. Bedford, a black charged with the theft of a horse, is lynched by whites.

October 18, Ash Fork, Arizona: An Indian is lynched on suspicion of rape.

October 26, Dalton, Georgia: Whites lynch a black man, James Wilson, without apparent motive.

October 30, New Monroesville, Alabama: Allen Parker, a black charged with arson, is lynched by whites.

November 2, Calahoula, Louisiana: The son and daughter of John Hastings, a black man sought on murder charges, are lynched by a white mob. Hastings is lynched by another mob on November 5.

November 11, San Jose, California: Henry Planz, a black man, is lynched without apparent motive.

November 15, Oxford, North Carolina: A black rape suspect, William Burnett, is lynched by whites.

November 18, Cheraw, South Carolina: Duncan McFatton, a black murder suspect, is lynched.

November 28, Quaker Creek, South Carolina: A black arson suspect, Nathan White, is lynched.

November 29, Hiawatha, Kansas: Whites lynch Commodore True, a black charged with murder.

December 5, Keystone, West Virginia: Cornelius Coffee, a black murder suspect, is lynched.

December 7, Newport, Arkansas: A black man named Lightfoot, accused of fraud, is lynched outside town.

December 7, Jellico, Tennessee: Two tramps, one of them black, are lynched on suspicion of rape.

December 14, Tennessee: Jesse Reed, a black murder suspect, is lynched.

December 15, Greenwood, Mississippi: A black convict, serving time on a murder charge, is taken from jail and lynched.

December 15, Nashville, Tennessee: A black rape suspect is lynched.

December 17, Shady Valley, Tennessee: Irwin Roberts, a black charged with murder, is lynched.

December 19, Guthrie, Kentucky: James Bond, a black man charged with attempted rape, is lynched by whites.

December 28, Bowling Green, Kentucky: A black accused rapist is lynched.

December 29, Luling, Louisiana: Whites lynch black murder suspects Lewis Fox and Adam Gripson.

1893

January 6, Brinkley, Arkansas: Two black men, Paul Scroggs and Henry Allen, are lynched on suspicion of murder.

January 6, Pocket Township, North Carolina: An unidentified black man is accused of murder and lynched.

January 12, Guston, Kentucky: Two black brothets, Edward and Richard Moorman, are lynched as murder suspects.

January 17, Honolulu, Hawaii: Armed Americans topple the native regime of Queen Liliuokalani, installing a white government that petitions for recognition by the United States. One Hawaiian policeman is wounded in the "bloodless" coup.

January 19, Pickens County, Alabama: James Williams, a black accused rapist, is lynched.

January 21, St. James Parish, Louisiana: Three black murder suspects are lynched by a mob.

January 25, Algiers, Louisiana: William Fisher, a black accused of murder, is lynched.

January 26, Quincy, Florida: Patrock Wills, a black arson suspect, is lynched by whites.

January 30, Kosciusko, Mississippi: Thomas Carr, a black man, is lynched without apparent motive.

January 31, Paris, Texas: Whites lynch Henry Smith, a black murder suspect.

February 1, Richmond, Virginia: Four black murder suspects are lynched.

February 9, Dickey, Mississippi: Two black arson suspects, Frank Harrel and a man named Felder, are lynched by whites.

February 11, Forest Hill, Tennessee: An unidentified black man is lynched on a charge of rape.

February 14, Chattanooga, Tennessee: Andy Blount, a black man suspected of rape, is lynched.

February 17, Hickory Creek, Texas: A mob lynches William Butler, a black man, without apparent motive.

February 18, Moberly, Missouri: John Hughes, a black man, is lynched for insulting whites.

February 21, Springfield, Missouri: Whites lynch Richard Mayes, a black man charged with attempted rape.

February 24, Asheville, North Carolina: Two black brothers, Thomas and Wilson Whitson, are lynched on accusations of murder.

February 26, Jellico, Tennessee: Joseph Hayne, a black rape suspect, is lynched.

March 1, Spring Place, Georgia: A mob lynches Thomas Hill, a black accused rapist.

March 1, Hot Springs, Virginia: Abner Anthony, a black rape suspect, is lynched.

March 19, Jellico, Tennessee: Jessie Jones, a black murder suspect, is lynched.

April 7, San Bernadino, California: Whites lynch Jesus Fulzen, a Mexican murder suspect.

April 14, Eufala, Alabama: Ed Only, a black charged with murder, is lynched by whites.

April 19, Morrillton, Arkansas: A mob lynches Flannegan Thornton, a black murder suspect.

April 20, Salina, Kansas: Dan Adams, a black man charged with murderous assault, is lynched by whites.

May 6, South Carolina: Whites lynch Sam Gaillard, a black arson suspect.

May 7, Los Lunas, New Mexico: Three Mexicans are lynched on suspicion of murder.

May 9, Bearden, Arkansas: Black prisoners John Stewart and "Doc" Henderson are lynched, together with a white suspect, on accusations of murder.

May 10, Columbia, South Carolina: Hayward Banks, a black accused rapist, is lynched.

May 12, Napoleonville, Louisiana: Whites lynch Israel Haloway, a black accused rapist.

May 12, Wytheville, Virginia: An unidentified black man is lynched on accusation of rape.

May 23, Hazelhurst, Georgia: Two blacks, Ephrim Muchlea and an unidentified man, are lynched on accusations of murder.

May 28, Cass Lake, Minnesota: An Indian is lynched on suspicion of murder.

May 30, Las Vegas, New Mexico: A Mexican murder suspect, Celio Lucero, is lynched by whites.

May 31, Jefferson Springs, Arkansas: Whites lynch John Wallace, a black accused rapist.

June 2, Ft. Madison, North Carolina: Isaac Lincoln, a black man, is lynched for "insulting white women."

June 3, Decatur, Illinois: Sam Bush, a black rape suspect, is lynched by whites.

June 8, Gleason, Tennessee: L.C. Dumas, a black rape suspect, is lynched.

June 13, Winchester, Virginia: A black rape suspect, William Shorter, is lynched by whites.

June 14, Waco, Texas: George Williams, a black accused rapist, is lynched outside of town.

June 24, Selma, Alabama: Whites lynch Dan Edwards, a black accused rapist.

June 27, Daleville, Alabama: Ernest Murphy, a black charged with rape, is lynched by a mob.

July 6, Poplar Head, Louisiana: Two unidentified blacks are lynched on suspicion of rape.

July 7, Bardwell, Kentucky: Charles Miller, a black suspected of rape, is lynched.

July 12, Ocala, Florida: Whites lynch Robert Larkins, a black rape suspect.

July 12, Columbus, Mississippi: A black burglary suspect, Richard Forman, is lynched by whites.

July 14, Lawrenceville, Illinois: Allen Butler, a black man, is lynched for performing an illegal abortion.

July 17, Brierfield, Alabama: An unidentified black man is lynched on an accusation of murder.

July 17, Georgia: A black rape suspect, Warren Dean, is lynched.

July 18, Memphis, Tennessee: Acting on rumors of an attempted rape, white vigilantes kill one black man and jail another. On July 22, suspect Lee Walker is dragged from the jail by a mob, stabbed repeatedly, hanged from a tree, then mutilated and burned.

July 18, Lexington County, South Carolina: Whites lynch Dyb Meetze, a black accused of stealing a horse.

August 14, Springfield, Louisiana: Monroe Smith, a black accused of rape, is lynched by whites.

August 18, Morganfield, Kentucky: Charles Walton, a black murder suspect, is lynched.

August 19, Paducah, Kentucky: A black hobo is lynched on suspicion of rape.

August 21, Leavenworth, Kansas: A mob lynches John Wilson, a black charged with rape.

August 21, Memphis, Tennessee: Charles Tait, a black murder suspect, is lynched outside town.

August 22, Lyons Station, Mississippi: Charles Hart, a black man, is lynched without apparent cause.

August 23, Greenwood, South Carolina: Jacob Davis, a black rape suspect, is lynched by whites.

August 28, Newcastle, Kentucky: Leonard Taylor, a black murder suspect is lynched.

August 31, Yarborough, Texas: An unidentified black man is lynched for no apparent reason.

September 1, Cadiz, Kentucky: Judge McNeal, a black charged with attempted rape, is lynched by whites.

September 2, McKinney, Kentucky: Whites lynch William Anderson, a black accused of rape.

September 6, Centerville, Alabama: An unidentified black is lynched for suspicion of rape.

September 8, Quincy, Mississippi: Benjamin Jackson, a black murder suspect, is lynched by whites.

September 11, Newton, Mississippi: Whites lynch Frank Smith, a black charged with attempted rape.

September 14, Jackson, Tennessee: John Williams, a black murder suspect, is lynched.

September 15, Carrolton, Alabama: Three blacks are lynched on an accusation of arson.

September 15, Jackson, Mississippi: Five blacks, including a woman, are lynched on accusations of poisoning a well.

September 22, Oklahoma: Five Indians are lynched without apparent cause.

October 2, Moore's Cross Roads, Virginia: George McFadden, a black accused rapist, is lynched.

October 22, Clayton County, Georgia: Whites lynch Edward Jenkins, a black murder suspect.

October 22, Pikeville, Tennessee: John Gamble, a black accused rapist, is lynched.

October 24, Knoxpoint, Louisiana: Two blacks are lynched on an accusation of theft.

November 1, Charlotte County, Virginia: Abraham Redmond, a black "desperado," is lynched by whites.

November 4, Lynchburg, Virginia: Three black men are lynched on accusations of barn-burning.

November 8, Spartanburg, South Carolina: A mob lynches Robert Kennedy, a black charged with attempted rape.

November 9, Ft. White, Florida: Henry Boggs, a black murder suspect, is lynched.

November 14, Varner, Arkansas: A black man named Nelson is lynched on suspicion of murder.

November 14, Lake City Junction, Florida: Three black murder suspects are lynched by whites.

November 29, Boxley, Arkansas: A black accused murderer, Newton Jones, is lynched by whites.

December 2, Concord, Georgia: Lucius Holt, a black murder suspect, is lynched.

December 7, Cross County, Arkansas: Robert Greenwood, a black man, is lynched without apparent motive.

December 8, Berlin, Alabama: Three black accused killers are lynched by whites.

December 10, Alabama: Whites lynch two blacks on an accusation of murder.

December 12, Selma, Alabama: Four blacks are lynched for attempted robbery.

December 16, Nebo, Kentucky: Henry Givens, a black charged with poisoning livestock, is lynched by whites.

December 19, Adel, Georgia: William Ferguson, a black man, is lynched for turning state's evidence against white criminals.

December 23, West, Mississippi: Sloan Allen, a black murder suspect, is lynched by whites.

December 23, Fannin, Mississippi: An unidentified black man is lynched on suspicion of robbery.

December 25, Georgia: Whites lynch Calvin Thomas, a black man, without apparent motive.

December 28, Brantley, Alabama: Mack Segars, a black man, is lynched without apparent motive.

December 28, Columbia, Louisiana: Tillman Green, a black, is lynched on a charge of "attempted assault."

1894

January 5, Lonoke County, Arkansas: Alfred Davis, a black man, is lynched on accusations of theft.

January 9, Greenville, Florida: Whites lynch Samuel Smith, a black charged with murder.

January 12, West Union, Ohio: Roscoe Parker, a black murder suspect, is lynched by whites.

January 14, Ocala, Florida: Charles Willis, a black "desperado," is lynched.

January 17, Valley Park, Missouri: Whites lynch John Buckner, a black accused rapist.

January 18, Bayou Sara, Louisiana: An unidentified black man is lynched on suspicion of arson.

January 21, Jellico Mines, Kentucky: M.G. Gumble, a black accused rapist, is lynched.

January 22, Verona, Missouri: An unidentified black man is charged with rape and lynched.

February 2, Neely, Nebraska: Whites lynch George Hurst, a black murder suspect.

February 9, Gulch County, Arkansas: Henry Bruce, a black murder suspect, is lynched by whites.

February 10, Athens, Georgia: A black man named Collins is lynched for enticing a servant away from her white employer.

February 10, Smokeyville, Texas: Jessie Dillingham, a black man, is lynched on suspicion of wrecking trains.

February 11, Pioneer, Tennessee: Henry McGreeg, a black accused rapist, is lynched.

February 15, Oglethorpe, Georgia: Whites lynch Robert Collins, without apparent motive.

March 2, Hariem, Kentucky: Len Tye, a black man arrested for kidnapping, is lynched by whites.

March 5, Collins, Georgia: A black murder suspect, Sylvester Collins, is lynched.

March 6, Marche, Arkansas: An unidentified black woman is lynched outside town, without apparent motive.

March 6, Bells Depot, Tennessee: Lampson Gregory, a black man, is lynched without apparent motive.

March 15, Pennsylvania: Richard Puryea, a black murder suspect, is lynched.

March 29, Montgomery, Alabama: Whites lynch Oliver Jackson, a black accused of murder.

March 30, Fishers Ferry, Mississippi: A black man named Saybrick is lynched on accusations of murder.

April 2, Bakerhill, Alabama: Holland English, a black charged with murder, is lynched.

April 5, Selma, Alabama: Two blacks, suspected of murder, are lynched outside town.

April 6, Greensboro, Georgia: Daniel Ahern, a black rape suspect, is lynched by whites.

April 14, Lamison, Alabama: Whites lynch William Lewis, a black man accused of murder.

April 14, Gatesville, Texas: Alfred Bren, a black man, is lynched without apparent motive.

April 15, Rushsylvania, Ohio: Seymour Neville, a black rape suspect, is lynched.

April 18, Lewisburg, Tennessee: Whites lynch Henry Montgomery, a black charged with larceny.

April 22, Tuscumbia, Alabama: Three blacks are lynched on suspicion of barn-burning.

April 24, Cherokee, Kansas: Whites lynch Jeff Luggle, a black murder suspect.

April 26, Georgia: Robert Evarts, a black jailed for rape, is lynched.

April 27, Tallulah, Louisiana: Seven black murder suspects are lynched.

April 27, Manassas, Virginia: Two blacks, James Robinson and Benjamin White, are lynched on suspicion of rape.

May 9, West Texas: An unidentified black man is lynched on a charge of "writing a letter to a white woman."

May 15, Ocala, Florida: Nim Young, a black accused rapist, is lynched by whites.

May 15, Pine Grove, Louisiana: Coat Williams, a black charged with murder, is lynched.

May 17, Jefferson, Texas: Henry Scott, a black murder suspect, is lynched by whites.

May 17, Gate City, Virginia: Samuel Wood, a black man, is lynched without apparent motive.

May 22, Miller County, Georgia: Whites lynch a black rape suspect.

May 23, Palestine, Arkansas: William Brooks, a black man, is lynched for proposing marriage to a white woman.

May 26, Hennessey, Oklahoma: Two Indian rape suspects are lynched.

May 29, Palatka, Florida: J.T. Burgis, a black man, is lynched by whites on accusations of "conspiracy."

May 29, Clinton, Mississippi: Whites lynch a black burglary suspect, Henry Smith.

June 1, Jackson, Tennessee: Frank Ballard, a black accused of attempted murder, is lynched.

June 2, Bethune, South Carolina: Jeff Crawford, a black charged with murder, is lynched by whites.

June 3, Lancaster, South Carolina: An unidentified black man is lynched on charges of robbery. The same mob also lynches a second black, Harry Gill, without apparent motive.

June 4, Monroe, Louisiana: Thomas Underwood, a black murder suspect, is lynched.

June 4, Yazoo City, Mississippi: A black accused rapist, Ready Murdock, is lynched by whites.

June 8, Cape Charles, Virginia: Isaac Kemp, a black murder suspect, is lynched.

June 9, Hewitt Springs, Mississippi: A mob lynches black rape suspect Lewis Williams.

June 10, Bienville, Louisiana: Mark Jacobs, a black man, is lynched without apparent motive.

June 10, Knoxville, Tennessee: A black man, James Perry, is lynched on accusation of introducing smallpox to the community.

June 13, Blackshear, Georgia: Whites lynch a black rape suspect.

June 13, Sweet Home, Texas: Two black murder suspects, Lon Hall and Bascom Cook, are lynched.

June 14, Monroe, Louisiana: A black arson suspect, J.H. Day, is lynched by whites.

June 15, Biloxi, Mississippi: Luke Thomas, a black murder suspect, is lynched.

June 18, Forsythe, Georgia: Owen Opietress, a black charged with rape, is lynched.

June 20–21, Mason County, Kentucky: Three members of the Haines family, who are black, are lynched for allegedly stealing horses.

June 22, Magnolia, Arkansas: Whites lynch Henry Capus, a black rape suspect.

June 24, Bowling Green, Kentucky: A black rape suspect, Caleb Godly, is lynched by whites.

June 28, Mitchell County, Georgia: Fayette Franklin, a black charged with rape, is lynched.

June 28, Brookhaven, Mississippi: George Linton, a black accused of attempted rape, is lynched by whites.

June 28, Hudson, Louisiana: Edward White, a black charged with attempted rape, is lynched.

June 29, Sulphur Springs, Texas: John Williams, a black accused murderer, is lynched.

June 29, Monett, Missouri: Ulysses Haydon, a black murder suspect, is lynched.

July 2, Hillers Creek, Missouri: Whites lynch Joseph Johnson, a black accused of rape.

July 6, Fulton, Mississippi: George Pond, a black jailed for attempted rape, is lynched.

July 6, Amite County, Mississippi: Mobs lynch two black prisoners, one accused of murder, the other of rape.

July 7, Tupelo, Mississippi: Augustus Pond, a black charged with attempted rape, is lynched.

July 7, Charlotte, Tennessee: Whites lynch James Ball, a black murder suspect.

July 14, Biloxi, Mississippi: An unidentified black man, accused of attempted rape, is lynched by whites.

July 14, Dixon County, Tennessee: William Bell, a black man, is lynched on accusations of barn-burning.

July 14, Abbeville, South Carolina: James Mason, a black man, is lynched for giving information against white criminals.

July 16, Scottsville, Kentucky: Whites lynch a black rape suspect, Marion Howard.

July 19, Oxford, Alabama: John Brownlee, a politically active black man, is lynched by whites.

July 20, Rankin County, Mississippi: Allen Myers, a black man, is lynched on an accusation of "conjuring."

July 24, Simpson County, Mississippi: An unidentified black woman is lynched without apparent motive.

July 26, Carlisle, Kentucky: William Tyler, a black charged with attempted rape, is lynched.

July 26, New Iberia, Louisiana: A mob lynches Vance McClure, a black man charged with attempted rape.

July 30, Woodville, Texas: Whites lynch black rape suspect William Griffith.

August, Beeville, Texas: Black farmhands attack Mexican laborers, who have been imported by white growers in an effort to lower black wages and create a labor surplus.

August 2, Elkhorn, West Virginia: Anderson Holliday, a black murder suspect, is lynched.

August 12, Rossville, Tennessee: William Nershbred, a black rape suspect, is lynched.

August 14, Frankfort, Kentucky: Marshall Boston, a black accused rapist, is lynched by whites.

September 1, Millington, Tennessee: Six black men are lynched on suspicion of barn-burning.

September 9, Minden, Louisiana: Link Waggoner, a black murder suspect, is lynched.

September 14, Starke, Florida: Whites lynch James Smith, a black charged with attempted rape.

September 14, Concordia Parish, Louisiana: Robert Williams, a black murder suspect, is lynched.

September 16, Oklahoma Indian Territory: Whites lynch In Ki Wish, an Indian peace officer.

September 19, Atlanta, Georgia: A mob lynches David Goosenby, a black rape suspect.

September 22, McGhee, Arkansas: Three black murder suspects are lynched by whites.

September 26, Lincoln, Oklahoma: An unidentified black man is lynched for allegedly stealing horses.

October 8, Fairfield, Texas: Henry Gibson, a black jailed for attempted rape, is lynched by whites.

October 15, Princeton, Kentucky: Willis Griffey, a black charged with attempted rape, is lynched.

October 20, Upper Marlboro, Maryland: A black man named Williams, charged with attempted rape, is lynched.

November 8, Jasper County, Georgia: Lee Lawrence, a black rape suspect, is lynched.

November 8, Blackford, Kentucky: Two black brothers, Gabe and Ulysses Nalls, are lynched on accusations of arson.

November 10, Tipton County, Tennessee: Needham Smity, a black rape suspect, is lynched by whites.

November 10, Lloyds, Virginia: Lawrence Younger, a black murder suspect, is lynched.

November 14, Dolimite, Alabama: Whites lynch Robert Moseley, a black accused of rape.

November 29, Landrum, South Carolina: An unidentified black man is lynched without apparent motive.

December, Geneseo, New York: A nativist orator, billing herself as an "escaped nun," is pelted with eggs during an anti-Catholic speech.

December 7, Ocala, Florida: William Jackson, a black rape suspect, is lynched.

December 14, Marion County, Florida: A black rape suspect is lynched by whites.

December 20, Brownsville, Texas: James Allen, a black arson suspect, is lynched.

December 23, Brooks County, Georgia: Whites lynch seven black murder suspects.

December 23, New Orleans, Louisiana: George King, a black prisoner charged with assault, is lynched.

December 26, Winston County, Mississippi: William Carter, a black murder suspect, is lynched by whites.

December 28, Morehouse Parish, Louisiana: Whites lynch Scott Sherman, a black man, without apparent reason.

1895

January 7, Flora, Mississippi: Whites lynch Spencer Costello, a black charged with murder and robbery.

January 9, Colquitt County, Georgia: A black murder suspect, George Coldhand, is lynched by whites.

February 26, Savannah, Georgia: A mob stones the Masonic temple where an anti-Catholic rally featuring lectures by a former priest is in progress.

March 2, Allendaletown, Georgia: Charles Robertson, a black charged with murder, is lynched.

March 11, Athens, Texas: Isaac Manion, a black murder suspect, is lynched.

March 14, Forsythe, Georgia: Whites lynch Armor Gibson, a black accused of rape.

March 19, Tyler, Alabama: Three blacks are lynched on suspicion of arson.

March 20, Petersburg, Tennessee: A black woman, Harriet Talley, is lynched on suspicion of arson.

March 29, Bluff Creek, Mississippi: A black arson suspect, Robert Betat, is lynched.

April 2, Florida: Whites lynch a black murder suspect, William Rawles.

April 12, Corsicana, Texas: A black rape suspect, Nelson Calhoun, is lynched.

April 15, Chilton County, Alabama: Manuel Dunegan, a black man, is lynched to prevent him from testifying in court against whites.

April 21, Greenville, Alabama: Five blacks, including three women, are lynched on suspicion of murder.

April 22, Cranberry, North Carolina: A black arson suspect, Robert Charmers, is lynched.

April 25, Parsons, Tennessee: An unidentified black man is lynched without apparent cause.

April 26, Gensonton, Kentucky: Whites lynch George Ray, a black accused of "being disreputable."

April 30, Devers, Texas: George Jones, an Indian, is lynched on accusations of assault.

May 2, Butts County, Georgia: Thomas Brownlee, a black man, is lynched for informing on white lawbreakers.

May 19, Coffee County, Alabama: Whites lynch Jerido Shivers, a black accused of rape.

May 19, Ellaville, Florida: Three blacks—Samuel Echols, Simeon Crowley, and John Brooks—are lynched by whites on suspicion of rape.

May 23, De Koven, Kentucky: Claude Johnson, a black charged with attempted rape, is lynched.

May 23, Rodney, Mississippi: An unidentified black rape suspect is lynched.

May 27, Elliot City, Maryland: Jacob Henson, a black murder suspect, is lynched.

May 30, Bartow, Florida: A group of whites lynch three blacks charged with rape.

May 31, Columbus City, Alabama: James Freeman, a black charged with rape, is lynched.

June 5, Alabama: James Powell, a black man, is lynched on an accusation of attempted rape.

June 9, Mayo, Florida: William Collins, a black charged with attempted rape, is lynched by whites.

June 11, Mayo, Florida: Two unidentified blacks are lynched on an accusation of hiding a fugitive.

June 11, Lufkin, Texas: William Johnson, a black rape suspect, is lynched by whites.

June 11, Keno, Texas: Two blacks, Alexander White and John Cherry, are lynched on suspicion of murder.

June 13, Tuskegee, Alabama: J.M. Alexander, a black man, is lynched for protecting other blacks from a mob.

June 18, Dublin, Georgia: George Harris, a black charged with attempted rape, is lynched outside of town.

June 19, Abbeyville, Mississippi: William Chandler, a black held on charges of attempted rape, is lynched.

June 20, Little Rock, Arkansas: Whites lynch a black murder suspect, Frank King.

June 26, Point Clear, Alabama: Thomas Browne, a black accused burglar, is lynched.

June 26, Colleton County, South Carolina: William Stokes, a black charged with attempted rape, is lynched by whites.

June 29, Brookhaven, Mississippi: Thomas Bowen, a black rape suspect, is lynched.

July 1, Trigg County, Kentucky: Mollie Smith, a black woman, is lynched on suspicion of murder.

July 2, Monroe, Georgia: A mob lynches Samuel Chandler, a black man, without apparent motive.

July 4, Lake City, Florida: Robert Bennet, a black charged with attempted rape, is lynched outside of town.

July 6, Jackson, Mississippi: Whites lynch Theodore Pickett, a black charged with larceny.

July 14, Hampton, Arkansas: Two blacks are lynched on suspicion of murder.

July 15, Winchester, Kentucky: Whites lynch Robert Huggard, a black suspected of rape.

July 15, Piedmont, South Carolina: Ira Jackson, a black accused of rape, is lynched.

July 18, Scranton, Mississippi: A black rape suspect, Andrew Thomas, is lynched.

July 20, Mant, Texas: Six blacks, including a woman and two of her children, are lynched during an outbreak of violence.

July 23, Brenham, Texas: An unidentified black woman is lynched without apparent motive.

July 24, Youngsville, Louisiana: Ovide Belzaire, a black, is lynched without apparent motive.

July 25, Hattiesburg, Mississippi: Thomas Johnson, a black accused of murder, is lynched.

July 28, Meridian, Mississippi: Whites lynch Charles Burwell, a black jailed for assault.

July 28–August 10, Muskogee, Oklahoma: Five Creek Indians led by Rufus Buck kill a deputy sheriff for "looking wrong." The murder launches a thirteen-day crime spree as they move toward Ft. Smith, Arkansas. During their spree they rape two white women, murder a black youth, and loot several homes. Captured after a gun battle with authorities on August 10, the five are transported to Ft. Smith and there sentenced to hang. The executions are carried out on July 1, 1896.

July 29, Lexington, Texas: Squire Loftin, a black rape suspect, is lynched by whites.

August 2, Dangerfield, Texas: A mob lynches a black couple, James Mason and his wife, without apparent cause.

August 12, Colquitt County, Georgia: William Harris, a black man, is lynched on an accusation of attempted assault.

August 12, Delta County, Texas: An unidentified black man is lynched for the color of his skin.

August 15, Fulton, Missouri: Emmett Divens, a black accused of murder, is lynched by whites.

August 18, Florida: Samuel Lewis, a black murder suspect, is lynched.

August 21, New Richmond, Ohio: Whites lynch Noah Anderson, a black charged with murder.

August 22, Wharton, Texas: An unidentified black man is lynched on accusation of murder.

August 22, Arkansas: James Jones, a black murder suspect, is lynched by whites.

August 26, Springfield, Kentucky: Harrison Lewis, a black accused of murder, is lynched.

August 26, Paris, Texas: Jefferson Cole, a black man, is lynched without apparent cause.

September 2, Hickman, Kentucky: Whites lynch William Butcher, a black murder suspect.

September 2, Simpson County, Mississippi: An unidentified black man is lynched on charges of miscegenation.

September 3, Farmington, Tennessee: Jerry Johnson, a black accused of insulting whites, is lynched.

September 6, Fayetteville, Tennessee: A black man, "Doc" King, is lynched on allegations of attempted rape.

September 10, Lunenburg, Virginia: Wesley Wingfield, a black charged with attempted rape, is lynched.

September 11, Osceola, Arkansas: Two blacks, William Caldwell and John Thomas, are lynched on accusations of murder.

September 19, Arkansas: An unidentified black man is charged with rape and lynched by whites.

September 22, Hammond, Louisiana: Whites lynch William Smith, a black murder suspect.

September 26, New Orleans, Louisiana: Felician Francis, a black man, is lynched outside of town for no apparent reason.

September 27, Bakersfield, California: William Archor, an Indian charged with murder, is lynched by whites.

October 4, Georgia: Neal Smith, a black accused of rape, is lynched.

October 5, Perote, Alabama: Whites lynch Tobe McGrady, a black accused of rape.

October 11, Jackson, Missouri: William Henderson, a black rape suspect, is lynched.

October 15, Manchester, Tennessee: Whites lynch Eugene Vancy, a black accused of rape.

October 15, Braden, Tennessee: A black murder suspect, Jeff Ellis, is lynched.

October 22, Hennessey, Oklahoma: Two Mexicans, James Umbra and "Mexican John," are lynched on suspicion of stealing cattle.

October 29, Tyler, Texas: Henry Hilliard, a black man, is publicly burned to death after confessing to the murder of a white woman.

November 4, Wynne, Arkansas: Albert England, a black accused of burglary, is lynched.

November 4, Homersville, Georgia: A mob lynches Lewis Jefferson, a black man charged with rape.

November 17, Frederick, Maryland: James Bown, a black charged with rape, is lynched by whites.

November 21, Henderson, Kentucky: Two unidentified black men are lynched on an accusation of rape.

November 20, Madison County, Texas: A black man is lynched on charges of riding his horse over a white girl and causing her serious injury. After the hanging, lynchers discover that their victim was innocent, the true culprit having fled town.

November 21, Wartburg, Tennessee: Charles Hurd, a black accused of murder, is lynched.

November 24, Abbeville, South Carolina: Two black murder suspects, John Richards and Thomas Watts, are lynched.

November 25, Gibson, Georgia: Whites lynch Balam Hancock, a black man charged with attempted rape.

November 25, Calvert, Kentucky: An unidentified black is lynched on a charge of wrecking a train.

November 29. Fayettville, Tennessee. Two black murder suspects, Joseph Robinson and Ozias McGahey, are lynched by whites.

December 2, Fairfax Court House, Virginia: Two blacks, named Poss and Henrip, are lynched by whites on an accusation of murder.

December 5, Colleton County, South Carolina: Whites lynch Isom Kearse, a black man, on suspicion of larceny. The same mob hangs his wife, Hannah, for allegedly having knowledge of his crime.

December 7, Hampton, South Carolina: William Blake, a black murder suspect, is lynched.

1896

January, Manatee County, Florida: Following a black boy's victory in a fight with the local sheriff's son, the sheriff leads a mob to seize the boy at home. The boy's father resists, killing the sheriff and fatally wounding two more men as they storm his house. When their intended victims escape, a reinforced mob spends the night shooting at black homes and burning several of them to the ground. Several blacks are killed, and others are forced to flee the area.

January, San Antonio, Texas: Aureliano Castellon is shot eight times, his body burned by "persons unknown." He had been courting a local Anglo girl, over the objections of her parents and brothers.

January 8, Lexington, Tennessee: Two black rape suspects, Frank Simpson and Harrison Fuller, are lynched.

January 10, Monroe, Louisiana: A.L. Smart, a black accused of murder, is lynched outside of town.

January 12, New Orleans, Louisiana: Patrick Morris, a black man, is lynched with a white couple on charges of miscegenation.

January 13, Alachua, Florida: Whites lynch Harry Jordan, a black murder suspect.

January 15, Ft. Holmes, Oklahoma: Four alleged highwaymen, including two Indians, are lynched.

January 18, Mitchelville, Iowa: An unidentified black man is charged with assault and lynched by whites.

January 28, Bluefield, West Virginia: Whites lynch Alexander Jones, a black murder suspect.

February 1, Bramwell, West Virginia: An unidentified black man suspected of murder is lynched.

February 17, Monticello, Kentucky: Fomit Martin, a black charged with barn-burning, is lynched.

February 29, St. Joseph, Louisiana: Gilbert Francis, a black jailed on charges of robbery and murder, is lynched.

February 29, Windsor, South Carolina: Whites lynch Melville Kennedy, a black rape suspect.

March 16, Rayville, Louisiana: A black robbery suspect, Bird Love, is lynched.

March 23, Shreveport, Louisiana: Isaac Pizer, a black charged with attempted rape, is lynched outside of town.

March 24, Carencro, Louisiana: Whites lynch Louis Senegal, a black accused of rape.

April 3, Teysels, Mississippi: Harvey Mayberry, a black rape suspect, is lynched.

April 12, Seale, Alabama: Reddrick Adams, a black accused of murder, is lynched by whites.

April 17, McMinnville, Tennessee: Whites lynch York Douglas, a black charged with arson.

April 20, De Land, Florida: John Brunt, a black prisoner charged with disorderly conduct, is lynched.

April 23, Westville, South Carolina: Thomas Price, a black charged with assault, is lynched.

May 3, Beaumont, Texas: William Benby, a black murder suspect, is lynched by whites.

May 7, MacClenny, Florida: Charles Jones, a black man, is lynched without apparent motive.

May 11, Madison County, Florida: Harry Wilson, a black man, is lynched for no apparent reason.

May 11, Fulton, Kentucky: An unidentified black murder suspect is lynched.

May 12, Nicols, Georgia: William Hardee, a black charged with assault, is lynched by whites.

May 19, St. Bernard Parish, Louisiana: Joseph Dazzele, a black man, is lynched on accusations of attempted rape.

May 21, Bossier Parish, Louisiana: An unidentified black man is lynched without apparent motive.

June 1, Columbus, Georgia: Two black rape suspects, Jesse Slayton and William Miles, are lynched.

June 10, Bryan, Texas: Two black rape suspects, Louis Whitehead and George Johnson, are lynched.

June 12, Baldwin, Louisiana: Walter Starkes, a black rape suspect, is lynched.

June 12, Martin, Tennessee: Samuel Clay, a black charged with attempted rape, is lynched.

June 20, Alabama: Whites lynch Leon Orr, a black accused of rape.

June 24, Montgomery, Alabama: A mob lynches William Westmoreland, a black man charged with murder.

June 27, Winona, Mississippi: A black rape suspect, Perry Young, is lynched.

June 30, Trenton, Tennessee: An unidentified black man is charged with rape and lynched outside of town.

June 30, San Antonio, Texas: The local paper publishes a note signed by twenty-five Mexicans, urging members of their race to rise and "slaughter the gringo." Blacks and Italians are included on the list of targets, but the uprising fails to materialize.

July 6, Madison County, Florida: Jacob Williams, a black charged with rape, is lynched.

July 6, Sardis, Tennessee: Nimrod Cross, a black accused rapist, is lynched.

July 6, Lincoln County, South Carolina: Whites lynch an unidentified black rape suspect.

July 13, Minden, Louisiana: Two black murder suspects, James Porter and Mond Dunley, are lynched.

July 13, Monroe, Louisiana: Courtney Rendrick, a black charged with murderous assault, is lynched.

July 15, Bayou Sara, Louisiana: A black murder suspect, Frank James, is lynched.

July 18, Ellenton, South Carolina: Daniel Dicks, a black accused of rape, is lynched by whites.

July 27, Homer, Louisiana: Isaac McGee, a black accused of rape, is lynched.

July 31, Clarendon, Arkansas: Whites lynch Gidfrey Gould, a black accused of rape.

August 1, Selma, Alabama: Isadore Moreley and William Hunter, two blacks charged with murder, are lynched outside town.

August 5, Franklin, Louisiana: Hiram Weightman, a black charged with attempted murder, is lynched by whites.

August 9, Halumlee, Louisiana: Three Italian murder suspects are taken from jail and lynched.

August 13, Hopkins County, Texas: Benjamin Gay, a black arson suspect, is lynched by whites.

September 14, Aurora, Kentucky: Thomas White, a black man, is lynched without apparent cause.

September 16, Terrell County, Georgia: Lem Warren, a black accused of rape, is lynched.

September 16, Watonga, Oklahoma: Whites lynch B.S. Morris, a black rape suspect.

September 16, Monroe, Louisiana: A black rape suspect, James McCauley, is lynched.

September 23, De Land, Florida: A mob lynches two black men, Charles Harris and Anthony Johnson, jailed for rape.

September 24, Gretna, Louisiana: Alexander Hawkins, a black man, is lynched on accusations of slapping a white child.

September 27, Alabama: Whites lynch John Fitch, a black charged with attempted rape.

September 27, Sparta, Georgia: Harrison Boone, a black man, is lynched for shooting at a policeman.

October 7, Georgia: Whites lynch Charles Williams, a black murder suspect.

October 9, Bossier Point, Louisiana: Louis Hamilton, a black accused of arson, is lynched.

October 10, Taylor Ferry, Alabama: James Anderson, a black suspected of murder, is lynched by whites.

October 10, Alabama: Whites lynch Henry Cyat, a black murder suspect.

October 12, Alabama: An unidentified black man accused of murder is lynched by whites.

October 14, Toadvine, Alabama: Whites lynch an unidentified black man suspected of murder.

October 15, Griffin, Georgia: Henry Miller, a black charged with rape, is lynched.

October 21, Sunnyside, Mississippi: An unidentified black man is lynched on suspicion of murder.

November 15, McKenzie, Tennessee: Charles Allen, a black rape suspect, is lynched.

November 18, Steenston, Mississippi: Mimms Collier, a black charged with attempted rape, is lynched by whites.

November 19, Huntingdon, Tennessee: A mob lynches Samuel Donald, a black man, for threatening whites.

December 7, Irondale, Alabama: William Wardley, a black man, is lynched for passing counterfeit money.

December 9, Milton, Arkansas: Jim Crazy, a black murder suspect, is lynched by whites.

December 17, Pine Bluff, Arkansas: An unknown black man is lynched on suspicion of murder.

December 21, Mayfield, Kentucky: James Stone, a black rape suspect, is lynched by whites.

December 22, Woodstock, Alabama: Whites lynch Joseph James, a black accused of rape.

December 22, Clio, Louisiana: Jerry Burke, a black man, is lynched on a charge of attempted murder.

December 22, Mayfield, Kentucky: George Finley, a black charged with theft, is lynched.

December 26, Owensboro, Kentucky: A mob lynches black murder suspect Alfred Holt.

1897

January 5, Georgia: Sidney Gust, a black man, is lynched without apparent motive.

January 6, Stilton, South Carolina: Whites lynch Lawrence Brown, a black suspected of arson.

January 8, Orangeburg, South Carolina: An unidentified black man is lynched on charges of arson.

January 8, Sumter, South Carolina: Simon Cooper, a black accused of murder, is lynched.

January 9, Unadilla, Georgia: A black murder suspect, Anthony Henderson, is lynched.

January 10, Vardaman, Mississippi: Two unidentified blacks are lynched on suspicion of murder and robbery.

January 17, White Castle, Louisiana: Whites lynch an unidentified black man, on accusations of robbery.

January 19, Amite City, Louisiana: Three blacks—Gus Williams, Archie Joiner, and Gus Johnson—are lynched on suspicion of murder.

January 20, Itta Bena, Mississippi: Peter Henderson, a black held on charges of assault and murder, is lynched.

January 22, Jeffersonville, Georgia: Two blacks charged with murder, William White and Charles Forsythe, are lynched.

January 24, Tallahassee, Florida: Whites lynch Pierce Taylor, a black man accused of attempted rape.

January 25, Bryan, Texas: Eugene Washington, a black rape suspect, is lynched.

January 27, Georgia: George Brannan, a black man charged with assault, is lynched.

January 31, Bibb County, Alabama: James Jackson, a black charged with murder, is lynched.

February 4, Rockford, Kentucky: Robert Morton, a black man, is lynched by whites for "writing insulting letters."

February 13, Saluda, South Carolina: Whites lynch an unidentified black man on charges of rape.

February 17, Webb City, Tennessee: Two blacks are lynched for arson.

February 26, Soddy, Tennessee: Charles Brown, a black charged with attempted rape, is lynched by whites.

March 2, Morganton, North Carolina: An Indian doctor is lynched without apparent motive.

March 5, Juliette, Florida: A mob lynches five black murder suspects.

March 5, Elgin, Texas: An unidentified black man is lynched on allegations of burglary.

March 8, Rock Springs, Kentucky: An unidentified black man is lynched on an accusation of theft.

March 14, Lynchburg, Virginia: William Clement, a black man charged with an unspecified felony, is taken from jail and lynched.

March 15, Juliette, Florida: Whites lynch three more blacks accused of murder.

March 18, Kennedy, Alabama: Andy Beard, a black man, is lynched for eloping with a white woman.

March 20, Scottsboro, Alabama: Whites lynch John Smith, a black accused of rape.

March 26, Pickens County, Alabama: John Marritt, a black man, is lynched on an accusation of assault.

March 28, Waynesboro, Mississippi: T.W. Hollinshead, a black named by whites as an "informer," is lynched.

April 2, Alexandria, Virginia: Joseph McCoy, a black rape suspect, is lynched.

April 3, Belen, Mississippi: A black man named Haines is lynched on suspicion of murder.

April 10, Vicksburg, Mississippi: An unidentified black is lynched outside of town, with no apparent motive.

April 16, Edwards, Mississippi: Black rape suspect Jesse Evans is lynched.

April 27, Harrison County, Texas: Three blacks—Hal Wright, Russell Wright, and Robert Brown—are lynched on charges of arson and robbery.

April 30, Sunnyside, Texas: Whites lynch seven blacks suspected of murder.

May 12, Jefferson, Alabama: Three blacks, including two women, are lynched on suspicion of murder.

May 14, Rosebud, Texas: Three black men—David Cotton, Henry Williams, and Sabe Stewart—are lynched on charges of attempted rape.

May 15, Redwood, Louisiana: Charles Jackson, a black suspected of train-wrecking, is lynched.

May 18, Lumpkin, Georgia: A black arson suspect known as Captain Lewis is lynched.

May 18, San Augustine, Texas: Three black murder suspects are lynched.

May 20, Arkansas: Whites lynch Presley Oates, a black man charged with theft.

May 23, Tyler, Texas: William Jones, a black accused of murder, is lynched.

May 27, Hemlock, Mississippi: James Cooper, a black charged with attempted murder, is lynched.

May 29, Concord, North Carolina: Two black murder suspects, Joseph Kiser and Thomas Johnson, are lynched by whites.

June 1, Lamar County, Alabama: John Hayden is lynched by whites after a mob mistakes him for a different black man.

June 4, Urbana, Ohio: Charles Mitchell, a black rape suspect, is lynched.

June 5, Orange Dale, Florida: Isaac Barrett, a black murder suspect, is lynched by whites.

June 9, Princess Anne, Maryland: Whites lynch William Anderson, a black accused of rape.

June 10, Muddy Creek, Nevada: An Indian known as Mouse is lynched on suspicion of murder.

June 23, Newcastle, Tennessee: An unidentified black murder suspect is lynched.

June 25, Crystal Springs, Mississippi: A black murder suspect, John Moses, is lynched by whites.

June 28, Aberdeen, Mississippi: Parry Gillam, a black charged with robbery and assault, is lynched.

July 9, Blossburg, Alabama: James Thomas, a black man, is lynched for refusing to testify in court.

July 10, Villa Ridge, Missouri: Erastus Brown, a black rape suspect is lynched.

July 13, Forest, Louisiana: Whites lynch Atticus Thompson, a black man, for insulting a white woman.

July 15, West Point, Tennessee: Tony Williamson, a black murder suspect, is lynched.

July 16, Elba, Alabama: A black man named Terrill is lynched on an accusation of murder.

July 20, Goose County, Alabama: James Daniel, a black man charged with attempted rape, is lynched by whites.

July 21, Riverton, Alabama: James Speak, a black accused of rape, is lynched.

July 22, Madison, Kentucky: Ephriam Brinkley, a black man of "bad reputation," is lynched.

July 23, Griffin, Georgia: A mob lynches Oscar Williams, a black charged with attempted rape.

July 23, Golboro, South Carolina: James Gray, a black rape suspect, is lynched.

July 24, Baldwin, Louisiana: Jack Davis, a black rape suspect, is lynched.

August 6, Nacodoches, Texas: Esseck White, a black rape suspect, is lynched.

August 10, Louisiana: A black murder suspect, John Gordon, is lynched by whites.

August 15, Meyers, Kentucky: George Wilson, a black man, is lynched without apparent motive.

August 20, Apalachicola, Florida: Whites lynch an unidentified black man on accusations of attempted rape.

August 23, Lovett, Georgia: A black murder suspect, Andrew Green, is lynched.

August 24, Rison, Arkansas: William Wyatt, a black murder suspect, is lynched.

August 26, Bellville, Texas: A black man named Bonner is lynched on charges of rape.

August 26, Baxter, Arkansas: Edward Williams, a black charged with rape, is lynched by whites.

August 30, Claiborne, Alabama: Whites lynch Jack Pharr, a black charged with robbery.

September 2, Excel, Alabama: An unidentified black man, suspected of murderous assault, is lynched by whites.

September 2, Echols County, Georgia: Whites lynch Ben Scott, a black accused of stealing cattle.

September 5, Robroy, Arkansas: An unidentified black man is lynched without apparent motive.

September 6, Friends Mission, Virginia: A black rape suspect, Henry Wall, is lynched by whites.

September 12, Mason, Georgia: Charles Gibson, a black accused of murder, is lynched by whites.

September 16, Hamilton, Arkansas: D.L. Watson, a black man, is lynched without apparent reason.

September 26, Hainesville, Kentucky: Whites lynch Raymond Bushrod, a black accused of rape.

October 1, Jefferson, Louisiana: William Oliver, a black, is lynched for "disobeying ferry regulations."

October 2, Georgia: A black rape suspect, Frank Johnson, is lynched.

October 2, Monroe, Louisiana: Washington Furran, a black accused of rape, is lynched.

October 6, Hernando, Mississippi: Henry Crower, a black rape suspect, is lynched by whites.

October 11, Brenham, Texas: Robert Carter, a black accused of murder, is lynched.

October 15, Kendall, Arkansas: Thomas Parker, a black man, is lynched for killing a member of the White Caps, a group of racist nightriders.

October 15, Quarantine, Louisiana: Douglas Bolte, a black, is mobbed and lynched for running in public.

October 16, Hamburg, Mississippi: William Williams, a black accused of rape, is lynched.

November 14, Williamsport, South Dakota: Two Indians, Alex Condout and Paul Track, are lynched on accusations of murder.

November 15, Osceola, Arkansas: Black murder suspect Henry Phillips is lynched by whites.

November 18, Gibson, Georgia: A black charged with rape, Joshua Ruff, is lynched.

November 18, Bryan, Texas: Thomas Sweat, a black murder suspect, is lynched by whites.

November 25, Starke, Florida: Whites lynch Hicks Price, a black charged with rape.

November 27, Town Creek, North Carolina: Nathan Willis, a black murder suspect, is lynched.

November 29, Montgomery, Alabama: Henry Abrams, a black accused of murder, is lynched outside of town.

December 10, Weason, Mississippi: Charles Jones, a black charged with murder, is lynched.

December 13, Plaquemine, Louisiana: Three black murder suspects—Charles Alexander, James Alexander, and Joseph Thomas—are lynched by whites.

December 16, Kennedy, Alabama: Two blacks, Louis and John Bonner, are lynched by White Caps for testifying in court.

December 16, Brookhaven, Mississippi: Thomas Waller, a black accused of murder, is lynched.

December 17, Carrolton, Alabama: Bud Beard, a black accused of rape, is lynched by whites.

December 27, Glendora, Mississippi: Whites lynch James Hopkins, a black murder suspect.

December 29, Kingstree, South Carolina: Sam Turner, a black accused of murder, is lynched.

1898

January 1, Sherrill, Arkansas: An unidentified black man is lynched on an accusation of theft.

January 1, Macon, Mississippi: James Jones, a black arson suspect, is lynched.

January 4, Clinton, South Carolina: Whites lynch David Hunter, a black man, for violating a contract.

January 7, Pea Ridge, Mississippi: Two black men, Sam Cole and James Watts, are lynched on a charge of insulting whites.

January 8, Maud, Oklahoma: Two Seminole teenagers, John McGeesey and Palmer Simpson, are burned alive by a lynch mob on suspicion of killing a white woman eight days before.

January 8, New Reader, Arkansas: Four black men are lynched on suspicion of murder.

February 1, Georgia: Whites lynch John Belin, a black murder suspect.

February 2, Galena, Missouri: A black man named Ward is lynched on accusations of murder.

February 20, Blanche, Alabama: John Kellog, a black charged with attempted rape, is lynched by whites.

February 22, Lake City, South Carolina: White residents riot over the appointment of a black postmaster, F.B. Baker. Baker and his wife Dora are lynched by the mob, which then burns their home to the ground.

February 23, Mayfield, Kentucky: Black prisoners Richard Allen and Thomas Holmes, charged respectively with robbery and murder, are lynched.

March 6, Lake Cormorant, Mississippi: William Jones, a black rape suspect, is lynched.

March 9, New Orleans, Louisiana: Black robbery suspects William Harris and Andrew Pigge are lynched outside town.

March 15, Marcella, Arkansas: An unidentified black man is lynched for murder.

March 20, Grenada, Mississippi: Alex Anderson, a black charged with attempted rape, is lynched by whites.

March 21, Calhoun County, Alabama: John Calloway, a black man, is lynched for "paying attention to a white girl."

March 21, Godson, Tennessee: John Collar, a black accused of attempted rape, is lynched by whites.

March 24, Moultrie, Georgia: Joseph Allen, a black charged with attempted rape, is lynched.

April 2, Amite, Louisiana: William Bell, a black accused of murder, is lynched by whites.

April 5, Brownsville, Texas: Whites lynch Carlos Guilen, a black murder suspect.

April 26, Lincoln Parish, Louisiana: Columbus Lewis, a black man charged with resisting arrest, is lynched.

May 6, New Orleans, Louisiana: Black murder suspect Dennis Burrel is lynched.

May 26, Salisbury, Maryland: Whites lynch Garfield King, a black murder suspect.

May 27, Donaldsonville, Georgia: Richard Olliver, a black charged with murder, is lynched by whites.

May 27, Rives, Tennessee: Black murder suspect Joseph Mitchell is lynched.

June 3, Texarkana, Arkansas: Levi Hayden, a black man, is lynched on a charge of assault.

June 3, Doyline, Louisiana: William Street, a black charged with attempted murder, is lynched.

June 6, Clarkville, Missouri: Whites lynch two black murder suspects, brothers Sam and Curtin Young.

June 6, Weimar, Texas: George Washington, a black murder suspect, is lynched.

June 15, Oak Ridge, Louisiana: An unidentified black man is lynched for assaulting a policeman.

June 16, Glasgow, Kentucky: Gams Calls, a black accused of rape, is lynched by whites.

June 17, Wetumpka, Alabama: Five blacks are lynched on an accusation of murder.

June 23, Mine Lick, Tennessee: Charles Washington, a black rape suspect, is lynched.

June 26, Russellville, Kentucky: George Scott, a black rape suspect, is lynched.

June 30, Macon, Missouri: A black accused of rape, Henry Williams, is lynched by whites.

July 1, Rison, Arkansas: A mob lynches black murder suspect Goode Gray.

July 12, Coaling, Alabama: Whites lynch Sidney Johnson, a black accused of rape.

July 12, Charlottesville, Virginia: John James, a black rape suspect, is lynched.

July 12, Leland, Mississippi: Wesley Gould, a black man, is lynched in what authorities call a case of "mistaken identity."

July 14, Monticello, Arkansas: Black murder suspects James Reid and Alexander Johnson are lynched by whites.

July 19, Westville, Mississippi: Whites lynch William Patterson, a black accused of murder.

August 8, Carmel, Georgia: John Meadows, a black man, is lynched on an accusation of attempted rape.

August 8, Ripley, Tennessee: Richard Thurmond, a black charged with attempted rape, is lynched by whites.

August 8, Palestine, Texas: Dan Ogg, a black accused of rape, is lynched.

August 9, Clarendon, Arkansas: A mob lynches four black murder suspects.

August 11, Corinth, Mississippi: Mulloch Walker, a black charged with robbery, is lynched by whites.

August 20, Americus, Georgia: An unidentified black man is lynched on suspicion of murder.

September 7, Fowlstown, Georgia: John Williams, a black accused of rape, is lynched.

September 11, Digbey, Georgia: Whites lynch George Burton, a black rape suspect.

September 13, Alabama: Albert Anderson, a black accused of murder, is lynched by whites.

September 26, Mountain City, Tennessee: John Williams, a black rape suspect, is lynched.

October 1, Edmond, Oklahoma: Peter Johnson, a black man accused of larceny, is lynched.

October 2, Lafayette, Alabama: John Anderson, a black charged with murder, is lynched.

October 2, Tompkinsville, Kentucky: Arch Bauer, a black charged with murderous assault, is lynched.

October 2, Annapolis, Maryland: Whites lynch Wright Smith, a black charged with attempted rape.

October 23, Lafayette, Alabama: An unidentified black man is charged with murder and lynched by a mob.

October 23, Edgefield Court House, South Carolina: Black murder suspects Joseph Mackie and Luther Sullivan are lynched by whites.

October 28, Morenci, Arizona: A Mexican, Juan Madera, is lynched on suspicion of murder.

November 6, Wellborne, Florida: Arthur Williams, a black murder suspect, is lynched.

November 7, Lacon, Illinois: Whites lynch F.W. Stewart, a black rape suspect.

November 8, North Carolina: Red Shirt vigilantes terrorize blacks on election day, acting under orders from Democratic spokesmen to "go to the polls, and if you find the Negro out voting, tell him to leave the polls, and if he refuses, kill him. Shoot him down in his tracks." Democrats win a decisive victory in the election.

November 9, Phoenix, South Carolina: Six blacks, including a woman, are lynched of allegations of murder. Black murder suspects Benjamin Collins and Essex Harrison are lynched by whites the next day.

November 10, Wilmington, North Carolina: Whites riot against blacks, burning the offices of a black-owned newspaper before launching a general massacre. Twenty to 100 blacks are killed in the outbreak.

November 17, Edgard, Louisiana: Charles Morrell, a black burglary suspect, is lynched by whites.

November 18, Greenwood, South Carolina: A black woman, Eliza Goode, is lynched without apparent cause.

November 19, Chapelton, Tennessee: John Smart, a black man, is lynched without apparent motive.

November 23, Monticello, Georgia: Edward Merriweather, a black man, is lynched on suspicion of rape.

November 27, Meridian, Mississippi: Three blacks are lynched outside of town, for allegedly assaulting a white man.

November 29, New Madrid, Missouri: An unidentified black man, accused of murder, is lynched outside of town.

December 6, Monticello, Georgia: A mob lynches Jacob Glover, a black murder suspect.

December 6, Arkansas: Newton Gaines, a black accused of rape, is lynched.

December 6, Benton, Louisiana: Two blacks named Hearn and Richardson are lynched on suspicion of murder.

December 6, Georgia: James Anderson, a black charged with murder, is lynched by whites.

December 6, Tallahatchie, Mississippi: A black man named White is lynched on suspicion of murder.

1899

January 5, Banks, Alabama: Marsal McGregor, a black man suspected of arson, is lynched.

January 11, Harps Cross, North Carolina: Whites lynch Henry Jones, a black murder suspect.

January 17, Lynchburg, Tennessee: Two blacks, John Shaw and George Call, are lynched on the basis of their "bad reputations."

February 1, Madison, Florida: Charles Martin, a black man, is lynched without apparent motive.

February 11, Leesburg, Georgia: Three blacks—George Bivins, William Holt, and George Foot—are lynched on allegations of rape.

March 11, McGee, Mississippi: Thomas Allen, a black man, is lynched without apparent motive.

March 16, Palmetto, Georgia: Five black arson suspects are lynched.

March 23, Little River County, Arkansas: A mob lynches seven black murder suspects.

March 23, Silver City, Mississippi: Three black men—Willis Boyd, C.C. Reed, and Minor Wilson—are lynched without apparent reason.

April 6, Brookfield, Mississippi: Whites lynch two black murder suspects, Forest Jameson and Moses Anderson.

April 23, Newman, Georgia: Samuel Holt, a black man charged with rape and murder, is mutilated and burned at the stake by a mob of 2,000 whites. After the lynching, pieces of the victim's charred body are sold as souvenirs.

April 24, Palmetto, Georgia: "Lije" Strickland, a black preacher implicated with Samuel Holt in a rape-murder in Newman, Georgia, on April 23 is found hanging from a tree near town.

April 25, Galena, Kansas: Whites lynch Charles Williams, a black charged with murder.

April 27, Leesburg, Georgia: Mitchell Daniel, a black man, is lynched for using "inflammatory language" in public.

May 1, Osceola, Arkansas: Willie Dees, a black charged with arson, is lynched.

May 11, Pitt County, North Carolina: Two black men are lynched on suspicion of murder.

May 22, Georgia: Thomas Linton, a black man, is lynched without apparent motive.

June 11, Sardis, Mississippi: Simon Brooks, a black charged with robbery, is lynched by whites.

June 13, Dunnellon, Florida: A white mob lynches three blacks, one a murder suspect and two men selected at random because of their race.

June 14, St. Peter, Louisiana: Whites lynch Edward Gray, a black man, without apparent motive.

June 16, Odum, Georgia: A black prisoner named Williams, accused of rape, is lynched outside of town. David Clark, another black inmate held on a charge of resisting arrest, is killed by the same mob.

June 18, Bayne, South Carolina: Louis Patrick, a black murder suspect, is lynched.

June 20, Scranton, Mississippi: Daniel Patrick, a black accused of rape, is lynched.

July 1, Waskom, Texas: Allie Thomas, a black rape suspect, is lynched.

July 14, Gilead, Texas: Whites lynch Abe Brown, a black charged with rape and murder.

July 14, Iola, Texas: An unidentified black murder suspect is lynched.

July 16, St. Charles Parish, Louisiana: George Jones, a black man, is lynched without apparent reason.

July 16, Navasota, Texas: Whites lynch Harry McGee, a black accused of murder.

July 21, Talullah, Louisiana: Five Italian immigrants, including three members of the Defalta family, are lynched on charges of complicity in murder.

July 23, Safford, Georgia: Five blacks are lynched on charges of robbery and murder.

July 23, Steinmetz, Missouri: Frank Embree, a black rape suspect, is lynched.

July 24, Wilmot, Arkanasa: Whites lynch Chich Davis, a black accused of rape.

July 24, Pushington, Mississippi: An unidentified black man is charged with rape and lynched by whites.

July 25, Safford, Georgia: Charles Mack, a black man, is lynched for alleged complicity in murder.

July 25, Navasota, Texas: Henry Hamilton, a black arson suspect, is lynched outside of town.

July 25, Hattiesburg, Mississippi: Whites lynch Henry Noark, a black man charged with attempted rape.

July 25, Leesburg, Georgia: An unidentified black man is lynched by whites for his involvement in a murder.

July 25, Lindsay, Louisiana: An unidentified black man is lynched in what authorities call a case of "mistaken identity." A mob was seeking Val Bages, suspected of attempting to rape a white woman, when they encountered a recent escapee from a nearby state hospital and instead lynched him.

July 26, Brandon, Mississippi: Stanley Hayes, a black jailed for attempted rape, is lynched outside of town.

August 1, Forrest, Georgia: Whites lynch Solomon Jones, a black charged with attempted rape.

August 3, Blakely, Georgia: Louis Henderson, a black accused of rape, is lynched.

August 8, Alexandria, Virginia: A black rape suspect, Benjamin Thompson, is lynched by whites.

August 9, Jasper, Florida: An unidentified black man is charged with rape and lynched by whites.

August 9, Amite City, Louisiana: Echo Brown, a black man, is lynched on accusation of "various crimes."

August 11, Clem, Georgia: A mob lynches William McClue, a black charged with attempted rape.

August 11, Bellbuckle, Tennessee: William Chambers, a black rape suspect, is lynched by whites.

August 11, Port Gibson, Mississippi: William Wilson, a black accused of attempted rape, is lynched.

August 11, Grant Point, Louisiana: Man Singleton, a black charged with attempted rape, is lynched by whites.

August 17, Brantley, Alabama: Charles Hunt, a black accused of attempted rape, is lynched by whites.

September 6, Rosemeath, Mississippi: William Stern, a black accused of murder, is lynched.

September 14, Ty Ty, Georgia: An unidentified black man is charged with rape and lynched.

September 20, Rawles Springs, Mississippi: Whites lynch William Otis, a black man, without apparent motive.

October 21, St. Anne, Mississippi: Joseph Luflore, a black charged with arson and murder, is lynched by whites.

October 24, Georgia: John Goosby, a black prisoner charged with attempted murder, is lynched by whites.

October 30, Wier, Kansas: George Mills, a black man, is taken from jail and hanged for the fatal shooting of a white bartender.

November 1, Fayette, Missouri: A black murder suspect, Thomas Hayden, is lynched outside town.

November 2, Courtland, Alabama: Albert Sloss, a black charged with attempted rape, is lynched outside town.

November 22, Pensacola, Florida: Lawrence West, a black accused of rape, is lynched outside of town.

November 23, Jackson, Georgia: An unidentified black man, charged with attempted rape, is lynched.

December 6, Maysville, Kentucky: Richard Coleman, a black accused of murder, is lynched.

December 13, Dunbar, Pennsylvania: Whites lynch David Pierce, a black murder suspect.

December 13, Jones, Louisiana: An unidentified black rape suspect is lynched by whites.

December 23, Bolton, Mississippi: Black murder suspects James Martin and Frank West are lynched.

1900

1900

January 9, Ripley, Tennessee: Black brothers Henry and Roger Giveney are lynched on accusations of murder.

January 11, West Springs, South Carolina: Whites lynch Rufus Salter, a black man, on suspicion of arson.

January 16, Henning, Tennessee: Anderson Ganse, a black man, is lynched for helping a murderer escape capture.

February 17, Basket Mills, South Carolina: William Burts, a black man, is lynched for threatening whites.

March 4, Tutwiler, Mississippi: James Crosby, a black, is lynched for threatening to kill whites.

March 4, Clyde, North Carolina: George Ratcliffe, a black accused of rape, is lynched.

March 10, Hernando, Mississippi: Thomas Clayton, a black rape suspect, is lynched.

March 11, Jennings, Florida: An unidentified black man is lynched on accusation of murder.

March 18, Marietta, Georgia: Whites lynch John Barley, a black man charged with attempted rape.

March 18, Lee County, Alabama: Charles Humphries, a black charged with attempted rape, is lynched.

March 22, Carthage, North Carolina: George Ritter, a black man, is lynched for informing on white lawbreakers.

March 23, Ripley, Tennessee: Louis Rice, a black man, is lynched after testifying in defense of another black charged with killing a white man.

March 24, Emporia, Virginia: Whites lynch two black murder suspects Walter Colton and Brandt O'Grady.

March 26, Belair, Maryland: Lewis Harris, a black rape suspect, is lynched.

March 27, Deep Creek, Mississippi: William Edward, a black murder suspect, is lynched.

April 3, Berryville, Georgia: Whites lynch Allen Brooks, a black rape suspect.

April 5, Southampton County, Virginia: An unidentified black arson suspect is lynched.

April 16, Tunica, Mississippi: A black accused of murder, Moses York, is lynched.

April 19, Brownsville, Mississippi: Henry McAfee, a black charged with attempted rape, is lynched.

April 22, Allentown, Louisiana: Two black men, John Hugerly and Edward Ames, are lynched for allegedly plotting to kill whites.

April 22, Tazewell, Virginia: John Peters, a black accused of rape, is lynched.

April 28, Marshall, Missouri: Whites lynch Munder Chowagee, a black murder suspect.

May 1, Gloster, Mississippi: Henry Ratcliffe, a black, is lynched for attacking a white man.

May 1, Albin, Mississippi: A black prisoner, George Gordon, is lynched on charges of assaulting a white man.

May 4, Douglas, Georgia: Marshall Jones, a black accused of murder, is lynched.

May 4, Liberty, Missouri: Whites lynch Henry Darley, a black rape suspect.

May 7, Geneva, Alabama: An unidentified black man is lynched on suspicion of rape.

May 7, Amite County, Mississippi: An unidentified black man is lynched without apparent motive.

May 11, Hinton, West Virginia: Whites lynch William Lee, a black charged with attempted rape.

May 13, Harlem, Georgia: Alex Whitney, a black murder suspect, is lynched.

May 14, Brooksville, Florida: Two black murder suspects are lynched.

May 14, Grovetown, Georgia: Whites lynch William Willis, a black charged with murder.

May 15, Lena, Louisiana: Henry Harris, a black man, is lynched on charges of attempted rape.

May 16, Cushtusha, Mississippi: Samuel Hinson, a black prisoner charged with assault, is lynched.

May 22, Pueblo, Colorado: Calvin Kunblern, a black murder suspect, is lynched.

May 26, West Point, Arkansas: An unidentified black man is lynched on charges of robbery.

June 3, Tutwiler, Mississippi: Whites lynch a black prisoner, known only as "Dago Pete," on suspicion of rape.

June 9, Columbus, Georgia: Simon Adams, a black murder suspect, is lynched outside of town.

June 9, Mississippi City, Mississippi: Henry Askey and Ed Russ, two blacks jailed in connection with the June 2 rape-murder of a thirteen-year-old girl, are taken from jail and lynched.

June 10, Sneads, Florida: A mob raids the home of John Sanders, a black man suspected of complicity in the beating death of a white farmer. Sanders and an unidentified male visitor are shot to death.

June 11, Metcalf, Georgia: Lenny Jefferson, a black, is lynched on charges of attempted rape.

June 12, Devail Bluff, Louisiana: Seth Cobb, a black man, is lynched for "making threats."

June 12, Lee County, Arkansas: Whites lynch John Brodie, a black man charged with attempted murder.

June 17, Earle, Arkansas: Nat Mullens, a black accused of murder, is lynched.

June 27, Mulberry, Florida: Whites lynch Robert Davis, a black murder suspect.

June 27, Molena, Georgia: Jordan Hines, a black man, is lynched without apparent motive.

June 27, Live Oak, Florida: Jack Thomas, a black charged with attempted rape, is lynched.

June 29, Panasoffkee, Florida: James Barco, a black man, is lynched without apparent motive.

July 23, Huntsville, Alabama: A mob smokes the sheriff out of jail and then lynches Elijah Clark, a black man charged with raping a thirteen-year-old girl.

July 25–28, New Orleans, Louisiana: White rioters launch a three-day rampage against blacks, leaving an unspecified number of victims dead in the wake of the outbreak.

August 13, Corinth, Mississippi: Whites lynch Jack Betts, a black rape suspect.

August 15, New York City: Race riots break out, with white mobs attempting to kill black entertainers in a theater. The performers escape.

September 1, Cheneyville, Louisiana: Thomas Amos, a black murder suspect, is lynched.

September 1, Forest City, North Carolina: An unidentified black murder suspect is lynched.

September 8, Thomasville, Georgia: Black prisoner Grant Welly is lynched for assaulting a white man.

September 10, Duplex, Tennessee: Logan Beams, a black charged with attempted rape, is lynched.

September 12, Tunica, Mississippi: Whites lynch Zed Floyd, a black murder suspect.

September 14, Tunica, Mississippi: Three blacks—David Moore, Frank Brown, and William Brown—are lynched on suspicion of murder.

September 19, Arlington, Virginia: An unidentified black rape suspect is lynched by whites.

September 21, Ponchatonia, Louisiana: Four black men are lynched on charges of burglary.

September 26, South Pittsburg, Tennessee: An unidentified black man is lynched outside of town on accusation of rape.

October 2, Eclectic, Alabama: Whites lynch Winfield Townsend, a black charged with attempted rape.

October 3, Tiptonville, Tennessee: A black man named Williams is lynched on suspicion of robbery.

October 18, Elliston, Kentucky: Fraten Warfield, a black charged with attempted rape, is lynched.

October 19, Willaston, Georgia: Frank Hardeman, a black accused of rape, is lynched by whites.

October 19, Baton Rouge, Louisiana: Nubry Johnson, a black murder suspect, is lynched outside of town.

October 23, Vicksburg, Mississippi: Gloster Barnes, a black accused of murder, is lynched outside of town.

October 24, Liberty Hill, Georgia: Whites lynch two black men, James Guer and James Caleaway, without apparent cause.

October 30, Duke, Alabama: A black man named Abernathy is lynched on charges of assault.

November 15, Jefferson, Texas: Three blacks are lynched on accusations of attempted murder.

December 8, Wythe County, Virginia: Daniel Long, a black accused of rape, is lynched.

December 16, Rockport, Indiana: Whites lynch two black murder suspects, Bud Rowland and Thomas Henderson.

December 17, Booneville, Indiana: A black prisoner, John Rollo, is lynched on charges of complicity in murder.

December 19, Arcadia, Mississippi: Two unidentified blacks are lynched on suspicion of murder.

December 20, Gulfport, Mississippi: A black man named Lewis is lynched on charges of murder.

December 21, Arkadelphia, Arkansas: An unidentified black man is lynched on allegations of rape.

December 28, Marion County, Georgia: George Fuller, a black arson suspect, is lynched.

1901

January 3, Rome, Georgia: Whites lynch George Reed, a black accused of rape, despite declarations of his innocence from the victim.

January 3, Wilsonville, Alabama: Louis McAdams, a black prisoner, is lynched on charges of murderous assault.

January 3, Campbell County, Georgia: Sterling Thomas, a black man, is lynched without apparent motive.

January 3, Neelyville, Missouri: Nelson Simpson, a black man, is lynched by White Caps without apparent cause.

January 5, Quitman, Georgia: An unidentified black man is lynched outside of town on accusations of rape.

January 7, Madison, Florida: James Denson and his stepson, both black, are lynched on suspicion of murder.

January 15, Leavenworth, Kansas: Frederick Alexander, a black charged with rape and murder, is lynched.

January 16, Dunnellon, Florida: Whites lynch Norman McKinney, a black man, on charges of train-wrecking.

January 16, Elko, South Carolina: Charles Robinson, a black accused of rape, is lynched.

January 24, Doyine, Louisiana: An unidentified black rape suspect is lynched.

February 1, Ocean Springs, Mississippi: Warner Matthews, a black accused of rape, is lynched.

February 6, Dade City, Florida: A mob storms the local jail, shooting black murder suspects Will Wright and Sam Williams to death in their cells.

February 11, Paris, Texas: George Carter, a black accused of rape, is lynched.

February 17, St. Peter, Louisiana: Whites lynch Thomas Jackson, a black murder suspect.

February 18, Macon, Mississippi: Black brothers Fred and Henry Isham are lynched on suspicion of arson.

February 18, Dyersburg, Tennessee: Fred King, a black charged with attempted rape, is lynched by whites.

February 20, Mena, Arkansas: Peter Berryman, a black, is lynched on charges of assaulting a white man.

February 21, Fenton, Louisiana: Thomas Vital, a black accused of rape, is lynched by whites.

February 26, Terre Haute, Indiana: Whites lynch George Ward, a black murder suspect.

February 28, Holdenville, Oklahoma: An Indian murder suspect, Johnson Miller, is lynched by whites.

March 2, Bryan County, Georgia: John Moody, a black man, is lynched by White Caps without apparent cause.

March 2, Richmond, Missouri: A black murder suspect, Arthur McNeal, is lynched.

March 5, Blanchard, Louisiana: William Davis, a black rape suspect, is lynched.

March 6, Moulton, Alabama: Bud Davis, a black man, is lynched without apparent motive.

March 13, Shellman, Georgia: Whites lynch Sherman Harris, a black murder suspect.

March 13, Corsicana, Texas: John Henderson, a black charged with killing a white woman, is taken from jail and publicly burned by a mob of 5,000. A jury later commends the mob for its action.

March 16, Rome, Tennessee: A black purse-snatcher named Crutchfield escapes from a mob bent on lynching him. Enraged, the mob storms his home and kidnaps his sister, Ballie, raping her repeatedly before she is shot and killed.

March 18, Randolph County, Georgia: An unidentified black murder suspect is lynched.

March 20, Terry, Mississippi: A black man, Terry Bell, is lynched without apparent cause.

March 22, Halifax County, Virginia: An unidentified black arson suspect is lynched.

April 15, Portal, Georgia: Kennedy Gordon, a black charged with attempted rape, is lynched by whites.

April 25, Winchester, Tennessee: Whites lynch Henry Noles, a black murder suspect.

April 29, Elberton, Georgia: A black prisoner, William Groulsby, is lynched on accusations of murderous assault.

April 29, Springfield, Tennessee: Wyatt Mallory, a black accused of murder, is lynched.

May 4, Rodessa, Louisiana: Whites lynch a black rape suspect, Felton Brigman.

May 4, Alden Bridge, Louisiana: Grant Johnson, a black man, is lynched on charges of running a gambling house.

May 6, Selma, Alabama: Three black men—Edward Mayes, "Dic" Mayes, and Robert Dawson—are lynched on charges of harboring a murderer.

May 10, Valdosta, Georgia: Whites lynch Henry Johnson, a black man charged with murderous assault.

May 11, Birmingham, Alabama: James Brown, a black man, is shot by a mob on charges of assaulting a white woman. The coroner later proclaims Brown innocent of the crime.

May 11, South Side, Alabama: William Williams, a black charged with theft, is lynched.

May 11, Leeds, Alabama: Whites lynch an unidentified black man in what authorities later describe as a case of mistaken identity.

May 13, Knoxville, Arkansas: A black man, Lee Key, is lynched without apparent motive.

May 13, Topeka, Kansas: A black doctor named Herman is lynched because of his race.

May 25, Pond Creek, Oklahoma: Whites lynch William Campbell, a black murder suspect.

May 30, Butler County, Alabama: Frank Reeves, a black charged with attempted rape, is lynched.

May 30, Bartow, Florida: Fred Rochelle, a black murder suspect, is lynched by whites.

June 5, Minden, Louisiana: Black murder suspect "Dic" Dickson is lynched by a mob.

June 16, Limestone County, Alabama: A black arson suspect, George Harris, is lynched by whites.

June 19, Benton, Louisiana: Whites lynch two black murder suspects, Prophet Smith and F.C. Moland.

June 29, Georgetown, Georgia: An unnamed black man, charged with attempted rape, is lynched.

July 1, Lawrenceville, Virginia: Whites lynch a black man named Walker on charges of rape.

July 10, California: A Chinese man, Tung Fook, is lynched by whites without apparent cause.

July 14, Thickety, South Carolina: A black man named Haines is lynched on suspicion of murder.

July 15, Courtland, Alabama: Whites lynch Alexander Herman, a black murder suspect.

July 15, Girard, Louisiana: Louis Thomas, a black man, steals six bottles of soda from a local store and is shot twice after striking a white man trying to arrest him. When neither wound proves fatal, Thomas is hanged by a white mob.

July 19, Crowley, Louisiana: An unidentified black man is lynched for resisting arrest.

July 21, Port Royal, South Carolina: Whites lynch William Cornish, a black murder suspect.

July 22, Elkins, West Virginia: William Brooks, a black accused of murder, is lynched.

July 25, Vidalia, Georgia: Frank Erle, a black robbery suspect, is lynched.

July 27, Hent's Ranch, Arizona: A Mexican, Ignacio Rivera, is lynched on a charge of stealing horses.

August 1, Carrolton, Mississippi: Three members of the McCray family, a black family, including two women, are lynched on allegations of involvement in a murder.

August 1, Mobile, Texas: An unidentified black is lynched for "insulting a white woman."

August 2, Leeds, Alabama: Charles Bentley, a black accused of murder, is lynched.

August 4, Carrolton, Mississippi: William Price, a black man, is lynched for complicity in murder.

August 5, Moscow, Iowa: Whites lynch William Heffen, a black murder suspect.

August 7, Enterprise, Alabama: John Pennington, a black suspected of attacking a white woman, is burned to death by a mob of 500.

August 10, Ways Station, Georgia: An unidentified black rape suspect is lynched.

August 19–20, Pierce City, Missouri: Three black murder suspects are lynched and several other blacks are injured as white rioters run amok. Indiscriminate gunfire also kills a white child and wounds several bystanders. At least five black homes are burned during the fifteen-hour rampage, with seventy-one-year-old Peter Hampton burned to death in one house. The entire black population leaves town, except for a handful of railroad porters "known to be respectable."

August 20, Dexter, Texas: Whites lynch Abe Wilder, a black murder suspect.

August 21, Wadesborough, North Carolina: Luke Hough, a black accused of murder, is lynched by whites.

August 25, Kenedy, Texas: A Mexican, Felix Martinez, is lynched without apparent cause.

September 1, East Louisiana Parish, Louisiana: Sam West, a black rape suspect, is lynched.

September 1, Philadelphia, Mississippi: Whites lynch Richard Hill, a black murder suspect.

September 3, Chestnut, Alabama: William Fournay, a black accused of rape, is lynched by whites.

September 7, Chipley, Florida: An unidentified black man is lynched on suspicion of rape.

September 12, Wickliffe, Kentucky: Whites lynch three blacks—Frank Howard, Sam Reed, and Ernest Harris—on charges of murder.

October 2, Shelbyville, Kentucky: Two black murder suspects, Jumbo Fields and Clarence Garnett, are lynched. A day after the lynching, the white jailer's wife dies from shock induced by the incident.

October 3, Harrison, Texas: Five blacks are lynched in an economic dispute over profit sharing.

October 4, Huntingdon, Tennessee: A black prisoner, Walter McClennon, is lynched on charges of assaulting a white man.

October 7, Caney Spring, Tennessee: Four blacks are lynched on suspicion of theft.

October 12, Balltown, Louisiana: Whites lynch William Morris, a black accused of rape.

October 21, Hampton, South Carolina: An unidentified black man is lynched on suspicion of burglary.

October 25, Quitman, Texas: A black murder suspect, Galner Gordon, is lynched by whites.

November 1, Allentown, Georgia: An unnamed black man is lynched on charges of attempted rape.

November 4, Perry County, Mississippi: An unidentified black is lynched on allegations of rape.

November 24, Shreveport, Louisiana: Frank Thompson, a black murder suspect, is lynched.

November 24, Anderson County, South Carolina: John Ladison, a black accused of murder, is lynched by whites.

December 6, Opp, Alabama: Three unidentified blacks are lynched without apparent motive.

December 7, Lake Charles, Louisiana: Whites lynch Sam Poydrass, a black charged with murderous assault.

December 25, Paris, Texas: J.H. McClinton, a black man, is lynched without apparent motive.

1902

Texas: A Texas Ranger shoots and kills Ramon de la Cerda on the King ranch, sparking angry Mexican protests along the border. Incensed by the Mexican reaction, Rangers soon gun down Ramon's brother, Albert de la Cerda, and whip a Mexican boy with a quirt in a separate incident.

January 11, Spyfield, Kentucky: Whites lynch James Mays, a black man charged with criminal assault.

January 18, Rosebud, South Dakota: An Indian, John Yellowwolf, is lynched on accusation of stealing horses.

January 26, West Carrol Parish, Louisiana: Two black men are lynched on accusations of murder.

February 6, Nicholasville, Kentucky: Thomas Brown, a black jailed for criminal assault, is lynched.

February 6, Lynchburg, Tennessee: Whites lynch Enless Whitaker, a black accused of murder.

February 7, Glen Jean, West Virginia: A black man named Williams is lynched on allegations of "conjuring."

February 15, Fulton, Kentucky: Bell Duly, a black murder suspect, is lynched.

February 17, New Madrid, Missouri: Black prisoner Louis Wright is lynched for assaulting a white man.

February 20, Winona, Louisiana: A black man, Oliver Bibb, is lynched as an accessory to murder.

February 26, Illinois: Woodford Hughes, a black man, is lynched on the basis of his "disreputable character."

March 10, Foreman, Arkansas: Horace McCoy, a black charged with criminal assault, is lynched.

March 11, Luling, Texas: Two blacks, Nathan Bird and his son, are lynched without apparent motive.

March 19, Vidalia, Louisiana: Whites lynch John Woodward, a black murder suspect.

March 20, Madrid Bend, Kentucky: Two blacks accused of larceny, James Stewart and Elijah Drake, are lynched.

March 24, Alabama: Whites lynch William Ziegler, a black charged with criminal assault.

March 25, La Junta, Colorado: Whites lynch Washington Wallace, a black man charged with assault.

March 25, Washington, North Carolina: James Walker, a black murder suspect, is lynched.

March 26, Higbee, Missouri: Oliver Wright, a black man, is lynched without apparent cause.

March 29, Savannah, Georgia: Richard Young, a black murder suspect, is burned alive by a posse. Subsequent investigation proves him innocent of any crime.

April 1, Rome, Georgia: Walter Allen, a black man, is hanged and riddled with bullets on suspicion of assaulting a fifteen-year-old girl.

April 1, Homer, Louisiana: George Franklin, a black charged with attempted murder, is lynched.

April 6, Tuscumbia, Alabama: William Reynolds, a black murder suspect, is lynched by whites.

April 6, Amherst, Virginia: James Carter, a black charged with murderous assault, is lynched.

April 10, Fulton, Kentucky: Thomas Blambard, a black accused of murder, is lynched.

April 10, Victoria, Louisiana: An unidentified black murder suspect is lynched.

April 22, Georgia: Whites lynch Harry Young, a black man, without apparent motive.

April 30, Brandenburg, Kentucky: Ernest Dewley, a black prisoner, is lynched on charges of murderous assault.

May 12, Decatur, Tennessee: James Underwood, a black man, is lynched for threatening whites.

May 13, Loreauville, Louisiana: Nicholas Dublano, a black jailed for attempted criminal assault, is lynched.

May 13, Cookamie, Mississippi: Horace Muller, a black charged with attempted murder, is lynched.

May 22, Lansing, Texas: Dudley Morgan, a black man charged with criminal assault, is burned at the stake by a mob of 4,000.

June 5, Ravenals, South Carolina: A black murder suspect, James Black, is lynched.

June 6, Toms Brook, Virginia: Wiley Gam, a black man, is lynched on charges of attempted rape.

June 11, Salisbury, North Carolina: Harrison Gillespie, a black accused of murder, is lynched.

June 11, Newport News, Virginia: An unidentified black man is lynched outside of town, without apparent cause.

June 25, Alabama: Willy Campbell, a black, is lynched on charges of attempted murder.

July 15, Clayton, Mississippi: Whites lynch William Ody, a black charged with attempted rape.

July 20, Cross Roads, Mississippi: Two blacks are lynched without apparent motive.

July 25, Elkins, West Virginia: Peter Jackson, a black man, is lynched in a case of "mistaken identity."

July 25, Wanelsdorf, West Virginia: Whites lynch four black murder suspects.

July 28, Pembroke, Georgia: John Wise, a black accused of rape, is lynched.

July 28, Bluff Springs, Florida: An unidentified black man is lynched without apparent motive.

July 28, Georgia: Whites lynch Arthur McCauley, a black murder suspect.

July 31, Leesburg, Virginia: Charles Craven, a black accused of murder, is lynched.

August 1, Arkansas: Lee Newton, a black charged with attempted rape, is lynched.

August 1, San Antonio, Florida: Alonzo Williams, a black accused of rape, is lynched.

August 4, Smithdale, Mississippi: John McDaniel, a black man, is lynched on accusations of "lawlessness."

August 12, Lexington, Missouri: Harry Gates, a black murder suspect, is lynched.

August 17, Walnut Grove, Mississippi: Whites lynch Charles Johnson, a black rape suspect.

August 25, Seven Springs, North Carolina: Thomas Jones, a black man, is lynched on charges of rape.

August 31, Monticello, Georgia: John Brosin, a black charged with attempted rape, is lynched.

September 1, Newberry, Florida: Two black murder suspects, Manny Price and Robert Scruggs, are lynched.

September 3, Stephens, Arkansas: Whites lynch Hog Wilson, a black rape suspect.

September 4, Illinois: Edward Brown, a black man jailed for attempted rape, is lynched.

September 4, Hempstead, Texas: Jesse Walker, a black rape suspect, is lynched.

September 8, Winona, Louisiana: William Morley, a black, is lynched on accusations of attempted rape.

September 28, Corinth, Mississippi: Clark Thomas, a black murder suspect, is lynched.

October 4, Columbus, Texas: Utt Duncan, a black charged with attempted rape, is lynched.

October 8, Newburn, Tennessee: Black murder suspects Garfield Burley and Curtis Brown are lynched.

October 17, Calcasieur Parish, Louisiana: Whites lynch an unidentified black murder suspect.

October 20, Forrest City, Arkansas: Charles Young, a black charged with rape and murder, is lynched.

October 20, Estabutchie, Mississippi: An unidentified black man is lynched on charges of attempted rape.

October 21, Hempstead, Texas: Black rape suspects Joseph Wesley and Reddish Barton are lynched by whites.

October 23, Tallapoosa, Georgia: Benjamin Brown, a black rape suspect, is lynched.

November 1, Darling, Mississippi: An unnamed black murder suspect is lynched.

November 3, Selma, Alabama: Samuel Harris, a black accused of murder, is lynched by whites.

November 13, Lewisburg, Tennessee: Whites lynch John Davis, a black murder suspect.

November 20, Wynne, Arkansas: Elijah Wells, a black charged with murderous assault, is lynched.

November 20, Summit, Mississippi: Two blacks, John Youngblood and an unidentified man, are lynched on charges of complicity in murder.

November 20, Sullivan, Indiana: James Dillard, a black accused of rape, is lynched by whites.

November 26, Francisville, Louisiana: Joseph Lamb, a black charged with attempted rape, is lynched.

December 20, Marbury, Alabama: A mob lynches Scott Bishop, a black murder suspect.

December 25, Pittsburg, Kansas: Montgomery Godley, a black accused of murder, is lynched.

December 27, Troy, South Carolina: A black couple, Oliver Wideman and his wife, are lynched on suspicion of murder.

1903

January 10, Drew, Mississippi: John Hollins, a black, is lynched on charges of "attempted assault."

January 14, Angleton, Texas: Black murder suspects Random O'Neal and Charles Tunstall are lynched by whites.

January 21, Leeper, Missouri: Andy Clark, a black murder suspect, is lynched.

January 26, Luling, Louisiana: Joseph Momas, a black accused of murder, is lynched.

February 4, Madison, West Virginia: Frank Brown, a black murder suspect, is lynched.

February 7, Wrightsville, Georgia: Whites lynch Lee Hill, a black murder suspect.

February 7, Plaquemine, Louisiana: Cornelius Lee, a black charged with murderous assault, is lynched.

February 24, Griffin, Georgia: William Fambro, a black man recently fined for "insulting a white woman," is killed by a white mob that fires over 1,000 shots into his rural home.

March 9, Parish, Florida: Henry Thomas, a black accused of rape, is lynched.

March 20, Bradley, Arkansas: Whites lynch Frank Robertson, a black arson suspect.

March 23, Oxnard, California: Luis Vasquez is shot and killed in a clash between white growers and members of the Japanese-Mexican Labor Association.

April 6, Warren, Arkansas: John Turner, a black charged with attempted rape, is lynched.

April 15, Joplin, Missouri: Thomas Gilyard, a black murder suspect, is lynched.

April 22, Gurdon, Arkansas: Alexander Thompson, a black jailed for murderous assault, is lynched by whites.

April 23, Bainbridge, Georgia: Whites lynch Andrew Rainey, a black arson suspect.

April 26, Bloomington, Indiana: A gang of thirty-eight men invade a home where two white sisters, Ida and Rebecca Stephens, have rented a room to Joe Shively, a black man. All three tenants are flogged.

April 26, Carthage, Texas: Hensley Johnson, a black charged with attempted rape, is lynched.

April 26, Thebes, Illinois: An unidentified black man is lynched on charges of attempted rape.

May 3, Mulberry, Florida: Whites lynch Dan Kennedy, a black murder suspect.

May 3, Vicksburg, Mississippi: Robert Bryant, a black accused of murder, is lynched.

May 3, Caruthersville, Missouri: Two blacks, D. Malone and W.J. Mooneyhon, are lynched without apparent motive.

May 20, Mulberry, Florida: Black murder suspects Amos Randall and Henry Gordon are lynched.

May 20, Corinth, Mississippi: Mose Hart, a black charged with murderous assault, is lynched by whites.

May 22, New Bainbridge, Georgia: William Hopkins, a black rape suspect, is lynched.

May 27, Kemp, Texas: An unidentified black is lynched for rape.

May 28, Woodville, Mississippi: An unidentified black man is lynched on suspicion of arson.

June 1, Georgia: A black accused of murder, Benjamin Gorman, is lynched by whites.

June 4, Greenville, Mississippi: Robert Dennis, a black accused of rape, is lynched.

June 6, Bellville, Illinois: Whites lynch David Wyatt, a black charged with murder.

June 8, Ft. Valley, Georgia: Banjo Peavey, a black murder suspect, is lynched.

June 8, Smith County, Mississippi: Five blacks, including a woman, are lynched for complicity in murder.

June 12, Forest Hill, Louisiana: Frank Dupree, a black accused of murder, is lynched.

June 12, Cleveland, Mississippi: George Kincaid, a black charged with murderous assault, is lynched outside of town.

June 22, Wilmington, Delaware: George White, a black man, is burned at the stake and riddled with bullets on suspicion of raping and killing a seventeen-year-old girl.

June 24, Scottsboro, Alabama: Andrew Diggs, a black charged with attempted rape, is lynched.

June 24, Concordia Parish, Louisiana: Two blacks, Jack Harris and Lamb Whittle, are lynched for assaulting a white man.

June 24, Elk Valley, Tennessee: Charles Jones, a black charged with rape, is lynched.

June 24, Newton, Georgia: Whites lynch three black murder suspects, Garfield McCoy, George McKinney, and Wiley Annett.

June 30, Norway, South Carolina: Charles Evans, a black prisoner charged with the murder of a one-armed Confederate war veteran, is taken from jail and lynched. Four other black inmates are beaten by the mob, with two reportedly dying of their wounds.

June 30, Piedmont, South Carolina: A black man, Ruben Elrod, is shot dead at his home by a mob of fifty whites. Three black women who lived with Elrod are also stripped, flogged, and ordered to leave the area. No reason is given for the attack.

July 7, Stouts Crossing, Mississippi: Cato Jarrett, a black accused of murder, is lynched.

July 14, Eastman, Georgia: Whites pursue a black man, thought to be rape suspect Ed Claus, across seven counties, hanging him and riddling his body with bullets after his capture. Claus is later found alive, the innocent victim remaining unidentified.

July 18, Lake Butler, Florida: Whites lynch a black named Adams, who has been accused of rape.

July 20, Aiken County, South Carolina: Two blacks, Jesse Butler and Dennis Head, are lynched in a case of "mistaken identity."

July 21, Pine Barren, Florida: Crane Green, a black rape suspect, is lynched.

July 22, Arkansas: Whites lynch two black prisoners, John Gilbert and an unidentified man, on suspicion of murder.

July 23, Danville, Illinois: I.D. Mayfield, a black murder suspect, is lynched.

July 23, Beaumont, Texas: Moony Allen, a black accused of murder, is lynched.

July 27, Shreveport, Louisiana: A black woman, Jennie Steers, is lynched outside of town on charges of using doctored lemonade to poison a white girl.

July 31, Alto, Texas: An unidentified black man, charged with assault, is lynched outside of town.

August 5, Lewisburg, Tennessee: Two unidentified black men are lynched without apparent motive.

August 12, Whitesboro, Texas: A black man charged with attempted rape is taken from jail and hanged, but officers arrive and cut him down, saving his life. The frustrated mob turns on local blacks, shooting at their homes and driving numerous families out of town.

September, Luxora, Arkansas: A black man named Hellem is lynched on charges of assaulting girls.

September, Lynchburg, Tennessee: Allen Small, a black held on charges of attempted rape, is lynched.

September, Mayersville, Mississippi: George Jones, a black arson suspect, is lynched.

September, Whigham, Georgia: Whites lynch an unidentified black man on suspicion of rape.

September, Centerville, Mississippi: Will Williams, a black murder suspect, is lynched.

September 17, Tonopah, Nevada: A Chinese man is lynched on account of his race.

October 1, Marshall, Texas: Black murder suspect Walker Davis is lynched by whites.

October 6, Sheridan, Arkansas: Edward McCollum, a black charged with murderous assault, is lynched.

October 9, Kevil, Kentucky: Whites lynch Thomas Hall, a black murder suspect.

October 16, Taylor Town, Louisiana: George Kenny, a black man, is lynched for threatening to kill whites.

October 16, Cordele, Georgia: An unidentified black man is lynched without apparent motive.

October 29, Hattiesburg, Mississippi: An unidentified black man is lynched on charges of attempted rape.

November 2, Taylor Town, Louisiana: Whites lynch Joseph Craddvels, a black murder suspect.

November 3, Lake Village, Arkansas: Henry Johnson, a black murder suspect, is lynched.

November 5, Pass Christian, Mississippi: Samuel Adams, a black accused of rape, is lynched by whites.

November 15, Alabama: Whites lynch Charles Young, a black charged with attempted rape.

November 24, Jefferson, South Carolina: A black rape suspect, Charles Nelson, is lynched.

November 28, Ross Station, South Carolina: John Fagler, a black charged with attempted rape, is lynched.

November 30, Alabama: Three blacks—Phillip Davis, Walter Carter, and Clinton Thomas—are lynched on charges of murder.

December 5, Tampa, Florida: Jackson Lewis, a black charged with attempted rape, is lynched outside of town.

December 10, Ripley, Tennessee: Whites lynch Joseph Brake, a black murder suspect.

December 24, Brookhaven, Mississippi: Eli Hilson, a black man, is lynched without apparent cause.

December 27, Millview, Louisiana: James Carr, a black murder suspect, is lynched.

1904

January 3, Ripley, Tennessee: Robert Alexander, a black man, is lynched without apparent cause.

January 14, Sussex County, Virginia: Elmer Moseley, a black accused of murder, is lynched.

January 14, Tallula, Mississippi: Bush Riley, a black murder suspect, is lynched.

January 15, High Springs, Florida: Whites lynch Jumbo Clark, a black rape suspect.

January 15, Dorchester County, South Carolina: A black man named "General" Lee is lynched on charges of attempted rape.

January 24, Guthrie, Kentucky: Lewis Radford, a black accused of murder, is lynched.

February 7, Doddsville, Mississippi: James Eastland, a white landlord, visits the shanty of black tenant farmer John Carr and orders a visitor, Luther Holbert, to leave. A quarrel erupts and turns violent, resulting in the deaths of Eastland, Carr, and another black man named Winters. A posse of white men searching for Holbert kills three blacks in a case of mistaken identity. The posse catches Holbert and his wife, and the couple is burned at the stake.

February 19, Crossett, Arkansas: Whites lynch Glenco Days, a black murder suspect.

March 7, Springfield, Ohio: A "race war" erupts after black prisoner Richard Dickerson is lynched for killing a white policeman.

March 12, Majane, California: An unidentified black man is lynched without apparent cause.

March 17, Saucier, Mississippi: An unnamed black man is lynched on suspicion of murder.

March 19, Cleveland, Mississippi: Two blacks, Fayette Sawyer and Burke Harris, are lynched as murder suspects.

March 26, Little Rock, Arkansas: Five black prisoners are executed by a vigilante firing squad.

March 26, St. Charles, Arkansas: Thirteen black men are lynched without apparent motive, in a savage outburst of racism.

April 16, Little River, Alabama: Whites lynch Ruben Sims, a black murder suspect.

April 29, Haywood, Tennessee: Thomas Seacey, a black rape suspect, is lynched.

May 1, Kingston, Alabama: Caines Hall, a black accused of rape, is lynched.

May 8, Alexandria, Louisiana: Frank Piper, a black man, is lynched for threatening whites.

May 15, Appling, Georgia: Jonathan Cummings, a black rape suspect, is lynched.

May 19, Seaboard, North Carolina: An unidentified black man is charged with rape and lynched by whites.

May 19, Virginia: Whites lynch a black rape suspect named Whitehead.

May 20, Mulberry, Florida: An unknown black man is lynched without apparent cause.

May 24, O'Neil, Mississippi: An unidentified black man is lynched on charges of murder.

June 1, Arlington, Georgia: Whites lynch Arthur Thompson, a black murder suspect.

June 3, Trail Lake, Mississippi: Two blacks, named Clark and Van Horne, are lynched on suspicion of murder.

June 4, Trail Lake, Mississippi: Mob violence continues, with the lynching of a black murder suspect named Mayfield.

June 14, Lebanon Junction, Kentucky: A black woman, Marie Thompson, is lynched on suspicion of murder.

June 22, Lamison, Alabama: Ephreim Pope, a black man, is lynched on accusations of rape.

June 26, Europa, Mississippi: Sterling Dunham, a black accused of rape, is lynched.

June 30, Scranton, South Carolina: Cairo Williams, a black murder suspect, is lynched.

July 1, Altoona, Alabama: Whites lynch Jonathan Jones, a black rape suspect.

July 5, Chesterfield County, South Carolina: John Taylor, a black charged with attempted rape, is lynched.

July 9, Mississippi: An unknown black man is lynched for attempted rape.

July 10, Houston, Mississippi: Jesse Tucker, a black charged with attempted rape, is lynched.

July 17, Kentucky: An unidentified black man is lynched on charges of murder.

July 30, Lockhart, Texas: Jonathan Larremore, a black man, is lynched without apparent cause.

August 4, Greenfield, Virginia: Andrew Dudley, a black charged with attempted rape, is lynched.

August 7, Selma, Alabama: Edward Bell, a black accused of murder, is lynched outside of town.

August 16, Statesboro, Georgia: Following their conviction and legal sentencing in the murder of a white family, black defendants William Cato and Paul Reed are dragged from the courtroom and burned alive by a mob.

August 17, Statesboro, Georgia: Two blacks, Albert Rogers and his son, are lynched without apparent motive. Several other blacks are whipped at the same time, one for riding a bicycle on the sidewalk, another "on general principles." Two black women are flogged for allegedly crowding a white woman off the sidewalk. Rioters invade and ransack black homes, continuing their murderous assault, beating a mother and killing her husband.

August 17, Thompson, Georgia: Whites lynch Rufus Lesuere, a black man, on accusations of assault.

August 22, Georgia: James Glover, a black rape suspect, is lynched.

August 28, Rebecca, Georgia: A black man named Scott is lynched on suspicion of murder.

August 30, Portal, Georgia: Sebastian McBride, a black man, is lynched without apparent cause.

August 30, Laramie, Wyoming: Whites lynch John Martin, a black charged with assault.

August 30, Hickman, Kentucky: Joe Bumpass, a black rape suspect, is lynched outside of town.

August 31, Stephens, Arkansas: Two unidentified blacks are lynched for "insulting a white woman."

August 31, Weimar, Texas: Oscar Turner, a black charged with attempted rape, is lynched by whites.

September 5, Crossett, Arkansas: An unidentified black man is lynched on charges of assaulting whites.

September 6, Bronson, Florida: Washington Bradley, a black accused of murder, is lynched.

September 7, Huntsville, Alabama: A mob storms the local jail and builds a fire in the hallway, forcing officers to surrender Horace Maples, a black jailed on suspicion of robbing and killing a white man. Once outside, Maples is hanged and riddled with bullets.

September 18, Royston, Georgia: Jonathan Wade, a black accused of murder, is lynched.

September 21, Talbotton, Georgia: Black murder suspect Jack Troy is lynched by whites.

September 24, Waterloo, South Carolina: An unidentified black man is lynched on charges of rape.

October 1, Clifton, Arizona: Forty children from a Catholic orphanage in New York are delivered to Mexican families for adoption. Rumors circulate that the Mexicans have "bought forty blond babies," and a mob of 300 Anglos descends on the Latino neighborhood, removing the children at gunpoint for placement in white homes.

October 2, Rawlins, Wyoming: Black murder suspect Frank Wigfall is lynched.

October 12, Tifton, Georgia: Whites lynch Moses Weaver, a black murder suspect.

November 29, Neal, Georgia: Hurbert Simmons, a black charged with murder, is lynched.

1905

January 4, Benoit, Mississippi: An unidentified black man is lynched without apparent motive.

January 4, Spring Hill, Arkansas: White Jetton, a black murder suspect, is lynched.

February 16, Dale, Texas: A Mexican rape suspect, Carlos Muñoz, is lynched outside of town.

February 17, Smithville, Texas: Whites lynch William Johnson, a black charged with rape.

February 20, Ingram, Virginia: Henry Henderson, a black man, is lynched without apparent motive.

March 5, Helm Station, Mississippi: An unknown black is lynched on charges of murder.

March 8, Tullahoma, Tennessee: Ronce Gwyn, a black charged with theft, is lynched by whites.

March 14, Pine Apple, Alabama: Two black brothers, Edward and William Plowly, are lynched on suspicion of murder.

March 14, Long View, Texas: Julius Stevens, a black charged with murderous assault, is lynched.

April 20, Askew, Arkansas: Whites lynch John Barrett, a black murder suspect.

May 12, Belmont, Missouri: Robert Pettigrew, a black charged with kidnapping, is lynched.

May 22, Waitman, Kentucky: Robert Shaw, a black accused of murder, is lynched.

June 1, Batchelor, Louisiana: Thomas Wilson, a black charged with murder, is lynched.

June 20, Riverside, Texas: Ford Simon, a black rape suspect, is lynched.

June 25, Meridian, Mississippi: A black murder suspect, Pierce Moberly, is lynched outside of town.

June 29, Watkinsville, Georgia: Eight black men—including one convicted of murder and seven prisoners awaiting trial—are dragged from jail and shot by a vigilante firing squad. One victim survives by feigning death.

July 1, Cottondale, Florida: Doc Peters, a black accused of murder, is lynched.

July 6, Arkansas: James Woodman, a black, is lynched for eloping with a white girl.

July 7, Normandy, Kentucky: Leon Beard, a black rape suspect, is lynched.

July 9, New York City: Three people are wounded by gunshots as whites besiege a ghetto tenement.

July 14, Golinda, Texas: A black accused of rape, Frank Mason, is lynched.

July 14, New York City: Police blame blacks for inciting racial clashes in two neighborhoods, San Juan Hill and The Gut. A small riot erupts in San Juan Hill on July 17.

July 19, Glendora, Mississippi: Whites lynch Henry Harris, a black accused of murder, outside of town.

July 20, New Braunfels, Texas: Sam Green, a black charged with rape, is lynched.

July 23, New York City: Police stand guard after blacks assault a white grocer. On July 24, officers rescue a black man from lynchers.

July 25, Glendora, Mississippi: William Harris, a black man, is lynched outside of town for his alleged involvement in a murder.

July 29, Avery, Texas: An unidentified black man is lynched on charges of rape.

July 30, Weehawken, New Jersey: Six blacks are jailed on charges of stabbing a white man in a racial altercation.

August 4, Hattiesburg, Mississippi: Two black men, Edward Lewis and Kid George, are lynched on charges of murder.

August 8, Waco, Texas: Whites lynch Sank Majors, a black rape suspect.

August 12, Eros, Louisiana: An unnamed black murder suspect is lynched.

August 14, Sulphur Springs, Texas: Thomas Williams, a black being held on charges of attempted rape, is lynched.

August 16, Lake Cormorant, Mississippi: Henry Young, a black accused of murder, is lynched.

August 22, Pittsburgh, Pennsylvania: An estimated 200 persons participate in a race riot at Luna Park.

August 23, Tunnel Springs, Alabama: Whites lynch Oliver Latt, a black murder suspect.

August 27, Clark, North Carolina: John Moore, a black charged with murderous assault, is lynched.

September 1, Rosetta, Mississippi: Alt Rees, a black rape suspect, is lynched.

September 2, Silver City, New Mexico: Whites lynch two black brothers, Arthur and Talcum Woodward, on charges of murderous assault.

September 7, Italy, Texas: Stephen Davis, a black charged with rape, is lynched.

September 14, Tallahatchie County, Mississippi: William James, a black man, is lynched for informing on white lawbreakers.

September 19, Rankin County, Mississippi: John McDowell, a black, is lynched without apparent motive.

September 20, Abbeville, South Carolina: Allen Pendleton, a black murder suspect, is lynched by whites.

September 22, Conway, Arkansas: Frank Brown, a black man, is lynched by whites in a case of "mistaken identity."

October 1, New York City: Irish and Italian laborers stone a crowd of 2,000 Jews on the East River, injuring several persons.

October 8, Bainbridge, Georgia: Whites lynch Thomas Seabright, a black accused of rape.

October 10, Woodville, Mississippi: John James, a black charged with attempted rape, is lynched by whites.

October 10, Brunswick, Tennessee: Luther Billings, a black held on charges of attempted rape, is lynched.

October 12, Elkton, Kentucky: Frank Leavell, a black jailed on charges of attempted rape, is lynched.

October 29, Bainbridge, Georgia: Augustus Goodman, a black murder suspect, is lynched.

November 11, Henderson, Texas: Whites lynch three black men— John Reese, Robert Askew, and an unidentified companion—on suspicion of murder.

November 22, Coahoma, Mississippi: David Simms, a black accused of murder, is lynched.

November 26, Tangipahoa, Louisiana: Monsie Williams, a black charged with attempted rape, is lynched.

December 11, Boyle, Mississippi: Whites lynch James Green, a black rape suspect.

December 20, Barnwell, South Carolina: Black brothers Frank and John Da Loach are lynched on suspicion of murder.

1906

January 1, Savannah, Georgia: Race riots disrupt an Emancipation Day parade.

January 10, Moscow, Texas: Whites lynch Benjamin Harris, a black murder suspect.

January 17, Penola, Mississippi: An unidentified black man, charged with attempted rape, is lynched by whites.

January 22, Cadiz, Kentucky: Ernest Baker, a black murder suspect, is lynched.

February 7, Elmarth, Arkansas: James Calton, a black accused of murderous assault, is lynched.

February 11, Gadsden, Alabama: Whites lynch Bunkie Richardson, a black charged with rape and murder.

February 20, Andalusia, Alabama: A black man named Pedigrie is lynched on accusations of rape.

February 24, Bienville, Louisiana: Wiltzie Page, a black rape suspect, is lynched.

February 27–March 1, Springfield, Ohio: Whites riot against black inhabitants, with militia units called out to quell the violence on March 1.

March 17, Plaquemine, Louisiana: Thirty vigilantes hang William Carr, a black man accused of stealing a white farmer's cow.

March 19, Chattanooga, Tennessee: Edward Johnson, a black convicted of rape, is taken from jail and hanged after the U.S. Supreme Court grants an appeal of his conviction.

March 28, Carrolle, Louisiana: A black rape suspect, known only as "Cotton," is lynched.

April 4, Springfield, Missouri: Harry Duncan, a black man, is lynched on allegations of rape.

April 14, Springfield, Missouri: James Copeland, a black rape suspect, is lynched.

April 15, Springfield, Missouri: A mob lynches black murder suspect William Allen.

April 24, Groesbech, Texas: An unidentified black man is lynched on suspicion of rape.

April 25, Oakwood, Texas: An unidentified black is charged with rape and lynched.

April 29, Rienzi, Alabama: Whites lynch William Brown, a black murder suspect.

May 7, Corvallis, Oregon: George Michel kills prophet Joshua II in an effort to break Joshua's hold on Michel's sister. Acquitted in court, Michel is subsequently murdered by his sister, and the woman is committed to an asylum for life.

May 8, Ethel, Louisiana: George Whitney, a black man, is lynched for "insulting a lady."

May 8, Jackson, Mississippi: Sam Simms, a black, is lynched for killing a white man's horse.

May 14, Eastman, Georgia: Whites lynch William Womack, a black rape suspect.

May 17, Inverness, Florida: A black murder suspect, Frank Jordan, is lynched.

May 23, Blanchard, Louisiana: Thomas Jackson, a black charged with robbery, is lynched by whites.

May 23, Columbus, Mississippi: George Younger, a black murder suspect, is lynched.

May 23, Choctaw Nation, Oklahoma: An unidentified black man is lynched on accusations of murder.

May 29, Tallulah, Louisiana: Black murder suspect R.T. Rogers is lynched.

June 8, Inverness, Florida: James Davis, a black accused of murder, is lynched.

June 11, Prentiss, Mississippi: A mob lynches black murder suspect Wood Ambrose.

June 14, Pocomoke City, Maryland: Edward Watson, a black charged with murderous assault, is lynched.

June 14, Union, South Carolina: Moses Hughes, a black man, is lynched on allegations of arson.

June 30, De Kalb, Mississippi: An unidentified black man is lynched on allegations of rape.

July 2, Chickasha, Oklahoma: An unidentified black rape suspect is lynched.

July 8, Pillar, Arkansas: Whites lynch William Anderson, a black rape suspect.

July 11, Swainsboro, Georgia: Edward Pearson, a black charged with murderous assault, is lynched.

July 12, Junction City, Arkansas: An unidentified black man, charged with attempted rape, is lynched outside of town.

July 27, Florida: Two black murder suspects, John Black and William Reagin, are lynched by whites.

July 31, Lakewood, Georgia: Floyd Carmichael, a black accused of rape, is lynched.

August, Brownsville, Texas: Following an altercation with a local merchant, a dozen black soldiers shoot up the town, killing one white man and wounding two others, including the police chief.

Rioting spreads to include members of three black infantry companies before white troops restore order. The three black companies are expelled from military service en masse by President Theodore Roosevelt, with all members receiving dishonorable discharges.

August 6, Salisbury, North Carolina: Three black men—Jack Dillingham, John Gillespie, and Nease Gillespie—are lynched on suspicion of murder.

August 18, Delaware: Authorities report an outbreak of racial rioting.

August 20, Greenwood, South Carolina: Whites lynch Robert Davis, a black man, on suspicion of rape.

August 20, Mont Willing, South Carolina: Robert Ethridge, a black charged with attempted rape, is lynched.

August 21, Mulberry, Florida: John Bapes, a black man charged with murderous assault, is lynched.

August 22, St. George, South Carolina: William Spain, a black held on charges of trying to enter a white person's house, is taken from jail, hanged by a mob, and has 500 bullets fired into his body.

August 26, Calhoun, Louisiana: Alfred Shaufilet, a black jailed for attempted rape, is lynched.

September 7, Laurel, Mississippi: Two black men are lynched on charges of attempted rape.

September 10, Culloden, Georgia: Whites lynch Charles Miller, a black charged with attempted rape.

September 12, New York City: A race riot breaks out in the neighborhood of San Juan Hill.

September 15, Rosebud, Texas: Mitchell Frazier, a black charged with murderous assault, is lynched.

September 22–25, Atlanta, Georgia: Whites riot against blacks for four days. Twelve blacks are killed, and seventy are wounded. Blacks are forcibly disarmed by authorities as the violence wanes on September 25.

October 6, Prichard, Alabama: Two blacks, Richard Robinson and Henry Peters, are lynched on charges of rape.

October 6, Basin, Mississippi: An unnamed black man is lynched for rape.

October 7, Argenta, Arkansas: A black prisoner charged with murderous assault, H. Blackburn, is lynched by whites.

October 8, Texarkana, Arkansas: Anthony Davis, a black charged with attempted rape, is lynched.

October 20, Alabama: Daniel Dove, a black charged with attempted rape, is lynched by whites.

October 25, Centerville, Mississippi: Thomas Crompton, a black murder suspect, is lynched.

October 26, Toyah, Texas: "Slab" Pitts, a black man, is lynched for marrying a white woman.

October 29, Hales Point, Tennessee: Whites lynch George Estes, a black accused of murder.

November 8, Lee County, Mississippi: A black murder suspect, "Jet" Hinks, is lynched by whites.

November 9, Madison, Florida: An unidentified black man is charged with rape and lynched.

November 15, Asheville, North Carolina: William Harris, a black murder suspect, is lynched outside of town.

November 15, Newberry, South Carolina: Mark Davis, a black held on charges of murderous assault, is lynched.

November 29, Hot Springs, Arkansas: Whites lynch an unidentified black man on accusations of attempted rape.

November 29, Lafayette, Louisiana: Anton Domingo, a black man, is lynched on charges of disorderly conduct.

December 5, Valley Park, Mississippi: Wesley Young, a black accused of murder, is lynched outside of town.

December 21, Annapolis, Maryland: Henry Davis, a black rape suspect, is lynched.

December 24–25, Meridian, Mississippi: U.S. troops are deployed on December 24 as blacks gather to avenge the shooting of two black men by whites. On Christmas Day, at least twelve blacks are murdered by white rioters.

1907

January 4, Midway, Alabama: An unidentified black man, charged with attempted rape, is lynched.

January 20, Beaufort, South Carolina: U.S. troops are deployed to prevent a "black uprising," after a black convict is killed by a white prison guard.

January 21, Columbus, Ohio: Fifty white soldiers raid a black neighborhood to avenge an attack on one of their friends by unidentified blacks.

January 23, Greenwood, Mississippi: Henry Bell, a black rape suspect, is lynched.

March 15, Monroe, Louisiana: Two black murder suspects, Flint Williams and Henry Gardner, are lynched.

March 20, Stamps, Arkansas: Two black women are lynched on charges of murderous assault.

March 24, Florence, Alabama: Whites lynch Cleveland Harding, a black charged with attempted rape.

March 26, Hartford, Alabama: An unidentified black rape suspect is lynched.

March 31, Colbert, Oklahoma: James William, a black held on charges of attempted rape, is lynched.

April 16, Bunkie, Louisiana: Charles Strauss, a black, is lynched on accusations of attempted rape.

April 17, Clinton, Louisiana: A black charged with attempted rape, Fred Kilbourne, is lynched by whites.

April 29, Pittsview, Alabama: Eben Calhoun, a black man, is lynched on charges of murderous assault.

May 3, Bossier City, Louisiana: A black rape suspect, Silas Ealy, is lynched.

May 7, Dearing, Georgia: Whites lynch Charles Harris, a black murder suspect.

May 7, Marion County, South Carolina: An unidentified black rape suspect is lynched.

May 21, Reidsville, Georgia: Five blacks are lynched by whites during a race riot.

June 1, Echo, Louisiana: Henry Johnson, a black held on charges of attempted rape, is lynched.

June 2, Trenton, South Carolina: Whites lynch George Hudson, a black charged with attempted rape and murder.

June 8–9, Yazoo City, Mississippi: Three blacks are lynched for their participation in a race riot, which left four white men wounded.

June 10, Gibsland, Louisiana: Whites lynch James Wilson, a black jailed for attempted rape.

June 28, Alexandria, Louisiana: Mathias Jackson, a black rape suspect, is lynched outside of town.

June 28, Ruby, Louisiana: Black rape suspect Ralph Dorans is lynched.

July 2, Cowen, Georgia: George Herbert, a black charged with murderous assault, is lynched.

July 4, New York City: One thousand blacks battle police over the attempted arrest of a black man who fired a pistol in the street. On July 5 a black man named Wright—who helped police during the riot—is found in the ghetto with his skull fractured.

July 7, Maryland: Forty whites armed with pistols and clubs attack 100 black excursionists at a railway junction on the Maryland-Washington, D.C., line.

July 7, New York City: Italians and blacks clash in the San Juan Hill neighborhood.

July 14, Del Rio, Texas: Fred Wilson, a black accused of murder, is lynched.

July 16, Oklahoma City, Oklahoma: Whites lynch Francis Bailey, a black murder suspect, outside of town.

July 20, Olive Branch, Mississippi: Andrew Trice, a black murder suspect, is lynched.

July 22, Lake County, Tennessee: Two blacks are lynched for fighting with a white man.

July 28, Crisfield, Maryland: Black murder suspect James Reed is lynched.

July 29, Vicksburg, Mississippi: Whites lynch Sam Washington, a black accused of murder, outside of town.

August 4, New York City: A race riot erupts in Harlem over an argument over a sports wager. On August 5, two blacks are beaten by whites, despite increased police patrols. Eight blacks are held on murder charges after a white riot victim dies.

August 6, Goliad, Texas: Thomas Hall, a black held on charges of "attempted assault," is lynched.

August 12, Onancock, Virginia: U.S. troops are requested to quell an outbreak of black rioting.

August 16, Maple Grove, Kentucky: William Clifford, a black charged with rape and murder, is lynched by whites.

August 27, Pickensville, Alabama: Jonathan Lipsey, a black accused of rape, is lynched.

September 3, Birmingham, Alabama: Whites lynch Jerry Johnson, a black rape suspect.

September 22, Prichard, Alabama: Moses Dossett, a black charged with attempted rape, is lynched.

October 5, Cumberland, Maryland: A black murder suspect, William Burns, is lynched.

October 11, Tunica, Mississippi: Three black burglars are lynched.

October 23, Van Vleet, Mississippi: Henry Sykes, a black man, is lynched for insulting a white woman.

October 27, Carrollton, Mississippi: A black man named Meyer is lynched for complicity in murder.

October 27, Byron, Georgia: Jonathan Wilks, a black robbery suspect, is lynched by whites.

October 27, St. Augustine County, Texas: Texas Rangers are sent to break up a "race war." Three persons are killed and numerous black families flee the county.

October 29, Belen, Mississippi: A black rape suspect, Charles German, is lynched outside of town.

November 2, Vinegar Bend, Alabama: Two blacks, Abram Sumroll and Henry Lucas, are lynched on charges of involvement in a murder.

November 3, Talladega, Alabama: Whites lynch Fred Quigleton, a black murder suspect.

November 4, Cameron, Texas: Alexander Johnson, a black held on charges of attempted rape, is lynched by whites.

November 30, Opp, Alabama: Newt Sanders, a black accused of rape, is lynched.

December 5, Augusta, Arkansas: Whites lynch Washington Mussay, a black murder suspect.

December 13, Mer Rouge, Louisiana: An unidentified black man is lynched on charges of murderous assault.

December 16, McHenry, Mississippi: Patrick Husband, a black rape suspect, is lynched by whites.

December 24, Muskogee, Oklahoma: Black murder suspect James Garden is lynched.

December 25, Norfolk, Virginia: White marines and black civilians riot.

December 26, Marquez, Texas: Whites lynch Anderson Callaway, a black charged with attempted rape.

December 31, New York City: A patrolman and a number of civilians are injured in clashes between armed bands of blacks and whites.

1908

January 2, Brookhaven, Mississippi: An unidentified black man is lynched on accusations of murder.

January 7, Bryson City, North Carolina: The courthouse is burned during a race riot.

January 9, Goldsboro, Georgia: Black prisoners Thomas Colen and Isaac Webb are lynched on accusations of murderous assault.

January 21, Morgan County, Tennessee: Whites lynch Walter Cole, a black murder suspect.

January 28, Commerce, Mississippi: Two unnamed blacks are lynched outside of town on suspicion of murder.

February 2, Greenville, Florida: Charles Pitman, a black man, is lynched on suspicion of murder.

February 5, Oak Grove, Louisiana: Whites lynch Robert Mitchell, a black murder suspect.

February 10, Brookhaven, Mississippi: Eli Pigatt, a black accused of rape, is lynched.

February 17, Statesboro, Georgia: An unidentified black man is lynched on allegations of rape.

February 24, Statesboro, Georgia: Gilbert Thomas, a black wrongly suspected of rape, is lynched by whites. The man actually accused of rape is identified a short time later.

February 26, Valdosta, Georgia: An unidentified black is lynched on charges of "conspiracy to do violence."

February 28, Conroe, Texas: Clem Scott, a black charged with attempted rape, is lynched.

March 6, Hawkinsville, Georgia: Black murder suspects Robertson Curry and John Henry are lynched.

March 10, Van Cleave, Mississippi: Four black men—David Poe, Thomas Ranston, and the Jenkins brothers—are lynched on suspicion of arson.

March 10, Navosota, Texas: John Campbell, a black charged with murderous assault, is lynched.

March 24, Conroe, Texas: An unidentified black man is lynched on charges of attempted rape.

March 24, Magnolia, Texas: Two unidentified blacks are lynched on accusations of attempted rape.

April 5, Wesson, Mississippi: John Burr, a black murder suspect, is lynched.

April 6, Bay Minett, Alabama: Whites lynch Walter Clayton, a black rape suspect.

April 9, Long View, Texas: Black rape suspect Albert Fields is lynched.

April 19, Atlanta, Texas: Jasper Douglas, a black accused of murder, is lynched by whites.

May 7, Naples, Texas: A mob lynches John Williams, a black murder suspect.

May 8, Pulaski, Tennessee: Elmo Garvard, a black held on charges of attempted rape, is lynched.

May 31, Providence, Kentucky: Jacob McDowell, a black accused of murder, is lynched.

June 20, Parkdale, Arkansas: Ernest Williams, a black man, is lynched for "using offensive language" to whites.

June 22, Hemphill, Texas: Nine black men are lynched on suspicion of murder.

June 27, Waycross, Georgia: Black rape suspects Walter Wilkins and Albert Baker are lynched.

June 27, Hickox, Georgia: An unidentified black rape suspect is lynched.

July 14, Middleton, Tennessee: Whites lynch Hugh Jones, a black charged with attempted rape.

July 15, Beaumont, Texas: An unidentified black man is lynched in what authorities call a case of mistaken identity.

July 18, Jonesville, Louisiana: Three unidentified blacks are lynched on suspicion of arson.

July 28, Greenboro, Texas: Tad Smith, a black rape suspect, is lynched by whites.

July 29, Pensacola, Florida: Leander Shaw, a black charged with attempted rape, is lynched.

July 29, Ohoopee, Georgia: Alonzo Williams, a black prisoner held on charges of attempted rape, is lynched.

August 1, Russellville, Kentucky: Four black men, including three members of the Jones family, are lynched for "expressing sympathy with the murder of a white man."

August 3, Bethany, Louisiana: Andrew Harris, a black charged with attempted rape, is lynched.

August 6, Brighton, Alabama: Whites lynch William Miller, a black man charged with setting off an explosive.

August 7, Tifton, Georgia: Charles Lokie, a black man, is lynched for "insulting a white woman."

August 14–16, Springfield, Illinois: At least two innocent black men, Scott Burton and George Donigan, are lynched by whites during a race riot. By the night of August 15, three persons are reported dead and at least seventy-five are injured. U.S. troops restore order on August 16.

August 15, Bellville, Texas: Moses Jackson, a black man, is lynched without apparent motive.

August 25, Louisville, Georgia: Vance Williams, a black accused of murder, is lynched.

August 28, Ittababa, Mississippi: John Williams, a black charged with arson, is lynched.

August 28, Murfreesboro, Tennessee: George Johnson, a black held on accusation of attempted rape, is lynched.

September 5, Damascus, Georgia: Whites lynch John Towne, a black man charged with rape.

September 8, Oxford, Mississippi: Lawson Patton, a black murder suspect, is lynched.

September 13, Brodeshire, Texas: Daniel Newton, a black accused of murder, is lynched by whites.

September 19, Louisiana: John Miles, a black held on charges of robbery and assault, is lynched.

September 20, Yazoo City, Mississippi: Whites lynch Charles Jones, a black accused of murder.

September 22, Ft. Gaines, Georgia: George Thomas, a black man, is lynched on allegations of murderous assault.

October 4, Hickman, Kentucky: Fifty nightriders kill a black man named Walker and his two children because he cursed a white woman and pulled a gun on a white man.

October 5, Florida: Benjamin Price, a black accused of rape, is lynched.

October 10, Hickory, Mississippi: Three black men—Dee Dawson, William Fuller, and Frank Johnson—are lynched for alleged complicity in murder.

October 11, Younker, Georgia: Whites lynch Henry White, a black man charged with murderous assault.

October 11, Lula, Mississippi: Black brothers Joseph and Frank Davis are lynched on charges of murder.

October 12, New Iberia, Louisiana: Nicholas Hector, a black "desperado," is lynched.

October 15, Hernando, Mississippi: W.J. Jackson, a black charged with theft, is lynched by whites.

October 19, Walnut Log, Tennessee: Nightriders lynch two black men, R.E. Taylor and Quentin Rankin.

October 21, Halselle, Alabama: A black man named Stover is lynched on accusations of attempted rape.

November 2, Union, Mississippi: Whites lynch William Hodges, a black charged with rape.

November 10, Biloxi, Mississippi: Black rape suspect Henry Leidy is lynched.

November 24, Tiptonville, Tennessee: Three members of the black Stineback family are lynched on accusations of murder.

December 26, Cuthbert, Georgia: Authorities prepare for a race riot after a white man fatally shoots two blacks.

1908–1925

Texas: Revolutionary violence in Mexico spills over the border, with military excursions, guerilla raids, and random murders leaving both Anglos and Mexicans in fear for their lives. Estimated body counts for the period range between 500 and 5,000 killed in the undeclared war between "gringos" and "greasers."

1909

January 6, Lexington, South Carolina: An unidentified black man is lynched on suspicion of rape.

January 6, Florence, South Carolina: Arthur Davis, a black man, is lynched following an argument with one of his white neighbors.

January 16, Poplarville, Mississippi: "Pink" Willis, a black prisoner charged with attempted rape, is lynched.

January 18, Hope, Arkansas: A black man named Hilliard is lynched for insulting a white girl.

January 22, Mobile, Alabama: Whites lynch Douglass Robertson, a black murder suspect.

January 24, Leighton, Alabama: A black man named Davenport, charged with barn-burning, is lynched.

February 1, Bolivar, Alabama: An unidentified black man is lynched on charges of attempted rape.

February 9, Houston, Mississippi: Robby Buskin, a black accused of murder, is lynched.

February 13, Lakeland, Florida: Whites lynch Jacob Nader, a black rape suspect.

February 19, Georgia: Rolley Wyatt, a black murder suspect, is lynched.

March 2, Blakely, Georgia: A mob lynches Joseph Fowler, a black charged with murder.

March 7, Rockwall, Texas: Whites lynch Anderson Ellis, a black rape suspect.

March 8, Rosedale, Maryland: William Ramsay, a black man, is lynched without apparent motive.

March 12, Greenwood, Mississippi: Joseph Gordon, a black murder suspect, is lynched.

April 5, Pensacola, Florida: David Alexander, a black accused of murder, is lynched.

April 9, Hopkinsville, Kentucky: Whites lynch Benjamin Brame, a black charged with attempted rape.

April 10, Arcadia, Florida: Jonathan Smith, a black rape suspect, is lynched by whites.

April 11, Mississippi: A mob lynches Horace Montgomery, a black man suspected of murder.

April 20, Paducah, Kentucky: A jury awards $25,000 each to two blacks beaten by nightriders. Forty-one white defendants in the case offer no defense to the charges.

April 25, Birmingham, Alabama: A black rape suspect named Thomas is lynched outside of town.

April 27, Marshall, Texas: Whites lynch James Hodges, a black murder suspect.

April 30, Marshall, Texas: Three black prisoners—Matthew Chase, "Pie" Hill, and "Mose Creole"—are lynched on suspicion of murder.

May 9, Duval County, Florida: An unnamed black man is lynched on charges of rape.

May 11, Waverly, Tennessee: Fourteen nightriders are convicted of flogging a black man in 1908, drawing $500 fines and ten-day jail terms.

May 24, Pine Bluff, Arkansas: Albert Aikens, a black rape suspect, is lynched by whites.

May 30, Portland, Arkansas: Whites lynch Joseph Blakely, a black murder suspect.

June 3, Frankfort, Kentucky: Jonathan Maxey, a black murder suspect, is lynched.

June 6, Tallahassee, Florida: Maik Morris, a black accused of murder, is lynched.

June 11, Branchville, South Carolina: Two black men, Frank Samuels and Tuillie Simmons, are lynched on allegations of murder.

June 15, Arcadia, Florida: Whites lynch an unidentified black man on charges of attempted rape.

June 22, Talbotton, Georgia: Joseph Hardy, a black charged with instigation of murder, is lynched. The same mob also kills another black man, William Cornaker, without apparent cause.

June 25, Cuthbert, Georgia: Albert Reese, a black man, is lynched on charges of murderous assault.

June 26, Wilburton, Oklahoma: Whites lynch Sylvester Shennien, a black accused of murder.

July 1, Barnett, Georgia: An unidentified black man is charged with burglary and lynched.

July 20, Gum Branch, Georgia: King Green, a black man, is lynched on accusations of "insulting women."

July 20, Paris, Tennessee: Albert Lawson, a black charged with murder, is lynched by whites.

July 29, Clarksville, Tennessee: Authorities report nighriders active against blacks in the area.

July 30, New York City: Police battle 5,000 blacks after trying to separate two women fighting in the street.

July 30, Grand Prairie, Louisiana: Two black murder suspects, Emile Antoine and Onexzime Thomas, are lynched.

July 31, Wellston, Georgia: Whites lynch Simon Anderson, a black charged with window-peeping.

August 1, New York City: A policeman is badly beaten by blacks in a fight in Harlem spurred by arguments over the ownership of a stray dog.

August 10, Cadiz, Kentucky: Wallace Miller, a black jailed for attempted rape, is lynched.

August 15, Morehouse Parish, Louisiana: An unnamed black is lynched for filing suit against a white man.

August 17, Greenville, Mississippi: William Robinson, a black man, is lynched without apparent motive.

August 24, Monroe, Louisiana: William Way, a black man, is lynched on charges of murderous assault.

August 27, Tarrytown, Georgia: Black murder suspects Benjamin Clark and John Sweeney are lynched.

September 4, Jackson, Alabama: Black murder suspects Joshua and Lewis Balaam are lynched.

September 8, Mangham, Louisiana: Whites lynch Henry Hill, a black rape suspect.

September 13, Bellamy, Texas: An unidentified black man is lynched on accusation of murder.

September 13, Sandy Point, Texas: Two unnamed blacks are charged with murder and lynched.

September 26, Perry, Florida: Charles Anderson, a black accused of murder, is lynched.

October 1, Greensburg, Louisiana: A black murder suspect, Aps Ard, is lynched.

October 27, Floyd, Louisiana: Black prisoners Joseph Gifford and Alex Hill are lynched on suspicion of murder.

October 28, Kemper County, Mississippi: Four unidentified black men are lynched on suspicion of murder.

November 3, Cairo, Illinois: William Jones, a black murder suspect, is lynched.

November 3, Sutton, West Virginia: Charles Lewis, a black rape suspect, is lynched outside of town.

November 20, Delhi, Louisiana: James Estes, a black accused of murder, is lynched.

November 24, Anniston, Alabama: Whites lynch Ray Rolston, a black charged with murderous assault.

November 27, Shreveport, Louisiana: Henry Rachel, a black rape suspect, is lynched.

December 1, Cochran, Georgia: Jonathan Harvard, a black murder suspect, is lynched by whites.

December 20, Magnolia, Alabama: Clinton Montgomery, a black murder suspect, is lynched.

December 20, Rosebud, Texas: Whites lynch Cope Mills, a black murder suspect.

December 20, Devil's Bluff, Arkansas: George Baily, a black accused of murder, is lynched by whites.

1910

February 2, Beaumont, Texas: An unidentified black man is lynched for rape.

February 20, Columbus County, Georgia: Daniel Lumpkin, a black man, is lynched for alleged complicity in a murder.

March 2, Vidalia, Georgia: An unidentified black man is lynched for attempted rape and murder.

March 3, Dallas, Texas: Holland Brooks, a black rape suspect, is lynched by whites.

March 7, Tampa, Florida: Two black brothers, Sam and Wade Ellis, are lynched on suspicion of murder.

March 8, Tampa, Florida: An unidentified black man is lynched for murder.

March 14, Rayville, Louisiana: Whites lynch Ely Denton, a black man, on suspicion of murder.

March 19, Marion, Arkansas: Black murder suspects Robert Austin and Charles Richards are lynched.

March 25, Pine Bluff, Arkansas: A mob of forty men drags black prisoner "Judge" Jones from his jail cell and lynches him for "improper conduct" with a young white woman.

April 5, Arkansas: Two blacks, Frank Pride and Laura Mitchell, are lynched on accusations of murder.

April 5, Centerville, Texas: Frank Bates, a black man, is lynched for murder.

April 11, Alamo, Georgia: James Tabor, a black rape suspect, is lynched.

April 15, Amboy, Georgia: Whites lynch two black men, Albert Royal and Charles Jackson, on charges of rape.

April 19, Meridian, Mississippi: Thomas O'Neil, a black murder suspect, is lynched.

May 14, Ashdown, Arkansas: "Dock" McLane, a black man, is lynched on charges of murderous assault.

May 26, Calera, Alabama: Whites lynch Jesse Matson, a black murder suspect.

May 26, Charlotte, North Carolina: An unidentified black man is lynched for rape.

May 27, Albany, Georgia: Charles Wilson, a black rape suspect, is lynched.

May 30, New Madrid, Missouri: An unidentified black man is lynched for murderous assault.

June 6, Orange, Texas: A black man is shot and killed during a race riot.

June 11, Florida: Robert Matthews, a black accused of rape, is lynched.

June 12, Mastadon, Mississippi: Whites lynch Elmer Curl, a black charged with murder.

June 14, Star City, Arkansas: William Hunter, a black man, is lynched for "insulting white women."

June 15, Durant, Mississippi: Otto Holmes, a black man, is lynched for attempted murder.

June 26, Rusk, Texas: Leonard Johnson, a black murder suspect, is lynched.

June 28, Braxton, Mississippi: A black man named Jones is lynched on accusations of murder.

July 3, Charleston, Missouri: Whites lynch black murder suspects Robert Coleman and Samuel Field.

July 3, Dothan, Alabama: Henry McKenny, a black man, is lynched on accusations of attempted rape.

July 5, Rodney, Texas: An unknown black man is lynched for attempted rape.

July 6, Huttig, Arkansas: Sam Powell, a black, is lynched on charges of robbery and arson.

July 9, Kathleen, Florida: Whites lynch Sam McIntosh, a black man, on charges of attempted murder.

July 15, Tampa, Florida: Three blacks are killed in church when white gunmen fire through the windows.

July 27, Georgia: Evan Ralent, a black man, is lynched for attempted rape.

July 30, Bonifay, Florida: Two unidentified blacks are lynched for murder.

July 30, Palestine, Texas: A mob of 200 whites opens fire on a group of unarmed blacks outside a local dance hall. The sheriff finds eighteen blacks dead in the woods and reports that they were killed "without any real cause at all."

July 31, Cairo, Georgia: An unidentified black man is charged with rape and lynched outside of town.

August 1, Axis, Alabama: William Wallace, a black accused of rape, is lynched.

August 2, Bonifay, Florida: Four unnamed blacks are lynched on charges of complicity in murder.

August 13, New York City: Three whites are shot and wounded in a race riot.

August 25, Monroe, Louisiana: Laura Porter, a black woman, is lynched for running a house of prostitution.

September 1, Armory, Mississippi: Whites lynch Nicholas Thompson, a black man, on charges of rape.

September 2, Graceville, Florida: Black murder suspects Edward Christian and Hattie Bowman are lynched.

September 6, Clark County, Georgia: Two blacks are lynched on charges of attempted burglary and murder.

September 13, Tiptonville, Tennessee: Two blacks, William Sharp and Robert Bruce, are lynched on charges of attempted rape.

September 14, Springfield, Louisiana: Isaac Glover, a black man, is lynched for murder.

September 20, Tampa, Florida: Two Italians, Castenego Ticoretea and Angelo Albano, are lynched for attempted murder.

October 4, Sanford, Alabama: Whites lynch Bush Rivers, a black rape suspect.

October 8, McFall, Alabama: An unidentified black man is lynched for rape.

October 8, Pelham, North Carolina: An unnamed black man is lynched for robbery.

October 9, Centerville, Alabama: Grant Richardson, a black accused of rape, is lynched.

October 9, Montgomery, Alabama: A black murder suspect, John Dell, is lynched by whites.

October 14, Huntington, West Virginia: An unidentified black is lynched for murder.

November 8, Montezuma, Georgia: Whites lynch two black men, John Walker and William Barnes, for murder.

November 8, Rock Springs, Texas: Antonio Rodriguez, a Mexican murder suspect, is taken from jail and burned at the stake.

November 15, Mannford, Oklahoma: An unidentified black man is lynched on suspicion of murder.

November 26, Mayo, Florida: Richard Lowe, a black charged with attempted rape, is lynched by whites.

November 26, Little Mountain, South Carolina: Flute Clark, a black man, is lynched for murder.

November 26, Gull Point, Florida: Whites lynch Robert Matthews, a black rape suspect.

November 30, Warren, Virginia: Mach Neal, a black charged with murder, is lynched.

December 29, Corsicana, Texas: Eighty prominent ranchers are indicted on charges of conspiring to drive blacks from the area.

1911

January, Rayne, Louisiana: A mulatto woman and her three children are axed to death in their beds. Authorities blame these and forty-five other subsequent ax murders of lighter-skin blacks on a cult dedicated to "purifying" the black race through human sacrifice.

January 14, Benton, Arkansas: One black man is killed and three injured during a riot following a minstrel show.

January 15, Shelbyville, Kentucky: Gene Marshall, a black murder suspect, is lynched by whites. The same mob also kills two other blacks, Wade Patterson and James West, on charges of "insulting women."

January 20, Opelousas, Louisiana: Oval Poulson, a black man, is lynched on suspicion of murder.

January 22, Georgia: William Johnson, a black murder suspect, is lynched.

January 23, Homing, Oklahoma: Armed whites reportedly drive all black residents from the area.

February, Crowley, Louisiana: Three members of the Crowley family—all mulattos—are hacked to death in their sleep, allegedly by black cultists.

February 6, Chicago, Illinois: Fifteen blacks are injured during a race riot.

February 12, Eufala, Alabama: Whites lynch Iver Peterson, a black man, for attempted rape.

February 25, Augusta, Georgia: Two blacks, Robert Jones and John Vease, are charged with murder and lynched.

March, Lafayette, Louisiana: A black family of four is massacred by an ax-wielding murderer as they sleep in their home.

March 5, Marianna, Florida: Galvin Baker, a black man, is lynched for threatening whites.

April, San Antonio, Texas: Five members of the Cassaway family, all mulattos, are axed to death in their sleep.

April 2, Union Springs, Alabama: An unidentified black man is lynched on charges of rape.

April 2, Seaford, Delaware: One white man is killed and three are wounded during a clash with armed blacks. Three blacks are jailed on murder charges.

April 7, Lawrenceville, Georgia: Whites lynch Charles Hale, a black man, on suspicion of rape.

April 8, Ellaville, Georgia: Three black murder suspects—Dawson Jordan, Charles Pickett, and Murray Burton—are lynched.

April 21, Livermore, Kentucky: William Potter, a black murder suspect, is lynched by whites.

May 18, Swainsboro, Georgia: John McLeod, a black accused of murder, is lynched.

May 21, Lake City, Florida: Following a shoot-out that leaves one white person dead, a black man named Norris and five of his friends surrender to the sheriff for protective custody. Lynchers impersonate a posse from Jacksonville and remove the men from jail "for safe keeping," and all six are shot on the outskirts of town.

May 21, Swainsboro, Georgia: Whites lynch Benjamin Smith, a black murder suspect.

May 22, Crawfordsville, Georgia: Joseph Moore, a black man, is lynched on charges of murder.

May 25, Okemah, Oklahoma: A black woman and her fifteen-year-old son being held for the murder of a deputy sheriff are taken from jail and hanged from a bridge. The woman is gang-raped by members of the mob before her death.

May 25, Gallatin, Tennessee: James Sweet, a black murder suspect, is lynched.

June 1, White Haven, Tennessee: Patrick Crump, a black man, is lynched for attempted rape.

June 8, Lafayette, Tennessee: Whites lynch John Winston, a black murder suspect.

June 16, Chunky, Mississippi: William Bradford, a black "desperado," is lynched by whites.

June 20, Thorndale, Texas: Antonio Rodriguez, age fourteen, stabs and kills an Anglo man who ordered him out of a store. Taken from jail by a mob, Rodriguez is beaten to death and dragged through town behind a buggy.

June 30, Monroe, Georgia: Thomas Allen, a black rape suspect, is taken from officers and shot by a mob, which then storms the jail and lynches Foser Watts, a black held on charges of "loitering in a suspicious manner." Prior to the lynchings, Judge Charles Brand rejected an offer of state troops, remarking that he "would not imperil the life of one man to save the lives of a hundred Negroes."

July, Saragos, Texas: Leon Martinez, accused of killing a white man, signs a confession at gunpoint. His family is run out of town by a mob, and Martinez is sentenced to die. His sentence is later commuted to a thirty-year prison term.

July 11, Baconton, Georgia: Whites lynch William McGroff, a black murder suspect.

July 24, Claibourne Parish, Louisiana: Miles Taylor, a black murder suspect, is lynched.

August 4, Demopolis, Alabama: Unable to locate Richard Verge, a black man suspected of killing a white planter, lynchers execute the suspect's brother, Samuel, in his place.

August 12, Farmersville, Texas: A black man, "Commodore" Jones, is lynched by whites for "insulting women."

August 13, Coatesville, Pennsylvania: Zacariah Walker, a black man charged with killing the town constable in a fight, is dragged from his hospital room and burned alive by a mob. Pieces of his charred bones are afterward distributed as souvenirs.

August 18, Durant, Oklahoma: An unidentified black person is lynched on charges of murder.

August 24, Purcell, Oklahoma: Peter Carter, a black accused of rape, is lynched.

August 29, Ft. Gaines, Georgia: Peter Davis, a black man, is lynched for murder.

August 30, Clayton, Alabama: An unnamed black man is charged with murder and lynched.

September 9, Augusta, Arkansas: Arthur Dean, a black man, is lynched for rape.

September 15, Winnsboro, Louisiana: Walter Byrd, a black charged with murderous assault, is lynched by whites.

October 5, Dublin, Georgia: An unidentified black man is lynched for attempted rape.

October 10, Greenville, South Carolina: Willis Jackson, a black man accused of molesting a white child, is hanged by his feet from a tree outside of town and then riddled with bullets. His severed fingers are distributed as souvenirs.

October 11, Georgia: Whites lynch Andrew Chapwan, a black charged with attempted rape.

October 11, Caruthersville, Missouri: Black prisoners A.B. Richardson and Benjamin Woods are lynched on charges of robbery and rape, respectively.

October 16, Forrest City, Arkansas: Nathan Lucy, a black rape suspect, is lynched.

October 19, Manchester, Georgia: Terry Lovelace, a black charged with murderous assault, is lynched.

October 20, Hope, Arkansas: Whites lynch Charles Lewis, a black man, for "insulting women."

October 22, Corneta, Oklahoma: Edward Suddeth, a black man, is lynched for murder.

October 28, Washington, Georgia: T.W. Walker, a black convicted and sentenced to die for killing the white man who raped his wife, is shot and wounded in court by the dead man's brother, then dragged outside and lynched by a mob.

October 29, Marshall, Texas: An unidentified black is lynched for attempted rape.

November, Anderson, South Carolina: A state representative leads the mob that lynches black prisoner Honea Path. The action is publicly praised by South Carolina's governor.

November 7, Lockhart, Mississippi: "Judge" Moseley, a black charged with murderous assault, is lynched by whites.

November 8, Delhi, Louisiana: William Nixon, a black man, is lynched for murder.

November 8, Clarksville, Texas: Whites lynch Riley Johnson, a black charged with attempted rape.

November 26, Lafayette, Louisiana: Six members of the Norbert Randall family, who are black, are hacked to death in their beds, allegedly by cultists seeking to "purify" the race.

December 3, Mannford, Oklahoma: Three whites and two blacks die in a race riot. On December 6 Bud Walker, one of the black rioters held on murder charges, is lynched by whites.

December 6, Clifton, Tennessee: While driving a load of cotton to the local gin, black farmer Ben Pettigrew and his two daughters are ambushed by four white men outside of town. Pettigrew is shot to death, his daughters hanged, with the load of cotton below their bodies set on fire. Two of the killers are later hanged for their part in the ambush.

December 21, Donald, Georgia: John Warren, a black murder suspect, is lynched by whites.

December 25, Brooklyn, Maryland: Whites lynch King Davis, a black charged with murder.

1912

Washington, D.C.: The Mexican ambassador files formal complaints over mistreatment of Mexicans in California and Texas, listing various assaults, lynchings, and murders to prove his case.

January 1, Muldrow, Oklahoma: Samuel Turner, a black murder suspect, is lynched.

January 15, Sucarnoochee, Mississippi: Neeley Giles, a black man, is lynched for murder.

January 18, Crowley, Louisiana: A black mother and her three children are axed to death in their beds.

January 20, Lake Charles, Louisiana: Five black members of the Felix Broussard family are killed in their sleep, with an ax or hatchet. The murderer leaves a cryptic note behind: "When He maketh the Inquisition for Blood, He forgetteth not the cry of the humble— human five." Police arrest several black members of the Sacrifice Church, but all are later freed for lack of evidence.

January 22, Hamilton, Georgia: Four blacks, including a woman, are dragged from jail and riddled with bullets on suspicion of killing a wealthy white farmer.

January 30, Cordele, Georgia: Albert Hamilton, a black man, is lynched for rape.

February 4, Macon, Georgia: Charles Powell, a black held on charges of assault and robbery, is lynched.

February 13, Marshall, Texas: Two blacks, George Saunders and Mary Jackson, are lynched for complicity in murder.

February 14, Starkesville, Mississippi: Mann Hamilton, a black rape suspect, is lynched.

February 15, Memphis, Tennessee: An unnamed black man is lynched for rape.

February 19, Dothan, Alabama: An unidentified black man is lynched on charges of murder.

February 19, Beaumont, Texas: A mulatto woman and her three children are axed to death in their beds.

February 19, Shelbyville, Tennessee: Three black murder suspects—Walter Grer, David Neal, and Green Boman—are lynched by whites.

March 13, Olar, South Carolina: Three black arson suspects—Peter Rivers, Alfred Dublin, and Richard Dublin—are lynched.

March 21, Cochran, Georgia: Whites lynch Homer Burk, a black accused of murder.

March 23, Arkansas: A black murder suspect, Sanford Lewis, is lynched.

March 27, Glidden, Texas: A family of six mulattos are slaughtered while asleep by an ax-wielding prowler.

March 29, Blacksburg, South Carolina: Two black prisoners, Joseph Bronson and Frederick Whisonant, are lynched.

April 3, Starkesville, Mississippi: Alexander Coleman, a black charged with attempted rape, is lynched by whites.

April 9, Shreveport, Louisiana: Thomas Miles, a black man, is lynched after a jury acquits him of writing "insulting letters" to a white woman.

April 11, San Antonio, Texas: Five mulatto members of the William Burton family are axed to death in their beds by black cultists.

April 14, Hempstead, Texas: Three mulattos die in an ax massacre, killed in their sleep. For the first time since January 1911, the killer misses three others in the house. None of the three, however, can describe the intruder.

April 15, Tampa, Florida: Whites lynch Sam Arline, a black accused of murder.

April 25, Delhi, Louisiana: An unidentified black man is lynched without apparent cause.

April 26, Jackson, Georgia: Henry Etheridge, a black man, is lynched for recruiting other blacks to found a colony in Africa.

May 3, Louisiana: Ernest Allums, a black youth, is flogged for "insulting a white woman," then lynched when he refuses to leave town.

May 7, Greenville, Mississippi: An unidentified black is lynched for attempted rape.

May 7, Macon, Mississippi: G.W. Edd, a black murder suspect, is lynched outside of town.

May 25, Tyler, Texas: Daniel Davis, a black man, is burned at the stake for attempted rape.

May 27, Robertson County, Tennessee: Whites lynch Jacob Samuels, a black charged with rape.

June 24, Pinehurst, Georgia: Anne Bostwick, a black servant subject to fits of violent delirium, is hanged and riddled with bullets after stabbing her female employer to death.

July 4, Bradentown, Florida: William English, a black man, is lynched for "insulting a white woman."

July 5, Plummerville, Arkansas: Jonathan Williams, a black accused of murder, is lynched by whites.

July 29, Plainville, Georgia: The sheriff and two other whites are wounded during a race riot.

July 30, Little Ferry, New Jersey: A race riot follows the stabbing of a white man by a black assailant.

August 5, Alabama: Whites lynch Sam Verge, a black murder suspect.

August 8, Richmond, Virginia: An unidentified black man is lynched for rape.

August 13, Columbus, Georgia: A black murder suspect, T.Z. Cotton, is lynched.

August 16, San Antonio, Texas: The home of mulatto James Dashiell is invaded by an ax-wielding black man, bent on mass murder. Dashiell's wife awakes, screaming, as the ax shears through her arm. Her cries alert the family and her assailant flees unrecognized. The bungled attack marks the end of cult-related serial slayings that have claimed forty-nine lives since January 1911.

August 20, Russellville, Arkansas: Monroe Franklin, a black accused of rape, is lynched by whites.

August 28, Gadsden, Alabama: An anonymous black murder suspect is lynched outside of town.

September 4, Bluefield, West Virginia: Robert Johnson, a black charged with attempted rape, is taken from jail by a mob, and tortured and hanged. Subsequent investigation proves him innocent.

September 10, Cumming, Georgia: Robert Edwards, a black man, is lynched for complicity in the murder of a white woman. Numerous other blacks are driven from the county at gunpoint, forced to surrender their homes and land.

September 11, Hackleburg, Alabama: Willis Perkins is lynched by whites "for being black."

September 13, Romeo, Illinois: James Winfield, a black man, is killed by whites during a race riot.

September 14, Atlon, Florida: A black man named Murphy is lynched for rape.

September 25, Grand Cane, Louisiana: Sam Johnson, a black accused of murder, is lynched by whites.

October 5, Americus, Georgia: A black named Yarborough is lynched on charges of rape.

November 2, Bessemer, Alabama: Whites lynch William Smith, a black murder suspect.

November 14, Ocala, Florida: Preech Nellis, a black accused of murder, is lynched.

November 18, Wetumpka, Alabama: A white man is shot and killed while trying to flog two blacks involved in a buggy collision with a white women. A mob lynches one of the blacks, named Berney, and another escapes after killing one of his pursuers.

November 19, Ocala, Florida: Jonathan Archer, a black murder suspect, is lynched.

November 23, Newberry, South Carolina: William Thomas, a black man, is lynched for murder.

November 28, Benton, Louisiana: Three blacks—Wood Burke, James Heard, and Silas Jimmerson—are lynched on charges of murderous assault.

November 30, Cordele, Georgia: Whites lynch Chesbley Williams, a black murder suspect.

December 7, Butler, Alabama: Azariah Curtis, a black accused of murder, is lynched.

December 17, Jackson, Mississippi: An unnamed black man is lynched on charges of murderous assault.

December 20, Cuba, Alabama: An unidentified black man is lynched for murder.

December 21, Norway, South Carolina: Henry Fitts, a black man, is lynched for failure to pay a debt.

December 28, Baton Rouge, Louisiana: Norm Cadore, a black murder suspect, is lynched.

1913

January 2, Wagoner County, Oklahoma: An unidentified black man is lynched for rape.

January 3, Selma, Alabama: A black man named Carson is lynched without apparent motive.

January 17, Paris, Texas: Henry Monson, a black murder suspect, is lynched.

January 23, Fullbright, Texas: Richard Stanley, a black man, is lynched for rape.

January 30, Drew, Mississippi: An unidentified black man is lynched on charges of murder.

February 7, Houston, Mississippi: Whites lynch Andrew Williams, a black murder suspect.

February 18, Houston, Texas: David Rucher, a black man, is burned alive for allegedly killing a white woman.

February 23, Drew, Mississippi: Willie Webb, a black man, is lynched on accusation of murder.

February 25, Marshall, Texas: A black murder suspect named Anderson is lynched outside of town.

February 25, Karnach, Texas: Robert Perry, a black man, is lynched on charges of stealing horses.

March 4, Cornelia, Georgia: Two unidentified blacks are lynched for murder.

March 12, Henderson, North Carolina: Nightriders set fire to the home of Joe Perry, a black man, shooting at people who run from the flames. Perry and his son are shot to death, while his wife and another child die in the fire.

March 21, Union City, Tennessee: John Gregson, a black man, is lynched on murder charges.

April 5, Mondak, Missouri: Whites lynch J.C. Collins, a black murder suspect.

May 5, Hogansville, Georgia: Samuel Owensby, a black accused of murder, is lynched by whites.

June 4, Beaumont, Texas: An unidentified black man is lynched for murderous assault.

June 5, Newton County, Texas: Richard Galloway, a black man, is lynched by whites during a period of racial unrest.

June 13, Anadarko, Oklahoma: Dennis Simmons, a black charged with murder, is lynched.

June 19, Hot Springs, Arkansas: William Norman, a black rape suspect, is lynched outside of town.

June 21, Atlanta, Georgia: A black prisoner, William Redding, is taken from jail and lynched for firing a shot at the officer who arrested him on charges of drunkenness. Four black bystanders are also shot by the mob, one of them fatally.

June 21, Americus, Georgia: An unidentified black man is lynched for murder.

June 27, Lambert, Mississippi: William Robinson, a black accused of murder, is lynched.

July 6, Yellow River, Florida: Whites lynch Roscoe Smith, a black murder suspect.

July 7, Bonifay, Florida: An unnamed black man is lynched for rape.

July 10, Blountstown, Florida: Kid Tempers, a black murder suspect, is lynched.

July 15, Alligator, Mississippi: Samuel Towner, a black man, is lynched for murder.

July 28, Georgia: John Shake, a black charged with murderous assault, is lynched by whites.

August 8, Spartanburg, South Carolina: Sheriff W.J. White stands off a mob intent on lynching a black prisoner.

August 12, Laurens, South Carolina: Richard Puckett, a black man, is lynched for rape.

August 14, Paul's Valley, Oklahoma: Whites lynch black murder suspects Sanders Franklin and Henry Ralston.

August 15, Morgan, Georgia: Robert Lovett, a black man, is lynched for murder.

August 18, Spartanburg, South Carolina: Three would-be lynchers are wounded while storming the jail in an effort to reach Will Fair, a black man charged with rape. Hundreds of shots are fired in the melee, with rioters using dynamite and a battering ram in their effort to enter the jail. Fair is found innocent at his trial on September 20.

August 24, Birmingham, Alabama: Wilson Gardner, a retarded black, is found hanged after he went door-to-door threatening residents in a white neighborhood.

August 25, Greenville, Georgia: Virgie Swanson, a black woman charged with murder (who is later proved innocent), is lynched.

August 26, Charlotte, North Carolina: Joseph McNeely, a black man, is lynched for murder.

August 27, Jennings, Louisiana: James Comeaux, a black held on charges of murderous assault, is lynched.

August 28, Kilgore, Alabama: An unidentified black is lynched without apparent cause.

September 5, Little Rock, Arkansas: Whites lynch Lee Simms, a black rape suspect.

September 13, Tamms, Illinois: Two unidentified blacks are lynched on charges of murderous assault.

September 21, Louisville, Mississippi: Henry Crosby, a black man, is lynched for "annoying a white woman."

September 21, Franklin, Texas: William Davis, a black accused of murder, is lynched.

September 28, Harriston, Mississippi: Whites lynch black murder suspects Walter and William Jones. On September 29, hundreds of blacks run amok in what police call a "cocaine joy riot," leaving ten persons dead and thirty-five injured.

October 15, Hinchcliff, Mississippi: Walter Brownlee, a black man, is lynched on a charge of attempted rape. Subsequent investigation proves him innocent of the crime.

October 22, Monroe, Louisiana: Warren Eaton, a black man, is lynched for "insulting a white woman."

November 4, Wewoka, Oklahoma: John Cudjo, a black murder suspect, is lynched by whites.

November 7, Dyersburg, Tennessee: Whites lynch John Talley, a black charged with attempted rape.

November 13, Rochester, Kentucky: Nightriders lynch ten blacks as part of a local terror campaign.

November 13, Hillside, Kentucky: Henry Allen, a black man, is lynched by nightriders without apparent motive.

December 6, Blanchard, Louisiana: Black brothers Frank and Ernest Williams are lynched on charges of murder.

1914

January 8, Jefferson, Texas: David Lee, a black charged with murderous assault, is lynched.

January 27, Wendell, North Carolina: Whites lynch James Wilson, a black man, on charges of murder.

January 27, Noble, Oklahoma: Benjamin Dickerson, a black man, is lynched for murder.

February 16, Love Station, Mississippi: Johnson McQuirk, a black accused of murder, is lynched.

February 24, Leland, Mississippi: Sam Petty, a black man sought for killing the deputy sheriff who tried to arrest him on a minor charge, is captured by a posse, set on fire, and shot when he attempts to run away.

March 13, Hearne, Texas: William Williams, a black murder suspect, is lynched by whites.

March 19, Fayette, Missouri: Dallas Shields, a black charged with murder, is lynched.

March 29, Clayton, Alabama: Whites lynch Charles Young, a black murder suspect.

March 30–31, Wagoner County, Oklahoma: Two white men attempt to rape Marie Scott, a seventeen-year-old black girl, at her rural home, but her brother intervenes and one of the attackers is killed. On March 31 a mob comes looking for her brother and, failing to find him, lynches the girl instead.

March 31, Santa Fe, New Mexico: A Mexican, Adolfe Padilla, is lynched on accusation of murder.

April 27, Marshall, Texas: Charles Fisher, a black youth accused of hugging and kissing a white girl, is abducted by whites, castrated, and has his ears severed and his lips slit.

May 7, St. James, Louisiana: An unidentified black man is lynched for murder.

May 12, Shreveport, Louisiana: Edward Hamilton, a black rape suspect, is lynched.

May 16, Grovetown, Georgia: Charley Jones, a black man, is lynched for shoplifting a pair of shoes.

June 7, Navasota, Texas: Whites lynch William Robertson, a black charged with murder.

June 17, West Plains, Missouri: A black woman, Paralee Collins, and her son Isaac are lynched without apparent motive.

July 13, Elloree, South Carolina: Rose Carson, a black woman, is lynched for murder.

June 30, Shaw, Mississippi: After killing Jennie Collins, a black woman suspected of complicity in murder, posse members scour the region for alleged murderer Jack Farmer. One of the posse members is accidentally shot to death by his companions.

July 14, Cormorant, Mississippi: Whites lynch Joseph Bailey, a black charged with murder.

August 7, Monroe, Louisiana: Black murder suspects Henry Holmes, Charles Griffin, and Presto Griffin are lynched by whites.

August 7, Eufala, Oklahoma: Crockett Williams, a black man, is lynched for murder.

August 9, Monroe, Louisiana: An unidentified black is lynched on suspicion of murder.

August 12, Slidell, Louisiana: A black man named Romeo is lynched for murder.

September 15, New York City: A black political rally erupts into rioting, and several people are jailed.

September 20, Rochells, Georgia: Nathan Brown, a black man, is lynched for murder.

October 17, Angleton, Texas: Whites lynch Joseph Durfee, a black charged with murder.

October 25, Aberdeen, Mississippi: Mayshe Miller, a black charged with murderous assault, is lynched by whites.

October 28, Newport, Arkansas: Howard Davis, a black murder suspect, is lynched.

November 3, Hernando, Mississippi: Thomas Burns, a black man, is lynched for murder.

November 14, St. Petersburg, Florida: Whites lynch John Evans, a black murder suspect.

November 24–25, Byhalia, Mississippi: A mob lynches Frederick Sullivan, a black man, on charges of arson. His wife is killed by another mob on identical charges the following day.

November 24, Shiloh, South Carolina: Dillard Wilson, a black murder suspect, is lynched.

December 2, Sylvester Station, Louisiana: Black prisoners Tobe Lewis and Munroe Durden are lynched on suspicion of killing the local postmaster.

December 3, Sylvester Station, Louisiana: Kane McKnight, an elderly black man, is burned at the stake for allegedly helping in the murder of the postmaster. Investigators find no evidence linking any of the three recent lynch victims to the crime.

December 4, Coward, South Carolina: William Grier, a black man, is lynched for "frightening women."

December 11, Mooringport, Louisiana: Whites lynch Bread Henderson and Charles Washington, two blacks suspected of murder.

December 12, Shreveport, Louisiana: Watkins Lewis, a black accused of murder, is lynched.

December 16, Hampton, South Carolina: Allen Seymour, a black man, is lynched for rape.

December 19, Ft. Deposit, Alabama: William Jones, a black man, is lynched on charges of murder.

1915

January 4, Wetumpka, Alabama: Two black brothers, Edwin and William Smith, are lynched on suspicion of murder.

January 15, Monticello, Georgia: Three blacks, including a woman, are lynched for resisting arrest on a charge of murderous assault.

January 18, Taylorsville, Alabama: Whites lynch Herman Deeley, a black murder suspect.

January 20, Vicksburg, Mississippi: Edward Johnson, a black man, is lynched on accusations of murder and stealing cattle.

January 23, Arlington, Georgia: Peter Morris, a black accused of murder, is lynched by whites.

February 4, Evens, Georgia: A.B. Culberson, a black man, is lynched on suspicion of rape.

February 10, Brookville, Mississippi: Whites lynch Alexander Hill, a black murder suspect.

February 17, Sparr, Florida: John Richards, a black man, is lynched for "insulting women."

February 20, California: The Mexican "Plan of San Diego" selects this date for a general revolt in which Hispanics will kill all white males above the age of sixteen. The plot fails, and no uprising takes place.

February 21, Mt. Pleasant, Missouri: W.F. Williams, a black charged with murder, is lynched by whites.

February 21–22, Bluff, Utah: Three people die as Paiute Indians clash with deputies and white posse members outside of town. On February 22, Paiute leader Tse-Ne-Gat is wounded and captured in a battle that leaves five Indians dead and six in custody.

February 24, Kissimmee, Florida: William Reed, a black man, is shot to death after publicly kissing a white woman he has dated for two years.

April 16, Valdosta, Georgia: Whites lynch Caesar Sheffield, a black charged with theft.

April 28, Somerville, Tennessee: Thomas Brooks, a black man, is lynched for murder.

May 2, Seaford, Delaware: A mob threatens the jail where two blacks are held on charges of stabbing a white man.

May 9, Norman, Oklahoma: A black physician, Dr. E.B. Ward, is lynched on suspicion of murder.

May 9, Big Sandy, Texas: An anonymous black murder suspect is lynched.

May 15, Louisville, Mississippi: An unidentified black man is lynched for "insulting a white woman."

June 4, Princeton, Kentucky: Arthur Bell, a black man, is lynched on suspicion of rape.

June 10, Johnson City, Illinois: Joseph Strands, a black murder suspect, is lynched.

June 14, Toccoa, Georgia: Samuel Hevens, a black man, is lynched for rape.

June 14, Winnsboro, South Carolina: Whites lynch Jules Smith, a black rape suspect.

June 15, Hope, Arkansas: Loy Haley, a black accused of murder, is lynched by whites.

June 28, Cedar Bluffs, Mississippi: An unidentified black man is lynched for attempted rape.

July, Texas: Mexican revolutionaries launch a series of border raids, totaling thirty attacks by July 1916. Twenty-one Anglos will die in the raids, while Americans retaliate by killing at least 300 Mexican suspects.

July 11, De Kalb, Mississippi: An unidentified black is lynched for theft.

July 16, Bunkie, Louisiana: Thomas Bunkie, a black held on charges of murderous assault, is lynched.

July 16, Sardis, Mississippi: William Mitchell, a black charged with murderous assault, is lynched by whites.

July 21, Cochran, Georgia: Two black men, Peter Flambe and a prisoner named Jackson, are lynched as accessories in a murder.

July 23, Trenton, Florida: Whites lynch H.M. Owens, a black man, without apparent cause.

July 29, Brownsville, Texas: A Mexican, Adolfo Munoz, is lynched on suspicion of murder.

August 6, Dade City, Florida: William Leach, a black rape suspect, is lynched.

August 6, Shawnee, Oklahoma: Edward Berry, a black man, is lynched for rape.

August 10, Alabama: James Fox, a black murder suspect, is lynched.

August 17, Milledgeville, Georgia: Leo Frank, a Jew convicted of killing a young girl employed at his pencil factory, is taken from prison and lynched by vigilantes. More than fifty years later, a posthumous confession reveals that the actual murderer was the prosecution's star witness against Frank.

August 17, Hope Hull, Alabama: Three black men are lynched on a charge of poisoning mules.

August 17, Bainbridge, Georgia: John Riggins, a black man, is lynched for rape.

August 20, San Benito, Texas: Six Mexicans are lynched on charges of pillage and murder.

August 21, Grand Bayou, Louisiana: An unidentified black man is lynched for attempted rape.

August 26, Conshama, Louisiana: An unnamed black is charged with attempted rape and lynched by whites.

August 29, Sulphur Springs, Texas: Whites lynch King Richmond, a black murder suspect.

September 1, Louisiana, Missouri: Rudd Lane, a black man, is lynched for theft.

September 3, Texas: Three Mexicans are lynched on allegations of murder.

September 4, Wagoner, Oklahoma: George Washington, a black man, is lynched on charges of attempted rape.

September 4, Dresden, Tennessee: Mallie Wilson, a black man, is lynched following his arrest after accidentally entering a white woman's hotel room.

September 12, Carlisle, Arkansas: Whites lynch Jacob Bowers, a black murder suspect.

September 14, San Benito, Texas: Six Mexicans are lynched on charges of banditry.

October 10, Brownsville, Texas: Ten Mexicans are lynched outside of town, on allegations of train-wrecking and murder.

October 11, Clarksdale, Mississippi: Two unidentified blacks are lynched for murder.

October 21, Wayside, Georgia: A black man, Alonzo Green, and his son are lynched on suspicion of murder.

November 12, Aberdeen, Mississippi: John Taylor, a black man, is lynched on charges of murderous assault.

November 26, Henderson, Kentucky: Ellis Buckner, a black rape suspect, is lynched.

December 3, Forrest City, Arkansas: William Patrick, a black accused of murder, is lynched.

December 8, Columbus, Mississippi: Cordella Stevenson, a black woman, is dragged from her home by whites who beat her husband unconscious and carried to a railroad depot, where she is gang-raped and hanged on accusation of barn-burning.

December 9, Hopeful, Virginia: Whites lynch an unidentified black man for theft.

December 20, Eastman, Georgia: Two blacks, Samuel Bland and William Stewart, are lynched without apparent cause.

December 27, Muskogee, Oklahoma: The militia rescues two black prisoners from would-be lynchers.

1916

January 1, Anderson County, South Carolina: Two black men are lynched and a third is badly beaten for saying "hello" to a white girl.

January 1, Blakely, Georgia: A rural black church is burned by nightriders. During the previous week, six blacks have been killed and a half-dozen lodge buildings burned in retaliation for the death of a white man killed by a black he was flogging.

January 3, Hayti, Missouri: Samuel Sykes, a black man, is lynched for attempted murder.

January 12, Goldsboro, North Carolina: John Richards, a black murder suspect, is lynched by whites.

January 21, Sylvester, Georgia: Five black men, including four members of the Lake family, are lynched on suspicion of killing the local sheriff. A sixth prisoner escapes from the mob and is later convicted of murder, drawing a life sentence. Subsequent investigation reveals that all six men are innocent.

January 28, Boyds, Alabama: Whites lynch Richard Burton, a black burglary suspect.

January 28, Ocala, Florida: Richard Anderson, a black accused of murder, is lynched.

February 12, Macon, Georgia: Harvin Harris, a black charged with murder, is lynched outside of town.

February 25, Cartersville, Georgia: Jess McCortele, a black man, is lynched for attempted rape.

March 1, Lebanon, Tennessee: Whites lynch William Whitley, a black murder suspect.

March 9, Columbus, New Mexico: Mexican revolutionary Pancho Villa, leading 1,500 guerillas, crosses the border and murders seventeen Americans. U.S. troops from a nearby cavalry base pursue Villa, killing fifty of his men on the U.S. side of the border and an additional seventy during a fifteen-mile penetration into Mexico.

March 19, Dyersburg, Tennessee: William Thomas, a black man, is lynched for shooting a police officer.

March 20, West Point, Mississippi: Jeff Brown, a black man, is lynched after bumping into a white girl as he runs to catch a train.

April 3, St. Charles, Missouri: Fayette Chandler, a black murder suspect, is lynched outside of town.

April 3, Idabel, Oklahoma: Oscar Martin, a black, is lynched for rape.

April 5, Kinston, North Carolina: A black youth, charged with attempting to kill a white child, is transported out of town for safekeeping. Frustrated lynchers vent their rage by hanging the suspect's father, Joseph Black.

April 9, Lawton, Oklahoma: Carl Dudley, a black prisoner held on murder charges, is lynched.

April 9, Del Rio, Texas: A black soldier, Pvt. J. Wade, is shot dead for "resisting arrest."

May 5, Hempstead, Texas: Thomas Dixon, a black accused of rape, is lynched.

May 15, Waco, Texas: Jesse Washington, a retarded black youth sentenced to hang for killing a white woman, is dragged from the courtroom by a mob, stabbed, mutilated, and burned alive while police stand and watch. The victim's teeth are later sold as souvenirs.

May 25, McNary, Louisiana: Whites lynch U.G. Tally, a black charged with attempted rape.

May 27, Prescott, Arkansas: Felix Gilman, a black murder suspect, is lynched by whites.

June 20, Brownsville, Texas: Jeronimo Lerma, a black man, is lynched on charges of murderous assault.

July 1, Pickensville, Alabama: Lemuel Weeks, a black accused of murder, is lynched.

August 7, Seymour, Texas: Whites lynch Stephen Brown, a black man charged with murder.

August 9, Stuttgart, Arkansas: An unidentified black man is lynched for rape.

August 19, Newberry, Florida: Unable to locate Boisy Long, a black charged with wounding a white farmer and killing the local sheriff, whites lynch Long's wife and five other blacks—including a pregnant woman—as accessories to the crime.

August 19, Rice, Texas: Edward Lang, a black murder suspect, is lynched.

August 21, Valdosta, Georgia: A black man named Lewis is lynched on allegations of burglary.

August 29, Vivian, Louisiana: Whites lynch Jess Hammett, a black charged with attempted rape.

August 31, Lima, Ohio: Sheriff Sherman Ely is beaten, slashed, and nearly lynched by a mob of 3,000 would-be lynchers, after he conceals Charles Daniels, a black rape suspect.

September 21, Durand, Georgia: Henry White, a black accused of rape, is lynched.

September 26, Cuthbert, Georgia: Black murder suspects Peter Hudson and Elijah Sturgis are lynched.

September 29, Bainbridge, Georgia: Moxie Shuler, a black man, is lynched for attempted rape.

September 29, Nowata, Oklahoma: Black prisoners John Foreman and a man named Powell are lynched as accessories to murder.

September 29, Gordon, Georgia: Two unidentified blacks are lynched as accessories to murder.

October 4, Leary, Georgia: Mary Connell, a black woman, is lynched by whites as an accessory to murder.

October 5, Graceton, Texas: William Spencer, a black man, is lynched on allegations of murder.

October 6, Greenwood, Mississippi: Allen Nance, a black man, is lynched for murderous assault.

October 7, Sandersville, Georgia: Charles Smith, a black murder suspect, is lynched outside of town.

October 9, Dewitt, Arkansas: Whites lynch Frank Dodd, a black man charged with attempted rape.

October 16, Paducah, Kentucky: Brock Henley, a black rape suspect, is lynched by a white mob, which then executes a second black, James Thornton, for "expressing sympathy with Henley."

October 21, Abbeville, South Carolina: After cursing a white cotton buyer, Anthony Crawford, a black man, is arrested and fined for disorderly conduct. Upon his release from jail, he is mobbed by whites, beaten, and stabbed after using a hammer to strike one of his assailants in self-defense. Rescued by the sheriff, he is soon dragged from jail by another mob, hanged from a tree, and riddled with bullets.

November 5, Bay City, Texas: Whites lynch Joseph Johnson, a black murder suspect.

November 29, Clarksville, Texas: Buck Thomas, a black man, is lynched on charges of murderous assault.

1917

January 10, Greeley, Alabama: An unidentified black man is lynched for rape.

February 8, Proctor, Arkansas: Whites lynch James Smith, a black murder suspect.

March 1, Meigs, Georgia: Linton Clinton, a black man, is lynched for rape.

March 1, Hammond, Louisiana: Emma Hooper, a black woman, is lynched on accusation of murder.

March 12, Maysville, Kentucky: William Sanders, a black robbery suspect, is lynched.

March 28, Pelham, Georgia: Whites lynch Joe Nowling, a black man, without apparent cause.

March 29, Kissimmee, Florida: S.G. Garner, a black farmer, is lynched for refusing to vacate his land on command of his white neighbors.

May 11, Shreveport, Louisiana: Henry Brooks, a black man, is lynched on charges of "intimacy with a white woman."

May 22, Memphis, Tennessee: Ell Pearson, a black man charged with killing a sixteen-year-old white girl, is taken from jail and burned to death by a mob of 15,000 whites.

May 26, New York City: One person is killed and seven are wounded when black rioters clash with the Home Defense Guard.

May 28–30, East St. Louis, Illinois: A bloody race riot erupts from white resentment over hiring of blacks in factories working on government contracts.

May 30, New York City: In Harlem, 200 blacks battle police in a riot sparked by a saloon brawl.

June 2, Columbia, Mississippi: Black murder suspects Van Haynes and Pratt Hempton are lynched by whites.

June 16, Holdenville, Oklahoma: Henry Conley, a black rape suspect, is lynched.

June 22, Courtney, Texas: Benjamin Harper, a black accused of murder, is lynched.

June 23, Reisel, Texas: Elijah Hays, a black man, is lynched for striking a white woman.

June 25, Punta Gorda, Florida: Shepherd Trent, a black man, is lynched for attempted rape.

June 25, Galveston, Texas: Charles Sawyer, a black rape suspect, is lynched.

June 29, Temple, Texas: Robert Jefferson, a black man, is lynched without apparent cause.

July 1–3, East St. Louis, Illinois: Rioting erupts after blacks, responding to attacks by white gunmen, accidentally fire on a police car and kill Det. Samuel Coppedge. Official casualty lists include nine whites and thirty-nine blacks killed during the outbreak, but police estimate black deaths at over 100. Four whites and eleven blacks are charged with murder. All charges against disorderly police are dropped after three patrolmen plead guilty to rioting and pay a total of $150 in fines.

July 3, Orange, Texas: Gilbert Guidry, a black prisoner, is lynched for attempted rape.

July 3, New York City: Blacks battle white police in the neighborhood of San Juan Hill.

July 10, Edgard, Louisiana: Whites lynch Marvel Ruffin, a black vagrant.

July 16, Reform, Alabama: An unnamed black is lynched for burglary.

July 23, Pickens County, Alabama: Poe Hibbler, a black man, is lynched on charges of attempted rape.

July 23, Elysian Fields, Texas: An unidentified black man is lynched for entering a white woman's room.

July 23, Letohatchee, Alabama: Black brothers William and Jesse Powel are lynched for threatening a white man.

July 25–28, Chester, Pennsylvania: At least five persons die in three days of racial rioting sparked by white attacks on blacks.

July 29, Amite, Louisiana: Black murder suspects Daniel and Jerry Rout are lynched.

July 30, Danville, Virginia: Black defendant Howard Grasty is fined for uttering remarks that touched off a recent race riot.

July 31, Garland City, Arkansas: Whites lynch Andrew Avery, a black charged with robbery.

August 9, Ashdown, Arkansas: Aaron Jimerson, a black charged with murderous assault, is lynched.

August 17, Lilian, Virginia: William Page, a black man, is lynched for attempted rape.

August 22, Marshall, Texas: Charles Jones, a black man charged with attempted rape, is lynched outside of town.

August 23, Houston, Texas: Seventeen whites and two blacks are killed as black soldiers clash with armed white civilians. Ten blacks are sentenced to death by a court martial, their sentences commuted to life imprisonment by President Woodrow Wilson.

August 24, York, South Carolina: W.D. Sims, a black man, is lynched on accusations of making a "seditious utterance."

August 24, Memphis, Tennessee: Lawrence Sheppard, a black charged with larceny, is lynched outside of town.

September 1, Lexington, Kentucky: National Guardsmen quell a riot between blacks and whites.

September 3, Beaumont, Texas: Whites lynch Charles Jennings, a black man, without apparent motive.

September 3, Newark, New Jersey: Thirty-three persons are injured in racial rioting.

September 13, England, Arkansas: Samuel Gates, a black man, is lynched for "insulting girls."

September 18, Whitehall, Georgia: A black rape suspect, Rufus Moncrief, is lynched by whites.

September 21, Goose Creek, Texas: Bertram Smith, a black man, is lynched for attempted rape.

October, Spartanburg, South Carolina: Black soldiers are beaten by local whites after seeking service in a segregated cafe.

October 8, Arkansas: An unidentified black man is lynched for robbery.

October 12, New Orleans, Louisiana: Whites lynch Fred Johnson, a black robbery suspect.

October 13, Danville, Virginia: Walter Clark, a black accused of murder, is lynched.

November, Chicago, Illinois: A bomb causes $1,000 damage to a home recently purchased by S.P. Motley, a black man.

November 4, St. Paul, Minnesota: Bombs damage the parish house of a local Catholic church.

November 16, Quitman, Georgia: Jesse Staten, a black man, is lynched for "insulting a white woman."

November 17, Sale City, Georgia: Black brothers Collins and D.C. Johnson are lynched for disputing a white man's word.

November 24, Milwaukee, Wisconsin: A bomb removed from the basement of the Italian Evangelical Church explodes at police headquarters, killing ten people and injuring several more.

December 2, Dyersburg, Tennessee: Ligon Scott, a black rape suspect, is lynched by whites.

December 15, Metter, Georgia: Claxton Dekle, a black man, is lynched for killing a white during a quarrel.

December 25, Ponvenir, Texas: Bandits raid a store outside of town, killing a stagecoach driver and two Mexican passengers who arrive during the robbery. The outlaws next assault a nearby ranch, but they are repulsed and suffer heavy losses. Capt. J.M. Fox of the Texas Rangers is assigned to investigate, recruiting a team of eight Rangers and four civilians, who proceed to terrorize the town's Mexican inhabitants in their search for suspects. Twenty-five Mexican men are rounded up and tortured, and two are gunned down in an effort to intimidate the rest. Finally, fifteen Mexicans are assembled and killed by the posse without a trial. Although no charges are filed, Fox and his men are dismissed from the Rangers for their "indiscretion."

1918

Chester, Pennsylvania: Five persons die during an outbreak of racial rioting.

January 17, Hazelhurst, Mississippi: Sam Edwards, a black prisoner, is lynched on charges of murdering a seventeen-year-old girl.

January 21, Chicago, Illinois: More than thirty homes owned by blacks are bombed.

January 26, Benton, Louisiana: Jim Hudson, a black man, is lynched for living with a white woman.

February 7, Fayetteville, Georgia: Whites lynch "Bud" Cosby, a black man, on charges of kidnapping and intent to rob.

February 7, Willacoochee, Georgia: Edward Dansy, a black charged with killing two policemen and wounding two, is lynched by whites.

February 10, Estill Springs, Tennessee: After Jim McIlheron, a black man, evades capture on charges of killing two whites who attacked him, Rev. G.W. Lych is shot and killed by a mob for aiding his escape. McIlheron is captured and tortured to death by a mob on February 12.

February 23, Fairfax, South Carolina: A black murder suspect, Walter Best, is lynched by whites.

February 26, Rayville, Louisiana: Three black men—Jim Lewis, Will Powell, and Jim Jones—are lynched on accusation of stealing hogs.

March 16, Monroe, Louisiana: Two black men, John Richards and George McNeel, are lynched for attacking a white woman.

March 22, Crawfordville, Georgia: Spencer Evans, a black man, is lynched for attempted rape.

March 26, Lewiston, North Carolina: Black prisoner Peter Bazemore is lynched for attacking a white woman.

April 4, New York City: White reserve troops battle black civilians during an outbreak of racial rioting in Harlem.

April 20, Poplarville, Mississippi: Claude Singleton, a black charged with killing a white man, is lynched.

April 22, Monroe, Louisiana: Whites lynch Clyde Williams, a black prisoner charged with shooting a white man.

April 22, Lexington, Tennessee: Black prisoner Berry Noyes is lynched for killing the local sheriff.

May 17–24, Georgia: A lynch mob in Brooks and Lowndes Counties spends a week hunting Sidney Johnson, a black man accused of killing a white farmer and wounding the farmer's wife. During the hunt, ten innocent blacks are lynched, including a pregnant woman hung by her heels, set afire, and riddled with bullets, the baby cut from her body and stomped to death. Johnson is caught near Valdosta and dies in a fierce duel with the posse, his body afterward mutilated. At least 500 blacks flee the area to escape further violence.

May 20, Erwin, Tennessee: Thomas Devert, a black prisoner, is lynched for killing a white girl.

May 22, Redlevel, Alabama: John Womack, a black man, is lynched for assaulting a white woman.

May 22, Miami, Florida: Henry Jackson, a black man, is lynched on charges of pushing a white man in front of a train.

May 23, Cordele, Georgia: James Cobb, a black prisoner, is lynched for killing a white woman.

May 25, Barnesville, Georgia: Whites lynch John Calhoun, a black man charged with murdering a white woman.

May 27, Beaumont, Texas: Kirby Goolsie, a black prisoner, is lynched for attacking a white girl.

June 4, Huntsville, Texas: Lynchers search for George Cabaniss, a black accused of threatening a white man. Unable to locate its victim, the mob lynches six other members of the Cabaniss family, including two women.

June 13, Earle, Arkansas: Allen Mitchell, a black, is lynched for wounding a white woman.

June 18, Mangham, Louisiana: George Clayton, charged with murdering a white man, is taken from jail and lynched by a mob.

June 29, Madill, Oklahoma: A black man named Magill is lynched for assaulting a white woman.

July 27, Benhur, Texas: Gene Brown, a black man, is lynched on charges of assaulting a white woman.

July 28, Philadelphia, Pennsylvania: Whites and blacks clash in a race riot. Four persons are killed during the outbreak, and sixty are injured.

August, Quincy, Florida: An unidentified black prisoner is lynched on charges of pushing a white man under a train.

August 7, Bastrop, Louisiana: Bubber Hall, a black man, is lynched for attacking a white woman.

August 11, Colquitt, Georgia: Whites lynch Ike Radney, a black man charged with killing one policeman and wounding another.

August 15, Natchez, Mississippi: Bill Dukes, a black man, is lynched without apparent cause.

September 3, Macon, Georgia: John Gilham, a black, is lynched on charges of attacking a white woman.

September 18, Buff Lake, Texas: Abe O'Neal, a black man, is lynched for shooting a white.

September 24, Waycross, Georgia: A black prisoner, Sandy Reeves, is lynched for assaulting a white girl.

October 4, Hopewell, Virginia: U.S. troops suppress rioting by black workers at the du Pont powder factory.

October 12, Brooklyn, New York: One black man is killed during rioting.

November 5, Rolesville, North Carolina: George Taylor, a black rape suspect, is lynched by whites.

November 11, Sheffield, Alabama: William Bird, a black man, is lynched for "creating a disturbance."

November 12, Sheffield, Alabama: Whites lynch George Whiteside, a black man, on charges of killing a policeman.

November 14, Ft. Bend County, Texas: Charles Shipman, a black, is lynched following an argument with a white man.

November 17, Winston-Salem, North Carolina: Five people die when a riot erupts from the attempted lynching of Russell High, a black man charged (and later acquitted) of assault. Because one of the casualties is a young white girl, fifteen would-be lynchers are convicted and sentenced to terms of fourteen months to six years in prison.

November 22, Welch, West Virginia: Whites lynch an unidentified black man on charges of attempted rape.

November 24, Culpeper County, Virginia: Allie Thompson, a black, is lynched for assaulting a white woman.

December 10, Green River, Wyoming: Edward Woodson, a black prisoner, is lynched on charges of killing a white railroad worker.

December 14, Rock Springs, Wyoming: Wade Hampton, a black man, is lynched for "annoying white women."

December 16, Hickman, Kentucky: Charles Lewis, a black man, is lynched for beating the local sheriff.

December 18, Newport, Arkansas: Willis Robinson, a black charged with killing a policeman, is lynched by whites.

December 21, Shubuta, Mississippi: Four blacks, including two pregnant sisters, are lynched on charges of killing a white dentist who sired their unborn children.

1919

Texas: A committee of the state legislature reports that Texas Rangers routinely violate the civil rights of Hispanic citizens, entering homes without warrants, making illegal arrests, employing deadly force without justification, and sometimes executing suspects prior to trial. Rangers admit to the mass execution of five alleged train robbers near Brownsville (two other suspects were spared when the local sheriff refused to deliver them on command). In Cameron County the sheriff threatens to arrest any Ranger confiscating weapons from Hispanic citizens without due cause or proper warrants.

March 15, Florida: A black prisoner named Johnson is publicly burned by a mob.

April 3, Blakely, Georgia: William Little, a black war veteran, is beaten to death for wearing his uniform in public. The mob ignores Little's protests that he has no other clothes.

April 14, Millen, Georgia: Five blacks and two policemen die in a race riot that leaves seven black lodges and five churches burned.

April 23, Maryland: U.S. troops are called to prevent the lynching of a black prisoner named Fountain.

April 28, Monroe, Louisiana: George Holden, an illiterate black man, twice escapes lynching on charges of writing an insulting note to a white woman. Shot in the leg during one attack, he is mobbed and beaten in a second incident the same day. Fleeing town on April 29, he is dragged from a train and shot to death outside of town.

May 10, Charleston, North Carolina: Six people die in a riot between black and white sailors.

May 14, Vicksburg, Mississippi: Lloyd Clay, a black man, is burned alive on charges of attempted rape.

May 26, Georgia: Perry Washington, a black man, is murdered for defending a black woman from a white man attempting to rape her.

May 28, Georgia: The burning of five black churches is described by authorities as a sign of renewed KKK activity.

May 28, Lamar, Missouri: Jay Lynch, a black prisoner, is taken from jail and hanged for killing the sheriff and his son.

June, Chicago, Illinois: A bomb wrecks the Hyde Park home scheduled for purchase by S.P. Motley, a black man. This is the second time within the previous year his home has been bombed.

June 26, Ellisville, Mississippi: Black prisoner John Hartfield is hanged and burned by a mob.

July 1, Twiggs County, Georgia: Cleveland Butler, an innocent black mistaken for a wanted fugitive, is shot and killed by four white vigilantes.

July 4, Bixbee, Arizona: Black soldiers clash with white civilians.

July 12, Longview, Texas: Several white men are wounded in a black neighborhood while seeking the author of a recent newspaper article condemning lynch mobs. Rioting erupts, and numerous black homes are burned, at least one man is killed, and a black school principal is flogged in the street. Martial law is declared on July 13, but violence sputters for several days, and many black families flee the area.

July 19, New York City: Two persons are shot and wounded during a race riot in Harlem.

July 19–22, Washington, D.C.: At least four persons are killed, seventy injured, and more than 100 arrested in a race riot sparked by false rumors of black men assaulting white women.

July 25, Gilmer, Texas: A black man named Jennings is taken from jail and hanged. Four whites are indicted for the lynching on August 2.

July 27, Chicago, Illinois: Race riots erupt after a black boy is stoned while swimming at a segregated beach, resulting in his death by drowning. U.S. troops are called in on the fourth day of the riot, but violence will continue through August 10, with a final toll of thirty-eight persons killed and 537 injured. At least 1,000 black families are left homeless after rioters burn their dwellings.

August 21, North Carolina: Walter Elliott, a black man, is lynched by whites.

August 28, Ocmulgee, Georgia: Eli Cooper, a black leader, is shot dead in church, and the building is burned. Other churches and a lodge building are set on fire in response to rumors of a planned "black uprising."

August 30–31, Knoxville, Tennessee: Rioting erupts after unsuccessful attempts to lynch a black prisoner charged with causing a white woman's death. Six persons are killed and at least twenty are injured, with property damage estimated at $50,000. U.S. troops shoot up a black neighborhood on the basis of false rumors that blacks have killed two white men.

August 31, Louisiana: Whites lynch Lucius McCarty, a black soldier.

September 1, Georgia: Several black schools and churches in outlying areas are burned.

September 7, Jacksonville, Florida: A mob seeking one black prisoner takes two others from jail and lynches them instead.

September 10, Athens, Georgia: Obe Cox, a black fugitive, is shot and burned by a posse outside of town.

September 13, Pueblo, Colorado: Two Mexicans are lynched for killing a policeman.

September 15, New York City: Arguments over the theft of a straw hat lead to a race riot.

September 22, Dooly County, Georgia: Ernest Glenwood, a black man charged with "inflaming local Negroes," is abducted from his home by three masked men. His body is pulled from the Flint River on October 2.

September 28, Omaha, Nebraska: Mayor Edward Smith is fatally injured while trying to save Will Brown, a black prisoner, from lynchers. The courthouse is nearly destroyed by fire as lynchers drag Brown out and shoot him more than 1,000 times, mutilating his body beyond recognition. Other blacks are assaulted and beaten before the mob disperses.

September 29, New Jersey: An armed mob pursues a black man who reportedly attacked a white woman.

September 29, Montgomery, Alabama: Two blacks, M. Phifer and R. Croskey, are taken from police custody and shot by a mob.

October 1–2, Elaine, Arkansas: A riot by white racists leaves numerous blacks dead in the streets, with one estimate placing the body count at over 200. Seventy-nine blacks are charged with murder and insurrection after the outbreak, with twelve convicted and sentenced to die. All the convictions are overturned on appeal.

October 3, Buffington, Indiana: A white picketer is shot and killed by black strike-breakers.

October 5, Washington, Georgia: One black is killed, two are whipped, and five are held for subsequent lynching as a mob seeks the alleged murderer of a white deputy sheriff.

October 6, Georgia: Two black men named Brown and Gordon are burned at the stake by whites.

October 7, Georgia: A black man named Hamilton, sentenced to ten years for assaulting a white farmer, is taken from custody and shot by a mob.

October 9, Donora, Pennsylvania: White strikers hurl bricks at their black replacements, who respond with gunfire.

October 10, Youngstown, Ohio: Two white strikers are shot and wounded by black strike-breakers.

October 31, Corbin, Kentucky: A white mob drives black families out of town.

November 16, Moberly, Missouri: A black murder suspect is lynched by 100 masked men.

November 25, Montgomery, Alabama: Twelve white men are fined on conviction for lynching a black man named Foukal the previous spring.

December 15, West Virginia: Two black men named Whitney and Whitfield are dragged from a train by lynchers and shot to death, their bodies dumped in a nearby river.

December 27, North Carolina: A black man named Green is abducted from jail, dragged through the streets behind a car, and then hanged.

December 29, Kentucky: White soldiers clash with black civilians near Camp Zachary Taylor.

1920

February 17, Ft. Worth, Texas: Pedro Torres, a Mexican youth, is arrested and beaten by police for allegedly stealing two pairs of trousers. Tried as an adult despite the fact that he is underage and speaks no English, Torres is sentenced to five years in state prison.

March 29, Paris, Kentucky: A black prisoner named Smith is abducted from jail and hanged by whites.

April 2, Laurens, South Carolina: A black man named Robertson is lynched.

April 20, Pittsburg, Kansas: Whites lynch an unidentified black man.

April 22, Indianapolis, Indiana: One person is shot and fifteen are arrested when whites try to lynch William Ray, a black accused of rape. Convicted and sentenced to die for his crime, Ray becomes the first person executed in Indiana's electric chair.

May 7, Lakeland, Florida: Henry Scott, a black Pullman porter who asked a white patron to wait while he made up her berth before going to bed is dragged from the train and shot sixty times by a lynch mob. A card left by the body reads: "This is what you get for insulting a white woman."

May 23, Alexandria, Virginia: U.S. troops foil the attempted lynching of black prisoner William Turner.

May 24, Frio County, Texas: Mexican laborer Bernadino Campos is murdered by an Anglo ranch foreman fifteen miles from Pearsall.

June 2, Waukegan, Illinois: Rioting breaks out after white soldiers try to demolish a hotel for blacks.

June 15, Duluth, Minnesota: Three black circus employees—Isaac McGhie, Elmer Jackson, and Nate Green—are lynched on suspicion of rape. Three other blacks are freed by the mob before state police arrive.

June 20, Chicago, Illinois: Two persons die and others are injured during a race riot that erupts after a group of black "Abyssinians" publicly burn the U.S. flag. Two black men are convicted of killing a white who tried to defend the flag, and both are hanged on June 24, 1921.

June 21, Rincon, Georgia: Philip Gathers, a black man, is lynched after confessing to the murder of a white girl.

July 4, Brooklyn, New York: One white man is shot and one black is stabbed during a race riot.

July 5, Mississippi: Whites lynch a black man named Spencer.

July 6, Paris, Texas: Black brothers Irving and Herman Arthur, suspected in a triple murder, are burned alive at the local fairgrounds.

July 7, Roxboro, North Carolina: Black inmate Edward Roach is taken from jail and lynched for rape.

July 8, Centerville, Missouri: A black man named Canafex is shot and killed by whites outside of town.

July 18, Graham, North Carolina: U.S. troops guard three black men accused of rape in the local jail. On July 19, one person is killed and two are wounded when soldiers shoot at would-be lynchers.

August 2, Centre, Texas: A mob wrecks the local jail and lynches a black prisoner named Daniels.

August 16, New York City: Fifty white longshoremen attack a group of twenty-five black strike-breakers.

August 29, Tulsa, Oklahoma: Whites lynch a black man named Belton.

August 30, Oklahoma City, Oklahoma: A black prisoner named Chandler is taken from jail and hanged.

September 3, New York City: White strikers riot against black workers on a local pier.

October 5, MacClenny, Florida: Four blacks accused of killing a local farmer are lynched.

October 14, Greenville, Alabama: A black man named Reid is killed by a mob outside of town.

October 27, Johnson City, Tennessee: Whites lynch Cooksey Dallas, a black man, without apparent motive.

October 27, Newport News, Virginia: Blacks attempt to lynch a white man named Cohen.

November 1, Montgomery, Alabama: Two blacks are killed and twelve are arrested after arsonists burn houses and a local cotton gin.

November 3, Florida: Whites lynch a black man during an election riot.

November 18, Douglas, Georgia: Three blacks, including a woman, are lynched outside of town.

November 23, Tylertown, Mississippi: Harry Jacobs, a black man, is abducted from court during his rape trial and lynched.

November 23, Dewitt, Georgia: Frustrated lynchers execute Curley McKelvey, brother of an elusive black murder suspect.

November 25, Texas: A black defendant named Lowe, twice rescued from lynch mobs, is acquitted of the assault charge that put him in jail.

December 5, Wise, Virginia: One person is killed and several are wounded when would-be lynchers storm the jail to reach a black prisoner. U.S. troops are dispatched to avert further violence.

December 5, Holdenville, Texas: A black prisoner is abducted from jail and hanged by whites.

December 23, Purvis, Mississippi: A black minister named Brown is found hanged. Authorities blame blacks for the murder.

December 26, Jonesboro, Arkansas: A black prisoner named Thomas is abducted from jail and hanged for killing a policeman.

1921

January 16, Jasper, Alabama: Seven National Guardsmen are arrested for the lynching of William Baird, a black man.

January 23, Warrenton, North Carolina: Two black prisoners named Bullock and Williams are dragged from jail and shot by whites in the wake of a race riot.

January 26, Nodena, Arkansas: Henry Lowry, a black charged with killing a white man and his daughter, is abducted from jail and burned at the stake.

January 31, Camilla, Georgia: Jim Roland, a black man, is lynched for firing a pistol at a white man who ordered him to dance at gunpoint.

February 12, Ocala, Florida: A black prisoner is abducted from jail and hanged by whites.

February 15, Clyde, Georgia: The tearful prayers of an intended lynch victim persuade the mob to let him live.

February 16, Ranger, Texas: Mexican workers are beaten by whites.

February 16, Clarke County, Georgia: J.L. Everhardt, a black man, is publicly burned at the stake.

March 11, Springfield, Ohio: Fourteen persons are shot and wounded during a race riot.

March 13, Versailles, Kentucky: Black defendant Richard James is hanged by a mob after jurors fail to reach a verdict in his murder trial.

March 14, Eagle Lake, Florida: William Bowles, a black man, is lynched for making remarks to a white woman.

March 15, Hope, Arkansas: Brownie Tuggles, a black man, is lynched on accusation of rape.

March 16, Lake Cormorant, Mississippi: Howard Hurd, a black railroad brakeman, is lynched after several warnings to quit his job. A note left with the body reads: "Take this as a warning to all nigger railroad men."

March 19, Water Valley, Mississippi: A black man named Ross is abducted from jail and hanged by a mob.

March 20, Hattiesburg, Mississippi: A black prisoner named Jennings is dragged from his cell and hanged.

March 22, Monticello, Arkansas: Whites lynch Phil Slater, a black man, after he confesses to rape.

March 24, Georgia: Jonathan Williams, a white farmer, is charged with murdering eleven blacks in a peonage case. Two more bodies are found at his farm on March 27.

April 2, Dallas, Texas: Klansmen use acid to brand the letters "KKK" on the forehead of Alex Johnson, a black man.

April 4, Langsford, Mississippi: A black man named Thompson is lynched by whites.

April 6, Lakeland, Florida: The local sheriff averts mob violence by swearing in a group of would-be lynchers as his deputies.

April 29, Missouri: A black prisoner named Hammonds is taken from a sheriff's custody and hanged.

May 10, Starke, Florida: Whites lynch a black man named Ballinger.

May 16, McGhee, Arkansas: A black man is lynched for attacking a white couple.

May 18, Georgia: Six blacks are shot and wounded in a race riot.

May 31, Tulsa, Oklahoma: Dick Rowland, a 19-year-old black man, is jailed and charged with attempted rape after he stumbles and falls against Sarah Page, a white 43-year-old divorcee, and steps on her foot. A group of armed black men appears at the jail after it is learned that a lynch mob of white men has gathered there, and a shoot-out results. White civilians then run amok, burning the mile-square black neighborhood. At one point, white men who have been deputized raid a nearby munitions dump for dynamite, commandeer some airplanes, and drop dynamite from the air on the black neighborhood. Twenty-five whites and at least sixty blacks lose their lives. (The director of a civilian burial detail reports that at least 150 blacks are dead.) Blacks who had left the area to avoid the riot are rounded up by local deputies and state militia as they return home and placed in a "camp" where the men, women, and children are separated. The black citizens are allowed to leave the camp to work, but now must carry a "green card" and produce it whenever requested by local law authorities. Thirty whites are charged with looting, and on June 25 a grand jury indicts seven civilians and five policemen–including the chief of police–on criminal charges linked to the riot.

June, Donna, Texas: Mexican Vidal Zamarripa is killed by a U.S. immigration officer. No charges are filed, but the same officer is tried—and acquitted—in early 1922 on charges of murdering Ventura Yanez in Brownsville.

June 11, Hoboken, New Jersey: A black gunman is mobbed and beaten after wounding two persons on a local pier.

June 13, Jersey City, New Jersey: Racial disorders erupt after a white man is stabbed by a black.

June 16, Autreville, Georgia: A black church is burned in retaliation for the unsolved murder of a white girl.

June 18, Moultrie, Georgia: John Williams, a black murderer sentenced to execution, is taken from custody and burned alive by a mob.

June 19, McCormick, South Carolina: A black man named Quarles is forced to climb a tree at gunpoint and is then riddled with bullets.

June 20, Jackson, Mississippi: A black man named Wimberly is hanged outside of town by white vigilantes.

June 23, Jersey City, New Jersey: A race riot erupts from a street fight between two boys.

June 24, Atlantic City, New Jersey: D.D. Murphy, a deranged black preacher, is shot and killed after wounding two persons inside his barricaded home.

July 17, Rayville, Louisiana: Four blacks are killed and one white man is wounded during an outbreak of racial violence.

July 18, Miami, Florida: A masked gang tars and feathers Rev. P.S. Irwin outside of town.

August 3, Lawrenceville, Virginia: A black prisoner is dragged from jail and hanged by whites.

August 7, Detroit, Michigan: A black man is nearly lynched after shooting and wounding two white boys.

August 15, Datura, Texas: Whites lynch Alexander Winn, a black man. On August 16, a second mob raids the funeral home and burns his corpse.

August 16–17, Augusta, Georgia: A race riot leaves at least five people dead. One victim, a black named Smalley, is dragged from his hospital room and burned alive by a lynch mob.

August 17, Abilene, Texas: Armed whites drive local blacks from their jobs.

August 18, Winston-Salem, North Carolina: Jerome Whitfield, a black rape suspect, is lynched by a mob of 2,000 whites. The lynchers ignore protests from Whitfield's alleged victim, declaring him innocent.

August 18, Barnstable, Massachusetts: A mob threatens two black prisoners charged with assaulting a white girl. U.S. troops are sent to protect the jail on August 19.

August 19, Knoxville, Tennessee: Deputies wound twenty-seven persons when a lynch mob storms the jail, intent on killing a black rape suspect.

September 8, Aiken, South Carolina: Two black men are tied to stakes and shot by a white mob.

September 12, North Carolina: Two black female prisoners are flogged by a white mob.

September 14, Montlake, Tennessee: The black population is forcibly driven from town following the shooting of a white girl by a black female assailant.

September 14, Columbia, Louisiana: A black man named Holmes is hanged by white lynchers.

September 21, McComb, Mississippi: A black named McDowell is hanged outside of town.

September 30, Pearl River, New York: White strikers clash with black replacements at a local factory.

October 1, Pinetta, Florida: Ray Newsome, a black man, is shot and killed for "insulting a white girl."

October 1, Lorena, Texas: The local sheriff and eight other persons are injured as violence erupts during a KKK parade. One of the injured, a stabbing victim, dies on October 5.

October 7, Dallas, Texas: A lynch mob is convinced to disperse without harming its chosen black target.

October 10, Leesburg, Texas: A black rape suspect, Wylie McNeely, is abducted from jail and burned alive by a mob of 500.

October 21, Texas: Klansmen abduct two black youths from prison and flog them.

October 23, Orange, New Jersey: A black pedestrian is shot three times when a white patrolman uses him as a human shield in a shoot-out with criminals.

October 24, Appleton, South Carolina: A black man named Kirkland is shot to death and burned by a lynch mob.

October 25, Baltimore, Maryland: One black is killed during a riotous disturbance.

October 27, Enid, Oklahoma: Masked nightriders warn local blacks to leave town.

November 18, Helena, Arkansas: Will Turner, a black charged with rape, is killed and publicly cremated by whites.

November 25, Lake Village, Arkansas: Robert Hicks, a black man, is lynched for allegedly writing a note to a white woman.

December 5, Oconee County, Georgia: Two blacks named Grove and Hale are lynched by a mob. A third victim, named Birdsong, is shot and killed by a vigilante posse.

December 6, Ft. Worth, Texas: Fred Rouse, a black strike-breaker at the local Armour plant, wounds two white strikers in a melee that leaves him hospitalized with a fractured skull. On December 11, Rouse is dragged from his hospital bed and lynched by a gang of thirty men. Three whites are charged with Rouse's murder on February 13, 1922.

December 26, Key West, Florida: A black murder suspect named Head is abducted from jail and lynched.

1922

January 8, Williamsburg County, South Carolina: Whites lynch a black man for having an affair with a white woman. A second black, driving the buggy in which he tried to escape, is shot and wounded by the mob.

January 15, Oklahoma City, Oklahoma: Jake Brooks, a black man, is snatched from his home by a mob. His body is found hanging outside of town on January 17.

January 16, Pearsall, Texas: Manuel Zapata is shot and killed by an Anglo gunman on the street. His slayer, released on $300 bail, is also linked with the previous murders of two Mexicans—Roberto Almos and Gregorio Escamilla—at Encinal.

January 17, Mayo, Florida: A black victim is lynched outside of town.

January 27, Harlingen, Texas: Members of the KKK approach Mexican farmhand Manuel Duarte, threatening him and ordering him to leave town. Authorities advise him to ignore the threats. On February 2 Duarte is assaulted and fired on by Klansmen while working at a local ranch.

January 29, Pontotoc, Mississippi: A black prisoner named Bell is taken from police custody and shot by whites.

February 2, Crystal Springs, Mississippi: Whites hang a black man named Thrasher.

February 13, Texarkana, Texas: A black man named Norman is lynched.

March 15, Pearsall, Texas: Mexican national Miguel Delgado is beaten by Anglos on the street.

March 21, Gulfport, Mississippi: Alex Smith, a black man, is lynched for running a whorehouse that employed white prostitutes.

April 30, Conroe, Texas: A black man named Winters is publicly burned by a lynch mob.

April 30, Allentown, Texas: Mose Bozir, a black man, is hanged outside of town by whites.

May 6, Kirvin, Texas: Three blacks—Mose Jones, John Curry, and "Shap" Curry—are burned at the stake on charges of killing a teenage girl. A fourth black suspect is found dead outside of town on May 7. Two white men are later convicted of the murder of the girl.

May 18, Davisboro, Georgia: Charles Atkins, a black man, is burned alive for murdering a white woman.

May 18, Plantersville, Texas: A black man named Early is hanged by white vigilantes.

May 24, Irwinton, Georgia: A black prisoner named Denson escapes from a lynch mob and is later recaptured by law authorities.

May 24, Bryan, Texas: A black man Wilson is whipped to death by white assailants.

May 26, Waco, Texas: Jesse Thomas, a black man charged with assaulting a white couple and raping the woman, is shot and killed by the father of his alleged victim. A mob publicly burns his body, and U.S. troops are dispatched on May 27 to guard five other blacks in the local jail.

May 29, Brentwood, Georgia: A black named Byrd, accused of murder, is lynched by whites.

June 23, New Dacus, Texas: Black rape suspect Warren Lewis is lynched.

July 1, Lanes Bridge, Georgia: Two black men named Harvey and Jordan are lynched outside of town. Five whites are indicted on September 22, but no convictions result.

July 18, Kissimmee, Florida: A black man named Mack is lynched on charges of killing two white women.

July 28, Guernsey, Arkansas: John West, a black man, is lynched after quarreling with his job foreman over the use of a drinking cup.

August 1, Hot Springs, Arkansas: Whites lynch a black murder suspect.

August 1, Macon, Georgia: A black man named Glover is lynched for killing the sheriff.

August 22, Yazoo City, Mississippi: Parks Banks, a black man, is found hanged outside of town. He has ignored warnings to leave town after verbal disagreements with local KKK leaders.

August 30, Shreveport, Louisiana: A black man named Rivers is lynched.

September 2, Athens, Georgia: J.R. Long, a black man, is hanged by white vigilantes.

December 11, Streetman, Texas: Failing to locate a black rape suspect, a posse lynches his uncle instead. Three blacks, including accused rapist George Gay, have been burned by mobs in Streetman during the previous three months.

December 14, Perry, Florida: Black prisoner Charles Wright, accused of killing a schoolteacher, is publicly burned by a mob.

December 28, Pilot Point, Texas: Two blacks suspected of stealing horses are snatched from jail and lynched. It is the second double-lynching of blacks in Pilot Point in recent months.

1923

January 1, Sapulpa, Oklahoma: One patrolman is killed and four are wounded in an ambush by black gunmen. A "dead line" is established to avert rioting. Black suspect W.M. Ragsdale is killed by vigilantes in Muskogee while en route to Sapulpa for arraignment on murder charges.

January 3, Shreveport, Louisiana: Leslie Legget is abducted from town and shot by a masked gang, on the accusation of "associating with white women." Investigation proves the victim was, in fact, a dark-skinned Caucasian.

January 5–7, Rosewood, Florida: The search for black escaped convict Jesse Hunter—charged with attacking a girl, killing two white men, and wounding four—erupts into general rioting when the fugitive evades capture. Several black homes are burned to the ground, and at least one innocent black man is shot by the mob.

January 11, Lillington, North Carolina: Klansman Mark Moore is sentenced to eleven months in jail for threatening critics of the KKK.

January 19, New Orleans, Louisiana: Police raid the offices of the United Negro Improvement Association, finding evidence of a "nationwide anarchist plot," reportedly linked to the recent murder of a black minister, Rev. J.W.H. Eason.

January 20, Blanford, Indiana: White miners begin driving blacks from the area after an attack on a young girl. All blacks have reportedly fled by January 25. On January 29, miners kill three persons and fire on a sheriff investigating reports of assaults on blacks.

February, Milledgeville, Georgia: A white grocer is accidentally shot and killed by police while chasing two black shoplifters. The blacks are later abducted from jail and lynched, with pieces of their bodies publicly displayed in town.

February 3, Milledgeville, Georgia: Two black robbery suspects are lynched after wounding a member of the arresting posse.

February 9, Baltimore, Maryland: An attempt is made to burn the local KKK headquarters.

February 15, Perry, Florida: Albert Young, a black man named as Charles Wright's accomplice in killing a white teacher, is ambushed and lynched while in transit to a safer jail.

February 27, Pawnee County, Oklahoma: Authorities jail twenty-two Klan nightriders for terrorizing local citizens.

April 1, Pittsburgh, Pennsylvania: Sixteen Klansmen are physically ejected from Bellevue Methodist Episcopal Church and have their masks and robes torn off by hecklers.

April 7, Chicago, Illinois: A bomb wrecks the publication office of *Dawn,* the KKK's national newsletter.

April 16, Pittsburgh, Pennsylvania: Sixteen persons are arrested during a race riot.

April 28, Columbia, Missouri: A mob that includes students from the University of Missouri lynches black janitor James Scott, who is accused of raping a professor's young daughter. When the professor tries to stop the lynching, he is driven away by the mob, with several members shouting, "Hang him, too!"

May 1, Bound Brook, New Jersey: A mob of 100 persons surrounds and threatens a church where Holy Rollers are meeting to form a new KKK chapter. Two persons are jailed as disorder erupts.

May 2, New Brunswick, New Jersey: Hecklers are threatened with guns at a Klan rally.

May 7, Atlanta, Georgia: White civilians clash with black railroad workers.

May 24, Irwinton, Georgia: A black prisoner under sentence of death escapes from a lynch mob, but is soon recaptured and returned to prison.

May 26, Texas: A white man shoots and kills a black accused of molesting his daughter.

June 4, Perth Amboy, New Jersey: A mixed group of blacks and whites physically disrupts a KKK meeting.

June 6, Plainfield, New Jersey: A Klan meeting is stoned by opponents.

June 12, Palm Beach Island, Florida: Henry Simmons, a black man, is lynched for publicly criticizing the treatment of blacks in the United States.

June 14, Bloomfield, New Jersey: A near-riot is averted after Klan participants in a Flag Day parade are pelted with eggs.

June 18, Holyoke, Massachusetts: Police use clubs against would-be lynchers, rescuing two blacks accused of insulting white girls.

June 19, Phoenix, Arizona: Two Klansmen are indicted for abducting and flogging Ira Haywood, a black man.

June 19, Savannah, Georgia: One person is killed and three are injured while storming the jail in an effort to lynch a black prisoner. Martial law is declared on June 20.

June 24, Long Branch, New Jersey: Three Klansmen are beaten during a street parade, with their attacker jailed for assault.

July 3, Bronson, Florida: Unable to locate a black rape suspect, lynchers vent their anger by shooting his father, Samuel Carter, instead.

July 4, Schulenberg, Texas: A black man named Bullock, accused of attacking a white girl, is taken from the marshal's custody and hanged by a mob.

July 8, Hackensack, New Jersey: A racial battle in the local shipyard leaves one person dead and eight in jail.

July 29, Macon, Georgia: Riots break out after a white deputy is shot and killed by a black man.

July 29, Yazoo City, Mississippi: Willie Minnifield, a black prisoner charged with axing a white woman to death, is publicly burned at the stake. By August 6, authorities estimate that 10,000 blacks have fled the area to escape further violence.

August 4, Iowa: An unidentified black is mobbed and beaten by 800 whites.

August 16, Steubenville, Ohio: One hundred Klansmen are mobbed by anti-Klan protestors, resulting in seven arrests and numerous injuries.

August 25, Jacksonville, Florida: Len Hart, a black "peeping tom," is shot and killed by white vigilantes.

August 25, Carnegie, Pennsylvania: One Klansman is shot to death and numerous persons are injured when an anti-Klan group attacks a KKK parade.

August 30, Perth Amboy, New Jersey: Police and firemen are overrun during an anti-Klan riot.

August 31, Johnstown, Pennsylvania: After a black riot leaves several policemen dead or injured, the mayor orders the expulsion of all blacks and Mexicans who have lived in Johnstown for less than seven years.

August 31, New Castle, Delaware: Five persons are shot when a KKK rally erupts into violence.

September 11, South Bend, Indiana: Blacks are reported fleeing the area after anonymous threats from whites.

September 18, Jackson, Mississippi: A lynch mob seizes and kills John Gray, a black man charged with shooting a local doctor.

September 27, Spruce Pine, North Carolina: Blacks are forced to leave en masse after an unsolved attack on a white woman.

October 10, Stowe Township, Pennsylvania: Blacks reportedly flee the area following the murder of a white man and the rape of a white girl.

October 13, Virginia: A black man named Carter, arrested on charges of attacking a white woman, is ambushed and shot on the way to jail.

October 24, Kansas City, Missouri: A mob stones a newly opened store of the KKK.

November 3, Eufala, Oklahoma: Dallas Sewell, a black man, is abducted by robed Klansmen and carried to the barn of a prominent KKK member, where he is "tried" and hanged from the rafters on charges of "passing for white and associating with white women."

November 5, New York City: Police stop the lynching of a black man who publicly kissed a white woman.

November 9, Springfield, Ohio: Thirty-two whites are arrested for assaulting police guards at a newly integrated school.

November 11, Weslaco, Texas: Mexican Elias Zarate is abducted from jail and lynched following his arrest for fighting with an Anglo.

November 15, Breckenridge, Texas: Blacks flee town en masse following threats of violence from the white community.

November 18, Texas: A national newspaper reports that "the killing of Mexicans without provocation is so common as to pass almost unnoticed" in the state.

December 18, Oklahoma: A.W. Birch, a black man, is killed for defending another black against would-be lynchers.

December 31, Florida: Two black men named Burman and Phillips are lynched.

1924

March 21, Long Island, New York: Dynamite planted under several burning crosses injures participants at a KKK rally.

April 3, Georgia: A black youth named Thrash, arrested on a charge of theft, is lynched after shooting the local police chief.

April 5, Lilly, Pennsylvania: Four persons are killed and at least thirteen are injured in a riot between Klansmen and anti-Klan demonstrators. On July 1, twenty-eight rioters are sentenced to jail terms of two years each.

April 21, South Carolina: Whites lynch a black rape suspect named Adams.

May 14, New York City: A black man named Walton is threatened with mob violence for allegedly attacking a white girl.

May 26, Florida: Whites lynch black prisoners named Williams and Wilson.

June 17, Leesville, Louisiana: One black is killed and numerous others are injured during an outbreak of racial rioting.

June 30, Berkeley, Michigan: Rev. Oren Van Loon is abducted from home. He is found delirious, near Battle Creek, on July 12, with the letters "KKK" branded on his back.

July 5, Binghamton, New York: Violent disturbances are recorded during a KKK meeting.

July 8, Darby, Pennsylvania: A policeman is fired for taking part in a KKK raid against an all-black Boy Scout camp.

July 19, Meridian, Mississippi: Whites lynch a black woman named Sheldon.

July 29, Massachusetts: Numerous persons are injured in anti-Klan riots in Lancaster and Spencer.

July 30, Haverhill, Massachusetts: Three persons are shot when a KKK rally erupts into violence. Thirteen of the rioters are convicted and sentenced to jail on August 18.

August 5, Blackstone, Massachusetts: A newsman is abducted and branded by KKK members.

August 8, Fairmont, West Virginia: Seven Klansmen, including a minister, are charged with conspiracy in the recent shooting of Rev. Daniel Washington. Three of the defendants are sentenced to prison on October 27.

August 11, Paxton, Illinois: Ralph Aaron, a Jew, is abducted by nightriders and branded with the letters "KKK."

August 16, Burlington, Vermont: Klansman W.C. Moyers is sought by police for looting a Roman Catholic church. He is captured in Tennessee on August 20.

October 9, Chicago, Illinois: William Bell, a black man, is beaten to death for accosting white girls on the street. Authorities believe him innocent of any crime.

October 11, Oakland, Michigan: A Roman Catholic seminary is terrorized by burning crosses and bomb explosions nearby.

October 18, Worcester, Massachusetts: Rioting breaks out during an anti-Klan protest.

October 21, Detroit, Michigan: A tear gas bomb scatters participants in an anti-Klan rally.

October 29, Niles, Ohio: The mayor's home is wrecked by a bomb after he denies the KKK a parade permit. Twelve persons are injured during a riot on November 1 between Klansmen and opponents, and a cache of weapons is seized at a KKK rally on November 4. On December 5, 105 persons are indicted for their participation in the November 1 riots, with ten defendants pleading guilty and accepting fines on March 25, 1925.

November 2, Henryetta, Oklahoma: Parading Klansmen are routed by angry miners.

November 6, Ft. Worth, Texas: The local KKK headquarters is damaged by arsonists.

November 10, Harrodsburg, Kentucky: Black workers on a local electric dam are threatened after the murder of a white man.

December 15, Nashville, Tennessee: A fifteen-year-old black boy named Smith is dragged from his hospital bed and lynched on charges of killing a white man.

December 18, Charleston, Missouri: A black man named Grigsby, charged with attacking a white girl, is hanged, shot, and dragged through the streets behind a car.

1925

Detroit, Michigan: A white mob stones the home of Dr. Alex Turner, a black physician, forcing him to flee the neighborhood.

Cleveland, Ohio: A mob tries to force Dr. Charles Garvin from his new home in a white section of town.

January 19, Chicago, Illinois: Bombers damage a synagogue recently sold to blacks.

February 15, Orange, Texas: Three white men are killed and two blacks are arrested after a business quarrel erupts into violence.

February 26, Benton, Louisiana: A black murder suspect named Airy is lynched.

March 20, Waverly, Virginia: Whites lynch a black rape suspect.

April 28, Northbridge, Massachusetts: Hostile crowds besiege and menace a KKK rally.

May 3, Berlin, Massachusetts: Klansmen and anti-Klan protestors clash at a rally.

May 3, Gardner, Massachusetts: The leader of a KKK parade is hurt by flying stones.

May 14, Longwood, Florida: A black rape suspect named West is dragged from a train and lynched outside of town.

May 19, Northbridge, Massachusetts: Riotous violence erupts at a KKK rally.

May 21, Dallas, Texas: One hundred persons are arrested for trying to lynch two black brothers charged with murder and criminal assault.

May 23, Pensacola, Florida: Five whites are convicted of flogging blacks and holding their victims in peonage.

May 30, South Carolina: Four whites are sentenced to prison in a peonage case.

June 11, Burlington, Massachusetts: Two persons are arrested when a KKK rally erupts into violence.

June 18, Salt Lake City, Utah: Whites lynch a black cop-killer named Marshall.

June 19, Newark, New Jersey: A fight between two boys sparks interracial rioting, and fifteen people are arrested.

June 20, Clinton, Massachusetts: Thirty-eight persons are held over for grand jury action following an anti-Klan riot.

July 22, Pittsburgh, Pennsylvania: Police suppress a race riot.

August 2, Westwood, Massachusetts: Three Klansmen are arrested for rioting after a KKK rally.

August 7, Excelsior Springs, Missouri: A black prisoner named Mitchell is lynched for attacking a white girl.

August 10, Framingham, Massachusetts: Five men are shot from ambush after a KKK meeting. A mob threatens the jail where sixteen Klansmen are being held on assault charges.

August 12, Reading, Massachusetts: Rioting breaks out at a Klan rally outside of town.

August 12, Mississippi: An insane black man named Towns is taken from prison and shot to death for killing a white man and woman.

August 18, Baltimore, Maryland: Samuel Krayer, a white man, is mobbed for allowing blacks to lease a home in a "white" district.

August 22, Long Island City, New York: A mob stones a carload of Klansmen whose vehicle has stalled on their way home from a rally in Freeport.

September 18, North Brookfield, Massachusetts: Two persons are jailed after a Klan riot.

September 20, New Albany, Mississippi: L.Q. Ivy, a black man, is burned at the stake after confessing to the rape of a white girl.

September 21, Asheville, North Carolina: A mob storms the local jail in an unsuccessful effort to lynch a black rape suspect.

December 19, Clarksdale, Mississippi: Whites lynch Lindsay Coleman, a black murder suspect, moments after his acquittal by a jury.

1926

Cleveland, Ohio: A bomb damages the home of Dr. Charles Garvin, who resides in what was formerly a "white" neighborhood.

February 1, Lexington, Kentucky: Soldiers fortify the courthouse to prevent mob violence during the rape trial of Ed Harris, a black man.

Sentenced to die on the basis of his confession, the execution is carried out on March 5.

February 7–8, Georgetown, Delaware: National Guardsmen use tear gas to scatter lynch mobs during the eight-minute long trial of Harry Butler, a black charged with raping a twelve-year-old white girl. Sentenced to die, Butler is hanged on February 26.

March 10, Royston, Georgia: Walton Adams is killed and Herman Bigby is fatally wounded during a KKK attack on Bigby's home.

April 22, Poplarville, Mississippi: A black prisoner named Jackson, charged with two murders, is taken from jail and forced to hang himself.

April 25, Carteret, New Jersey: One white man is killed and another is wounded during a clash with six blacks. On April 26 a white mob sets fire to a black church and drives 100 black families out of town in revenge.

June 2, Osceola, Arkansas: Albert Blades, a black man, is lynched on charges of raping a white girl. Subsequent medical examination of the "victim" proves that no rape occurred.

June 27, Beverly, New Jersey: State police are called to break up street fighting between blacks and whites.

August 15, Wytheville, Virginia: A masked gang storms the jail and kills Raymond Bird, a black rape suspect.

August 30, Coffee County, Georgia: Dave Wright, a black man charged with killing a white woman, is taken from jail and lynched. One of the lynchers is sentenced to life on February 4, 1927.

September 11, Charlotte, North Carolina: A police riot squad curbs a violent demonstration by blacks angered by mass baptisms conducted by Rev. B. Grace.

October 8, Aiken, South Carolina: A mob enters the jail and shoots three blacks suspected of killing the local sheriff. One victim, Demon Lowman, has already been acquitted by a jury. The other two, his sister and cousin, are believed to have been innocent.

November 2, Marinette, Wisconsin: Six men are convicted of inciting a riot at a June 1925 KKK rally.

December 16, Media, Pennsylvania: Three black prisoners are removed to a safer jail after threats of lynching.

December 19, Mississippi: A black man named Coleman is lynched after jurors acquit him of killing a white storekeeper. Five days later, the sheriff is indicted on misdemeanor charges for permitting the violence.

1927

Indiana: Bus driver Glen Branoski, assigned to the Indianapolis-Cincinnati run, is sentenced to twenty days in jail and a $50 fine for assaulting a black woman on his bus while attempting to enforce his own personal Jim Crow law.

Coffeeville, Kansas: Armed blacks dig trenches to bar white mobs from the local ghetto and prevent the lynching of a black rape suspect. Two days of fighting leave ten white men dead and thirteen persons wounded before National Guardsmen arrive to restore order.

March 2, Miami, Florida: Four patrolmen shoot and kill a black man named Kier. Critics of the police department accuse Police Chief H.L. Quigg of secretly approving the execution-style slaying. A year later, on March 24, 1928, Quigg and eight patrolmen are indicted for the murder of Kier.

March 9, Mobile, Alabama: Attorney Clarence Darrow is menaced by a mob and escorted out of town under guard, after giving a public speech against lynching.

May 4, Little Rock, Arkansas: Jonathan Carter, a black man, is burned alive after confessing to the rape-murder of an eleven-year-old white girl. Thousands of blacks flee the community after the lynching.

May 20, Macon, Mississippi: Dan Anderson, a black man, is taken from police custody and executed by a "firing squad" for killing a white man.

May 23, Braggadocio, Mississippi: Whites lynch Will Sherod, a black man accused of raping a white woman.

May 30–June 1, Tampa, Florida: Four persons are killed and thirty-three are wounded during three days of rioting, after National Guardsmen prevent the lynching B.F. Levins, a black man charged with the massacre of a white family.

May 31, Queens, New York: Klansmen battle police after they are ordered to withdraw from a Memorial Day parade.

June 2, Boyce, Louisiana: Whites hang David and Lee Blackman, the brothers of a black who had been recently shot by police after murdering a white man.

June 13, Louisville, Mississippi: Black brothers Jim and Mark Fox are burned alive on charges of killing their white foreman at work.

June 17, Paris, Tennessee: Joseph Upchurch, a black suspected of killing the local sheriff, is executed by a white posse.

June 20, Houston, Texas: A black murder suspect, Robert Powell, is dragged from his hospital bed and hanged by whites.

June 27, Beaufort, South Carolina: National Guardsmen protect seven black prisoners charged with killing a white woman.

June 27, Hickory Grove, South Carolina: U.S. troops are dispatched to protect the black community from violence after a series of attacks on white women.

June 29, Brookhaven, Mississippi: Vigilantes execute two blacks charged with attacking white men.

June 29, Queens, New York: Police rescue a black man from would-be lynchers.

July 2, Mississippi: Whites lynch "Shug" McEllee, a black jail inmate.

July 22–23, New York City: Twenty-five hundred blacks clash with 150 police in a riot in Harlem sparked by the arrest of a black man. Violence continues the following day, with one officer stabbed.

July 24, Grand Prairie, Texas: Rioting erupts during a KKK march.

August 15, New York City: A black man is stabbed by a white during an argument over a ball game.

August 25, Virginia: One Klansman is killed when nightriders attack the home of C.W. Wilson during a "morality" raid.

September 3, Geneva, New York: A Klan parade is marked by rioting.

September 10, Jefferson County, Alabama: J.L. Bolton is flogged by Klansmen, and his home is burned to the ground.

September 11, Berlin, Maryland: Police are called to quell a race riot.

November 11, Columbia, Tennessee: Henry Choate, a black rape suspect, is hanged from the courthouse balcony by a lynch mob.

November 30, Kentucky-Virginia border: A black named Woods, charged with killing a white man, is abducted from jail and murdered.

1928

Authorities report a total of nine blacks lynched during the year.

1929

Gastonia, North Carolina: Police attack a group of integrated strikers at a local textile mill. The police chief and three officers are killed, with seventy-one strikers beaten and jailed, fifteen of whom will face murder charges.

Lincoln, Nebraska: In the wake of a policeman's shooting, white rioters drive 200 blacks out of town.

Chicago, Illinois: Claude Green, a disciple of cult leader Noble Drew Ali, is shot and killed by gunmen from the rival Moorish Temple of America. Police battle with members of the Moorish Temple. One policeman and one cultist die before the cultists surrender.

March 17, Mayflower, Massachusetts: Sen. Tom Heflin is pelted with mud and stones while delivering a speech on behalf of the KKK.

March 18, Brockton, Massachusetts: A policeman is injured when a heckler throws a bottle at Sen. Tom Heflin's car following a pro-Klan address.

April 20, Missouri: Fred Allen, a black man accused of robbing homes and assaulting two housewives, is abducted from jail by a mob, flogged, and then returned to police custody.

May 17, Lake City, Florida: N.G. Romey, a black man jailed after a fight with police that left his wife dead, is dragged from his cell and executed by a vigilante firing squad.

May 29, Alamo, Tennessee: A teenage black is lynched by whites.

June 23, New York City: Seven persons are injured and eight are arrested after members of the Garvey Club and the UNIA clash over the use of a meeting hall.

July 3, Detroit, Michigan: Voodoo cultist Benjamino Evangelista, his wife, and four children are found dead in their home, their bodies savagely mutilated. Evangelista's body is propped upright at a desk, his severed head beside him on the floor. The case remains unsolved.

July 13, North Platte, Nebraska: Blacks flee the area as white mobs gather in response to a policeman's murder.

July 14, Princess Anne, Maryland: Rioting erupts, with blacks and whites clashing in the streets. Three hundred blacks flee the town to escape further violence.

July 22, Eufala, Alabama: National Guardsmen are deployed to protect Lester Bouyer, a black jailed on charges of killing a white man and raping his victim's girlfriend.

August 11, New York City: Blacks and whites clash in a riot on East 100th Street.

August 21, New York City: Police quell a riot in Harlem between Puerto Ricans and Southern blacks.

August 23, Baltimore, Maryland: Twenty people are injured in racial street fighting.

November 28, Colorado: Investigation of a riot at the state prison reveals that white inmates have organized a KKK chapter.

1930

Detroit, Michigan: W.D. Fard founds the Black Muslim religion, which is based on doctrines of black separatism and the inherent evil of white "devils." Ironically, some students of the movement believe that Fard—who vanished without a trace in 1934—may actually have been a dark-skinned Caucasian.

January 1, Gadsden County, Florida: A black accused of rape is smuggled out of jail to avoid a lynch mob.

January 1, Alexandria, Virginia: National Guard units are deployed to prevent the lynching of a black man charged with killing a patrolman.

January 6, Vicksburg, Mississippi: Three blacks charged with wounding a policeman are removed from town to avoid lynchers.

January 9, Wallace, North Carolina: A black murder suspect is transferred from jail to avoid lynching.

January 23, Evansville, Indiana: A black murder suspect is removed from jail after threats of lynching.

January 28, Bolivar, Tennessee: Force is used to repel a mob bent on lynching a black accused of rape.

February 1, Ocilla, Georgia: James Irwin, a black accused of killing a white girl, is tortured, mutilated, and burned alive by a lynch mob.

February 20, Laurel, Mississippi: A black accused of rape is transferred to another jail after threats of lynching.

February 20, Bolivar, Tennessee: A black murder suspect is removed from jail to avert lynching.

March 4, New Orleans, Louisiana: One person dies in a Mardi Gras riot between white sailors and black civilians.

March 23, Devall Bluff, Arkansas: Officers transfer a black prisoner, accused of attempted rape, to distant a jail after threats of mob action.

April, Union City, Tennessee: National Guardsmen are called to protect a black accused of rape from lynchers.

April 2, Troy, Alabama: Force is used to repel a lynch mob seeking to hang a black accused of rape.

April 5, Luverne, Alabama: A black man accused of wounding a white boy is removed to a distant jail after threats of lynching.

April 8, LaGrange, Georgia: A black man charged with attempted rape is removed from jail to avoid lynching.

April 21, Blountstown, Florida: A black prisoner charged with killing a policeman is spirited out of jail to escape lynchers.

April 23, Waxhall, Mississippi: Dave Harris, a black murder suspect, is captured and shot more than 200 times by a white mob.

April 24, Walhalla, South Carolina: A mob of 200 whites invades the county jail, clubs the sheriff unconscious, and abducts Allen Green, a black man charged with raping a white woman. Green is driven into the countryside, tied to a tree, and shot to death. Seventeen whites are indicted for the lynching, but all are acquitted. In October 1932, one of the defendants publicly confesses his role in leading the mob.

April 27, Sylvania, Georgia: A black inmate accused of attempted rape is transferred to another jail after threats of lynching.

May 9, Sherman, Texas: A white mob scatters militiamen and torches the courthouse, killing George Hughes, a black prisoner charged with raping a white woman. The jail vault is blasted open and Hughes's body is dragged through the streets before public cremation. Rioters afterward burn down the black business district. On May 10 another mob sets on fire three blocks of homes owned by blacks.

May 16, Honey Grove, Texas: After fatally wounding his white employer, Sam Johnson, a black man, is shot and killed by police. A mob seizes his corpse and drags it through the streets in celebration.

May 18, Graniteville, South Carolina: Two blacks charged with rape are removed from jail to escape lynchers.

May 22, Granbury, Texas: A black prisoner charged with wounding a man is removed from jail to avert lynching.

May 31, Chickasha, Oklahoma: Henry Argo, a black accused of rape, is shot and stabbed to death in his jail cell by lynchers.

June 10, Edgefield, South Carolina: A black accused of rape is smuggled out of jail to avoid mob action.

June 17, Bryan, Texas: Will Roan, a black accused of trying to rape a white woman, is abducted and shot to death. His body is discovered two days later.

June 21, Santuc, South Carolina: Dan Jenkins, a black accused of raping one white woman and attempting to rape another, is shot to death by a mob of 150 whites.

June 27, Port Arthur, Texas: A black accused of rape is moved to a more secure jail in the face of lynching threats.

June 28, Concord, North Carolina: National Guardsmen are called to protect seven blacks accused of rape from a white lynch mob.

July 4–5, Emelle, Alabama: Grover Boyd, a white planter, is killed by members of the Robinson family, who are black, in an altercation over a secondhand car battery. A white mob retaliates by raiding the Robinson home and hanging Esau Robinson and shooting John Robinson to death before burning the house. A member of the mob, Charlie Marrs, is accidentally shot to death by fellow lynchers at the same time. Members of a posse kill black suspect Winston Jones on July 5 at nearby Narkeeta, Mississippi. Viola Dial, a black woman, is killed when white vigilantes fire on her car near the Mississippi border.

July 13, Erick, Oklahoma: White mobs drive black families from their homes in retaliation for a white woman's murder.

July 14, Shamrock, Texas: A black murder suspect is removed from jail to avoid a lynch mob.

July 29, Ailey, Georgia: S.S. Mincey, an elderly black man active in the Republican party, is abducted and beaten by masked whites. He dies of head injuries on July 30.

August 7, Marion, Indiana: Tom Shipp and Abe Smith, two blacks accused of killing a white man and raping his girlfriend, are abducted from jail and lynched.

August 15, Dublin, Georgia: Officers used force to prevent a mob from lynching a black man involved in a traffic accident.

August 15, Raymond, Mississippi: George Robinson, a black accused of resisting arrest, is shot and killed by lynchers.

August 19, Tarboro, North Carolina: Oliver Moore, a black man accused of trying to rape two white girls, is abducted from jail, hanged, and shot at the scene of the crime.

September, Pueblo, Colorado: Three black men charged with rape are smuggled out of town to avoid being lynched.

September, Lawrenceburg, Tennessee: A black rape suspect is removed from jail to avoid mob action.

September 8, Darien, Georgia: George Grant, a black man accused of killing the local police chief, is shot to death in his cell while under the "protection" of National Guardsmen. A second black suspect, Willie Bryan, is killed by a white posse.

September 10, Scooba, Mississippi: Two blacks, Pigg Lockett and Holly White, are taken from custody and hanged on an accusation of robbing white tourists.

September 15, Cartersville, Georgia: Armed force is used to repel a mob bent on lynching Willie Clark, a black accused of killing the local police chief. No resistance is offered on October 1, however, when a second mob invades the jail and carries Clark to the fairgrounds and hangs him.

September 25, Thomasville, Georgia: Willie Kirkland, a black man accused of attempting to rape a white girl, is taken from custody and shot by a mob. His body is then dragged through the business district of town.

September 25, Helena, Arkansas: A black accused of attempted rape is removed to a distant jail after lynching threats.

September 28, Thomas County, Georgia: Lacy Mitchell, a black prosecution witness against two white men charged with raping a black woman, is shot and killed at his rural home.

September 29, Huntsville, Alabama: National Guardsmen are deployed to prevent the lynching of two blacks charged with murder.

October 1, Centersville, Georgia: John Clark, a black man, is lynched by whites.

October 15, St. Genevieve, Missouri: Three black murder suspects, one of whom is a woman, are removed from jail after threats of lynching.

October 20, Waycross, Georgia: A black man and woman suspected of murder are removed from jail after threats of lynching.

October 20, Clarksdale, Mississippi: National Guardsmen are deployed to protect a black accused of rape from lynchers.

October 22, Mobile, Alabama: A black accused of murder is moved to a distant jail after threats of lynching.

December 7, Pawnee, Oklahoma: Force is used to prevent the lynching of a black accused of murder.

December 7, Arlington, Texas: A black murder suspect is smuggled out of jail to avoid lynchers.

1931

January, Bucyrus, Ohio: National Guardsmen are called to prevent the lynching of three black murder suspects.

January 2, Quitman, Mississippi: A black murder suspect is removed from jail to escape lynching.

January 5, Lexington, South Carolina: Threats of mob action force the removal of a black murder suspect from jail.

January 12, Maryville, Missouri: Raymond Gunn, a black man charged with the rape and murder of a teacher in the local schoolhouse, is abducted from jail by a mob and carried to the scene of the crime. Chained to the rooftree, he dies when the building is burned down.

January 14, West Chester, Pennsylvania: National Guard units are called to prevent the lynching of a black accused of murder.

January 18, Shreveport, Louisiana: National Guardsmen are deployed to protect a black murder suspect from lynch mobs.

January 18, Anderson, South Carolina: A black murder suspect is removed from jail after lynching threats.

January 20, Mayfield, Kentucky: Two blacks accused of robbery are removed from jail to avoid lynching.

January 20, Lexington, South Carolina: National Guardsmen are called to prevent the lynching of six black murder suspects.

January 21, Hopkinsville, Kentucky: Force is used to repel a lynch mob after a black man is accused of murder.

January 26, Bogalusa, Louisiana: A black murder suspect is removed from jail after lynching threats.

January 31, Mt. Pleasant, Texas: National Guard units are summoned to protect a black murder suspect from lynchers.

February, Los Angeles, California: Authorities begin their task of "getting Mexicans off relief" by forcibly "repatriating" Hispanics to Mexico. Mexicans are rounded up in groups and placed aboard southbound trains, with 11,000 making the trip in 1932. By 1936 it is estimated that over 150,000 Mexicans have been "repatriated," some without regard to their nation of birth.

February 2, Rome, Georgia: A black accused of murder is smuggled out of jail to avoid lynchers.

February 24, Ocean Springs, Mississippi: A black rape suspect is removed from jail to escape lynchers.

March, Poplar Bluff, Missouri: A black prisoner charged with attempted rape is smuggled out of town to avoid lynching.

March, Southport, North Carolina: A black accused of rape is removed from jail to escape lynchers.

March 12, Caddo Parish, Louisiana: A black prisoner charged with rape is smuggled out of town to avoid lynchers.

March 17, Marshall, Texas: National Guardsmen are called to prevent the lynching of a black accused of rape.

March 21, Cassia, Florida: Lynching threats force the removal of a black murder suspect from the local jail.

March 22, Inverness, Mississippi: Steve Wiley, a black charged with attempted assault, is taken from jail and hanged by a mob.

March 25, Scottsboro, Alabama: National Guardsmen protect nine black youths accused of rape from a white lynch mob and convicted by an all-white jury. The case was ordered retired by an appeals court. Even though the two "victims" repudiated the charges before the retrial, an all-white jury again found the youths guilty.

March 25, Ocala, Florida: A black accused of rape is smuggled from jail to avoid lynchers.

March 29, Vicksburg, Mississippi: Eli Johnson, a black man accused of attacking a white woman, is shot and killed by a vigilante firing squad.

April 5, Campbell County, Georgia: A black prisoner charged with murder is removed from jail to prevent a threatened lynching.

April 17, Union City, Tennessee: George Smith, a black accused of attempting to rape a white girl, is lynched in jail by a mob of several hundred persons.

April 19, Trenton, Tennessee: A black murder suspect is transferred to another jail after being threatened with lynching.

April 20, Hickman, Kentucky: A black accused of rape is removed from jail to avoid lynchers.

April 28, Elizabethtown, Kentucky: Force is used to repel a white mob bent on lynching a black accused of murder.

April 30, Mobile, Alabama: Force is used to repel a white mob attempting to lynch a black man accused of rape.

May 6, Water Valley, Mississippi: Force is used against a white mob bent on lynching a black accused of murder.

May 19, Elberton, Georgia: National Guardsmen are called to protect six blacks accused of rape from a lynch mob.

June 25, Wetonja, Oklahoma: National Guardsman are deployed to prevent the lynching of a black murder suspect.

July 8, Anderson, Indiana: Two blacks, charged with murder and robbery, are removed from jail to escape lynchers.

July 17, Camp Hill, Alabama: Violence erupts from black protests over recent verdicts in the Scottsboro "rape" case. One black is killed and five persons are injured, and seventeen people are arrested. Rioting whites retaliate by burning the home of a black family.

July 21, Springfield, Tennessee: Force is used to prevent the lynching of a black prisoner charged with wounding a policeman.

July 22, Hampton, South Carolina: Force is used to prevent the lynching of a black prisoner charged with wounding a white man.

August 2, Point a La Hache, Louisiana: Oscar Livingston, a black accused of rape, is abducted from jail by a white mob and shot to death.

August 5, Hayneville, Alabama: Neal Guinn, a black man suspected of attempted rape, is captured by a citizens' posse and shot thirty-two times.

August 10, Pine Bluff, Arkansas: A black man accused of firing at a picnic party is removed from jail and hidden after threats of lynching.

August 17, Conroe, Texas: National Guardsmen are deployed to prevent the lynching of two black murder suspects.

August 18, Quitman, Mississippi: A black prisoner charged with robbery and wounding a man is removed from jail to avoid mob action.

August 20, Douglas, Georgia: A black murder suspect is removed from jail to avoid lynchers.

August 20, Pittsburgh, Pennsylvania: Rioting breaks out after white toughs assault black picnickers.

August 27, East Felicia Parish, Louisiana: A black murder suspect is smuggled out of town to escape lynching.

August 28, Blountstown, Florida: Richard and Charles Smoke, a black father and son free on bond from charges of attacking a forest ranger, are shot to death by a white mob.

September 7, Anoka, Minnesota: A black man accused of attacking a girl is removed from jail to escape a lynch mob.

September 12, McGhee, Arkansas: A black accused of murder is transferred to a distant jail in response to lynching threats.

September 12, Honolulu, Hawaii: Thalia Massie, wife of a navy officer, accuses five native men of rape. In the absence of solid evidence, the five are acquitted in December, a verdict that sparks two days of white rioting on December 13 and 14. A few days later, one former suspect, Horace Ida, is abducted and whipped by sailors seeking to force his confession. A short time later, former suspect Joe Kahahawi is abducted by Thomas Massie, two enlisted men, and Thalia Massie's mother. Kahahawi is "accidentally" shot to death when he refuses to confess. On May 4, 1932, the four killers are sentenced to ten years each, but their sentences are commuted to one hour spent in the office of Gov. Laurence Judd.

September 14, Lockhart, South Carolina: Force is used to repel a white mob bent on lynching a black accused of murder.

October 1, Greensboro, North Carolina: A black murder suspect is spirited out of town to avoid lynching.

October 13, Snow Hill, Maryland: A black prisoner accused of murder is smuggled out of town to avoid lynching. On November 5 the suspect's three white lawyers are driven from town after being threatened.

October 22, Liberty, Mississippi: Force is used to protect a black murder suspect from lynchers.

November 6, Columbus, Mississippi: A white mob invades the local convict camp and lynches Coleman Franks, a black prisoner accused of wounding a white man during an argument.

November 8, Greenville, Texas: A black rape suspect is removed from jail after lynching threats.

November 15, York, South Carolina: Three black prisoners are smuggled out of town following threats of mob action.

December 4, Salisbury, Maryland: Mack Williams, a black accused of killing his employer, is taken from his hospital room by a mob of 2,000, who hang him outside the courthouse and then cremate his body.

December 10, Lewisburg, West Virginia: Tom Jackson and George Banks, black men charged with killing two white constables, are abducted from jail and hanged by a mob, their bodies then riddled with bullets.

December 26, Richmond, Kentucky: A black murder suspect is smuggled from jail to avoid lynchers.

1932

Illinois: White workers on the Illinois Central Railroad murder ten black trainmen in an effort to drive blacks out of railroad jobs.

February 13, Massilon, Ohio: Two blacks charged with attempted rape are smuggled out of jail to prevent their lynching.

February 19, Hiseville, Kentucky: A black prisoner accused of wounding a white man is removed from jail to avoid lynching.

February 27, Jenkins, Kentucky: A black murder suspect is smuggled from jail after threats of lynching.

April, Little Rock, Arkansas: A black man accused of murder is transferred to a distant jail after threats of lynching.

April 1, Crockett, Texas: Dave Tillis, a black man, is hanged by a small group of whites, on the accusation of entering a white woman's bedroom. Five whites are arrested in the case, but none is convicted.

April 6, Talladega, Alabama: A black inmate charged with attempted rape is removed to a distant jail after threats of lynching.

April 6, Ashland, Alabama: A black charged with attempted rape is transferred after threats of lynching.

April 20, Rawls Springs, Mississippi: A black prisoner accused of threatening a woman is removed from jail to escape lynching.

May, Coushatta, Louisiana: Force is used to repel a white mob bent on lynching a black accused of murder.

May 7, Gastonia, North Carolina: Two black murder suspects are removed from town to escape lynching.

May 15, Albany, Georgia: Force is used to protect a black prisoner, charged with attempted rape, from a white lynch mob.

May 19, Marion, Indiana: Force is used to protect a black prisoner accused of rape from a white lynch mob.

May 24, Walterboro, South Carolina: A black accused of rape is removed from jail to escape lynching.

June 6, Jasper, Florida: Henry Woods, a black suspected of murder and robbery, is killed by a white posse, his body riddled with bullets and afterward burned.

June 11, Ironton, Ohio: Luke Marion, a black man, is beaten to death by a mob after pulling a knife on two whites, his body dumped in a nearby river. Six whites are indicted in the case, but no convictions result.

June 14, Winnsboro, South Carolina: The sheriff is killed and six deputies are wounded in an attempt to prevent the lynching of a black prisoner.

June 18, Bainbridge, Georgia: A black inmate charged with murder is smuggled out of jail to escape a lynch mob.

June 20, Amory, Mississippi: A black accused of rape is removed from jail to avert mob action.

July, Radford, Virginia: National Guard units are called to prevent the lynching of a black rape suspect.

August, Poplar Bluff, Arkansas: A black man charged with attempted rape is removed to a distant jail after lynching threats.

August 7, Rome, Georgia: A black man accused of wounding a woman is spirited out of jail to avoid lynchers.

August 8, Lake Charles, Louisiana: A black accused of murder is smuggled out of town to escape lynching.

August 9, New Madrid, Missouri: A black prisoner charged with attempted rape is removed from jail to avoid mob action.

August 29, Texarkana, Texas: A black accused of rape is smuggled from jail to avoid lynchers.

September 5, Lebanon, Tennessee: Officers use force to disperse a mob bent on lynching five black prisoners charged with killing two policemen.

September 7, Waynesville, North Carolina: Force is used to prevent the lynching of a black suspect accused of insulting a woman and killing the policeman who tried to arrest him.

September 15, Crossett, Arkansas: Frank Tucker, a black man accused of stabbing a deputy sheriff, is abducted from jail and hanged in the main business district.

September 15, Linden, Virginia: Searchers find the body of Shadrick Thompson, a black man accused of assaulting a white couple on July 12, hanging from a tree. Authorities surrender the corpse to a mob, which burns Thompson's body, distributing teeth as souvenirs and placing his severed head on exhibition in the town of Warrenton.

September 23, Philadelphia, Mississippi: A black murder suspect is removed from jail in the face of lynching threats.

October 3, McComb, Mississippi: A black accused of rape is smuggled out of jail to escape lynching.

October 9, Damascus, Georgia: A black murder suspect is transferred to another jail after lynching threats.

October 18, Crystal Springs, Mississippi: A black prisoner accused of wounding a man is removed from jail because of mob threats.

November, Blytheville, Arkansas: A black prisoner charged with attempted rape is transferred to a distant jail after threats of lynching.

November 7, Birmingham, Alabama: Klansmen rout black crowds gathered to protest the Scottsboro "rape" verdicts.

November 19, Wisner, Louisiana: William House, a black arrested for insulting two white women, is abducted from police custody by a gang of whites. His body is found hanging from a tree the next day.

December 20, Yuma, Arizona: A black man suspected of murder is moved to a distant jail after threats of lynching.

December 20, Tallapoosa, Alabama: Three blacks are killed by police during an "uprising" of a local tenant farmer's union. A fourth victim dies of his wounds on December 27.

1933

January 12, Homer, Louisiana: A black man, Fell Jenkins, is flogged to death by three whites. No motive is discovered, and no arrests are made.

February 19, Ringgold, Louisiana: Nelson Nash, a black, is taken from jail by a mob after confessing to burglary, murder, and attempted rape. He is hanged at the scene of his crime with fifty shots fired into his body.

February 19, Aiken, South Carolina: George Jeter, a black man, is flogged to death by four whites who accuse him of stealing and selling their bootleg liquor.

May 11, Warrenton, Georgia: One white man is killed during a shoot-out between four whites and two black tenant farmers. A mob of fifty whites pursues the alleged killer, Will Kinsey, to a doctor's office where he is seeking treatment for gunshot wounds, and there he is shot to death.

May 23, Carthage, Texas: W.C. Lovell, a black suspected of attacking a white woman, is cornered and killed by police and members of a large mob.

June 12, Newton, Georgia: T.J. Thomas, a black man, is taken from his home and hanged and shot a week after an interracial shoot-out left one white man dead. Thomas was not a participant in the gunfight. Two blacks arrested at the time of the shooting are removed from jail for safekeeping.

June 17, Newton, Georgia: Richard Marshall, a black man, is abducted from jail by a mob and transported to the site where a white man was killed in December 1932, and there he is hanged and shot by his captors. Mob members describe the Thomas lynching on June 12 and Marshall's lynching as "examples" to local blacks.

July 4, Clinton, South Carolina: Black prisoner Norris Dendy is abducted from jail by four white men and then beaten, hanged, and shot.

July 10, Caledonia, Mississippi: An unnamed black tenant farmer accused of "improper conduct" toward a white woman is kidnapped from work and hanged. His weighted body is found in a creek ten days later.

July 18, Louisville, Mississippi: Following an altercation with a white man, Reuben Moore is abducted from his home by a mob and flogged and shot to death before his body is dumped in a canal.

August 13, Tuscaloosa, Alabama: Dan Pippen and A.T. Hardin, two blacks arrested for the murder of a white girl, are abducted from custody by a white mob and shot to death.

August 27, Willard, North Carolina: Following a violent altercation with a white bootlegger, black farmer Doc Rogers is killed by a posse in a shoot-out that also leaves one deputy wounded. The suspect's body is dragged around the courthouse square, and arsonists burn down his house.

September 18, Minter City, Mississippi: Richard Roscoe, a black farmer accused of striking a white man and "being too smart," is taken from his home by a mob and shot to death, his body then dragged through the streets behind a car.

September 24, Tuscaloosa, Alabama: Dennis Cross, an invalid black, is lured from his home by whites and shot to death. At the time, Cross is free on bond on a charge of assaulting a white woman.

September 26, Opelousas, Louisiana: John White, a young black accused of rape, is seized from police custody and shot to death by a mob.

Fall, Kern County, California: A strike by Mexican farm workers is broken by wholesale police and vigilante violence. As one deputy sheriff tells federal investigators: "We protect our farmers here in Kern County. They are our best people, but the Mexicans are trash. They have no standard of living. We herd them like pigs."

October 9, Ninety-Six, South Carolina: Bennie Thompson, a black jailed for pulling a gun on a white man, is abducted from custody and beaten to death by four whites.

October 11, Labadieville, Louisiana: Freddie Moore, a black man charged with killing a white girl, is taken from jail and hanged by a mob. A second black, Norman Thibodeaux, escapes death a short time later after being flogged by the mob.

October 11, Arvin, California: Anglo growers open fire on a picket line of Mexican workers, killing Pedro Subia and wounding several other strikers.

October 11, Pixley, California: Armed growers assault a Mexican workers' union hall, killing Dolores Hernandez and Delfino D'Avila and wounding eleven others. Eight gunmen are tried and acquitted on murder charges.

October 18, Princess Anne, Maryland: George Armwood, a black accused of attacking an elderly white woman, is abducted from jail by a mob of 5,000, dragged through town for a mile, and then hanged on main street. His body is later burned.

October 23, Lumpkin, Georgia: Cephus Davis, a black man charged with assaulting a patrolman while drunk, is abducted from jail by a white mob, beaten, and shot to death.

November 16, Greenville, South Carolina: George Green, a black man, is abducted from home and shot to death by a gang of robed, masked whites. Authorities could ascertain no motive.

November 29, Salisbury, Maryland: A mob of 500 whites besieges the Wicomico Hotel hoping to lynch "Yankee" newsmen, and vent their frustration by burning one reporter's car.

November 29, St. Joseph, Missouri: Lloyd Warner, a black accused of rape, is abducted from jail and hanged by four men, his body burned while a mob of 7,000 looks on. Carl Fisher, leader of the hanging party, is sentenced to prison on an unrelated charge of attempted rape in February 1936.

December 7, Kountze, Texas: David Gregory, a black accused of raping and murdering a white woman, is killed by police while resisting arrest. A mob of 400 seizes the body, dragging it around town for two hours before dismembering and burning it in a black neighborhood.

December 15, Columbia, Tennessee: Cord Cheek, a black man charged with assaulting a white girl and freed for lack of evidence, is kidnapped from home and hanged near the scene of the crime.

1934

January 12, Imperial Valley, California: Police attack a peaceful CAWIU meeting, killing an Hispanic adult and child.

January 24, Tampa, Florida: Robert Johnson, a black man arrested for stealing chickens, is abducted from jail and shot to death by a mob of whites.

January 24, Hazard, Kentucky: Rex Scott, a black man jailed for punching a white, is abducted from his cell by coal miners, hanged, and shot to death outside a rural graveyard.

January 30, Georgia: An interracial commission requests an inquiry into recent beatings and murders of black citizens by whites.

February 11, Mississippi: National Guard units are called to protect three black rape suspects. The defendants plead guilty on February 12 and are sentenced to die. On March 7 state legislators pass a bill permitting the rape victim's father to hang her attackers. The execution is carried out on March 16.

February 19, Imperial Valley, California: Police raid a CAWIU shanty town, burning shacks and evicting 2,000 mostly Hispanic tenants, effectively crushing a farm workers' strike.

March 17, New York City: Five thousand blacks riot during a rally held in Harlem to protest the Scottsboro "rape" case.

June 8, Lambert, Mississippi: Two blacks charged with attempted rape, Joe Love and Isaac Thomas, are seized from custody and hanged by a mob.

June 21, Newton, Georgia: Sonny Griggs, a black man, is hanged by a mob of several hundred whites, on charges of "associating with a white girl."

June 24, Manchester, Tennessee: Eight white men invade a black dance, provoking an argument in which one of them is struck by a black man, Richard Wilkerson. As Wilkerson returns home, the whites attack him and shoot him, strip his body, and crush his skull with an ax. Wilkerson's killers are sentenced to jail terms on conviction of manslaughter.

July 9, Bastrop, Louisiana: Andrew McLeod, a black man charged with attempted rape, is taken from jail by a mob. He is hanged on the courthouse square, his throat slashed.

July 16, Bolton, Mississippi: James Sanders, a black man, is shot to death by three whites on accusation of "writing an indecent letter to a white girl." Three relatives of the girl confess to the murder, but their case is dismissed at the request of local prosecutors.

July 24, Pelahatchee, Mississippi: Henry Bedford, a black, is taken from home and flogged by whites for "speaking disrespectfully to a young white man." He dies on July 25. Four whites are arrested, but no indictments are returned.

August 3, Bethany, Louisiana: A black man, Grafton Page, is flogged to death by vigilantes on a charge of drunk and disorderly conduct.

August 13, Michigan City, Mississippi: Two blacks awaiting trial for murder, Robert Jones and Smith Houey, are abducted from custody and hanged by a mob.

August 23, Birmingham, Alabama: White men pursue and shoot to death an unidentified black who is accused of trying to rob three white women on their way to church.

August 27, New York City: Racial fighting breaks out at a meeting held to raise funds for the legal defense of Alphonso Davis, a black rape suspect.

September 8, Princess Anne, Maryland: White rioters drive the entire black population out of town.

October 9, Darien, Georgia: A mob of fourteen bootleggers surround the home of a black man, James Curtis, and engage him in a gunfight. Curtis is later reported missing and presumed dead.

October 26, Brewton, Alabama: Claude Neal, a black man accused of rape and murder in Marianna, Florida, is abducted by a gang of white men from the jail where he has been transported for safekeeping. The mob returns Neal to Marianna, where he is tortured to death and hanged in front of the courthouse.

November 6, Holland, Missouri: One white man dies, two are wounded, and several blacks are beaten when vigilantes try to prevent blacks from voting.

November 19, Shelbyville, Tennessee: A lynch mob threatens E.K. Harris, a black rape suspect.

1935

January 11, Franklinton, Kentucky: Jerome Wilson, convicted of killing a police officer, is shot to death in his cell after the U.S. Supreme Court grants his appeal for a new trial. The sheriff says: "There wasn't any lynching. There wasn't any mob. There were just about six or eight men who were going about their business."

March 3, Maringuoin, Louisiana: Anderson Ward, a black jailed for beating a white man who pulled a gun on him, is abducted from his cell and shot dead by a mob, his body hanged from a tree.

March 12, Slayden, Mississippi: Ab Young, a black suspected of killing a white man, is hanged in a local schoolyard after his capture in Rossville, Tennessee.

March 19, New York City: The arrest of a black shoplifter, one week after another was beaten and blinded by police, leads to angry street demonstrations in Harlem. Full-scale rioting erupts after patrolmen assault protest leaders, with one black man killed by police and snipers firing back in retaliation. Looters destroy more than 200 shops, and over 100 persons are injured. Property damage is estimated in excess of $2 million.

March 21, Poinsett County, Arkansas: A mob of forty nightriders, including peace officers and planters, raids the home of Rev. A.B. Brookins, an elderly black active in the STFU. The house is riddled with bullets and the minister's daughter killed. Brookins and his wife escape injury.

March 21, Hernando, Mississippi: Rev. T.A. Allen, a black union organizer, is shot to death and dumped in the Coldwater River, his body weighted with chains.

March 22, Marked Tree, Arkansas: STFU organizers Clay East and Mary Hilliard are besieged by a mob in their office, then escorted out of the county by armed vigilantes, under threat of death if they return.

March 22, Poinsett County, Arkansas: Whites terrorize W.H. Stultz, president of the STFU, and attempt to blow up his home.

March 22, Mississippi County, Arkansas: Mary Green, wife of a black union member, dies of fright when armed vigilantes invade her home seeking to lynch her husband.

March 23, Marked Tree, Arkansas: Nightriders fire on the home of STFU attorney C.T. Carpenter, then move on to raid the homes of several black union members.

March 24, Marked Tree, Arkansas: Armed vigilantes invade STFU attorney C.T. Carpenter's office, threatening to kill him if he does not sever his association with the STFU.

March 25, Lawrence County, Mississippi: R.J. Tyrone, a prosperous black farmer, is ambushed and riddled with bullets in the woods near his home. Earlier he had been threatened by a mob because of his financial difficulties with a white neighbor.

March 27, Cross County, Arkansas: STFU secretary John Allen escapes from a mob of planters and deputies bent on lynching him. Numerous blacks are beaten in the resultant search, including one woman whose ear is severed by a pistol-whipping.

March 28, Hernando, Mississippi: An unidentified black man is found in a gully near town, a rope around his neck and several bullets in his body. The coroner rules his death a "suicide."

March 30, Marked Tree, Arkansas: Whites mob a group of blacks returning home from church outside of town. Men, women, and children are beaten indiscriminately in the raid.

March 30, Hitchiecoon, Arkansas: Arsonists destroy a black church that had lately been used for union meetings.

April, Gallup, New Mexico: Hispanics riot after the arrest of Exiquio Navarro, leader of a local miner's union. The sheriff and three miners die in the melee; three Hispanics are convicted of second-degree murder and sentenced to sixty-year prison terms. One defendant is freed on appeal; the other two are pardoned in 1939.

April 2, Poinsett County, Arkansas: Vigilantes raid the home of Rev. E.B. McKinney, vice president of the SFTU, firing 250 machine-gun bullets into his house.

April 22, Mt. Vernon, New York: A patrolman is mobbed by blacks after arresting one of them for drunkenness.

June 22, Wiggins, Mississippi: R.D. McGee, a black accused of sexually assaulting a white child, is captured by a mob of 300 whites, hanged from a tree, and riddled with bullets.

July 15, Columbus, Mississippi: Two blacks charged with attempted rape, Dooley Morton and Bert Moore, are seized from custody and hanged by a mob of thirty-five white men.

July 19, Ft. Lauderdale, Florida: Reuben Stacey, a black accused of murderous assault on a white woman, is abducted from police custody by a mob of 100 masked men. Stacy is hanged and shot seventeen times.

August 3, Louisburg, North Carolina: Govan Ward, a retarded black accused of axing a white farmer to death, is dragged from his home by an integrated mob, hanged, and shot to death.

August 5, Pittsboro, Mississippi: Bodie Bates, a black charged with attempted rape, is taken from jail and hanged from a nearby bridge.

September 17, Oxford, Mississippi: Elwood Higgenbotham, a black defendant awaiting the jury's verdict in his trial for killing a white man, is taken from jail and hanged by a mob.

September 28, Vienna, Georgia: Lewis Harris, a black prisoner charged with resisting arrest, is taken from custody, hanged, and riddled with bullets by a white mob.

October 17, Moultrie, Georgia: Bo Bronson, a black man, is beaten and shot by a posse seeking another black suspected of killing a white man. Bronson, innocent of all involvement in the crime, dies in a local hospital.

November 1, Gretna, Louisiana: Two unidentified black men jailed on charges of attempted rape are shot to death in their cell by three whites.

November 4, White Bluff, Tennessee: Baxter Bell, a black accused of striking a white woman, is abducted from police custody and shot to death by five whites. The killers are tried and acquitted in court.

November 11, Columbus, Texas: Two blacks accused of rape and murder, Ernest Collins and Benny Mitchell, are seized from custody and hanged by a mob of 700 whites. A local prosecutor calls the lynching "an expression of the will of the people."

1936

January 10, Delaware: Three blacks are publicly flogged on conviction of larceny.

March 7, Wilmington, Delaware: Two blacks receive fifteen lashes each, on conviction of stealing chickens.

March 14, Cusseta, Georgia: Philip Baker, a black accused of attacking two white women, is abducted from custody, hanged, and riddled with bullets.

March 29, Huntsville, Alabama: National Guardsmen are called out to protect four black murder suspects from lynchers.

Spring, Los Angeles County, California: Police marshal 1,500 armed men to break a strike by Mexican celery pickers. Protest marchers are attacked on three successive days, with strikers pursued to their homes and tear-gassed there. One striker is badly burned by a tear gas projectile fired at point-blank range. In the Domingues Hills, near San Pedro, a battle erupts when police surround a barn with Mexican workers barricaded inside. Arrests are so numerous that neither police nor the union can keep an accurate tally.

April 10, St. Petersburg, Florida: Klansmen are accused in the 1935 abduction and mutilation of Robert Cargell.

April 28, Danielsville, Georgia: A mob of forty men invades the jail, fatally shooting Lint Shaw, a black awaiting trial on charges of criminal assault.

April 29, Lepanto, Arkansas: Willis Kees, a black charged with attempted rape, is abducted from custody and shot dead by a masked gang.

April 30, Huntsville, Alabama: National Guardsmen use tear gas to disperse a mob bent on lynching four black murder suspects.

May 3, Pavo, Georgia: A mob of 200 men seizes John Rushin, a black accused of murder, from custody and shoots him to death.

May 18, New York City: Blacks riot against Italians in Harlem in a show of sympathy for Ethiopia's struggle against Mussolini. Looters wreck two Italian-owned stores.

June 17, El Campo, Texas: Prevented from lynching nine black murder suspects, a mob of 300 vigilantes burns the white-owned cafe where the killing took place.

June 19, New York City: Blacks riot after the defeat of boxer Joe Louis by a white opponent.

Summer, Orange County, California: Police and civilians mount late-night raids against striking Mexican farm workers. After one clash a local newspaper reports that "old vigilante days were revived in the orchards of Orange County yesterday as one man lay near death and scores nursed injuries."

July 13, New York City: Police quell another outbreak of rioting in Harlem.

July 31, Anniston, Alabama: Militia units are deployed to supervise the hunt for a black man accused of insulting a white girl.

August 12, Anniston, Alabama: National Guardsmen from Huntsville are dispatched to guard three black prisoners accused of wounding white men in a gunfight.

August 16, Welch, West Virginia: Fifteen blacks are gunned down by whites. Four are critically wounded.

September 6, Dalton, Georgia: A.L. McCamy, a black charged with attempted rape, is abducted from jail and hanged by a mob of 150 whites.

September 12, Atlanta, Georgia: Tom Finch, a black hospital orderly, is abducted from his home on the pretense of a lawful arrest, then shot to death and dumped outside the hospital where he worked. Police initially claim that Finch was shot while fleeing after he assaulted a patrolman, but an autopsy reveals five bullet wounds in his chest.

September 11, Greenville, Florida: Buckie Young, a black accused of rape, is shot to death by a mob. The coroner refuses to convene an inquest.

December 4, Tampa, Florida: Joseph Shoemaker, a socialist labor leader friendly with blacks, is beaten, castrated, and tarred by a KKK raiding party. He dies a week later. Eight men are indicted for murder—including six policemen—and several are convicted.

December 23, Roswell, Georgia: The handcuffed, bullet-riddled body of Mack Brown, a black janitor, is pulled from a local river several weeks after he was accused of insulting a white woman by kissing her hand.

1937

February 2, Abbeville, Alabama: Wes Johnson, a black accused of rape, is taken from jail, hanged, and shot by a mob. Impeachment proceedings are brought against the sheriff after state investigators announce that "the wrong Negro was lynched."

April 13, Duck Hill, Mississippi: Black prisoners Roosevelt Towns and Bootjack McDaniels, charged with killing a white man, are taken from custody and tortured to death with blow torches.

May 24, Bainbridge, Georgia: Willie Reed, a black charged with murdering two white women, is killed by police officers escorting him back from Alabama. A mob of 100 invades the mortuary and seizes Reed's corpse, then drags it through town before burning it.

August 2, Tallahassee, Florida: Two blacks, Richard Hawkins and Ernest Powders, charged with stabbing a police officer, are abducted from jail and shot by four masked men.

August 17, Covington, Tennessee: Albert Gooden, a black accused of killing a patrolman, is abducted from custody and hanged by six whites.

September 3, Mt. Vernon, Georgia: A black man named Kirby is shot and killed during the search for an elusive rape suspect. The mayor and another white man are wounded while trying to save Kirby's life.

October 4, Milton, Florida: J.C. Evans, a black man, is lynched by whites.

October 19, Delaware: Three blacks convicted of robbery are publicly flogged.

November 16, Miami, Florida: Klan raiders close a local nightclub.

1938

June 10, Columbus, Mississippi: Washington Adams, a black man, is lynched.

July 6, Arabi, Georgia: John Dukes, a black man severely wounded by police sent to arrest him on a disorderly conduct charge, is seized by a mob of several hundred whites and burned alive.

July 6, Rolling Fork, Mississippi: Tom McGehee, a black man suspected of killing his white employer, dies in a shoot-out with a posse. Later, a mob seizes his body, sets it on fire, and drags it through town behind a car.

July 16, Pittsburgh, Pennsylvania: Two persons are shot and forty are arrested during a race riot.

July 29, Canton, Mississippi: Black motorist Claude Brooks is shot to death by police for ignoring a command to stop his car. Officers were searching for a suspect in the murder of a white man, a crime in which Brooks is later found not to have been involved.

August 9, Perry, Florida: Otis Price, a black accused of rape, is abducted from jail and shot by a vigilante firing squad.

September 19, Snow Hill, Maryland: A white riot over jobs leaves one person dead and twenty-five arrested. Unemployed blacks are warned to leave town.

October 3, Milton, Florida: J.C. Evans, a black accused of robbery and an "unnatural crime" against a white boy, is abducted from custody and shot by four whites.

October 13, Ruston, Louisiana: R.C. Williams, a black charged with killing a white man and raping the victim's girlfriend, is abducted from jail, hanged, shot, and cremated.

October 17, Smyrna, Georgia: A black school is burned, with several persons beaten by whites, after a black prisoner confesses to a double murder. The riot's leader is jailed on November 19.

November 21, Wiggins, Mississippi: Wilder McGowan, a black accused of choking and robbing an elderly white woman, is hanged by a mob of 200 whites. The sheriff calls it "an orderly lynching," with "no shooting and no disorder in the mob."

December 8, Mt. Holly, New Jersey: Eight blacks are held for beating white children on a school bus.

1939

April 29, Daytona Beach, Florida: Lee Snell, a black taxi driver held for accidentally striking and killing a white boy, is abducted from custody and shot by two of the boy's relatives.

May 8, Canton, Mississippi: Joe Rogers, a black sawmill worker, vanishes after an argument with his white foreman. His body, with hands and feet tied, is pulled from a nearby river days later.

August, San Antonio, Texas: During a strike by Hispanic pecan shellers, a mob of 7,000 Anglos storms an auditorium with 100 strikers inside. The intended victims escape through a rear exit.

August 20, Jersey City, New Jersey: One person is injured when white gangs assault blacks on the street.

1940

February 13, Snow Hill, Maryland: A black woman and her daughter, held for questioning in a local murder, are saved from would-be lynchers by police.

May 9, Fairfield, Alabama: Black prisoner O'Dee Henderson, jailed after an altercation with a white man, is beaten and shot to death in his cell by three police officers and a civilian.

June 22, Brownsville, Tennessee: Elbert Williams, a black man, disappears after trying to register to vote. His bullet-riddled body is found in a nearby river days later.

June 28, Luverne, Alabama: Jesse Thornton, a black man, disappears after "speaking disrespectfully" of a local peace officer. His body, riddled with bullets, is pulled from a nearby stream a week later.

September 8, LaGrange, Georgia: Austin Callaway, a black charged with attempted rape, is abducted from jail and shot by six whites.

1941

February 20, Andrews, South Carolina: Bruce Tisdale, a black man, is severely beaten in a fight with five whites. He dies on February 25, and three of his assailants are later convicted of manslaughter.

April 13, Cherryville, North Carolina: A black man, Robert Melker, is shot dead while fighting four whites near his rural home. All four gunmen are convicted, drawing sentences of ten to twenty-five years in prison.

May 6, Blakely, Georgia: Robert Sapp, a black accused of stealing from his employer, is fatally beaten by three white men. He dies several days later.

May 13, Quincy, Florida: A.C. Williams, a black accused of trying to rape a twelve-year-old white girl, is beaten and shot to death by vigilantes.

1942

January 25, Sikeston, Missouri: Cleo Wright, a black man jailed on suspicion of attempting to rape a white woman, is abducted from jail and lynched by a mob of 300 whites. His body is afterwards dragged through the streets of a black neighborhood and publicly burned.

February 28, Detroit, Michigan: Scores of persons are injured when 1,200 armed whites repel black tenants from the federally funded Sojourner Truth housing project. On April 16 a federal grand jury indicts three leaders of the mob for conspiracy. Two thousand policemen and National Guardsmen protect fourteen black families when they move into the project on April 30.

March 12, New York City: Police disperse black demonstrators protesting the death of Wallace Armstrong, a black man shot by a police officer he tried to stab.

April 2, Ft. Dix, New Jersey: One white soldier and two blacks are shot to death and five are wounded during racial violence sparked by an argument over the use of a telephone.

May, Los Angeles, California: Chepe Ruiz, a Hispanic youth, is pistol-whipped by police during his arrest for "suspicion of robbery." Jurors later acquit Ruiz of the charge.

May 3, Hempstead, New York: Three patrolmen are mobbed and beaten by blacks while trying to arrest a suspect on the street.

July 2, St. Louis, Missouri: Hispanic inmate Edward Melendes is beaten and kicked to death by policemen in the city jail.

July 13, Texarkana, Texas: Whites lynch Willie Vinson, a black rape suspect.

August 1, Los Angeles, California: Hispanic youths crash a party at the Williams ranch, and brawl with the guests. The next morning, an invited guest is found dead on a nearby road, and twenty-two

Hispanics are held for trial in the "Sleepy Lagoon" murder case. Some of the defendants are beaten by police in an effort to obtain confessions. On January 12, 1943, the defendants are convicted of charges ranging from assault to first-degree murder.

August 10–11, Los Angeles, California: Police blockade the streets leading to several barrio neighborhoods, stopping and searching all cars with Mexican occupants. Of 600 persons arrested in the sweep, 425 are later released without charges. One hundred seventy-five are held for possession of various "weapons," ranging from pocket knives to tire irons, jack handles, and other automotive tools.

August 14, Houston, Texas: Federal officers initiate the prosecution of two policemen who beat a black soldier after ordering him out of a "white" bus seat.

September 14, New York City: One white man and four black leaders of the Ethiopian Pacific Movement in Harlem are indicted on federal sedition charges. Prosecutors claim they planned to sponsor a black revolt in the United States, thus helping the Japanese establish a "dark-skinned empire."

October, Paris, Illinois: J.E. Person, a black man, is lynched by whites outside of town. On July 13, 1943, thirteen lynchers are indicted on federal charges.

October 11, New York City: Three white youths are injured in a fight with forty blacks over possession of a scrap pile.

October 12, Shubuta, Mississippi: A white mob lynches two fourteen-year-old black boys after they plead guilty to the attempted rape of a white girl.

October 17, Laurel, Mississippi: Convicted the previous day of killing his white employer, black prisoner Howard Wash is abducted from jail and lynched. Three whites are charged with the lynching and are acquitted by a federal jury on April 24, 1943.

October 18, New York City: A detective is beaten by blacks while attempting to ease a black-white dispute.

October 19, Brooklyn, New York: Police guard local schools after a twelve-year-old white boy is attacked by blacks.

November 2, Los Angeles, California: Police rough up ten Hispanic youths, arrested for the "crime" of wearing zoot suits.

November 7, New York City: A white patrolman is attacked and beaten by five blacks.

November 16, New York City: A detective is assaulted by three blacks, wounding one of his assailants and taking the man into custody.

November 27, Phoenix, Arizona: A black soldier and a black civilian are killed and twelve persons are wounded in a shoot-out between black GIs and military police.

December 6, Manzanar, California: One persons is killed and nine are wounded when troops fire on a riotous mob at a Japanese relocation camp. Violence began the previous night, between factions supporting and opposing a celebration of the Pearl Harbor attack.

December 27, New York City: John Hartigan, a white man, is beaten by five blacks on a public street.

1943

January 30, Newton, Georgia: Robert Hall, a black man, is lynched by whites.

May 8, Venice, California: Police stand idly by as white sailors beat Hispanic youths at the Aragon Ballroom.

May 25, Mobile, Alabama: National Guard units are deployed after a race riot at the Alabama Drydock & Shipbuilding Company injures eight persons.

May 25, Los Angeles, California: Four Anglos are attacked and beaten by members of a Hispanic zoot-suit gang.

June 1, Orange County, California: Five persons are reported injured in zoot suit attacks.

June 3–7, Los Angeles, California: Following an attack on white sailors by a group of Hispanic youths, rioting servicemen and civilians spend five days attacking Hispanics and blacks on the streets, singling out youths in zoot suits for special attention. Violence peaks on June 7, when more than 1,000 rioters invade theaters, streetcars, and homes dragging out Hispanics to be stripped and beaten. Police stand idly by, confining their arrests to battered victims of the mob. More than 600 Hispanics are jailed in a series of "preventive" arrests.

June 10, Camp Stewart, Georgia: Black troops riot on base, killing one white MP and wounding four others.

June 12, Pennsylvania: Four black zoot-suiters are beaten by whites and then jailed by police.

June 16, Beaumont, Texas: Rioting erupts after reports of a black man assaulting a white woman. Two persons die and eleven are injured before martial law is declared.

June 16, Marianna, Florida: Cellos Harrison, a black prisoner charged with killing a white man, is abducted from jail by a mob and beaten to death.

June 16, Chester, Pennsylvania: Five black shipyard workers are shot and wounded in a clash with white guards.

June 20–21, Detroit, Michigan: A race riot leaves twenty-five blacks and nine whites dead, with more than 700 persons injured and over 600 arrested. Black spokesmen charge that police used lethal force against blacks, while ignoring white violence or actively aiding white rioters. On October 22, two blacks are convicted of inciting the riot.

June 27, Evansville, Indiana: White soldiers clash in the streets with black zoot-suiters.

August 2, New York City: A twelve-hour riot in Harlem leaves five blacks dead and 500 injured, with another 500 in jail. Hundreds of shops are wrecked and looted. Property damage is estimated at $5 million.

August 3, New York City: A black youth stabs a white youth who ridiculed his zoot suit.

December 29, New York City: Two white youths are assaulted and stabbed by a gang of five blacks.

1944

January 14, Ash Hill Township, Missouri: Fifty-five white farmers are indicted for driving black workers out of the area.

March 1, Albany County, New York: A black witness in a criminal case says he was beaten and terrorized by state police.

March 14, New York City: Two blacks are injured when military police quell a riot in a restaurant.

March 18, Helena, Arkansas: A white defendant, A.S. Johnson, is sentenced to prison for the brutal treatment of his black employees.

March 26, Amite County, Mississippi: Angered by the refusal of Rev. Isaac Simmons, a black man, to sell his oil-rich land, whites abduct him and shoot him to death, afterward breaking his bones and cutting out his tongue. The minister's son is also beaten and ordered to leave the county.

May 9, New York City: One person is injured during racial fighting at a city high school.

June 16, New York City: Two hundred whites assault blacks on the street, injuring three persons. Two rioters are jailed in the outbreak.

October, Hart, Michigan: Nineteen-year-old Jose Davilla, a Hispanic, is beaten and shot to death by the county sheriff after hiding an Anglo girl's glasses as a practical joke.

November 23, Pikesville, Tennessee: J.T. Scales, a black man held on suspicion of killing a white woman, is dragged from jail and shot by a vigilante firing squad.

1945

January 18–19, Placer County, California: Vigilantes attempt to burn buildings on the property of Sumio Doi, a Japanese-American farmer.

March 25, San Quentin, California: Prisoners riot over the mixing of black and white inmates at mealtime.

May 13, California: Federal officers report twenty-four cases of anti-Nisei violence in the previous four months.

August, DeKalb County, Georgia: Porter Turner, a black cab driver, is stabbed to death and dumped on a doctor's lawn. KKK members publicly boast of their role in the murder.

September 21, Jacksonville, Florida: Sam Askins, a black farmhand, jumps in the Suwanee River and drowns after being pistol-whipped and flogged by Constable Tom Crews. On October 3, 1946, Crews is convicted of violating federal civil rights laws.

1946

Los Angeles, California: School administrators in the Belvedere district are reprimanded for forcing Hispanic girls to parade nude through the gym as a "disciplinary measure."

February 13, Atlanta, Georgia: Nightriders flog a black navy veteran.

February 25, Los Angeles, California: Pfc. Daniel Elizalde, a Mexican-American home on leave from the army, is shot and killed without cause by an Anglo night watchman.

February 26, Columbia, Tennessee: Riots erupt after an altercation between blacks and a white store owner. Three hundred guns are seized in door-to-door searches of the black community, with homes and shops vandalized by whites. Ten persons are injured and seventy are arrested during the outbreak. On February 28, two blacks are shot to death during "questioning" at police headquarters. On October 4, two blacks are convicted of attempted murder, with twenty-three others cleared of all charges.

March 30, Los Angeles, California: Mexican Tiofilo Pelagio is shot and killed by an Anglo private detective during a cafe argument. On the same day complaints are filed against police for using "third degree" tactics to obtain criminal confessions from four Hispanic boys.

June 9, Gordon, Georgia: Willie Dudley, a black laborer, is abducted and beaten with rubber hoses for joining a labor union.

June 21, Atlanta, Georgia: FBI agents report a "well-organized plot" by local Klansmen to murder Gov. Ellis Arnall in revenge for his efforts to revoke the KKK's charter.

July 21, Monterey Park, California: An unarmed Hispanic honor student, thirteen-year-old Eugene Montenegro, is shot in the back and killed by a white sheriff's deputy investigating a complaint of prowlers.

July 22, Lexington, Mississippi: Leon McTatie, a black man, is flogged to death for allegedly stealing a saddle. Six whites are charged with the crime on July 30, but all are acquitted.

July 26, Monroe, Georgia: A gang of twenty whites stop Roger Malcolm, George Dorsey, and their wives on the highway, dragging the four blacks out of their car and shooting them to death.

July 30, Hattiesburg, Mississippi: A white deputy is held on preliminary murder charges in the shooting death of Buddy Wolf, a black father of 10.

July 31, Georgia: FBI agents report that Klansmen in one county have been firing into homes as a warning to blacks against voting in elections.

August, Soperton, Georgia: A white political rally erupts into violence when participants storm and destroy a black church.

August 4, Brooklyn, New York: Two persons are injured in racial street fighting.

August 5, Miami, Florida: Roosevelt Winfield, a black CIO shop steward, is forced off the road and threatened by hooded Klansmen.

August 6, Minden, Louisiana: John Jones, a black man accused of breaking into a white woman's house, is taken from jail by a mob. His hands are severed and he is burned to death with a blow torch. A second black man, Albert Harris, is beaten in the same incident.

On October 18, federal charges are filed against six men, including three peace officers charged with handing Jones and Harris over to the mob.

August 10, Athens, Alabama: Fifty to 100 blacks are injured during a race riot, with ten whites jailed on various charges. Sixteen rioters are formally indicted on August 23.

August 12, Elko, South Carolina: James Walker, a black man, is shot and killed by a white gunman.

August 20, Magee, Mississippi: White mobs assault black residents.

August 26, Crowley, Louisiana: Authorities report mob attacks on blacks.

September, Tallahassee, Florida: State police are dispatched to avert the lynching of a black motorist who caused a white woman's death in a car accident.

September 19, Florence, South Carolina: Blacks are targeted by whites in an outbreak of mob violence.

September 29, Philadelphia, Pennsylvania: One person is killed and many injured during a riot between blacks and whites. Eleven persons are arrested.

October 17, Mt. Pleasant, Tennessee: Seventy-five would-be lynchers disperse after two black robbery suspects are smuggled out of town.

October 30, Atlanta, Georgia: The mayor orders a probe of recent racial attacks, including shots fired and rocks thrown at black-owned homes. One victim, black youth Clifford Hines, is blackjacked by a member of the Columbians, Inc. (a neo-Nazi group) "on patrol." On October 31, a black home in a formerly all-white neighborhood is bombed. Police arrest four members of the Columbians on November 2, charging them with inciting a riot. Two members are convicted in February 1947.

November 3, Athens, Alabama: Police quell a near-riot between blacks and whites.

November 14, Atlanta, Georgia: The Columbians, Inc., are evicted from their meeting hall after a gas bomb explodes during one of their gatherings.

December, Elba, Alabama: CIO organizer James Harden is abducted and beaten by nightriders.

1947

January 23, Oxnard, California: Two police officers are dismissed for beating four Mexican farm workers.

February 17, Pickens, North Carolina: Willie Earle, a black man accused of stabbing a white cab driver, is abducted from jail and tortured to death. Thirty-one whites are charged with the crime following an FBI investigation. A judge directs acquittal for three defendants on May 19, while jurors acquit the remaining twenty-eight on May 22.

April 23, La Junta, Colorado: Charles White, a Hispanic war hero, is murdered by Anglos for seeking service in a white-only nightclub. Authorities refuse to take action against the club's owner.

May 3, Ft. Leavenworth, Kansas: Tear gas quells a riot sparked by the desegregation of a mess hall in the army's disciplinary barracks.

May 16, San Fernando, California: Civil rights activists complain that police habitually break into Mexican-American homes without warrants, beating and threatening juvenile occupants, while conducting "wholesale roundups and arrests of Mexican-American boys without previous inquiry as to the arrested boys' connection—if any—with the crime in question."

May 23, Jackson, North Carolina: Godwin Bush, a black prisoner accused of attempted rape, escapes from white lynchers after they drag him from jail. He surrenders to the FBI on May 25, and seven whites are arrested two days later. A grand jury releases them all without charges on August 5.

June 10, Huntsboro, Alabama: Mayor Hugh Vann rescues Jimmy Harris, a black prisoner, from members of a white lynch mob. Convicted of attempted rape on June 18, Harris is sentenced to twenty years in prison.

July 11, Glynn County, Georgia: Eight black inmates at a state prison camp are shot and killed by guards during an "escape attempt." Witnesses maintain that only one prisoner was trying to climb the fence. Four of the victims are found under camp buildings, where they had sought cover from gunfire. A federal grand jury indicts the warden and four guards.

July 26, Tuskegee, Alabama: The Tuskegee Institute reports thirteen blacks were lynched in the first half of 1947.

August 23, Atlanta, Georgia: Gov. M.E. Thompson announces a probe of recent floggings, including the attack on a CIO organizer and his wife, at LaGrange. On the night of Thompson's announcement, bombs strike the home of a local reporter active in covering KKK political affiliations.

September, Los Angeles, California: Patrolmen beat Bruno Cano, a Mexican-American, when he tries to stop them from clubbing two Hispanic youths in a tavern. One officer, William Keyes, was investigated for shooting two Hispanics earlier in the year.

1948

February 20, Lakeview, Georgia: Walter Bowland, a high school athletic coach, loses his job after a month-long campaign of KKK harassment.

March 2, Wrightsville, Georgia: Three hundred robed Klansmen parade, announcing that "blood will flow in the streets of the South" if blacks seek equality. On March 3, election day, none of the towns 400 registered blacks attempt to vote.

March 9, Swainsboro, Georgia: Cardboard coffins, labeled "KKK," are left on the porches of black homes overnight. On March 10, less than a third of the area's 1,500 registered blacks vote in the Democratic primary.

March 10, Los Angeles, California: While drinking at a local tavern, patrolman William Keyes and his partner arrest a seventeen-year-old Hispanic, Agustino Salcido, and transport him to a vacant building, where he is riddled with bullets. The officers accuse their victim of trying to sell stolen watches, but none are found at the scene. Witnesses to the encounter are beaten and run out of town by police. Keyes is tried and acquitted on manslaughter charges.

March 13, Columbus, Georgia: Three newsmen covering a Klan rally are seized by KKK members, given injections, forced to drink liquor, and then are jailed for intoxication.

March 21, Mt. Vernon, Georgia: The NAACP charges that KKK threats prevented 480 blacks from voting in the recent election.

May 9, Jackson, Mississippi: Gov. Fielding Wright, in a radio address, urges blacks seeking equality to "make your home in some state other than Mississippi."

May 13, Suffield, Connecticut: White neighbors rebuild the home of a black family destroyed by arsonists.

May 15, New York City: Three persons are jailed in racial disorders after a black woman is ejected from a store.

August 31, North Carolina: Speeches in Charlotte and Hickory by presidential candidate Henry Wallace are cut short by whites hurling eggs and tomatoes. Racists are angered by Wallace's refusal to address a segregated audience.

September 8, Alston, Georgia: Isiah Nixon, a black man, is shot and killed by two whites for the "crime" of voting. Jurors acquit one of the killers on November 5, accepting his plea of self-defense.

September 27, Georgia: Leaders of the Progressive Party ask for federal protection, charging that groups of campaign workers have been abducted and threatened on two successive days.

November 1, Nashville, Tennessee: Mayor Thomas Cummings says local black neighborhoods have been "flooded" with threats against voting in tomorrow's election.

November 2, Montgomery, Georgia: NAACP president D.V. Carter is beaten while escorting blacks to the polls.

November 2, Mississippi: Three armed whites prevent a black minister, Rev. William Bender, from voting.

November 20, Lyons, Georgia: Robert Mallard, a black, is ambushed and shot eighteen times by robed (but unmasked) white men. Two white men identified by Mallard's widow, are indicted on December 10, but both are later acquitted.

December, Milledgeville, Georgia: Three whites are arrested for firing into a black man's home, the shootings being a part of a campaign to drive blacks from the area.

1949

February 18, Chattanooga, Tennessee: A local Klansman is indicted on nine criminal counts related to floggings and other terrorist activities.

February 24, Columbus, Georgia: Three black high school students are abducted at gunpoint and driven to the jail in Phoenix City, Alabama, for questioning about their alleged ties to the NAACP. Afterward, they are beaten and dumped from the car, with shots fired over their heads as they flee.

March, Dallas, Texas: Bombs strike a black-owned home in a previously all-white neighborhood.

March 26, Birmingham, Alabama: Three black homes are bombed by nightriders.

April 2, Hooker, Georgia: The local sheriff hands seven blacks over to a KKK flogging squad after complaints of a "wild party." The sheriff and one of his deputies are convicted of civil rights violations on March 9, 1950.

April 8, Memphis, Tennessee: Six white policemen are indicted for beating a black prisoner.

April 9, Chattanooga, Tennessee: Investigators report that nightriders have flogged sixteen local residents in the past four months.

May, Birmingham, Alabama: Klansmen abduct two white men without explanation, flogging one of them while the other, a cripple, is threatened and forced to watch.

May 21, Soperton, Georgia: Two Klansmen are jailed for assaulting the mayor. Moments later, two others flee under police fire.

May 30, Irwinton, Georgia: Calif Hill, a black man held for firing a shot at the sheriff, is abducted from jail and killed by lynchers.

June 3, Dora, Alabama: Klansmen flog five local residents, including two women, with prayers recited between the beatings.

June 11, Birmingham, Alabama: Klansmen drag a woman from her home, flog her, and threaten her with burning at the stake. The same night, terrorists kidnap and threaten a white cafe owner who serves black customers.

June 15, Birmingham, Alabama: Billy Stovall, a white Navy veteran, is kidnapped from his home and flogged by KKK nightriders on charges of "immorality."

June 21, St. Louis, Missouri: Two hundred whites attack fifty black youths at a public swimming pool. The pool is subsequently closed by order of the mayor.

June 28, Alabama: Gov. James Folsom signs an anti-mask law, inspired by reports of KKK violence around the state. On July 1 a grand jury convenes to examine reports of Klan violence around Birmingham.

June 29, Washington, D.C.: Three persons are injured and five are arrested in racial clashes at the newly desegregated Anacostia Park swimming pool.

July 2, Praco, Alabama: Residents report at least a dozen Klan floggings in the past month.

July 16, Birmingham, Alabama: A grand jury indicts seventeen Klansmen on forty-four criminal counts related to recent acts of terrorism.

July 16–19, Groveland, Florida: Whites terrorize local blacks during four days of racial violence, burning several homes and firing shots into others. The violence is sparked by reports of four blacks raping a white woman. National Guard units restore order on July

19. One of the rape suspects, Ernest Thomas, is shot and killed by a white posse near Perry, Florida, on July 26.

July 17, Iron City, Georgia: Eight carloads of armed Klansmen are greeted with gunfire at the home of Mayor C.L. Drake. The raiders flee, with no casualties suffered on either side.

July 19, Goodwater, Alabama: Two men—one white, one black—are kidnapped and flogged by Klansmen.

July 23, Chattanooga, Tennessee: The first black-owned home in a formerly all-white neighborhood is bombed.

July 24, Sandy Bottoms, South Carolina: Four blacks are beaten and shot by hooded whites, who tell them, "This is your civil rights."

July 25, Polk County, Florida: Four police officers are indicted on federal charges of beating two black prisoners.

July 28, Birmingham, Alabama: Five white men wreck the new steel tower of black radio station WEDR, causing $5,000 damage.

August 2, Rome, Georgia: Officers deliver seven black prisoners to a KKK flogging party. Sheriff John Lynch and three of his deputies are indicted by a federal grand jury on August 3, with a mistrial declared in their case on December 17.

August 4, Ozark, Alabama: Four blacks are the first persons arrested under the new anti-mask law, charged with forming their own "klavern" to frighten black women away from dating whites. One defendant is sentenced to six months, another to sixty days, while a third is referred to juvenile authorities.

August 7, Iron City, Georgia: Mayor Drake and friends exchange shots with a sixteen-car KKK motorcade.

August 8, Chattanooga, Tennessee: A local Klan chapter is ejected from the "Invisible Empire" because of involvement in floggings and armed intimidation. At the same time, other units are stripped of their charters for similar reasons in Trenton and Lafayette, Georgia.

August 13, Birmingham, Alabama: Two black homes are damaged by bombs in a neighborhood zoned for white occupancy. Blacks fire on one of the cars from which bombs were thrown.

September 3, Bainbridge, Georgia: Hollis Riles, a black man, is lynched by whites.

September 4, Peekskill, New York: White rioters, including policemen and members of the American Legion, stone and beat spectators leaving a concert performance by black singer Paul

Robeson. While claiming to be anti-communists, the rioters shout racist, anti-Semitic epithets at their victims during the assault.

November 3, New York City: Blacks assault policemen in Harlem during a celebration for black city councilman Benjamin Davis, seeking reelection despite his conviction on federal conspiracy charges. Six patrolmen are injured and six people are arrested in the melee.

November 5, Montgomery, Alabama: Former police chief Thomas Gantt is sentenced to two years in jail on conviction of beating five blacks in order to obtain criminal confessions.

November 21, Birmingham, Alabama: A black man is shot and seriously wounded by a street car conductor after refusing to sit in segregated seats. Two other blacks are also wounded in the burst of gunfire.

December 17, New Orleans, Louisiana: Two policemen are fired after their conviction for beating black prisoners.

1950

January, Nashville, Tennessee: Plans for a new black housing project are abandoned after a bomb blast and a cross-burning in the area.

January 9, Kosciusko, Mississippi: Black resident Thomas Harris and his daughter are wounded and three other children—ages four, seven, and thirteen—are murdered by three escaped convicts. The killers, all white, were serving time on charges brought by Harris: burglary, robbery, and the attempted rape of his daughter. The three convicts escaped from custody on December 30, 1949, and all are recaptured by January 11.

February 18, Lafayette, Alabama: Black teenager Willie Carlisle is beaten to death while in police custody. One white officer is convicted by a federal jury on October 31, receiving a ten-month prison term. Another officer, who pleads guilty, is sentenced to six months in prison.

February 22, Pell City, Alabama: Retired storekeeper Charlie Hurst, an outspoken opponent of the Klan, is killed and his son is wounded in an exchange of fire with KKK nightriders at his home. Four days later one of the Klansmen—a Methodist minister—shoots himself to death in nearby Talladega. Another member of the raiding party is convicted of manslaughter on June 28.

March 2, Eastman, Georgia: Jessie Goodman, a black farmhand, is abducted and beaten by Klansmen on suspicion of theft. A white farmer comes to his aid, trading shots with the floggers and forcing them to release Goodman.

April, Birmingham, Alabama: A black minister's home is bombed for the second time in less than a year. Nine days later a bomb causes $11,000 damage to the home of a black dentist.

May, Chattanooga, Tennessee: A black home in a previously all-white neighborhood is bombed for the second time, nearly killing two children.

July 25, Soperton, Georgia: Will Robinson, a black man, becomes the latest victim in a series of Klan floggings that have prompted some residents to leave town.

August 5, Colonial Beach, Virginia: Whites assault black swimmers at a public beach.

August 17, Carrollton, Georgia: A Communist party official is beaten and threatened with lynchings by inmates in jail while serving a term for passing out leaflets condemning the recent conviction of a black murder suspect.

August 26, Myrtle Beach, South Carolina: A uniformed policeman is mortally wounded while riding with other Klansmen against a black dance hall. Some 300 shots are exchanged in the battle before the nightriders retreat.

September, Philadelphia, Pennsylvania: The walls of Independence Hall are defaced with anti-Semitic slogans and obscenities.

September 1, Pell City, Alabama: A Klansman and defendant in the Hurst murder case of February 22, 1950, is stabbed while attending a local carnival.

Fall, Boston, Massachusetts: A series of anti-Semitic incidents leads to a near-riot by Jewish residents.

October 9, Charleston, South Carolina: Nightriders stone the home of J. Waites Waring, a federal judge who struck down the state's "white primary" in 1947.

October 31, Basile, Louisiana: A black man is shot and wounded by a white gunman in a dispute over segregation.

November 1, Washington, D.C.: A White House security guard is shot and killed and two others are wounded when two Puerto Rican nationalists attack Blair House in an attempt to assassinate President Harry Truman. Gunman Griselio Torresola is killed in the exchange of gunfire; Oscar Collazo survives his wounds and is sentenced to death, but President Truman commutes the sentence to life imprisonment. Collazo's release from prison is ordered by President Jimmy Carter on September 6, 1979.

November 9, Conway, South Carolina: Klansmen raid a black family's rural home, beating Rufus Lee and his two sons.

December, Birmingham, Alabama: Bombers strike at the home of a black woman who led a court fight against racial zoning laws. The incident marks Birmingham's fifth racist bombing since the spring of 1949.

December 5, Greenwood, South Carolina: Clayton Moore, a black man, is flogged by Klansmen on charges of "showing a photograph to a white woman." Moore's son opens fire on the raiders, killing one man before they escape. On February 12, 1951, thirteen whites plead guilty to conspiracy in the case.

1951

January 17, Conway, South Carolina: Klansmen flog two disabled war veterans.

January 18, Chadbourn, North Carolina: Nightriders invade the home of Evergreen Flowers, a black woman, beating her with sticks and pistols.

January 22, Columbus County, Virginia: A black woman reports being beaten by nightriders.

March, Nashville, Tennessee: A dynamite charge explodes in the yard of a house recently sold to blacks.

March 31, Winter Garden, Florida: Melvin Womack, a black man, is dragged from his bed, beaten, and shot to death by nightriders.

May, Birmingham, Alabama: Arsonists destroy two black homes that have been targeted by bombers during recent years.

May 26, Norfolk, Virginia: Rev. Joseph Mann, a black, is abducted by nightriders who tell him, "We want you to help us run some niggers out." Mann is driven to a black-owned home and tossed inside after his abductors set the house on fire. He dies of burns on May 29, after making a statement to police.

May 26, Los Angeles, California: Responding to complaints of noise, police raid a Hispanic baptismal party, assaulting guests, throwing a pregnant woman and a crippled man to the floor, and breaking the leg of one guest who tries to intervene.

June, Atlanta, Georgia: A "white" home recently sold to blacks is bombed by nightriders. A high-ranking Klansman is indicted on July 27, his case ending with a mistrial on January 25, 1952.

June 5, Miami, Florida: A Jewish community center is bombed.

July, Mobile, Alabama: Two whites are arrested for beating a black co-worker who drank from a "white" water fountain.

July 5, Houston, Texas: An Egyptian newsman touring the United States complains of gestapo-like treatment by local police because of his skin color.

July 10–12, Cicero, Illinois: Whites riot for three days when a black resident, Harvey Clark, Jr., tries to occupy his newly rented apartment. National Guardsmen are deployed on July 12 to disperse a mob of 3,500 rioters. Ninety-nine persons are arrested and seventeen are hospitalized (including five treated for bayonet wounds). On June 23, 1952, Cicero's police chief is fined $2,000 for denying Clark's civil rights by failing to protect him adequately. Two patrolmen are fined $250 each on the same charge.

July 20, New York City: Three persons are injured in a series of black-white street clashes.

July 24, Indianola, Mississippi: The sheriff frees three black murder suspects, reporting that their confessions were obtained through torture by arresting officers.

July 27, Atlanta, Georgia: Charles Klein, the number-two man in the local KKK, is indicted for bombing a black-owned home.

August 11, Dallas, Texas: Authorities report that black-owned homes have been the targets of thirteen bombings in the past seventeen months.

August 25, Columbia, South Carolina: Two men are blackjacked at a Klan rally while police stand by and watch.

August 31, Pike County, Mississippi: Five policemen are indicted for beating black prisoners.

September 6, Swainsboro, Georgia: A black man named Jordan is flogged by nightriders.

September 11, Orange, Texas: Four policemen, including the local police chief, are indicted for abusing black prisoners.

September 22, Miami, Florida: A black housing project, Carver Village, is bombed by nightriders.

September 30, Miami, Florida: A synagogue is vandalized with anti-Semitic graffiti. On October 1, congregants at another temple discover two sticks of dynamite, the explosion negated by a faulty fuse.

October 2, Dublin, Georgia: A black couple, Willie Brinson and his wife, are hospitalized after robed Klansmen beat them with ax handles and a leather strap.

October 6, Fair Bluff, North Carolina: Ben Grainger and Dorothy Martin are abducted by Klansmen, driven across the state line into South Carolina, and flogged. On February 16, 1952, ten KKK members are arrested on federal kidnapping charges.

October 8, Miami, Florida: Two sticks of dynamite are thrown at a Hebrew school, but the fuse extinguishes on impact.

November 6, Groveland, Florida: Sheriff Willis McCall shoots two black rape suspects, killing one and severely wounding the other. Both men are handcuffed at the time.

November 14, Chadbourn, North Carolina: Esther Floyd, a pregnant black woman, is attacked by Klansmen, who shear off her hair as punishment for "going with white men." FBI agents arrest eleven nightriders on February 27, 1952.

November 25, Tallahassee, Florida: Two patrolmen are suspended pending results of a federal probe into charges of beating a black man.

November 30, Miami, Florida: Carver Village, a housing project, is again bombed, causing $20,000 damage.

December 1, Whiteville, South Carolina: Klansmen perpetrate the first of six floggings in less than two months.

December 2, Miami, Florida: Bombs explode at Carver Village (a housing project), a Jewish school, and a black-owned home in a "white" neighborhood.

December 8, Whiteville, North Carolina: Woodrow Johnson is dragged from his home and beaten by Klansmen.

December 19, Columbus County, North Carolina: Nightriders flog Greer Wright, a local tenant farmer.

December 23, Miami, Florida: A stick of dynamite is found outside a local Catholic church, the fuse extinguished.

December 24, Los Angeles, California: In the "Bloody Christmas" case, seven Hispanic juveniles are beaten by police officers in jail. Several patrolmen are convicted and imprisoned for assault.

December 25, Mims, Florida: NAACP official Harry Moore and his wife are killed by a bomb planted in their bedroom. In 1978, an ex-marine confesses to placing the bomb as part of a murder contract commissioned by KKK members and Sheriff Willis McCall. No prosecutions have resulted.

December 30, Ft. Payne, Alabama: A woman's home is bombed after she has driven away white men attempting to burn a cross in her yard.

1952

January 12, Orlando, Florida: Nightriders beat Arthur Holland, a black man, and graze his scalp with a bullet "as a lesson to other Negroes."

January 13, Dallas, Texas: A bomb explodes in the parking lot of a black nightclub. Authorities call it the third "pointless" bombing in less than a month.

January 30, Cairo, Illinois: A black home is bombed. Four whites are arrested on February 2.

February 12, Gaffney, South Carolina: Black candidate C.L.C. Glymph withdraws from the race for a town council seat, citing death threats from the KKK.

April 17, Mobile, Alabama: Two white men are held for beating a black who drank from a water fountain at work. Both are acquitted.

July 30, Whiteville, North Carolina: Klan wizard Tom Hamilton is sentenced to four years in prison for conspiracy in the flogging of a black woman. Sixty-three other Klansmen draw terms ranging from ten months to six years in the beatings of ten victims.

August 15, Macon, Georgia: Three policemen are indicted for beating black prisoners.

August 16, Lynchburg, Virginia: FBI agents investigate a black man's charges of false arrest and beatings at the hands of white police.

November 11, Yanceyville, North Carolina: Mack Ingram, a black defendant, is convicted of assault for "leering" at a white woman from an estimated distance of sixty feet. He is sentenced to six months in jail, suspended, with five years probation. The conviction is overturned by an appeals court on February 15, 1953.

1953

May 3, New York City: The NAACP and the American Jewish Council report no lynchings in 1952, but they record at least ten race- or religion-inspired bombings of homes, public buildings, and houses of worship during the year.

May 5, Cleveland, Ohio: A black minister's home is bombed by nightriders, while another bomb planted at the home of a black next-door neighbor fails to explode. Two miles away, a bottle containing a threatening note, signed "KKK," is tossed through the window of another black-owned dwelling.

May 8, Los Angeles, California: Sheriff's deputies beat David Hidalgo, a fifteen-year-old Hispanic, in front of his mother. In 1955, two of the officers are ordered to pay their victim $1,000 in damages.

June 3, Miami, Florida: A federal grand jury indicts six Klansmen for perjury, based on their testimony concerning acts of violence around Apopka, Florida, in the summer of 1950. Specific incidents include at least two floggings and the burning of a shanty occupied by a black child-molestation suspect.

August, Houston, Texas: Black-owned homes are targeted in a series of bombings.

August 3, Live Oak, Florida: A white dentist, a member of the KKK, is shot and killed in his office by a black woman, the mother of his illegitimate child.

August 24, Norfolk County, Virginia: Nightriders bomb a black home.

September 11, Norfolk County, Virginia: Authorities log the county's third racist bombing in eighteen days.

September 16, Ft. Worth, Texas: Violence erupts when an Anglo patrolman delivers a child custody order to a Hispanic home. Asked for a warrant, the officer draws his pistol, threatening members of the family and shooting Ernest Garcia in the chest. A grand jury indicts the officer for aggravated assault.

1954

March 1, Washington, D.C.: Four Puerto Rican nationalists, including a woman, open fire on congressmen from the gallery of the House of Representatives, wounding five persons. The terrorists are given life sentences, but President Jimmy Carter, in September 1979, commutes their sentences to time served.

June 27, Louisville, Kentucky: A black home in a formerly all-white neighborhood is bombed. A cross was previously burned at the house, with stones hurled and shots fired in the preceding days.

July, Holmes County, Mississippi: Henry Randle, a black youth, is shot by the sheriff and left to die along a country road where he had been talking to friends.

July 11, Indianola, Mississippi: The first White Citizens Council is organized to oppose court-ordered school desegregation by "all lawful means."

August–September, Norfolk County, Virginia: Three bombs explode on property owned by blacks.

October 1, Baltimore, Maryland: Thirty-six black high school students are pursued by a mob of white adults.

October 14, Ocilla, Georgia: A black candidate for city office reports being harassed and terrorized by white police.

December 2, Alabama: A black murder suspect is transferred to an unnamed jail after threats of mob violence.

December 31: Media sources report 195 racially motivated bombings and arson incidents during the preceding year.

1955

May 7, Belzoni, Mississippi: Rev. George W. Lee, a black NAACP officer, is shot and killed by nightriders on a rural highway.

June 21, Wadley, Alabama: An armed white mob disrupts an integrated meeting.

August 13, Brookhaven, Mississippi: Lamar Smith, a black man, is shot dead on the lawn of the county courthouse. Smith had urged blacks to register to vote.

August 14, Florence, South Carolina: A local newspaper editor is punched after trying to question a group of men burning a cross.

August 28, Money, Mississippi: Emmett Till, a fourteen-year-old black boy, is kidnapped, shot, and dumped in a river for allegedly whistling at a white man's wife. His killers are acquitted by a jury, then sell their confessions to a national magazine.

September, Lake City, South Carolina: A Klan motorcade circles the home of Rev. Joseph Delaine, a black minister, smashing windows with bricks and bottles. Delaine had moved to Lake City from Summerton, South Carolina, where his home was earlier burned by nightriders. Delaine has become a target for helping to initiate a lawsuit that overturned school segregation.

October 6, Lake City, South Carolina: Arsonists destroy Rev. Joseph Delaine's church. On October 10, the minister exchanges gunfire with a party of Klansmen.

October 22, Mayflower, Texas: Sixteen-year-old John Reese is killed and two other blacks are wounded when white gunmen shoot at a local cafe. The attack is linked to an ongoing terror campaign aimed at discouraging blacks from building a new school.

November 25, Erath, Louisiana: Two white women beat the instructor of an integrated Sunday school class. The women, both Catholics, are briefly excommunicated for their actions, but are reinstated with the church after they apologize.

November 26, Belzoni, Mississippi: Gus Courts, a black civil rights activist, is shot and wounded in his store.

December 3, Glendora, Mississippi: Clinton Melton, a black gas station attendant, is shot dead by a white customer who received more gas than he ordered.

December 7, Gonzales, Texas: NAACP leader H. Johnson is beaten to death. Authorities deny that race was the motive.

December 22, Heathsville, Virginia: Jurors acquit a white defendant of murder charges in the death of H. Bromley, a black man, accepting the prisoner's plea of self-defense. Evidence shows that Bromley was shot three times in the back.

1956

January 19, Pensacola, Florida: Two policemen are charged with various crimes committed against blacks while off duty.

January 30, Montgomery, Alabama: A bomb explodes at the home of Rev. Martin Luther King, Jr.

February 1, Montgomery, Alabama: The home of black civil rights worker E.D. Nixon is bombed.

February 3–4, Tuscaloosa, Alabama: Klansmen and white students riot for two days at the University of Alabama, protesting the admission of black coed Autherine Lucy. Another outbreak is recorded on February 6, leading to Lucy's suspension on February 7 and her eventual expulsion from the university.

February 18, Columbus, Georgia: Dr. Thomas Brewer, a black NAACP leader, is shot dead by a white gunman. Authorities deny that race was the motive.

March 25, Atlanta, Georgia: A black home in a mixed neighborhood is bombed.

April 11, Birmingham, Alabama: Six KKK members assault singer Nat "King" Cole during a performance at the city's municipal auditorium.

April 11, Harris County, Texas: A white man beats a black demonstrator during an attempt to integrate the county courthouse cafeteria.

April 22, Huntsville, Alabama: Rev. L.C. Baldwin, a black man, is fatally injured by a stone-throwing white assailant. The attacker is charged with second-degree murder.

May 3, Chattanooga, Tennessee: A white man assaults a black who refuses to sit in the back of a city bus.

May 5, Roanoke, Virginia: One person is injured and five are arrested in racial fighting after a bottle is thrown at blacks from the white gallery at a dance.

May 28, Tallahassee, Florida: A cross is burned at the home of a black coed arrested for refusing to sit at the back of a city bus.

June, Centerville, Mississippi: Nine members of the Taplin family, a black family, die when arsonists mistakenly set their home on fire, attempting to burn the home of a neighbor who keeps a white mistress.

June 3, Knoxville, Tennessee: Three whites are jailed after firing a shotgun into a black home, in a dispute over a stolen baseball.

June 6, Memphis, Tennessee: A cross is burned at the home of a black plaintiff in a bus desegregation case.

June 15, Kingstree, South Carolina: Nightriders fire on a black religious meeting.

July 2, Atlanta, Georgia: A black home in a nearly all-white district is bombed.

July 13, Camden, South Carolina: Following proposals for an integrated work camp on the campus of Methodist-run Mather School, a cross is burned on campus and anonymous callers threaten to destroy the building.

July 23, Americus, Georgia: A dynamite charge wrecks the roadside vegetable stand operated by members of Koinonia Farm, an integrated commune.

August, Clinton, Tennessee: Five bombs explode in black neighborhoods.

August 25, Montgomery, Alabama: A bomb explodes at the home of Rev. Bob Graetz, a civil rights activist.

August 28, Mansfield, Texas: Three black dummies with racist placards attached are hanged on Main Street and at a local high school. On August 31, a white mob threatens to bar blacks from entering the school.

August 30–31, Clinton, Tennessee: Police clear the streets after racial brawls involving 1,000 people. Fighting continues on August 31, with three whites arrested. Segregationist agitator John Kasper is jailed for violation of a court restraining order.

September 2, Clinton, Tennessee: Civilian volunteers use tear gas to disperse a mob of rioting segregationists. Shots are fired into the home of Judge Yarnell, who ordered John Kasper's arrest, and state troopers are sent to restore order. On September 3, National Guardsmen deploy seven tanks to restrain unruly mobs.

September 4, Oliver Springs, Tennessee: Violence erupts over rumors of school integration. Two bombs explode in a black neighborhood, and a mob of 250 armed whites terrorize black motorists. One white man is shot by a black driver, and a deputy is wounded by members of the mob. National Guardsmen are dispatched from Clinton, and one soldier is stabbed by white thugs. Guardsmen disperse another armed mob on September 5, as whites maul seven newsmen, destroying their equipment and threatening their lives.

September 5, Mansfield, Texas: White mobs once more prevent black students from entering a local high school.

September 5, Alvarado, Texas: A mob gathers on the opening day of the local high school, drawn by rumors of desegregation. Six effigies are hanged, and a cross is burned in a black neighborhood.

September 5–6, Sturgis, Kentucky: Mob violence flares at the prospect of school integration. National Guardsmen charge the crowd, to clear a path for a black student leaving the school, and a plainclothes state officer is beaten by two white men. Nightriders tour the black district on September 8, warning against school desegregation.

September 6, Clinton, Tennessee: Several whites are released on bond after being arrested on riot charges. After leaving the courtroom, they pummel newsmen waiting outside.

September 6, Clay, Kentucky: A mob bars two black children from attending a local grade school, threatening newsmen in the process. The scene is repeated on September 7 and 10, with protestors rocking a black motorist's car. After September 10, black parents abandon their plans to enroll children in the white school.

September 8, Mt. Gay, West Virginia: One hundred twenty-five whites attempt to bar teachers and pupils from a newly integrated grade school, shoving one black parent down a flight of stairs.

September 10, Texarkana, Texas: A mob of 300 whites bars two black students from entering a local junior college.

September 18, Clarendon County, South Carolina: NAACP organizer Bill Fleming reports that nightriders have fired twice on his home in recent days, and arsonists have burned his uncle's church.

September 27, Mobile, Alabama: Arsonists set fire to a "white" home briefly occupied by blacks. The occupants have already gone, driven out by shooting and rock-throwing incidents.

September 27, San Francisco, California: A bottle containing a racist threat is hurled through the window of a black-owned home in a nearly all-white area. A cross is burned in the yard as well.

October 6, Newton, Georgia: A black woman, Mrs. M.A. Rigdon, is shot and killed by a white gunman.

October 27, Wildwood, Florida: Jesse Woods, a black jailed for public drunkenness and insulting a white woman, is taken from jail and flogged. Seven whites are acquitted on December 12, after witnesses recant their testimony.

November, Summerville, Georgia: KKK threats result in the closing of a white high school's football field when two black teams are scheduled to play.

December, Kershaw, North Carolina: Arsonists burn a black home.

December, Americus, Georgia: Shotgun blasts cause $300 damage to the roadside vegetable stand at Koinonia Farm, an integrated Socialist community.

December 4, New Orleans, Louisiana: Rev. Paul Turner, a white minister, is severely beaten while escorting black children to a newly integrated school.

December 5, Montgomery, Alabama: Nightriders fire a shotgun blast into the home of Rev. Martin Luther King, Jr.

December 7, Zebulon, Georgia: Maybelle Mahone, a black mother of six, is shot dead after "sassing" a white man.

December 19, Birmingham, Alabama: Two white men fire shots at an integrated bus.

December 24, Birmingham, Alabama: The home of Rev. Fred Shuttlesworth, a black activist, is bombed. Neighboring homes are also damaged.

December 25, Montgomery, Alabama: A fifteen-year-old black girl is beaten by whites while waiting to board a city bus.

December 27–28, Montgomery, Alabama: White gunmen fire on three integrated buses, wounding a black female passenger on December 28. Seats are re-segregated to avoid further violence, but the same bus draws more sniper fire in a new attack. A black girl is beaten by whites while disembarking from another bus.

December 28, Camden, South Carolina: The band director of a local high school is flogged by hooded Klansmen.

December 31, Montgomery, Alabama: Snipers fire on a segregated city bus.

December 31, Birmingham, Alabama: A black-owned home in a formerly all-white neighborhood is bombed.

1957

January, Beaumont, Texas: A segregationist bomb damages the city auditorium.

January 1, Montgomery, Alabama: Nightriders fire on a store owned by relatives of a black leader of boycotts. More shots are fired into the home of Rev. C.K. Steele, an integrationist, and a cross is burned at Steele's church.

January 5, Montgomery, Alabama: Four white youths are arrested for throwing spark plugs at an integrated city bus.

January 5, Clinton, Tennessee: Police report the fourth recent bomb blast near an integrated high school.

January 9, Montgomery, Alabama: Bombs damage four black churches and the homes of two civil rights leaders. KKK members are charged with the bombings and later released without prosecution.

January 9, Charleston, Missouri: A white mob attempts to bar five black students from entering a local high school.

January 10, Mobile, Alabama: A black home is bombed, with attempts on two other homes. Crosses are burned at three other black homes.

January 11, Chattanooga, Tennessee: Two firebombs damage an interstate bus from which segregation signs have been removed.

January 15, Tallahassee, Florida: Bottles are hurled through the windows of a black-owned grocery store.

January 15, Americus, Georgia: Bombers cause $5,000 damage to a roadside market maintained by integrated residents of Koinonia Farm.

January 23, Montgomery, Alabama: Willie Edwards, a black deliveryman, is waylaid by Klansmen, interrogated on suspicion of accosting white women, and forced to leap from a river bridge at gunpoint. His body is recovered three months later, and his death is considered accidental until 1976, when one of the nightriders confesses. Three other Klansmen are indicted, but charges are dismissed when the prosecution fails to pinpoint a specific cause of death.

January 23, Birmingham, Alabama: Klan leader Asa Carter is arrested for shooting two of his followers during a KKK meeting.

January 23, Chattanooga, Tennessee: A bomb explodes outside a home recently shown to black prospective buyers.

January 27, Montgomery, Alabama: A black home is bombed, and nightriders fire shots at a television newscaster.

January 28, Montgomery, Alabama: Bombs damage a taxi stand owned by blacks and the home of a black hospital worker. An unexploded bomb is found on the porch of Dr. Martin Luther King, Jr.'s home.

January 28, Birmingham, Alabama: Asa Carter and his brother scuffle with police during a KKK meeting.

February, Knoxville, Tennessee: Segregationists bomb the city auditorium.

February, Charlottesville, North Carolina: Bombers attempt to destroy a black school.

February 7, Jackson, Mississippi: A black man, O. Moore, is shot dead by a white assailant during an altercation over a traffic accident.

February 14, Clinton, Tennessee: A suitcase bomb explodes on the street in a black neighborhood, injuring two persons and shattering windows in twenty homes. The blast, audible for twenty miles, is Clinton's eighth racial bombing in recent months.

March, Mobile, Alabama: A black home in a mixed neighborhood is bombed.

March, Beaumont, Texas: Bombs damage a truck, home, and church owned by white "moderates."

March 6, Birmingham, Alabama: White thugs assault an integrationist at the railroad station.

March 22, Americus, Georgia: Shots are fired at Koinonia Farm, an integrated Socialist farm.

April 7, Wilmington, Delaware: A black home is bombed.

April 16, Montgomery, Alabama: A white man assaults three black women on a city bus.

April 16, Miami, Florida: A white bus driver assaults a black passenger who refuses to ride in the back.

April 26, Richmond, Virginia: Six black youths are wounded by shotgun blasts fired by whites from a passing car.

April 28, Bessemer, Alabama: Bombs damage a black church and the home of a black labor leader.

May, Chattanooga, Tennessee: A black home in a white neighborhood is bombed.

May 1, Alexandria, Louisiana: A black rape-murder suspect is removed from jail and hidden to protect him from lynchers.

May 2, Tallahassee, Florida: Four white youths rape a black coed at Florida A&M University.

May 19, Americus, Georgia: Explosions damage three stores, two of which have done business with Koinonia Farm, an integrated Socialist farm.

July, Birmingham, Alabama: A black home is bombed in the district nicknamed "Dynamite Hill."

July 23, Greenville, South Carolina: A black man baby-sitting white children is flogged by fifteen Klansmen.

August, Jersey, Tennessee: A black home is bombed.

August 2, Wilmington, Delaware: A black home is bombed.

August 8, Evergreen, Alabama: Four blacks, including a minister, are beaten by KKK members. The incident marks Alabama's second flogging in a week.

August 9, Maplesville, Alabama: Six blacks are beaten by nightriders.

September 2, Birmingham, Alabama: Edward "Judge" Aaron, a black man, is abducted and castrated by Klansmen as part of a KKK initiation ceremony. Four suspects are convicted of mayhem and sentenced to twenty-year prison terms. All win early parole after the inauguration of Klan-backed Governor George Wallace.

September 4, Little Rock, Arkansas: National Guardsmen bar black students from Central High School while a white mob jeers. A cross is burned outside the mayor's home on September 6.

September 5, Prattville, Alabama: Nightriders fire shots at a black motorist, Rev. J.W. Bonner, who was active in the recent Montgomery bus boycott.

September 9, Nashville, Tennessee: Black students and their parents are jeered and stoned by a white mob outside a newly integrated school. That night, the school is destroyed by dynamite blasts. Seven Klansmen are charged with the bombing.

September 9, Birmingham, Alabama: Rev. Fred Shuttlesworth is beaten by whites while attempting to enroll his daughters and two other black children in a white school. Bomb threats are phoned to one high school on September 10.

September 10, Little Rock, Arkansas: Thirty whites bar black students from entering a local high school.

September 23–25, Little Rock, Arkansas: Riotous mobs protest the enrollment of black students in Central High School. President Dwight Eisenhower dispatches federal troops to protect the children after Gov. Orval Faubus refuses to intervene.

October, Greensboro, North Carolina: A black home is bombed.

October, Chattanooga, Tennessee: Bombs damage two black homes.

October 2, Matoaka, West Virginia: Six black students are attacked by 100 whites at a local high school.

November, Ringgold, Georgia: The wife of a black civil rights activist is killed when her home is bombed.

November, Charlotte, North Carolina: Nightriders attempt to bomb a synagogue.

November, Chattanooga, Tennessee: A black home is bombed.

November 1, Bessemer, Alabama: The home of a black integrationist is bombed.

November 20, Gaffney, South Carolina: A bomb damages the home of a white woman who advocated racial moderation. On November 23, a cross is burned near the same woman's house. Five whites are charged with the bombing on December 7.

December, Cowpens, South Carolina: A black home is bombed.

December, Birmingham, Alabama: Bombs damage five black homes.

1958

January, Little Rock, Arkansas: The home of an NAACP official is bombed.

January 1, Charlotte, North Carolina: A bomb damages the marquee of an integrated drive-in theater.

January 2, Greensboro, North Carolina: Guards are stationed at the school superintendent's home after attacks linked to recent desegregation.

January 3, Columbus, Georgia: A white patrolman is charged with murder in the beating death of a black minister, Rev. C.H. Pickett.

January 8, Houston, Texas: A white youth is stabbed after trying to drag a black passenger from his seat on a city bus.

January 18, Maxton, North Carolina: Armed Lumbee Indians disrupt a KKK rally protesting integration of whites and Indians in Robeson County. Klansmen escape on foot as Indians shoot at their cars and confiscate KKK regalia. On May 4, 1959, Klan leader James Cole is fined for inciting the riot.

January 18, New York City: Seven young members of the United Nordic Confederation are arraigned on weapons charges after police foil their plot to secure money for "the cause" by robbing a bank in Queens.

January 19, Chattanooga, Tennessee: A bomb explodes near a black school, causing $1,000 damage.

January 19, Tulsa, Oklahoma: Bombers damage a black-owned home.

January 20, Little Rock, Arkansas: A black high school student is assaulted by a white classmate. Police find a dynamite bomb at the school.

January 27, Chattanooga, Tennessee: Explosions damage an integrated YWCA building.

January 27, Columbus, Georgia: A bomb shatters windows at a black-owned home.

February, Chattanooga, Tennessee: A newly integrated school is bombed.

February 9, Gastonia, North Carolina: An unexploded bomb is found outside a local synagogue.

February 15, Charlotte, North Carolina: Six Klansmen are arrested while planting a bomb at a local school. Three of the defendants are sentenced to prison on March 20.

February 17, Atlanta, Georgia: A black home in a formerly all-white neighborhood is bombed.

February 20, Birmingham, Alabama: Nightriders bungle an attempt to bomb a black church.

March 16, Miami, Florida: Bombers damage a local synagogue.

March 16, Nashville, Tennessee: A synagogue is bombed.

March 17, Atlanta, Georgia: An unoccupied home, newly purchased by blacks in a "white" neighborhood, is damaged by a bomb.

April 20, Dawson, Georgia: James Brazier, a black prisoner, is beaten to death in police custody. His killer is later promoted to chief of police.

April 27, Jacksonville, Florida: Bombs damage a synagogue and a black school.

April 28, Birmingham, Alabama: An unexploded bomb is found at a local synagogue.

May, Yalobusha County, Mississippi: A black prisoner, Woodrow Daniel, is beaten to death in jail by Sheriff Buck Treolar. After his acquittal on manslaughter charges, Treolar stops to retrieve his blackjack from the prosecutor's table, remarking, "Now I can get back to rounding up moonshiners and niggers."

May 3, Jacksonville, Florida: Officials from twenty-nine Southern cities convene to discuss the epidemic of hate bombings. Forty-six blasts have been recorded since January 1, 1957.

May 17, Bessemer, Alabama: A black home is bombed.

May 29, Birmingham, Alabama: Vandals smear a black-owned radio station with KKK graffiti.

June 13, New Orleans, Louisiana: A white man assaults a black passenger on an integrated city bus.

June 21, Beaumont, Texas: A bomb damages the home of a white professor at an integrated college.

June 29, Birmingham, Alabama: A bomb explodes outside Rev. Fred Shuttlesworth's church, shattering windows in a four-block radius. Twenty years will pass before KKK leader J.B. Stoner is convicted and imprisoned for his involvement in the crime.

July 2, Columbus, Georgia: A black home is bombed.

July 7, Durham, North Carolina: A bomb damages the home of a white minister in charge of the Human Relations Committee.

July 17, Birmingham, Alabama: A black home is bombed, and two Klansmen are captured and beaten by blacks for their role in the bombing.

August 1, Birmingham, Alabama: Three whites are held on charges of attempting to bomb two black homes in July.

August 5, Memphis, Tennessee: Bombers damage a black church.

August 24–25, Deep Creek, North Carolina: Arsonists burn two rural schools scheduled for racial desegregation.

September 9, Ozark, Arkansas: Three black girls are assaulted during lunch hour at a newly integrated high school. All three withdraw from school on September 11.

September 27, Saraland, Alabama: Seven whites, including the local police chief, are charged with burning crosses to intimidate blacks. Prosecutors say the arrests are also linked to the August 6 murder of Saraland's mayor.

October 1, Wheelwright, Kentucky: A jeering, stone-throwing white mob forces the closing of a newly integrated school.

October 5, Clinton, Tennessee: Three dynamite blasts virtually destroy an integrated high school.

October 8, Greensboro, North Carolina: Two Klansmen are fined for damaging property owned by an NAACP leader and another black.

October 12, Atlanta, Georgia: Explosions damage a synagogue. Several members of the NSRP are charged in the case, but all are acquitted at trial.

October 13: ADL spokesmen report forty-six racially motivated bombings or attempted bombings since January 1. Over the next seven weeks, the ADL will record ninety-eight cases of anti-semitic vandalism in twenty-five states.

October 14, Chicago, Illinois: Bombs destroy two black-owned homes.

October 14, Peoria, Illinois: A local synagogue is bombed.

October 15, Boston, Massachusetts: A hand grenade explodes in the front yard of a meeting house used by Jehovah's Witnesses.

October 25, Clinton, Tennessee: An integrated school is bombed.

November 10, Osage, West Virginia: A bomb explodes at an integrated school.

1959

April 7, Wilmington, Delaware: Bombers strike at a black home in a formerly all-white suburb.

April 10, Birmingham, Alabama: Rev. Charles Billups, a black minister active in civil rights work, is abducted by nightriders and beaten with tire chains.

April 25, Poplarville, Mississippi: Mack Parker, a black rape suspect, is taken from jail and lynched by whites. A county prosecutor refuses to accept FBI evidence naming several of the lynchers. (At the time of Parker's arrest, a state trooper offered his pistol to the rape victim's husband, so that he could shoot Parker on the spot, but the man refused on the basis of his wife's uncertain identification.)

April 27, Richmond, Virginia: Six black youths are wounded by shotgun blasts in a drive-by shooting. Six white youths are arrested the following day.

May 1, Alexandria, Louisiana: Authorities remove Ora Rogers, a black rape-murder suspect, from jail and hide him from would-be lynchers.

May 1, Norfolk, Virginia: Two white servicemen—a Navy captain and a Marine Corps private—are assaulted by blacks. Six youths are fined $50 each and sentenced to jail terms on May 4.

May 2, Tallahassee, Florida: Four white youths are arrested for raping a black university coed. All four are convicted on June 14 and sentenced to life imprisonment on June 22.

May 29, Selma, Alabama: Rev. Horace Bell, a black minister missing for nearly a week, is found dead on the shore of a lake outside of town. The cause of death is listed as a heart attack, but civil rights activists point out that white gangs have twice attacked blacks near the lake in the past seven days.

June 9, Little Rock, Arkansas: Arsonists set fire to the porch of a home owned by C.G. Hall, Arkansas secretary of state and an outspoken opponent of the KKK.

August 2, Wilmington, Delaware: A black family's home is bombed for the second time since May. Thirteen whites are jailed on various charges by August 8, with white residents of Wilmington contributing cash for a legal defense fund.

August 12, Little Rock, Arkansas: Authorities use fire hoses to disperse a pro-segregationist mob outside the state capitol.

August 24, Wake Forest, North Carolina: A white defendant pleads no contest in the "accidental" shooting death of a black man, William Person. The defendant claims he fired at Williams "as a joke," to make him run. The court orders a cash payment of $2,750 to the victim's wife and four children.

August 25, Little Rock, Arkansas: Two white youths are jailed after a bomb explodes in front of a newly integrated high school.

August 27, Little Rock, Arkansas: Two white women break up a school board meeting with tear gas grenades.

September 7, Little Rock, Arkansas: Bombs destroy the local school board office and damage the fire chief's car and property owned by the mayor. Five members of the White Citizens Council are charged in the series of bombings, with one defendant pleading guilty on September 18. A second suspect is convicted at trial on November 28.

September 12, Montgomery, Alabama: J.B. Peek, Jr., a white tavern owner, is charged in the death of a KKK member. Klansmen had earlier threatened Peek's life for his refusal to fire black employees.

September 27, Pickens County, Alabama: The local sheriff reports that a dozen blacks have been flogged by nightriders during the past year.

October, Philadelphia, Mississippi: Luther Jackson, a black man, is shot and killed by Patrolman Lawrence Rainey, later county sheriff and a member of the KKK. When a female friend of Jackson denounces the killing as unprovoked, she is beaten by Rainey and the town's police chief.

December 26: ADL investigators mark the beginning of a nine-week long "swastika epidemic," logging 643 incidents of anti-Semitic vandalism in forty-two states by late February 1960. One hundred sixty-seven vandals are arrested in the outbreak, with 70 percent of them identified as juveniles.

1960

January 7–8: Several teenage vandals are arrested in a wave of anti-Semitic incidents. Racist graffiti is scrawled on synagogues and other buildings in New York City, Philadelphia, Chicago, Boston, and at least thirteen other cities. In New York City a Protestant and an Episcopal church are defaced with stars of David and pro-Jewish slogans on January 7 in apparent retaliation for the swastika attacks.

January 14, Queens, New York: Three youths are arrested for organizing the National American Socialist Renaissance Party and plotting attacks on Jews in the Fresh Meadows district. On January 15, the three are charged with treason, which carries a possible death sentence upon conviction.

January 14, Detroit, Michigan: A series of anti-Semitic incidents climaxes when police break up a small Nazi club boasting a fourteen-year-old führer.

January 15, Park Forest, Illinois: Several graves are vandalized with anti-Semitic graffiti.

January 15, Columbus, Ohio: Two university students are suspended for painting swastikas on the Jewish student's center.

January 28, Kansas City, Missouri: A bomb explodes outside a local synagogue. Police investigation reveals neo-Nazi groups active in two area high schools. On January 30, two youths are arrested for painting swastikas on four synagogues.

February 6, Greensboro, North Carolina: A department store closes after receiving bomb threats sparked by sit-in demonstrations at its segregated lunch counter.

February 8, Durham, North Carolina: Bomb threats close another department store during sit-in protests.

February 9, Little Rock, Arkansas: The home of a black student at Central High School is bombed.

February 26, Henderson, North Carolina: A bomb threat clears a department store targeted by civil rights protestors.

February 27, Montgomery, Alabama: Klansmen armed with baseball bats assault blacks outside two variety stores where lunch counter sit-ins are scheduled.

March 1, Rock Hill, South Carolina: A dormitory at Friendship Junior College is evacuated after racist bomb threats.

March 2, Nashville, Tennessee: Bomb threats are phoned to the Greyhound bus depot during civil rights demonstrations.

March 6, Montgomery, Alabama: Scattered fighting erupts after white mobs heckle a black protest meeting.

March 7, Houston, Texas: Felton Turner, a black man, is kidnapped by four masked whites who tell him that they were hired for the job.

Beaten with chains and the letters "KKK" carved on his stomach and chest, he is left hanging upside-down in a tree.

March 22, Petersburg, Virginia: A bottle containing a threatening note signed "KKK" is thrown at the home of a minister active in the NAACP.

March 25, Gadsden, Alabama: A synagogue is firebombed during services and shots are fired at worshippers as they emerge. Two persons are wounded, one of them seriously. A white youth confesses responsibility for the attack to police.

March 27, Anniston, Alabama: A bomb is tossed into the yard of a black-owned home. On the same day, twelve whites are arrested in a series of cross-burning incidents.

May 31, Montgomery, Alabama: Defendant James Peek, charged with murder in the shooting of a Klansman who threatened his life, is acquitted on grounds of self-defense.

April 2, Baton Rouge, Louisiana: A black faculty member, Professor Lee, is murdered at Southern University.

April 12, Atlanta, Georgia: A black home in a formerly all-white neighborhood is bombed.

April 15, Chattahoochie, Florida: Arsonists burn the home of a black rape-murder suspect.

April 19, Nashville, Tennessee: The homes of a black city councilman and a NAACP lawyer are bombed.

April 19, Charleston, South Carolina: A white gang attacks blacks picketing a local department store.

April 24, Biloxi, Mississippi: Five blacks are wounded in attacks by whites at a segregated beach.

May 19, Ringgold, Georgia: A black housewife, Mrs. J. Green, dies when a bomb is set off at her home by nightriders.

July 1, Knoxville, Tennessee: White mobs attack black picketers.

July 12, Little Rock, Arkansas: Three whites are arrested by the FBI while planting a bomb at a Philander Smith College dorm. Two hours later, another bomb damages the city's public school warehouse and black homes nearby.

July 15, Chattanooga, Tennessee: The home of a black teacher is burned by arsonists. A vacant house owned by the teacher was burned in 1956, and a restaurant owned by his sister was bombed in 1958.

August 13, Chattanooga, Tennessee: Another bomb explodes in a racially mixed neighborhood.

August 17, Chattanooga, Tennessee: Two bombs explode near the home of a white realtor who advertised houses for sale to blacks.

August 21, Chattanooga, Tennessee: A black home is bombed.

August 26, Union, Mississippi: A white minister is beaten while helping to build a black ministerial college. The mob chases away four black workers and the town constable. Several attackers are recognized as members of the local White Citizens Council.

August 27, Jacksonville, Florida: Klansmen riot against blacks on "Axhandle Saturday," so-called for the number of such weapons in evidence. One white youth is stabbed and two blacks are wounded by gunshots. More than 100 persons are arrested.

August 30, Buford, Georgia: Whites clash with black picketers and five bombs are hurled at stores and cars during an outbreak that local police blame on out-of-town racists.

September 9, Chattanooga, Tennessee: Arsonists burn a home in a racially mixed neighborhood.

October 2, Little Rock, Arkansas: A bomb wrecks the car of a leading segregationist. Police deny that the motive is racial.

October 7, Whitesburg, Georgia: Nightriders flog a black couple.

October 27, Jackson, Tennessee: White gangs assault black picketers.

November 10, Nashville, Tennessee: Black sit-in demonstrators are sprayed with water, powder, and insecticide at a segregated lunch counter.

November 12, Nashville, Tennessee: A white restaurant owner uses a gun to rout sit-in protestors.

November 15, New Orleans, Louisiana: Rioting erupts during a rally of the White Citizens Council, and seven whites are arrested during violent demonstrations at a desegregated school. On November 17, 250 persons are jailed during new outbreaks of rioting. Incidents include stabbings, firebombings, and a clash between 200 white and black longshoremen on the waterfront. One black is arrested for attempted murder after firing shots at two white men.

November 18, Atlanta, Georgia: Bombs damage the homes of two blacks and two whites in an integrated neighborhood.

November 23, Montgomery, Alabama: Five whites are arrested for making threats of violence at a football game between two black teams. On November 24, a dummy bomb and a KKK banner are found at the stadium.

November 29, New Orleans, Louisiana: White mobs harass a priest and students at an integrated Catholic school. A white woman is also assaulted while escorting her child to school. On November 30 mobs demonstrate at the homes of the priest and the woman who defied the white boycott.

November 29, Austin, Texas: A bomb explodes outside the building where members of the Texas University Religious Council are discussing integration of local restaurants.

December 3, St. Petersburg, Florida: KKK leader Bill Hendrix is ejected from town after trying to organize demonstrations.

December 5, New Orleans, Louisiana: White rioters stone vehicles carrying black children home from school. The home of a white integrationist minister is also damaged. On December 7, stone-throwing hoodlums attack the home of a white woman who has defied the school boycott.

December 12, Atlanta, Georgia: A black elementary school is bombed – the city's eighteenth racial bombing in four years. Damage is estimated at $5,000.

1961

January 1, Greenville, Mississippi: Two blacks are wounded by white motorcyclists in a drive-by shooting.

January 5, Anniston, Alabama: Whites assault black protestors outside the courthouse during the trial of a white man accused of beating a black.

January 11, Athens, Georgia: Six hundred whites riot at the University of Georgia, hurling rocks and firecrackers at the dormitory housing a black coed. Of the nine rioters arrested, eight are admitted KKK members.

January 15, Athens, Georgia: Security guards disarm a white man who invaded the university campus searching for a black student.

May, Jackson, Mississippi: White youths, while riding in a convertible, lasso and drag a nine-year-old black girl.

May 9, Rock Hill, South Carolina: Whites attack a busload of integrated freedom riders sponsored by CORE to desegregate Southern bus depots.

May 13, Talladega, Alabama: Three white residents are flogged for allowing a black maid to discipline their children. Eight Klansmen are arrested on May 23. On October 8, one of the floggers is sentenced to eight years in prison.

May 14, Anniston, Alabama: The occupants of a CORE freedom bus are mobbed and beaten by whites. Tires are slashed on a second integrated bus, and then the bus is surrounded and firebombed. Nine whites are charged in the case, six of whom plead "no contest" on January 16, 1962. One is sentenced to jail; five others receive one-year probations after promising to sever all ties with the KKK.

May 14, Birmingham, Alabama: Freedom riders are mobbed and severely beaten by KKK members at a local bus terminal. FBI informants report that police have granted the Klan permission to assault the demonstrators with impunity.

May 20, Montgomery, Alabama: Freedom riders are beaten by white mobs at the bus station. Federal marshals are dispatched to protect a black church after whites surround the building and threaten to burn it down with the worshippers inside. Injunctions are issued forbidding further violence by the KKK and NSRP.

May 22, Montgomery, Alabama: Two white high schools soon to be integrated are evacuated after anonymous bomb threats.

May 25, Montgomery, Alabama: Rev. S. D. Seay, a black civil rights leader, is shot and wounded by a gunman in a passing car. Six white youths are arrested for the crime on May 27, then released to the custody of their parents.

May 25, LaGrange, Georgia: Five KKK members are jailed for trying to block passage of a CORE freedom bus between Georgia and Alabama. On May 29, three are fined for inciting a riot.

June 16, Ocala, Florida: Two whites attack freedom riders at the local bus depot. The victims are arrested for assault.

June 16, Montgomery, Alabama: Gov. John Patterson warns highway patrolmen that any officer who cooperates with FBI probes of racial violence will be dismissed from his job.

June 17, Washington, D.C.: Two bombs explode in a streetside trash can. Anonymous calls link the blasts to the recent freedom rides.

June 20, Montgomery, Alabama: Two bomb threats are phoned to the city's bus terminal as more freedom riders arrive.

July 5, Jackson, Mississippi: Police beat Jesse Harris, a black man, for refusing to leave the white section of a bus depot. On conviction of his "crime" Harris is sentenced to four months in jail, with a $500 fine.

July 13–15, Chicago, Illinois: Blacks riot for three nights after police kill a black youth, Matthew Tolbert, on July 12. At least twenty-one whites are beaten by roving gangs, and sixty-five blacks are jailed during the outbreak.

July 22, Griffin, Georgia: Two whites are arrested for burning a cross in a black family's yard.

September 4, Atlanta, Georgia: Angry participants in a KKK rally mob a car driven by the local police chief, mistaking him for an FBI agent. Visiting Pennsylvania Klan leader Roy Frankhouser is charged with assaulting an officer.

September 5, McComb, Mississippi: A black man attempting to register to vote is beaten by a mob of white men.

September 7, Walthall County, Mississippi: A black voter applicant is pistol-whipped by the white registrar.

September 25, Liberty, Mississippi: Herbert Lee, a black civil rights worker, is shot to death by state legislator E.H. Hurst.

October 11, McComb, Mississippi: Whites beat two newsmen covering a black protest march.

November 28, Anniston, Alabama: L.M. Parker, a member of a jury that failed to reach a verdict in the case of nine whites charged with burning a freedom bus, is jailed for perjury after his KKK membership is revealed. (All jurors denied affiliation with the Klan when they were sworn in for the trial.)

November 29, McComb, Mississippi: A white mob beats five freedom riders at a segregated lunch counter. On December 1, an estimated 700 whites menace the protestors, beating four out-of-town newsmen. A carload of freedom riders are attacked by whites on December 2, and a segregationist assaults the editor of a local "moderate" newspaper on December 3.

December 26, Jackson, Mississippi: Following a traffic collision with a white female motorist, black driver Rafford Johnson is beaten so severely by police that he later requires brain surgery.

1962

January 16, Birmingham, Alabama: Three black churches are bombed, and damage is suffered by adjacent homes and a police car parked near the scene of one blast.

January 22, Huntsville, Alabama: Sit-in demonstrators are beaten and sprayed with chemicals at a segregated lunch counter.

February 6, Clarksdale, Mississippi: Bessie Turner, a black woman jailed on suspicion of theft, is forced to strip and lie on her back while patrolmen whip her with belts.

February 18, Shreveport, Louisiana: A home under construction for NAACP leader C.O. Simpkins is bombed.

March 22, Jackson, Mississippi: Jesse Harris, a black man, is sentenced to thirty days in jail for sitting on the "white" side of a courtroom. Over the next two weeks, he is beaten once by deputies in jail and twice by guards at the county work farm.

April 9, Taylorsville, Mississippi: A black soldier, Roman Ducksworth, is shot to death by a white policeman for refusing to sit in the back of a bus.

April 24, Shreveport, Louisiana: A black Masonic temple is bombed.

April 25, Talladega, Alabama: Whites assault black picketers, destroying their signs. Tear gas bombs are hurled at the demonstrators from a passing car.

April 26, Bossier City, Louisiana: Fire damages the summer home of NAACP official C.O. Simpkins.

April 27, Los Angeles, California: Two patrolmen are attacked when they stop and question a black man outside a Black Muslim mosque. Reinforcements arrive to suppress the riot, and gunfire erupts, leaving one Muslim dead and fourteen persons wounded (including eight policemen). Sixteen Muslims are indicted for assault and resisting arrest, eleven of the defendants are convicted and sentenced to prison on June 14, 1963.

May, Philadelphia, Mississippi: Willie Nash, a black epileptic, is riddled with bullets while handcuffed and in police custody. Two of the gunmen—Sheriff Hop Barnett and Deputy Lawrence Rainey—are later identified as KKK members and are indicted on various civil rights charges.

June 20, Jackson, Mississippi: The editor of a black newspaper is beaten by police en route to Forest, Mississippi, to investigate reports of a black man killed by whites.

July, Greenwood, Mississippi: Sam Block, a black SNCC volunteer, is beaten by whites on a city street. In a later incident, Block is nearly killed by a white hit-and-run driver.

July 23, Albany, Georgia: The pregnant wife of a black civil rights worker is beaten while visiting her husband in jail. The beating results in a miscarriage.

July 28, Albany, Georgia: A black attorney is assaulted with a cane by the sheriff after requesting medical aid for jailed civil rights workers.

July 30, Charlottesville, Virginia: Two white youths are convicted and sentenced for kidnapping one black man and assaulting others on the street.

August, Greenwood, Mississippi: Police beat a black youth with clubs and blackjacks, then strip off his clothes and continue to flog him on the floor of the police station.

August 16, Greenwood, Mississippi: A black civil rights worker is beaten by whites.

August 17, Greenwood, Mississippi: An armed mob raids and vandalizes the office of the SNCC.

August 25–27, Monroe, North Carolina: One freedom rider is wounded in a drive-by shooting, two others are beaten by whites on the street, and a fourth is beaten by cellmates in jail. On August 26, black picketers are attacked by whites armed with knives and bottles, and a few stray shots are fired during the melee. Demonstrators are mobbed again on August 27, with several blacks injured and one policeman shot in the leg. Black residents exchange fire with nightriders until dawn.

August 29, Birmingham, Alabama: Two white policemen are indicted on federal civil rights charges after breaking into the home of black resident Phillip Travis without a warrant, shooting him in the leg, and beating his two sons.

August 31, Lee County, Georgia: Shots are fired into the homes of four blacks active in a voter registration drive. One house is struck by twenty-seven rounds from high-powered rifles.

August 31, Buras, Louisiana: A Catholic school closes after threats of violence against black students.

September 5, Dawson, Georgia: Nightriders fire into a black home, wounding a civil rights worker. Six whites are arrested for the shooting on October 19.

September 5, Dallas, Georgia: Masked nightriders storm the rural home of a family black, but retreat after one of the masked white men is shot and killed by return fire.

September 7, New Orleans, Louisiana: Shots are fired through the door of an integrated Catholic school. Several other schools receive bomb threats.

September 9, Sasser, Georgia: A black church is burned.

September 9, Chickasawhatchee, Georgia: Arsonists burn a black church. A white farmer is arrested for assaulting two FBI agents sent to investigate the fire.

September 17, Dawson, Georgia: Nightriders burn a black church. Three whites plead guilty to arson on September 20.

September 19, Marksville, Louisiana: Two whites are jailed for illegal cross-burning and assault.

September 28, Birmingham, Alabama: A member of the American Nazi Party assaults Dr. Martin Luther King, Jr., at a local NAACP convention.

September 30, Oxford, Mississippi: Whites riot through the night to protest enrollment of a black student, James Meredith, at the University of Mississippi. One of the rioters, Ray Gunter, is killed by a stray bullet. Paul Guihard, a French journalist, is shot to death, execution-style, behind one of the campus dormitories.

October, McComb, Mississippi: Eli Brumfield, an unarmed black driver, is shot to death by a white patrolman "in self-defense."

October 13, Birmingham, Alabama: A white man is beaten at a KKK rally after announcing that "mob violence is no answer to anything."

November 1, Pascagoula, Mississippi: Nightriders fire a shotgun blast through the window of a "liberal" newsman's office.

December 14, Birmingham, Alabama: A black church is bombed.

1963

January 11, Natchez, Mississippi: A carload of whites pursue two SNCC workers, twice forcing their vehicle off the road and firing four shots into the car before the SNCC workers escape.

February 7, Bossier City, Louisiana: Four men are arrested after painting thirty "KKK" signs on sidewalks and buildings in town.

February 24, Greenville, Mississippi: Four black civil rights workers are wounded, one of them seriously, when whites riddle their car with machine-gun fire.

February 28, Leflore County, Mississippi: James Travis, a black civil rights worker, is wounded by white gunmen in a drive-by shooting.

March, Greenwood, Mississippi: Shotgun blasts damage the home of a black man whose son is attending the state university.

March 2, Greenwood, Mississippi: Nightriders fire shotgun blasts into a carload of blacks parked outside SNCC headquarters.

March 6, Greenwood, Mississippi: Four black voter registration workers are shot and wounded by whites. The shooting occurs hours after the release of white gunmen jailed for the February 24 shooting at Greenville.

March 24, Birmingham, Alabama: Two persons are injured in the bombing of a black home.

March 24, Greenwood, Mississippi: Arsonists damage a black voter registration headquarters.

March 26, Greenwood, Mississippi: Shots are fired into the home of a black student who applied to the state university.

April 1–2, Macon, Georgia: White mobs attack black demonstrators at a segregated public park, touching off rock- and bottle-throwing. One black protestor is stabbed by whites on April 2.

April 12, Clarksdale, Mississippi: A firebomb damages the home of black civil rights worker Aaron Henry. Two white men are arrested the following day.

April 15, Clarksdale, Mississippi: Larry Johnson, a black man, is arrested, stripped, and beaten by five officers who force him to sign a confession to car theft. Sentenced to one year in jail, he serves eight months and is flogged with a strap by white guards on at least four occasions.

April 23, Attalla, Alabama: A white northerner, William Moore, is shot and killed during a one-man civil rights march from Tennessee to Mississippi. A local white man is charged with murder on April 27.

April 23, Clarksdale, Mississippi: Vera Pigee, a black NAACP secretary, is beaten by a white gas station attendant. Police arrest Pigee on charges of "disturbing the peace."

May 3, Attalla, Alabama: Whites harass newsmen filming the arrest of civil rights protestors.

May 3, Birmingham, Alabama: Fire hoses and attack dogs are used to disperse civil rights marchers. The demonstrators remain nonviolent until a state police investigator deliberately swerves his car into the crowd. Blacks retaliate with rocks and bottles, injuring two firemen and a photographer. Hoses are turned on the crowd to suppress the disturbance. Four hundred fifty persons are arrested during the demonstration and subsequent riot.

May 3, Rising Fawn, Georgia: Whites stone and assault black civil rights protesters on the highway leading to Alabama.

May 4, Clarksdale, Mississippi: The sheriff blames "lightning" for explosions that damage a store owned by an NAACP officer.

May 7, Birmingham, Alabama: High-pressure hoses are turned on black protesters a second time, sending one man to the hospital. Blacks retaliate by stoning police, touching off an hour-long battle. Twelve persons are injured in the melee, and more than forty are arrested.

May 12, Birmingham, Alabama: The home of Rev. A.D. King and the black-owned Gaston Motel are bombed shortly after a KKK rally. One witness claims that uniformed patrolmen planted the motel bomb.

May 12, Anniston, Alabama: Shots are fired into a black church and two black homes.

May 13, Nashville, Tennessee: White youths stone black protestors, touching off rock fights. Shots are fired into the home of a civil rights activist. On May 14 a white man attacks black demonstrators on the street.

May 27, Jackson, Mississippi: A firebomb explodes in the carport of NAACP leader Medgar Evers.

May 28, Jackson, Mississippi: Whites, including one ex-policeman, beat three civil rights workers at a segregated lunch counter.

June 1, Jackson, Mississippi: Police assault black civil rights worker David Green on the street. A witness to the beating, James Jones, is clubbed and arrested without charges and is beaten again in the squad car and on his arrival at jail where officers book him for "resisting arrest."

June 2, Gainesville, Florida: One person is shot and two are beaten in attacks on civil rights protestors at a local theater.

June 5, Chattanooga, Tennessee: Three black demonstrators are beaten by whites.

June 6, Lexington, Tennessee: Five hundred whites raid a black neighborhood and meet resistance from black residents. One white man is killed and a journalist is wounded by gunfire. A state of emergency is declared on June 7, with ten whites and seven blacks arrested on various charges.

June 8, Winona, Mississippi: Five whites, including the county sheriff and Winona's police chief, are indicted on federal charges of brutalizing black prisoners. On June 9, six blacks—including two women—are jailed and beaten after trying to desegregate the local bus depot.

June 8, Clarksdale, Mississippi: Nightriders shoot at the home of NAACP secretary Vera Pigee.

June 11, Selma, Alabama: A SNCC field secretary is beaten by whites.

June 11, Cambridge, Maryland: Whites and blacks clash during a black protest march, and two men are wounded by shotgun blasts.

June 12, Jackson, Mississippi: Medgar Evers, a black NAACP leader, is killed by a sniper's bullet in the driveway of his home. An FBI investigation names the killer as Byron de la Beckwith, a member of the KKK and White Citizen's Council, but three murder trials result in hung juries. Beckwith continues his racist career by running for governor in 1967 with Klan backing.

June 14, Linden, Alabama: A cross is burned and rocks are thrown at the home of a white minister who resigned rather than exclude blacks from his church.

June 17, Itta Bena, Mississippi: A black church is firebombed.

June 18, Gillett, Arkansas: A black church is bombed.

June 23, Biloxi, Mississippi: A white man is arrested for threatening black demonstrators with a gun.

June 24, Canton, Mississippi: Five blacks are wounded by shotgun blasts after a COFO voter registration rally.

June 26, Gulfport, Mississippi: A bomb explodes at the office of a black doctor active in the NAACP.

June 30, Jackson, Mississippi: A black home is bombed.

June 30, New York City: Police blame Black Muslims after eggs are thrown at Martin Luther King's car in Harlem en route to a speech.

July, New York City: Several NSRP members are arrested for brawling with black picketers outside a restaurant. A search of their vehicle turns up several knives, an ax, and a crossbow.

July 1, St. Augustine, Florida: Nightriders trade shots with black guards at the home of a black civil rights activist. Police arrest three blacks in the incident.

July 11–12, Savannah, Georgia: Whites riot against black protesters for two consecutive days. On July 13, a racist spokesman declares that "the white people have shown remarkable restraint in not killing niggers wholesale."

July 13, Rosman, North Carolina: White rioters rout campers from Camp Summerlane, an integrated facility. The camp's gymnasium is burned and gasoline is poured on the lake and set afire. One man is stabbed, and a camp bus is riddled with gunfire.

July 16, Charleston, South Carolina: A nocturnal march by black civil rights demonstrators ends in a riot. Six patrolmen and one fireman are injured.

July 20, Emporia, Virginia: the American Nazi Party leader George Rockwell is jailed for conspiring to incite racial violence.

July 20–21, Parchman, Mississippi: As punishment for "singing," black civil rights worker Willie Carvell is hanged by his wrists from the bars of his cell at the state prison farm for a period of thirty hours.

July 28, Ocala, Florida: Two whites fire shotgun blasts through the windows of the home of Dr. L.R. Hampton, a black NAACP leader.

August 2, Chicago, Illinois: Whites riot, injuring several persons, when three black families move into a "white" neighborhood.

August 9, Clarksdale, Mississippi: Arrested for "littering," black civil rights worker Lafayette Surney is beaten by six officers in jail.

August 10, Jersey City, New Jersey: Two whites are jailed after a fourteen-year-old black youth is killed in a drive-by shooting. The incident follows racial arguments outside a local bar.

August 15, Birmingham, Alabama: A tear gas bomb explodes in a newly integrated department store.

August 18, Parchman, Mississippi: Sentenced to hang by his wrists for forty-eight hours, without charges, black civil rights worker Douglas Cotton is released after two hours in irons.

August 20, Birmingham, Alabama: The home of a black attorney is bombed.

August 27, Columbia, South Carolina: A bomb explodes near the home of a black woman scheduled to enter the state university.

August 27, Buras, Louisiana: An integrated Catholic school is bombed.

August 29, Clarksdale, Mississippi: Percy Atkins, a black civil rights activist, is arrested while walking home from work and charged with "parading without a permit." He is beaten twice by officers in jail, and is finally released on September 2 after paying a $16 fine.

August 29–30, Folcroft, Pennsylvania: White rioters prevent a black couple from occupying their new home. A firebomb damages the house on August 29, and seven whites are arrested the next day when a mob stones passing cars. Order is restored on August 31.

August 31, Jackson, Mississippi: Bombers demolish a black home.

September 1, Clarksdale, Mississippi: Jailed on charges of disturbing the peace, James Atkins, who is black, is beaten by officers in his cell.

September 4, Birmingham, Alabama: The home of black attorney Arthur Shores is bombed for a second time, touching off a riot that leaves one person dead and eighteen injured. Elsewhere, 125 NSRP members scuffle with police outside a newly integrated school.

September 4, Little Rock, Arkansas: Vandals damage the home of a white woman who enrolled her son in a black school.

September 8, Birmingham, Alabama: The home of black businessman A.G. Gaston is bombed.

September 9, Northport, Alabama: Three students from Ghana mistaken for civil rights workers are forced from their car and beaten by whites.

September 10, Birmingham, Alabama: Twelve whites are arrested during an unruly demonstration at a local high school. A concussion grenade explodes outside a black-owned home.

September 15, Anniston, Alabama: Two black ministers are attacked by a white mob while trying to desegregate a local library.

September 15, Birmingham, Alabama: A bomb explodes at the 16th Street Baptist Church during Sunday services, killing four black girls and blinding another. Black violence erupts in response, and state troopers are dispatched under the command of Col. Al Lingo, a self-described "good friend" of the KKK. During the outbreak, black youth Johnny Robinson is killed when a policeman "accidentally" shoots him in the back. Another black, thirteen-year-old Virgil Ware, is shot dead by two white youths on a motorcycle.

September 16, Calhoun, Florida: Klansmen beat a sixty-two-year-old white man for "having affairs" with black women.

September 16, Birmingham, Alabama: Two suburban high schools scheduled for desegregation receive bomb threats

September 18, St. Augustine, Florida: Four blacks are beaten at a KKK rally after they are caught spying on the gathering. The sheriff arrives and arrests the four for assaulting the Klansmen.

September 23, Birmingham, Alabama: Eight members of the NSRP are indicted for violent interference with school integration.

September 25, Birmingham, Alabama: Two bombs with scrap metal for shrapnel explode in a black neighborhood while police are searching for clues in the recent church bombing.

October 2, Birmingham, Alabama: A black-owned butcher shop is bombed.

October 25, St. Augustine, Florida: A Klansman is shot and killed during an armed raid on a black neighborhood.

October 28, St. Augustine, Florida: Nightriders fire shots into five black homes, tossing a hand grenade (which fails to explode) through the window of a sixth house.

November 16, Tuscaloosa, Alabama: Two bombs explode on the campus of the state university—one near an integrated dorm, the other in a parking lot.

November 19, Tuscaloosa, Alabama: A bomb detonates near a university dorm housing a black coed. Five National Guardsmen are charged with the bombing on December 22.

December, Wilkinson County, Mississippi: Three blacks, including a woman, are found dead in their car, ten miles north of Woodville. The press attributes their death to carbon monoxide, but a black undertaker reports finding broken bones and gunshot wounds in the bodies.

December 8, Dawson, Georgia: Gunfire and an explosion damage the home of a black civil rights worker. Fifty shots strike the house before a bomb is thrown inside.

December 22, Hot Springs, Arkansas: The Roanoke Baptist Church is burned after its pastor complains to the White House about local segregation.

1964

January, St. Augustine, Florida: A black family's car is burned outside a PTA meeting after they enroll their child in a newly integrated school.

January 6, Birmingham, Alabama: Prosecutors say they will not charge a National Guardsman who has confessed to detonating a bomb in a black neighborhood the previous October. Residents did not report the blast, and no physical evidence remains.

January 8, Tuscaloosa, Alabama: Five National Guardsmen are indicted for setting bombs around the state university campus in October 1963, at the height of the desegregation crisis.

January 19, Atlanta, Georgia: Klansmen pack a restaurant to keep out black demonstrators and scuffle with the protesters as they leave.

January 25, Atlanta, Georgia: Klansmen clash with black students during civil rights demonstrations.

January 31, Liberty, Mississippi: Louis Allen, a black witness to the 1961 murder of Herbert Lee, is shot and killed in his front yard.

February, Natchez, Mississippi: Black mortician Archie Curtis is lured to a rural highway with false reports of a dying woman, then ambushed and beaten by hooded whites.

February, Charleston, Mississippi: Two black youths are hospitalized after being pistol-whipped and beaten with ax handles in a white-owned grocery store.

February, St. Augustine, Florida: Arsonists destroy the home of a black family whose child is enrolled in an integrated school. In a separate incident, a black man enrolled in adult classes at a white school is accosted and beaten on his way home.

February 8, St. Augustine, Florida: Nightriders fire four shotgun blasts into the home of NAACP leader R.N. Hayling, killing the family dog.

February 12, St. Augustine, Florida: Klansmen burn a black minister's car.

February 16, Jacksonville, Florida: Bombers strike at the home of a black family whose grandson has enrolled in a formerly all-white school. One Klansman pleads guilty on March 13 and is sentenced to seven years in prison; five others are acquitted at trials in June and November.

February 21–22, Princess Anne, Maryland: Fighting erupts during black civil rights demonstrations at Maryland State College.

February 24, Princess Anne, Maryland: A black home is bombed.

February 29, Centreville, Mississippi: A black motorist is shot and killed by nightriders.

March, St. Augustine, Florida: Vandals smash windows in the home, car, and office of John Kalivos, a restaurant owner who served black patrons during a sit-in.

March 23, Jacksonville, Florida: Ghetto rioting erupts after a black woman, Mrs. Johnnie Mae Chappell, is killed by nightriders in a drive-by shooting. The triggerman is convicted of first-degree manslaughter on December 2.

April 5, Natchez, Mississippi: Black farm worker Richard Butler is shot and wounded. Two whites are jailed on October 26, with police confiscating guns and blackjacks.

April 7, Cleveland, Ohio: Rev. Bruce Klunder is crushed to death by a bulldozer while protesting the construction of a segregated school.

April 18, Notasulga, Alabama: Macon County High School is burned by arsonists on the eve of court-ordered desegregation.

April 18, Bogalusa, Louisiana: Klansmen abduct, flog, and pistol-whip a local mill worker, an integrationist.

April 19, Jackson, Louisiana: Newsman Bob Wagner is seized and beaten near a Klan rally.

April 28, McComb, Mississippi: The home of a black NAACP leader is bombed.

May, McComb, Mississippi: Windows of the COFO headquarters are smashed two times in three days. In the second attack, a female occupant of the building is struck in the head by a brick.

May 2, Meadville, Mississippi: Black teenagers Henry Dee and Charlie Moore are abducted by Klansmen. Two months later their bodies are pulled from a river near Tallulah, Louisiana. Murder charges filed against two KKK members are later dismissed.

May 10, Laurel, Mississippi: Klansmen bomb the offices of a local "moderate" newspaper.

May 28, St. Augustine, Florida: White rioters, including many Klansmen, mob black demonstrators downtown.

May 29, St. Augustine, Florida: Nightriders shoot at a beach cottage used by SCLC staff members. In a separate incident, gunmen fire at one of Dr. Martin Luther King's aides on the highway, narrowly missing him. Newsman Gary Hanes is assaulted twice in the space of four hours while covering black demonstrations.

June, Canton, Mississippi: White gunmen stop a car driven by Rev. Edwin King, the white dean of predominantly black Tougaloo College, outside of town. They debate killing King, but decide against it because they would then have to kill his wife and a Pakistani student riding in the car. In the months to come, King is stopped and harassed so frequently by police around Jackson that many of the citations simply describe his car as "King's Rambler."

June 8, McComb, Mississippi: Three carloads of nightriders stop three blacks on the highway outside of town, dragging them from their car, and beating them with guns and brass knuckles.

June 9, St. Augustine, Florida: Several blacks are beaten when Klansmen attack protest marchers.

June 10, St. Augustine, Florida: A white mob hurling bricks and sulphuric acid breaks through police lines to attack black demonstrators. Tear gas and police dogs are used to disperse the rioters.

June 16, Philadelphia, Mississippi: Klansmen beat black worshippers at the Mt. Zion Methodist Church, afterward burning the church to the ground.

June 17, Jackson, Mississippi: Hooded nightriders abduct and flog a black man.

June 20, Fayette, Mississippi: A black civil rights worker is chased from his car by white thugs.

June 20, McComb, Mississippi: Bombs strike two black homes, a black-owned barbershop, and the homes of two white moderates who have spoken out against Klan violence.

June 21, Brandon, Mississippi: A black church is bombed.

June 21, Maben, Mississippi: Armed whites surround a car occupied by six black civil rights workers, cursing, threatening, and spitting on the passengers.

June 21, Athens, Georgia: Two blacks are wounded when Klansmen fire shotgun blasts into their apartment.

June 21, Philadelphia, Mississippi: Civil rights workers Michael Schwerner, James Chaney, and Andrew Goodman are arrested for allegedly speeding, then released to a waiting gang of Klansmen. Murdered on a rural road, they are afterward buried in an earthen dam. Their bodies are recovered on August 4. The state refuses to file murder charges, but seven Klansmen are convicted of federal civil rights violations in October 1967.

June 22, McComb, Mississippi: Bombs strike the homes of two black civil rights workers. Seven sticks of dynamite are found on the lawn of a third home.

June 22, Brandon, Mississippi: A black youth is killed by a white hit-and-run driver. Black residents believe the hit-and-run was intentional, but police rule it an accident.

June 23, Jackson, Mississippi: Nightriders fire into a black-owned cafe, wounding one customer, and shoot at a black minister's home. In the latter attack, the gunmen escape in a truck with municipal license tags.

June 23, Moss Point, Mississippi: A firebomb causes slight damage to a Knights of Pythias hall used for black voter registration meetings.

June 23, Ruleville, Mississippi: Two Northern newsmen covering a civil rights meeting are chased out of town by nightriders at speeds topping eighty-five miles per hour.

June 24, Ruleville, Mississippi: Nine black-owned homes and cars are damaged by bottles thrown from passing vehicles.

June 24, Canton, Mississippi: A shot is fired into a civil rights worker's car.

June 25, Ruleville, Mississippi: A black church is firebombed, causing slight damage. Eight plastic bags of gasoline are found outside the building.

June 25, St. Augustine, Florida: White mobs repeatedly assault black demonstrators throughout the afternoon and evening. On one occasion, five white prisoners are released by police in response to demands from the mob.

June 25, Itta Bena, Mississippi: Armed whites escort two civil rights workers to the bus station, ordering them to leave town.

June 25, Longdale, Mississippi: A black church is damaged by a firebomb.

June 26, Clinton, Mississippi: Arsonists burn a black church.

June 26, Holly Springs, Mississippi: Local whites throw beer cans at civil rights workers and slash the tires on their car.

June 27, McComb, Mississippi: A Molotov cocktail, bearing a note signed "KKK," is hurled against the door of a local, anti-Klan newspaper.

June 27, Doddsville, Mississippi: Highway patrolmen shoot and kill an unarmed black man with a history of mental illness.

June 28, Jackson, Mississippi: Civil rights worker Steven Smith is attacked and beaten by whites near the downtown railroad station.

June 28, Batesville, Mississippi: A local black man is abducted and beaten by whites.

June 29, Hattiesburg, Mississippi: Nightriders fire into two cars owned by civil rights workers, causing $100 damage to each car.

June 30, Holly Springs, Mississippi: White youths stone the local COFO office. Later in the day, a civil rights worker is assaulted and threatened with a shotgun by a white man.

July 2, Vicksburg, Mississippi: Nightriders pursue and fire on a black motorcyclist.

July 2, Meridian, Mississippi: A bottle is thrown at civil rights workers outside a local church. One woman is cut by flying glass.

July 2, Gulfport, Mississippi: Two black voter registration workers are assaulted by whites.

July 3, Soso, Mississippi: A black-owned cafe is bombed, causing minor damage.

July 3, Americus, Georgia: Whites mob and beat an integrated party emerging from a local theater.

July 3, Tougaloo, Mississippi: Four civil rights workers en route to Canton are pursued by two carloads of whites in a high-speed chase, finally stopping in Jackson for their own protection.

July 4, Atlanta, Georgia: Three blacks are mobbed and beaten with chairs at a rally where Gov. George Wallace shares the podium with segregationist Lester Maddox and the grand dragon of the Georgia KKK.

July 4, Laurel, Mississippi: Two whites and two blacks are injured when blacks attempt to integrate a local cafe.

July 4, Jackson, Mississippi: A black woman is punched by a white man while waiting for service at a newly desegregated lunch counter.

July 5, Greenwood, Mississippi: Black civil rights worker Silas McGhee is assaulted by whites outside a newly integrated theater.

July 5, Columbus, Mississippi: A black visitor from St. Louis is mistaken for a civil rights worker and beaten by whites. The visitor is then fined $75 on trumped-up charges by authorities.

July 5, Jackson, Mississippi: A black woman is injured by a bottle thrown at the local COFO office.

July 6, Jackson, Mississippi: A black church is damaged by arsonists. In a separate incident, a black youth is assaulted by whites on the street.

July 6, Moss Point, Mississippi: A black woman is wounded twice when nightriders fire on a voter registration rally. Three blacks are arrested while pursuing the gunmen.

July 6, Raleigh, Mississippi: Two black churches are burned to the ground.

July 7, Bovina, Mississippi: A black recreation center is burned by arsonists. Despite a smoldering torch found at the scene, the sheriff dismisses it as an accidental rubbish fire.

July 8, McComb, Mississippi: Two persons are injured in the bombing of a SNCC Freedom House.

July 9, Vicksburg, Mississippi: Black students are stoned by whites en route to the local Freedom School.

July 10, Hattiesburg, Mississippi: Segregationists armed with metal clubs beat three rabbis active in black voter registration. One of the victims is hospitalized. On August 8, two white men plead guilty to assault, paying $500 fines and receiving ninety-day suspended sentences.

July 10, Colbert, Georgia: Klansmen fire at and miss a black traveling salesman from South Carolina.

July 11, Shaw, Mississippi: Whites offer a local black man $400 to bomb a SNCC Freedom House.

July 11, Canton, Mississippi: A firebomb explodes on the lawn of the local Freedom House.

July 11, Colbert, Georgia: Klansmen ambush a carload of black army reserve officers bound for home after summer training exercises. Lt. Col. Lemuel Penn is killed by shotgun blasts, and his companions escape unharmed. Two KKK members are acquitted of murder charges, but both are sentenced to prison in 1966 for federal civil rights violations.

July 11, Greenwood, Mississippi: A black civil rights worker is assaulted by whites on the street.

July 11, Browning, Mississippi: A black church is burned.

July 12, Kingston, Mississippi: Arsonists burn two black churches. No arrests are made, despite eyewitness identification of several suspect vehicles.

July 12, Jackson, Mississippi: White youths slash a civil rights worker's tires and spit in a black woman's face when demonstrators attempt to integrate a drive-in restaurant. In a separate incident, a black woman is beaten by an elderly white man at the Greyhound coffee shop. She is then arrested on charges of disturbing the peace after she receives medical treatment for her injuries.

July 12, Itta Bena, Mississippi: A black baby-sitter is attacked and slashed on both arms by two white youths.

July 12, Natchez, Mississippi: A black contractor's home is firebombed and a black church is burned to the ground.

July 13, Elm City, North Carolina: Three whites are arrested for attempting to burn a black church. Klan leaders had earlier warned the congregation against letting white students help paint the building.

July 14, Laurel, Mississippi: Gasoline bombs are thrown at a black home.

July 14, Canton, Mississippi: Nightriders pursue a carload of civil rights workers on the highway.

July 16, Greenwood, Mississippi: Following an FBI interview, Silas McGhee, a black civil rights activist, is abducted by whites at gunpoint and beaten with a board and a piece of pipe.

July 17, McComb, Mississippi: A black church is burned and two black bystanders at the scene are assaulted by whites.

July 17, St. Augustine, Florida: Four blacks, while seeking service in a segregated restaurant, are beaten by a gang of white men. One of the victims is hospitalized.

July 17, Philadelphia, Mississippi: A civil rights worker and a writer are beaten by two whites armed with chains.

July 18, Batesville, Mississippi: The county sheriff holds eight civil rights workers in jail for ninety minutes without charges, then releases them to a waiting mob. One of the prisoners is knocked down and beaten on the sidewalk.

July 18, Laurel, Mississippi: A rock with a threatening note signed "KKK" is thrown through a window of a doctor's office, one floor below the office of a dentist affiliated with the NAACP.

July 18–21, New York City: Blacks riot in Harlem following the fatal police shooting of fifteen-year-old James Powell on July 16. The outburst of violence leaves one black dead and five wounded. Eighty-one civilians and thirty-five policemen are injured, and 185 persons are arrested and 112 businesses are damaged.

July 19, Madison County, Mississippi: Arsonists destroy a rural black church.

July 19, Brooklyn, New York: Blacks and Puerto Ricans battle in the streets for five hours, leaving two men shot and another scarred by acid thrown in his face. Twelve persons are injured less seriously, and seven people are arrested.

July 20, Greenville, Mississippi: Nine shots are fired into a civil rights worker's car.

July 20, Hattiesburg, Mississippi: A civil rights worker is beaten on the public street. Both he and his assailant are charged with assault.

July 20, Greenwood, Mississippi: Two shotgun blasts are fired into a civil rights worker's car.

July 20–21, New York City: Race riots erupt in Harlem after police shoot and wound a twelve-year-old black child.

July 21, Tchula, Mississippi: A SNCC volunteer is assaulted on the street.

July 21, Lexington, Mississippi: A black voter registration worker is beaten outside the courthouse.

July 21, Greenwood, Mississippi: Nightriders smash the windows of three black-owned cafes and a civil rights worker's car.

July 21–23, New York City: Blacks riot in Bedford-Stuyvesant, leaving three civilians and two policemen injured. Over 200 store windows are smashed during the first night of violence.

July 22, Jackson, Mississippi: Two whites armed with clubs attack a civil rights worker in a major downtown intersection.

July 22, McComb, Mississippi: A black church is burned.

July 23, McComb, Mississippi: For the second night in a row a black church is burned.

July 24, St. Augustine, Florida: A firebomb is thrown into the integrated Monson Motor Lodge. Later in the day, five Klansmen are jailed for burning a cross on private property.

July 24–26, Rochester, New York: Five persons die during an outbreak of black rioting, with 350 injured and 750 arrested. Three of the dead are killed when an observation helicopter crashes.

July 25, Greenwood, Mississippi: Police stand by and watch as SNCC volunteers are harassed and assaulted by whites. That night, gunmen fire shots into the home of civil rights worker Silas McGhee.

July 25, Hattiesburg, Mississippi: A home occupied by black FDP activists is firebombed before dawn.

July 26, McComb, Mississippi: Nightriders make two bombing attacks on the home of a black civil rights activist. After the first blast, occupants of the house fire shots at the escaping bombers.

July 26, Batesville, Mississippi: A tear gas bomb explodes behind a home housing five civil rights workers, forcing the occupants to evacuate the house.

July 26, Mileston, Mississippi: A SNCC car is burned outside a home housing civil rights volunteers.

July 26, Canton, Mississippi: Four white civil rights workers are turned away from a local church, then mobbed outside, their car damaged in the attack.

July 26, Greenwood, Mississippi: Silas and Jake McGhee, black civil rights activists, are mobbed by 200 whites while leaving a local theater. Inside their car, both are cut by flying glass when a bottle is thrown through a window. At the county hospital, they are besieged by armed whites blocking all the exits. The sheriff waits three hours before responding to calls for assistance.

July 27, Canton, Mississippi: Five Northern ministers and two black women are cornered in an alley behind the downtown bus station and harassed and threatened by whites for two hours before their tormentors leave.

July 27, Itta Bena, Mississippi: Vandals strike at the local voter registration headquarters, smashing windows and tearing the door from its hinges. Porch supports are ripped out leaving the roof sagging dangerously.

July 29, Meridian, Mississippi: A black church is burned.

July 30, Gulfport, Mississippi: A black COFO volunteer is abducted at gunpoint and driven to Biloxi. There he is alternately threatened with death and offered bribes by white men seeking information on his civil rights activities.

July 30, Batesville, Mississippi: Nightriders fire three shots at the same house that was tear-gassed on July 26.

July 30, Brandon, Mississippi: A black church is burned to the ground by arsonists, with flames detonating a nearby butane tank.

July 31, Brandon, Mississippi: Two white civil rights workers are beaten by ten men in a local doctor's office. Attempting to flee the building, the civil rights workers are met outside by a deputy sheriff and jailed for disturbing the peace.

August 2, Greenwood, Mississippi: Nightriders fire four shots into the local SNCC office.

August 2, Natchez, Mississippi: Shots are fired at the black-owned Archie Curtis Funeral Home.

August 2, Canton, Mississippi: Nightriders fire on the local Freedom House.

August 4, Jackson, Mississippi: After being denied service at a segregated cafe, a civil rights worker is pursued and fired on by a white gunman in a pickup truck.

August 4, Natchez County, Mississippi: Arsonists burn a black church.

August 5–6, Tallahatchie County, Mississippi: Four members of the first black family to register as voters in several decades are threatened and harassed by truckloads of armed whites circling their rural home

August 7, Jackson, Mississippi: Two civil rights workers are pursued by a white assailant while canvassing a neighborhood for potential black voters.

August 9, Mileton, Mississippi: Nightriders detonate a bomb forty yards from a black community center, leaving a crater six feet wide and one foot deep.

August 9, Aberdeen, Mississippi: Three tear gas grenades are found on the lawn of the COFO Freedom House. Police dispose of the bombs before FBI agents can examine them for fingerprints.

August 10, Gluckstadt, Mississippi: A church meeting hall used for civil rights rallies is burned, marking the seventeenth attack on a Mississippi church since mid-June.

August 10, Marigold, Mississippi: Neimiah Montgomery, an elderly, unarmed black man, argues with a white gas station attendant about alleged overcharging. A policeman arrives and settles the dispute by shooting Montgomery to death.

August 11, Brandon, Mississippi: Arsonists burn a black church that has been used as a Freedom School.

August 11, Laurel, Mississippi: Eugene Keys, a black man, is assaulted by Klansmen in a local department store.

August 12, Oak Ridge, Mississippi: Robed, hooded raiders invade the home of an FDP activist, beating three occupants and firing several rounds at the house. The three victims require hospital treatment for their injuries.

August 12, Hattiesburg, Mississippi: Nightriders pepper a black home with bullets in a drive-by shooting.

August 12, Ocean Springs, Mississippi: Nightriders fire on two local black men in separate incidents. In yet another attack, whites in a pickup truck try to run down a black female pedestrian.

August 13, Ocean Springs, Mississippi: White gunmen narrowly miss a black man in the third shooting within twenty-four hours.

August 13, Cleveland, Mississippi: A local black reports that Police Chief W.H. Griffin, of Shaw, Mississippi, has offered him $300 to "get rid of" three voter registration workers.

August 14, McComb, Mississippi: A black-owned supermarket across the street from a COFO Freedom School is bombed.

August 14, Greenwood, Mississippi: The white proprietress of a grocery store fires a shotgun at black picketers, narrowly missing her target.

August 14, Columbus, Mississippi: A civil rights attorney is jailed for "reckless driving" after his parked car is deliberately rammed by a local white resident driving a pickup. One passenger is injured.

August 14, Canton, Mississippi: Nightriders fire on the local Freedom House.

August 14, Natchez, Mississippi: Bombers demolish a nightclub and grocery next door to a COFO Freedom School. The tavern is owned by a racially mixed couple.

August 15, Greenwood, Mississippi: Black civil rights activist Silas McGhee is shot and wounded while sitting in a parked car.

August 15, Jackson, Mississippi: Nightriders club a white civil rights worker, wound two persons with gunfire in scattered raids, and burn at least six crosses around town.

August 15, Jasper County, Mississippi: Two SNCC volunteers are fired on, the windows of their car broken, while investigating the beating of two black women several weeks earlier.

August 15, Laurel, Mississippi: Four civil rights workers are mobbed and beaten with fists and baseball bats at a department store lunch counter.

August 16, Tupelo, Mississippi: A civil rights worker is attacked and beaten with a baseball bat outside COFO headquarters. His white assailant escapes.

August 16, Dixmoor, Illinois: One thousand blacks battle police in the streets. Fifty people—most of them white—are injured during the outbreak. Thirty-one people are arrested. Two houses are burned by the rioters, and fifty cars are damaged or destroyed. Sporadic violence resumes on August 17.

August 16, Laurel, Mississippi: Two white civil rights workers, male and female, are attacked and beaten at a gas station, leaving the man unconscious.

August 17, Gulfport, Mississippi: A civil rights worker is attacked and severely beaten outside the city library.

August 17, Laurel, Mississippi: Another civil rights worker is assaulted on the street.

August 18, McComb, Mississippi: A bungled firebombing causes minor damage to the home of a black civil rights activist. In a separate incident, whites in a pickup truck pursue a civil rights worker on the highway.

August 18, Vicksburg, Mississippi: A bottle is hurled through the window of a barbershop owned by an FDP delegate.

August 18, Natchez, Mississippi: A five-gallon gasoline bomb is found under a black-owned tavern. A Louisiana bar owned by the proprietor's brother was bombed the previous weekend.

August 19, Collinsville, Mississippi: Arsonists burn a black church.

August 20, Canton, Mississippi: Blacks foil an arson attempt on the local Freedom House, causing nightriders to drop the firebomb and set their own pickup on fire as they flee.

August 21, Itta Bena, Mississippi: A black church is burned to the ground.

August 22, Jones County, Mississippi: Fifteen Klansmen attack a picnic of local blacks and civil rights volunteers near Laurel, beating two persons with sticks and chains and firing shots at two others.

One of the attackers is freed on bail after assaulting a civil rights activist on August 17.

August 23, McComb, Mississippi: Hooded Klansmen abduct a white man who has befriended blacks, holding him captive for three hours.

August 23, Tupelo, Mississippi: Arsonists damage a black voter registration office.

August 25, Madison, Florida: Five shotgun blasts are fired into a car owned by civil rights workers.

August 26, Canton, Mississippi: A voter registration worker en route to the local Freedom House is fired on three separate times. He identifies the gunman's vehicle as a police car.

August 27, Jackson, Mississippi: Bombs strike the office of a small weekly paper whose editor openly opposes the Klan.

August 28–29, Keansburg, New Jersey: One hundred whites and blacks brawl at a local amusement park, with twelve white youths arrested at the scene. Police blame the violence on "local white punks" who attacked black passengers on a charter bus from New York City.

August 28–30, Philadelphia, Pennsylvania: Blacks riot over three nights, leaving 248 persons injured, including sixty-six policemen and two firemen. Hundreds of shops are looted or damaged during the outbreak, which is sparked by a routine traffic arrest.

August 29–30, New York City: Blacks clash with Puerto Ricans on the Lower East Side after a black gunman wounds a Puerto Rican man. Thirty persons are arrested in the ensuing riot.

August 30, Mt. Sterling, Kentucky: Arsonists burn the black DuBois School and a storage building owned by a local NAACP leader.

August 31, Meridian, Mississippi: A shotgun blast is fired into a black home housing civil rights workers.

September 1, Holly Springs, Mississippi: A firebomb destroys the black Baptist College.

September 6, Canton, Mississippi: A white-owned grocery store in a black neighborhood is bombed.

September 7, Bogue Chitto, Mississippi: Klan bombers strike at a black-owned pool hall in a white neighborhood.

September 7, Auburn, Mississippi: A black church is bombed.

September 7, Magnolia, Mississippi: The home of a black school principal is damaged by a bomb.

September 7, Summit, Mississippi: Predawn explosions damage a black-owned home, store, and tool shed.

September 7, Pickens, Mississippi: A fourteen-year-old black boy named Herbert Oarsby disappears, and his body is pulled from a nearby river two days later. Authorities attribute his death to accidental drowning and deny reports that Oarsby was active in civil rights work, despite the fact that he was wearing a CORE T-shirt when he died.

September 9, McComb, Mississippi: A black minister's home is bombed.

September 10, Jackson County, Mississippi: Bombs cause minor damage to a black church.

September 13, Vidalia, Mississippi: A bomb explodes in the yard of a white resident known to support the Democratic ticket.

September 14, Natchez, Mississippi: White segregationists lob stink bombs at several businesses owned by "moderates."

September 17, Canton, Mississippi: Two black churches used in civil rights activities are burned. Estimates place the total number of Mississippi churches destroyed since June at twenty-four.

September 19, Coy, Mississippi: A black church is destroyed by arsonists.

September 19, Kemper County, Mississippi: A rural black church is burned.

September 20, McComb, Mississippi: A black home and church are bombed.

September 23, McComb, Mississippi: Bombs strike two black homes, including one owned by an ex-policeman.

September 25, Natchez, Mississippi: Bombs explode at a black home and on the "moderate" mayor's lawn. Two weeks earlier the mayor's supermarket was bombed.

September 25, Laurel, Mississippi: A fifty-year-old black man "armed" with a cane is shot and killed by a white grocer firing in "self-defense."

September 26, Farmville, North Carolina: A minister attending a KKK rally is threatened and abused by Klansmen.

September 27, Jackson, Mississippi: A bomb wrecks the carport of a black businessman's home.

October 4, Vicksburg, Mississippi: A black church used for voter registration work is bombed, injuring two persons.

October 4, Meridian, Mississippi: Nightriders fire into a black home housing civil rights workers.

October 12, Magnolia, Mississippi: Four Klansmen are indicted for their role in recent bombings around McComb; five more indictments are issued October 13, with charges covering nine defendants in sixteen bombings and the burning of several churches. All nine Klansmen are convicted on October 23, but a sympathetic judge releases them on probation, citing his belief that they were "unduly provoked" by civil rights activists.

October 20, Indianola, Mississippi: A Freedom Democratic Party worker is punched and kicked by a white assailant. Outside of town a SNCC photographer is beaten while covering an FDP rally.

October 20, Lambert, Mississippi: Five civil rights workers are run out of town by whites while canvassing for the Democratic Party.

October 21, Marks, Mississippi: Four whites force an FDP activist off the highway, beat him unconscious, and urinate on his body. The victim suffers a concussion.

October 22, Indianola, Mississippi: A small plane from the "Klan Air Force" makes several passes over an FDP rally, dropping flares and explosives.

October 24, Tchula, Mississippi: Four shots are fired into the home of a black FDP activist.

October 24, Ruleville, Mississippi: Vandals stone the shop of a black merchant displaying Democratic campaign posters.

October 26, Indianola, Mississippi: An FDP volunteer is assaulted while escorting black voters to the courthouse.

October 28, Indianola, Mississippi: A tear gas bomb is thrown into a black home housing civil rights workers. Arsonists attempt to burn the local SNCC Freedom School.

October 29, Ruleville, Mississippi: Nightriders shoot out the windows of a black-owned shop displaying Democratic campaign posters.

October 31, Ripley, Mississippi: Nightriders burn a black church being used as a COFO Freedom School.

November, McComb, Mississippi: Shots are fired into a local newspaper office following an editorial against racial violence.

November 2, Vicksburg, Mississippi: A fourteen-year-old black youth is shot and wounded for failing to call a white man "sir."

November 3, Laurel, Mississippi: A civil rights worker is assaulted by a KKK member.

November 17, Laurel, Mississippi: Masked Klansmen kidnap a black union official at gunpoint and carry him outside of town to be flogged.

November 29, Montgomery, Alabama: A bomb damages the carport of a black home in a previously all-white neighborhood.

November 30, Laurel, Mississippi: Klansmen assault a civil rights worker in a local department store.

December 10, Ferriday, Louisiana: Klansmen set fire to a local shoeshop and force black proprietor Frank Morris to remain inside by threatening him with guns. Morris dies of burns on December 14.

December 13, Montgomery, Alabama: Explosives are detonated outside a black church. Three whites—including a Klansman arrested for racial bombings in 1957—are sentenced to six months in jail.

1965

January, Charlotte, North Carolina: A bomb demolishes the car of a black civil rights worker.

January 5, Bogalusa, Louisiana: A public address by ex-congressman Brooks Hays is canceled after KKK threats.

January 15, Selma, Alabama: Dr. Martin Luther King is assaulted by a member of the NSRP, while checking into a hotel.

January 15, Laurel, Mississippi: A civil rights worker is assaulted in a downtown parking lot by two Klansmen.

January 17, Jonesboro, Louisiana: Two black churches are burned.

January 22, Jackson, Mississippi: Allie Shelby, an eighteen-year-old black convicted of making an indecent gesture to a white woman, is shot dead by officers inside the county jail.

January 22, Brandon, Mississippi: A black church is burned.

January 24, New Bern, North Carolina: Two bombs explode outside a black church where an NAACP meeting is in progress. Another blast damages a mortuary owned by a black civil rights activist. The FBI arrests three Klansmen on January 29.

January 29, Soso, Mississippi: Arsonists attempt to burn a black home.

February, Atlanta, Georgia: FBI agents foil a KKK plot to murder Dr. Martin Luther King, Jr., at SCLC headquarters.

February 3, Bogalusa, Louisiana: Five Klansmen assault a civil rights worker.

February 9, Marion, Alabama: An FBI informant reports KKK plans to kill Dr. Martin Luther King during a scheduled visit to town on February 15. The trip is canceled.

February 9, Laurel, Mississippi: Nightriders fire into COFO headquarters.

February 10, Selma, Alabama: Deputies armed with electric prods drive civil rights marchers out of town, leaving them stranded and injured a mile from Selma.

February 14, Queens, New York: Firebombs destroy the home of ex-Black Muslim leader Malcolm X. Malcolm first blames rival Muslims, then suspects the U.S. government. Muslims insist that Malcolm burned the house himself to gain publicity.

February 15, Bogalusa, Louisiana: Klansmen attack five local blacks and damage their car after the blacks seek service at a gas station. In a separate incident, whites attack two civil rights workers on the street.

February 16, Mobile, Alabama: Two black youths are shot and wounded by whites.

February 16, Selma, Alabama: Civil rights leader C.T. Vivian is beaten and arrested during a voter registration protest.

February 17, Laurel, Mississippi: COFO headquarters is set on fire by members of the KKK.

February 18, Marion, Alabama: Jimmy Lee Jackson, a black civil rights worker, is beaten and fatally shot when state troopers attack 400 black demonstrators. While in a Selma hospital he is served with an arrest warrant listing charges of assault with intent to kill. Jackson dies on February 26.

February 18, Bessemer, Alabama: Striking Klansmen, unwilling to work with blacks at the W.S. Dickey Clay Co., damage large pipe couplings at the plant and shoot up the car of a nonstriking worker.

February 19, Bessemer, Alabama: Another black worker's car is hit by gunfire at the W.S. Dickey Clay Co.

February 21, New York City: Malcolm X is assassinated during a speech at the Audubon Ballroom. Three people are wounded during the exchange of gunfire between his bodyguards and killers. Two assassins, one of them shot in the leg, are beaten by members of the audience and held for police and are eventually convicted of murder and sentenced to prison on March 10, 1966. Reports of two other suspects in custody are later "corrected" by police and the media, prompting charges of conspiracy from various quarters.

February 23, New York City: A Black Muslim mosque in Harlem is burned by arsonists, apparently in retaliation for the murder of Malcolm X.

February 23, San Francisco, California: A second Black Muslim mosque is destroyed by fire, as the internecine war continues.

February 24, Mobile, Alabama: Nightriders fire on the homes of Mobile's mayor and a black civil rights worker.

February 28, Lowndes County, Alabama: Armed whites invade a church during services, warning the "moderate" minister to leave town by sundown or die.

March, Laurel, Mississippi: The local Freedom House is set on fire by arsonists.

March, Vicksburg, Mississippi: Two Klansmen assault an elderly black man in a local restaurant, smashing eggs in his face and knocking him to the floor. A few days later they return and lob two firebombs through the cafe windows, causing extensive damage inside.

March 2, Bessemer, Alabama: Klansmen stone a black employee leaving the W.S. Dickey Clay Co., pursuing his car down the highway and firing several shots that miss the employee.

March 4, Ellisville, Mississippi: A black home is burned by Klansmen.

March 5, Indianola, Mississippi: Nightriders burn a Freedom School and assault a white civil rights worker on the street.

March 6, Bessemer, Alabama: Klansmen fire shots at a black employee leaving the W.S. Dickey Clay Co., blasting holes in the trunk of his car.

March 7, Selma, Alabama: A planned civil rights march from Selma to Montgomery is blocked by state troopers and mounted deputies. Officers scatter the marchers with clubs, whips, and tear gas, sending sixty-six persons to the hospital. Hours later, several whites, including NSRP members, beat a black man on Highway 80 outside of town and assault an FBI agent who tries to intervene.

March 8, Bessemer, Alabama: Striking Klansmen fire on a black employee leaving the W.S. Dickey plant, peppering his car with buckshot.

March 9, Selma, Alabama: White thugs attack three ministers active in civil rights, fatally beating Rev. James Reeb. Charged with Reeb's murder, the defendants are acquitted after Sheriff Jim Clark, an avowed racist, visits jurors to "discuss" their verdict.

March 10, Bessemer, Alabama: A black worker from the W.S. Dickey Clay Co. is attacked by Klansmen while running an errand for his employers, damaging a company car before he escapes. In a separate incident, Klan strikers stone several trucks entering the factory grounds, smashing their windows with rocks and bottles.

March 16, Montgomery, Alabama: Mounted police "mistakenly" attack a civil rights parade, wielding clubs, knotted ropes, and electric prods. Eight marchers are hospitalized in the incident, which results in a public apology.

March 21, Vicksburg, Mississippi: An integrated cafe is firebombed.

March 21–22, Birmingham, Alabama: Six time bombs are discovered in the black community. All are defused before they explode.

March 25, Lowndesboro, Alabama: Viola Liuzzo, a white civil rights worker, is ambushed and shot to death by Klansmen on a rural highway. One member of the hit team is an FBI informant, who identifies the gunmen for police. Three defendants are acquitted on state murder charges and subsequently convicted of federal civil rights violations on December 3.

March 28, Meridian, Mississippi: Firebombs are thrown into two black churches.

March 29, Bogalusa, Louisiana: Klansmen hurl a tear gas grenade at a group of blacks.

April 1, Birmingham, Alabama: A bomb wrecks the home of a black accountant. Two other bombs are found and defused at the homes of the mayor and a city council member.

April 2, Bessemer, Alabama: A rifle shot is fired into the W.S. Dickey Clay Co. plant as the violent Klan strike against black workers continues.

April 5, Prosperity, South Carolina: Robed, hooded men drag a black man from his jail cell, slapping and threatening him.

April 7, Bogalusa, Louisiana: Nightriders exchange gunfire with civil rights workers at a black home. Thirty bullets strike the house and damage a parked car. In a separate incident, two armed Klansmen threaten blacks at a civil rights meeting.

April 8, Prosperity, South Carolina: Two police officers are charged with second-degree lynching after dressing in Klan robes and beating a black youth in jail.

April 9, Bogalusa, Louisiana: White mobs assault civil rights marchers and newsmen. One white man is struck and injured by a police car. An FBI agent is attacked by members of the mob.

April 10, Jonesboro, Louisiana: A black motorist trades shots with a carload of nightriders.

April 11, Pittsburgh, Pennsylvania: A cross is burned in Point State Park, where vandals have twice smashed windows of a newly opened COFO Freedom Center during the previous week.

April 15, Bogalusa, Louisiana: A black man, released from jail after a scuffle with whites, claims he was interrogated in his cell by men wearing KKK hoods over police uniforms.

April 17, Hamburg, Arkansas: Klansmen threaten a police officer and steal the car of a newsman who took "unauthorized" photos during a KKK rally.

April 18, St. Augustine, Florida: White spectators pelt black marchers in an Easter parade with rocks and eggs. Other blacks are egged while entering a white church.

April 23, Ellisville, Mississippi: Klansmen burn a black-owned home.

April 25, Atlanta, Georgia: Police detour a march by 2,000 white racists after one marcher sets off a smoke bomb.

April 30, Columbia, South Carolina: Two whites are fined for beating a white student who joined a black protest march.

May 1, Somerville, Tennessee: Six civil rights workers are injured by whites during protests at local restaurants.

May 1, Indianola, Mississippi: Firebombs destroy two black homes. Arsonists also damage another home, a store, and the local COFO freedom house.

May 2, Lexington, Mississippi: Maggie Gordon, a black woman, is beaten in the Holmes County jail. She files suit in federal court, and on July 13, 1966, a white deputy sheriff is ordered to pay his victim $1,500 in damages.

May 9, Bogalusa, Louisiana: A white mob led by a Klansman uses clubs, belts, and other weapons to attack blacks during an attempt to integrate a city park.

May 11, New Orleans, Louisiana: A Unitarian church is firebombed by nightriders.

May 12, New Orleans, Louisiana: Firebombs damage a car owned by an ACLU member.

May 13, Oxford, Alabama: A black church is wrecked by a bomb blast.

May 16, Mt. Olive, Mississippi: Arsonists burn a black-owned grocery.

May 16, Laurel, Mississippi: Klansmen set fire to a black-owned grocery, a community recreation center, and a baseball park.

May 17, Laurel, Mississippi: Nightriders set fire to a gas station and a motel owned by outspoken opponents of the KKK.

May 24, Bogalusa, Louisiana: Three hundred whites tear down the gates of a city park closed to avert racial demonstrations.

May 26, Crawfordsville, Georgia: A black civil rights worker is abducted and beaten by Klansmen, who then deliver him to the local sheriff.

June 3, Bogalusa, Louisiana: Two black deputies, O'Neal Moore and Creed Rogers, are ambushed on patrol. Moore dies, and Rogers is wounded. On June 5 shots are fired at the home of an officer investigating the murder. A KKK member is charged in Moore's death, but no prosecution results.

June 14, Vicksburg, Mississippi: Firebombs damage the home of a Westinghouse officer who hired black secretaries for the local plant.

June 16, Laurel, Mississippi: Klansmen shoot at a black-owned nightclub and fire shots at the state vice president of the NAACP in separate incidents.

June 19, Jones County, Mississippi: Arsonists burn a rural black home.

July 1, Philadelphia, Pennsylvania: One hundred fifty persons are injured during a race riot, with 165 jailed for looting and assaulting police officers.

July 1, Laurel, Mississippi: Klansmen burn COFO headquarters and thirteen houses occupied by civil rights activists.

July 1, Jones County, Mississippi: Nightriders burn an integrated restaurant.

July 1, Sharon, Mississippi: Bombs destroy the barn of a white Klan opponent.

July 1, Mt. Olive, Mississippi: The homes of three white moderates are set on fire by arsonists.

July 3, Jackson, Mississippi: A white man assaults a black minister leading a civil rights march.

July 3, Laurel, Mississippi: Arsonists attempt to burn the home of a black civil rights activist.

July 7, Long Island, New York: Four white youths are held for smashing windows and burning a cross at the home of an interracial couple.

July 8–11, Bogalusa, Louisiana: White racists repeatedly assault black demonstrators. One white attacker is shot and wounded. Klansmen are observed distributing clubs to white youths along the route of a civil rights march on July 11.

July 15, Anniston, Alabama: Willie Brewster, a black man, is shot and killed by nightriders after a rally sponsored by the NSRP.

July 16, Bogalusa, Louisiana: White mobs stage six assaults on black protestors while police idly watch. Two whites are finally arrested during the seventh attack. On July 17 whites spray black demonstrators with hoses, and pelt them with stones and fruit.

July 16, Jonesboro, Louisiana: Whites harass a newsman covering a civil rights demonstration.

July 16, Greensboro, Alabama: Seventy-five black demonstrators are attacked by a white mob armed with clubs, rubber hoses, and hammers. Seventeen protesters require hospital treatment after the assault.

July 18, Elmwood, Alabama: A black church is burned.

July 18, Greensboro, Alabama: Arsonists burn two black churches.

July 18, Jackson, Mississippi: Addressing a KKK rally, Imperial Wizard Sam Bowers boasts that the Klan is responsible for more than sixteen arson fires in his hometown of Laurel, Mississippi

July 19, Laurel, Mississippi: Klansmen set fire to the home of a white attorney hostile to the KKK.

July 21, Newton, Georgia: A black civil rights worker is assaulted while picketing the courthouse.

July 27, Ferriday, Louisiana: Two black homes are firebombed.

July 27, New Orleans, Louisiana: A bomb damages the local CORE office.

July 28, Americus, Georgia: White mobs stone black motorists. A white youth is shot and fatally wounded while attacking one car.

July 31, Columbia, Mississippi: A civil rights headquarters is riddled with bullets and damaged by fire.

July 31, Americus, Georgia: Five black demonstrators are assaulted.

August, San Francisco, California: Authorities report several buildings and fences defaced with anti-Semitic graffiti.

August 2, Americus, Georgia: Two blacks are beaten while picketing a supermarket.

August 3, Slidell, Louisiana: Two black churches are burned.

August 7, Jackson, Alabama: Three blacks and one white are wounded by shots fired at a restaurant where blacks seek service.

August 7, Jackson, Mississippi: A black youth is stabbed while picketing a shopping center.

August 8, West Point, Mississippi: Nightriders fire shotgun blasts into a home housing civil rights workers.

August 8, Valewood, Mississippi: Arsonists burn the local Head Start office. Several crosses are also burned nearby.

August 10, Sharon, Mississippi: Nightriders set fire to the home of a white moderate whose barn was bombed on July 1. In a second attack, the home of a white anti-Klan minister is riddled with bullets and burned.

August 12–15, Chicago, Illinois: Three nights of black rioting are sparked by an accident in which a black woman is struck and killed by a fire truck on August 12. By the predawn hours of August 15, eighty persons are injured, and 140 are in custody.

August 12–16, Los Angeles, California: A drunk-driving arrest sparks widespread rioting in the Watts section, involving an estimated 7,000 to 10,000 rioters. Authorities record thirty-five riot-related deaths during the outbreak, most of the victims shot dead while looting. Six hundred buildings are damaged or demolished, and damages are estimated at $40 million. Police arrest 3,400 adults and 500 juveniles during the riot.

August 12, Baton Rouge, Louisiana: Bombs explode at a hotel and motel housing civil rights workers.

August 13, Springfield, Massachusetts: Two white-owned stores are burned by blacks protesting alleged police brutality. Their grievance stems from an incident on July 17, when seventeen black men and one white woman were arrested in a disturbance at a black bar.

August 14, Ft. Deposit, Alabama: A crowd of white men armed with heavy walking sticks harass civil rights demonstrators. A cross is burned on the courthouse lawn, and a large swastika is painted on the town's water tower.

August 15, Charlottesville, Virginia: A white man is arrested for shooting a black.

August 16, Meadville, Mississippi: An ex-Klansman, suspected of supplying information to authorities, is beaten to death near his home.

August 16, North Philadelphia, Pennsylvania: Black mobs riot overnight, smashing store windows and burning a car on the street.

August 18, Los Angeles, California: Four persons are hospitalized and fifty-nine are arrested after a shoot-out between police and Black Muslims at the local mosque. Two small fires are set inside the building, ostensibly to destroy Muslim records before they fall into police hands.

August 20, Hayneville, Alabama: Jonathan Daniels, a white seminary student active in civil rights work, is shot and killed by a KKK member and part-time deputy sheriff. A Catholic priest is critically wounded in the same attack. The gunman is charged with manslaughter, but laughing jurors acquit him on September 30, accepting his plea of "self-defense."

August 20, Greenwood, Mississippi: Freddie Thomas, a black man, is found dead on the outskirts of town, an apparent hit-and-run victim. Activists charge that his death is deliberate murder, designed as a warning to black voters.

August 22, Greensboro, Alabama: Perry Small, an elderly black man, is found beaten to death in his home with his tongue cut out.

August 23, Jackson, Mississippi: Rev. D.A. Thompson, a Unitarian minister active in civil rights work, is seriously wounded in a shotgun ambush.

August 25, Baton Rouge, Louisiana: Bombs wreck a black-owned nightclub.

August 26, Plymouth, North Carolina: Klansmen and hecklers clash at a KKK rally outside of town. Twenty-seven black protesters are beaten.

August 27, Natchez, Mississippi: George Metcalfe, a black NAACP leader, is maimed by a car bomb. FBI agents identify the KKK faction responsible, but no prosecutions result.

August 29, Anniston, Alabama: A black man is killed by a shotgun blast, his white assailant held in jail.

August 30, Americus, Georgia: Six whites armed with bricks and stones assault black demonstrators at the courthouse.

August 31, Augusta, Georgia: Three white youths are arrested for stealing grenades and anti-riot bombs from an army base and using explosives to terrorize blacks.

August 31, Plymouth, North Carolina: One Klansman is shot and another is slashed with a knife when whites mob black demonstrators outside police headquarters.

September 2, Laurel, Mississippi: A bomb destroys a COFO truck.

September 5, Forrest, Mississippi: Nightriders fire on the home of a black family whose child attends a newly integrated school. One occupant is wounded in the arm.

September 7, Sandersville, Mississippi: Klansmen burn a local black home.

September 9, Greenwood, Mississippi: Blacks ask federal authorities to investigate the recent murder of F. L. Thomas, suggesting that he was killed as a warning against black voter registration.

September 14, Sandersville, Mississippi: Nightriders burn a black home.

September 16, Laurel, Mississippi: Shots are fired at the home of the state NAACP vice president. A white gunman is arrested on September 17.

September 26, Jones County, Mississippi: A rural black church is burned by arsonists.

September 30, Ovett, Mississippi: Klansmen bungle an attempt to burn a black-owned home.

October, Jones County, Mississippi: Authorities report more than forty racially motivated cases of assault, bombing, and arson in the county since May 1964.

October 4, Crawfordsville, Georgia: Calvin Craig, grand dragon of the KKK, assaults a black demonstrator.

October 7, Crawfordsville, Georgia: A white integrationist is dragged from his car and beaten by whites during a black protest.

October 10, Lakewood, New Jersey: Arsonists damage two homes under construction for black families in a previously segregated neighborhood.

October 11, Laurel, Mississippi: A black home, first targeted by nightriders in April, is riddled with bullets and burned in a second attack.

October 12, Crawfordsville, Georgia: An SCLC photographer is assaulted by a Klansman.

October 16, Montgomery, Alabama: Attorney General Richmond Flowers issues a report that links the KKK to forty of Birmingham's forty-five racist bombings, and twelve of the South's seventeen civil rights murders since 1963.

October 17, Crawfordsville, Georgia: Armed Klansmen force a black motorist off the road, assault him, and threaten him with guns.

October 22, Lincolnton, Georgia: Thirty whites assault civil rights marchers. On October 23, seven civil rights workers are injured when their car overturns, allegedly during a high-speed chase by nightriders.

October 26, Laurel, Mississippi: A shotgun blast is fired through the door of a black school.

October 30, Montgomery, Alabama: State attorney general Richmond Flowers, an opponent of the KKK, is assaulted by two white men while attending a football game.

October 31, Reading, Pennsylvania: Daniel Burros, New York leader of the KKK, commits suicide after newspaper articles reveal his Jewish background.

November 7, Wilmington, Delaware: Delaware's top-ranking Klansman is arrested for a shooting in Hartley two weeks before.

November 7, Detroit, Michigan: Black janitor Eddie Cook is killed by a shotgun blast, fired from a car occupied by five white youths. The same boys were seen earlier, throwing bottles at a black teenager on the street.

November 8, Jones County, Georgia: Nightriders burn an abandoned home and a vacant black church.

November 8, Twiggs County, Georgia: A black church is burned. Police file charges against a white Florida physician for this fire and the Jones County fire the same evening.

November 11, Hattiesburg, Mississippi: For the first time in state history, a white youth is convicted of raping a black girl.

November 11, Chicago, Illinois: Five days after its occupation by black tenants, a home formerly owned by a white family is damaged by stones and Molotov cocktails.

November 12, Lakeland, Florida: A four-foot cross is jammed through the screen door of a home occupied by Phyllis Johnson, daughter of a ranking Klansman, who supplied information about the KKK to congressional investigators.

November 18, Victoria, Virginia: Shots are fired at four civil rights workers, wounding one.

November 21, Ferriday, Louisiana: A gasoline bomb damages the home of a black civil rights activist.

November 22, Charlotte, North Carolina: Bombs explode at the homes of four blacks active in civil rights work.

November 29, Vicksburg, Mississippi: Three persons are injured when a car bomb explodes near a black-owned grocery store rumored to be the site of an integrationist meeting.

December 1, New Orleans, Louisiana: A federal injunction is issued against "acts of terror and intimidation" by the KKK in Bogalusa.

December 4, Bogalusa, Louisiana: A visiting Italian musician, mistaken for a civil rights worker, is beaten by three white women.

December 6, Greenville, Alabama: Black protest marchers stone police after three of them are arrested for carrying weapons.

December 15, Hamburg, Arkansas: Lee Culbreath, a black paper boy, is shot and killed by white gunmen. Police charge two KKK members with his murder.

December 22, Natchez, Mississippi: A black picket is assaulted and shoved through a store window by a white attacker.

December 31, Natchez, Mississippi: Arsonists destroy a market owned by Mayor John Nosser, an opponent of the KKK.

1966

January 2, Newton, Georgia: A black church is burned. Anonymous callers threaten to kill the sheriff if he investigates the fire.

January 3, Mississippi: Crosses are burned in nine counties, with shots fired at two FBI agents observing one incident.

January 3, Tuskegee, Alabama: Samuel Younge, Jr., a black civil rights worker, is shot and killed by a white gunman for trying to use a segregated rest room.

January 10, Hattiesburg, Mississippi: Black civil rights activist Vernon Dahmer is fatally burned when Klansmen firebomb his home. Several nightriders are sentenced to life in 1968 on conviction of murder.

January 23, Camden, Alabama: David Colston, a black man, is shot and killed outside a church. His assailant is identified as a local white man.

January 30, Atlanta, Georgia: The Southern Regional Council reports that Southern whites killed a total of fourteen local blacks and civil rights workers in 1965 and three local blacks thus far in the new year.

February 2, Kosciusko, Mississippi: Two people are wounded by shotgun blasts fired into a home housing civil rights workers. On February 3 nightriders fire shots into a COFO Freedom House.

February 6, Zachary, Louisiana: A black home is bombed.

February 19, Birmingham, Alabama: A white racist "bomb factory" is found in the woods outside of town. One timing device is identical to those found on unexploded bombs in April 1965.

February 21, Birmingham, Alabama: Five blacks are wounded when a white gunman fires on a roadside crowd. The gunman later claims that the blacks obstructed his car.

February 24, Elba, Alabama: Two dynamite blasts damage a newly integrated high school.

February 25, Hamburg, Arkansas: A state trooper testifies that a white defendant, charged with killing a black man in 1965, confessed Klan membership at the time of his arrest.

March 11, Bogalusa, Louisiana: A black army captain is shot in the neck by a sniper while using a public phone booth. Two whites are charged in the attack.

April 2, Baton Rouge, Louisiana: Bombs explode at two swimming pools scheduled to open on an integrated basis.

April 9, Ernul, North Carolina: Bombs demolish a black church.

May 26, Fayette, Mississippi: A white man is arrested in the shotgun wounding of a sixteen-year-old black boy, shot outside the gunman's home.

June 1, Waterloo, Iowa: Black prisoner Eddie Sallis, jailed on a charge of public intoxication, is found hanged in his cell. The coroner rules his death a suicide, but protesters call it a case of police murder.

June 6, Hernando, Mississippi: James Meredith is wounded by three shotgun blasts, during a one-man "march against fear." A white man is charged in the attack. The hospital treating Meredith receives bomb threats from a man describing himself as a KKK member.

June 9, Mississippi: Other blacks take over James Meredith's "march against fear," and white mobs harass newsmen along the line of the march.

June 10, Natchez, Mississippi: Ben White, an elderly black, is kidnapped and shot to death by Klansmen, who believe that his death will attract Dr. Martin Luther King to the area. Klansmen are acquitted of murder charges on December 9, 1967, but White's relatives file a civil suit for wrongful death. On November 13, 1968, the KKK is ordered to pay $1,021,500 in damages.

June 17, Greenwood, Mississippi: Newsmen covering a civil rights rally escape injury after two poisonous snakes are tossed in their vehicle. Klansman Byron de la Beckwith circulates through the crowd, seeking the whereabouts of Charles Evers, brother of the civil rights leader that Beckwith is charged with murdering in 1963.

June 19–20, Jersey City, New Jersey: Blacks and Puerto Ricans clash in the streets on two consecutive nights. One person is arrested during the outbreak.

June 21, Philadelphia, Mississippi: Civil rights marchers are stoned and assaulted by white mobs while police stand by watching. That evening nightriders stage four shooting attacks in the black community. A white man is shot and wounded while firing on FDP offices.

June 22, Canton, Mississippi: A white man is wounded shortly after a firebomb attack on the local civil rights headquarters.

June 24, Philadelphia, Mississippi: Whites pelt Dr. Martin Luther King and other black demonstrators with eggs and bottles.

June 24, Carthage, Mississippi: Arsonists destroy a Catholic church.

June 28, Cordele, Georgia: A crowd of twenty-five to thirty armed whites gathers at a black-owned gas station. Some in the crowd open fire after a black youth throws a bottle toward their cars. Blacks return the fire in a shoot-out that lasts ninety minutes.

July 1, Milwaukee, Wisconsin: Klansmen bomb a linoleum store owned by the former president of the Wisconsin Civil Rights Congress.

July 3, Lebanon, Ohio: Klansmen pelt police with stones after two KKK members are arrested for violation of the state's anti-mask law.

July 3–5, Omaha, Nebraska: Blacks riot for three nights following a clash with police on July 3. The incident begins after a citizen complaint of illegal fireworks and black youths hurl bottles and firecrackers at patrolmen sent to investigate. Most white-owned stores in the local ghetto are damaged, with windows smashed by vandals. One hundred twenty-two persons are arrested, most of whom are released by July 7 with all charges dropped.

July 10, Grenada, Mississippi: Two whites are arrested after firing submachine gun bursts at a federal officer and two civil rights workers outside a black church.

July 13, Jackson, Mississippi: A black woman is awarded $1,500 in the out-of-court settlement of a lawsuit filed against a deputy sheriff who assaulted her. Police, swinging clubs and gun butts, scatter black demonstrators.

July 16, Troy, New York: The arrest of a black woman and subsequent charges of police brutality spark angry black protests. Violence erupts on the night of July 20, with three firebombing incidents and two reports of window-smashing. Three blacks are arrested in a car containing Molotov cocktails.

July 17, Cordele, Georgia: Seven Klansmen are arrested for illegal possession of riot equipment at the site of a KKK rally.

July 18, Jacksonville, Florida: A race riot erupts after jeering whites assault civil rights marchers. One white man is arrested while trying to serve a "Klan warrant" on a local NAACP leader.

July 20, Jacksonville, Florida: A black-owned store is bombed.

July 28, Baltimore, Maryland: White gangs invade a black neighborhood after an NSRP rally. Three NSRP leaders are charged with inciting a riot. Convicted on November 21, each one draws a two-year prison term.

July 30, Bogalusa, Louisiana: Clarence Triggs, a black man, is shot to death by two white gunmen.

July 30–August 2, Omaha, Nebraska: Four persons are arrested during three nights of black rioting.

July 31, Raleigh, North Carolina: Klansmen brawl with blacks at a KKK rally.

July 31, Chicago, Illinois: Fifty-four persons are injured, including two patrolmen, when white mobs stone a civil rights procession led by Dr. Martin Luther King.

August 3, Minneapolis, Minnesota: Eleven teenage blacks are arrested during an outbreak of youth violence, with blacks stoning white motorists.

August 5, Chicago, Illinois: Dr. Martin Luther King is struck in the head by a brick while leading civil rights marchers past crowds of violent racists. Another marcher is struck in the neck by a thrown knife aimed at King. Black motorists are also stoned by whites during the demonstration.

August 7–8, Lansing, Michigan: Eleven persons are injured and thirty-one people are arrested during two nights of rioting after violence erupts when white youths taunt blacks and are pelted with stones in return. Several firebombings are reported on the second night of rioting.

August 8, Grenada, Mississippi: Police use tear gas, clubs, and gunfire to disrupt black protests.

August 9, Grenada, Mississippi: An estimated 175 whites hurl bricks, stones, bottles, steel pipes, and firecrackers at black protest marchers. Police stand by, laughing, as a riot erupts.

August 9, Milwaukee, Wisconsin: Klansmen bomb the local NAACP office.

August 9–11, Detroit, Michigan: Rioting erupts after a streetcorner incident in which a patrolman is knifed while trying to arrest three black men for loitering. At least fourteen stores are damaged by looters the first night. On August 10 a black pedestrian is wounded by white gunmen in a drive-by shooting, and two firebombings are reported. Forty persons are arrested on August 10, including seven white youths armed with Molotov cocktails. On August 11, there are three more reports of firebombing, and fifteen arrests.

August 11, Carthage, Mississippi: The home of a black civil rights activist is bombed.

August 12, Chicago, Illinois: White mobs stone civil rights marchers in Marquette Park.

August 12, Muskegon, Michigan: Police responding to a report of two white men being assaulted by blacks at a downtown location are surrounded by a black mob. Reinforcements clash with 1,500 blacks in a club-swinging melee that leaves five persons injured and twenty-seven in custody. After the mob is dispersed, seven men are arrested for trying to loot a nearby jewelry store.

August 13, Ypsilanti, Michigan: Eleven black youths, ages twelve to nineteen, are arrested for stoning white motorists on the highway.

August 14, Chicago, Illinois: Assaults by white mobs on black demonstrators are repeated in Bogan and Gage Parks. White rioting continues in Marquette Park, with one car burned and two others damaged. Two policemen and several blacks are injured before the violence subsides.

August 15, Providence, Rhode Island: Four Molotov cocktails are thrown at a black church that has recently opened in a white neighborhood.

August 19–29, Wauwatosa, Wisconsin: Black picketers at the home of Circuit Judge Robert Cannon are repeatedly attacked by white mobs. National Guard units are sent to protect the demonstrators on August 26.

August 21, Chicago, Illinois: A civil rights procession is stoned by white rioters.

August 23, South Deering, Illinois: White rioters stone black civil rights demonstrators in a Chicago suburb.

August 26–28, Waukegan, Illinois: Fourteen persons are injured and eighty are arrested during an outbreak of black rioting. The worst violence is reported on August 28, when firebombs trap several motorists inside their burning cars.

August 28–31, Benton Harbor, Michigan: Blacks riot over four nights, allegedly protesting "a lack of recreational facilities and bullying by local police." Thirteen blacks and three whites are jailed during the outbreak. On August 30, Cecil Hunt, a black pedestrian, is shot by white gunmen in a drive-by shooting. He dies on August 31 and a suspect is arrested on September 1 but is later released when ballistics tests on his gun prove him innocent.

September, Old Claiborne, Alabama: A local Jewish cemetery is repeatedly vandalized during the month.

September 1–2, Dayton, Ohio: Blacks riot for two nights after Lester Mitchell, a black man, is killed by white gunmen in a drive-by shooting. Fifty stores are looted during the outbreak, and another black is shot by white residents while throwing stones at their home. National Guard units are briefly deployed, with the last troops removed by September 6.

September 6, Atlanta, Georgia: Rioting erupts after police wound a black suspected of auto theft. Militant leader Stokely Carmichael harangues the crowd before it runs amok, leaving sixteen persons injured and seventy-three in custody. Mayor Ivan Allen is toppled from the hood of a car at one point while calling for an end to violence. At least twenty cars are damaged during the outbreak, with sporadic violence and firebombings reported on September 7. Carmichael and fourteen others are indicted on September 13 for inciting a riot.

September 10–12, Atlanta, Georgia: A riot erupts after white gunmen kill Hubert Vorner and wound another black youth in a drive-by shooting. A brief melee on September 10 is followed by two nights of more extensive violence. Twenty persons are injured on September 11, including a policeman wounded by gunfire and a television journalist whose skull is fractured. Sixty-five persons are arrested during the outbreak, with five reports of firebombing on September 12.

September 12–13, Grenada, Mississippi: A mob of 200–400 whites riots over two days in opposition to local school integration. Police take no action as blacks and newsmen are beaten with ax handles, chains, and steel pipes. Two black youths are hospitalized with serious injuries.

September 24, Cleveland, Ohio: Arsonists destroy a home purchased by Rev. John Compton, a black minister.

September 28, St. Louis, Missouri: Violence erupts after police kill Russell Hayes, a black robbery suspect who confronted officers with a tear gas gun. Fourteen persons are injured during the outbreak. There are no arrests.

September 29, San Francisco, California: National Guard units are summoned to cope with an outbreak of rioting.

October 5, Richmond, Virginia: A black church is bombed.

October 8, Waukesha, Wisconsin: A shotgun blast strikes the home of KKK Grand Dragon David Harris.

November 8: Incidents of election-time violence against blacks are reported in Lowndes County, Alabama, and in Amite County, Mississippi.

November 20, Wetumpka, Alabama: James Motley, a black man, is beaten to death in the local jail. Jurors acquit Sheriff Harvey Conner of murder charges on April 12, 1967.

1967

January 1, Richmond, Virginia: Five whites, including a woman and a state prison employee, are arrested for illegal cross-burning.

January 10, New Orleans, Louisiana: Vandals strike at two Jewish cemeteries and desecrate over 100 graves.

January 13, Wetumpka, Alabama: A coroner described the jailhouse death of J.E. Motley, a black prisoner, as the result of "accidental falls," even though several officers have admitted to beating him.

January 14, Rosebud Reservation, South Dakota: An Indian girl, Jancita Eagle Deer, informs police that she has been raped by attorney William Janklow, who is later elected state attorney general and governor of South Dakota. An FBI probe fails to resolve the incident, and the young woman makes her accusation public in November 1974. Janklow files libel suits against an author and a magazine who report the charges, but the suits are thrown out of court in the spring of 1983.

January 15, New York City: Arsonists torch an unoccupied home recently purchased by a black family.

January 21, Collins, Mississippi: Nightriders burn a black church.

January 23, Grenada, Mississippi: A black church used for civil rights activities is damaged by an "accidental" fire.

January 29, Atlanta, Georgia: Mrs. L.C. Briley, the wife of a black minister, is shot and killed in her home. Nightriders had made an attempt to burn her husband's church.

February 11, Meridian, Mississippi: Nightriders fire on the home of Rev. Delmar Dennis, a former Klansman turned FBI informant. Dennis returns fire, driving away the raiders.

February 27, Natchez, Mississippi: Wharlest Jackson, a black factory worker recently promoted to a job formerly held by a white man, is killed by a bomb in his pickup. FBI agents identify the KKK faction responsible, but no prosecutions result.

March 4, Grenada, Mississippi: A black church is burned.

March 8, Prattville, Alabama: Four school buses are damaged during violent protests against school integration.

March 9, Pascagoula, Mississippi: Two Klansmen, including an attorney, are charged with abducting and threatening a witness in the Vernon Dahmer case.

March 12, Hayneville, Mississippi: A black church is burned.

March 13, Ft. Deposit, Alabama: Arsonists burn a black church.

March 13, Hayneville, Alabama: An Episcopal church, lately converted into a federal anti-poverty headquarters, is burned.

March 13, Liberty, Mississippi: The local Project Head Start office is bombed.

April 8–10, Nashville, Tennessee: Seventeen persons are injured and eighty are arrested during an outbreak of racial rioting. The violence erupts after the black manager of a local restaurant calls police to eject a black patron.

April 10–20, Louisville, Kentucky: White mobs repeatedly stone and assault black demonstrators over an eleven-day period of racial turmoil.

April 17, Massilon, Ohio: Three black youths and two whites are jailed after a racial fight outside of Washington High School.

April 22, Atlanta, Georgia: Rock-throwing erupts, sparked by rumors of a black man shot and wounded by a white storekeeper.

April 25, Birmingham, Alabama: Bombs damage the home of Judge Frank Johnson's mother. Johnson, an opponent of the KKK, has issued several rulings in favor of school integration.

May 10–11, Jackson, Mississippi: Students riot at all-black Jackson State College following the arrest of a speeder by black campus police. Black deliveryman Benjamin Brown is killed on the night of May 11 and two people are wounded when police open fire on a riotous crowd. National Guardsmen restore order on May 12 and withdraw the following day.

May 14, Cleveland, Ohio: A black-owned home in a nearly all-white suburb is bombed.

May 14, San Francisco, California: Fourteen persons are injured and twenty-nine are arrested during a racial brawl at an amusement park. On May 15 blacks riot in the Hunter's Point area, assaulting two white youths, hurling firebombs at a junior high school, stoning cars, and smashing store windows.

May 16, Houston, Texas: One patrolman is killed and two officers and one student are wounded during a shoot-out at mostly black Texas Southern University, the scene of sporadic disorders since March 28. Four hundred eighty-eight students are arrested during the disturbance, which is sparked by protests over alleged unequal punishment of white and black students involved in a fight. Scattered violence continues on May 17, but 472 of those arrested are freed without charges the following day. Five students are indicted for murder on June 2.

May 21, Chicago, Illinois: Thirty persons are arrested during a two-hour clash between blacks and police following a memorial service for Malcolm X.

June 2–5, Boston, Massachusetts: More than seventy-five persons are injured and over 100 are arrested when blacks riot. Authorities report that twenty-five stores are looted on the first day of the outbreak, and a fireman is wounded by snipers on June 3.

June 5, Tierra Arvarilla, New Mexico: Hispanic militant Reies Tijerina leads an armed occupation of the local courthouse, claiming ownership of the property under ancient land grants. Tijerina later draws a prison term of two to ten years for his part in the raid.

June 11, Prattville, Alabama: Violence erupts after a speech by militant Stokeley Carmichael. Four people are wounded in a duel between police and black snipers. Ten suspects are arrested at a home from which shots were fired, and the home's owner is treated for injuries sustained in a police beating.

June 11–13, Tampa, Florida: Blacks riot for three nights after police kill robbery suspect Martin Chambers. One policeman dies of a heart attack during the riot, at least sixteen people are injured, and more than eighty people are arrested. Property damage is estimated at $1.5 million.

June 12, Dayton, Ohio: Violence erupts during a speech by militant Rap Brown when blacks begin beating a white woman in the audience. More violence is reported on June 15, and order is restored the following day.

June 12–15, Cincinnati, Ohio: Rioting erupts from a demonstration at a local junior high school protesting the recent death sentence imposed on black serial slayer Posteal Laskey. Numerous injuries are reported, with over 300 persons arrested and property damage estimated at $1 million. Violence spreads to the Cincinnati Workhouse on June 15, when 400 black inmates battle guards. Rap Brown appears for a speech that day, but the riots have already begun to subside.

June 14–15, Lansing, Michigan: Two patrolmen are injured in a four-hour clash with black youths that leaves several cars damaged and seventeen persons in jail.

June 19, Atlanta, Georgia: Blacks riot for an hour following a speech by Stokeley Carmichael. Four patrolmen and two civilians are injured during the outbreak. On June 20 black mobs stone police, and officers respond by firing shots "in the air," killing Timothy Ross and wounding three others, including a nine-year-old boy.

June 21, New York City: Fifteen black members of RAM are arrested for plotting to kill moderate civil rights leaders. Police seize thirty guns, 1,000 rounds of ammunition, and 275 packets of heroin during the raids. (A sixteenth suspect is arrested the same day, in Philadelphia.) Two of the defendants are convicted on June 15, 1968, drawing maximum prison terms of seven years.

June 27–30, Buffalo, New York: More than 100 persons are injured and 205 arrested during an outbreak of violence that begins when black youths throw stones at a city bus. Damage from arson and looting is estimated at $100,000.

June 28, Mobile, Alabama: The home of a black civil rights leader is bombed.

June 30, Wadesboro, North Carolina: Bombs damage property owned by five school board members who favor desegregation. Targets include three homes, a business office, and a lodge.

July 2, Des Moines, Iowa: Seven black youths are arrested during an outburst of racial violence.

July 3, Atlanta, Georgia: Nine blacks are jailed after a crowd throws bottles at store windows and police, leaving two patrolmen hurt. One of those arrested is an officer of the SNCC.

July 3–4, Cincinnati, Ohio: Two nights of racial violence leave twenty-one persons injured and eleven arrested. Damage from the twenty-six arson fires is estimated at $1 million.

July 9, Waterloo, Iowa: Black youths smash windows and set fires during an outbreak of racial violence.

July 9, Tampa, Florida: A curfew is imposed after blacks loot and firebomb local shops.

July 9, Kansas City, Missouri: Police use tear gas to rout a mob of 150 rock-throwing blacks in Swope Park. One person is hurt and eleven are arrested during the two-hour clash, sparked by the arrest of three blacks for a liquor-law violation. Those arrested are fined $50 each and released on July 10.

July 11–12, Erie, Pennsylvania: Two persons are injured and eight are arrested during a black riot. Police use attack dogs to quell the disorder on July 12.

July 12–13, Hartford, Connecticut: The arrest of a black man for cursing a cafe waitress sparks rioting, with several stores damaged by firebombs and stones.

July 12–17, Newark, New Jersey: Blacks riot, the violence at its peak covering ten of the city's twenty-three square miles. The outbreak leaves twenty-six persons dead, more than 1,500 injured, and 1,397 in jail. Authorities report more than 300 arson fires, twelve of which are major. Sparked by the arrest and alleged police beating of a drunken black cab driver, the outbreak results in an estimated $15 million to $30 million in damages.

July 14–18, Plainfield, New Jersey: Five days of rioting erupt on July 14, with black mobs stoning police cars and shops. Twenty-five blacks and thirteen whites are jailed during the first night of violence. On July 16 white traffic officer John Gleason is mobbed by black rioters, disarmed, beaten, and shot to death. Forty-six rifles are stolen from a Middlesex arsenal the same day, and authorities search house-to-house for the weapons. Order is restored on July 19. Two blacks are convicted of Gleason's murder on December 23, 1968; the jury recommends life imprisonment.

July 15–17, Jersey City, New Jersey: Authorities report incidents of sniper fire, firebombing, and rock-throwing during a three-day riot by blacks. More than fifty persons are arrested during the outbreak, and one black is fatally burned by a Molotov cocktail thrown at a taxi in which he is riding.

July 16, Des Moines, Iowa: Seventeen blacks are arrested during a window-smashing spree.

July 16–17, Fresno, California: Eight persons are jailed and one youth is wounded by police during an outbreak of black violence and vandalism.

July 17, New Brunswick, New Jersey: At least fifty shop windows are smashed during an outburst of rock and bottle-throwing by blacks. Police make fifty arrests.

July 17, Paterson, New Jersey: Twelve black youths are jailed for smashing windows during a brief, unprovoked riot.

July 17, Elizabeth, New Jersey: Two hundred black youths run the streets, setting fires and looting a dozen shops.

July 17, Cairo, Illinois: Violence erupts after reports that a black prisoner has hanged himself in jail. That night, a white-owned warehouse is burned by arsonists, and three stores and a vehicle are damaged by other fires. Snipers fire on police from a black housing project on July 18, with firebombs hitting a lumber yard and cotton warehouse. National Guard units arrive on July 19 to enforce a curfew.

July 18, North Carolina: FBI agents arrest twelve whites, including at least seven Klansmen, for acts of racist terrorism spanning the previous twenty-one months in Rowan and Cabarrus counties. In a separate incident in Greensboro, two Klansmen are jailed for a cross-burning incident.

July 18, Erie, Pennsylvania: Eight blacks are jailed during a new eruption of rioting. Arson damage is estimated at $150,000.

July 19, Port Allen, Louisiana: A bomb explodes outside the home of a black woman active in the civil rights movement.

July 19, Durham, North Carolina: Two persons are injured when a black protest march degenerates into window-smashing and street-fighting.

July 19, Baton Rouge, Louisiana: Bombs destroy one car and damage another at the home of a labor leader who has actively opposed the KKK.

July 19–21, Atlanta, Georgia: Authorities confirm twenty-two arson fires, causing nearly $1 million damage, during a black riot that leaves fifty-six persons jailed and at least nine injured. National Guard units remain on duty until July 25, and a local tavern is firebombed soon after their departure.

July 21–23, Englewood, New Jersey: Five persons are jailed and eight patrolmen are injured during three nights of random violence by blacks.

July 22, Youngstown, Ohio: Two buildings are dynamited and three others are burned in a race riot. Three persons are injured, and two blacks and five whites are arrested.

July 22, Birmingham, Alabama: Blacks riot and loot local shops after a white patrolman wounds a black robbery suspect. Eleven persons are injured and more than seventy are arrested. National Guard units are called to restore order.

July 22–23, New Britain, Connecticut: Blacks stone passing cars in scattered incidents of violence. One white motorist is dragged from his car, beaten, and robbed.

July 23, Kalamazoo, Michigan: Police quell a disturbance involving some 200 blacks, which is sparked after unknown gunmen wound a black girl on the street.

July 23–24, Rochester, New York: Blacks riot for over two days. The riot is sparked by the stoning of a city water truck that hose down a street to prevent drag racing. More than fifty persons are jailed during the outbreak, and two blacks are wounded by white gunmen in a drive-by shooting. Thomas Wright, a black driver, is killed July 24 when he tries to ram through a police barricade.

July 23–25, New York City: Puerto Ricans riot in East Harlem for three days after police kill Renaldo Rodriguez, a knife-wielding resident who has already stabbed one of his neighbors. Two more civilians are shot dead during the riot, which leaves thirty-six persons injured and thirteen in custody.

July 23–30, Detroit, Michigan: The nation's worst race riot in decades leaves forty-three persons dead, more than 2,000 injured, and over 5,000 jailed. Authorities report 1,442 arson fires, with 477 buildings destroyed or heavily damaged, leaving another 5,000 persons homeless. Property damage is estimated between $250 and $500 million. On August 7, two white patrolmen are charged with murdering two black youths during the riot (both are later acquitted), and two blacks are charged with the murder of officer Jerome Olshove. On August 13, Michael Lewis, a black man, is charged with three counts of rioting and incitement, and is blamed for playing a major role in launching the catastrophic outbreak.

July 24, Flint, Michigan: More than 100 blacks are jailed during a rampage of firebombing and window-smashing. National Guardsmen arrive on July 25 to restore order.

July 24–25, Grand Rapids, Michigan: At least forty persons are injured and over 200 are jailed during two days of rioting in the black community. Snipers wound three black members of a task force designed to "cool down" the violence, and authorities report forty arson fires during the outbreak. National Guard units arrive on July 25. Scattered looting is reported through July 26.

July 24–25, Pontiac, Michigan: Two blacks are killed and one policeman is wounded by sniper fire during a riot that leaves eighty-seven people under arrest. Seventeen-year-old Alfred Taylor is shot by a member of the state legislature after he hurls a trash basket through the window of a market. National Guard units arrive to restore order on July 25.

July 24–26, Toledo, Ohio: One hundred thirty-seven persons are arrested during an outbreak of black rioting. National Guard units are summoned on July 25. At least twenty arson fires are reported during the first night of violence, with damage estimated at $75,000.

July 24–26, Cambridge, Maryland: SNCC militants descend on the city after one patrolman is shot and wounded during a July 24 race riot. On July 25 a black school is burned following a speech by Rap Brown, who informs his audience that "you should've burned it down long ago." Arson fires rage through the black business district and destroy twenty shops while white firemen refuse to intervene.

Police use tear gas to disperse unruly crowds on July 26, and Brown is charged with inciting a riot.

July 24–28, Mt. Vernon, New York: Blacks smash windows and destroy property over five nights. A state of emergency is declared on July 26.

July 25–26, Phoenix, Arizona: Black arsonists destroy a laundromat and several cars during violence that leaves forty-eight persons in custody.

July 25–26, Saginaw, Michigan: Eight persons are wounded by gunfire and seventy are arrested during two days of black rioting.

July 25–28, South Bend, Indiana: Four nights of racial violence leave seven persons wounded by police gunfire at a west side recreation center on July 26. National Guard units are placed on standby, but are recalled on July 29 without seeing active duty.

July 26, Lorain, Ohio: National Guard units arrive in the wake of several firebombings by blacks.

July 26, New York City: Twenty-two persons are arrested when blacks loot exclusive shops on 5th Avenue.

July 26, Cincinnati, Ohio: Blacks stone firemen at the scene of an arson blaze. More fires are set and several shops are looted. One person is wounded in the hip when police "fire in the air" to disperse the crowd.

July 26, Philadelphia, Pennsylvania: Black rioting erupts, and a state of limited emergency is declared the following day. The order forbids the gathering of twelve or more persons for purposes other than recreation until August 15.

July 26–August 1, Chicago, Illinois: Blacks riot for a week on the south and west sides, with over 100 persons arrested. At least six shops are firebombed in Hyde Park on July 26, and ten persons are injured when rioters stone a passing bus. A black man, Herman Hancox, is shot to death on July 28 while trying to stab a black patrolman. Julius Worth, another black man, is killed August 1 during an argument with the owner of a liquor store.

July 27, Poughkeepsie, New York: Eleven persons are jailed after blacks run amok downtown.

July 27–28, Passaic, New Jersey: More than fifty black youths are jailed in an outbreak of rioting, with reports of window-smashing and firebombing. Most of the property damage is to two liquor stores.

July 27–28, Peekskill, New York: Twenty-one persons are jailed and more than forty-four shops are looted during an overnight riot by 200 blacks.

July 27–28, San Francisco, California: Police arrest thirty-seven persons during a riot by black youths.

July 28, Long Beach, California: Fourteen persons are jailed after blacks riot. Two patrolmen are cut by flying glass in a duel with snipers.

July 28, Marin City, California: Three blacks are wounded during a five-hour rampage by twenty-five to thirty youths. The violence includes sniper fire directed at firemen.

July 28, Memphis, Tennessee: Blacks hurl rocks and set small fires.

July 28, Palmyra, New York: Racial violence erupts after a tavern brawl, with one person stabbed and ten arrested.

July 28–29, Wilmington, Delaware: Seven persons are wounded by gunfire and eighty to 100 people are arrested during a four-hour riot by blacks.

July 29, Springfield, Ohio: Two persons are injured when black rioters firebomb two adjacent homes.

July 29, Brooklyn, New York: Police suppress a minor riot in a black community.

July 29, Hamilton, Ohio: One person is injured in clashes between black and white gangs.

July 29–30, Rockford, Illinois: Forty-three persons are arrested during two nights of black rioting, with several reports of sniping and firebombing.

July 29–30, Newburgh, New York: Blacks riot for two days following an NSRP rally at the local courthouse. Seventy persons are arrested.

July 29–30, New Castle, Pennsylvania: Blacks smash store windows and assault white pedestrians. Two firebombings are reported.

July 30, Portland, Oregon: Thirty blacks and seventeen whites are arrested during an outbreak of racial rioting. At least nine firebombings are reported, with a black youth wounded by police while fleeing the scene of one explosion. Sporadic stoning and firebombing continues through July 31.

July 30–31, West Palm Beach, Florida: National Guard units are summoned to disperse black rioters after incidents of window-smashing, firebombing, and sniper fire directed at police.

July 30–31, San Bernadino, California: Two persons are arrested during a two-day outburst of sniping and firebombing in black and Hispanic neighborhoods.

July 30-August 3, Milwaukee, Wisconsin: Rioting leaves four black persons dead and more than 100 injured and 705 arrested. The violence begins with disorderly youths and is quelled by a rainstorm in the early hours of July 31 after one policeman and one elderly white woman are killed. National Guard units arrive later that day when rioting resumes.

July 31, Rivera Beach, Florida: Forty-six blacks are arrested during a riot that breaks out simultaneously with arson fires in a white-owned lumber yard and plastics factory. Angered by the arrest of two blacks at a fire scene, rioters stone police until tear gas is used to disperse the mob. Fire damage is estimated at $350,000.

July 31, Wichita, Kansas: Nineteen persons are arrested during an outbreak of firebombing and rock-throwing by black youths.

July 31–August 2, South Providence, Rhode Island: White and black gangs clash in this mostly black town. Police intervene on July 31 after blacks charge a white-owned lemonade stand and the proprietor defends himself with gunfire, wounding two rioters. Twenty persons are wounded when police duel with snipers on August 1, and white gangs repeatedly invade the town, looking for "action." Most of the seventy-two persons jailed by early August 2 are white.

August 1, Birmingham, Alabama: Firebombs damage a white cafe in a black neighborhood.

August 1, Chicago, Illinois: Fifty-four blacks are jailed for mob action at a liquor store, after the white proprietor shoots a black ex-convict in self-defense.

August 1, Washington, D.C.: Rioting begins when blacks stone firemen at the scene of a four-alarm blaze. Thirty-four persons are arrested, with eleven reports of arson and windows smashed in fifty shops.

August 2, Peoria, Illinois: Snipers concealed in a black housing project fire on police directing traffic at the scene of a grocery store torched by arsonists. Two persons are jailed on weapons charges during the outbreak. Witnesses report that a mixed gang of three blacks and two whites set fire to the store.

August 2–4, Wyandanch, New York: Eight persons are jailed during three nights of random firebombing and rock-throwing in this mostly black Long Island community.

August 3–5, Wichita, Kansas: Racial violence erupts. Two stores are firebombed and several patrolmen are injured by thrown objects. Twenty persons of both races are wounded in random shotgun attacks on August 4, and four white youths are charged with the shootings the following day.

August 5, Elgin, Illinois: Three persons are jailed during an outburst of arson and window-smashing by blacks. Fire causes $135,000 damage to a local Sears store.

August 12, Milwaukee, Wisconsin: Arson fires damage thirteen buildings in a black neighborhood, including the NAACP Youth Council headquarters. A white man is charged on August 13.

August 15, Sastsuma, Louisiana: Fifteen whites assault black demonstrators.

August 16, Holden, Louisiana: Seventy-five whites attack civil rights marchers.

August 16–19, Syracuse, New York: One hundred persons are jailed during sporadic outbreaks of black rioting, which is sparked by the arrest of a black teenager for loitering.

August 18, Denham Springs, Louisiana: White crowds stone and heckle black marchers.

August 19–23, New Haven, Connecticut: Four hundred fifty persons are jailed during a race riot sparked by a white cafe owner's shooting of a knife-wielding patron. Arsonists destroy at least two stores and several cars, and dozens of shops are looted during the riot.

August 21, Baton Rouge, Louisiana: Racial violence erupts, with black gangs throwing firebombs and white vigilantes patrolling the streets.

August 24, Philadelphia, Mississippi: A black school boycott erupts in violence when whites fire shotgun blasts at two busloads of black students. Two of the children are cut by flying glass.

August 25, Chicago, Illinois: Snipers harass firemen at the scene of a blaze on the South Side. A black youth then opens fire on the crowd of spectators and is arrested on charges of attempted murder.

August 28, Milwaukee, Mississippi: NAACP demonstrators are stoned by white mobs shouting "We want slaves!" and "Get yourself a nigger!" Marchers are attacked again on August 29 while arsonists destroy a Freedom House in the black district, and snipers harass firefighters summoned to quench the blaze.

September 10–13, East St. Louis, Illinois: At least six persons are jailed during a black riot that follows a speech by militant Rap Brown. Roosevelt Young, a black youth, is killed while trying to disarm the patrolman who stopped him on suspicion of auto theft. Two blacks are hospitalized with burns and gunshot wounds during the outbreak.

September 14, Chicago, Illinois: Black violence erupts during a SNCC rally held to protest the alleged police beating of a woman arrested two days before. Eleven persons are injured during the riot, including five patrolmen, and more than fifty persons are arrested.

September 17, Dayton, Ohio: Robert Barbee, a black civil rights activist, is shot and killed by a white off-duty patrolman. Blacks riot September 19 and 20. One hundred thirty-one people are arrested and more than fifty are injured.

September 18, Jackson, Mississippi: Nightriders bomb the Temple Beth Israel. As FBI agents pursue a suspect in a car, the FBI vehicle is rammed from behind by a carload of armed Klansmen. The KKK members are jailed after threatening the agents.

September 18, Hartford, Connecticut: Violence breaks out during a protest march by blacks and Puerto Ricans demanding stricter enforcement of fair-housing laws. Twenty-five rioters are jailed, and windows are smashed in at least twenty-four shops. Rioting resumes on September 19. Fourteen patrolmen are injured while restoring order.

October 1, Youngstown, Ohio: Arsonists set fire to a suburban home under construction for black owners. On October 3 the house is set on fire a second time.

October 6, Jackson, Mississippi: A bomb explodes at the home of the white dean of mostly black Tougaloo College.

October 6, Carthage, Mississippi: Nightriders fire into the home of a black NAACP activist.

October 8, Bastrop, Louisiana: Two hunters are injured by an explosive booby trap when they attempt to enter a rural KKK hangout.

October 28, Oakland, California: Patrolman John Frey is killed and a second officer is wounded during a shoot-out with Huey Newton, founder of the Black Panther Party. Newton, also wounded in the exchange, is convicted of manslaughter on September 8, 1968, but the verdict is overturned on appeal, after the disclosure of evidence that Frey apparently provoked the shooting in an attempt to kill Newton.

November 2, Winston-Salem, North Carolina: Violence erupts after the funeral of James Eller, a black prisoner beaten to death while in police custody. Two hundred seventy persons are jailed before order is restored on November 4, with fifty injuries and property damage estimated at $350,000.

November 8, Selma, Alabama: Three whites are charged with the murder of black tenant farmer J.A. Langdon. One defendant is convicted of manslaughter on January 20, 1968.

November 13, Wilberforce, Ohio: Black rioting erupts at Central State University, when police try to arrest a student who had been suspended earlier for threatening to kill a school administrator. Nine patrolmen are injured during the outbreak, and ninety students are arrested. The school closes on November 14, but reopens on November 27.

November 15, Laurel, Mississippi: A bomb damages the parsonage at St. Paul's Church, where the pastor doubles as a local NAACP leader.

November 17, Oceanside, New York: A bomb tossed through the window of a black-owned home fails to explode. Three white youths are arrested on December 7.

November 17, Philadelphia, Pennsylvania: At least twenty-two persons are injured and fifty-seven are arrested during a clash between 400 policemen and 3,500 students from ten mostly black schools. The violence erupts during a protest demonstration at the board of education's office.

November 19, Jackson, Mississippi: Bombs damage the home of a white family that sometimes entertains black guests.

November 19, Nyack, New York: Eighteen persons are jailed when black youths protest against alleged police abuse.

November 21, Jackson, Mississippi: The home of Rabbi Perry Nussbaum is bombed for the second time. The homes of two civil rights workers had been bombed a few nights before.

November 21, Chicago, Illinois: False rumors of racial violence spark fighting at Waller High School, leaving twelve students injured and eighty-four arrested. Administrators close the school, but the rioters march on two other schools, setting fires along the way, their ranks swell to an estimated 2,000 persons.

December 6, San Francisco, California: Outbreaks of race-related violence are reported from the campus of San Francisco State College, where BSU members are pressing demands for a minority studies program.

December 21, Collins, Mississippi: Two Klansmen stopped for reckless driving are arrested when police find a submachine gun in their car.

December 25, Louisburg, North Carolina: Nightriders fire on the home of a black civil rights activist.

1968

New York City: The Jewish Defense League is organized by militant members of a synagogue in the borough of Queens. Trained in martial arts, demolitions, and marksmanship, JDL members spend the next three years harassing Russians, Arabs, neo-Nazis, black militants, and moderate Jews with a campaign of assaults, sniping, bombings, and vandalism.

January 15, Dayton, Ohio: Black students go on a rampage in the cafeteria at Roth High School, throwing food and other objects at whites. The outbreak is sparked by anger over the principal's decision to let a white girl stay at home because she displays "intense racial feelings."

January 16, New York City: Black demonstrators scuffle with police and chase a busload of athletes outside of Madison Square Garden while picketing against alleged discrimination by the New York Athletic Club.

January 16, Nashville, Tennessee: Patrolman Thomas Johnson is shot and killed and his partner is wounded after stopping a carload of black militants following a merchant's complaint of stolen money orders. Four defendants are later convicted of murder and sentenced to ninety-nine years in prison.

January 19, Brooklyn, New York: Four persons are injured and one is arrested after four Black Muslims assault the principal and two staff members at Junior High School No. 117. One of the assailants is captured by teachers and held for police. He says the assault is due to alleged mistreatment of black and Puerto Rican students.

January 19, East St. Louis, Illinois: One person is injured when ten black youths smash windows along State Street, assaulting a white pedestrian and stealing his wallet. Authorities describe the incident as retaliation for the city's failure to issue a business license to a black teenage club.

January 20, Philadelphia, Pennsylvania: A white youth is stabbed by blacks at South Philadelphia High School. One hundred patrolmen rush to the scene when two racial brawls erupt after the stabbing. Eleven persons are injured and seven are arrested.

January 22, Cambridge, Maryland: Leon Lewis, a black man, is sentenced to six years in prison for shooting a police officer during 1967 racial disorders.

January 22, San Diego, California: Two hundred black youths stone cars and hurl firebombs at four local schools. Twelve persons are arrested.

January 22, Washington, D.C.: The U.S. Supreme Court refuses to hear the appeal of New York PLP leader William Epton, who had been sentenced to one year in prison for conspiracy to commit anarchy during the 1964 Harlem riot.

January 25, Springfield, Massachusetts: Ten black youths are surrounded and assaulted by whites from a rival high school. One person is reported injured during the assault.

February, Hattiesburg, Mississippi: Nightriders fire on the home of NAACP activist Kaley Duckworth.

February 1, Brooklyn, New York: Circulation of false rumors sparks racial fighting between black, Puerto Rican, and Italian youths, leaving four persons arrested. On February 2 black students brawl in the corridors and set off false fire alarms at a high school.

February 3, Miami, Florida: A white patrolman resigns after charges of stripping a black youth to his shorts and dangling him from a freeway overpass.

February 3, Wilmington, Delaware: Five persons are injured and nine are arrested in racial fighting at a teenage dance.

February 3, Syracuse, New York: Four white youths are assaulted in separate incidents by a mob of blacks.

February 5, New Haven, Connecticut: Black and white students clash at Hillhouse High School. A similar brawl erupts at Lee High School on February 6, leading to five arrests and several minor injuries.

February 5, Chicago, Illinois: Three persons are arrested when black students riot at Dunbar Vocational High School.

February 6, Milwaukee, Wisconsin: Black students riot at North Division High School, vandalizing rooms, smashing windows, and setting at least two fires. One police officer is struck on the head with a rock before the outbreak is controlled.

February 8, Orangeburg, South Carolina: Three blacks are killed and at least thirty-four are wounded when state police fire on rioters at South Carolina State College. The campus has witnessed continued unrest since February 5, with demonstrations aimed at a segregated bowling alley nearby. Federal charges are filed against nine police officers on December 20; all nine are acquitted on May 27, 1969.

February 9, Washington, D.C.: A week of racial fighting at Douglass Junior High School peaks when six black students mob and beat a policeman without apparent provocation. Two are arrested.

February 9, Lackawanna, New York: Four students are injured and five are suspended when racial brawling closes a local high school.

February 14–15, Social Circle, Georgia: Seven persons are injured and forty-six are arrested when police clash with black demonstrators.

February 15, Durham, North Carolina: Firemen turn high-powered hoses on black demonstrators protesting the February 8 shootings at Orangeburg, South Carolina. Protestors stone authorities, smash thirteen storefront windows, and burn a simulated coffin and an effigy of South Carolina's governor.

February 16, Mt. Vernon, New York: One person is injured when racial fighting caps three days of protests at Mt. Vernon High School.

February 19, Milwaukee, Wisconsin: Demands for black history classes at Riverside High School lead to racial fighting, with two fires set in restrooms and one school bus damaged. Two hundred fifty students are suspended following the outbreak.

February 19, Newark, New Jersey: Seventeen persons are arrested when black picketers clash with police and assault white employees outside Newark Hospital.

February 20, Cambridge, Maryland: Black militant James Lewis is convicted of assaulting an officer after a speech by Rap Brown.

February 21, Chicago, Illinois: Violence erupts at Calumet High School during an unauthorized memorial service for Malcolm X in the cafeteria. Three students are arrested.

February 21, Lorman, Mississippi: Police fire tear gas and bullets into disorderly crowds on the campus of all-black Alcorn A & M College. In a second flare-up, 200 students pelt police with rocks and bottles.

February 23, Memphis, Tennessee: Six persons are jailed after black demonstrators surround and rock a city police car.

February 25–26, Milwaukee, Wisconsin: Three persons are injured and six are arrested during two days of black rioting and vandalism at Wells Street Junior High.

February 27, Chicago, Illinois: Forty-eight persons are arrested after racial fighting at Roosevelt High School.

February 28, Trenton, New Jersey: Thirty-six persons are injured and four are arrested following racial fighting at Trenton High School.

March 2, Carteret, New Jersey: Blacks assault four white students at a high school dance, they smash the windows of four nearby shops and one home.

March 3, Jackson, Mississippi: Guards at the home of black leader Charles Evers exchange shots with nightriders. A white youth is arrested the following day.

March 4–5, Mt. Clemens, Michigan: Four persons are injured and one is arrested during two days of racial fighting near Mt. Clemens High School. The windows of several passing cars are also smashed.

March 4–6, Omaha, Nebraska: Rioting erupts after police clash with violent demonstrators at a George Wallace political rally. One person is killed, sixteen are injured, and eighteen are jailed. At least eleven stores are looted, six other buildings are vandalized, and twelve cars are damaged.

March 6, Birmingham, Alabama: W.A. Maxwell, a black man, wins a $45,000 damage suit against the SCLC. Maxwell filed the suit after receiving gunshot wounds during a 1965 demonstration.

March 7, El Dorado, Arkansas: Police use Mace and tear gas to disperse a crowd of rock-throwing blacks. One person is arrested.

March 7, Maywood, Illinois: Black students go on a rampage at Proviso East High School, damaging five cars and two city buses, and smashing windows of a nearby grocery store. Four students are jailed.

March 8, Gainesville, Florida: Three white-owned businesses are firebombed after an appeals court upholds the conviction of two civil rights activists. Firebombings of white shops and homes multiply on March 15, and six blacks—including Irvin Dawkins, one of the original defendants—are arrested for possessing Molotov cocktails on March 17.

March 9, Knoxville, Tennessee: Two persons are arrested after rioting erupts at mostly black Knoxville College. The riot begins after campus police impound a car with two black occupants. A white taxi driver is shot to death by the rioters and his cab is burned.

March 12, Maywood, Illinois: Police use Mace to quell racial fighting between eighty white students and forty blacks at Proviso East High School. Eleven students are expelled, and the school is closed for two days.

March 13, Gainesville, Florida: Six persons are arrested after two white-owned stores are firebombed in a black neighborhood. Authorities report that seventeen white-owned businesses have been set on fire since January 1.

March 14, Cincinnati, Ohio: Two persons are arrested after black teenagers stone white motorists and white-owned houses.

March 19, Tampa, Florida: One hundred fifty blacks riot after the arrest of a drunken black woman. Nine persons are arrested.

March 21, Washington, D.C.: Police scuffle with black protest marchers near the South African embassy.

March 21, Chicago, Illinois: Two black students from Harper High School are shot and wounded by white gunmen. Racial clashes occur at the school on March 22 and escalate into street violence when blacks smash the windows of several nearby stores.

March 22, Cheyney, Pennsylvania: Cheyney State College is closed after black demonstrators assault the college president and vandalize the administration building.

March 22, Chicago, Illinois: Eight persons are arrested after black youths stone white motorists near Cregier Vocational High School.

March 25, Hartsdale, New York: The appearance of racist graffiti at Woodlands High precipitates a series of clashes between black and white students.

March 26, Linden, New Jersey: Several students at Linden High are suspended after fights between white youths sporting Nazi armbands and black youths.

March 27–28, Pittsburgh, Pennsylvania: Two persons are arrested and three businesses are damaged during an overnight outbreak of black violence.

March 28, Memphis, Tennessee: Violence erupts during a black protest march led by Dr. Martin Luther King. Larry Payne, a black youth, is killed by police and more than 150 persons are arrested. The windows of at least 155 shops are smashed.

March 29, Seat Pleasant, Maryland: Eleven persons are arrested after black youths hurl bricks and bottles at police during a party sponsored by the Black Defenders.

March 31, Notasulga, Alabama: The city's police chief and a state trooper go on trial for beating a black prisoner.

April, Soledad, California: Black inmate Clarence Causey is stabbed to death while "attacking" six Mexican convicts at the state prison. Other blacks maintain that racist guards marked Causey for death and deliberately opened his cell for hostile gang members.

April 2, White Plains, New York: Racial fighting at White Plains High School results in all area schools being closed the following day.

April 2, Chicago, Illinois: Hirsch High School is closed after black students vandalize the cafeteria and set the building on fire.

April 2, Washington, D.C.: Two persons are jailed after blacks stone police and smash store windows following a confrontation between black youths and a commercial security guard.

April 3, New York City: One person is arrested after black demonstrators invade and vandalize a state welfare office.

April 4, Memphis, Tennessee: Rev. Martin Luther King, Jr., is assassinated by a sniper on the eve of a scheduled protest demonstration. An overnight riot in Memphis leaves more than thirty persons injured, with reports of sniping and at least three major fires. Nationwide, rioting erupts in 125 cities over the next week, leaving forty-six persons dead (one of them in Memphis, on April 6), 2,600 injured, and 21,270 arrested. Damage from arson and vandalism is estimated at $45 million, while taxpayers spend another $5.38 million to deploy 36,000 federal troops in urban riot zones. Insurance companies report a total loss of $67 million in the riots. In addition to riots described below in some detail, black violence is also reported from the following states and cities from April 4–11: Arkansas: El Dorado; California: Vallejo; Iowa: Knoxville and Marshalltown; Minnesota: Minneapolis; Mississippi: Clarksdale,

Cleveland, Crystal Springs, Holly Springs, and Oxford; North Carolina: High Point; Pennsylvania: Chester.

April 4, Tampa, Florida: Violence erupts in the wake of Dr. Martin Luther King's murder.

April 4, Winter Haven, Florida: Following the announcement of Dr. Martin Luther King's death, white youths stone the home of a local NAACP leader. Blacks retaliate that night by stoning white motorists and smashing the windows of three white-owned stores. Violence resumes on April 6, with more stonings and the burning of a grocery store and a vacant house. Police retrieve a firebomb from the doorway of a diner frequented by blacks.

April 4, Ithaca, New York: Black students at Cornell University invade the economics department and hold its white chairman hostage for seven hours.

April 4, Erie, Pennsylvania: Twelve persons are injured and fifteen are arrested during racial clashes at a local high school.

April 4, Houston, Texas: A firebomb causes heavy damage to a furniture store in a black neighborhood.

April 4, Itta Bena, Mississippi: Two black youths are shot and wounded during a violent clash with police.

April 4, Tyler, Texas: Fifty blacks stone police cars.

April 4, Charleston, South Carolina: Black mobs stone, assault, and fire on white motorists in the wake of Dr. Martin Luther King's death. Police record at least eleven incidents of rock-throwing at cars or shops, with one grocery store firebombed and one person reported injured.

April 4, Dallas, Texas: Black firebombers target a vacant building and a white-owned grocery store.

April 4, Jackson, Mississippi: Blacks burn a white-owned supermarket and two cars and loot at least three other stores, smashing hundreds of windows. Calm is restored on April 5, although there are sporadic reports of sniper fire on April 6.

April 4, St. Louis, Missouri: News of Dr. Martin Luther King's assassination sparks a riot by black inmates at the city jail. The riot is quelled with tear gas and smoke grenades after several fires are set inside the building. Rioting spreads to the streets from April 5 through April 14, with sixty firebombings, one person injured, and six arrested. Property damage is estimated at $60,000.

April 4, New Bern, North Carolina: Eleven persons are arrested after black demonstrators stone white-owned businesses, damaging twenty-two stores and five delivery trucks.

April 4–5, New York City: Sporadic outbreaks of violence in Harlem and Bedford-Stuyvesant follow announcements of Dr. Martin Luther King's murder. Thirty persons are injured, including ten patrolmen, with ninety-four arrested on various charges. Authorities report 158 incidents of arson, looting, and rock-throwing.

April 4–5, Greensboro, North Carolina: National Guardsmen are deployed during two nights of violence around mostly black A&T State University, trading fire with snipers on campus. At least five persons are injured and twenty-two are arrested during the riot.

April 4–5, Albany, Georgia: Seven persons are injured and nine are arrested during an outbreak of overnight violence. Two white-owned stores are looted, with two more set on fire by blacks.

April 4–5, Birmingham, Alabama: Overnight violence leaves one grocery store looted and burned, and three blacks in jail for illegal entry. Two firebombs are thrown on April 5, but no damage is reported.

April 4–5, Savannah, Georgia: Three persons are injured during overnight violence with sporadic incidents of firebombing by blacks. Damage is estimated at $300,000.

April 4–5, Newark, New Jersey: Authorities report sporadic looting, window smashing, and several small fires in black communities.

April 4–5, Battle Creek, Michigan: One person is injured and thirty-three are arrested when police clash with black protesters.

April 4–5, San Francisco, California: Sporadic looting and four firebombings are reported overnight. On April 5 black youths vandalize cars at a city garage and invade nearby stores, scuffling with clerks. Two area high schools are closed after racial incidents.

April 4–5, Tallahassee, Florida: National Guard units are deployed during two nights of violence. On May 25 three black youths are charged with killing a white youth during the riots. Seven other persons are reported injured.

April 4–5, Syracuse, New York: At least one person is injured when black gangs drag white motorists from their cars and beat them, and set fires in two abandoned houses.

April 4–5, Winston-Salem, North Carolina: One person is injured and six are arrested in black violence that includes window-smashing and at least five arson fires.

April 4–5, Tampa, Florida: Eight people are injured and two are arrested in sporadic outbreaks of black rioting and arson.

April 4–6, Boston, Massachusetts: National Guard units are placed on standby when blacks stone and loot shops. Twenty-one persons are injured and thirty are arrested. Property damage is estimated at $50,000.

April 4–6, Denver, Colorado: Police report at least fifteen incidents of firebombing, rock-throwing, and racial fighting.

April 4–7, Washington, D.C.: Ten persons die and 1,191 are injured during one of the month's four worst riots. Speeches by Stokeley Carmichael urge blacks to arm themselves when 13,600 federal troops are deployed. Authorities report 1,130 arson fires during the riot.

April 4–8, Pittsburgh, Pennsylvania: National Guard units are deployed to suppress black rioting. One person is killed, forty-five are injured, and 1,265 are arrested. Property damage is estimated at $2 million.

April 4–8, Raleigh, North Carolina: Twenty persons are injured and 105 are arrested during black rioting sparked by Dr. Martin Luther King's death. Damage from arson fires is estimated at $40,000.

April 4–8, Greenwood, Mississippi: Seven persons are arrested during sporadic outbreaks of black violence. White motorists are stoned by blacks, several store windows are smashed, and two homes are firebombed.

April 4–8, Hartford, Connecticut: At least three persons are injured and forty are arrested during rioting in the black community.

April 4–9, New Bedford, Massachusetts: Sporadic violence is reported in the wake of Dr. Martin Luther King's murder.

April 4–10, Philadelphia, Pennsylvania: At least thirty-seven persons are injured and 100 are arrested during black rioting sparked by Dr. Martin Luther King's assassination. Police report sporadic looting, with over 300 windows smashed, twelve arson fires, and thirty attacks on individuals by black mobs.

April 4–10, Lexington, Kentucky: Two persons are injured and twenty are arrested during seven nights of sporadic violence in the black community. At least a dozen arson fires are reported, with numerous windows smashed.

April 4–10, Macon, Georgia: One hundred persons are arrested over seven nights of sporadic violence sparked by Dr. Martin Luther King's murder. Property damage is estimated at $35,000.

April 4–10, Rockford, Illinois: Seven days of sporadic violence by blacks includes at least six firebombings and windows smashed by hit-and-run vandals. Police report no gatherings of major crowds.

April 5, Wilmington, Delaware: Racial fighting is reported at area schools after administrators deny permission for a memorial march on behalf of Dr. Martin Luther King.

April 5, Greenville, Mississippi: Two persons are injured when black youths stone police cars and white motorists.

April 5, Helena, Arkansas: Five black youths are arrested (and later convicted) for disorderly conduct following an outbreak of racial unrest.

April 5, Grand Rapids, Michigan: Two persons are injured during sporadic outbreaks of black violence against whites.

April 5, Spokane, Washington: One black is arrested after gangs smash windows in eleven stores.

April 5, Portland, Oregon: Racial fighting and incidents of arson close an area high school at noon. Violence spreads to the streets after students are dismissed, with blacks stoning shops and passing cars. The school is firebombed on April 7.

April 5, Prairie View, Texas: Authorities respond in force after fifty black youths stone passing cars on the street.

April 5, Niles, Michigan: One hundred fifty black youths riot downtown, smashing at least 100 windows during a half-hour rampage.

April 5, Trenton, New Jersey: Racial fighting breaks out at Central High School and spills into the streets, several shops are looted by blacks. One bystander is accidentally shot and wounded when a policeman trips while chasing looters.

April 5, Wichita, Kansas: Two white students are attacked and beaten by black students at an area high school.

April 5, East Palo Alto, California: Four hundred black youths smash seventy-five windows and overturn and burn a car at a local shopping center.

April 5, Pittsburgh, California: Three persons are injured during racial fighting at an area high school. Forty-five black students are suspended.

April 5, Dayton, Ohio: One black youth is wounded by gunfire as scattered rioting and rock-throwing erupt in the black community.

April 5, South Bend, Indiana: Three persons are injured and at least four businesses are damaged or looted after a black demonstration downtown turns violent.

April 5, New Haven, Connecticut: Richard C. Lee High School is closed after black students go on a window-smashing rampage.

April 5, Buffalo, New York: One person is injured and two are arrested after racial fighting at two local schools.

April 5, Freeport, New York: Freeport High School closes after black students smash a window and burn the American flag to protest Dr. Martin Luther King's assassination.

April 5, Greenburgh, New York: Area schools are closed after 200 black youths loot four stores, smash the windows of twenty-three others, and burn a car and a grocery store.

April 5, Jefferson City, Missouri: Window-smashing and vandalism erupt during a black protest march. Authorities blame rioters for the robbery of a gun shop later that night.

April 5, Monticello, New York: Fifty blacks smash store windows in the wake of Dr. Martin Luther King's assassination.

April 5, Mt. Vernon, New York: The local high school is closed after outbreaks of racial fighting.

April 5, Ossining, New York: Area schools are closed after racial fighting spills into the streets, with black gangs blocking traffic and damaging a neighborhood liquor store.

April 5, Niagara Falls, New York: One person is injured and six are arrested after black rioters stone police cars and smash windows in at least a dozen homes. Violence resumes on April 7, with assaults on police and minor damage reported from several inept firebombings.

April 5, Braddock, Pennsylvania: Fifteen blacks are jailed following firebombings and scattered reports of window-smashing.

April 5, Johnstown, Pennsylvania: A mixed group of twenty-four teenagers led by a black adult smash windows downtown and loot a jewelry store in the wake of Dr. Martin Luther King's death. One person is arrested.

April 5, North Little Rock, Arkansas: Police impose strict security on black neighborhoods after rioters firebomb a local store.

April 5, Alton, Illinois: One person is injured during racial fighting at a local high school. New outbreaks are reported on April 8, and several people are arrested.

April 5, East St. Louis, Illinois: Black rioters smash windows in eleven stores, damage several cars, and burn one car.

April 5–6, New Rochelle, New York: Four persons are arrested after blacks launch an overnight spree of window-smashing downtown.

April 5–6, Berkeley, California: Police report scattered incidents of looting, window-smashing, and rock-throwing by blacks.

April 5–6, Flint, Michigan: Thirteen persons are injured and thirty-four students are suspended after blacks assault and rob whites at two area high schools. Violence spreads into the streets at night, with two reported firebombings and scattered incidents of sniper fire and window-smashing.

April 5–6, Port Chester, New York: Black rioters loot several stores and smash windows.

April 5–6, Lancaster, Pennsylvania: One person is injured and one is arrested during an outbreak of rioting by blacks. At least thirty incidents of rock-throwing are reported, and one patrolman narrowly escapes injury when a sniper's bullet glances off his holster.

April 5–6, Springfield, Missouri: Five black youths are jailed for vandalizing a white-owned restaurant. Other blacks smash windows at Drury College and five local stores.

April 5–6, Pine Bluff, Arkansas: Three persons are injured and twenty-nine are arrested after outbreaks of rioting by blacks. Authorities report six arson fires, with property damage estimated at $200,000. Three hundred fifty-four blacks are taken into custody and marched to City Hall for questioning following a duel between snipers and police at a local nightclub.

April 5–6, West Chester, Pennsylvania: Thirty-five to forty black youths are involved in sporadic acts of street violence and arson fires before a state of emergency is declared.

April 5–6, Aliquippa, Pennsylvania: Thirty-one persons are jailed following rioting.

April 5–6, Oakland, California: Police report scattered incidents of looting and vandalism, sparked by racial fights at area high schools. Property damage is $265,000. On the night of April 6, Bobby Hutton, a teenage Black Panther, is killed during a ninety-minute shoot-out with police that leaves four others wounded and eight persons in custody.

April 5–7, Chicago, Illinois: Black rioting leaves eleven persons dead, more than 500 injured, and 3,000 in custody. One hundred sixty-two buildings are destroyed by arsonists and more than twenty are damaged for an estimated loss of $11 million. Scattered incidents continue through April 11, without further serious injury.

April 5–7, Toledo, Ohio: Fifty-eight blacks are arrested during three days of rock-throwing and window-smashing. Four arson fires are reported.

April 5–7, Alexandria, Virginia: Three persons are jailed after black youths run the streets, smashing windows and setting off false fire alarms.

April 5–7, Fayetteville, Arkansas: Authorities tighten security in black neighborhoods after scattered outbreaks of violence.

April 5–7, Tucson, Arizona: Two persons are jailed during three nights of violence by blacks. Eight arson fires are reported. Property damage is estimated at $12,900.

April 5–7, Paris, Arkansas: Police report scattered incidents of arson and window-smashing by blacks.

April 5–7, Malvern, Arkansas: Police impose tight security on black districts after reports of violence, including sniper fire at a patrol car.

April 5–8, Evanston, Illinois: Eight persons are injured and six arson fires are reported during four nights of black rioting.

April 5–8, Mobile, Alabama: Three persons are injured and 362 arrested during three days of black rioting. Property damage is estimated at $5,000.

April 5–8, Goldsboro, North Carolina: Seventy-one persons are jailed during four days of rioting.

April 5–8, Charlotte, North Carolina: At least twelve people are injured and seventy-three are arrested during four nights of black rioting.

April 5–9, Detroit, Michigan: Two looters are killed when National Guardsmen and state police attempt to suppress riots in the black community. Twelve persons are reported injured, with 1,525 arrests and 378 reports of arson.

April 5–9, Nashville, Tennessee: Four thousand National Guardsmen are deployed to suppress black rioting. The campus of mostly black A&I State College is sealed off after two students are wounded on April 5. More than 100 persons are arrested during the outbreak. A curfew remains in effect until April 14.

April 5–9, Atlanta, Georgia: Police record numerous incidents of black violence between the time of Dr. Martin Luther King's assassination and his funeral. A white prisoner is murdered by blacks in the city jail on April 6, with a jailer reporting that they "just beat and stomped him to death for being white."

April 5–10, Durham, North Carolina: Twenty-four persons are arrested during sporadic black violence, with National Guard units placed on standby. Property damage is estimated at $50,000.

April 5–11, Baltimore, Maryland: Six persons are killed and 900 injured during rioting. Thirty-nine hundred federal troops are deployed to suppress the outbreak, with 14,000 arrests and over 1,000 arson fires reported. A curfew remains in effect until April 14. Property damage is estimated at $14 million.

April 6, East Orange, New Jersey: Two Main Street businesses are firebombed by blacks.

April 6, Lakeland, Florida: Black arsonists firebomb two grocery stores.

April 6, Weldon, North Carolina: Sixteen persons are jailed after blacks smash windows in at least five shops.

April 6, Peoria, Illinois: Twelve blacks are arrested for looting and window-smashing.

April 6, Prince Georges County, Maryland: Black arsonists set fire to a local elementary school, and a policeman is wounded by sniper fire. One person is arrested during the outbreak, and a second arson fire is reported early on April 8.

April 6–7, Wilmington, North Carolina: Fourteen persons are injured during violence by blacks marked by looting and sniper fire.

April 6–7, Decatur, Illinois: Black arsonists attempt to burn a local high school during overnight violence that leaves two men in custody for smashing windows.

April 6–7, Rockville, Maryland: Four blacks are arrested after a series of local firebombings.

April 6–7, Takoma Park, Maryland: Three firebombs start minor brush fires in a black neighborhood overnight. At the scene of one blaze firemen are pelted with stones by black youths.

April 6–7, Wilson, North Carolina: One hundred forty-six blacks are arrested in an overnight spree of window-smashing. Property damage is estimated at $10,000. National Guardsmen arrive on April 7 and remain for three days.

April 6–7, Hot Springs, Arkansas: Black violence flares overnight, with three arson fires and one report of sniper fire at motorists. Property damage is estimated at $25,000.

April 6–7, Frederick, Maryland: Two persons are injured and two are arrested afters blacks loot stores and stone police.

April 6–7, Fairfax County, Virginia: An estimated dozen buildings are firebombed in the black community of Gum Springs.

April 6–7, Joliet, Illinois: Eight persons are injured and fifty-seven are jailed following black rioting. Property damage is estimated at $500,000.

April 6–8, Frankfort, Kentucky: Black students riot near Kentucky State College, stoning two auto dealerships and blocking white students from the campus.

April 6–8, Gainesville, Florida: Two persons are injured and at least twenty-four are arrested during an outbreak of black rioting marked by firebombings and sniper attacks. Property damage is estimated at $2,500.

April 6–8, Columbia, South Carolina: One person is injured and twelve are arrested when students riot near two mostly black colleges. Thirty arson fires are reported, with property damage estimated at $18,000. National Guardsmen begin enforcing a curfew on April 9.

April 6–8, Gary, Indiana: Thirty-two persons are arrested during three nights of racial unrest. Four major fires are reported.

April 6–9, Benton Harbor, Michigan: Fourteen persons are jailed after blacks riot. An eight-year-old boy is wounded by sniper fire.

April 6–9, Lexington, North Carolina: Six persons are jailed when blacks stone passing cars, smash store windows, and set an abandoned school on fire.

April 6–9, Richmond, Virginia: One hundred twenty-two persons are jailed following an outbreak of black rioting. Thirty-two arson fires are reported. Property damage is estimated at $220,000.

April 6–10, Pomona, California: Four persons are arrested during sporadic black violence marked by numerous small fires.

April 7, Ft. Pierce, Florida: National Guardsmen are sent to quell incidents of firebombing by black youths. Statewide, black arsonists are blamed for causing $750,000 damage in five cities.

April 7, Tacoma, Washington: Six persons are jailed during a one-hour rampage, during which blacks smash store windows, loot one shop, and firebomb two others.

April 7, Chicago Heights, Illinois: More than twenty persons are jailed during a black riot marked by window-smashing, looting, and arson.

April 7, Des Moines, Iowa: Two persons are injured and twenty-one are taken into custody when violence erupts during a memorial march for Dr. Martin Luther King. Blacks scuffle with police, stab a white pedestrian, smash store windows, and firebomb at least six shops. Damage is estimated at $35,000.

April 7, Topeka, Kansas: Black arsonists cause an estimated $40,000 damage downtown.

April 7, Cambridge, Maryland: Two blacks are arrested after a night of window-smashing and arson fires.

April 7, Hagerstown, Maryland: Three guards and one inmate are injured after black prisoners attack white prisoners at the Maryland Correctional Institution.

April 7, Wheeling, West Virginia: Fifty blacks burn two homes and smash windows in six others.

April 7, Hampton, South Carolina: National Guardsmen are deployed after black arsonists burn five houses in the predawn hours.

April 7, Tuskegee, Alabama: Twelve college trustees are held captive for thirteen hours by black students at Tuskegee Institute.

April 7, Hamilton, New York: Thirty-five black students at Colgate University invade the Sigma Nu fraternity house after a white student threatens two blacks with a starter's pistol.

April 7, Orangeburg, South Carolina: Black arsonists burn a warehouse valued at $250,000.

April 7, Ft. Valley, Georgia: Blacks on a rampage smash several windows and set two stores on fire.

April 7–8, York, Pennsylvania: One person is injured and two blacks are jailed following a window-smashing spree accompanied by three arson fires.

April 7–8, Albion, Michigan: Eight persons are injured and one is arrested during black rioting marked by arson and sniper attacks. Property damage is estimated at $200,000.

April 7–8, Ft. Pierce, Florida: Fifty-eight blacks are arrested during an overnight outbreak of window-smashing and arson.

April 7–8, Aurora, Illinois: A group of ten to fifteen black youths detonate explosives at a gas station, firebombing three businesses, and stoning several others. Property damage is estimated at $1,350.

April 7–8, Carbondale, Illinois: Black arsonists set ten fires and ring in three false alarms overnight.

April 7–8, Lorman, Mississippi: A theater and a vacant house are firebombed following the official cancelation of a memorial march for Dr. Martin Luther King.

April 7–10, New Orleans, Louisiana: Black rioters burn at least four cars and attempt to firebomb a grocery store during sporadic incidents of racial violence.

April 8, Cincinnati, Ohio: Rioting spreads after James Smith, a black security guard, accidentally kills his own wife while trying to protect a jewelry store from looters. Rumors circulate that she has been killed by white police, and blacks retaliate with attacks on white motorists and pedestrians. Noel Wright, a white student, is dragged from his car and stabbed to death by blacks, who also beat his wife. More than twenty persons are injured during the riot, with 284 arrests. Property damage is estimated at $250,000.

April 8, Battle Creek, Michigan: The vocational training center at Battle Creek High is firebombed by blacks at noon. Moments later, a firebomb is hurled at a nearby grocery store.

April 8, Pensacola, Florida: Black youths stone cars and policemen after a memorial service for Dr. Martin Luther King.

April 8, Pompano Beach, Florida: One black is arrested during a three-hour rampage that includes three arson fires, the looting of two stores, and the stoning of ten other shops.

April 8, Bridgeton, New Jersey: Six persons are jailed after blacks riot, marked by window-smashing and firebombing.

April 8, Rahway, New Jersey: One student is hospitalized at Rahway High School after black students run the halls, angry over administrative refusals to close the school in honor of Dr. Martin Luther King.

April 8, Michigan: Authorities report scattered outbreaks of black violence in Benton Harbor, Grand Rapids, Kalamazoo, Lansing, and Niles.

April 8, North Merrick, New York: Six persons are injured when forty black students riot at a junior high school, assaulting white students and teachers.

April 8, Milwaukee, Wisconsin: Black youths smash store windows during a protest march downtown.

April 8, Hammond, Indiana: Police report fifty incidents of blacks stoning shops and white motorists around town.

April 8, Gifford, Florida: Nine blacks are arrested during an outbreak of window-smashing and firebombing.

April 8–9, Jacksonville, Florida: Police record twenty-nine incidents of looting, firebombing, and sniper attacks when blacks riot. A black youth is shot and killed by nightriders on April 9, and a second black is shot by whites the following day. A white man is charged with the first murder on April 12.

April 8–9, Sacramento, California: The barbershop owned by a black minister who organized a parents' patrol to keep youths off the street is firebombed twice in two days. On April 9, six more arson fires are reported in the black neighborhood of Del Paso Heights.

April 8–9, Middletown, Ohio: Two persons are injured when blacks stone and burn cars, and smash windows in three shops and one home.

April 8–9, Youngstown, Ohio: Three persons are injured and 144 are arrested during two nights of black rioting. National Guard units are deployed on April 9, and a curfew remains in effect until April 11. Property damage is estimated at $50,000.

April 8–9, Kalamazoo, Michigan: Violence erupts during a black protest march. Five persons are arrested in scattered incidents of looting, firebombing, and window-smashing.

April 8–9, Buffalo, New York: Twenty-four persons are injured and thirty-five are arrested during rioting by blacks, that includes window smashing, looting, firebombing, and sniper attacks. Property damage is estimated at $88,000.

April 8–9, Providence, Rhode Island: One person is injured when black rioters burn several shops and homes, stoning firemen at the scene of one blaze.

April 8–9, Stamford, Connecticut: Twenty-eight blacks are jailed during two nights of window-smashing and firebombing.

April 8–9, East St. Louis, Illinois: Twenty-one fires are reported during twelve hours of rioting. Firemen are stoned by black mobs at the scene of two different fires.

April 8–10, Harrisburg, Pennsylvania: Black rioters stone vehicles and shops, burn cars, and set fire to twenty-three buildings. Damage is estimated at $250,000.

April 8–10, New York City: Authorities log seventy-seven injuries, 461 arrests, and 592 incidents of arson, burglary, and disorderly conduct during outbursts of violence in black communities.

April 8–12, Trenton, New Jersey: Two hundred thirty-five persons are arrested and thirty are injured during sporadic outbursts of violence by blacks. Dozens of shops are looted or damaged by fire during the riots. On April 9 Harlan Joseph, a black divinity student, is shot and killed by police on the street, sparking further violence. National Guard units are summoned the same day, and remain on duty until April 12. Property damage is estimated at $600,000.

April 8–14, Wilmington, Delaware: Rioting by blacks prompts a declaration of emergency, with National Guard units deployed. Forty-two persons are injured during the outbreak, and 504 people are arrested. Property damage is estimated at $162,835.

April 8–15, Lower Chichester, Pennsylvania: Black vandals smash windows and set several fires in sporadic outbreaks of racial violence.

April 9, Newark, New Jersey: Three hundred ninety-two arson fires are reported, leaving 600 persons homeless, when blacks riot in the streets. Three hundred windows are smashed, and more than fifty shops are looted. Violence continues on April 10, with sporadic looting and fifty-eight fires. Six persons are reported injured, and fifteen are arrested during the outbreak.

April 9, Bridgeport, Connecticut: Fifteen blacks are arrested during a riot marked by several arson fires, with mobs stoning firemen at the scene of several fires.

April 9, New Brunswick, New Jersey: Black rioters loot one tavern, smash windows in fifteen other shops, and trigger ten false fire alarms.

April 9, Hempstead, New York: Nine persons are jailed during an outbreak of rioting, with five shops firebombed and fifteen other incidents of black mob violence reported.

April 9, Long Beach, New York: Two blacks are jailed after violence and window-smashing break out on a march sponsored by CORE and the NAACP.

April 9, Newburgh, New York: Black youths vandalize several shops, and hurl three firebombs that fail to explode.

April 9, New Cassel, New York: Fourteen persons are jailed during an outbreak of black rioting, with at least ten arson fires reported. Damage is estimated at more than $100,000.

April 9, Reading, Pennsylvania: Two persons are arrested after white bikers and black youths clash outside a black teen club.

April 9, Sharon, Pennsylvania: One white man is beaten outside a tavern after loitering blacks shoot at the building.

April 9, Waterloo, Iowa: Property damage is estimated at $6,400 when black youths smash windows, and rob shops and white pedestrians.

April 9, Jackson, Michigan: Black rioters stone passing cars and hurl several firebombs, causing property damage estimated at $20,000.

April 9, Lansing, Michigan: Black youths stone white motorists in scattered incidents of violence.

April 9, South Haven, Michigan: Black rioters damage four white-owned homes and two cars with stones and Molotov cocktails.

April 9, Somerville, New Jersey: Blacks smash the windows of three white-owned businesses.

April 9, Homestead, Florida: Police disperse a memorial march for Dr. Martin Luther King when blacks in the procession begin hurling rocks through shop windows along the parade route.

April 9–10, Lincoln, Nebraska: Authorities report seven arson fires in a black neighborhood following a protest march by black youths. Property damage is estimated at $1,000.

April 9–10, Oberlin, Ohio: Black gangs beat two white students at Oberlin College, firebomb a nearby elementary school, and light several other fires.

April 9–10, Louisville, Kentucky: Eight persons are arrested during black rioting, with property damage estimated at $6,000.

April 9–10, Flint, Michigan: Blacks riot overnight, smashing windows in a synagogue, a theater, three stores, and one home. At least one car is struck by sniper fire.

April 9–11, New Haven, Connecticut: Police log forty arson fires in black neighborhoods, with damage estimated at $50,000.

April 9–11, Dallas, Texas: One person is injured and six are arrested during three days of scattered looting and firebombing by blacks.

April 9–12, Chattanooga, Tennessee: Twenty-two persons are arrested during three nights of scattered violence in black communities. One fireman dies of smoke inhalation at the scene of an arson blaze. Property damage is estimated at $3,000.

April 9–12, Kansas City, Missouri: Six blacks are killed, seventy-nine people are injured, and 991 are jailed following riots. Authorities report at least 155 arson fires, and 3,000 National Guardsmen are deployed to suppress the violence. Scattered sniping and firebombing are reported through April 13, with no further injuries. Property damage is estimated at $500,000.

April 10, Manhasset, New York: One person is injured when black rioters firebomb a white woman's home in a mostly black neighborhood. Store windows are smashed and several businesses are set on fire. At some of the blazes, firemen are met with stones and pellets fired from air guns. Property damage is described as "extensive."

April 10, Columbus, Ohio: BSU members scuffle with whites at the administration building of Ohio State University over an attempt to lower the flag in honor of Dr. Martin Luther King.

April 10, New York City: Three white girls are injured and twelve black girls are arrested for subway attacks around Queens. Victims report their attackers chanted "We want black power" during the assaults.

April 10, Milford, Delaware: A carload of blacks follows a white couple to their home outside of town, shouting racial slurs against "white trash" and firing at least one gunshot before they depart.

April 11, Meridian, Mississippi: A black church damaged by arsonists on two previous occasions is burned to the ground.

April 13, Passaic, New Jersey: Twenty-nine persons are jailed after a feud between blacks and Puerto Ricans erupts into street fighting, firebombing, and the looting of shops.

April 15, Berkeley, California: Black and white students clash in racial fighting at Garfield Junior High School.

April 16, Pittsburgh, California: Responding to tenant complaints, fifteen sheriff's deputies enter a black housing project to raid an illegal crap game. Two officers and one black resident are shot after a crowd gathers and attacks the deputies. Ten persons are arrested during the outbreak.

April 17, Washington, D.C.: Three hundred blacks stone policemen during the arrest of a black heroin dealer.

April 18, Cartaret, New Jersey: Black mobs stone police and firebomb three businesses and several unoccupied buildings.

April 18–25, Denver, Colorado: Police report numerous calls for assistance as racial incidents erupt in area high schools and junior high schools, with several incidents deliberately instigated by non-students.

April 19, Boston, Massachusetts: A gang of twenty white youths taunt eight blacks with racial slurs, then drag them from their car and attack them with fists and knives. One black is stabbed to death in the assault, and nine persons are injured before police intervene. One white youth is immediately jailed on murder charges; two more are identified and seized at his preliminary court hearing.

April 20, Newark, New Jersey: An arson fire in the black community, described as the worst fire in city history, leaves 500 persons homeless. Thirty-four buildings are destroyed in the Central Ward.

April 20, New Bedford, Massachusetts: A laundromat recently picketed by several black groups is firebombed, with minor damage. Police report other outbreaks of vandalism and firebombing at two mostly black schools.

April 21–22, Seaside, California: Black violence erupts at a neighborhood carnival and spreads to the streets. Two policemen are wounded by shotgun fire. Six persons are jailed.

April 22, Montclair, New Jersey: Three persons are injured when blacks firebomb a liquor store and an automotive shop.

April 22, Stockton, California: A black protest march dissolves into violence when militant youths vandalize and loot shops. One white man is arrested for brandishing a pistol at rioters.

April 22, San Antonio, Texas: Two white soldiers are assaulted on the street by a gang of eight black and Hispanic youths. Police arrest several of the attackers, while a crowd of several hundred blacks and Hispanics gathers, with several fights breaking out. At least eight persons are injured and thirty-four are arrested in the outbreak. One man is jailed for shooting a boy in the leg.

April 22–23, Hartford, Connecticut: A mixed group of 200 students capture the administration building at Trinity College, holding the president and seven trustees hostage for over twenty-four hours, demanding new courses in black history and "the psychology of the ghetto." (At the time, Trinity has twenty nonwhites out of a total student population of 1,160.)

April 25, Brooklyn, New York: Fifteen black students hold the provost of Long Island University hostage for nine hours while demanding a greater role for blacks on campus.

April 26, Providence, Rhode Island: One person is injured when white youths invade Esek Hopkins Junior High School, assaulting black students with fists and rocks.

April 26, Seaside, California: White youths wearing swastikas clash with militant blacks at Seaside High School and at a nearby restaurant.

April 27, Washington, D.C.: Five white youths disrupt a black party, injuring one person before police are summoned. The youths then turn on a white police sergeant, calling him a "nigger-lover" before they beat him unconscious. Later, at the hospital, two of the youths are arrested for threatening the officer's wife.

April 27–30, East St. Louis, Illinois: Four persons are injured and seven are arrested during four days and nights of racial violence around area schools. A school attorney is beaten by blacks on April 27, and an elementary school is seriously damaged by a bomb that night. On April 28 a black youth hurls a firebomb into a high school auditorium occupied by 400 persons. Five area schools are closed on April 30, following bomb threats, and hand grenades explode at five separate locations, injuring three persons.

April 27–30, Omaha, Nebraska: At least ten persons are injured and forty-one are arrested when black violence is sparked by a police raid on an illegal crap game. A total of twenty-six stores are looted or burned, with thirty-seven vehicles damaged.

April 28, Newark, New Jersey: Two patrolmen are mobbed and beaten by 100 blacks during the arrest of a black bicycle thief. Six rioters are arrested.

April 30, New York City: One hundred forty-eight persons are injured and 720 are arrested when police rout student demonstrators from five occupied buildings at Columbia University. The protest is aimed at university plans to erect a gym on land used for recreational purposes by Harlem blacks. On May 1 eleven students are injured when police storm a protest rally on campus.

May 10, Washington, D.C.: Local papers report that black vandals and arsonists have caused property damage in excess of $300,000 in various outbreaks since late April. At least forty-two persons have been arrested in the incidents.

May 15, Hattiesburg, Mississippi: Black civil rights activist Kaley Duckworth is injured by a bomb wired to the horn of his car.

May 18–20, Salisbury, Maryland: Riots erupt after police kill a black deaf-mute burglary suspect. A patrolman is charged with manslaughter on May 19, while a state of emergency is declared and National Guard units are dispatched to the city.

May 21–22, New York City: Sixty-eight persons are injured and 191 are arrested when police clash with demonstrators at Columbia University. The latest sit-ins are held to protest the suspension of students involved in earlier racial demonstrations.

May 27–30, Louisville, Kentucky: National Guardsmen are deployed to suppress ghetto rioting. Two persons are shot and 100 others are injured on May 27. One black is shot and forty-two are arrested the following day. On May 29, two blacks are killed in separate incidents by police and a white shop owner. Scattered looting and numerous fires are reported on May 30, with twenty arrests bringing the four-day total to 350.

May 28, Meridian, Mississippi: Nightriders bomb the Temple Beth Israel.

June 6, Florence, Mississippi: One person is injured when bombs strike the home of a black civil rights worker's widow.

June 12, Brooklyn, New York: Three detectives are injured while trying to disperse crowds after a clash between black and Puerto Rican youths. In Manhattan a grand jury indicts six blacks who allegedly planned to kill one patrolman per week in the interest of "black liberation."

June 14, New York City: RAM leaders Herman Ferguson and Arthur Harris are convicted of plotting to murder moderate black leaders. On October 4 both defendants draw seven-year jail terms, the maximum.

June 24, Washington, D.C.: Blacks riot over the arrest of demonstrators during the SCLC Poor People's March on Washington. National Guard units are deployed, and 316 persons are jailed overnight.

June 29, Meridian, Mississippi: Police ambush two KKK terrorists when they attempt to plant a bomb in a Jewish businessman's home. Klanswoman Kathy Ainsworth is killed by police gunfire, and her male companion, Thomas Tarrants, is wounded in a battle that also leaves a policeman and an innocent bystander gravely injured. On November 27 Tarrants is sentenced to thirty years in prison.

July 3–6, Paterson, New Jersey: Rumors of police brutality spark violence in the Puerto Rican community. Sixteen persons are injured and fourteen are arrested on July 3. Firebombings are reported on July 5 and 6, with 114 arrests logged during the outbreak. On

December 18, federal authorities indict eight patrolmen on charges of civil rights violation.

July 9, Brooklyn, New York: Angry crowds gather after police wound a black youth who, with another suspect, was threatening pedestrians with a gun.

July 17–18, Akron, Ohio: More than 100 persons are jailed during two days of black rioting. National Guard units are deployed in the face of firebombings, with order restored on July 22.

July 19–22, Brooklyn, New York: Blacks and Puerto Ricans clash with police over four nights in the vicinity of Coney Island. Two patrolmen are beaten on July 21, with a firebomb hurled at two others on July 22.

July 22, New York City: Black mob violence erupts on the Lower East Side. Eight persons are arrested after a tavern is firebombed. Three hundred persons throw bottles at police on July 23; ten more are arrested.

July 23, Cleveland, Ohio: A shoot-out between police and black militants, later described by federal investigators as "armed guerilla warfare," leaves three patrolmen, two militants, and one bystander dead. The fifteen wounded include twelve officers, one militant, and two bystanders. Blacks riot over the next five days, and Clifford Miller, a black, is killed by white gunmen in a drive-by shooting. By July 26, at least forty-seven shops have been burned or looted, with property damage estimated at more than $2.6 million. Fred Evans, leader of the militant group involved in the shoot-out, is convicted of murder and sentenced to death on May 12, 1969.

July 27–30, Gary, Indiana: Two hundred thirty-five persons are jailed during an outbreak of black rioting, with three whites and three blacks wounded by sniper fire. Property damage is estimated at $35,000.

July 27–30, Goldsboro, North Carolina: Scattered ghetto violence erupts after police arrest a black "leader" for disorderly conduct at the local Playboy Club. One black is wounded by gunfire, his assailants unknown, while authorities log reports of sniper fire and looting.

July 28, Cincinnati, Ohio: Three persons are injured and six are jailed after blacks mob patrolmen responding to complaints of a loud party. Officers report sniper fire and respond with shotgun blasts fired in the air to disperse the rock-throwing crowds.

July 29–31, Seattle, Washington: Scattered rioting breaks out, including rock-throwing and reports of sniper fire, after police raid the local Black Panther headquarters, arresting two men and impounding stolen office equipment. At least thirteen persons are injured in the riots, with 101 arrested. Damage is estimated in excess of $220,000.

July 30, Peoria, Illinois: Ten patrolmen and a reporter are wounded after a clash with rock-throwing blacks escalates into an exchange of shotgun fire. Thirteen persons are jailed.

July 30, San Francisco, California: Snipers pump six shots into a police car when officers approach a house recently firebombed in the Hunter's Point neighborhood.

July 31, Pittsburgh, California: Two persons are injured and twenty-six are arrested when residents of a black housing project pelt patrolmen with rocks and bottles. Snipers open fire when police reinforcements arrive, hitting several squad cars.

August 1, Brooklyn, New York: Police clash with Panthers after interrupting an unauthorized street rally.

August 2, St. Petersburg, Florida: A black patrolman's car is firebombed.

August 2, Pulaski County, Arkansas: A black inmate at the county penal farm is beaten to death by a white trusty.

August 2, Brooklyn, New York: Patrolmen Thomas Dockery and Leonard Fleck are wounded by black snipers in a deliberate ambush while responding to a false distress call. Authorities blame Black Panthers for the shooting.

August 4–8, Inkster, Michigan: Black gunmen terrorize this suburb of Detroit, wounding two patrolmen and a passing motorist on August 7, and killing Det. Robert Gonser on August 8. A black youth, James Mathers, is shot and killed by police while fleeing the scene of Gonser's murder. Property damage is estimated in excess of $500,000.

August 4–11, York, Pennsylvania: Racial violence flares after a white resident fires shots from his home at a group of blacks on the street. Eleven persons are wounded in a shoot-out on the first night of what authorities term "a planned operation" by young blacks. Property damage in the riot is estimated at $40,000.

August 5, Charlotte, North Carolina: The home of a known KKK member is bombed.

August 5, Jackson, Michigan: Blacks fire an estimated thirty shots at two white patrolmen outside a Catholic youth center where previous incidents were reported in late July, when militants tried to take over the center.

August 5, Los Angeles, California: Three Black Panthers are killed and two patrolmen are wounded during a gas station shoot-out. Each side blames the other for firing first.

August 6, Los Angeles, California: The opening day of the Watts Summer Festival is marred by the wounding of four persons in a drive-by shooting incident, with several members of the crowd returning fire.

August 6, Chicago, Illinois: Police blame a militant group, the Black Elephants, for shotgun attacks that leave six officers wounded in the suburbs of Harvey and Dixmoor. Race relations in the area have been strained since police killed a black youth several weeks earlier. A total of ten persons are injured and thirty-three arrested.

August 7–9, Miami, Florida: Three blacks are killed, forty-eight injured, and 222 arrested during three nights of rioting. Property damage is estimated at $250,000.

August 7–12, Little Rock, Arkansas: Scattered violence in the black community erupts in response to the August 2 death of an inmate at the county prison farm. At least six persons are injured, including two policemen and a National Guardsman, and 193 are arrested.

August 8, Woodside, New York: Six black youths are charged with the murder of Thomas Syron, a white youth selected at random in retaliation for a white truck driver beating a black. The trucker in question is jailed on assault charges.

August 10, East Point, Georgia: Black youths stone policemen after officers are called to eject party crashers from an all-black social gathering. One officer is injured and three persons are arrested, while snipers fire an estimated fifty shots at police.

August 11, Los Angeles, California: Three blacks are killed and fifty persons are injured—including six patrolmen—in a clash at the Watts Summer Festival. Thirty-five persons are jailed in the latest outbreak of violence. Firebombings are reported through the night of August 13. Property damage is estimated in excess of $40,000.

August 11–13, Chicago, Illinois: Five persons are injured and thirteen are arrested during outbreaks of arson and sniper fire by blacks in the suburbs of Chicago Heights and East Chicago Heights. Damage is estimated at $500,000.

August 12, New York City: Black snipers fire three shots through the windshield of a police car on routine patrol.

August 14, Louisville, Kentucky: Rev. A.D. King's church is bombed. Police disperse an angry crowd after one white man is mobbed and beaten.

August 16–17, Cincinnati, Ohio: Violence erupts after two white men shoot and kill the black female proprietor of a local tavern. Rock-throwing and sniper fire are reported in the outbreak that leaves four persons injured and six in custody. One black youth is shot and critically wounded while stoning police cars.

August 17, Waterloo, Iowa: Blacks stone police cars, puncturing six vehicles with gunfire, during a two-hour outbreak of violence. One black is wounded by police.

August 19, Shelby, North Carolina: A bomb explodes at a chemical plant owned by a KKK leader.

August 19–20, Owensboro, Kentucky: Blacks stone cars and vandalize shops during two nights of violence.

August 21, Brooklyn, New York: Three Black Panthers are jailed for assaulting a policeman.

August 22–24, Evansville, Indiana: Four persons are injured, including two firemen and a police officer wounded by sniper fire, in a riot sparked by the arrest of two black auto thieves. White racists compound the problem by driving through black neighborhoods and firing bullets and arrows from their cars on both nights. Seventy-nine persons are jailed during the outbreak, including forty-two whites. Property damage is estimated at $275,000.

August 22–24, Wichita, Kansas: Rioting erupts after a white youth shoots a black in a mostly black neighborhood. At least sixty-three persons are jailed before order is restored, with police reporting thirteen shooting incidents.

August 24–25, Memphis, Tennessee: Riots erupt, marked by firebombing and sniper fire, after the arrest of a black militant charged with threatening the lives of two whites. One person is injured, and eleven are arrested during the outbreak.

August 30–31, St. Paul, Minnesota: Racial violence erupts after two off-duty patrolmen confiscate a pistol from a black youth at a teenage dance. Gunfire erupts from the crowd, with twenty-two patrolmen and thirty civilians injured during the ensuing melee. Fifteen persons are jailed on various charges, with firebombings and vandalism continuing into the next day.

September 1, Newport News, Virginia: Fifteen blacks assault a patrolman, beating him unconscious, with one of them using his sidearm to fire on police reinforcements. Floyd Price, a black man, is killed when police return fire, and blacks riot in protest, causing $2 million damage to black-owned businesses. Police seal off the district at sundown on September 2, and the riot soon ends.

September 1, Los Angeles, California: Hispanic Jess Dominguez, looking for his teenage children in the predawn hours, is stopped and beaten on the street by fifteen policemen.

September 2, Berea, Kentucky: One white man and one black man are killed in a shoot-out after three carloads of blacks open fire on an NSRP rally. Seven whites and seven blacks are held on murder charges.

September 3, Wilmington, Delaware: Police seize guns and ammunition in raids on BLA strongholds.

September 4, Brooklyn, New York: One hundred fifty off-duty policemen mob three Black Panthers emerging from a court hearing on assault charges relating to the August 21 assault on an officer.

September 4, Lexington, Kentucky: A bomb wrecks the home of Dr. Z.A. Palmer, a member of the Kentucky Human Rights Commission. Palmer and members of his family are injured.

September 8, Fairfield, California: Police Sgt. David Huff, earlier disciplined for pistol-whipping a prisoner, fatally shoots Jose Alvarado, a one-armed Hispanic. The department refuses to censure Huff, insisting that Alvarado assaulted a group of five officers who were unable to restrain him without deadly force.

September 10, Oakland, California: Two white patrolmen are fired and jailed after drinking on duty and firing twelve rifle shots into the headquarters of the Black Panther Party.

September 12, Brooklyn, New York: The FBI arrests four Black Panthers as fugitives from an arson charge in Baltimore, where they allegedly conspired to burn a supermarket. On the same day, Sgt. Peter Kunik and Patrolman James Rigney are wounded by a black sniper while waiting for a traffic light to change.

September 22, Cleveland, Ohio: William McWilliam, a white attorney, is fatally stabbed in a clash between white and black youths at a Democratic Party campaign rally.

September 24, Brooklyn, New York: Three hundred Hasidic Jews clash with 100 Puerto Ricans outside a synagogue. One patrolman is injured during the riot.

October 8, Washington, D.C.: Elijah Bennett, a black man, is shot and killed by the white patrolman who stopped him for jaywalking.

Tear gas is used to disperse angry crowds at the scene. A coroner's jury describes the shooting as willful homicide on October 16, but state and federal grand juries refuse to issue indictments.

October 11, New York City: Two white men are charged with conspiring to kill 158 civil rights workers and "active leftists."

October 14, Santa Barbara, California: BSU members seize a classroom building at the state university, barricading themselves inside for nearly ten hours.

October 23–24, Berkeley, California: Two hundred persons are arrested in rock-throwing incidents sparked by the cancelation of scheduled lectures by Eldridge Cleaver, a Black Panther spokesman.

November 2, Washington, D.C.: A white patrolman wounds a black woman who allegedly threatened him with a knife, and one of his stray bullets strikes an innocent bystander. Blacks riot in protest, burning three cars and beating several whites. Thirteen persons are jailed during the outbreak.

November 4, San Fernando, California: A three-hour demonstration by members of the BSU and SDS includes seizure of the administration building at San Fernando State College, with militants holding the president hostage to protest alleged racial discrimination in campus athletic programs. On December 20, twenty-eight students are indicted on charges ranging from assault to kidnapping.

November 6, San Francisco, California: Members of the BSU and SDS call for a student strike at San Francisco State College, demanding creation of an ethnic studies program. Violent incidents close the school November 13–18, and the president resigns on November 26.

November 9, Los Angeles, California: Thirteen-year-old Salvador Barba is beaten by police, and requires forty stitches to close his head wounds.

November 13, Berkeley, California: One patrolman and one Black Panther are wounded in a shoot-out following a traffic stop. Three blacks are jailed on charges of attempted murder.

November 13, Boston, Massachusetts: Three blacks are killed and two are wounded when black gunmen invade the offices of the New England Grass Roots Organization (NEGRO), a black self-help group. The dead include NEGRO's founder, Guido St. Laurent.

November 19, San Francisco, California: Three patrolmen are wounded in a gunfight with eight Black Panthers whose van was stopped in connection with a nearby service station robbery. Two of the suspects are indicted on December 2.

November 25, New York City: A suspicious fire at the Bronx Hebrew School marks the tenth attack in New York City on Jewish facilities in the previous three months.

November 27, New York City: Fire destroys the Yeshiva of Eastern Parkway synagogue. Two teenagers are charged with the Yeshiva fire on November 29.

November 28, Newark, New Jersey: Seven Black Panthers are arrested on weapons charges.

November 29, Jersey City, New Jersey: Police blame Black Panthers for a drive-by shooting at the local police station. Three Panthers are charged with the crime on December 5.

December 1, Jersey City, New Jersey: Black Panther headquarters is firebombed by persons unknown, injuring three occupants. Party spokesmen blame police for the attack.

December 5, San Francisco, California: Police use Mace and drawn guns to defend the administration building at San Francisco State College from violent BSU and SDS demonstrators. Twelve persons are injured and eighty-five are arrested in riotous outbursts before acting president S.I. Hayakawa closes the school for an early Christmas on December 13.

December 8, San Fernando, California: BSU arsonists set fire to the state college president's office, causing $100,000 damage.

December 13, San Mateo, California: Minority students riot on a local college campus following a joint rally of the Third World Liberation Front and the New Black Generation demanding an autonomous ethnic studies program.

December 16, Brooklyn, New York: Three Black Panthers plead guilty to assault charges stemming from a clash with firemen and police at a rubbish fire in August 1968.

December 24, Monroe, Louisiana: Shots are fired into the home of a black OEO administrator, narrowly missing his wife. A Klansman is arrested in the shooting, but legal technicalities set him free in February 1969.

1969

January 2, Brooklyn, New York: The Manhattan Beach Jewish Center is damaged by five small arson fires.

January 3, Far Rockaway, New York: Shaary Tefila Synagogue is destroyed by a suspicious fire.

January 3, St. Louis, Missouri: Racial tensions erupt into black-white fighting at Normandy High School. Police fire warning shots to stop the brawl, and 300 students walk out of classes in protest. On January 7 a white female student is beaten by three blacks. Two white youths are stabbed by blacks in separate incidents on January 9. On January 15 a white youth is beaten by black students.

January 5, New York City: The mayor reports that thirty-two religious institutions were torched in 1968, including fourteen synagogues.

January 9, Pittsburgh, Pennsylvania: Racial brawling erupts at Gladstone High School during a parents' meeting where blacks demand the principal's resignation, following an incident with a black student. On January 10 vandals damage the school's heating system during a walkout by 100 black students.

January 10, Denver, Colorado: Six youths are arrested after a gang of twenty blacks attacks two white teachers at a local high school.

January 13, New York City: Fifteen black youths invade the office of the SEEK program director at Queens College, vandalizing the rooms and tossing furniture through the windows.

January 15, Waltham, Massachusetts: Five black women students disrupt the library at Brandeis University, dumping 2,500 periodicals from their shelves. The action is linked to disputes over the creation of a black studies program.

January 15, Chicago, Illinois: Chairs are thrown during a racial brawl in the University of Illinois cafeteria. The violence erupts after blacks try to expel white students from a memorial service for Dr. Martin Luther King. Eleven perons are injured before campus police intervene.

January 15, Colfax, Washington: Black students with guns invade a white frat house at Washington State University. Fighting breaks out, and two rifle shots are fired. Five persons are arrested, and confined for thirty to sixty days in the county jail.

January 16, Chester, Pennsylvania: Black students smash furniture and throw books through windows at Pulaski Junior High School after the school board refuses to close schools for Martin Luther King Day. Eleven persons are arrested.

January 17, Los Angeles, California: Black Panthers John Huggins and Alprentice Carter are shot and killed during a meeting with rival black militants at UCLA.

January 20, Brooklyn, New York: Two suspicious fires are reported at different synagogues. Both result in little or no damage.

January 20, New York City: A white teacher is beaten and set on fire by black students during a period of racial unrest at Franklin K. Lane High School.

January 23, Jacksonville, Florida: Scattered incidents of stoning and firebombing are reported after jurors acquit a white suspect for the 1968 slaying of a black man, Rudolph Hargett.

January 24, Hamden, Connecticut: Racial fighting erupts at Hamden High School during a campus dance. More violence is reported in the school cafeteria on January 27, with one patrolman and one student injured.

January 26, Seattle, Washington: Edwin Pratt, black director of the local Urban League, is shot and killed at his home —presumably by a white assailant—following a series of racist death threats.

January 31, Las Vegas, Nevada: Racial tension erupts into fighting at three schools, resulting in thirty arrests and over $2,000 property damage. During the outbreak a group of ten to fifteen blacks raid a local gun store for weapons and money.

January 31, Brooklyn, New York: Arsonists cause $1,000 damage to a Jewish school.

February 3, Miami, Florida: Five black non-students invade the campus of Edison High School and beat three white students.

February 4, Minneapolis, Minnesota: Black defendant Clarence Underwood draws a life sentence for killing a white man in April 1968. The murder was carried out after Underwood learned of Dr. Martin Luther King's assassination.

February 4, Providence, Rhode Island: A white boycott sparked by alleged black intimidation and preferential treatment of blacks erupts into fighting at Esek Hopkins Junior High School.

February 5, New York City: Eight blacks ransack the dean's office at Queens College while fifty others occupy the office of the controversial SEEK program director.

February 5, Mt. Vernon, New York: Fighting erupts during a demonstration promoting black studies at Mt. Vernon High School.

February 8, Columbus, Georgia: Racial fighting erupts during a high school basketball game and spreads to the streets, with blacks pelting motorists. One car is damaged by sniper fire. Six persons are reported injured.

February 9, Itta Bena, Mississippi: Windows are smashed during a six-hour demonstration at all-black Mississippi Valley State College.

February 10, Edwardsville, Illinois: Fighting erupts in the auditorium at Southern Illinois University, after whites attending a lecture by author LeRoi Jones are ordered to vacate seats "reserved" for blacks.

February 12–13, Pittsburgh, Pennsylvania: A fight between two girls on February 12 sparks brawling by 350 black and white students at Oliver High School the next day. Two persons are stabbed and two others are arrested during the outbreak.

February 13, Durham, North Carolina: Black protestors attack a police car at Duke University after a black girl claims officers tried to run her down. Fighting rages for two hours, with twenty-five persons injured and eight arrested before tear gas disperses the mob.

February 14, Columbia, South Carolina: Fighting erupts after black students burn a Confederate flag on the university campus. Officers make one arrest as they restore order.

February 15, Springfield, Illinois: Southeast High School closes early after two students are injured in racial fighting sparked by Black Awareness Week. On February 17 police disperse campus gangs armed with bricks, boards, and other weapons.

February 17, New York City: Blacks and Puerto Ricans demonstrate at City College of New York, spray-painting blackboards and setting small fires in a protest demanding a separate school for nonwhites.

February 17–18, Pittsburgh, Pennsylvania: Racial violence at Gladstone High School spreads to the streets with two days of rioting and stoning of nearby homes. Two persons are stabbed on February 18, six are injured, and sixteen are arrested.

February 18, Memphis, Tennessee: Three members of the Invaders, a black militant group, are charged with attempted murder for the August 1968 shooting of Patrolman R.J. Waddell. The ambush was allegedly planned in retaliation for a clash between police and Black Panthers in Oakland, California.

February 19, Harrisburg, Pennsylvania: Violence erupts when schools reopen, following recent closings due to racial tension. Two students are stabbed and a teacher is assaulted at John Harris High School. Students roam the halls and smash windows at William Penn High School, and several other schools report arson fires.

February 19, Detroit, Michigan: Nine black youths invade mostly black Butzel Junior High School, smashing windows and beating teachers in an effort to close the school.

February 20, New Haven, Connecticut: Racial fighting erupts at Lee High School after an assembly celebrating Brotherhood Week. Six students are injured, and school closes early.

February 20, Brooklyn, New York: Black and white students fight over the use of a water fountain at Canarsie High School. On February 25, six persons are injured and four are arrested in a cafeteria riot. On February 26, school is canceled for the rest of the week.

February 20, San Francisco, California: Racial brawling erupts after a black non-student enters Lincoln High School and threatens a white student with a knife. Violence rages for 45 minutes, spreading into the streets before police intervene. Two whites are stabbed, four students are injured, and four are arrested. On February 26 police intercept a gang of black non-students en route to the campus and arrest three. Violence resumes after two white girls are assaulted by fifteen blacks in the cafeteria. Two more are injured and one is arrested in the February 26 outbreak.

February 20, Warrensburg, Missouri: Black students riot at Central Missouri State College after administrators order a halt to unauthorized meetings between students and Black Panthers. Seven students are suspended in the incident, with property damage listed at $2,300.

February 21, Middletown, Connecticut: Black students occupy and vandalize a classroom building at Wesleyan University, following faculty rejection of a proposal to close the school in memory of Malcolm X.

February 21, Fayetteville, North Carolina: Several arson fires are lit on the campus of Fayetteville State College during demonstrations held in memory of Malcolm X.

February 25, Detroit, Michigan: Four black girls attack three white girls at Cooley High School, forcibly cutting their hair. One of the attackers is arrested, the three others are sent home for the day.

February 25, Waltham, Massachusetts: Racial unrest continues at Brandeis University, with eight incendiary fires causing $5,000 damage on campus.

February 25, San Francisco, California: Anti-bussing activists disrupt a school board meeting, assaulting persons who criticize their tactics. Ten whites assault two members of the Progressive Labor Party in the lobby. Four persons are injured in the melee, but the police make no arrests because victims of the beating refuse to cooperate, claiming that police already know the attackers.

February 25, Little Rock, Arkansas: Racial fistfights and rock-throwing result in the arrest of sixteen black youths after a high school basketball game. Black parents charge unequal treatment by police.

February 26, Leland, Mississippi: A protest by blacks against white merchants erupts into violence, with demonstrators smashing windows and patrolmen firing tear gas to disperse the mob.

February 26, New Brunswick, New Jersey: Bomb threats, detonation of smoke bombs, and racial fighting are reported from Rutgers University, where black students have occupied a classroom building since February 21.

February 26, Chicago, Illinois: Twenty members of the Black Student Alliance vandalize Central YMCA Community College, overturning furniture in the student union and cafeteria. The outbreak is sparked by false rumors that a black faculty member was threatened with dismissal over his ties with the Alliance.

February 27, Queens, New York: Sporadic racial fighting is reported at Jackson High, and escalates after school when black students mob white students waiting in line for their buses.

February 27, Chicago, Illinois: Arson fires cause $500 damage at all-black Harlan High School during protests over the dismissal of a black teacher.

February 27, Minneapolis, Minnesota: Thirty black students from Lincoln Junior High, some armed with sticks and pipes, invade the campus of Sheridan Junior High, smashing windows and injuring three whites. The raid is allegedly mounted in retaliation for the beating of black Lincoln students by whites from Sheridan.

February 27, Wilmington, North Carolina: Police are summoned to Hoggard High School after racial fighting leaves eight students injured and one suspended.

February 27, Big Rapids, Michigan: Interracial fighting rages for four hours after a false fire alarm at Ferris State College. Twenty-two persons are injured, and one knife-wielding student is jailed before police restore order in the predawn hours of February 28.

February 27–28, Claremont, California: Violence erupts on three college campuses, sparked by Black Student Union demands for creation of a black studies department. On February 27 bombs explode at Scripps College and Pomona College, while blacks smash windows at Southwest College. On February 28 a bomb explosion rocks the Southwest campus.

March 1–2, Jackson, Tennessee: Four weekend arson fires are set on the campus of mostly black Lane College. The violence follows a two-day boycott by 1,100 black students, which results in the school closing for a week to relieve racial tension.

March 3–4, Gainesville, Florida: Police record two nights of rioting and arson fires in the black community.

March 4, Evanston, Illinois: Twenty black students invade a white frat house at Northwestern University, smashing furniture, windows, and dishes. Four persons are injured and two are arrested in the raid, allegedly designed as retaliation for white harassment of a black coed.

March 4, Brooklyn, New York: Canarsie High School reopens, with more racial fighting reported a block from the campus. Two persons are arrested during the melee, and seven more students are suspended.

March 5, San Francisco, California: Sixty black youths attack a white baseball coach and fourteen members of his team at Ocean View Playground, shouting, "This is our park! Go away, whitey!" Four persons are injured during the melee.

March 7, Trenton, New Jersey: Racial fighting erupts after a church dance, with fifty teens involved. Witnesses say that blacks from outside the neighborhood attacked whites leaving the dance.

March 7, Los Angeles, California: Black students at Carver Junior High smash windows when police disperse a sit-in demonstration sponsored by the BSU. The protest leader is a BSU officer arrested on March 6 at Southwest College.

March 7, New Orleans, Louisiana: Three persons are injured and one is arrested during racial fighting at Frontier High School. The violence is sparked by demands for a black studies program.

March 10, Passaic, New Jersey: Two white students are assaulted by black students at Passaic High School during a demonstration demanding the creation of a black studies program.

March 10, Los Angeles, California: Violence, including arson and window-smashing, is reported from eighteen different schools in black neighborhoods. On March 12 twenty-six fires are reported at Vars Junior High School alone.

March 12, Van Nuys, California: The dean's office at Valley College is firebombed by blacks.

March 12, Culver City, California: Violence erupts at Venice High School after black and Hispanic students are denied permission for a special assembly. Twelve students raid the main office at noon, and fighting spreads across the campus, resulting in widespread vandalism. Six persons are injured and thirty-nine are suspended.

March 12, Atlanta, Georgia: Twelve black non-students invade the gym at Georgia Tech during a basketball game. One student is stabbed and another beaten. Six are arrested.

March 14, New Brunswick, New Jersey: New Brunswick High School closes at noon after black students riot in the cafeteria and several classrooms. On March 18, 100 black students invade a junior high school meeting on race relations, hurling chairs, smashing windows, and assaulting white students. Eight persons are injured during the melee.

March 14, Lawrence, Kansas: Racial slurs spark a brawl involving fourteen white and black students at Lawrence High.

March 15, Washington, D.C.: A black youth is stabbed during a fight between seven blacks and three whites. Around the same time, but in a different area, six black youths assault a fifty-six-year-old white man.

March 17, Houston, Texas: Three hundred black students ransack the student center at the University of Houston after Gene Locke, head of the Afro-Americans for Black Liberation, claims he was beaten by three white men.

March 18, Lorain, Ohio: A white student is beaten by fifteen blacks on the campus of Clearview High during the school's second week of racial unrest.

March 18, Orange, New Jersey: Classes are suspended at Orange High School after racial fighting in the halls and a protest march by black students.

March 18, Geneva, New York: Four black youths draw fifteen-day jail terms for participating in street violence.

March 19, Chicago Heights, Illinois: Twelve black youths, including one armed with a gun, invade the student union at Prairie State College, injuring several students, and smashing windows and furniture.

March 19, Los Angeles, California: New violence erupts at Carver Junior High. Windows are smashed and racial brawls erupt on campus. City-wide, police report seven injuries, forty-two arrests, and $4,500 damage from racially motivated campus violence.

March 20, Reading, Pennsylvania: Police intercept a gang of whites en route to the YMCA's House of Soul recreation center. Blacks emerge from the building to stone patrolmen, and eighty blacks march toward city hall, smashing windows along the way. One person is injured and fifteen are arrested when police disperse the crowd using Mace.

March 20, Forrest City, Arkansas: Rioting blacks smash all the windows at Lincoln Junior High and vandalize hallways to protest the firing of a popular black teacher.

March 21, Zion, Illinois: Police are called to break up racial fighting at Zion-Benton Township High School. Officials report at least three later outbreaks, and two white students are arrested for fighting on March 26.

March 23, St. Louis, Missouri: Several hundred blacks assault two policemen, preventing the arrest of a black man armed with an illegal pistol. Backup police units are stoned by the mob, and three persons are arrested.

March 23, Brooklyn, New York: Vandals cause $1,000 damage to the Young Israel synagogue.

March 25, Summit, Illinois: Racial violence at Argo Community High School results in the closing of the school for two days.

March 27, Chicago, Illinois: Chicago Vocational High School closes at mid-day after outbreaks of racial fighting. Two students are suspended for assault.

March 26–29, Monrovia, California: Police respond to racial violence at three area high schools, sparked by efforts to organize the

Black Students Union. Fourteen persons are arrested and at least eight are injured during the various outbreaks.

March 29, Detroit, Michigan: Officer Michael Czapski is killed and his partner is wounded after they stop twelve armed members of the Black Legion of the Republic of New Africa for questioning. Backup police units draw fire from the New Bethel Church, where Black Legion members are holding a conference. Officers storm the church, wounding five persons and arresting 147, all but two of whom are later released without being charged.

March 31, Cairo, Illinois: Nightriders invade a black neighborhood, firing at motorists and wounding a black man in front of a church. Police exchange fire with snipers who flee into a black housing project. The snipers had been responding to the white shooters.

April, Tucson, Arizona: Multiple firebombings mark a period of protest by the BSU at the University of Arizona.

April 1, Riverside, California: Black and Hispanic youths hurl food in the cafeteria at Ramona High School. Police are called as black-white fighting spreads across the campus.

April 1, Lorman, Mississippi: White arsonists damage farm and shop buildings at all-black Alcorn A&M College. A classroom building and the college president's home were earlier targets for firebombs.

April 2, Levittown, Pennsylvania: Delhaas High School is closed after racial fighting erupts, with one boy stabbed. On April 3 a Delhaas student is suspended for striking a teacher who tried to disperse gangs in the hallway.

April 2, New York City: Twenty-one Black Panthers are indicted for conspiring to inaugurate a reign of terror, which allegedly included scheduled bombings and assassinations of policemen. On the same day, two patrolmen are shot and killed in a Brooklyn ambush. Three Panthers are charged with the murders on April 18.

April 2, Chicago, Illinois: FBI provocateurs spark an armed clash between Black Panthers and members of a violent street gang, the Blackstone Rangers.

April 3, Kalamazoo, Michigan: Black youths riot, hurling rocks and overturning cars, after memorial services for Dr. Martin Luther King are canceled at Central High School.

April 3, Chicago, Illinois: Three area high schools close after black youths smash windows and set off fire alarms. Two hundred seventy-one persons are injured during the outbreak, which results in ninety arrests. On the South Side white youths are arrested for firing shotguns at blacks.

April 3, Pittsburgh, Pennsylvania: Black-white fighting in the cafeteria of Columbus Middle School spills into the streets after school. A brick is hurled through the window of a school bus.

April 3–4, Baltimore, Maryland: Blacks riot for two nights, and 340 persons are arrested. Three stores are firebombed on April 3, and many others are vandalized and looted. On April 4 black youths rampage through Mondawmin Shopping Center, throwing rocks and smashing windows.

April 4, Memphis, Tennessee: Violence flares during a black memorial service for Dr. Martin Luther King, held on the first anniversary of his assassination. At least four incidents of firebombing are reported.

April 5, Anniston, Alabama: Violence erupts after four weeks of black demonstrations against hiring discrimination. A white-owned grocery store is burned after its owner pistol-whips a black man, and firebombs damage a white-owned gas station in the same neighborhood. Fifty persons are arrested.

April 6–7, York, Pennsylvania: Two nights of looting and firebombing lead to a declaration of emergency on April 8 and a curfew imposed on minors.

April 7–9, Haddon Heights, New Jersey: Three nights of racial gang-fights leave five persons in jail. Blacks claim the violence began after white thugs harassed black children.

April 7, Waycross, Georgia: Students at three mostly black schools overturn furniture, then move into the streets, stoning cars and firebombing several stores before National Guardsmen arrive. The outbreak is sparked by announcements that classes will meet during spring vacation to make up for time lost during recent black boycotts. More incidents of arson and vandalism are reported on April 9 and 10.

April 9, New Orleans, Louisiana: Six students at predominantly black Southern University overpower security guards, lowering the U.S. flag and raising a "black power" flag in its place. Crowds stone police after one of the men is arrested; three persons are injured and twenty-seven are arrested.

April 9, Port Gibson, Mississippi: The assistant police chief fatally wounds a black man, Roosevelt Jackson, during his attempt to arrest Jackson on charges of "interfering with an officer." Black protestors march on the court house, smashing windows en route, and denounce the shooting as deliberate murder.

April 10, Beaumont, Texas: Fifty members of the Afro-American Students Association invade the campus of Lamar State College of Technology, destroying books and other property to protest the administration's refusal to lower entrance requirements for blacks.

April 11, New York City: Four blacks are arrested for assault and disorderly conduct in the Criminal Courts Building while protesting the high bail set for twenty-one Black Panthers charged with conspiracy.

April 11, Gainesville, Florida: A black gang roams the University of Florida campus and stabs white students in two separate attacks. Authorities cite thirteen similar incidents in the preceding two weeks. Three suspects are charged on April 28.

April 13, Des Moines, Iowa: Violence erupts after police arrest a Black Panther for using a loudspeaker without a permit. Stone-throwing spreads over a two-block area, and fourteen are arrested.

April 13, St. Louis, Missouri: Twelve members of the militant Black Egyptians are arrested for looting a clothing store and are held on charges of mob action and resisting arrest.

April 16, Chicago, Illinois: Black students riot in and around the cafeteria at Calumet High School. One person is injured, and eleven are arrested.

April 16, Moorhead, Minnesota: Three persons are arrested after blacks draw guns in a confrontation with white students at Moorhead State College. Sporadic violence continues for a week, with shots fired at a black student driving home from a date on April 19.

April 16, San Mateo, California: San Mateo High School is closed due to racial fighting. A reopening is canceled on April 17 after four persons are hurt in new clashes.

April 17, Chicago, Illinois: Vincennes Upper Grade School is closed after rampaging black students cause $1,800 damage.

April 17, Homestead, Florida: Angered by a racial fight at Homestead Junior High, 200 black students leave campus, stoning cars and overturning trash cans as they roam the streets. Six persons are arrested.

April 18, Glen Cove, New York: Racial fighting breaks out in rest rooms at Glen Cove High School. Two white students are beaten by black students while walking home.

April 18, New Brunswick, New Jersey: Fighting erupts when sixty uninvited blacks are barred from a frat party at Rutgers University. Twelve persons are injured and two are arrested.

April 18, Syracuse, New York: A white youth is beaten by black students at Smith Junior High. Two more injuries are recorded at Levy Junior High before police are summoned to break up racial fighting.

April 18, Providence, Rhode Island: Forty black inmates at a state reform school smash windows and burn a truck to protest the firing of three black employees. Twenty other inmates, including sixteen whites, take advantage of the diversion to escape custody.

April 18, Madison, Wisconsin: Racial fighting erupts outside a church dance, and three people are arrested.

April 18, Port Gibson, Mississippi: The assistant police chief, who fatally wounded another black man nine days before, is charged with murder after a black prisoner dies in custody. The release the following day of the assistant police chief on $5,000 bond sparks incidents of brick-throwing by angry black protesters.

April 20, Menlo Park, California: A feud between white and black families leads to violence, with 250 blacks besieging the white home. Police responding to the call are pelted with rocks, pipes, and bottles.

April 20, Baltimore, Maryland: Roving black gangs assault white pedestrians after a protest demonstration at Memorial Stadium. One hundred thirty-eight persons are injured in the riot, and 130 are arrested.

April 21, San Antonio, Texas: SNCC members lead 500 blacks on a window-smashing rampage, looting stores during an annual parade. Two persons are injured and nine are arrested.

April 21–23, Ocala, Florida: Twelve students are suspended from Ocala High School during racial violence sparked by the suspension of a black boy who pinched a white girl.

April 21–23, St. Petersburg, Florida: Thirty-seven students are suspended from Boca Ciega High School during three days of racial brawls involving over 100 youths.

April 22, Yonkers, New York: Eleven persons are injured when 400 black youths invade city hall and clash with police in an effort to present the city manager with a list of demands.

April 23, Racine, Wisconsin: An emergency is declared after blacks and police clash during demonstrations over a new city park. Six persons are injured and twenty-five are arrested during the outbreak.

April 23, New York City: Fighting erupts when blacks and Puerto Ricans bar white students from the South Campus of CCNY. By April 25 racial violence has resulted in the closing of four area high schools and over 100 arrests.

April 23, Chicago, Illinois: A white patrolman is killed by black sniper fire on the West Side. Violence continues on April 24, when police trade fire with snipers and five persons are injured.

April 23–24, Racine, Wisconsin: Black protests over the placement of a new park lead to rock-throwing and clashes with police.

April 24, Newburgh, New York: Three black youths meet with the principal at Newburgh Free Academy, demanding school holidays in honor of Dr. Martin Luther King and Malcolm X. Two of the blacks draw pellet guns, theatening administrators before they are disarmed. All three are arrested, with one person injured.

April 24, Freeport, New York: Two black students and one white student are stabbed during racial fighting at Freeport High, sparked by demands for the hiring of more black teachers. Ten persons are arrested on April 25 when black students riot on campus, beating three whites, smashing windows, and tearing down the U.S. flag.

April 25, Linden, New Jersey: Racial clashes at a carnival climax with black mobs roaming the city, damaging cars and homes in a rampage that leaves six people injured and thirty arrested. A curfew is imposed when new violence erupts on April 29.

April 25, Roosevelt, New York: After a liaison between police and black youths is stabbed at a local youth center, two hundred blacks roam the business district, assaulting whites and smashing windows. At least three shops are wrecked and four persons are hospitalized.

April 25, Chicago, Illinois: Eight persons are injured and fourteen are arrested when racial fighting spreads from the campus of Tilden Technical High School into the streets.

April 25, Cleveland, Ohio: John F. Kennedy Junior High School is closed after black outsiders attempt to enter the school to protest the transfer of a black teacher. An armed student drops his gun, which fires accidentally on impact.

April 25, St. Louis, Missouri: Five black youths are wounded by white snipers. Violence continues through May 9, with three more blacks shot and one beaten by whites with iron pipes. White gangs roam the streets, stoning blacks, and black youths respond in kind.

April 26, Chicago, Illinois: Two patrolmen are shot and wounded while responding to calls for help at the scene of a racial disturbance.

April 26–28, Cairo, Illinois: Violence flares during a black boycott of white merchants, with three white-owned stores and one black home firebombed. Incidents of sniper fire are also reported, and National Guardsmen arrive to enforce a curfew on April 29.

April 27, Des Moines, Iowa: Black Panther headquarters is demolished by an explosion, with four persons arrested in the ensuing melee. Four firebombings are reported after the blast and dispersal of an angry crowd.

April 27, Winston-Salem, North Carolina: Street violence erupts after police wound a black suspect. National Guardsmen are called to enforce a curfew on April 29 after several stores are looted and snipers shoot at firefighters. Six persons are arrested.

April 28, Oakland, California: After police use tear gas to disrupt an unruly Black Panther demonstration, black youths attack cars and beat white pedestrians.

April 28, Chicago, Illinois: Racial disorders, including the beating of a white professor by black students, close the southeast branch of Chicago City College.

April 28, San Francisco, California: A police raid on Black Panther headquarters touches off bottle-throwing by a crowd of 600 blacks.

April 28, Cairo, Illinois: Eleven black youths are jailed after four firebombing incidents. National Guard units are deployed on April 29, as arson and sniper fire continue. Police draw sniper fire while guarding firefighters, and nightiders fire shots into a Roman Catholic rectory.

April 29, Linden, New Jersey: An emergency is declared after black snipers fire on police. Four persons are arrested, including a Black Panther charged with threatening the mayor's life.

April 29, Cairo, Illinois: National Guardsmen enforce a curfew after eight additional firebombings.

April 30, Brooklyn, New York: Two hundred black and Puerto Rican students invade the president's office at Brooklyn College and present a list of demands. Furniture is destroyed and several small fires are reported during the three-hour disturbance.

April 30, Pasadena, California: Pasadena High School is closed after a window-smashing rampage by fifty black students protesting administrative rejection of demands from the Black Cultural Organization.

April 30, Detroit, Michigan: Firebombings and student rioting close Martin Luther King, Jr., High School.

April 30, Richmond, California: The principal at Pinole Valley High School blames racial fighting on white harassment of blacks.

May 1, New York City: Two Black Panthers are arrested for assaulting a white Transit Authority patrolman.

May 1, Jackson, Michigan: Police are called to Jackson High School when black students roam the halls assaulting white students.

May 1, San Francisco, California: Forty-five blacks leave a parade organized to protest the jailing of Black Panther Huey Newton, smashing windows and display cases of stores along the route. The group disperses when police arrive.

May 1, Flint, Michigan: Fifty black youths armed with chains and iron bars invade DeWaters Art Institute, smashing windows and destroying works of art, to protest alleged racism in the school choir.

May 1, Highland Park, Michigan: Racial fighting erupts during a black demonstration at a community college.

May 1, Springfield, Missouri: Racial fighting erupts at a local college after the student senate reverses its appointment of two black coeds to the pep squad.

May 2, New York City: Five hundred police are deployed when bands of black students roam the campus at Queens College, smashing windows and disrupting classes.

May 2, North Little Rock, Arkansas: Arsonists damage a white-owned grocery store picketed by blacks since March for alleged abuse of black customers.

May 3, Long Beach, New York: The arrest of one black youth prompts twelve others to smash windows in the police station and white-owned shops. A second youth is arrested during the outbreak.

May 4, Mobile, Alabama: Blacks stone firemen responding to arson blazes in the city's black neighborhood. Three hundred fourteen persons are arrested.

May 4, Long Beach, New York: The arrest of a black youth sparks a rock-throwing rampage in the downtown business district.

May 4, Chicago, Illinois: A Puerto Rican member of the militant Young Lords is killed by police during a racial clash.

May 4, Beaumont, Texas: A black woman is killed when white gunmen, angered by a near-collision with a black motorist, open fire on black pedestrians.

May 5, Chicago, Illinois: Black students stone buildings and set off false fire alarms at Vincennes Upper Grade School.

May 5, Los Angeles, California: Patrolman Thomas Parkham, twice disciplined by his superiors for drinking on duty and aiming his pistol at a minor, shoots Frank Gonzalez, an unarmed Hispanic truant. Parkham is allowed to resign in lieu of criminal prosecution.

May 5, Raleigh, North Carolina: Violence erupts during a black rally called to discuss allegations of police brutality. Parked cars are vandalized, and five arson fires are reported. Three persons are arrested. On May 7 a truck and two stores are firebombed by blacks.

May 5–6, Beaumont, Texas: Blacks hurl eighteen firebombs at white-owned shops, causing $10,000 damage. Seventeen persons are arrested.

May 6, Brooklyn, New York: A synagogue is firebombed, and police arrest a twenty-three year old male suspect. On the same day, one person is injured at Pratt Institute during a BSU protest against alleged police brutality.

May 6, Lorain, Ohio: Twenty-five black students smash glass doors, overturn furniture, and light at least one incendiary fire at Clearview High School.

May 6, West Haven, Connecticut: A patrolman is summoned to break up racial fighting at Gianotti Junior High. A crowd of 200 blacks gathers, and several girls assault the officer. Police reinforcements scatter the crowd with Mace.

May 6, Camden, New Jersey: A local high school is closed after racial fights involving 200 students. Scattered firebombing is reported that night, with further incidents on May 7. Thirteen persons are arrested during the outbreak.

May 6, Central Islip, New York: Central Islip High School is closed for two days after racial fighting erupts during demands for the hiring of black teachers and counselors.

May 6, New York City: Two hundred black and Puerto Rican students riot at George Washington High School, protesting the arrest of a black minister who tried to enter the campus for an unauthorized speech. One student is arrested.

May 6, Chicago, Illinois: The dismissal of a militant black teacher prompts seventy-five black students to invade the principal's office at Englewood High School, smashing windows and setting off fire alarms.

May 7, Richmond, California: Racial fights and window-smashing are reported at two area high schools.

May 7–8, New York City: Racial violence continues at City College of New York over a two-day period. Twelve blacks armed with clubs disrupt classes and harass whites in the library on May 7, while seven whites are beaten for attempting to enter the campus. On May 8 black protests erupt into general rioting, and ten campus buildings are damaged by fire.

May 7–8, Washington, D.C.: Outbreaks of racial violence are reported around Howard University Law School, with blacks stoning cars and buses, and hurling rocks and bottles at police. A major fire damages one classroom building, and rioters inflict extensive damage on a responding fire truck. One patrolman is injured, three newsmen are assaulted, and twenty-one persons are arrested during the riots.

May 8, New York City: Racial brawls erupt in the cafeteria at Franklin K. Lane High School, with several small arson fires reported during the afternoon. Another racial clash at Brooklyn Technical High School injures thirteen students.

May 9, Walnut, California: Mt. San Antonio College is closed after five persons are injured in racial fighting sparked by a fund-raising drive for the BSU and United Mexican-American Students.

May 10, New York City: A minor riot erupts in Harlem, with scattered reports of looting after two arson fires are extinguished. Fourteen persons are arrested, with two patrolmen, one fireman, and one civilian reported injured.

May 11, Tacoma, Washington: Rioting breaks out after the arrest of two blacks for a traffic infraction. Shops are looted and one patrolman is wounded by gunfire. A curfew is imposed on May 12.

May 12, Chicago, Illinois: A shoving incident precipitates racial brawling, with rock- and bottle-throwing, at Gage Park High School. One person is injured and twelve are arrested during the outbreak.

May 12–13, Trenton, New Jersey: Two years of racial tension erupt into violence at Trenton High School, with one student injured in sporadic brawling.

May 13, Providence, Rhode Island: Black demonstrators vandalize the auditorium at Hope High School. Five white students are hurt in assaults by blacks.

May 13, Des Moines, Iowa: Eight shots are fired into the home of a police lieutenant who supervised dispersal of unruly blacks at East High School five days earlier.

May 13, Baton Rouge, Louisiana: Black students at Southern University hurl stones and firebombs at police, who respond with tear gas and shotguns. Thirty persons are injured and seventeen are arrested.

May 14, Atlanta, Georgia: Black Muslim demonstrators assault four patrolmen following the arrest of two disorderly picketers. The Muslim attackers escape in a milling crowd of black spectators.

May 14, Chattanooga, Tennessee: Forty black students walk out of Central High School after police are called to suppress racial fighting.

May 15, Newark, New Jersey: Racial fighting erupts during a protest meeting at Essex County College.

May 16, Chicago, Illinois: Four white students are injured and eighteen persons are arrested when black youths invade Fenger High School, hurling bricks and assaulting whites at random until police intervene. Two more whites are beaten by blacks at Chicago Vocational High School, and two black students are arrested for stoning cars. Fenger High is closed on May 21, following new racial outbreaks the day before.

May 16, Steubenville, Ohio: Steubenville High School is closed due to racial fighting.

May 16–17, Burlington, North Carolina: Blacks riot overnight after students at an integrated high school fail to elect black cheerleaders. Police kill one black youth and wound three others on May 16, and National Guard units are deployed the next day. One hundred fifty persons are arrested during the outbreak.

May 17, Glassboro, New Jersey: Black and white students clash at Delsea Regional High School, the day after forty-five students are suspended for participating in a protest demonstration. Street violence, including vandalism and at least one stabbing, resumes on May 18, and fifty-five rioters are arrested.

May 18, Waycross, Georgia: One black youth is wounded when a racial argument over a motorcycle erupts into gunfire. Three persons are arrested, and sporadic shooting continues into the early hours of May 19.

May 19, Freehold, New Jersey: State police are deployed to quell black looting and vandalism. Two youths are wounded by shotgun pellets, and a curfew is imposed on May 20. Four persons are arrested in the outbreak.

May 19, Newark, New Jersey: Looting breaks out in the 1967 riot area after Dexter Johnson, a black youth, is shot dead by a black policeman. Twenty-two stores are damaged, and twelve persons are injured and 200 are arrested.

May 19, Big Rapids, Michigan: Racial fighting erupts at Ferris State College, a day after the student newspaper refers to black cafeteria patrons as "pigs." Two hundred whites and seventy-five blacks battle with clubs, rocks, and bottles, leaving fifteen persons injured and thirteen in custody.

May 19, Niles, Michigan: Patrolmen with dogs are dispatched to quell racial fighting at a drive-in restaurant after two whites are beaten by blacks. Six persons are arrested, with one black man killed after firing a shot at police.

May 19–20, Eugene, Oregon: An overnight series of bombings strike a bank, a church, a newspaper office, a state office building, and a structure on the university campus. Damage is estimated at $12,000, and blacks blame white racists for the blasts, allegedly meant to discourage a scheduled speech by Black Panther leader Bobby Seale. Four other bombings have shaken Eugene in the previous nine months.

May 20, Cincinnati, Ohio: Black demonstrators at the University of Cincinnati hurl chairs through windows of the science and administration buildings.

May 20, Portland, Oregon: Police break up racial fights at Roosevelt High School. Further incidents, including vandalism and threats from outsiders, alleged to be Black Panthers, are recorded on May 23. Six persons are injured and twelve are arrested—including one adult—in the latter outbreak.

May 21, Oxford, Pennsylvania: Racial fighting erupts at a local high school.

May 21, Providence, Rhode Island: Windows are smashed during a black protest at Roger Williams Middle School.

May 21, Saginaw, Michigan: Ricker Junior High is closed for the rest of the week after black-white brawls and extensive vandalism.

Five persons are injured and three are arrested during the three-hour melee.

May 21–23, Greensboro, North Carolina: Violence erupts after police use tear gas to quell a demonstration by black high school students. Outbreaks of sniper fire are reported at mostly black A&T State University. Honor student Willie Grimes is killed by a sniper on May 22, and five patrolmen are wounded during the exchange of gunfire. National Guardsmen clear the campus on May 23, using tear gas, rifle fire, and smoke sprayed from aircraft. Two hundred persons are jailed during the outbreak, with eight guns confiscated from a university dorm.

May 21, Nashville, Tennessee: Racial fighting erupts at Central High School after a black athlete fails to receive a sport letter. Police make five arrests on May 22 when the violence resumes and passing cars are stoned by blacks.

May 22, New Haven, Connecticut: Eight Black Panthers are charged with the torture-slaying of alleged police informant Alex Rackley. The first defendant to face trial pleads guilty to second-degree murder on December 1.

May 22, Brookville, New York: Racial fighting breaks out at C.W. Post College. A white student is stabbed on May 24, and more brawling and several bomb scares are reported that afternoon.

May 26, Cairo, Illinois: Black snipers fire more than seventy-five shots at police headquarters during a ten-minute period.

May 27, Hempstead, New York: Three hundred whites clash with 150 supporters of the Organization of Black Collegians, smashing glassware and furniture in the cafeteria at Hofstra University. Police are summoned to break up the fight.

June 1, New York City: Six members of the Jewish Defense League are arrested for beating uniformed members of the neo-Nazi National Renaissance Party.

June 1–2, New York City: Violence erupts in the Bronx when Puerto Rican youths attack police at a street carnival. Seven persons are arrested, and Molotov cocktails are seized from the gang.

June 4, Chicago, Illinois: FBI agents raid Black Panther head-quarters searching for wanted fugitives, and seize guns and ammunition. Panthers charge deliberate vandalism and theft of party documents. Eight persons are arrested in the raid.

June 5, Pittsburgh, Pennsylvania: Racial fighting breaks out in the cafeteria at Oliver High School and spreads into the streets after school. Gangs roam the neighborhood, smashing windows of homes and parked cars. More than twenty persons are injured and three are arrested.

June 5, Carson National Forest, New Mexico: Reies Tijerina and other Hispanic militants attempt to occupy federal land, claiming ownership under colonial land grants. Tijerina and others are jailed on June 7 for assaulting a federal officer.

June 5–6, Hartford, Connecticut: Blacks riot for two consecutive nights. Two persons are shot and wounded by police, and nine other injuries are reported.

June 6–7, Indianapolis, Indiana: A brawl at a black housing project erupts into two nights of racial violence, with snipers firing on police. Six persons are injured on June 7, including a patrolman wounded by gunfire; eighty-two persons are arrested, including thirty at Black Panther headquarters, where a policeman is beaten.

June 7, New York City: Black militant C37X Kenyatta, leader of the local Mau Mau faction, is shot and wounded in the Bronx, and blames the attack on rival Black Muslims.

June 12–13, Trenton, New Jersey: Puerto Ricans riot for two nights after police wound a Puerto Rican burglary suspect.

June 13, New York City: Clarence Jowers, an ex-Muslim and founder of the youth-terrorist gang the Five Percenters, is found murdered in his apartment.

June 15, Cairo, Illinois: Snipers drive police and firemen from a burning warehouse. Three more nocturnal firebombings are reported on June 16.

June 15–16, Utica, New York: Two nights of rioting erupt after blacks stone police cars. Twenty-one persons are arrested on June 15, with two patrolmen and two civilians injured. On June 16 police intercept a gang of white youths "looking for trouble" in a black neighborhood, arresting eight and confiscating six guns.

June 16, New York City: One hundred fifty Puerto Ricans storm a Bronx police station in an attempt to free three prisoners, but they are driven away by warning shots.

June 16, Sacramento, California: Racial disorders erupt when police order cars off the grass at a city park. Black youths stab a newsman and snipers fire at police, leaving thirteen officers wounded and thirty-seven rioters arrested. Authorities use tear gas in a raid on Black Panther headquarters.

June 17, Oakland, California: Black Panther Willie Brent, free on bail for a November 1968 shoot-out with San Francisco police, hijacks an airliner bound for New York City to Cuba.

June 18, Portland, Oregon: Black snipers harass firemen, and arson fires cause $500,000 damage.

June 19, Cairo, Illinois: State troopers replace members of the White Hats vigilante gang on street patrol after four incidents of arson, including a fire at a local lumber yard.

June 20–22, Red Bank, New Jersey: Three nights of racial violence are sparked by rumors of a police shooting. One man is wounded after threatening patrolmen in an incident that the authorities call unrelated to the riots. A curfew is imposed to quell the violence.

June 21, Charleston, South Carolina: Black protest marchers pelt police and National Guardsmen with rocks, bricks, and bottles, and overturn several parked cars along their route.

June 23–25, Harrisburg, Pennsylvania: Blacks clash with police during three nights of rioting. Fifteen persons are injured and eight are arrested in a rock-throwing incident on June 23. Authorities report two arson fires and ten false alarms the same night. On June 24 Charles Scott, a black youth, is killed by police while lighting a firebomb. A limited state of emergency is declared on June 25.

June 24–27, Omaha, Nebraska: National Guardsmen are called to quell four nights of rioting sparked by the fatal police shooting of a black girl. Sixty persons are arrested.

June 27, Kokomo, Indiana: At least two firebombs are thrown and police cars are damaged by gunfire during an outbreak of black rioting.

June 27, North Little Rock, Arkansas: A firebomb causes minor damage to a white-owned grocery targeted by black boycotts and a prior arson attempt in the preceding three months.

June 27, Cairo, Illinois: Blacks and whites stone each other after a "mother's march" on police headquarters demanding equal rights for whites. A warehouse arson fire forces evacuation of 3,000 residents from the immediate area.

June 29, Hartford, Connecticut: Black youths riot and snipers fire at police, leaving five persons injured and thirty-five arrested.

June 30, Middletown, Connecticut: A curfew is imposed and four persons are arrested for looting during racial outbreaks sparked by a clash between black and white youths.

July 1, Waterbury, Connecticut: A curfew is imposed and forty-five persons arrested during an outbreak of rioting by blacks.

July 5, Middletown, North Carolina: One woman is wounded in a series of drive-by shootings that follow a local KKK rally. Seventeen Klansmen are charged with inciting a riot.

July 5, Ft. Wayne, Indiana: One man is shot and a girl is injured when violence erupts after a black dance. Police use tear gas to disperse a mob of 250 blacks and arrest eight persons.

July 6, Tampa, Florida: Rioting erupts after police raid an illegal dice game in a black neighborhood. Twenty-five persons are jailed and four are injured when blacks stone police cars and white motorists.

July 11–12, Evansville, Indiana: Blacks riot for two nights after a sniper kills Jeffrey Taylor, a black youth. Incidents of firebombing are recorded, and four persons are wounded by sniper fire. Twenty are arrested.

July 14, Brooklyn, New York: Black and white youths are dispersed by police after a rock-throwing melee.

July 14, San Diego, California: Rioting erupts after police try to arrest black rock-throwers. Three persons are killed during the outbreak and three people are wounded. Sixty-four arrests are made.

July 15–17, Youngstown, Ohio: Blacks riot for three nights after a black woman claims she was kicked by a white store owner. National Guardsmen are dispatched on July 16 after two patrolmen are injured by thrown stones. Snipers join the melee on July 17. Five persons are injured and twenty are arrested.

July 16, Chicago, Illinois: Black Panther Larry Robeson is killed and six other people are arrested in a clash with police.

July 16–17, Bridgeport, Connecticut: Black youths riot for two nights, pelting police with stones and firebombs. A firebomb thrown into a bakery on July 17 injures two employees.

July 17–22, York, Pennsylvania: Blacks riot for eight consecutive nights, leaving thirty-seven persons injured and nineteen—mostly whites—convicted of curfew violations. Sales of liquor, guns, and gasoline are banned on July 19 after snipers wound a patrolman. A black woman is killed by sniper fire on July 21 while driving through the riot zone, and National Guardsmen are dispatched on July 22.

July 17, Jamesburg, New York: A curfew is imposed after racial scuffles at an ice cream shop erupt into street violence and angry demonstrations. More fighting is reported on July 20.

July 18, Rayne, Louisiana: A white restaurant owner is indicted by federal authorities for assaulting four black customers.

July 20, Camp Lejeune, North Carolina: Cpl. Edward Bankston is killed and two other white marines are injured in an attack by blacks and Puerto Ricans at the local Marine Corps base. Three blacks and two Puerto Ricans are charged with murder, riot, and assault. Two of the defendants are convicted by year's end.

July 21, Farrell, Pennsylvania: A curfew is imposed after black youths smash windows and toss firebombs into downtown stores.

July 21, Columbus, Ohio: Rioting erupts after a black man is shot and killed in an argument with a white man. The gunman is held on murder charges as the violence spreads. George Stulz, a white man, is killed by sniper fire while directing traffic. Thirty-six persons are injured and 434 are arrested during the outbreak. Authorities report four major arson fires before National Guard units arrive.

July 25, Freehold, New Jersey: Six persons are arrested during a racial clash outside a delicatessen being picketed by blacks after the white owner allegedly abused black customers.

July 26, Brooklyn, New York: Three persons are killed and three are wounded in a series of shootings between blacks and Puerto Ricans.

July 26, Blythe, California: Authorities raid a commune occupied by members of a black magic cult, Ordo Templi Orientis, and charge several persons with child abuse after a young boy is found locked in a cage, exposed to the desert sun.

July 30, Chicago, Illinois: Gunfire erupts when police investigate reports of an armed man outside Black Panther headquarters. Two patrolmen are fatally wounded and three other officers sustain less serious injuries. Black gunman John Soto is killed at the scene, and three other blacks are held on charges of attempted murder. After the raid, a fire razes one floor of the Panther building.

July 30–August 1, Baton Rouge, Louisiana: Twelve arson fires are recorded during two nights of violence. The riots erupt during protests over the police shootings of two black youths earlier in July.

August, Blythe, California: A member of the OTO cult is found dead near a commune recently raided by police. Authorities suspect homicide, but leaders of the cult have fled to Mexico, where they evade arrest.

August 3–8, Passaic, New Jersey: A forced eviction from a local housing project sparks five nights of rioting by Puerto Ricans. At least 131 persons are arrested, with two stores firebombed and property damage listed at $150,000.

August 10, Honolulu, Hawaii: Sixteen marines are injured during a racial brawl at the Kaneohe Marine Corps base outside of town.

August 12, Somerville, Tennessee: A white father and son assault two black women, sparking a protest march that erupts into general rioting. One hundred forty-one persons are jailed during the outburst. The father and son are arrested on August 15.

August 14, Freehold, New Jersey: Three schools and three commercial buildings are firebombed after the conviction of four blacks and two whites charged in connection with a July 25 racial brawl. On August 15 a suspicious fire destroys a railroad freight station.

August 16–19, Lakewood, New Jersey: Three nights of arson and looting result in forty-five arrests and $100,000 in property damage.

August 17–18, Tacoma, Washington: An argument over a parking space erupts into racial street fighting and reports of sniper fire. Twenty persons are arrested during two nights of rioting.

August 17–20, Niagara Falls, New York: Racial fighting at a theater spreads into the streets on August 17, leading to a declaration of emergency the next day. Looting and vandalism are reported through August 20.

August 25, Florence, North Carolina: Rioting is sparked by reports that a white storekeeper has insulted and manhandled black customers.

August 27, Forrest City, Arkansas: A white mob storms the jail in an attempt to lynch three black rape suspects. State police and National Guardsmen disperse the mob.

August 29, Willingboro, New Jersey: Racial fighting erupts at a dance after a white youth allegedly strikes a black girl. Nine persons are arrested and eight are injured, including three patrolmen.

August 30–September 3, Ft. Lauderdale, Florida: Five nights of black rioting are sparked by false rumors of policemen shooting a black woman. One hundred fifteen persons are arrested and at least ten are injured.

September 1–5, Hartford, Connecticut: Violence erupts after an August 31 newspaper article quotes a fireman referring to Puerto Ricans as "pigs." Puerto Ricans storm a local fire station on September 1, and blacks join the violence on September 3, with 155 arrests pushing the two-day total over 300. The violence tapers off by September 5, with scattered firebombings and police gassing black mobs at a housing project. A total of 516 persons are arrested during the riots, with two wounded by police gunfire and one by a sniper. More than seventy shops are destroyed.

September 2, Parkesburg, Pennsylvania: Harry Dickinson, a black man, is killed, and eight blacks are wounded during a racial clash outside a local hotel. Four white men are charged with murder in the case, while reports of the violence spark window-smashing by blacks in Coatesville, seven miles away.

September 2–5, Camden, New Jersey: Blacks riot for four nights. On September 2 Patrolman Rand Chandler and Rose McDonald, a black girl, are killed by sniper fire. A second officer is wounded.

September 5, Sarasota, Florida: A patrolman is shot and wounded while investigating disturbances caused by a mob of 150 blacks.

September 5, St. Louis, Missouri: Three policemen are wounded while dueling with snipers at a black housing project.

September 8, Hightown, New Jersey: A curfew is imposed after clashes between black and white youths.

September 8, Camden, New Jersey: Police raid the Martin Luther King Memorial Center to confiscate a cache of weapons. Five members of the militant Black People's Unity Movement are arrested.

September 9, New York City: Four Black Panthers arrested in August are formally charged with conspiracy to kill a police detective, conspiracy to commit robbery, and weapons violations.

September 9, Fayette, Mississippi: Three Klansmen are arrested with a carload of weapons outside a store owned by newly elected black mayor Charles Evers.

September 13–14, Kokomo, Indiana: Two nights of black violence leave four patrolmen wounded by sniper fire. The home of alleged KKK leader Paul Brook is one of three buildings destroyed by arson.

September 14, Chicago, Illinois: Angered by the recent shooting of a Puerto Rican high school student, Hispanic youths skirmish with police in the streets.

September 16, Cairo, Illinois: A black woman is wounded when white gunmen strafe a housing project. On September 17 a black boy is wounded in a drive-by shooting.

September 29, Dallas, Texas: Black sniper J.L. Thomas is killed by police after wounding three patrolmen and three black women in a shooting rampage. Another black man is also killed in the same incident, and black crowds respond by stoning police.

October 3, Los Angeles, California: Douglas Freed and Shirley Sutherland, both white, are arrested by federal officers on charges of purchasing ten hand grenades for the Black Panther Party.

October 4, Chicago, Illinois: One patrolman is wounded during a shoot-out on the roof of Black Panther headquarters. Seven blacks are jailed on various charges.

October 5–8, Las Vegas, Nevada: Blacks riot for four nights after the routine traffic arrest of a black taxi driver by black patrolmen. Two persons are killed during the riot, and 142 are arrested.

October 10, Chicago, Illinois: Police pursue three black youths who allegedly beat and robbed a white man. A shoot-out erupts, with nine officers wounded and Michael Soto, brother of a black gunman killed on July 30, shot dead by police.

October 13, Sanford, North Carolina: Racial disorders close local schools.

October 13, Pacoima, California: Forty-two persons are arrested when blacks and Hispanics clash outside a home where the Hispanics are having a party. One person is reported injured in the violence that erupts when blacks begin to stone the vehicles of party-goers.

October 14–18, Springfield, Massachusetts: The arrest of black demonstrators at a welfare office sparks five nights of rioting. Thirty persons are arrested and three patrolmen are injured.

October 20, Winston-Salem, North Carolina: Rioting erupts and a curfew is imposed following the acquittal of a white deputy sheriff charged with assaulting two black youths.

October 29, Oakland, California: A Black Panther is sentenced to fifteen years in prison for his role in a 1968 shoot-out with police.

October 31, Chicago, Illinois: Police raid and ransack the local Black Panther office.

October 31, Jacksonville, Florida: Riots erupt after a white trucker wounds one of three blacks caught looting his truck. The gunman is charged with assault, but the violence continues despite his arrest. A black security guard is shot and the owner of a gas station dies from heart failure before the riot subsides.

November 10, Memphis, Tennessee: Fifty-three persons are arrested when police disperse a riotous march by 2,000 blacks protesting local school conditions. Marchers pelt police with rocks and bottles before tear gas scatters the crowd.

November 13, Chicago, Illinois: Patrolmen Francis Rappaport and John Gilhooley are killed in a shoot-out at Black Panther headquarters. Black gunman Spurgeon Winters also dies during the exchange of fire.

November 26, Sandersville, Georgia: Nightriders fire on the home of a black civil rights leader.

December 4, Jackson, Michigan: Charles Cade, the editor of a black newspaper, is found dead in his apartment, with "Black Niger" painted in blood on the walls.

December 4, Chicago, Illinois: Police raid Black Panther headquarters and kill Fred Hampton and Mark Clark, wound four others, and arrest seven persons. Two officers are also injured in the raid, which NAACP investigators describe as a deliberate "search and destroy" mission. Law enforcement officers are charged with conspiracy, but win acquittal in court.

December 5, Kansas City, Missouri: Four Black Panthers are clubbed and arrested after trying to invade the police chief's office.

December 8, Los Angeles, California: A four-hour battle erupts when police stage a predawn raid of Black Panther headquarters seeking two fugitives charged with assault. Three patrolmen and three blacks are wounded in the shoot-out, with eleven Panthers arrested and an arsenal of weapons seized.

December 9, Pell City, Alabama: Arsonists damage the auto dealership of a white man who sold land to the Black Muslims.

December 10, Los Angeles, California: Black state senator Mervyn Dymally charges that police beat him during a protest march outside Black Panther headquarters.

December 21, New York City: Puerto Rican terrorists detonate three bombs at a local bank and department store.

December 28, Sandersville, Georgia: An armed white man is shot and wounded while attempting to force his way inside the home of a local SCLC leader. Occupants of the home find a sputtering dynamite bomb in the yard and extinguish its fuse.

1970

January, Clay County, Mississippi: The county courthouse is bombed by white egregationists.

January 1, Cairo, Illinois: The local police chief resigns after a black sniper attack on police headquarters.

January 13, Oakland, California: Three Black Panthers are arrested after a brawl with police.

January 13, Soledad, California: Three black convicts are shot and killed by guards during a racial brawl in the state prison's exercise yard. A white guard is murdered by blacks in retaliation on January 16.

January 16, New Haven, Connecticut: A second Black Panther pleads guilty to second-degree murder for the death of Alex Rackley, a police informer tortured to death by Black Panthers.

January 19, New York City: Fire damages a Bronx synagogue that has been vandalized four times in the past year.

January 20, Jersey City, New Jersey: Black Panther headquarters is firebombed and riddled with bullets by persons unknown.

January 28, Selma, Alabama: A police captain is charged with first-degree murder in the December 1969 shooting of Lloyd Bizzell, a black man.

January 28, New York City: Vandals paint swastikas and light a small fire at the Intervale Jewish Center in the Bronx.

February 1, Philadelphia, Pennsylvania: Police shoot two black youths fleeing the scene of an alleged car theft, killing Harold Brown. Two patrolmen are charged with aggravated assault on April 6, prosecutors alleging that they beat the wounded victims before the ambulance arrived.

February 21, New York City: Three firebombs damage the home of Justice John Murtagh, who is presiding over the conspiracy trial of twenty-one Black Panthers.

February 28, Montgomery, Alabama: A black activist is convicted of trying to burn a radio station that fired him for leading a local black boycott.

March 3, Lamar, South Carolina: Rioting whites armed with ax handles attack school buses carrying black students to schools formerly segregated. Three of the rioters are convicted on February 17, 1971.

March 10, Bel Air, Maryland: Two black militant associates of H. Rap Brown are killed when a bomb explodes in their car two miles from the courthouse where Brown is standing trial on riot charges.

March 11, Cambridge, Maryland: A bomb damages the courthouse where H. Rap Brown's trial was originally scheduled to be held.

March 13, Miami, Florida: Members of the Black Afro Militant Movement firebomb a store and attempt to burn a lumberyard.

March 15, Ashville, Alabama: The sheriff says that sixty-three cows on a farm owned by Black Muslims have been poisoned with cyanide since October 1969. KKK members are named as the probable culprits.

March 26, Inwood, New York: Three white volunteer firemen are charged with setting fires at a black youth meeting house, the target of repeated attacks since 1969.

April 6, Buffalo, New York: A black man and two infants are injured when police respond to reports of shots fired from a housing project. On June 2, sixty-two patrolmen are ordered into a lineup in a futile effort to identify the attackers.

April 20, Atlantic City, New Jersey: Two hundred black youths riot in the streets following racial clashes at a local high school. Five persons are arrested and two patrolmen are injured.

April 20–21, Lawrence, Kansas: National Guardsmen are placed on standby following reports of gunfire exchanged between white and black gangs. Arsonists cause $2 million damage at the state university, and a local high school is firebombed. Most of the troops withdraw by April 24.

April 24, Baltimore, Maryland: Patrolman Donald Sager is killed and his partner is seriously wounded in an ambush by black militant snipers.

April 25, Seattle, Washington: Four bombs explode in black neighborhoods. The city is divided by the recent police killing of Larry Ward, a black man, during the alleged attempted bombing of a real estate office. The official inquest on Ward's death reports that he died "by criminal means," and later evidence reveals he was hired for the bombing run by a black FBI informant. More than twenty bombs have rocked Seattle in the preceding four months.

April 27, Baton Rouge, Louisiana: The state senate chamber is bombed in apparent retaliation for local police killing three blacks. A note at the scene links the incidents and threatens several patrolmen by name.

April 27–28, River Rouge, Michigan: Seventeen persons are injured and twenty-nine are arrested after racial fighting at a high school spreads into general rioting by blacks. Property damage is estimated at $250,000.

April 30, Baltimore, Maryland: Ten persons are arrested when police raid Black Panther headquarters seeking suspects in the October 1969 torture-slaying of Panther Eugene Anderson. One of those arrested is convicted and sentenced to life imprisonment on December 10.

May 5, Miami, Florida: Members of the Black Afro Militant Movement firebomb a computer center at the state university. Three are indicted by federal authorities on December 16.

May 10, Sacramento, California: Officer Bernard Bennett is critically wounded by sniper fire while patrolling a black district.

May 11, Augusta, Georgia: Violence erupts during a black protest march sparked by the death of Charles Oatman, recently beaten to death by two fellow inmates in jail. The riot leaves six black looters dead and sixty other persons injured. Two more persons are killed on May 12 before National Guard units arrive. On September 1, two policemen are indicted on federal civil rights charges concerning the deaths of two black looters.

May 13, Athens, Georgia: Rioting erupts and seventy-two persons are arrested after police use tear gas to disperse black protest marchers at the local school board.

May 13–14, Syracuse, New York: Black youths vandalize a ten-block area, firebombing four shops and terrorizing two hospitals. A black youth is shot and wounded near one of the hospitals.

May 14, Jackson, Mississippi: Black youths Phillip Gibbs and Earl Green are killed when state police spray bullets into a student dormitory at Jackson State College following a night of disorderly demonstrations.

May 17, Lake Providence, Louisiana: A curfew is imposed after the defeat of two black political candidates sparks riots.

May 17, Hot Springs, Arkansas: Blacks riot and loot local stores after hearing reports of a black man allegedly shot by a white merchant.

May 20, Hardeeville, South Carolina: Black suspects Martin Rutrell and Ben Chaney—brother of murdered civil rights worker James Chaney—are jailed on charges of killing four whites and wounding four others since April 15 in a series of racially motivated attacks spanning three states. In the latest attack, a white businessman and black gunman L.L. Thompson are reported killed during an exchange of gunfire. Rutrell is convicted of murder on November 25, and Chaney is convicted at a later date.

May 20–23, Rahway, New Jersey: Twenty-seven persons are arrested and five patrolmen are hospitalized during four nights of rioting by blacks. Fifty-one persons are jailed during the outbreak.

May 24, Jackson, Georgia: Arson damages two stores during a night of turbulent racial disorders.

May 25–26, Oxford, North Carolina: Black arsonists destroy five white-owned businesses, climaxing a week of racial disorders sparked by the shooting death of a black man. Two white civilians are charged with murder in that incident, with riot damage estimated at $1 million.

May 27–28, Melbourne, Florida: Three persons are injured and sixty are arrested during a rampage by black youths.

May 29–June 5, Alexandria, Virginia: The fatal shooting of a black youth by a white man touches off black rioting, with one death and scores of shops looted before order is restored.

June 10–13, Jersey City, New Jersey: Puerto Rican youths riot for four nights to protest alleged police brutality. On the final night of violence, a local library is firebombed and sustains minor damage.

June 11, Aliquippa, Pennsylvania: Police fire tear gas and warning shots to disperse a mob of 250 whites demanding the release from jail of four youths arrested during racial disturbances at a local high school. Twelve persons are arrested and one is injured.

June 11, Bridgeport, Connecticut: A local Black Panther leader is arrested for threatening patrolmen with a gun.

June 11–12, Brooklyn, New York: Black youths riot for two nights, lighting garbage fires in the streets and torching a vacant building. Small groups continue sporadic violence on June 13, with two patrolmen injured by flying rocks.

June 11–12, Detroit, Michigan: Blacks riot for two nights in the Highland Park ghetto following reports of a black man shot by a white bartender.

June 14, New York City: Puerto Rican youths riot after a Young Lords rally in Harlem. Nine persons are arrested, and twelve firemen and seven patrolmen are injured.

June 15–18, Miami, Florida: Fifty persons are arrested when riots erupt in three neighborhoods. On the night of June 16 police wound eight blacks and two whites in a series of clashes with snipers. A total of thirteen persons are injured, with more than sixty arrested.

June 16, Detroit, Michigan: Two blacks are acquitted of killing Patrolman Michael Czapski and wounding his partner outside the Republic of New Africa headquarters in 1969.

June 18, Des Moines, Iowa: Rioting breaks out after police kill a black escaped convict. Twelve whites are injured by stone-throwing blacks.

June 21, Pittsburgh, Pennsylvania: Ernest Caldwell, a black youth, is killed when a white man fires shots into his home in a mostly black neighborhood. The shooting touches off a riot, leaving six persons injured and eight under arrest.

June 27, Brooklyn, New York: Black and Puerto Rican youths assault and stone Hasidic Jews after a black girl is accidentally killed by a Jewish truck driver. On June 28, three patrolmen are injured during a JDL demonstration protesting the lack of police protection afforded to Jews against blacks. Meyer Kahane and two other JDL members are charged with throwing bottles at police.

June 28, Detroit, Michigan: Two patrolmen are wounded in an ambush shooting. Five associates of the Black Panther Party are charged in the attack on June 29.

June 29, Cleveland, Ohio: Violence erupts when police serve warrants on a group of black nationalists charged with threatening their black neighbors. A patrolman and a black youth are wounded and three persons are arrested.

June 30, Plainfield, New Jersey: A patrolmen is killed and his partner is wounded at the scene of a fire deliberately set to lure targets for black snipers. Minor racial disturbances continue through July 1.

July 4, Philadelphia, Pennsylvania: Twenty-nine guards and eighty-four inmates are injured during three hours of racial rioting at Holmesburg Prison. Twenty white inmates are beaten by blacks in the initial assault, and twelve inmates are wounded by gunfire before order is restored.

July 4, Los Angeles, California: Twenty-two persons are arrested during a riotous demonstration outside a sheriff's substation protesting the killing of six Hispanics in the preceding five months.

July 4–8, Asbury Park, New Jersey: Scores are arrested during five nights of rioting by blacks, with at least sixty-three persons reported injured.

July 5, Longview, Texas: Two dozen bombs explode, damaging thirty-six school buses scheduled for use in court-ordered school desegregation.

July 7, Freehold, New Jersey: Blacks riot in the streets, setting fires and looting stores.

July 8–13, New Bedford, Massachusetts: Six nights of racial violence leave one black youth dead and three others wounded in drive-by shootings. Three white men are charged with the attacks on July 11, and a curfew is imposed the following day.

July 10–12, Michigan City, Indiana: Rioting breaks out after police arrest three drunken blacks in a local tavern. Fifteen persons are arrested and nine are injured before National Guard units arrive on July 12.

July 14, Brooklyn, New York: Four hundred black and white youths brawl at a local night school, resulting in four arrests and the injury of one patrolman.

July 15, Kansas City, Missouri: A black congressman, Leon Jordan, is killed by shotgun blasts from a passing car. Jordan is in the midst of his fourth campaign for reelection at the time.

July 16, Los Angeles, California: Two Hispanic men are killed when police raiders storm the wrong tenement searching for fugitives. Seven officers are charged with manslaughter on July 22.

July 16–20, Lawrence, Kansas: Rioting breaks out after police kill black teenager Rick Dowdell on July 16. Several sniping and firebombing incidents are reported during the riots, with one policeman seriously wounded. Student Harry Rice is shot and killed on July 20 when violence erupts near the state university campus.

July 17, Chicago, Illinois: Police Sgt. James Severin and Patrolman Anthony Rozzato are killed by sniper fire from a black housing project, with backup teams pinned down by gunshots. On July 18 three black youths are jailed on murder charges, and a fourth suspect is arrested the following day.

July 18, Brooklyn, New York: Police patrols are increased after whites stone school buses carrying black children.

July 19, Hagerstown, Maryland: One hundred black youths riot in the streets after a series of racial brawls erupt into general violence.

July 19, Newark, New Jersey: Police clash with members of the Young Lords at a Puerto Rico Day parade. Five persons are arrested, with five civilians and two patrolmen injured.

July 20, Lawrence, Kansas: Donald Dowdell, a black college student, dies when police return sniper fire on the East Side. White student Harry Rice is killed and a black companion is wounded during subsequent street violence aimed at police.

July 20, Brooklyn, New York: The Crown Heights Jewish Community Council building is damaged by a bomb.

July 23–24, New Brunswick, New Jersey: Thirty-three persons are arrested and a state of emergency declared during two nights of rioting by blacks.

July 23, Pittsburgh, Pennsylvania: Black and white patrolmen brawl at a police department picnic held at an amusement park. The fight is allegedly triggered by a black officer dancing with a white woman.

July 23–24, Providence, Rhode Island: Twenty white youths are attacked and beaten by blacks at a theater.

July 23–24, Peoria, Illinois: Twenty-seven persons are arrested during two nights of black rioting. Police report that members of a small militant group, the "FBI Rangers," is responsible for firing shots into a patrol car and two local taverns during the riot.

July 25–26, West Chester, Pennsylvania: Two nights of violence between Puerto Ricans and police erupt in the wake of false rumors alleging that a Puerto Rican man has been killed by a white bartender.

July 26, New York City: Puerto Rican youths riot in the streets, looting a drug store and pelting police from the rooftops. Officers disperse the crowd by firing into the air, and making two arrests.

July 27, Houston, Texas: Violence erupts following a rally by a militant group, People's Party Two. Sniper fire is reported after police arrest two armed youths near party headquarters. Party chairman Carl Hampton is killed and another black is wounded when police trade shots with snipers. Twelve persons are arrested.

July 28–August 3, Hartford, Connecticut: Puerto Ricans riot for seven nights after the acquittal of an ex-policeman charged with murdering a Puerto Rican. Efraim Gonzales is killed by gunfire on August 1, and police blame his death on snipers. New reports of sniper fire on August 2 result in a police raid on Black Panther headquarters, with seven persons arrested.

July 29–31, New Bedford, Massachusetts: New rioting erupts in black neighborhoods, with cars burned in the streets and police pinned down by sniper fire. Fifty-two arrests include nineteen Black Panthers charged with conspiracy to commit murder and anarchy.

August 1, Asbury Park, New Jersey: Blacks burn two buildings in the downtown business district, chanting "Burn, baby, burn!" four youths are charged with arson on August 2.

August 5, Lima, Ohio: Rioting breaks out after police kill a black woman, Christine Ricks. Several persons, including a deputy sheriff and a white television newsman, are wounded during a shoot-out at Black Panther headquarters, but raiders find the building empty when they enter. Twenty-four arrests and five arson fires are reported on August 6, with National Guard units deployed on August 7 to quell sputtering violence. Seventy-eight persons are arrested before order is restored on August 8.

August 7, Bridgeport, Connecticut: Twelve policemen are injured and eighteen persons are jailed for assault during the attempted arrest of a Black Panther. On August 8, five Molotov cocktails are thrown from a black housing project, causing minor damage. Four black youths are burned when a sixth firebomb explodes before it can be thrown.

August 7, San Rafael, California: Gunfire erupts when black militant Jonathan Jackson attempts to rescue three black defendants from the local courthouse during their trial on murder charges. Jackson, the white judge, and two of the defendants die in the shoot-out, with the deputy district attorney severely wounded.

August 9, Jersey City, New Jersey: Twelve persons are injured and firemen are pelted with stones during an outbreak of rioting by Puerto Ricans.

August 11, San Bernadino, California: Police trade shots with snipers at a black housing project. One person is wounded by gunfire, with five others injured and ten arrested in the ensuing melee. A short time later, the community recreation center is damaged by firebombs.

August 14, Chicago, Illinois: Det. J.A. Alfano is fatally wounded by a black sniper, the fourth Chicago officer killed under these circumstances since June. Police raid the headquarters of a major street gang, the Black P. Stone Nation, and arrest twenty persons. By September 3, seven gang members are charged with the murder. All are acquitted on January 17, 1971.

August 15, West Point, Mississippi: Johnny Thomas, a black political activist, is shot to death. A white man is charged with his murder.

August 15–16, Waterbury, Connecticut: Thirty-seven persons are jailed during a weekend of sporadic racial violence.

August 15–17, Pompano Beach, Florida: Blacks riot for three successive nights.

August 17, Atlanta, Georgia: Firebombs damage three stores in a black neighborhood, following rumors that police have killed a black youth.

August 17, Omaha, Nebraska: Patrolman Larry Minard is killed and seven officers are wounded after being lured to an abandoned house booby-trapped with explosives. Fifteen blacks, including members of the Black Panther Party, are arrested on August 24, with six Panthers facing murder charges by August 28.

August 18, Ft. Lauderdale, Florida: Eleven youths are jailed, and one is wounded during violent protests over the police slaying of a local black. On August 19 police kill a black robbery suspect and arrest nineteen rioters. Two buildings are burned.

August 20, Berkeley, California: Patrolman Ronald Tsukamoto is shot to death by a black gunman during a routine traffic stop. Police describe his murder, and the recent slayings of Patrolmen Richard Huerta and Richard Radetich, as political assassinations conducted by black militants.

August 27, Hoboken, New Jersey: Puerto Rican youths riot, leading to twenty arrests, after a militant leader is jailed on drug charges.

August 28, Rocky Mount, North Carolina: Bombs rock a school scheduled for desegregation.

August 29, Los Angeles, California: Rioting erupts during a Hispanic anti-war rally. Sixty persons are arrested and forty-eight are injured, including twenty-five patrolmen. Violence continues the following day, with another 140 arrests. Hispanic newsman Rueben Salazar is killed by a tear gas shell fired into a tavern after police receive reports of armed men inside.

August 29–31, Philadelphia, Pennsylvania: Police Sgt. Frank Van Colln is killed and six other officers are wounded in separate shootings. Information gathered from a suspect leads police to raid Black Panther headquarters on August 31. Shots are traded with militants before fifteen are arrested.

August 31, Trenton, New Jersey: A curfew is imposed after a melee between Black Panthers and police.

September 1, New Haven, Connecticut: Another Black Panther is convicted of conspiracy in the Rackley murder case.

September 1, Blytheville, Arkansas: A curfew is imposed after violence—including two shootings and six arson fires—erupts in the wake of funeral services for a black man killed by a white shop owner.

September 3, New Jersey Turnpike: Police stop four Black Panthers in a stolen truck. One patrolman is wounded during the ensuing shoot-out.

September 14, Bogalusa, Louisiana: White and black students brawl at a newly integrated school. Fourteen persons are arrested.

September 14–15, New Orleans, Louisiana: One black is killed, twenty-one persons are injured, and fourteen are arrested during the twenty-four-hour police siege of a black housing project. The violence erupts after two black undercover officers are beaten in the office of a militant group affiliated with the Black Panther Party.

September 16, Los Angeles, California: Two thousand Hispanic youths clash with police and hurl rocks and firebombs. Sixty persons are arrested, and six patrolmen are injured.

September 17, Syracuse, New York: A fireman is suspended for deliberate failure to dispatch trucks to a September 13 fire at a black home in which one black woman died. Firetrucks were ninety minutes late arriving at the fire, which injured seven other persons, including patrolmen and firefighters.

September 18, Toledo, Ohio: Patrolman W.A. Miscannon is shot and killed in his cruiser near Black Panther headquarters. Two Panthers are wounded in the ensuing police raid on their office.

September 19, Sumter, South Carolina: Grand Dragon Robert Scoggins and nine KKK members are charged as accessories to murder, with additional charges of conspiracy to commit robbery, after security guards kill victim W.L. Odom at a Klan rally.

September 19, Birmingham, Alabama: Deputies fire on members of the Alabama Black Liberation Front while trying to serve an eviction notice on the group.

September 21, Houma, Louisiana: Gov. John McKeithen declares a state of emergency after a weekend of racial clashes that began following a high school football game.

September 27, Seattle, Washington: A Black Panther official is wounded when his shotgun explodes.

September 28, Cleveland, Ohio: Black gunmen kill Patrolman Joseph Tracz and wound his partner, Fred Fulton, during a routine traffic stop.

October 5, Pontiac, Michigan: Four white students are beaten and wounded by gunshots in a schoolyard attack by twenty black youths. Racial fights continue for the next two days, including rock- and bottle-throwing. One black student is shot on October 7, while another is struck by a car. Police use tear gas to rout 500 brawlers from the scene.

October 10, Brooklyn, New York: Jews and Puerto Ricans brawl in the streets after fifty Puerto Ricans attack a synagogue with Yom Kippur services in progress. Windows are smashed in the temple, and six Jews are reported injured.

October 10–11, Quincy, Florida: Blacks riot for two nights, protesting the police wounding of a black man.

October 18, Cordele, Georgia: Police Sgt. Hiram Watson is killed with his own gun while trying to arrest a Black Muslim.

October 21, Cairo, Illinois: Black snipers fire on the police station and other targets around town. On the night of October 24 carloads of black gunmen repeatedly strafe the police station over a six-hour period.

October 24, Detroit, Michigan: One patrolman is killed and another is wounded during a shoot-out at Black Panther headquarters. Fifteen blacks are charged with murder and conspiracy.

October 28–30, Trenton, New Jersey: Violence erupts on the third day of school desegregation, and continues for three nights. Two hundred persons are arrested, with more than twenty-five reported injured.

October 31, Daytona Beach, Florida: Clashes between black and white youths on Halloween spark a weekend of racial violence, with firebombing of stores and sniper attacks on police.

November 1, New Castle, Pennsylvania: Ronald Mitchell, a black man, is killed in a drive-by shooting at a local tavern. Subsequent riots leave nine persons injured, including five patrolmen.

November 5, Bridgeport, Connecticut: A public meeting on police-community relations erupts into violence, with blacks and whites brawling in the aisles.

November 6, Henderson, North Carolina: National Guard units are deployed after a night of sniper fire and arson sparked by local school desegregation policies. One fireman is shot to death and 104 persons are arrested by November 8. Local schools reopen on November 9, with two receiving telephone bomb threats.

November 7–8, Daytona Beach, Florida: Blacks riot after the arrest of nineteen persons in a downtown protest march. At least a dozen shops are firebombed, and one black youth is wounded by gunfire.

November 8, Cairo, Illinois: Wiley Anderson, a black soldier, is wounded by sniper fire. Two other persons are reported injured by shots fired into a black housing project. The same night arsonists burn the city's biggest lumberyard, owned by the founder of the vigilante White Hats, a group of white racists.

November 12, Buffalo, New York: FBI agents seize an arsenal of guns and ammunition in a raid on Black Panther headquarters.

November 12, Carbondale, Illinois: Ten persons are wounded, including four patrolmen, in a series of shoot-outs between police and gunmen claiming to be Black Panthers.

November 12, Las Vegas, Nevada: Blacks riot downtown after a high school football game, leaving twelve persons injured and three in jail.

November 14, Hartford, Connecticut: Two patrolmen, one black and one white, come to blows during the arrest of a Puerto Rican girl.

November 18, Greenville, South Carolina: National Guard units are deployed after racial desegregation leads to fighting at six area schools. Whites fire shots into an empty school bus and at two school security guards on the night of November 19.

November 20–21, Cummins, Arkansas: Two days of racial fighting at a state prison farm stems from inmate demands for segregated housing. State troopers restore order on November 22.

November 21, Chapel Hill, North Carolina: James Cates, a black youth, dies in a clash between black students and white members of the Storm Troopers motorcycle gang at a university dance. Two gang members are charged with murder. It is the second recent incident of violence involving gang members.

November 22–30, Englewood, New Jersey: Police blame racial tensions for an outbreak of fifteen arson fires in a black neighborhood. A fire on November 30 leaves thirty-eight families homeless.

November 26, New Orleans, Louisiana: One person is wounded and six are arrested during a shoot-out at Black Panther headquarters. The violence erupts when police try to serve an eviction notice filed against Panthers by the city housing authority.

December 5, Cairo, Illinois: Police begin deputizing members of a militant white racist group, the White Hats, after a white deputy is wounded by sniper fire. Twelve blacks are arrested after the shooting, including four men who are charged with attempted murder on December 6.

1971

January, West Point, Mississippi: John Thomas, a black civil rights worker, is shot and killed. His assailant pleads self-defense, and is acquitted by an all-white jury on October 11.

January 9, Los Angeles, California: Thirty-two Hispanics are arrested in a riotous demonstration outside police headquarters. Chief Ed Davis blames the incident on militant Brown Berets and "swimming pool communists."

January 12, Winston-Salem, North Carolina: Police and militants exchange gunfire at Black Panther headquarters after snipers inside the building pin down patrolmen.

January 12, New Orleans, Louisiana: Fire destroys two buildings occupied by Black Panthers in a housing project. Tenants of the project block firefighters from reaching the scene.

January 13, Tampa, Florida: Violence erupts after an off-duty policeman fatally wounds a black youth who attacked him on the street.

January 17, Memphis, Tennessee: Thirteen Black Panthers are arrested and two are charged with assault to murder during their unauthorized occupation of a newly constructed housing project.

January 28, New York City: The conspiracy trial of thirteen Black Panthers is delayed following a clash between the defendants and their jailers.

January 31, Los Angeles, California: Violence erupts during a Hispanic protest demonstration, with windows smashed along the route of march. Deputies intervene when shooting breaks out, and fire shotguns to disperse the mob. One rioter is killed, nineteen others are wounded by buckshot, and two persons are stabbed. Property damage is estimated at $200,000.

February 1, Los Angeles, California: One Mexican is killed and many others are injured when youth gangs attack a neighborhood sheriff's station. Rioting erupts during a protest rally against alleged police brutality sponsored by the Chicano Moratorium.

February 4, Chapel Hill, North Carolina: Arsonists cause $50,000 damage to the office of J.L. Chambers, a black lawyer active in civil rights.

February 5, Wilmington, North Carolina: Violence breaks out after bomb threats are received by a local black church. Armed youths fortify the church against attack and trade shots with white gunmen. One white man is killed by sniper fire and a black youth is slain by police before National Guardsmen restore order on February 8.

February 15, Atlanta, Georgia: One hundred riot officers quell violence between Black Muslims and Black Panthers when the two groups battle over rights to sell their newspaper on a particular corner.

February 21, Ft. Pierce, Florida: Rioting, including arson fires, spreads over a thirteen-block area, leaving three black youths wounded and twenty-nine jailed before a curfew is imposed.

February 23, Princeton, New Jersey: Three white men are arrested for burning a cross at a local football field in violation of state law.

March 4, Los Angeles, California: Four patrolmen are indicted for the deaths of newsman Rueben Salazar and another Hispanic killed during August 1970.

March 6–7, Texarkana, Texas: White arsonists attack four black churches in two days.

March 9, New York City: Robert Webb, "field marshal" of the Black Panther Party, is shot dead by three gunmen while selling party newspapers on the street.

March 12, Houston, Texas: Klansmen bomb the offices of a local socialist political group.

April 3, Ypsilanti, Michigan: Dr. R.W. Brownlee, principal of Willow Run High School, is stopped on the highway by KKK members, abducted at gunpoint, and tarred and feathered. Brownlee was targeted by Klansmen for promoting racial harmony at his school.

April 17, Corona, New York: Sam Napier, a West Coast Black Panther official, is found dead in the party's burned headquarters. By September 24, four New York Panthers have pled guilty to arson and murder in the case.

April 20, Santa Cruz, California: The charred remains of Black Panther Fred Bennett are found in the ruins of a remote bomb factory. Authorities estimate that he died around January 6.

April 23, New York City: A JDL bomb explodes in a downtown office building housing the Soviet trade mission. A phone call prior to the blast demands freedom for Soviet Jews.

May 5, Brooklyn, New York: Rioting erupts in the Brownsville section, with over 120 arson fires reported. Fourteen policemen, thirteen firemen, and six civilians are reported injured, with property damage estimated at $100,000.

May 12, New York City: Seven JDL members are arrested for violation of firearms and explosives legislation. On July 9 leader Meyer Kahane and two other defendants plead guilty to the illegal manufacture of bombs.

May 13, New York City: Four black militants are convicted of illegally possessing firearms and explosives, part of their avowed scheme to "kill a cop a week."

May 13, Chicago, Illinois: Three patrolmen are wounded by snipers firing from a building occupied by Black Panthers. Four gunmen are charged with attempted murder.

May 17, Brooklyn, New York: Disorder breaks out in the Bedford-Stuyvesant section after police kill a knife-wielding black man.

May 19, New York City: Two policemen assigned to guard the home of District Attorney Frank Hogan are wounded by black gunmen firing from a passing car. A member of the Black Panther Party is convicted for the shooting on March 7, 1973, and sentenced to life in prison.

May 21, New York City: Patrolmen Waverly Jones and Joseph Piagentini are ambushed and killed by BLA gunmen.

May 21, Ecru, Mississippi: A black man is shot and killed during an argument with a white grocer.

May 21–25, Chattanooga, Tennessee: Four nights of racial violence erupt after the cancellation of a rock concert. One black youth is shot and killed on May 25 while stoning police cars. Heavy damage is reported to local stores before National Guardsmen are called to enforce a curfew.

May 22, Marysville, California: Three black servicemen are held in custody after a brawl with whites at Travis Air Force Base. Black protests over the arrests lead to further violence on May 24, leaving ten airmen injured and nintey-seven arrested. One fireman dies of a heart attack while fighting an arson fire on the base.

May 26, Drew, Mississippi: A black teenager, Jo Etta Collier, is killed following her high school graduation ceremony in an unprovoked drive-by shooting. Three whites are charged in the case, and the triggerman is convicted of manslaughter on October 30.

May 30, Cairo, Illinois: Three policemen are wounded during a shoot-out with black militants.

June, Marianna, Arkansas: In the midst of a black economic boycott a white county official tries to run down two black protesters with his car. When they enter the courthouse to file charges, he follows, and chases them out with a pistol.

June 1, New York City: One policeman is stabbed and three people are injured when black and Puerto Rican youths clash. One of the Puerto Rican youths is charged with the stabbing.

June 3, New York City: Two JDL members are arrested after homemade bombs and other weapons are found in their car.

June 5, New York City: Four blacks, including two Black Panthers, are arrested for the attempted robbery of a black social club. The two Panthers are also suspected in the recent ambush shootings of New York policemen.

June 8, Houston, Texas: Police arrest six persons and draw sniper fire during a raid on the headquarters of a black militant group, the People's Party II.

June 10, Jacksonville, Florida: A fifteen-year-old black youth is shot and killed by a white police officer. The patrolman is later indicted for manslaughter.

June 12, Houston, Texas: KKK leader Louis Beam and three others are indicted for bombing Pacifica network radio station KPFT and the local offices of the Socialist Workers Party.

June 13, New York City: A Puerto Rico Day parade erupts into violence sparked by members of the Young Lords and other militant groups. Twenty persons are arrested and many are injured, including nineteen patrolmen.

June 13–14, Albuquerque, New Mexico: Black and Hispanic youths riot for two consecutive nights following the cancellation of a scheduled rock concert. Property damage is estimated at $2 million, with fifty persons arrested and fifty-eight injured, including eleven police officers. Order is restored by the National Guard.

June 14, Newburgh Heights, New York: More than twenty-five persons are hurt, with two shot by snipers, during an outbreak of violence. Fifteen persons are arrested during the riot.

June 14, Star City, Arkansas: A white patrolman is charged with murder in the death of a black motorist, killed during a routine traffic arrest.

June 16–20, Jacksonville, Florida: Blacks riot for five nights over a June 10 police shooting. Two hundred seventy-four persons are jailed during the outbreak, with sniper fire and firebombing reported after the youth's funeral on June 19. Property damage is estimated at $250,000.

June 19–22, Columbus, Georgia: Violence rages for three nights after eight black patrolmen are dismissed from the local police force. The situation is aggravated when police kill a black robbery suspect on June 21.

July 22, Syracuse, New York: Three black youths are arrested when gangs pelt white motorists. Firebombing incidents are reported on August 6.

July 22–24, Rochester, New York: Three nights of racial disturbances erupt after police attempt to ticket illegally parked cars. Nine persons are jailed.

July 25, Coumbus, Georgia: More violence, including arson and sniper fire, erupts in local black neighborhoods.

July 26, New Orleans, Louisiana: Two deputies are held hostage for eight hours by black prisoners, including several Black Panthers facing trial on charges of attempting to murder policemen. Twelve Panthers are acquitted of those charges on August 6.

August 1, Cincinnati, Ohio: Interracial street fights are reported on the fringe of the local black neighborhood.

August 6, Ayden, North Carolina: An unarmed black man, William Murphy, is shot and killed by a white policeman "during a struggle."

August 12, Denver, Colorado: The fire department reports a recent epidemic of firebombings, linked to tension between police and militant minorities.

August 16–23, Camden, New Jersey: Protest demonstrations by Puerto Rican residents at city hall erupt into eight nights of violence, with reports of arson and looting, rock-throwing, and sniper fire. Triggered by the alleged police beating of a forty-year-old Puerto Rican man, the riots leave 200 persons jailed, twenty injured (including four patrolmen), and two youths wounded by gunfire. On the second night of violence six major fires are reported burning out of control.

August 18, Jackson, Mississippi: Police raid the booby-trapped headquarters of the Republic of New Africa. Two policemen are shot, and Lt. Louis Skinner dies from head wounds on August 19.

Eleven blacks are charged with murder in the case, two of whom are convicted and sentenced to life on May 3 and September 14, 1972.

August 21, San Quentin, California: Violence erupts at the state prison, with five white guards and three black inmates killed in an apparent escape attempt. One of the dead convicts is "Soledad Brother" George Jackson, a militant reportedly marked for execution by racist guards. Three other guards and two inmates suffer nonfatal wounds during the outbreak. Weeks later, a police informant reports that Jackson has been deliberately "set up" for assassination by law enforcement officers. The source of a pistol, allegedly carried by Jackson in the maximum-security cell block, remains unknown. Jackson's lawyer, accused of smuggling the gun into prison, is later acquitted on all counts.

August 30, Pontiac, Michigan: Bombs destroy ten school buses scheduled for use in desegregation. Six Klansmen are arrested, and Grand Dragon Robert Miles is eventually convicted and sentenced to prison.

September, Wilmington, North Carolina: Sand is poured into the gas tanks of nineteen buses scheduled for use in school desegregation.

September 4–5, Hoboken, New Jersey: Rioting erupts after two Puerto Rican men are arrested for threatening a local grocer. Two stores are firebombed, and eight patrolmen are injured by rock-throwers.

September 7, New York City: One youth is shot and four others are hurt during a clash between black and Dominican gangs.

September 7–8, Utica, New York: Fourteen blacks and four whites are arrested during two nights of racial violence. Several arson incidents are also reported.

September 9–10, Lubbock, Texas: Rioting breaks out after Willie Ray Collier, a sixteen-year-old black, is shot and killed by a white youth at a local high school. Angry blacks stone police headquarters, and three gunmen are charged with wounding a patrolman. On September 11 police raid a private dwelling and arrest seven blacks on charges of shooting at officers.

September 10, Jacksonville, Florida: A bomb with fourteen sticks of dynamite is found under a school bus and defused.

September 11, Butler, Alabama: Margaret Knott is struck and killed by a car during a peaceful civil rights demonstration at the county courthouse. Sheriff Leon Clark witnesses the incident, but makes no effort to arrest the driver because protestors "didn't have any business in the street." A grand jury clears the driver on September 23, accepting his story that he was trying to flee from demonstrators who attacked his car.

September 11, Los Angeles, California: Police and Black Panthers exchange seventy-five shots after a routine traffic stop, leaving one officer and three Panthers wounded.

September 17, Madison, Arkansas: Five persons are wounded by gunshots during a black-white clash.

September 24, Detroit, Michigan: A white woman is arrested with dynamite at the local airport attempting to hijack a plane as part of a plot to help two Black Panthers flee the country.

September 24–28, Springfield, Massachusetts: Racial violence spills over from local high school incidents into the streets. Two whites are injured and nine are arrested on September 27. Six persons are arrested for stoning shops and motorists on September 28.

September 30, Springfield, Massachusetts: Police intervene when white and Puerto Rican youth gangs brawl in the streets. Thirty-five persons are arrested and at least thirty-one injured during a series of clashes spanning several days.

September 30–October 2, Jacksonville, Florida: Police log three nights of rioting. A member of the U.S. Air Force is wounded by gunshots and further injured when his car is firebombed in the riot zone.

October 1–5, Wilmington, North Carolina: Racial violence spreads following fights at a local football game. Police dodge sniper fire while members of a racist group, the Rights of White People, mount private patrols of the streets. One white man is killed by a black in a neighborhood shooting.

October 7, New York City: Black Panther Donald Weems, facing trial for bank robbery, pleads guilty to firing at local police in January 1969.

October 9, Arkansas: Reports from Marianna, Madison, and Forrest City suggest that the rapid growth of the KKK has been accompanied by widespread violence. In the preceding year one black has been killed by police, several buildings have been burned by arsonists, and at least ten persons have been wounded in racially motivated shootings.

October 16, New York City: H. Rap Brown and three other black militants are captured during a shoot-out with police following the robbery of a local tavern.

October 18, Memphis, Tennessee: Twenty-three policemen are suspended after the beating death of Elton Hayes, a black man who at first is listed as the accidental victim of a high-speed chase. Five nights of rioting erupt after the Hayes funeral on October 19, with seven persons injured in sniper fire and firebombing incidents. A two-year-old black boy is struck and killed by a patrol car in the riot zone. On the last night of violence, October 23, police log twelve arrests and nine firebombings. On December 9 four officers—including a lieutenant—are indicted for first-degree murder in the Hayes slaying.

October 20, New York City: A JDL sniper fires several shots into the Russian Mission, narrowly missing four children sleeping in bed.

October 23, Washington, D.C.: Hispanic militant Reies Tijerina, recently released from prison, declares that a New Mexico state policeman raped his wife while he was incarcerated.

October 23–24, Southern Pines, North Carolina: Two nights of violence erupt after blacks stone a caravan of nightriders and shots are exchanged.

November 21, Ayden, North Carolina: Authorities report that three months of racial violence, including several dynamite blasts, have followed the August killing of a black sharecropper by a white state trooper.

November 25, Rochester, New York: Bombs damage a black church and an Islamic mosque nearby.

December 3, Roosevelt, New York: Rocks and bottles are thrown during a demonstration calling for the suspension of a patrolman who shot and killed Lawrence Blaylock, a black car thief, on December 2.

December 14, New York City: Two Puerto Rican students are convicted of possessing bombs with intent to destroy various department stores. They are sentenced to jail terms of five and seven years, respectively.

December 20, Queens, New York: Two policemen are injured when black militants hurl a hand grenade under their patrol car.

December 28, Jacksonville, Florida: Rioting erupts after police try to prevent black children from roller skating on the street.

1972

January 10, Baton Rouge, Louisiana: Five persons are killed, including two sheriff's deputies, when gunfire erupts following a Black Muslim rally. Thirty-one persons are wounded during the exchange, including fifteen policemen, four innocent bystanders, and a television newsman. A curfew is imposed against the possibility of further violence. Thirteen Muslims are charged and ultimately convicted of inciting a riot and sentenced to lengthy prison terms.

January 19, New Orleans, Louisiana: KKK Imperial Wizard H.R. Thompson is injured by blacks armed with bricks during a parade honoring the birthday of Confederate Gen. Robert E. Lee.

January 19, Memphis, Tennessee: The mayor promises new guidelines on the use of deadly force after police shoot and kill a third black youth in recent days.

January 26, New York City: JDL arsonists set fire to two offices linked with Soviet cultural exchange projects. Iris Jones, an office worker, dies in one of the fires.

January 27, Brooklyn, New York: Patrolman John Bauer is wounded by black militant gunmen after stopping their car for a routine traffic violation.

January 28, New York City: Patrolmen Gregory Foster and Rocco Laurie are fatally wounded in an ambush carried out by members of the BLA.

February 4, High Point, North Carolina: Three Black Panthers are convicted of wounding policemen in a February 1971 shoot-out, drawing prison terms of seven to ten years each.

February 14, Baltimore, Maryland: Attorney A.F. Turco pleads guilty to assault, bargained down from murder charges in the 1969 torture-slaying of Black Panther and alleged police informant E.L. Anderson.

February 15, St. Louis, Missouri: Black militants open fire on police during a routine traffic stop. One of the blacks is killed at the scene, and one of his companions and one patrolman are wounded.

February 27, Wilmington, North Carolina: Street violence and sniper fire erupt in a black neighborhood, with arsonists torching the local headquarters of a white supremacist organization.

March, San Jose, California: James Carr, a black militant friend of "Soldedad Brother" George Jackson, is shot and killed by two white gunmen in his front yard.

March 5, Drew, Mississippi: Murder charges are dismissed against two whites for the May 26 murder of Jo Etta Collier. The confessed trigger man is already serving twenty years on conviction for manslaughter.

April 12, Cobleskill, New York: Racial violence erupts on a local college campus, with white students hurling bricks and Molotov cocktails at a dorm housing twenty-five blacks. Authorities estimate damages at $10,000.

April 13, Los Angeles, California: A hijacked airliner initially bound from Albuquerque to Phoenix lands at Los Angeles International Airport. The Hispanic gunman on board surrenders after making a statement to the media about discrimination suffered by minorities in the United States.

April 14, New York City: A Black Panther is convicted of murder and arson in the Sam Napier case. Four other defendants go on trial for the same charges on May 22.

April 14, New York City: Five policemen and three blacks are injured after brawling and gunfire erupt at a Black Muslim temple in Harlem, sparking three hours of street violence. Two Muslims are indicted on felony charges on May 19.

April 17, Cobleskill, New York: A series of arson fires at a racially troubled college knock out campus power.

May 19, Blythe, California: Hispanics riot after Mario Barreras is shot and killed by an off-duty policeman.

May 27, Wilmington, North Carolina: A night of violence includes sniper fire and the burning of a white militant organization's headquarters. Rioting continues on May 28 and is finally controlled by the imposition of a curfew the following day.

June 7, Alton, Illinois: Police and black snipers exchange shots while firemen battle an arson blaze.

June 20, Texarkana, Texas: A black church burned by arsonists in 1971 reopens.

October, Texas: An Hispanic woman submits to being raped by an Anglo border patrolman after he threatens the lives of her two children.

October 4–7, Newburgh, New York: Rioting erupts, leaving sixteen persons injured and nine in jail when police try to disperse gangs of black youths loitering outside a local store.

October 24–25, Dallas, Texas: Two nights of angry demonstrations are sparked by police shootings of three blacks in the preceding two weeks.

December 31, New Orleans, Louisiana: Black sniper Mark Essex kills one police cadet and wounds two patrolmen in unprovoked shootings. One of the wounded officers dies two months later.

1973

January 1, New Orleans, Louisiana: Black gunman Mark Essex sets fire to two downtown warehouses. The flames burn for five days, requiring 200 firemen to bring them under control.

January 7, New Orleans, Louisiana: Mark Essex, a black man responsible for shooting police officers on December 31, 1972, wounds a white grocer before stealing a car and driving to a nearby Howard Johnson Motel, where he begins setting fires and randomly shooting white guests. Seven persons are killed—including two guests, two motel employees, and three policemen—and another sixteen are wounded before Essex is shot by police.

January 12, New Jersey: A Klansmen is sentenced to six months in jail and two others are fined $500 each for burning a cross at a black family's home.

January 12, Rochester, New York: Arson destroys a black church closed since being bombed by whites in November 1971.

January 19, Brooklyn, New York: Four Sunni Muslims invade a local gun shop, looting it for weapons, and are captured in a shoot-out with police. All four are convicted on June 21, 1974, and sentenced to twenty-five-year prison terms on August 5.

January 21, Buffalo Gap, South Dakota: Indian Wesley Bad Bull Heart is stabbed to death by a white man at a local gas station. His assailant is charged with second-degree manslaughter, sparking angry demonstrations by AIM.

January 25, Brooklyn, New York: Two patrolmen are wounded by machine gun fire from a passing car occupied by blacks.

January 28, Queens, New York: Two policemen are wounded by black gunmen in an unprovoked drive-by shooting.

February 6, Custer, South Dakota: Rioting erupts when police use clubs and tear gas to disperse an AIM protest march. Thirty-seven persons are jailed, and the courthouse and chamber of commerce offices are damaged by firebombs.

February 9, Rapid City, South Dakota: More than forty Indians are arrested in clashes with whites at a local tavern.

February 17, Denver, Colorado: Police kill Luis Martinez during a raid on the office of the Mexican Crusade for Justice. Martinez had been the target of a recent bombing at his home.

February 27, Wounded Knee, South Dakota: Two hundred armed AIM supporters raid the village trading post for arms and supplies, then lay siege to the hamlet. One of the militants is wounded in a duel with police on February 28, while seventeen others are jailed on charges of looting. Eleven hostages are released on March 1, and the reservation home of an AIM member is firebombed by opponents the same day. AIM militants burn the local trading post on April 29, and the siege continues until May 5, with four Indians killed and five persons wounded—including two federal agents—in various gun battles.

April 7, Middletown Township, New Jersey: Sixty-five patrolmen from various New Jersey communities disrupt a fundraiser featuring a guest speaker accused of killing a policeman in the 1967 Plainfield riots.

April 20, Brooklyn, New York: Two Hasidic Jews are assaulted and beaten on the street.

April 28, Queens, New York: Violence erupts after a policeman fatally shoots ten-year-old Clifford Glover, a black child. The officer responsible is charged with murder on June 13.

May 2, New Brunswick, New Jersey: A state trooper and a Black Panther are killed during a shoot-out on the New Jersey Turnpike. BLA leader Joan Chesimard is wounded and captured in the same incident, and a second trooper is injured. The gunfight begins after a routine traffic stop, with Chesimard sought on multiple charges of murder, armed robbery, and attempted murder. A BLA fugitive from the shoot-out is arrested on May 3, following a thirty-six-hour manhunt. Convicted and sentenced to life imprisonment, Chesimard escapes from custody on November 2, 1979, and is believed to be living in Cuba.

May 31, Holmesburg, Pennsylvania: Black Muslim Fred Burton, serving a life sentence for the August 1970 murder of a policeman, attempts to escape from state prison with Joseph Bowen, a black prisoner facing trial for the February 1971 killing of a police officer. The convicts fatally stab the warden and deputy warden and critically injure a captain of the guards before both are shot and wounded by sentries.

June 2, Brooklyn, New York: A black physician is assaulted by Hasidic Jews while escorting a patient past a Jewish mob. Police respond and a riot erupts. Three Jews are jailed on charges of assault, inciting a riot, and possessing dangerous weapons.

June 6, New York City: Transit Patrolman Sidney Thompson is killed by BLA gunmen in the Bronx.

June 8, New York City: Police and FBI agents arrest Andrew Jackson, a member of the BLA, on charges of bank robbery. He is also suspected in the deaths of four policemen and a rival Black Panther.

June 20, Queens, New York: Four Black Panthers are sentenced to prison terms of three years each for their guilty pleas to the murder of Panther Sam Napier. One defendant is already serving a life term for shooting two policemen in May 1971.

June 27, Brooklyn, New York: Violence between Italian and Hispanic youths leaves twelve persons injured, including five policemen and five teenagers suffering from gunshot wounds.

July 27, Dallas, Texas: Santos Rodriguez, a twelve-year-old Hispanic, is "accidentally" shot in the head by a policeman trying to extort a robbery confession. Hispanics riot on July 28, and four persons are injured and twelve are arrested. The officer is convicted of "murder without malice" on November 16, drawing a five-year prison term.

July 30, Newark, New Jersey: Shots are fired into the office of a black nationalist group, the Committee for Unified Newark. Sniper fire damages a city patrol car a short time later.

August 6, Queens, New York: Violence flares for several hours after police kill a black man suspected of stealing a bus. Ten persons are injured and five are arrested during the outbreak.

August 23, Long Branch, New Jersey: One thousand black and Puerto Rican youths stone police and firemen responding to the scene of an arson fire at a local warehouse.

September 4, Newark, New Jersey: Black Muslim leader Min Shabazz is shot dead on his driveway. On October 24 eleven members of the rival New World of Islam are arrested on murder charges. A total of fourteen Muslims are charged by October 27.

September 17, New York City: Three policemen are wounded in a shoot-out with BLA members at a Bronx apartment. The captured gunmen are sought on charges of bank robbery and multiple murder in New York.

September 26, New Orleans, Louisiana: Klansman Byron De La Beckwith is arrested with firearms and an armed time bomb in his car. He was allegedly planning a raid on the home of a local Jewish leader. Federal charges of transporting explosives across state lines are filed on October 9, and the Louisiana KKK begins fundraising efforts for Beckwith's defense on October 10. A jury acquits Beckwith of all charges on January 16, 1974.

September 27, New York City: BLA member Henry Brown, facing charges for the murder of two police officers, escapes from Kings County Hospital. He is never recaptured.

October 2, Boston, Massachusetts: Evelyn Walker, a white woman, is doused with gasoline and burned to death by black youths after her car breaks down in a black neighborhood.

October 4, Boston, Massachusetts: Ludovico Barba is stoned and stabbed to death by black youths while fishing near a violence-ridden housing project.

October 6, Boston, Massachusetts: White cab driver Kirk Miller becomes the third victim of racially motivated homicide within a week.

October 17, Pine Ridge, South Dakota: AIM member Pedro Bissonette, facing indictments from the February 1973 siege of Wounded Knee, is killed when he pulls a gun on reservation police officers.

October 19, San Francisco, California: Prospective members of a Black Muslim splinter group, the Death Angels, assault white victims Richard and Quita Hague with machetes, killing the woman and leaving her husband gravely injured in the first of twenty-three random attacks in the so-called Zebra case. Sect members reportedly earn their "angel wings"—symbols of acceptance in the cult—by killing a specified number of white men, women, or children.

October 22, San Francisco, California: A white woman is kidnapped and sexually abused by one of the Zebra gunmen.

October 29, San Francisco, California: Frances Rose, a white woman, is shot dead in another Zebra attack. Muslim Jessie Cooks, arrested near the scene, is eventually sentenced to life in jail for her murder.

November 2–8, Washington, D.C.: Militant AIM members occupy and barricade the Bureau of Indian Affairs office. Five of the demonstrators are jailed for theft of government property on November 22, after FBI agents recover stolen items in a raid at Lawrence, Kansas.

November 6, Oakland, California: Marcus Foster, the black superintendent of schools, is shot and killed by radical SLA gunmen.

November 12, Fort Lauderdale, Florida: An interracial couple is abducted by black hoodlums, who set the white husband on fire and then release his black wife unharmed.

November 14, New York City: BLA member Twyman Myers is killed in a shoot-out with detectives.

November 21, New York City: The Sephardic Institute for Advanced Learning is damaged and one employee is killed when arsonists set fire to the building. A second fire destroys the Institute on November 23, causing $1 million damage.

November 25, San Francisco, California: Merchant Saleem Erakat is bound and shot to death in a Zebra attack.

November 26, Gadsden, Alabama: Rev. Edward Pace, a black minister, is shot and killed at his home. A Klansman is convicted of the murder on March 9, 1974.

November 27, Pontiac, Michigan: Five white students are wounded when black gunmen open fire at an area high school.

December 11, San Francisco, California: Paul Dancik is shot and killed in a Zebra attack.

December 13, San Francisco, California: Arthur Agnos and Marietta DiGirolamo are fatally shot by Death Angel candidates in two separate Zebra attacks.

December 20, San Francisco, California: Ilario Bertuccio and Angela Roselli are shot on city streets in separate Zebra incidents.

December 22, San Francisco, California: Neal Moynihan and Mildred Hosler are shot down by Death Angel candidates in two separate attacks.

December 23, San Francisco, California: Assembled Death Angels torture and dismember a white transient during one of their periodic gatherings. The victim has never been identified.

December 31, Odessa, Florida: Black Panther Frank Fields, sought for the murder of fellow militant Sam Napier, is shot and killed by FBI agents. Companions of Fields are arrested on bank robbery charges.

1974

January 3, Asbury Park, New Jersey: An appeals court upholds the conviction of a KKK member jailed for burning a cross at a black family's home.

January 10, Concord, California: Fire damages a house occupied by SLA fugitives.

January 18, Washington, D.C.: Seven Hanafi Muslims are massacred in their communal home by members of a rival sect. Five Black Muslims from Philadelphia are charged with the crime. Four defendants are convicted on May 17, with the fifth found guilty on November 20.

January 28, San Francisco, California: Death Angel gunmen kill four whites and wound a fifth in random, racially motivated attacks linked to the Zebra case. Police agree that members of the Muslim splinter group have killed at least seventy whites in California during the preceding eighteen months.

February 4, Brooklyn, New York: Four men are killed and one wounded in a shoot-out between rival Black Muslim factions in the Bedford-Stuyvesant section.

February 5, Berkeley, California: Newspaper heiress Patricia Hearst is kidnapped from her home by SLA gunmen in their bid to dramatize the plight of American blacks.

February 7, Whiteclay, Nebraska: A sniper's bullet narrowly misses AIM member Milo Goings and strikes a nine-year-old boy in the face.

February 17, Tampa, Florida: One person is killed and four are wounded after two Black Muslims exchange gunfire with an off-duty policeman moonlighting as a commercial security guard.

March 1, Manderson, South Dakota: The reservation home of Aaron De Sersa is firebombed by GOON arsonists.

March 15, Ossining, New York: Three teenagers are arrested after a night of scattered racial violence. As many as 200 youths are involved in the brawls that had erupted after various high school incidents earlier in the week.

April, Pine Ridge, South Dakota: GOON members launch a three-month terror campaign against opposition spokesman Severt Young Bear, shooting at his home repeatedly through late June.

April 1, San Francisco, California: Thomas Rainwater is killed and Linda Story wounded in random Zebra attacks by Death Angel gunmen.

April 14, San Francisco, California: Ward Anderson and Terry White are shot by Zebra gunmen at a bus stop.

April 16, San Francisco, California: Nelson Shields becomes the twenty-third victim—and the thirteenth fatality—in random attacks committed by black Zebra gunmen.

April 19, San Francisco, California: Frank Carlson, a white grocer, is murdered and his wife is beaten and raped by a black man who claims to be one of the Zebra killers. Police arrest seven Death Angel suspects on May 1; three are released for lack of evidence, while four others are convicted and sentenced to life imprisonment in March 1976. Police declare that an estimated fifteen Death Angels remain at large, and are responsible for the murders of over eighty people.

May 15, New York City: A demonstrator is shot outside Lincoln Hospital's detoxification center while picketing to protest the program's alleged involvement with members of the BLA.

May 30, Cleveland, Ohio: Three Sunni Muslims invade an apartment, tying up the tenants and stealing $2,000 before they flee with hostage Andrew Jackson. The gunmen are cornered by police in a nearby house, where they hold nine more captives at gunpoint. They surrender after a ninety-minute shoot-out that leaves six patrolmen and two hostages wounded.

June 19, Pine Ridge, South Dakota: Brothers Clarence and Vernal Cross, both members of AIM, are shot by GOON opponents while sitting in their car. Clarence dies of his wounds.

June 22, Little Falls, New Jersey: Francine Feldman blames anti-Semitic attacks for her daughter's withdrawal from public school.

July 27, Kokomo, Indiana: Shooting incidents are reported during a local KKK recruiting drive.

August 13, Staten Island, New York: Black and white youths fight in the streets for two hours. One teenager is arrested with a Molotov cocktail.

August 17, Kokomo, Indiana: More shootings are reported as the Klan recruiting drive continues.

August 31, New York City: FALN terrorists claim credit for the bombing of Lincoln Center.

September 2, Newark, New Jersey: Puerto Ricans David Perez and Fernando Rodriguez are shot to death by police after violence erupts during a celebration in Branch Brook Park. The shootings provoke four days of rioting, and incidents of looting and arson. A grand jury investigating the disturbance in February 1975 indicts one policeman for the murder of Perez, charging that police officers joined in a "conspiracy of silence" to cover up the crime. The defendant is cleared by a jury on December 12, 1975.

September 20, Boston, Massachusetts: Klan-led anti-busing demonstrations erupt into sporadic violence at several points in the city, with mobs stoning school buses and battling police. One man is arrested for assaulting an officer. Incidents continue through September 22, when armed whites invade a black housing project and harass occupants.

September 28, Newark, New Jersey: FALN terrorists claim credit for a bomb explosion in the alley between city hall and police headquarters. The bomb is in retaliation for the Labor Day shootings of Perez and Rodriguez.

October 7–8, Boston, Massachusetts: Twenty-four whites and fourteen blacks are injured during various outbreaks of violence linked with the controversy over forced busing to desegregate schools. National Guard units are mobilized on October 15, as sporadic incidents continue. Calm is restored by October 22.

October 21, Pine Ridge, South Dakota: AIM supporter Agnes Lamont is hospitalized after a carload of armed GOONs deliberately ram her vehicle at a stop sign.

October 24, Montgomery, Alabama: Members of a Black Muslim splinter sect open fire on police, killing a retired officer who tries to help patrolmen under fire. Five Muslims are held on murder charges.

October 26, New York City: FALN terrorists claim responsibility for bomb explosions at five banks and business establishments.

November 7–8, New York: Racial violence is reported from Newburgh and Beacon Heights, with blacks stoning vehicles and setting at least one fire.

November 10, Pine Ridge, South Dakota: AIM member Phillip Little Crow is beaten to death on the reservation. A GOON member is held on charges of voluntary manslaughter, then released without prosecution.

November 15, Pine Ridge, South Dakota: Pat Hart, an outspoken opponent of GOON, is wounded in the stomach by sniper fire.

November 18, Beacon Heights, New York: Schools close after black and white youths armed with clubs and knives clash in the halls.

November 20, Pine Ridge, South Dakota: AIM member Allison Little Fast Horse is found shot to death in a ditch on the reservation.

November 30, Pensacola, Florida: Five black fishermen are found drowned, the anchor rope on their boat apparently cut with a knife. The deaths are officially listed as accidental, but black leaders charge that the victims were murdered following an altercation with the white owner of a bait shop.

December 9, Boston, Massachusetts: Four white girls are injured during an outbreak of racial fighting at a local high school. Schools in South Boston and Roxbury are closed on December 11, after white mobs angered by the stabbing of a white student trap 135 black students inside South Boston High School for four hours. The schools remain closed through December 17 to avert further violence.

December 11, New York City: Anonymous callers lure rookie patrolman Angelo Poggi to an abandoned tenement, where a bomb blast leaves him permanently disabled. FALN terrorists claim credit for the attack.

1975

January, Pensacola, Florida: Simmering racial animosities and local KKK activity erupt into violence, and arrests for the month of January total fifty. Shots are fired into the state attorney's home, and a brick is hurled through the window of a local black leader.

January 9, Boston, Massachusetts: New outbreaks of mob violence are reported as the controversy over school busing continues.

January 10, Atlanta, Georgia: Black job-seekers riot outside the local unemployment office.

January 14, Boston, Massachusetts: Authorities report new outbreaks of racial fighting in area schools.

January 24, New York City: FALN terrorists bomb the Fraunces Tavern on Wall Street, killing four persons and wounding fifty-five.

February 27, Pine Ridge, South Dakota: GOON members shoot at an airplane that has brought two attorneys to the reservation on a probe of alleged violence by Indian vigilantes.

March 3, Pine Ridge, South Dakota: GOONs shoot at the home of opposition spokesman Matthew King.

March 5, Pine Ridge, South Dakota: GOONs torch the home of Chief Fools Crow, a vocal opponent, burning the house to the ground.

March 9, Pine Ridge, South Dakota: GOON member William Steele is killed on the reservation. AIM member Jerry Shield is charged with the killing, but is later cleared.

March 21, Custer County, South Dakota: Edith Eagle Hawk, her four-year-old daughter, and her three-year-old grandson are killed when GOONs force their car off Highway 44, between Scenic and Rapid City. The dead woman was scheduled to testify as a defense witness for AIM member Jerry Shield in the March killing of a GOON vigilante.

March 22, Pine Ridge, South Dakota: AIM supporter Stacy Cottier is shot and killed by GOON hoodlums.

March 27, Pine Ridge, South Dakota: Jeanette Bissonette is killed by sniper fire while walking home from AIM supporter Stacy Cottier's funeral.

March 31, Baton Rouge, Louisiana: The state supreme court overturns convictions of nine Black Muslims sentenced to twenty-one years for inciting a 1972 riot that left five persons dead.

April 2, New York City: FALN bombs strike at three office buildings, causing extensive damage and injuring two pedestrians.

April 3, New York City: FALN terrorists bomb a restaurant, causing massive damage.

April 4, Valentine, Nebraska: An Indian woman, Jancita Eagle Deer, is murdered and dumped along a rural highway, five months after airing charges that South Dakota's current governor, William Janklow, raped her in January 1967. The case still remains unsolved. Janklow's various libel suits against media sources reporting the charge are dismissed in the spring of 1984.

April 26, New York City: Police in Chinatown allegedly beat a male prisoner after his arrest during a street demonstration. Departmental investigation of the charge leads to the May 23 transfer of the captain in charge of the Chinatown precinct.

June 6, Hamlet, North Carolina: Violence is sparked by reports that police have beaten and shot a black woman. Windows of the mayor's car are shattered by rioters, and three persons are hurt and $24,000 damage is reported in four arson fires. Rioting continues for two more nights, despite the imposition of a curfew. Two arson fires are reported on June 8, and a white patrolman is charged with assaulting a black female prisoner in the incident that started the violence.

June 8, Pine Ridge, South Dakota: AIM leader Russell Means is "accidentally" shot in the back when a reservation policeman tries to arrest him for "rowdy behavior."

June 14, New York City: A bank and office building are seriously damaged by FALN bombers.

June 17, Elizabeth, New Jersey: Cubans clash with police after the arrest of two Cuban men in a traffic incident on June 16. One hundred forty-three persons are arrested and seven are injured, including five policemen. On June 19 rioters stone one police car and try to burn two civilian vehicles, and a telephone bomb threat causes an evacuation of city hall.

June 26, Pine Ridge, South Dakota: FBI agents Jack Coler and Ronald Williams are killed during a shoot-out with AIM militants. Indian gunman Joseph Stuntz also dies in the exchange of gunfire.

July 2–August, Boston, Massachusetts: An estimated 100 whites, including some armed with baseball bats, attack six black Bible salesmen at Carson Beach. Two whites are arrested on charges of assault with a deadly weapon. On July 29 two more persons are injured in racial clashes, and rock fights are reported at the public beach on August 10. Seventeen persons are arrested and nine injured when black youths attack white motorists on August 12. On August 13, two more persons are arrested and seventeen are injured, including six policemen. By August 14, a total of thirty-six persons are injured and eighty-three are jailed. Three civilians are injured on August 15. On August 26, ten persons are arrested in racial clashes, including one who is charged with assaulting an officer.

July 2, Pine Ridge, South Dakota: FBI agents raid and ransack the home of AIM supporter Wallace Little, Sr.

July 4, Pine Ridge, South Dakota: Indian gunmen shoot down a helicopter carrying FBI agents over the Sioux reservation.

July 28–29, Detroit, Michigan: Blacks and police clash for two consecutive nights at a tavern where eighteen year old Obie Wynn was earlier shot and killed by the white proprietor. The tavern owner is charged with second-degree murder, while sixty-three other persons are jailed on riot charges. White motorist Marian Pyszko is dragged from her car and beaten to death by blacks during the riot.

August 12–13, Elyria, Ohio: Rioting flares for two nights after patrolmen shoot a black burglary suspect.

August 14, Riverside, California: An Hispanic mob drags a white motorist from his truck and beats and stabs him. Gunfire erupts when police arrive, leaving two officers and three Hispanics wounded. Gunfire forces down a police helicopter and damages a sheriff's department airplane during the search for the escaped gunmen.

August 16, Greenville, Alabama: Judge Arthur Gamble, who signed murder indictments against three Klansmen in the 1965 Viola Liuzzo case, is injured by a car bomb.

August 21, Wilmington, Delaware: Police use tear gas and arrest two persons when demonstrators protest the release of a white woman on bail for the shooting of a thirteen-year-old black girl.

August 30, Stone Mountain, Georgia: Five men, including two blacks and one Asian, are assaulted and expelled from a KKK convention.

September 5, Louisville, Kentucky: Opponents of school busing riot in two white neighborhoods, leaving fifty persons injured and 200 in jail. National Guard units are deployed on September 6.

September 10, Pine Ridge, South Dakota: AIM supporter Jim Little is stomped to death by four GOONs.

September 14, Castroville, Texas: Hispanic prisoner Richard Morales is taken into an isolated field and murdered by the chief of police. The chief is convicted and sentenced to ten years in jail before FBI agents open a civil rights probe in February 1977. (The chief's wife has also received a year's probation for helping to hide the corpse.) On February 23, 1977, federal civil rights charges are filed against the chief, his wife, and his sister-in-law. All three defendants are convicted on September 29, 1977.

September 19, Dayton, Ohio: Dr. Charles Glatt, employed by the city to prepare plans for local school desegregation, is shot and killed in his office. Police arrest white racist Neal Long, and an FBI investigation links Long to a series of shootings that have killed six Dayton blacks and wounded fourteen others in the early 1970s.

October 27, New York City: FALN bombs strike at four banks and the U.S. mission to the United Nations.

October 27, Chicago, Illinois: The FALN claims credit for bombing one bank and four office buildings.

October 27, Washington, D.C.: An FALN bomb explodes outside the U.S. State Department building.

November, Huntington Park, California: Lorenzo Verdugo, an Hispanic prisoner, is found hanging in his jail cell. A coroner's report states that the cause of death—a ruptured trachea—was not produced by hanging, but appears to have resulted from a beating.

November 1, Anderson, South Carolina: Black youths pelt white motorists with rocks and bottles. Four whites are arrested on charges of attempted murder after wounding four blacks in a drive-by shooting.

November 9, New York City: FALN bombers damage a downtown bank.

November 11, Brooklyn, New York: Firebombs are thrown at two synagogues, a Jewish school, and the homes of two Hasidic Jews in Boro Park, an area where tension has been reported between Jews and Hispanics.

November 17, Oglala, South Dakota: GOON member Jesse Trueblood, also employed as a Bureau of Indian Affairs policeman, fires an automatic rifle into the home of AIM supporter Chester Stone, wounding Stone, three members of his family, and a male visitor. Authorities find Trueblood in his car hours later, dead from a self-inflicted bullet wound.

1976

January 30, Pine Ridge, South Dakota: Sioux attorney Byron De Sersa is killed in a high-speed chase by GOONs on the reservation. GOON leader Dale Janis is convicted of manslaughter and sentenced to two years in prison.

February 24, Wanblee, South Dakota: AIM member Anna Aquash is found outside the reservation village, killed by a gunshot wound to the head.

February 26, Montgomery, Alabama: Four KKK members are indicted for the 1957 murder of black victim Willie Edwards. Charges are dismissed for lack of evidence on April 14.

March 1, Sharps Corners, South Dakota: AIM member Hobart Horse is murdered by unidentified gunmen.

March 14, Brooklyn, New York: Three policemen are injured in an attack by militant Hasidic Jews.

April 6, Boston, Massachusetts: A white youth armed with a pole bearing the U.S. flag beats a black lawyer on the steps of City Hall.

April 19, Boston, Massachusetts: Black youths drag a white motorist from his car and beat him severely, while others stone a railroad crew trying to clear debris from nearby train tracks. On April 21 one suspect is charged in the beating and robbery.

May 6, Wagner, South Dakota: GOONs attack AIM leader Russell Means and one of his followers in a housing project on the Yankton Sioux Reservation.

June 7, Chicago, Illinois: FALN bombs strike two banks, an office building, and police headquarters, wounding five persons.

June 15, Chicago, Illinois: Racial violence erupts after floods and tornados cause white motorists to detour from major highways and through a local black community. Phyllis Anderson is shot dead after her husband refuses to pay black youths $10 to guide his car through a flooded viaduct. At least fifteen other persons are reported injured during the outbreak.

June 25, New York City: FALN terrorists bomb two banks, an office building, and a police precinct house.

July 7, Birmingham, Alabama: Eight whites, including at least one Klansman, are arrested on weapons charges after firing guns in a racially troubled neighborhood. Sporadic violence marked by rock-throwing and assaults has been reported in the area since police killed a black woman at a local convenience store in June.

July 12, New York City: FALN terrorists detonate multiple incendiary devices in six downtown department stores.

July 17, Chicago, Illinois: One hundred fifty civil rights marchers clash with whites in Marquette Park, leaving twenty-eight injured and sixty-two jailed.

August, Douglas, Arizona: A white rancher and his two sons kidnap three Hispanic migrant workers, stripping them naked, slashing them with knives, and burning them with hot irons before they are dragged through the desert. One of the victims is also wounded by buckshot, with another subjected to a mock hanging. A local judge, friendly with the attackers, refuses to issue arrest warrants in the case. The three Anglos are finally indicted on federal charges in 1979, with the father dying before his sons are tried and convicted of civil rights violations in 1981.

August 9, Brooklyn, New York: The bombing of an apartment house leads FBI agents to launch an investigation of local violence between blacks and whites.

August 21, Chicago, Illinois: Eleven persons are arrested during racial clashes in Marquette Park.

September 6, Atlanta, Georgia: Racist Joseph Paul Franklin follows a black man and his white date for ten miles before stopping the couple and spraying them with Mace. The future serial slayer is jailed for assault.

September 8, New York City: White youths armed with pipes, bats, and chains randomly assault nonwhite pedestrians in Washington Square Park. One victim is killed, and thirteen others are injured. Convicted of various charges on May 12, 1978, five of the youths are sentenced to prison terms ranging from three to twenty-five years.

September 21, New York City: FALN bombs strike a downtown hotel.

November 5, New Jersey: The state KKK leader is sentenced to six months in jail for carrying an unlicensed firearm.

November 13, Camp Pendleton, California: Black marines raid a barracks occupied by members of an on-base KKK chapter.

December 6, Camp Pendleton, California: KKK leader David Duke is assaulted by anti-Klan picketers during a public demonstration. Six whites are hospitalized with wounds from clubs and screwdrivers. Fourteen blacks are charged with conspiracy and assault.

1977

February 14, New Rochelle, New York: Suspended from his job after an altercation with a Jewish supervisor, self-styled neo-Nazi Fred Cowan returns to work with a small arsenal, killing five persons and wounding five before he commits suicide. Investigation reveals that Cowan was a member of the violent NSRP.

February 18, New York City: FALN bombs cause extensive damage to the offices of two international oil companies.

March, San Antonio, Texas: Hispanic prisoner Juan Zepeda is beaten to death in police custody.

March 21, New York City: FALN bombs strike the local FBI field office, wounding one pedestrian outside. The Puerto Rican terrorists are credited with fifty-one bombings since August 31, 1974.

April, Los Angeles, California: Three Klansmen are jailed on charges of plotting to kill local JDL leaders. All three are convicted in December 1978.

April 15–17, Elwood, Indiana: A weekend outbreak of Klan violence includes cross-burnings, garbage scattered on lawns, and a shotgun blast fired into the mayor's home.

May, Hudspeth, Texas: Sheriff Claymon McCutcheon beats Hispanic prisoner Juan Zuniga to death with a pool cue in his cell.

Arrested as a drunk, Zuniga enraged the sheriff by weeping in custody.

May 10, Salt Lake City, Utah: Rulon Allred, an excommunicated Mormon and leader of a polygamist splinter group, is murdered by followers of rival cult leader Ervil LeBaron. Six members of LeBaron's Church of the Lamb of God are jailed on September 28.

May 20, Philadelphia, Pennsylvania: Black members of the MOVE nature cult erect armed barricades to prevent health inspectors from touring their garbage-strewn, rat-infested homes. The siege is lifted with a mass surrender on May 7, 1978.

June 1, Brooklyn, New York: A feud between rival Hasidic factions climaxes in street violence and the burning of a Jewish newspaper office.

June 4, Humboldt Park, Illinois: FALN terrorists claim credit for a bombing at the Cook County Building. News of the explosion sparks violence at a nearby Puerto Rico Day celebration, where one member of the crowd opens fire on police, missing his targets and killing a bystander. Police return fire, killing the gunman. Forty-nine people are injured as rioting spreads.

July 2, Plains, Georgia: Motorist Buddy Cochran deliberately steers his car into the crowd at a KKK rally, injuring thirty-nine persons. Convicted of assault on October 28, he is sentenced to twelve years in prison.

July 4, Columbus, Ohio: A KKK rally at the state capitol erupts into violence when hecklers assault Klansmen.

July 4, New York City: Luis Robinson, a U.S. Navy seaman said to be "very upset with the racial situation" in the United States, hijacks a bus at JFK International Airport and demands $6 million and an airplane in which to flee the country. Two hostages are killed before Robinson surrenders.

July 10, Brooklyn, New York: Blacks demonstrate against recent acts of violence committed by Jewish "anti-crime patrols."

July 10, Ramapo Township, New Jersey: Eleven youths are arrested on charges of harassing Hasidic Jews.

July 11–13, Jamesburg, New Jersey: Three nights of racial violence are reported, including cross-burnings, rock-throwing incidents, and assaults.

July 23, Chicago, Illinois: Nineteen persons are injured and twenty-seven are arrested when whites attack black demonstrators in Marquette Park.

July 29, Chattanooga, Tennessee: Racist serial killer Joseph Paul Franklin bombs a local synagogue.

August 7, Madison, Wisconsin: A racially mixed couple, Alphonse Manning and Toni Schwenn, are shot and killed by a sniper. Evidence links the murders to racist serial killer Joseph Paul Franklin.

September 5, Columbus, Ohio: Klansmen battle hecklers at an anti-busing rally.

September 5, Jonesville, North Carolina: A white youth wearing a Nazi armband fires on black picnickers, killing two men and wounding three before he commits suicide. A third victim dies on September 7.

September 24, Mobile, Alabama: Violence erupts between Klansmen and hecklers at a KKK rally.

October, South Tucson, Arizona: Hispanic motorist Joe Sinohui, Jr., is killed by a policeman "firing at his tires" when Sinohui drives away from the scene of a racial disturbance.

October 6, Houston, Texas: Two patrolmen are convicted of negligent homicide in the death of Hispanic prisoner J.C. Campos. On October 7 the officers are fined $1 each, and released on terms of probation. Federal authorities respond on October 21, indicting four policemen on civil rights charges.

October 8, San Jose, California: American Nazi demonstrators are stoned and assaulted by hecklers on the street.

October 8, St. Louis, Missouri: A sniper kills Gerald Gordon as he leaves a bar mitzvah in suburban Richmond Heights. Evidence suggests that racist killer Joseph Paul Franklin is involved.

November 18, Birmingham, Alabama: Ex-KKK member Robert Chambliss is convicted of murder for the 1963 church bombing that killed four black girls and blinded another.

November 18, Wilkes County, Georgia: Four rural black churches are burned by arsonists. A white man pleads guilty on April 28, 1978, and is sentenced to six years in prison.

1978

Salt Lake City, Utah: Rachel Longo, one of several wives claimed by polygamist cult leader Immanual David, hurls seven of their children from the upper story of a downtown hotel before leaping to her death.

January, Boston, Massachusetts: The police department establishes a special Community Disorders Unit to deal with cases of racial violence. By December 31 the unit has investigated 660 reported cases.

January 30, New York City: FALN terrorists bomb a downtown office building and a parked police car.

March 11, St. Louis, Missouri: Police battle protesters during an American Nazi parade.

April 2, Carbon County, Utah: Ervil LeBaron and two members of his polygamist cult are charged with the murder of Robert Simmons. The three members had contested Simmons' leadership.

April 27, Lakeside, California: Everett Henson, a KKK member, is murdered by a fellow Klansman. His killer is sentenced to life on June 15, 1979, in a case authorities describe as drug-related.

May 3, Highland Park, Illinois: Michael Gerschenson is shot and killed by members of De Mau Mau, a black racist group.

May 7, Houston, Texas: Barrio violence erupts on the anniversary of Joe Campos Torres' beating/drowning death at the hands of white policemen. Twelve persons are hospitalized, including two newsmen, and four patrolmen are reported injured.

May 10, Salt Lake City, Utah: A polygamist cult member pleads guilty to the murder of Verlan LeBaron, killed on orders from his brother, cult leader Ervil LeBaron.

May 22, New York City: FALN terrorists detonate bombs at JFK International and LaGuardia airports.

May 22, Newark, New Jersey: The FALN bombs a local airport building.

May 22, Washington, D.C.: FALN terrorists explode a bomb outside the U.S. Department of Justice.

June, Brooklyn, New York: On June 18, black community leader Arthur Miller dies in a struggle with police. Victor Rhoades, a black teenager lying comatose after a beating by Hasidic vigilantes, dies on June 20. A policeman is arrested on June 22 for striking a black during a traffic altercation. On June 23 two Hasidic Jews are charged with the Rhoades homicide.

June 20, Chicago, Illinois: Mau Mau gunmen murder Kathleen Fiene in her home. The Mau Mau were black racists who randomly killed whites.

June 26, Prince Georges County, Maryland: Two white patrolmen are shot and killed by a black looting suspect.

July, Lochearn, Maryland: Three Klansmen are arrested for plotting to bomb a local synagogue and the home of a black congressman. All are convicted.

July 10, Birmingham, Alabama: Former KKK member Gary Rowe says he killed a black man during a 1963 race riot and covered up the crime on orders from FBI agents who paid him to infiltrate the Klan.

July 12, New York City: FALN bombmaker William Morales is injured in an accidental explosion, and afterward jailed on federal weapons charges.

July 16, Plainview, Texas: Federal prosecutors say that they will not charge a white policeman presently serving five years for the 1973 murder of Santos Rodriguez, a twelve-year-old Mexican boy.

July 23, Reidsville, Georgia: Racial violence at the state prison leaves one guard and two white inmates dead. Another guard survives ten stab wounds suffered in the melee.

July 30, Oxnard, California: Three hundred Mexicans brawl with police outside a theater where KKK members are screening *Birth of a Nation.* Dozens are injured and thirteen are arrested.

August 4, Barrington Hills, Illinois: Paul Corbett, his wife, and their daughter are executed in their home by Mau Mau gunmen.

August 8, Philadelphia, Pennsylvania: One patrolman is killed and seven perons are injured when police evict MOVE cultists from their trash-filled commune. A crane is used to level the three-story building.

August 16, Reidsville, Georgia: New racial violence at the state prison leaves one black convict stabbed to death by whites.

September 2, Highland Park, Illinois: Mau Mau gunmen murder William Richter on the street, afterward firing shots at a white truck driver who escapes unharmed.

September 3, Monroe, Illinois: Stephen Hawtree, his wife, and their son are murdered in their home by members of the Mau Mau.

September 9, Grand Island, Nebraska: Two white victims are slain as Mau Mau gunmen invade their home. Eight members of the terrorist clique are jailed by Chicago police in mid-October, ending their reign of terror.

October 15, Boston, Massachusetts: Demonstrators with placards assault two KKK members at a Klan-sponsored anti-busing rally.

October 30, Camp Pendleton, California: A white marine, identified as a member of the KKK, is "accidentally" shot and killed in his barracks by an Hispanic marine.

November 24, Vineland, New Jersey: Twenty-two Klansmen and neo-Nazis are arrested on weapons charges prior to a scheduled public rally. Police seize twenty weapons, including guns, clubs, and knives.

November 26, Algiers, Louisiana: A KKK member is charged with firing shots at policemen after officers were dispatched to investigate complaints of unusual noise at a Klan rally.

December 2, Brooklyn, New York: Angered by the recent stabbing death of an old man in a street robbery, hundreds of Hasidic Jews invade a local police station, led by a rabbi and a Jewish member of the state assembly. Sixty-two officers and eight demonstrators are injured in the resultant clash.

1979

January 7, Brooklyn, New York: Five Hasidic Jews are arrested for their roles in the December 1978 attack on a local police station. One of the defendants is fined $250 for damages to city property on February 22.

January 18, Utah: Polygamist cult leader John Singer is shot and killed by police while resisting arrest on charges of refusing to send his numerous children to public school.

February 23, Queens, New York: A white man is convicted of burning a cross at the home of a black neighbor.

April–May, Decatur, Alabama: A robed KKK member is shot and wounded while "patrolling" a black neighborhood. On May 3 shots are fired into a white home, and gunman shoot at a black family's home on May 5. Local tensions have mounted since the arrest of a retarded black man on charges of raping three white women, with Klansmen using the incident for publicity to launch a membership drive. On May 26, four persons are wounded by gunshots, including two KKK members and a black woman. On May 28 a black man is charged with wounding the Klansman shot on April 29. By May 29 three KKK members are charged with assaulting police in the May 26 melee.

April 4, Birmingham, Alabama: Twenty-one KKK members—including a policeman—are indicted for firing shots into the homes of interracial couples and NAACP members in Childersburg and Sylacauga. Twelve of those charged are convicted on June 14.

April 14, Selma, Alabama: Klansmen and blacks clash during a KKK parade.

May 20, Red Lake, Minnesota: An Indian occupation of the Chippewa Reservation law enforcement center erupts into gunfire and arson. Two persons are killed during the outbreak, and two stores, two homes, several government buildings, and dozens of cars are destroyed by fire.

May 26, Decatur, Alabama: Four persons are hospitalized, three of them with gunshot wounds, after Klansmen and blacks clash. The riot occurs during street demonstrations over the case of a retarded black man recently convicted of rape.

June 4, Birmingham, Alabama: Loyal Bailey, prosecution witness in the upcoming trial of seventeen Klansmen, is found dead near the federal courthouse. A KKK member is charged with his murder on June 5.

June 4, Attica, New York: A white inmate is stabbed to death at the state prison during a racial brawl involving sixty convicts. The riot was provoked by the stabbing of a black inmate.

June 13, Lake County, Illinois: Mau Mau defendants Nathaniel Burse and Edward Moran are strangled in their cells by persons unknown. Six other defendants in the series of racist murders are later convicted and sentenced to life.

June 18–20, Philadelphia, Pennsylvania: Three days of violence follow the fatal shooting of a black youth by city police officers.

June 25, Birmingham, Alabama: Officers break up a protest march sparked by the fatal police shooting of Bonita Carter, a black woman, on June 22. The shooting followed Carter's violent argument with a white gas station proprietor. New violence erupts on July 5, when a group of whites—including KKK members—are arrested for bullying blacks on July 6.

June 30, Vineland, New Jersey: Two KKK members are charged with raping a female member of the JDL, whom they caught spying on one of their chapter meetings. Both defendants are acquitted on March 1, 1980.

July 19, Birmingham, Alabama: Two white gunmen are jailed for firing shots into black homes.

July 22, Doraville, Georgia: Black victim Harold McIver is killed by sniper fire at a local cafe. Evidence points to the involvement of racist serial killer Joseph Paul Franklin.

August 11, Selma, Alabama: Weapons are confiscated and eleven persons are arrested during a KKK demonstration.

August 19, Castro Valley, California: One person suffers a head injury when Klansmen and hecklers clash.

September 13–14, Plainfield, New Jersey: White assaults on six area blacks touch off two nights of sporadic violence.

September 25, Plainfield, New Jersey: Two white men appear in court and are charged with firing shots at a black family's home.

October 21, Oklahoma City, Oklahoma: Jessie Taylor and Marion Bresette, a racially mixed couple, are shot and killed in a parking lot. Racist serial slayer Joseph Paul Franklin is later charged in the case, but indictments are dismissed in January 1983.

November 3, Greensboro, North Carolina: Members of the Revolutionary Communist Party stage a "Death to the Klan" rally, seeking publicity for their cause. Armed Klansmen and American Nazis attack the marchers, killing four and wounding eight in a burst of gunfire recorded by television news cameras. A fifth wounded marcher dies of his wounds on November 5. Thirteen white supremacists are indicted for murder on December 13.

November 24, Vineland, New Jersey: Twenty-two Klansmen and U.S. Nazis are arrested on weapons charges prior to a scheduled public demonstration.

November 29, Metairie, Louisiana: KKK leader David Duke is sentenced to six months (suspended) and one year probation following his conviction for inciting a riot in 1976.

December 17, Miami, Florida: Black motorcyclist Arthur McDuffie is hospitalized in critical condition after an altercation with police. He dies on December 21, with authorities describing his wounds as the result of a high-speed chase and crash. Four officers are indicted for murder when other patrolmen describe McDuffie's beating while in custody. All four are acquitted in May 1980.

1980

January, Muscle Shoals, Alabama: Two Klansmen plead guilty to assaulting black ministers in a local restaurant.

January 1, St. Paul, Minnesota: A black family's New Year's party is invaded and disrupted by a white mob.

January 8, Indianapolis, Indiana: Racist sniper Joseph Paul Franklin kills Larry Reese, a black man, at a local fast-food restaurant.

January 14, Indianapolis, Indiana: Joseph Paul Franklin kills his second black victim in a week, gunning Lee Watkins down at a neighborhood market.

January 17, Greensboro, North Carolina: Fourteen whites are indicted in the shooting deaths of five victims at an anti-KKK rally in November 1979. Only six defendants remain by November 17, and they are all acquitted of murder charges.

January 20, Idabel, Oklahoma: Rioting erupts after a black youth is killed near a whites-only private club. Police report $100,000 property damage during the outbreak, which leaves two people dead and at least four injured. A white man is charged with first-degree murder in the original victim's death.

February, Dutton, Alabama: An interracial couple is assaulted by whites.

February 5, Oakland, California: Darline Cromer, a white woman, admits strangling Reginald Williams, a five-year-old black, expressing her belief that "it was the duty of every white woman to kill a nigger child."

February 17, Barnegat, New Jersey: Police seek a teenage KKK organizer on charges of firing shots into a neighbor's home. Police recover an arsenal from his attic.

February 27, Brooklyn, New York: Two Hasidic Jews are acquitted on charges of beating a black youth unconscious in 1978.

March, Hayden, Alabama: A KKK member is indicted for raiding the home of a racially mixed couple and injuring a black man in the attack.

March 3, Orlando, Florida: Twenty armed men disrupt a KKK rally, firing shots at Klansmen as they flee. Police arrive to find two Klansmen handcuffed and badly beaten. One of the raiders is arrested.

March 15, Oceanside, California: Thirty Klansmen brawl with 150 hecklers when a KKK rally erupts into violence.

April, Jersey City, New Jersey: Bombs explode at the local office of Jesse Jackson's Operation PUSH.

April 1, North Carolina: The KKK grand dragon and one of his followers are sentenced to prison for cross-burning.

April 8, Wrightsville, Georgia: Rioting by whites erupts when two hundred whites attack a group of black demonstrators. Buildings are set on fire in the black neighborhood, and whites trade gunfire with blacks. A nine-year-old black child is shot and wounded by two Klansmen following a black demonstration on April 19.

April 19, Chattanooga, Tennessee: Three Klansmen are arrested after firing into a crowd of blacks and wounding five women. One Klansman is acquitted on July 22, and two others are convicted on reduced charges. The outcome of their trial sparks three nights of racial violence in Chattanooga.

April 22, Wichita, Kansas: Two hundred blacks riot after an altercation between a white patrolman and a black civilian at a laundromat.

April 29, Las Vegas, Nevada: The home of black comedian Redd Foxx is vandalized with KKK graffiti.

May, New Britain, Connecticut: Klansmen are blamed for acts of racist vandalism in this town.

May 2, Greensboro, North Carolina: Eight persons are indicted on riot charges from the anti-Klan rally held in November 1979. Scuffles erupt in court on June 16 as the trial begins.

May 3, Boston, Massachusetts: William Kelly, a black man, is murdered by white youths in the mostly white Charlestown district. One of his attackers is jailed on May 4.

May 3, Tomah, Wisconsin: Racist serial killer Joseph Paul Franklin murders Rebecca Bergstrom and dumps her body outside of town.

May 17–19, Miami, Florida: Sixteen persons are killed, 300 are injured, and nearly 1,000 are arrested during black rioting sparked by the acquittal of four policemen charged with murder in the 1979 death of Arthur McDuffie, a black man. Miami is declared a disaster area in the wake of the riots, with property damage estimated at $100 million. Five police officers involved in the outbreak are suspended for various acts of misconduct on May 22.

May 19, Wrightsville, Georgia: Three persons are shot—including a policeman, a fireman, and a white civilian—during rioting by blacks. At least twenty-five persons are arrested. Blacks accuse the police of indiscriminately breaking into homes to search for snipers.

May 20, Tampa, Florida: Police seal off black neighborhoods during a second night of rioting sparked by violence in Miami. A white patrolman is wounded by sniper fire on May 21 while erecting a street barricade to divert traffic.

May 22, Wrightsville, Georgia: A black man is shot and critically wounded by white gunmen on a highway outside of town.

May 29, Ft. Wayne, Indiana: Vernon Jordan, black leader of the National Urban League, is wounded by a sniper while sitting in a parked car with a white woman outside a local motel. Racist serial killer Joseph Paul Franklin is charged in the case, but is later acquitted.

June 8, Cincinnati, Ohio: Two blacks, Darrell Land and Dante Brown, are killed by sniper fire while crossing a railroad trestle. Evidence points to racist killer Joseph Paul Franklin as the gunman.

June 10, San Francisco, California: A local theater is mobbed and vandalized for showing *The Birth of a Nation*, a film that glamorizes the original KKK.

June 15, Johnstown, Pennsylvania: Arthur Smothers, a black man, and his white fiancee, Kathleen Mikula, are killed by shotgun blasts. Racist serial killer Joseph Paul Franklin is later charged with the murders.

June 16, Greensboro, North Carolina: Three members of the Communist Workers Party are arrested during courtroom clashes with police at the trial of Klansmen accused of killing party members in November 1979.

June 24, Long Beach, New York: Two hundred black and white youths brawl in the street following an exchange of racial slurs at a sports event. At least three persons are injured, including two policemen, and three people are arrested.

Summer, Boston, Massachusetts: A black soldier is assaulted and stabbed by whites. In a separate incident, bombs damage a black family's home.

July, Forsyth County, Georgia: White gunmen fire shots at a black fireman during a picnic.

July, Muncie, Indiana: A bomb damages a black-owned home.

July, Chicago, Illinois: A white mob stones the home of an elderly black woman.

July, Indianapolis, Indiana: A home is bombed and eight black people are killed. Klansman Clifford Redwine is arrested after boasting that he had "killed eight niggers."

July 1, Fontana, California: A black telephone lineman is wounded by a white gunman in an unprovoked drive-by shooting.

July 4, Wrightsville, Georgia: Mike Salter, an elderly civil rights activist, is murdered. Unofficial reports state that "KKK" was scrawled on his body.

July 13, Flint, Michigan: Five hundred blacks stone policemen investigating the shooting of two nightclub employees in an apparent holdup. Tension has increased since the death of a black youth, shot by a white policeman. The latest outbreak leaves two patrolmen and one civilian injured.

July 15–17, Miami, Florida: Five patrolmen are shot and wounded, and fifteen others are injured during black rioting. Violence erupts after police try to arrest robbery suspects at a housing project in the Liberty City section and continues for two more nights despite the imposition of a curfew on July 16.

July 22–24, Chattanooga, Tennessee: Black protest marches are banned after stones and firebombs are hurled at buildings, cars, and firetrucks the previous night. A curfew is posted on July 24, but the violence continues, leaving eight policemen shot and wounded. More than fifty persons are arrested.

July 29–31, Orlando, Florida: Blacks riot for three nights, hurling rocks and firebombs, following the arrest of a black man in a local bar.

August, Detroit, Michigan: Klansmen fire shotguns at a black man in a drive-by shooting. On learning that he is not hurt, the gunmen return, and shoot at his home.

August 1, Boston, Massachusetts: Five persons are injured and one is arrested when black youths stone white motorists outside a low-income housing project.

August 4, Greensboro, North Carolina: The widows of two communists killed in November 1979 are arrested for disrupting the trial of Klansmen charged in the case.

August 20, Salt Lake City, Utah: Racist serial killer Joseph Paul Franklin fatally shoots two black joggers, David Martin and Ted Fields. He is sentenced to life for the crime on September 23, 1981.

August 26, Philadelphia, Pennsylvania: Five hundred protesters demonstrate outside police headquarters after the fatal shooting of a black youth by a white patrolman. Seven policemen and one fireman are injured, and similar outbreaks are recorded on August 27. Murder charges are filed against the officer in question on August 29.

September, Polk County, Georgia: Ramirio Lopez is shot and killed by white gunmen. Three years later, "persons unknown" murder Tyrus Cazzort, the prosecution's star witness.

September, Windham County, Connecticut: Klansmen and hecklers clash on the highway near a KKK rally, leaving six persons injured and eight in custody.

September 3, New Orleans, Louisiana: Police officers pursuing a hit-and-run suspect are driven from a local housing project by angry blacks. Tension has run high in the neighborhood since two officers shot and killed a black man in the project on September 1.

September 16, San Diego, California: Klansman and political candidate Tom Metzger is the target of an assassination attempt at one of his campaign rallies by an anti-Klan assailant armed with a pistol.

September 20, Orange County, Florida: Two KKK leaders are acquitted on charges of beating three dissident Klansmen.

September 22, Buffalo, New York: Glenn Dunn, a black man, is shot and killed by a white gunman outside a local market.

September 23, Buffalo, New York: Two more black men, Harold Green and Emmanuel Thomas, are shot in separate attacks by a gunman using the same weapon used to kill Glenn Dunn.

September 24, Niagara Falls, New York: A black man, Joseph McCoy, is fatally shot. The killing is linked to the deaths of black men on September 22 and 23 in nearby Buffalo, and the murderer is dubbed the ".22-caliber killer."

October, Manchester, Connecticut: A black-owned home is firebombed.

October, St. Paul, Minnesota: Two white men attempt to abduct black children in a racially tense neighborhood, striking one child with a club when he runs away.

October, Bennington, Vermont: Three white men abduct and stab a black teenager.

October 10, Buffalo, New York: Collin Cole, a black man, is assaulted and nearly strangled in his hospital bed by a white man matching descriptions of the ".22-caliber killer," whom police believe is responsible for the deaths of black men in Buffalo on September 22 and 23 and in Niagara Falls on September 24.

October 22, Powderly, Alabama: Police defuse a bomb planted at a local black church.

October 31, Youngstown, Ohio: White gunmen fire at two black girls as they walk home from a party, narrowly missing both. As the gunmen round a streetcorner, they open fire on two black adults, killing Vernoica Vaughn.

November, Pensacola, Florida: Three blacks are assaulted by white men armed with iron pipes and sharpened pieces of steel. The leader of the attack is identified as a KKK member.

November, Tara Hills, California: Black families are the targets of violent harassment that includes armed assaults, shotgun blasts fired into homes, and near-miss hit-and-run attacks on pedestrians. Burning gasoline is dumped on one family's lawn on December 2. Three days later a white youth is arrested for deliberately ramming a car parked outside a black resident's home.

November, Jackson, Mississippi: Black students on a school bus are tear-gassed by two white youths, one of whom is the son of a KKK member.

November, Harvey County, Missouri: Stephen Harvey, a black musician, is beaten to death in Liberty Memorial Park by a bat-wielding white man.

November, Detroit, Michigan: Three Klansmen plead guilty to shooting a black man who entered a "white" tavern. A fourth KKK member pleads guilty to harassing a black family in nearby Romulus in an attempt to drive them from their home.

November, Port Jefferson, New York: A mob of stone-throwing whites besiege and vandalize a black woman's home.

November, Norfolk, Virginia: A white man is convicted of burning a cross at the home of an interracial couple.

November 8, Algiers, Louisiana: White patrolman Gregory Neupert is shot and killed at a black housing project. Officers kill four blacks—including one woman—during their search for suspects in the case.

November 19, Maiden, North Carolina: One of the Greensboro murder defendants from the November 1979 deaths of communist worker party members trades shots with an unknown gunman at his home.

December, Tuscaloosa, Alabama: James Herrod, Jr., a twelve-year-old black boy, is beaten to death at a housing project where racial tensions have run high. His body is discovered in March 1981. Shots are fired at search parties hunting for the child, and a cross is burned at the project shortly before the discovery of Herrod's body.

December, San Pablo, California: A black woman's home is set on fire by whites. Assaults are reported against an Hispanic person and the wife of a politician running for office against a KKK member.

Informants report that local Klansmen boast of decapitating an unidentified Hispanic.

December, West Palm Beach, Florida: A black man is shot and wounded by white youths.

December, Montgomery County, Maryland: The Maryland Human Rights Commission logs twenty-five acts of racist violence in the area during 1980.

December 14, Los Angeles, California: Two American Nazis are arrested for the predawn arson fire that caused $100,000 damage to Temple Beth David.

December 22, New York City: Racist serial killer Joe Christopher, the ".22-caliber killer," stabs five blacks and one Latino victim in separate attacks that span thirteen hours. Four of his victims die.

December 29, Rochester, New York: A black man, Wendell Barnes, is stabbed to death by an assailant matching Joe Christopher's description.

December 30, Buffalo, New York: Albert Menefee, a black man, is wounded in an unprovoked stabbing assault by Joe Christopher, the ".22-caliber killer."

1981

January, Contra Costa County, California: The home of an interracial couple is vandalized with KKK graffiti and a sledge hammer is thrown through a window.

January 1, Smithburg, West Virginia: Methodist Rev. Michael Curry is reportedly in hiding after a six-month reign of terror that began when he refused to let the KKK hold meetings in his church.

January 1, Buffalo, New York: Black victims Larry Little and Calvin Crippen are wounded in separate stabbing incidents. Their assailant matches descriptions of racist serial killer Joe Christopher, the ".22-caliber killer."

January 6, Miami, Florida: Trial opens in the case of four blacks charged with beating and stomping three white victims to death during a 1980 riot. Charges are dismissed against two of the defendants on March 11. The other defendants are convicted on March 26 and receive long prison terms.

January 6, Ft. Benning, Georgia: Federal agents announce a break in the recent New York murders after Pvt. Joe Christopher is arrested for stabbing a black soldier on the post.

February, Tuscaloosa, Alabama: Shots are fired into a black-owned home.

February, Contra Costa County, California: Blacks and Hispanics are reportedly the targets of two vandalism incidents, an assault, and an arson attack.

February, Denver, Colorado: A local KKK leader is charged with harassing and threatening a black family.

February 25, Salt Lake City, Utah: A bomb scare disrupts the murder trial of racist serial killer Joseph Paul Franklin.

February 28, Queens, New York: Five white youths are charged with attempted murder after trying to run down three black women with their car.

March 1, Brooklyn, New York: Hundreds of Hasidic Jews stone a rival synagogue.

March 21, Mobile, Alabama: Michael Donald, a black teenager, is found hanged from a tree. One member of the KKK is convicted and sentenced to death for the murder, and another KKK member is jailed for life.

Spring, Jefferson County, Kentucky: A black youth is assaulted by a white teenager affiliated with the local "Junior Klan."

Spring, Montgomery County, Maryland: Authorities report twelve cases of racially motivated vandalism, assault, and harassment.

April, Merced, California: A KKK member is convicted of boarding a school bus and menacing an interracial group of students with a gun.

April, Hamilton, Georgia: Four whites abduct and threaten a black man.

April 1, Sacramento, California: One person is arrested when Klansmen and hecklers clash at a KKK rally.

April 11, Barnegat Township, New Jersey: Two ex-Klansmen are sentenced to six months for shooting at a black home.

April 11, San Jose, California: Twenty-three people are arrested for stoning KKK demonstrators.

April 16, Queens, New York: Patrolman John Scaranella is killed in an ambush, his partner wounded. A black militant suspect, also linked with a major robbery in October, is indicted for murder on January 9, 1982.

May, San Bernadino, California: A black coed's dormitory room is set on fire following a series of racist death threats.

May, Roslyn, Pennsylvania: White racists attempt to bomb the homes of a black family and their white next-door neighbors.

May, Brooklyn, New York: A black woman narrowly escapes injury while being shot at by white gunmen.

May 14, Houston, Texas: A federal court orders Klansmen and local fishermen to cease the harassment of Vietnamese refugees on the Gulf Coast. The KKK is specifically ordered to halt "armed boat patrols" in which robed Klansmen brandish weapons to intimidate the Asian fishermen.

May 27–28, Nashville, Tennessee: FBI agents arrest six Klansmen for conspiring to bomb a synagogue, a television tower, and several Jewish businesses.

Summer, Atkinson County, Georgia: Following threats from the KKK against "race-mixing trash," shots are fired at the homes and cars of interracial families on at least three occasions.

June 4, Petros, Tennessee: James Earl Ray, convicted and sentenced to ninety-nine years in prison for the murder of Martin Luther King, is stabbed by a black inmate at the state prison.

July, Rodeo, California: The sheriff blames Klansmen for firing shots into a black housing project.

July, Massachusetts: A pipe bomb is found at an NAACP office.

July, West Babylon, New York: A Puerto Rican family returns from vacation to find their home and yard extensively vandalized, including KKK hate messages.

July, Rhode Island: Racists steal and burn the car of an NAACP official, then phone a warning to him: "Nigger, you're next."

July, Suffolk County, New York: A black home is firebombed by white racists, and a cross is burned nearby.

July 9, New Orleans, Louisiana: Federal authorities indict seven white policemen on civil rights charges stemming from the beating and harassment of four black men suspected of killing an officer in November 1980. Three of the officers are convicted and sentenced on March 28, 1983, to five years without parole.

July 11, Meriden, Connecticut: Two persons are injured and four are arrested after a mob attacks a local KKK meeting.

July 11, Miami, Florida: Calm is reported after a violent melee between police and blacks. One resident, Thaddis Jackson, is shot dead by patrolmen.

August 5, Miami, Florida: A white man is charged with killing a black during the 1980 riots. Charges are dismissed on January 18, 1982.

August 29, Baltimore, Maryland: A local KKK leader is convicted of attempting to bomb an NAACP office.

September, Clayton County, Georgia: Authorities log four incidents of racist vandalism against blacks.

September 26, Baltimore, Maryland: A KKK leader is sentenced to fifteen years in federal prison for attempting to firebomb the local NAACP headquarters.

October, Bakersfield, California: Racist vandals terrorize a black family in a previosly all-white neighborhood, burning a cross on their lawn and hurling a pumpkin through a window of their home. The attacks continue through December, with reports of the house being stoned, trees cut down, and fireworks set off late at night.

October 21, Nyack, New York: Two policemen and a security guard are killed in the robbery of a Brink's armored truck conducted by black and white radicals that include former members of the BLA and the Black Panther Party.

October 23, Queens, New York: An ex-Black Panther is killed by police and a companion is wounded when police corner the suspects for the Brink's robbery on October 21.

October 29, Trenton, New Jersey: A local physician is arrested for plotting to kill one of his sons who has testified against his brother, a Klansman, in a February 1980 shooting incident at Barnegat. Black neighbors were the target of the shooting which resulted in three arrests and the discovery of an arsenal at the young KKK member's home.

November 22, Meriden, Connecticut: Twenty-five persons are injured, including nineteen patrolmen, when protesters assault the participants in a KKK rally.

December, Talladega, Alabama: A Klansman is charged with stabbing three blacks.

December, Jackson, Mississippi: Klansmen fire thirty-two shots into a local newspaper office.

December, Pipe, Wisconsin: Members of the Posse Comitatus burn a Department of Natural Resources building at Columbia Park.

December 8, Walton County, Georgia: Lynn Jackson, a black soldier missing since August, is found hanging from a tree. Despite persuasive evidence of lynching, his death is ruled a suicide.

December 9–10, Gainesville, Florida: Rioting flares for two nights after police wound a black youth during of a drug arrest.

December 12, Detroit, Michigan: Four Klansmen are sentenced to prison for firing shots into a black resident's home and plotting to burn another black family's home.

December 16, Yuma, Arizona: A Klansman from San Bernadino, California, is held as a fugitive from justice pending his extradition on charges of arson, assault with a deadly weapon, and issuing terrorist threats.

December 19, Clearwater, Florida: White supremacist Harold Reifsnyder is sentenced to thirty years for murder and assault following his conviction for a September 1981 attack on two black men.

1982

January, Jackson, Mississippi: Two Klansmen are charged with firing eighty-four shots into a newspaper office.

January, Iredell County, North Carolina: Fifteen Klansmen attempt to "bail out" a black rape suspect, but he rejects their offer.

January 3, Raleigh, North Carolina: Robed Klansmen protest the recent conviction of their regional leader in a firebombing case.

January 5: The ADL reports that anti-Semitic incidents have more than doubled in 1981, increasing for the third consecutive year.

January 22, Jackson, Mississippi: A KKK member surrenders on charges of firing shots into a black newspaper office.

February, Atlanta, Georgia: Frederick York, a black man, is found hanging from a tree downtown. The initial ruling of suicide is later reversed.

February, Knoxville, Tennessee: Two white gunmen invade a black neighborhood, threatening a child and shooting at a school bus before they are disarmed.

February, Springfield, Missouri: Racist serial killer Joseph Paul Franklin is stabbed fifteen times in prison. He survives the attack and refuses to name his assailants.

February, North Carolina: White racists fire on black homes in Iredell and Alexander counties.

February, Cleveland, Ohio: Nazi Frank Spisak launches a series of "search and destroy" missions, killing three blacks and one Jew before his September arrest. Prior to his August 1983 conviction and death sentence, the leader of a neo-Nazi splinter group announces that Spisak was "acting under orders from the party." His instructions: "Kill niggers until the last one is dead."

February 8, Petros, Tennessee: Two black inmates are killed and two are injured in attacks by white convicts at the state prison. Armed with a pistol, the whites take four guards as hostages, relieve them of their keys, and then shoot the black prisoners in their cells.

February 20, Monroe, Georgia: Demonstrators demand an investigation into unsolved black deaths dating from 1946, including one that was ruled a suicide in December 1981.

February 27, Chattanooga, Tennessee: Federal jurors award $5.35 million in damages to five blacks shot and wounded by Klansmen during three nights of rioting in 1980.

February 28, Brooklyn, New York: Arson destroys a Hasidic school and synagogue.

March, Baltimore County, Maryland: Two black men are assaulted by a pair of knife-wielding Klansmen. One black family leaves the county after repeated incidents of racist vandalism.

March 7, Miami, Florida: Ira Picket is convicted of murder and arson in the death of a 1980 black riot victim.

March 13, Dorchester, Massachusetts: White youths attack William Atkinson, a black man, and his white companion on the street, pursuing Atkinson until he is struck and killed by a train. A bystander is assaulted in the same incident, which results in several arrests.

April, Burke County, North Carolina: Ranson Connelly, an elderly black motorist, is shot and killed by a white driver

April 16, Houston, Texas: Seven patrolmen are fired and six are suspended for beating blacks at a party in November 1981.

April 17, Limestone County, Texas: Jurors acquit three former deputies charged with drowning three black youths in June 1981. The victims were in custody when a police boat capsized on Lake Mexia.

April 24, Hannibal, Missouri: Black protesters violently disrupt a KKK rally.

March, New Hampshire: A Puerto Rican child is struck and killed by a car. Driver Gerald Gerlock is convicted of manslaughter after witnesses describe him as deliberately swerving the car toward his target.

May, Cobb County, Georgia: A group of blacks and American Indians are assaulted by armed Klansmen in a national park. In 1983 one assailant pleads guilty and two others are convicted in federal court.

May, Seattle, Washington: Wendell Dixon, a black man, is beaten by a white gang that includes two Klansmen.

May, Brooklyn, New York: Three black men are assaulted by a white mob.

May, Gloucester, Rhode Island: The Guardian Knights of Justice, a white supremacist group, violently harass a local resident with gunfire and bombing attempts.

May, Milton, Massachusetts: Arson destroys the Torahs at a local synagogue.

May 6, Denham Springs, Louisiana: The local NAACP asks Louisiana's governor to investigate the "nightrider, KKK-type" murder of a black man.

June, North Carolina: White gunmen fire on an interracial couple, killing Curtis Anderson, a black man, and wounding his white girlfriend.

June, Cumberland County, North Carolina: Gunmen fire eight shots at an officer investigating cross-burnings at a black housing project.

June, Burlington, Vermont: Whites hurl a bottle at Melvin Smith, a black man targeted by racist threats in recent weeks.

June, Louisville, Kentucky: Two women—a Puerto Rican and a white with dark-skinned children—are hospitalized after assaults by white men claiming to be KKK members.

June, Menomonie, Wisconsin: Sani Tela, a Nigerian student, is beaten to death after dating a white woman.

June 1, Boston, Massachusetts: Several black families abandon their Dorchester homes following incidents of racial violence.

June 19, Detroit, Michigan: Vincent Chin, a Chinese-American, is beaten to death by a white father and son who reportedly mistook him for Japanese. The father and son blamed the Japenese for the loss of U.S. jobs. The killers are sentenced to three years probation and fines of $3,000 each in 1983. A later trial on federal civil rights charges ends in acquittal.

June 21, Brooklyn, New York: Three black transit workers are attacked on the street by a gang of twenty whites. One of the victims, William Turks, is fatally injured.

July, Knoxville, Tennessee: Klansmen are accused of burning a black family's home.

July, Dallas, Texas: A Cambodian refugee is murdered by whites.

July, Alexander County, North Carolina: Nightriders fire on a black home.

July, Stevens Point, Wisconsin: Three Nigerian men are assaulted by whites.

July, Meridian, Mississippi: Beverly Parnell, a black teenager missing since June, is found dead in an abandoned warehouse with KKK graffiti painted on the floor beside her body.

September, Chico, California: Joseph Hoover, a white teenager, is shot and killed for giving police information on an NSWPP splinter group, the Chico Area National Socialists. A leader of the faction is convicted of the murder.

September, Edinburgh, Indiana: Frank McGrone, a black Job Corps supervisor, is abducted by whites and branded with "KKK" on his chest and a single "K" on his forehead. Earlier in the same month, McGrone's house and car had been set on fire in separate incidents.

September, Montgomery County, Maryland: Authorities log incidents of shooting and vandalism aimed at Jewish residents.

September 30, Oroville, California: A black teenager disappears and his body is discovered on October 13 with two bullet wounds in the skull. A local nazi activist is charged with the murder.

October, Baltimore County, Maryland: Incidents of vandalism and arson against black families are reported.

October, Buchanan, Michigan: A black woman's apartment and car are firebombed in two separate attacks.

October, Oxford, Mississippi: Five cases of physical harassment against blacks are reported during a controversy over displays of Confederate symbols at the state university.

October 14, Boston, Massachusetts: A Klan leader is pelted with eggs and fighting breaks out in the audience during the broadcast of a live television program.

October 23, Miracle Valley, Arizona: Two persons are killed and nine are wounded during a shoot-out between deputies and members of the all-black Christ Miracle Healing Center and Church. The violence erupts when officers try to serve traffic warrants on three cult members, and 100 blacks rush to the attack with firearms, clubs, and other weapons.

November, Amelia County, Virginia: KKK leader William Church is charged with raping a seven-year-old girl.

November, North Carolina: The White Knights of Liberty launch a two-month campaign of terror against black families that includes gunfire attacks on four homes.

November 23, Waco, Georgia: A white woman, Peggy French, is beaten for socializing with black friends. On December 18, 1984, three KKK members are sentenced to forty years for the assault and for the flogging of a black man who married a white woman.

December, Colorado Springs, Colorado: A KKK member is convicted of robbery.

December, Salem, Oregon: Fire guts the home of an interracial couple. Graffiti painted on a nearby fence reads: "KKK Merry Christmas Niggers."

December, Oakdale, Louisiana: A local Klan leader launches a two-month campaign of terrorism against an interracial couple. On April 3, 1984, a KKK member draws three years in federal prison for his role in plotting the harassment.

December, DeKalb County, Georgia: A Klansman fires rifle shots at blacks in a restaurant, wounding one man.

December, Montgomery County, Maryland: The Human Rights Commission reports 185 incidents of racist vandalism and harassment in 1982.

December 7, Chicago, Illinois: Three whites are indicted on federal charges for firebomb attacks on the home of a suburban black family.

December 28–31, Miami, Florida: Violence flares for two hours after a black, Nevell Johnson, Jr., is accidentally shot and killed by police chasing narcotics suspects in an amusement arcade. One looter is killed in the riot, and twenty-six persons are reported injured. Forty-three people are arrested, and property damage is estimated at $50,000. The officer who shot Johnson is acquitted of reckless conduct on March 15, 1984.

December 31, New York City: The FALN detonates four bombs, including one at police headquarters and another at the federal courthouse in Brooklyn. One patrolman loses a leg, and two others are injured.

1983

January 12, Memphis, Tennessee: Members of a black religious cult take two police officers hostage, torturing one of them to death before raiders storm the house on January 13. Cult leader Lindbergh Sanders, a former mental patient, is shot to death with six of his followers in the ensuing battle.

February, Tallapoosa, Georgia: Six masked men invade an interracial family's home, beating Warren Cokely, a black man. Four KKK members are later convicted on federal charges.

February, Sturgis, Indiana: A Klansman is arrested for the armed harassment of a local woman.

February 1, Dublin, Georgia: A federal jury rejects the $21.3 million suit filed by blacks against the local sheriff and ten whites accused of leading a mob that attacked civil rights demonstrators outside the courthouse in 1980.

February 17, Miami, Florida: A white policeman is indicted for manslaughter in the 1982 death of black prisoner Nevell Johnson, Jr.

February 19, Austin, Texas: At least ten persons are injured when police and demonstrators clash at a KKK rally.

March 13, Miami, Florida: Rioting erupts after police try to break up a loud party in the Liberty City section. Thirty-one persons are arrested and three are injured when officers clash with looters. Twenty more arrests are recorded in similar incidents on March 14.

April, Cedartown, Georgia: Casiano Zamudio, an Hispanic, is murdered, and his killer, a white man, acquitted despite several eyewitness accounts of the crime.

April 2, Houston, Texas: Eggs are hurled and six persons arrested when violence erupts at a KKK rally.

April 10, Montgomery, Alabama: Blacks stone police cars after a white detective wounds a black suspect.

May, Davis, California: Whites mob four Vietnamese students at Davis High School, beating them and fatally stabbing Thong Hy Huynh.

May, Miami, Florida: A Cuban radical group, Omega 7, claims responsibility for bombing a local bank.

May, Ceres, California: Arsonists attempt to burn a black woman's home.

May 22, Farmington, Connecticut: Three persons are arrested when anti-Klan zealots assault KKK members. Three patrolmen are injured.

June, Rowland Heights, California: Two Native American lesbians are the targets of vandalism, arson, and two separate assaults.

June, Buford, Georgia: White men try to abduct the mulatto child of a black woman who has been threatened by racists.

June, Polk County, Georgia: A Hispanic man is assaulted by three whites, and shots are fired into a restaurant patronized by Hispanics.

June 20, Brooklyn, New York: Rabbi Mendel Wechter is forced into a van and shorn of his beard in an attack that leaves him with a broken ankle. Wechter blames members of a rival Hasidic sect, who have allegedly harassed Satmar and Lubavitcher Jews in the area since May.

June 22, New York City: Gunmen wound three Jewish students in a drive-by shooting that police describe as "a bias incident."

June 25, New Britain, Connecticut: Four persons are jailed during anti-KKK violence.

July, Cobb County, Georgia: Authorities report racist vandalism and harassment aimed at black families.

July, Santee, California: White racists vandalize the home of a black policeman.

July, Muscogee County, Georgia: White racists bomb three black churches and a black woman's home.

July, Greeley, Colorado: A black woman is terrorized during the night by white youths shouting and throwing fireworks at her home.

July 4, Brooklyn, New York: A Jewish yeshiva is firebombed. A teenager is charged on July 6.

July 7, Texas: Morris Moss, a white man, is charged with burning six black churches in the central part of the state.

July 8, Allegan, Michigan: Police remove sixty-six children from the House of Judah religious commune, where a twelve-year-old boy has been beaten to death for refusing to do his chores. Authorities say at least ten other children were also abused by the cult.

July 28, Montgomery, Alabama: The Southern Poverty Law Center is damaged by a fire allegedly set by members of the KKK to destroy Project Klanwatch legal records in pending lawsuits.

August, Carroll County, Georgia: Two black men are abducted by three armed whites after a KKK rally. Vandalism is reported at the homes of two black families.

August, Bloomington, Indiana: CSA members burn a Jewish community center.

August 11, West Hartford, Connecticut: Arsonists damage a synagogue.

September 16, Asheville, North Carolina: Six American Nazis are convicted following their third trial on charges of conspiracy to firebomb targets in Greensboro during 1979. The arson incidents were conceived to support other racists facing trial on homicide charges at the time.

September 18, New York City: A female pedestrian is killed by stray rounds from a sniper firing on Jewish high school students. Authorities report that Lucille Rivera has been slain with the same rifle used in four other shootings since June 22.

September 22, Brooklyn, New York: Nine patrolmen are injured in a melee with Hasidic Jews outside a synagogue. On December 7 a rabbi and two other Jews are indicted on felony assault and riot charges.

October, Sacramento, California: Four blacks and two firefighters are hospitalized after breathing fumes from a chemical powder, scattered by vandals in the blacks' apartment. KKK graffiti is found at the scene.

October, Cedartown, Georgia: Three whites are caught attempting to booby-trap the apartment of Casiano Zamudio's widow. Casiano Zamudio was an outspoken critic of racist organizations.

October, Cobb County, Georgia: Shots are fired into a black family's home and car, tires are slashed, their dog is poisoned, and fireworks are set off in their yard to protest the desegregation of a formerly all-white neighborhood.

November, Pittsboro, North Carolina: KKK leader David Wallace is shot and killed by one of his followers at a Klan meeting. On July 14, 1984, the gunman is sentenced to eighteen years in prison.

November, Goulds, Florida: A grocery patronized by blacks is targeted for bomb threats and assaults by callers claiming membership in the KKK.

November, Arkansas: Six CSA members bomb a natural gas pipeline along the Red River.

1984

January, Grand Prairie, Texas: Robed Klansmen harass worshippers at a Buddhist temple.

January, Dallas, Texas: A bomb kills Ward Keeton, an informant against the KKK and American Nazi Party. Two Klansmen are charged with the murder.

February, New York City: Ly Yung Cheung is killed when a white man shoves her in front of a subway train. The killer tells police he has a "phobia" about Asians.

February, Orange County, California: A black-owned home is bombed.

March 8, Chattanooga, Tennessee: Racist Joseph Paul Franklin is indicted in the July 1977 bombing of a local synagogue. Jurors convict him on July 12.

March 15, Miami, Florida: Violence erupts after the acquittal of a police officer charged with manslaughter in the 1982 death of black prisoner Nevell Johnson, Jr. Three hundred blacks are arrested.

Spring, Chicago, Illinois: The home of one black family is bombed, with a swastika painted on an outbuilding. A second family is victimized by arson and vandalism.

Spring, Baltimore County, Maryland: Two black men are assaulted by armed Klansmen.

April, Cedartown, Georgia: Tim Carey, a black youth, is sprayed with Mace and beaten with brass knuckles for riding his bike past a KKK meeting. A Klansman is charged with the assault on May 8, 1985.

April, Guilford County, North Carolina: Shots are fired into an elderly black man's home, with a cross—topped by a dog's severed head—burned on the property.

April, Muscogee County, Georgia: A black church is bombed.

April, Boise, Idaho: A member of The Order, a white supremacist group, bombs a local synagogue.

April, Henderson County, North Carolina: A black-owned home is bombed.

April, Baltimore, Maryland: Two Klansmen are held on attempted murder charges after trying to stab two blacks in a bar.

1984

May, Garden Grove, California: Jesse Jackson's presidential campaign office is bombed.

May 17, Decatur, Alabama: Nine Klansmen are indicted for violating the civil rights of black demonstrators attacked in 1979.

June, San Francisco, California: Two cars owned by a black dance company are vandalized, and an unexploded bomb is found in one vehicle.

June, Danbury, Connecticut: Street fighting erupts after whites attending a Klan party taunt black pedestrians.

June, East County, California: A black man is assaulted by KKK members.

June, Indianapolis, Indiana: A black woman's new home is burned one day after she receives a threat signed "KKK."

June 18, Denver, Colorado: Alan Berg, a Jewish radio personality, is assassinated by The Order. Several members are later convicted of his murder.

July, Lancaster, South Carolina: Three rural black churches are burned by arsonists. Two white men are arrested while trying to burn a fourth church.

July, Enterprise, Alabama: A known Klansman assaults two boys in a local parking lot. The attacker is sentenced to one year in jail.

August, Hickory Hills, Illinois: An unexploded firebomb is found at the home of Rev. Enell Hall, a black minister. A Chicago Klansman is indicted for planting the bomb on June 20, 1985.

August, Daytona Beach, Florida: A local newspaper office is targeted for bomb threats and vandalized with KKK graffiti following publication of anti-Klan editorials.

August 8–10, Lawrence, Massachusetts: Three nights of Hispanic rioting lead to imposition of a curfew from August 10–13.

August 10, Georgia: Five Klansmen are arrested on federal charges for invading the homes of interracial couples and attacking the couples. The new FBI crackdown has jailed twenty-nine Klansmen since October 1982.

August 18, Waynesboro, Georgia: Street violence and arson erupt after the death of a black prisoner in police custody. Officers seal off the town, impose a sundown curfew, and arrest eleven rioters.

September, Jackson, Mississippi: A hooded white man terrorizes black children in a series of incidents.

September, Mapleton, Georgia: A black businessman receives racist bomb threats.

September, Carroll County, Georgia: Arsonists torch the home of an interracial couple.

September 19, Huntsville, Texas: Calvin Williams, a black prison inmate, is severly burned when two members of the Aryan Brotherhood ignite a flammable liquid in his cell.

Fall, Louisville, Kentucky: A black-owned home is set on fire by arsonists.

October, Fontana, California: A black man is paralyzed from the waist down after being beaten by three whites.

October, Doraville, Georgia: White racists burn a black family's car and burn a cross on their property.

October, Franklin, Tennessee: Racial fighting breaks out after whites wound four blacks in a drive-by shooting.

October 18, Sandpoint, Idaho: A member of The Order flees his home after a shoot-out with FBI agents. The weapon used in the June 1984 murder of Alan Berg in Denver is found in the suspect's home.

October 23, Cairo, Nebraska: Arthur Kirk, a neo-Nazi member of Posse Comitatus, mistakes police officers for members of the Israeli Mossad and dies in the subsequent shoot-out.

October 31, Brooklyn, New York: Arson is blamed after explosions and fire severely damage the Mapleton Park Hebrew Institute. On November 1 arsonists attempt to burn a synagogue one block away.

November, Frederica, Delaware: Arsonists damage a store being converted to a church for Puerto Ricans. Days later, the building is sprayed with KKK graffiti and threats.

November, Chicago, Illinois: A white mob attacks the home of an interracial couple. A black-owned home is firebombed and an attempted firebombing is foiled at the home of an Hispanic family.

November, Oregon: A young white man, Michael Fehrer, kills a black jogger and then shoots himself. Police report that the victim, Chris Braithwaite, was killed because of his race.

November 9, Atlanta, Georgia: Three Klansmen are convicted on federal charges in a series of 1982 floggings throughout western Georgia. Another Klansman is convicted of perjury in the same case.

November 20, Baltimore, Maryland: Five Klansmen are sentenced to jail for two cross-burning incidents.

December, Rutherford County, North Carolina: Klansmen arrested for shooting a black man defend their actions by claiming they are waging a war against local narcotics dealers.

December, Cleveland, Ohio: The local Community Relations Board logs 24 cases of racially motivated violence in the preceding year. Statewide, authorities report fourteen cases of anti-Semitic vandalism and harassment.

1985

January, Cobb County, Georgia: Two firebombs are tossed through the window of a home purchased by blacks in a formerly all-white neighborhood.

January, Flint, Michigan: Members of the SS Action Group are held responsible for extensive anti-black and anti-Semitic vandalism.

January, Tallapoosa, Georgia: White racists fire shots into a black woman's car.

January 15, Scottsboro, Alabama: Bomb threats from Klansmen evacuate a radio station, the courthouse, and city jail on Martin Luther King Day.

January 16: The ADL reports 715 acts of anti-Semitic vandalism in 1984, a 6.7 percent increase after two years of declining violence.

January 28, Rochester, Indiana: A white youth is sentenced to six months probation after his conviction for a series of racial harassment incidents.

February, Ulster County, New York: Six white prisoners dressed in KKK-style robes assault a black jail inmate.

February, Weslaco, Texas: Racist groups are blamed for a bombing attack against Mayor Hector Farias.

February, Iredell County, North Carolina: White racists shoot at a black-owned home, injuring three of its occupants.

March, Long County, Georgia: After a brawl between black and white youths at a local high school, Klansmen come into the area for a recruiting drive.

March, Louisville, Kentucky: Alleged KKK members phone bomb threats to a local motel, the Braden Memorial Center, and the offices of the Kentucky Alliance Against Racist and Political Repression.

March, Chicago, Illinois: Members of the Uptown Rebels, a racist gang affiliated with the American Nazi Party, murder police informant Kevin Zornes.

Spring, San Diego, California: Two white men set fire to a truck owned by black residents in a "white" neighborhood.

Spring, Ft. Worth, Texas: A dozen white youths, calling themselves the Legion of Doom, carry out more than thirty racial assaults, including several shootings and bombings.

April, Detroit, Michigan: A black man narrowly escapes after two white co-workers attempt to hang him.

April, Long County, Georgia: A black home is damaged by fire of "suspicious" origin.

April, Northbrook, Illinois: A pipe bomb explodes at a synagogue.

April 9, St. Petersburg, Florida: Five Klansmen are arrested for plotting to bomb property owned by blacks and Jews.

April 9, Murfreesboro, Tennessee: A KKK member pleads guilty to shooting at a suspected "drug house" in December 1984.

April 15, Ridgedale, Missouri: State trooper Jimmie Linegar is shot and killed and his partner is wounded by a fugitive member of the neo-Nazi Bruder Schweigen group.

April 25, Evansville, Indiana: Two KKK/Nazi activists are jailed for firing a rifle into a teenager's car.

April 27, Detroit, Michigan: Two whites threaten to lynch a black janitor after demanding to know when he "last had sex with a white woman."

May, Chicago, Illinois: Two whites overturn a black man's car.

May, Long Island, New York: Arsonists set fire to the South Baldwin Jewish Center.

May, New Hanover County, North Carolina: Racial fighting breaks out at a local high school after the discovery of a racial slur published in the yearbook.

May, South Boston, Massachusetts: A white mob stones the home of a Vietnamese family. Three men invade the house and assault family members.

May, Cheltenham, Pennsylvania: An Arab activist and his wife are stabbed to death in their home.

May, Houston, Texas: Local KKK members are charged with arson attacks on black citizens' homes.

May, Clayton County, Georgia: A black woman is knocked down and beaten during a streetcorner altercation with Klansmen.

May 12, Philadelphia, Pennsylvania: Authorities lay siege to a building occupied by MOVE cultists after snipers fire on patrolmen. On May 13 explosives dropped from a police helicopter ignite a fire that destroys more than fifty houses, leaving 300 persons homeless. Property damage from the fire is estimated at $5 million.

June, Louisville, Kentucky: A black-owned home is burned to the ground by white arsonists.

June, Sharon, Massachusetts: Three whites launch a six-month campaign of terrorism against a black banker's home and family, repeatedly vandalizing the property, uprooting shrubs, scattering garbage and feces over the lawn, and making anonymous telephone threats after midnight.

June, Houston, Texas: Bombs destroy a local mosque.

June, Cleveland, Ohio: A firebomb kills Mabel Gant, an elderly black woman, and leaves the rest of her home and family homeless. Three whites are charged with the crime.

June 7, Florida: The NAACP calls for an investigation after two black men, Walter Jones and Louis Wright, are found dead on the highway between Panama City and Wewahitchka.

July, East Point, Georgia: A black policeman is assaulted while trying to enter a right-wing cult church.

July, Iredell County, North Carolina: A member of the White Knights of Liberty pleads guilty to several incidents of racial violence in Iredell and an adjoining county. He turns state's evidence for a trial that results in the conviction of other group members.

July, Boston, Massachusetts: Three Asian teenagers are assaulted by whites.

July, Chicago, Illinois: Two blacks are beaten by three whites armed with baseball bats.

July, Belle Glade, Florida: Three members of the White Patriot Party are charged with a series of violent acts against blacks. The list of charges includes three assaults, several shootings, the stoning of blacks, and the slashing of car tires.

July, Providence, Rhode Island: Arson fires strike at the homes of six Asian-Americans.

July 10, Montgomery, Alabama: A KKK member is sentenced to one year in jail for a 1983 cross-burning incident.

July 11, Dunlap, Tennessee: Rocky Coker, a Klansman jailed for illegal possession of explosives in 1980, is sentenced to die for the murder of a local black businessman.

August, Clark, New Hampshire: The first black-owned home in this all-white community is targeted by racist vandalism, cross-burning, and arson threats.

August, Guilford County, North Carolina: Glen Hampton, a black motorist, narrowly escapes death in a drive-by shooting committed by white youths.

August, Erwin, North Carolina: Whites fire shots at Prenetta Savoy, a black motorist driving through town.

August, Revere, Massachusetts: Two Cambodian men are beaten, one of them fatally, by a white gang.

August, Hayden Lake, Idaho: An Aryan Nations security officer is charged with paying $1,800 to arrange the murder (by decapitation) of a suspected police informant.

August, Boston, Massachusetts: Arab residents are the targets of two separate bombing attacks.

September, Villa Rica, Georgia: A black youth is assaulted by a Klansman on the street.

September, Corry, Pennsylvania: Authorities report a new outbreak of anti-Catholic vandalism.

September, Chicago, Illinois: Henry Hampton is beaten to death by neo-Nazi members of the Uptown Rebels.

September, New Rochelle, New York: A synagogue is evacuated on Rosh Hoshanah after bomb threats are recieved.

September, Iredell County, North Carolina: Whites shoot at the home of a black policeman.

September, Monroe, Louisiana: J.L. Williams, a black man, is shot to death by a white gunman alleged to be his employer.

September 30, Ashbury, Georgia: Vandalism erupts during a protest march after the death of a black prisoner shot by police while fleeing a court hearing. Ashbury's mayor imposes a curfew on teenagers the following day.

October, California: Lisa Bonilla is charged with killing an elderly Hispanic man. At her trial she reads aloud from the Bible and chants KKK slogans in court.

October, Atlanta, Georgia: A black-owned home is vandalized and firebombed.

October, Santa Ana, California: A bomb kills one man and injures eight persons at the office of the American Arab Anti-Discrimination Committee.

October, Dallas, Georgia: A black woman is abducted and threatened by four hooded whites.

October 25, Arlington, Virginia: Robert Bloom is fatally beaten during an exorcism.

October 31, Robeson County, North Carolina: Joyce Sinclair, a black woman, is kidnapped, raped, and murdered by "a white man wearing white." Her body is discovered in a field beside a KKK rally site.

November, Concord, California: Timothy Lee, a black homosexual, is found hanged two blocks from the site where robed Klansmen assault two other blacks. Civil rights leaders reject the official verdict of "suicide" in Lee's death.

November, Forest Hills, Pennsylvania: A black home is bombed.

November, Wren, Mississippi: Arson destroys a black man's home in a nearly all-white neighborhood.

November, Dover, Delaware: An NAACP office is firebombed.

November, Venice, California: A fake bomb is planted at the home of a Moslem family previously targeted by threats.

November 20–21, Philadelphia, Pennsylvania: A black family leaves town after their home is attacked by a mob of 400 whites. White mobs also gather outside the home of an interracial couple.

November 25, Philadelphia, Pennsylvania: A black couple deserts their new home in a "white" neighborhood following acts of vandalism and mob demonstrations by white neighbors. An interracial couple, also targeted by bullies, pledges to remain. The newly vacant house is set on fire by arsonists on December 12.

November 28, DeKalb County, Georgia: Four firebombs are tossed through the window of a home purchased by blacks in a "white" neighborhood. Rain-dampened fuses prevent the bombs from exploding.

December, Cleveland, Ohio: Black families are the targets of racist vandalism. The Cleveland Community Relations Board logs fifty incidents of racial violence for the preceding year, nearly double the total for 1984.

December, Milwaukee, Wisconsin: Three men enter a synagogue and torture Buzz Cody, the sexton. A short time later Cody's apartment is vandalized.

December 18, Statesville, North Carolina: Four whites, including two KKK leaders, plead guilty to violation of federal civil rights laws. The four are charged with burning crosses at the homes of interracial couples.

December 24, Seattle, Washington: Neo-Nazi David Rice massacres a family of four after mistaking them for "Jew communists." He is sentenced to prison for life.

1986

January, Polk County, Georgia: A Hispanic man is assaulted by whites.

January, Chicago, Illinois: Members of the KKK and neo-Nazi groups disrupt an interracial meeting.

January 7, Boise, Idaho: Federal jurors convict an Aryan Nations member of tampering with witnesses and trying to arrange a contract murder. On March 21 he is sentenced to twelve years in prison.

February, Springfield, Illinois: Bombs strike a housing project where several black families reside.

February, Nash County, North Carolina: A white farmer shoots a black man who is dating the farmer's stepdaughter.

February, Austin, Texas: Black student activist Randy Bowman narrowly escapes death when two armed whites attempt to push him through an eighth-floor window at the state university.

February, Boulder Creek, California: A black man is assaulted by whites.

February, Cobb County, California: A black staff member of the Center for Democratic Renewal is assaulted by members of the KKK and NSRP.

February 6, Kansas City, Missouri: Racist Carl Rosendahl launches a campaign to rid his neighborhood of a black family and fires shots into their home. The shooting is repeated on February 21, February 22, and March 14. Rosendahl is finally jailed after detonating a bomb in the family's back yard on April 29.

February 14, Madison, Wisconsin: Racist serial killer Joseph Paul Franklin is convicted and sentenced to life imprisonment in the 1977 murder of a racially mixed couple.

March, Hayden Lake, Idaho: Bombers attack a Jewish-owned business.

March, Philadelphia, Pennsylvania: Four white racists stone the home of an Asian family.

March, Cicero, Illinois: A black man is assaulted by six whites.

March 16, Dallas, Texas: Black civil rights leader Fred Finch and his wife are murdered in their home, each victim stabbed over thirty times. Two brothers are charged with the crime on March 18.

Spring, Orange County, California: Seventeen cases of anti-Semitic vandalism are reported.

Spring, Watertown, New York: Black soldiers are assaulted by a mob of whites.

Spring, Albuquerque, New Mexico: A local home is bombed following numerous threats from callers claiming to represent a neo-Nazi group.

Spring, Contra Costa County, California: Two blacks are assaulted by whites. Ten black families have been recent targetes of racist vandalism.

April, Tuscaloosa, Alabama: Three Arab students are assaulted by whites on the state university campus.

April, Pittsburgh, Pennsylvania: A rabbinical student is shot and killed by two white youths outside a Jewish community center.

April, Philadelphia, Pennsylvania: Two whites shouting racial epithets run down a black man with their car.

April, Atlanta, Georgia: Neo-Nazi skinheads are blamed for one racist assault and two cases of vandalism.

April, Baltimore, Maryland: A black man is assaulted by a group of white racists.

April, Revere, Massachusetts: Several Asians and a white associate are terrorized by a bombing, assault, and vandalism.

April, Cleveland, Ohio: Three black families suffer repeated acts of vandalism over a nine-day period.

April, Leavenworth, Kansas: A window is smashed at a home where a cross is burned in the yard.

April 14, Columbus, Indiana: Two whites hurl a smoke bomb into a black family's home. The attackers are sentenced to one year in prison and $1,000 fines.

May, Baltimore, Maryland: An anti-apartheid exhibit is firebombed at Johns Hopkins University, injuring one student.

May, Vance County, North Carolina: A black woman is shot and wounded by a white store owner. When other blacks try to picket the store, they are also fired on.

May, Kansas City, Missouri: Arsonists burn a lakeside cabin owned by blacks.

May, Winston-Salem, North Carolina: Two black men are assaulted by whites.

May 26, Staten Island, New York: A teenage son of the borough president is charged with assault after beating a black youth with a hammer.

May 28, New York City: A black cyclist, Samuel Spencer III, is fatally beaten and stabbed by whites near Coney Island. One of his assailants pleads guilty in 1987; another is convicted and sentenced to prison in March 1988.

June, Cedartown, Georgia: Authorities report six racially motivated assaults by white attackers.

June, Mt. Airy, North Carolina: Klansmen attack a heckler at one of their rallies.

June, Otto, North Carolina: A security guard fires on tourists who accidentally trespass on the property of the neo-Nazi Church of the Creator.

June, Rock Springs, Wyoming: Three masked whites approach a black traveler and call out epithets and order him out of the area before firing a shot at his car.

June, Baltimore, Maryland: A black-owned home is bombed.

June, Zion, Illinois: Fighting erupts between blacks and Klansmen in a state park.

June, Cleveland, Ohio: A black family leaves their home after three months of threats and vandalism that have culminated in several days of mob gatherings outside.

June, Nash County, North Carolina: A member of the White Knights of Liberty interrupts an NAACP parade and threatens marchers with a gun.

June 1, Brooklyn, New York: An Asian youth is stabbed by Hispanics in a racially motivated attack. One of his assailants is charged the following day.

Summer, Tuckerton, New Jersey: Nine whites assault a black couple and vandalize their car.

July, Arizona: Members of the Civilian Materiel Assistance mount armed patrols of the Mexican border for five days, holding a group of illegal aliens at gunpoint for several hours on one occasion.

July, Charlotte, North Carolina: Klansmen are blamed for vandalizing a black woman's home.

July, Philadelphia, Pennsylvania: A black woman flees her home after receiving threats of mob violence. Three other cases of racist vandalism are also reported.

July, Scott County, Iowa: A nearly all-black church is set on fire by arsonists two weeks after an incident of vandalism.

July, Presidio County, Texas: An Hispanic man is assaulted by three whites dressed in military fatigues.

July, Zion, Illinois: Fahim Ahmad, a black teenager, is shot and killed by a white man shouting, "Klan! Klan! Klan!"

July 4, New York City: A Puerto Rican man is dragged from his car and beaten by whites in the Bronx. A similar attack, days later, leaves another Puerto Rican with a broken arm.

August, Hayden Lake, Idaho: Bombs nearly destroy a Jewish-owned business.

August, Philadelphia, Pennsylvania: A black man is beaten by two whites.

August, Toledo, Ohio: Four whites are jailed for firing shotguns into the homes of two black families in mostly white areas. Windows are smashed at a third home, and a cross is burned outside a fourth.

August, Baltimore, Maryland: Kenneth Shray, an associate of white supremacists, is shot to death execution-style. A member of the Aryan Nations later pleads guilty to his murder.

August, Federal Way, Washington: Bomb threats from a caller claiming membership in the Aryan Nations close the same bank twice in one week.

August, Gaithersburg, Maryland: Arson damages an Asian-owned business.

August, Chicago, Illinois: A small anti-Klan demonstration is disrupted by hundreds of whites in Marquette Park.

August 4, New York City: Two hundred additional police are dispatched to the Bronx after an outbreak of racial violence sparked by recent black-Hispanic influx into the formerly all-white Belmont district. On August 5, two Puerto Rican youths are charged with beating two Yugoslavian brothers in retaliation for earlier incidents. On September 11 six youths are indicted for recent racial assaults.

September, Summit Township, Michigan: Black families are victimized by arson, shootings, and vandalism.

September, Cumberland County, North Carolina: Members of the White Patriot Party are charged with conspiring to rob a local business in order to purchase weapons for racist attacks.

September, New York: Synagogues in Manhattan and Greenport receive bomb threats on Rosh Hoshanah.

September 15, Coeur d'Alene, Idaho: An explosion damages the home of Rev. William Wassmuth, an outspoken opponent of the Aryan Nations.

September 29, Coeur d'Alene, Idaho: Aryan Nations bombs strike three downtown businesses.

October, Florence, Arizona: The murder of Paul Engle, a convict and member of the Aryan Brotherhood, touches off rioting at the state prison, leaving two black prisoners seriously injured.

October, Tacoma, Washington: An arson fire leaves several Cambodian refugees homeless.

October 30, Miami, Florida: Rudolph Broussard and Anthony Brown, two vocal critics of the all-black Hebrew Israelite cult, are shot to death at their apartment complex. Cult member Robert Rozier is later convicted of their slayings and sentenced to prison. Authorities suspect Rozier in five other Miami homicides, in addition to violent crimes in St. Louis and New York City, allegedly committed in his capacity as a "Death Angel" serving the whims of cult leader "Yaweh Ben Yaweh."

November, Robeson County, North Carolina: A Lumbee Indian is shot and killed by police after being stopped for a traffic violation.

November, Philadelphia, Pennsylvania: Three black men are beaten by whites armed with clubs.

December, Ozone Park, New York: Two Hispanic men are assaulted by whites in a mainly white neighborhood. Their attackers are arrested.

December, Stoughton, Massachusetts: Three white men are arrested for beating three Vietnamese immigrants.

December 26, Howard Beach, New York: Three black men are attacked and beaten by a gang of whites. One of the victims, Michael Griffith, is struck and killed by a car while trying to flee. On December 21, 1987, three white youths are convicted of manslaughter in the case and a fourth defendant is acquitted.

1987

January 11, New Iberia, Louisiana: An eight-year-old girl is killed in an exorcism.

January 17, Cumming, Georgia: A white mob attacks an integrated brotherhood parade, injuring four marchers, and eight whites are arrested.

January 20, Buffalo, New York: Joseph Christopher, "the .22-caliber killer," is sentenced to twenty-five years for manslaughter in the racially motivated stabbing deaths of three local blacks.

January 24, Cumming, Georgia: Whites menace a new March Against Fear, but police prevent any violence from occuring. KKK leader David Duke is among the fifty-five whites arrested. On February 10 seven whites are indicted for racial incidents spanning the preceding month.

February 15: Project Klanwatch reports forty-five cross-burnings and arson incidents over the preceding two years directed at minority residents in "white" neighborhoods across America.

February 19–20, Tampa, Florida: Two nights of racial violence follow the death of a young black man. His death occurred while being subdued by a "choke hold" in police custody.

March 11, Maplewood, New Jersey: Vandals slash auto tires at the homes of two witnesses who testified against a white man accused of harassing black neighbors and vandalizing their property.

March 24, Queens, New York: A black man is found stabbed to death in the racially tense Howard Beach area.

April 7, Tampa, Florida: Violence erupts after police kill their fourth black suspect since November 1986.

May 8, New York City: Three members of the JDL are arrested for a series of bombings dating back to 1984. With a fourth defendant, they plead guilty to federal charges on August 13. On October 26, two are sentenced to ten-year prison terms, one is sentenced to five years, and one receives a three-year suspended sentence with six months house-arrest.

July 21, Montgomery, Alabama: State police investigate a local murder linked with a black magic cult, Children of the Light, said to be affiliated with the OTO. Authorities suspect the group in twenty-four other homicides.

September 10, Atlanta, Georgia: Eddie Callahan, a black man, is shot and killed by police, with five wounds in his back. On October 14 one of the officers involved is indicted for involuntary manslaughter.

September 21, Jackson, Georgia: Convicted killer Timothy McCorquodale is executed for the 1974 murder of a teenage white girl whose neck he broke after seeing her talk to a black man.

October 16, Utah: Daniel Jordan, polygamist cult leader and son-in-law of Ervil Lebaron, a polygamy cult leader, is shot and killed at a mountain camp site. Authorities link the slaying to a fifteen-year feud between Mormon splinter groups, which may have claimed a dozen lives in several western states and Mexico.

November, Robeson County, North Carolina: Local Indians charge police brutality after one of them is killed during a shoot-out with police.

November 3, Berkeley, California: Administrators report that black students are leaving the University of California "in droves" following a series of racial incidents and attacks.

November 11, Chicago, Illinois: Jewish stores are vandalized on the North Side, with windows smashed and swastikas painted on the walls, a reminder of the November 1938 *Kristalnacht* pogroms in Nazi Germany.

November 26, Brooklyn, New York: Two blacks collecting discarded cans are pursued and beaten by a gang of whites armed with rocks and bottles. The attackers shout, "This is our Howard Beach!"

November 28, Wappingers Falls, New York: Tawana Brawley, a black girl, is found behind her apartment complex wrapped in plastic trash bags, smeared with animal feces, her hair shorn in uneven tufts, and with "KKK" and "nigger" chalked on her stomach and chest. She accuses six white men, including a uniformed policeman, of raping and abusing her, but she refuses to identify her attackers before a grand jury. Authorities ultimately term her accusations a hoax and publicity stunt.

December 15, Raleigh, North Carolina: Authorities report forty-five attacks on racial or religious minorities in North Carolina during 1987, an increase from thirty-seven incidents in 1986 and thirty-one in 1985.

December 23, Columbia, South Carolina: State representative Tee Ferguson is arrested for slapping a black caucus worker.

December 25, Hemphill, Texas: Loyal Garner, Jr., a black prisoner, is fatally beaten in the county jail and dies two days later. On March 5, 1988, three officers—including the police chief and county sheriff—are indicted on murder charges. A federal jury acquits all three of civil rights violations on July 15, 1988.

December 25, Brooklyn, New York: Two black men are beaten by a gang of whites. One of their assailants is jailed on December 31.

December 27, Cambridge, Massachusetts: A church nativity scene is burned by arsonists, who leave behind a dead sparrow, a severed cow's tongue, and a note reading: "How many more fires before you realize your God is dead?" Authorities say voodoo cultists may be linked to a series of recent church arsons in eastern Massachusetts.

December 29, New York City: Alfred Sanders, a black man, is shot eleven times by two patrolmen on the street after allegedly pulling a knife. Witnesses insist that the dead man was unarmed, but the killing is ruled justifiable on February 1, 1988.

1988

January, New York City: Rafael Guttierez is mobbed and beaten by thirty blacks in the Bronx. During the same month, black educator Theodore Carelock accuses white patrolmen of assaulting him on the street.

January 16, Kamas, Utah: A bomb blast causes $1 million damage to a local Mormon church. Authorities surround a polygamist compound at nearby Marion, seeking suspects in the case, but cultists stand off police with gunfire for twelve days. The siege ends on January 28 in a shoot-out that leaves one officer dead and cult leader Addam Swapp wounded. On May 10 Swapp and three other cult members are convicted on multiple felony charges.

January 23, Dallas, Texas: A black vagrant, urged on by members of a mob, fatally shoots Patrolman John Chase after taking the officer's service revolver. The incident increases the existing tension between blacks and police.

January 26, Lincoln City, Indiana: A cross is burned to intimidate black members of a local basketball team. Three whites plead guilty to the "prank" on June 28.

January 28, New York City: The ADL reports a 17 percent increase in anti-Semitic incidents during 1987, with 207 violent acts logged in New York alone.

January 31, New York City: Juan Garcia dies of a "heart attack" while in police custody. A private autopsy reveals evidence of being fatally beaten.

February 1, Lumberton, North Carolina: Two militant Cherokees invade a newspaper office, holding seventeen hostages at gunpoint for ten hours and demanding a probe of local discrimination against Indians.

February 7, Amherst, Massachusetts: Five whites assault two black men walking with a white woman on the local university campus. Two hundred blacks retaliate by occupying the campus New Africa Hall on February 14, demanding better security and the expulsion of the attackers from the school.

February 7, New York City: Relatives of Alfred Sanders, a black man shot and killed by police, on December 29, 1987, call for a special grand jury to investigate possible racist motives in the shooting.

February 17, Harahan, Louisiana: Two blacks file a $1.5 million federal suit against a deputy sheriff who beat them in 1987. The deputy, Sgt. Edwin McClendon, had been fined $1,000 and placed on three years probation following his conviction.

February 24, Chicago, Illinois: James Kalafut, a white man "taught to hate black people," is sentenced to perform 200 hours of community service for the NAACP after he admits chasing two blacks with a baseball bat.

March, Starkville, Mississippi: University officials strip the Sigma Alpha Epsilon fraternity of its charter after members threaten to take an Hispanic pizza delivery man hostage in retaliation for Cuban uprisings in Georgia and Louisiana prisons.

March, St. Paul, Minnesota: Threatening letters with racial slurs are mailed to Tina Edwards, an American Indian who serves as student body president of local college.

March 22, Lumberton, North Carolina: Lumbee Indian activist John Godwin is killed in a car crash that friends term "suspicious."

March 26, Lumberton, North Carolina: Julian Pierce, an Lumbee attorney running for county judge, is shot and killed by two white gunmen, climaxing weeks of racial tension. Lumbee tribesmen call the murder a political assassination; police term it a "domestic dispute."

April, Berkeley, California: Vandals strike the dormitory room of a black university coed, prompting demonstrations by the African Student Association.

April 19, Hobart, Indiana: Two whites are convicted of burning a cross at a black family's home in October 1984.

April 20, Parma, Ohio: Vandals spray-paint the Catholic church once attended by John Demjanjuk after he is convicted of Nazi war crimes in Israel. Police in nearby Akron guard synagogues after receiving anonymous threats related to the case.

April 23, Bloomington, Indiana: Vandals set fire to a black student's dormitory room at the state university, scrawling "KKK" and "nigger" on the door.

May 5, Louisville, Kentucky: David Price, a black teenager, is shot and killed by a carload of white youths who toured his neighborhood shouting racial insults.

June 10, Perth Amboy, New Jersey: A night of rioting by Hispanics follows the funeral of Carmen Coria, one of two Mexican brothers shot by an off-duty patrolman.

June 22, Staten Island, New York: Six young white men shouting racial slurs assault a black pedestrian and his two white companions and beat them with baseball bats.

June 23, New York City: A black pedestrian is accosted and beaten by four white men armed with clubs.

June 27, Texas: Four defectors from Ervil Lebaron's Church of the Lamb of God are murdered execution-style. On July 14 Texas and Utah officers question five polygamist cult members, including Lebaron's son, about unsolved murders spanning two states.

August 4, Oxford, Mississippi: Arson is suspected in the fire that destroys a building scheduled to house the first black fraternity at the University of Mississippi.

August 4, Washington, Missouri: Londell Williams, a member of The Order and other racist groups, pleads guilty to plotting the murder of black presidential candidate Jesse Jackson.

September 10, Portland, Oregon: Two skinheads are charged with assaulting a black security guard. Both attackers are subsequently jailed for the beating death of another black in November.

September 18, New York City: Vandals spray-paint a synagogue and set fire to the building, destroying five valuable Torahs. Two youths, ages 12 and 15, are charged.

September 20, Shreveport, Louisiana: Blacks riot, looting and burning three stores, after two white women are arrested in the shooting death of William McKinney, a black man. At least fifty shots are fired at police during the riot, and four persons are arrested. Sporadic violence and shooting continues on September 21.

September 28, Clinton, Mississippi: The FBI investigates charges that police beat three black adults during a clash with high school students at a pizza parlor.

September 28, Philadelphia, Pennsylvania: Two hundred black youths riot following the shooting death of an alleged gang member. At least two cars are overturned and burned during the outbreak.

October 1, Shreveport, Louisiana: A white youth is shot and wounded by a group of blacks. Authorities deny any link to two other racial shootings in recent months.

October 9, Belleville, Illinois: Two white youths are convicted of burning a cross outside a black family's home.

October 11, Terre Haute, Indiana: Two white university students are charged with beating Shawn Pruitt, a black youth, in his dormitory room the previous week.

October 30, New York City: Four skinheads are jailed for beating William Stump, a white man who objected to their use of racial epithets, and for trying to throw his infant child down a flight of stairs.

November 3, New York City: Fighting between blacks and skinheads erupts in a television studio during the taping of Geraldo Rivera's daily talk show. Rivera suffers a broken nose when he is struck by a flying chair.

November 13, Portland, Oregon: Ethiopian national Mulugeta Seraw is beaten to death with a baseball bat. Skinhead Kenneth Menske, alias "Ken Death," pleads guilty to the murder and is sentenced to life.

November 13, Staten Island, New York: Two white youths are attacked by a black gang, and one of the assailants is shot and wounded by mistake when a gang member opens fire on the intended victims.

1989

January 1, Long Beach, California: Video cameras record the public beating of Don Jackson, a black off-duty police officer, by white patrolmen.

January 11, Howard Beach, New York: White youths armed with baseball bats attack a car carrying two black men, just blocks from the scene of the fatal 1986 incident.

January 15, Longmont, Colorado: Five white supremacists are arrested with 300 pounds of plastic explosives, several weapons, and a large supply of ammunition. One prisoner tells detectives that the group planned to blow up local police stations.

January 16–17, Miami, Florida: Rioting erupts after a black motorcyclist is shot and killed by an Hispanic policeman. At least 250 persons are arrested, one is killed, and seven are wounded in scattered shooting incidents.

February 1–2, Tampa, Florida: Blacks riot for two nights over the death of a local drug dealer killed in a scuffle with police while resisting arrest.

February 26, Anne Arundel County, Maryland: A racial brawl erupts outside a local tavern.

March 2, Maryland: Two white men receive the maximum one-year jail sentence for smashing windows in a black family's home.

May 28, LaVerne, California: Four skinheads are arrested for beating an Iranian couple that they mistook for Jews. A black school security guard is injured in the same attack.

June 24, Brighton Beach, New York: Max Kowalski, a Jewish holocaust survivor, is stabbed to death in an argument with a neighbor who drew a swastika on the door of Kowalski's apartment.

July, Philadelphia, Pennsylvania: A young Hispanic man is killed by white racists in the Feltonville district.

August 22, Atlanta, Georgia: White supremacists issue a declaration of war against the Eleventh Circuit of the U.S. federal courts, threatening poison gas attacks at unspecified locations. On the same day a tear gas parcel bomb arrives at local NAACP headquarters and injures eight persons.

August 23, Brooklyn, New York: A white gang armed with baseball bats and guns pursues four black youths on a street in Bensonhurst. Black teenager Yusuf Hawkins is beaten and shot to death in the attack, and seven whites are arrested. Marchers protesting the murder are met by white mobs shouting "Niggers go home!" while brandishing signs that read "We Are Not Racists."

October 7, Wellesley, Massachusetts: Two men are arrested on charges of malicious mischief after an outbreak of anti-Semitic vandalism.

October 8, New York City: Three Jewish youths are attacked and beaten by a gang of twenty hoodlums shouting ethnic slurs. Two of the victims are hospitalized.

October 10, Dothan, Alabama: SCLC demonstrators march on city hall, accusing police of brutalizing two black prisoners.

October 11, Adamsville, Alabama: Racial fighting leaves the principal and one student injured at Minor High School. A teacher faces disciplinary action for firing shots in the air during the melee.

October 11, Little Rock, Arkansas: Three hundred students at Central High skirmish in racial fighting that leaves several persons injured after a disorderly pep rally.

December 16, Birmingham, Alabama: A parcel bomb kills U.S. Circuit Judge Robert Vance, known for his decisions favoring black civil rights groups and his opposition to the KKK.

December 18, Atlanta, Georgia: Authorities evacuate a federal courthouse after a parcel bomb is discovered. The bomb, described as identical to that which killed Judge Robert Vance in Birmingham two days earlier, is defused before it explodes.

December 18, Savannah, Georgia: A parcel bomb stuffed with nails kills Robert Robinson, a black lawyer active in civil rights work.

December 19, Jacksonville, Florida: A nail bomb is delivered to NAACP headquarters but is deactivated by police before it explodes. FBI spokesmen link the four-day series of attacks with an August "declaration of war" by Southern white supremacists.

BIBLIOGRAPHY

Literally hundreds of books, official reports, newspaper clippings, and magazine articles were reviewed in preparation of this volume. A selected list of the more significant books consulted over two years of research is offered in the following pages.

AMERICAN INDIANS
Andrist, Ralph. *The Long Death*. New York: Macmillan, 1964.
Bird, Harrison. *War for the West 1790–1813*. New York: Oxford University Press, 1971.
Brown, Dee. *Bury My Heart at Wounded Knee*. New York: Holt, Rinehart and Winston, 1970.
Dillon, Richard. *North American Indian Wars*. New York: Facts on File, 1983.
Downey, Fairfax. *Indian Wars of the U.S. Army, 1776–1865*. New York: Doubleday, 1963.
Dunn, Jacob. *Massacres of the Mountains*. New York: Archer, 1958.
Ellis, Edward. *The Indian Wars of the United States*. New York: Cassell, 1892.
Frost, John. *Indian Wars of the United States*. Philadelphia: J.B. Smith, 1857.
Glassley, Ray. *Pacific Northwest Indian Wars*. Portland, Ore.: Binfords, 1953.
Longstreet, Stephen. *War Cries on Horseback*. New York: Doubleday, 1970.
Marrin, Albert. *War Clouds in the West*. New York: Atheneum, 1984.
Mayhall, Mildred. *Indian Wars of Texas*. Waco, Tex.: Texian Press, 1965.
Oehler, C.M. *The Great Sioux Uprising*. New York: Oxford University Press, 1959.
Schellie, Don. *Vast Domain of Blood*. Los Angeles: Westernlore, 1968.
Schmitt, Martin. *Fighting Indians of the West*. New York: Scribner, 1948.
Stone, William. *Border Wars of the American Revolution*. New York: Harper, 1845.
Sylvester, Herbert. *Indian Wars of New England*. Boston: Clarke, 1910.
Tebbel, John. *The American Indian Wars*. New York: Harper & Row, 1966.
Thompson, John. *History of the Indian Wars and War of the Revolution of the United States*. Philadelphia: Lippincott, 1873.
Vestal, Stanley. *Warpath and Council Fire*. New York: Random House, 1948.
Weems, John. *Death Song*. New York: Doubleday, 1976.
Wellman, Paul. *Death in the Desert*. New York: Macmillan, 1935.
———. *Death on Horseback*. Philadelphia: Lippincott, 1947.
———. *Death on the Prairie*. New York: Macmillan, 1934.

ASIANS
Daniels, Roger. *Anti-Chinese Violence in North America*. New York: Arno, 1978.
McWilliams, Carey. *Prejudice—Japanese Americans: Symbol of Racial Intolerance*. Boston: Little, Brown, 1944.

Miller, Stuart. *The Unwelcome Immigrant*. Berkeley: University of California Press, 1969.

Sandmeyer, Elmer. *The Anti-Chinese Movement in California*. Urbana, Ill.: University of Illinois Press, 1939.

Saxton, Alexander. *The Indispensible Enemy*. Berkeley: University of California Press, 1971.

ASSASSINATION

Clarke, James W. *American Assassins*. Princeton, N.J.: Princeton University Press, 1987.

Donovan, Robert. *The Assassins*. New York: Harper & Row, 1955.

Kirkham, James. *Assassination and Political Violence*. New York: Bantam,1970.

McKinley, James. *Assassination in America*. New York: Harper & Row, 1977.

Miller, Tom. *The Assassination Please Almanac*. Chicago: Regnery, 1977.

BLACKS

Aptheker, Herbert. *American Slave Revolts*. New York: Columbia, 1944.

Belfrage, Sally. *Freedom Summer*. New York: Viking, 1965.

Berlin, Ira. *The Destruction of Slavery*. New York: Cambridge University Press, 1985.

Boskin, Joseph. *Urban Racial Violence in the Twentieth Century*. Beverly Hills: Glencoe, 1976.

Carroll, Stanley. *Slave Insurrections in the United States, 1800–1865*. NewYork: Negro Universities Press, 1938.

Diggs, Ellen. *Black Chronology*. Boston: Hall, 1983.

Filler, Louis. *The Crusade Against Slavery*. New York: Harper & Row, 1960.

Foner, Eric. *Reconstruction*. New York: Harper & Row, 1985.

Franklin, John Hope. *From Slavery to Freedom*. New York:Vintage, 1969.

Grimshaw, Allen. *Racial Violence in the United States*. Chicago: Aldine, 1970.

James, C.L.R. *A History of Negro Revolt*. London: Fact, 1938.

Lincoln, Charles. *The Black Muslims in America*. Boston: Beacon, 1961.

Marine, Gene. *The Black Panthers*. New York: Signet, 1969.

Newton, Michael. *Bitter Grain*. Los Angeles: Holloway, 1980.

———. *The King Conspiracy*. Los Angeles: Holloway, 1988.

Nichols, Alice. *Bleeding Kansas*. New York: Oxford University Press, 1954.

Oates, Stephen. *To Purge This Land With Blood*. New York: Harper & Row, 1970.

Quarles, Benjamin. *Allies for Freedom: Blacks and John Brown*. New York: Oxford University Press, 1974.

Rawley, James. *Race And Politics: "Bleeding Kansas" and the Coming of the Civil War*. Philadelphia: Lippincott, 1969.

Ratner, Lorman. *Powder Keg: Northern Opposition to the Anti-Slavery Movement*. New York: Basic, 1968.

Robinson, Charles. *The Kansas Conflict*. New York: Harper & Row, 1892.

CATHOLICS

Billington, Ray. *The Protestant Crusade*. New York: Rinehart, 1938.

Desmond, Humphrey. *The A.P.A. Movement*. New York: Arno, 1912.

Gohman, Mary. *Political Navitism in Tennessee to 1860*. Washington, D.C.: Catholic University of America, 1938.

Leonard, Ira. *American Nativism, 1830–1860*. New York: Arno, 1971.

McGann, Agnes. *Nativism in Kentucky to 1860*. Washington, D.C.: Catholic University of America, 1944.

Noonan, Carroll. *Nativism in Connecticut, 1828–1860*. Washington, D.C.: Catholic University of America, 1938.

Schmeckbier, Laurence. *History of the Know Nothing Party in Maryland*. Baltimore: Johns Hopkins, 1899.

Thomas, Evangeline. *Nativism in the Old Northwest, 1850–1860.* Washington, D.C.: Catholic University of America, 1936.

CULTS/WITCHES
Boyer, Paul. *Salem Possessed.* Cambridge, Mass.: Harvard University Press, 1974.
Demos, John. *Entertaining Salem.* New York: Oxford University Press, 1982.
Hansen, Chadwick. *Witchcraft at Salem.* New York: Braziller, 1969.
Kahaner, Larry. *Cults that Kill: Probing the Underworld of Occult Crime.* New York: Warner, 1989.
Newton, Michael. *Hunting Humans.* Port Townsend, Wash.: Loompanics, 1990.

HISPANICS
Clendenen, Clarence. *Blood on the Border.* New York: Macmillan, 1969.
Gregg, Robert. *The Influence of Border Troubles on Relations Between the United States and Mexico, 1871–1910.* Baltimore: Johns Hopkins, 1937.
Mazon, Mauricio. *The Zoot-Suit Riots.* Austin: University of Texas Press, 1984.
McWilliams, Carey. *North From Mexico.* Philadelphia: Lippincott, 1949.
Mirande, Alfredo. *Gringo Justice.* Notre Dame, Ind.: University of Notre Dame Press, 1987.
Prago, Albert. *Strangers in Their Own Land.* New York: Four Winds, 1973.
Vanderwood, Paul. *Border Fury.* Albuquerque, N.M.: University of New Mexico Press, 1988.

JEWS
Dinnerstein, Leonard. *Uneasy at Home.* New York: Columbia University Press, 1987.
Du Bois, Rachel. *The Jews in American Life.* New York: Nelson, 1935.
Epstein, Benjamin. *"Some of My Best Friends . . ."* New York: Farrar, Straus & Giroux, 1962.
Forster, Arnold. *A Measure of Freedom.* New York: Doubleday, 1950.
Hendrick, Burton. *The Jews in America.* New York: Doubleday, 1923.

KU KLUX KLAN
Chalmers, David. *Hooded Americanism.* New York: New Viewpoints, 1981.
Hass, Ben. *K.K.K.* San Diego: Regency Books, 1963.
Newton, Michael and Judy. *The Ku Klux Klan: An Encyclopedia.* New York: Garland, 1991.
Sims, Patsy. *The Klan.* New York: Stein & Day, 1978.
Trelease, Allen. *White Terror.* Westport, Conn.: Greenwood, 1971.
Wade, Wyn C. *The Fiery Cross.* New York: Simon & Schuster, 1987.

LYNCHING
Ames, Jessie. *The Changing Character of Lynching.* Atlanta: Commission on Interracial Cooperation, 1942.
Caughey, John. *Their Majesties, the Mob.* Chicago: University of Chicago Press, 1960.
Ginzburg, Ralph. *100 Years of Lynchings.* New York: Lancer, 1962.
National Association for the Advancement of Colored People. *Thirty Years of Lynchings in the United States.* New York: NAACP, 1919.
Raper, Arthur. *The Tragedy of Lynching.* Chapel Hill, N.C.: University of North Carolina Press, 1938.
White, Walter. *Rope and Faggot.* New York: Knopf, 1929.

MILITARY ENGAGEMENTS

Adams, Henry. *The War of 1812* (9 vols.). Washington, D.C.: Infantry Journal Press, 1944.

Catton, Bruce. *The American Hertitage Picture History of the Civil War.* New York: American Heritage, 1960.

Coles, Harry. *The War of 1812.* Chicago: University of Chicago Press, 1965.

Connelly, William. *Quantrill and the Border Wars.* Cedar Rapids, Iowa: Torch, 1910.

Henry, Robert. *The Story of the Mexican War.* New York: Ungar, 1961.

Joseph, Alvin. *The Patriotic Chiefs.* New York: Viking, 1961.

Leckie, Robert. *The Wars of America.* New York: Harper & Row, 1968.

Parkman, Francis. *France and England in North America* (10 vols.). Boston: Little, Brown, 1887–1888.

Smith, Justin. *The War with Mexico.* Gloucester, Mass.: Smith, 1963.

Ward, Christopher. *The War of the Revolution.* New York: Macmillan, 1953.

MORMONS

Codman, John. *A Solution to the Mormon Problems.* New York: Putnam, 1885.

Gunnison, John. *The Mormons.* Toronto: Maclear, 1853.

Hickman, William. *Brigham's Destroying Angel.* Salt Lake City: Shepard, 1904.

Lee, John. *The Mormon Menace.* New York: Home Protection Publishing Company, 1905.

NEO-NAZIS

Bell, Leland. *Hitler's Shadow.* New York: Kennikat, 1973.

Carlson, John. *Under Cover.* New York: Dutton, 1943.

Coates, James. *Armed and Dangerous.* New York: Hill & Wang, 1987.

Higham, Charles. *American Swastika.* New York: Doubleday, 1985.

Schonbach, Morris. *Native American Facism During the 1930s and 1940s.* New York: Garland, 1985.

Singular, Stephen. *Talked to Death.* New York: Berkley, 1987.

POLICE

Council of Federated Organizations. *Mississippi Black Paper.* New York: Random House, 1965.

Newton, Michael. *The FBI Plot.* Los Angeles: Holloway, 1981.

O'Reilly, Kenneth. *"Racial Matters."* New York: Macmillan, 1989.

Porambo, Ron. *No Cause for Indictment.* New York: Holt, 1971.

Stark, Rodney. *Police Riots.* Belmont, Calif.: Wadsworth, 1972.

Turner, William. *The Police Establishment.* New York: Tower, 1969.

RIOTS

Archer, Jules. *Riot!* New York: Hawthorn, 1974.

Cook, Adrian. *The Armies of the Streets.* Lexington, Ky.: University Press of Kentucky, 1974.

Feldberg, Michael. *The Turbulent Era.* New York: Oxford University Press, 1983.

Grimshaw, Allen. *A Study in Social Violence.* Philadelphia: University of Pennsylvania Press, 1959.

Headley, Joel. *The Great Riots of New York.* New York: Dover, 1873.

Methvin, Eugene. *The Riot Makers.* New York: Arlington, 1970.

Mitchell, J. Paul. *Race Riots in Black and White.* Englewood Cliffs, N.J.: Prentice-Hall, 1970.

Monte, Anita. *Riots.* New York: Washington Square, 1970.

Richardson, Leonard. *Gentlemen of Property and Standing.* New York: Oxford University Press, 1970.

Rossi, Peter. *Ghetto Revolts.* New York: Dutton, 1973.

Waskow, Arthur. *From Race Riot to Sit-in.* New York: Doubleday, 1966.

Wills, Garry. *The Second Civil War.* New York: New American Library, 1968.

VIOLENCE

Bingham, Jonathan. *Violence and Democracy.* New York: World, 1970.

Brown, Richard. *Stain of Violence.* New York: Oxford University Press, 1975.

Buhle, M.J., Buhle, P., and Georgakas, eds. *Encyclopedia of the American Left.* New York: Garland, 1990.

Crawford, Fred. *Violence and Dissent in Urban America.* Atlanta: Southern Newspaper Publishers, 1969.

Daigon, Arthur. *Violence USA.* New York: Bantam, 1978.

Fogelson, Robert. *Violence as Protest.* New York: Doubleday, 1971.

Hersch, Herbert. *Violence as Politics.* New York: Random House, 1970.

Hofstadter, Richard. *American Violence.* New York: Vintage, 1970.

Jeffreys-Jones, Rhodri. *Violence and Reform in American History.* New York: New Viewpoints, 1978.

Parker, Thomas. *Violence in the United States.* New York: Facts on File, 1974.

Rose, Thomas. *Violence in America.* New York: Vintage, 1970.

Skolnick, Jerome. *The Politics of Protest.* New York: Simon & Schuster, 1969.

Sloan, Irving. *Our Violent Past.* New York: Random House, 1970.

INDEX